# PEARSON
# myeducationlab™

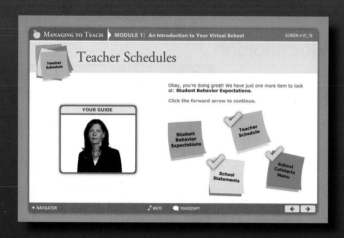

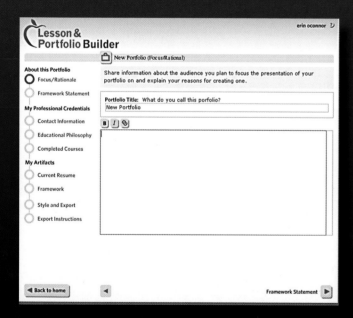

## Videos and Practical Tools for Your Classroom and Career!

*MyEducationLab* helps bring the classroom to life with a wealth of resources to help you prepare for practice teaching and the job of teaching itself.

## Managing To Teach

An interactive, virtual learning environment, Managing To Teach has been designed to help teachers-in-training develop effective classroom management skills. Users will watch videos of classroom scenarios, complete interactive assignments, assume the role of decision maker in simulated teaching experiences, and receive valuable feedback from the Program Guide on their classroom decisions. Based on the three cornerstones of effective classroom management—prior planning, establishing constructive behaviours, and exhibiting desired modes of behaviour—**Managing to Teach** is the *MyEducationLab* resource that soon-to-be teachers have been waiting for!

## Canadian Link Library

A comprehensive aggregation of provincial- and board-level links, the Canadian Link Library will provide you and other students across the country with valuable information about programs and standards that will start you on the right path to becoming a teacher!

## Portfolio Builder and Sample Lesson Plans

Use the portfolio-building wizard to build a print or e-portfolio, and sample a rich array of lesson plans that can be used during your practicum or when you start teaching.

## Save Time. Improve Results. www.myeducationlab.com

# INCLUSION OF EXCEPTIONAL LEARNERS IN CANADIAN SCHOOLS

## A PRACTICAL HANDBOOK FOR TEACHERS

### THIRD EDITION

NANCY L. HUTCHINSON

QUEEN'S UNIVERSITY

**Pearson Canada**
Toronto

Dedicated to the memory of my mother,
Ailene Holts, 1921–2007

**Library and Archives Canada Cataloguing in Publication**

Hutchinson, Nancy Lynn
Inclusion of exceptional learners in Canadian schools : a practical handbook for teachers / Nancy L.
Hutchinson. — 3rd ed.

Includes bibliographical references and index.
ISBN 978-0-13-241883-6

1. Inclusive education—Canada.    I. Title.

LC3984.H88 2010              371.9'0460971      C2008-906037-7

ISBN-13: 978-0-13-241883-6
ISBN-10: 0-13-241883-5

Vice President, Editorial Director: Gary Bennett
Editor-in-Chief: Ky Pruesse
Acquisitions Editor: David S. Le Gallais
Marketing Manager: Loula March
Associate Editor: Brian Simons
Production Editor: Patricia Jones
Copy Editor: Martin Townsend
Proofreader: Sally Glover
Production Coordinator: Avinash Chandra
Composition: Macmillan Publishing Solutions
Art Director: Julia Hall
Cover Designer: Hands Design/Kerrin Hands
Interior Designer: Gail Ferreira Ng-A-Kien
Cover Image: Veer Incorporated

4 5      13 12 11 10

Printed and bound in the United States of America.

# Brief Contents

# Contents

**Chapter 3**

# Preface

Preparing the third edition of *Inclusion of Exceptional Learners in Canadian Schools* has taught me many things. Some things I learned by doing background research in areas with which I was less familiar. Other things I learned through discussions with colleagues, graduate students, parents, teacher candidates, and individuals with exceptionalities. In particular, I have learned by challenging my assumptions about teaching exceptional children and adolescents. I believe that when we accept the challenges of teaching exceptional students in inclusive settings, we must be prepared to challenge assumptions about what exceptional students can and cannot do and to find new ways to help them reach their potential. Therefore, I hope this book helps you to challenge your assumptions and to reflect critically on what it means to include exceptional students in the classroom.

I am frequently reminded of the way the rest of the world views Canadian approaches to inclusion and inclusive education. Educators in other countries look to Canada's commitment to inclusion as a model and an inspiration. The organizing body for the Commonwealth Games has committed to inclusive games in the future, modelled on the games held in Victoria in 1994. Our 1982 *Constitution Act* has served as a model for countries developing constitutions since the early 1980s. Even Britain's charter of rights, approved by its upper and lower chambers in 2000, was compared with our *Charter of Rights and Freedoms* (1982) and found to contain fewer guarantees of individual rights. I recently interviewed adolescents with disabilities and their co-operative education employers about how they negotiate accommodations in the workplace. They reminded me forcefully that, to be effective, inclusion during the school years must mean inclusion in the community as well as in the school. Through all of this, I am aware of the incredible challenges facing parents, educators, employers, and exceptional individuals in making inclusion a reality. My hope in writing this book is that it may serve as a research-based, practically focused resource on inclusive education for teacher educators and pre-service and in-service teachers.

This book contains many references to Canadians—exceptional individuals, schools, educators, and educational researchers—including their locations in the country. I believe that it is critical that we know our history, stories, legislation, and heroes. We live next to a massive and influential power on the international stage. However, citizens, educators, and lawmakers in many countries respect us as a role model. Perhaps we are too self-effacing—I have observed that Canadians are among those least likely to be aware of how we lead by example in our field. I have tried to point to the contributions of individuals such as Terry Fox and Rick Hansen, heroes and leaders of advocacy for the disabled, and of organizations such as the Canadian National Institute for the Blind, winner of national and international awards for advocacy and service. I believe that Aboriginal students, learners from diverse cultures, and students at risk can benefit from inclusive environments and differentiated teaching. I have tried to draw attention to significant recent developments in Aboriginal education that coexist with the crisis of disappearing Aboriginal languages. Whenever possible, I have used Canadian examples and, at times, I may be guilty of citing Canadian research without including references to major research programs in other countries. I hope that the extensive listings of Canadian books, websites, and programs will help teacher candidates, teacher educators, and parents to locate our resources and our experts, of which there are many.

# Perspective

For many years I have organized my pre-service and in-service teaching about exceptional learners around topics such as planning, classroom organization and climate, and differentiating teaching and assessment—a *non-categorical* approach. I am reminded each year, as I work in the university and in schools in our community, how much is expected of beginning teachers. If they are to meet these expectations, I think they must begin, from the first lesson they plan, by thinking about the range of individuals in the class. The question they need to ask is not, "How do I individualize for these students?", an impossible task, but, "How do I differentiate my teaching to include these exceptional individuals?" That is the perspective you will find in this book. I have tried to focus on the kinds of information, skills, and strategies that recent teacher candidates have found both thought-provoking and practical. I have taught in both elementary and secondary schools, and I often teach classes with teacher candidates from both panels; I have tried to acknowledge the different challenges in these two settings.

# Organization

This textbook is informally divided into two main sections. The first section provides fundamental background knowledge in the field of exceptional education in Canada. Chapter 1 describes the current situation in Canada and provides a brief history of how we came to be where we are. It also includes a step-by-step strategy for adapting instruction, called *ADAPT*, that will help teachers to meet the needs of exceptional students. Chapter 2 describes the role of the classroom teacher in the education of exceptional learners and the kinds of partnerships that teachers forge with parents, paraeducators, and other professionals. Chapter 3 focuses on characteristics and strategies to meet the learning needs of exceptional students with six high-incidence exceptionalities (from giftedness to learning disabilities). Students with low-incidence exceptionalities and a range of health conditions are the focus of Chapter 4; the characteristics of these students and strategies to meet their learning needs are discussed. Chapter 5 turns attention to equity and diversity. There are strategies for differentiating teaching for Aboriginal students; culturally diverse students; those who have English as a second language; and students at risk for a variety of reasons, including poverty, abuse, and divorce.

The second section of the book presents the heart of any course on inclusive practices: instructional approaches that emphasize teaching students effectively regardless of exceptionality or other forms of diversity. Chapter 6 focuses on the climate, organization, and management of inclusive classrooms. Chapter 7 provides approaches to differentiating teaching, and Chapter 8 provides approaches to adapting assessment. There are many examples representing a range of grades, exceptionalities, and teaching subjects. In Chapter 9, you will find information on enhancing social relations of exceptional students. Chapter 10 deals with strategies for independent learning and independent living. The Conclusion turns the focus from exceptional learners to those who teach them most successfully and how they thrive on challenges and cope with stress in their professional lives.

# Features

This book offers the following features designed to help readers learn effectively:

- Chapter-opening vignettes serve as introductory cases to help readers relate the chapter content to the real world of Canadian schools.
- Learner objectives at the beginning of each chapter point to key content within that chapter.
- Key terms throughout the chapters appear in boldface type, and easy-to-understand definitions often appear in the text and always appear in the Glossary at the back of the book.
- Chapter summaries highlight important information in the chapters.
- Margin notations are designed to stimulate critical reflection and to introduce additional resources, including weblinks that have been researched and tested for quality and relevance.
- *Focus* boxes offer readers inspiring examples of Canadian families, communities, schools, programs, and educators that may serve as models.
- *Theory and Research Highlights in Educational Psychology* boxes provide a theoretical grounding in the psychology that informs the education of exceptional students and their inclusion in Canadian society.
- NEW! *Challenges* boxes at the end of each chapter present review questions to help students apply what they have learned in the chapter.
- Canadian references throughout help students locate practical supports, resources, research, curricula, people, and websites within the exceptional education community in Canada.

# Student Supplement

**MyEducationLab** Discover where the classroom comes to life! From video clips of teachers and students interacting to sample lessons, portfolio templates, and standards integration, MyEducationLab gives students the tools they will need to succeed in the classroom—with content easily integrated into existing courses. MyEducationLab gives students powerful insights into how real classrooms work and also gives them a rich array of tools that will support them on their journey from their first class to their first classroom.

# Instructor Supplements

The following supplements are available to instructors on Pearson Education Canada's password-protected online catalogue (http://vig.pearsoned.ca):

**Instructor's Manual** Each chapter of the Instructor's Manual includes an overview outline, teaching ideas, activities, discussion questions, transparency masters, and handout masters.

**MyTest** Over 450 test questions, including multiple-choice, matching terms, and essay, are provided in MyTest format. A powerful assessment generation program, MyTest helps instructors easily create and print quizzes, tests, and exams. Questions and tests can all be authored online, allowing flexibility and the ability to efficiently manage assessments at any time, from anywhere. MyTest is compatible with both Windows and Macintosh software.

**Technology Specialists** Pearson's Technology Specialists work with faculty and campus course designers to ensure that Pearson technology products, assessment tools, and online course materials are tailored to meet your specific needs. This highly qualified team is dedicated to helping schools take full advantage of a wide range of educational resources, by assisting in the integration of a variety of instructional materials and media formats. Your local Pearson Education sales representative can provide you with more details on this service program.

**CourseSmart** CourseSmart is a new way for instructors and students to access textbooks online anytime from anywhere. With thousands of titles across hundreds of courses, CourseSmart helps instructors choose the best textbook for their class and give their students a new option for buying the assigned textbook as a lower cost eTextbook. For more information visit www.coursesmart.com.

# Acknowledgments

Many people have contributed to the completion of this project, so many that, out of necessity, I will name only a few. First, thank you to Hugh Munby for seeing me through yet another big project with encouragement and laughter. To my family— Jen, Deb, Jim, and Sandy—for understanding. And then to my outstanding research assistants, Wanda Beyer, Toni Thornton, and Kate Walker, for their persistence in locating elusive references and their positive perspectives no matter how much work was left to be done. Derek Berg has been a great collaborator in the writing of the Instructor's Manual for this text. For the previous editions, library research was conducted diligently by Nicole Lévesque, Jenny Taylor, Shelley Gauthier-McMahon, Cinde Lock, Lara Smith, Karin Steiner-Bell, Beth Noble, Cheryl Schmid, Jolene Wintermute, and Jenn deLugt. All our library searches were made easier by the excellent work of our reference librarian, Brenda Reed. Many thanks to the professionals at Pearson Education Canada—to Cliff Newman, who started me on this odyssey, and to Christine Cozens, Brian Simons, Patricia Jones, and Peggy Brown, who guided me at every stage of the journey. I am also grateful to Martin Townsend for his expert copy-editing. Special thanks go to the reviewers in the field who provided valuable feedback on this edition:

Carolyn Crippen, University of Manitoba
Sonja Grover, Lakehead University
Jacki Oxley, Queen's University
Wayne Sheldrick, University of Ottawa
Lantana Usman, University of Northern British Columbia

Finally, thank you to thousands of parents, pre-service and in-service teachers, and exceptional students. You have been my teachers. I hope I have learned well and that this book does justice to your fine practice and your high ideals for including exceptional students in Canadian society and in Canadian classrooms.

Nancy L. Hutchinson
Queen's University
Kingston, Ontario, Canada
March 2009

# Introduction

## So You Want to Be a Teacher

> One teacher's perspective: "I wish I had been made more know-ledgeable about and sensitive to the realities of teaching real kids in a real school."
>
> Seymour B. Sarason (*You Are Thinking of Teaching? Opportunities, Problems, Realities*, 1993, p. xii)

A teacher voices a concern that is shared by many educators and administrators in Canadian schools. It can take this form: "I didn't realize there would be so many exceptional students in my classes." Or, "I wanted to teach English litera-ture, not special education." Allow me to begin here the process of talking directly with teachers, using the second person "you"—so *you* want to be a teacher. One of the purposes of this book is to help you become more know-ledgeable about the realities of teaching all the students who show up at school these days. In Canada, early in the twenty-first century, being a classroom teacher means you are certain to have exceptional children or adolescents in your classes, and you may feel like a special education teacher some days—even if you were hired to teach classes in advanced physics. This is because, as a country, we have made a commitment to the inclusion and participation of per-sons with disabilities in Canadian society. This commitment is expressed for-mally through federal and provincial legislation and supported by many court decisions of the past few years. Although you and your teaching colleagues were not consulted directly about inclusion, all Canadian citizens have been repeat-edly consulted and informed indirectly—through elections, public debates, polls, and research.

The polls and research studies suggest that Canadians support inclusion, but individuals who must fulfill these expectations, whether they are employers or teachers, report that they need guidance and support. They repeatedly express that, while they want to treat everyone fairly, they simply don't know enough about disabilities and about the changes that must be made in schools, workplaces, and the rest of society.

My intent in writing this book has been to help you and your fellow educators to access the information you need to be confident and competent when you teach in inclusive classrooms. Recent research shows that when regular classroom teach-ers used differentiated teaching practices within inclusive science classes, the result was increased achievement for typical students, low achievers, and students with learning disabilities (Palincsar et al., 2001). The differentiated teaching practices they used included guided inquiry, group work, monitoring and facilitating student thinking, and recursive opportunities for students to develop and refine investiga-tive processes. Although the students had different amounts of knowledge at the beginning of the unit, all the students made gains. The authors reported that some of the actions they took and that you can take to differentiate instruction include attending to the dynamics of students working effectively with peers; conferencing with students about how they are thinking and why they are making specific decisions; providing a variety of presentation and practice opportunities for students so they have choices; and accepting multiple methods for students to show what they know. A number of studies point to the same conclusion: the teaching approaches used to increase the learning of students with disabilities also increase the learning of students who are low achievers, average achievers, or gifted (e.g., Baker et al., 2002; Montague & Applegate, 2000; King-Sears, 2008).

These teaching approaches represent a paradigm shift from educators' belief that "one size fits all" to ensuring that variety and flexibility for diverse learners, including exceptional learners, are built into instructional design, delivery, and assessment. No one would say that such approaches are without dilemmas or that we have all the research we need to inform our teaching decisions. However, a host of researchers—of whom Anne Marie Palincsar of the University of Michigan, Lesly Wade-Woolley of Queen's University, and Judy Lupart of the University of Alberta are but three—are focused intently on advancing our understanding of the issues associated with these approaches to teaching. You are joining the profession at an exciting time for advances in practice and in research in the field of inclusion.

## The Role of Classroom Teachers

As you can imagine, schools and classroom teachers have a pivotal role in the creation of an inclusive society. First, unlike other institutions, schools are legally responsible for preparing children and adolescents with disabilities to participate meaningfully as educated adults in a democratic society. This means that as teachers we are expected to teach exceptional children and adolescents the same kinds of knowledge and skills that we teach all other students, but in ways that are meaningful to them. We have in recent years adopted policies in every jurisdiction in Canada that reflect our commitment to carrying out this teaching in regular classrooms alongside peers without exceptionalities whenever possible. (This topic is explored fully in Chapter 1.) Second, schools have a legislated responsibility to prepare all children and adolescents to participate in an inclusive society and to accept individuals with disabilities as peers, co-workers, employees, employers, etc. This responsibility follows from one of the primary purposes of public education: preparing citizens to live in the democratic society that we have shaped, with its values, laws, and high expectations for participation. This means that Canadian educators, educational researchers, and policy-makers have to direct their efforts to understanding and reconciling these potentially conflicting responsibilities. As the discussion below suggests, it is impossible to hold dialogues in Canada about inclusive education without acknowledging and matching the extensive efforts of other institutions to include persons with disabilities.

While teachers are central to the Canadian project of inclusion, it is important for you as an individual teacher to remember that you are neither the cause of nor the solution to all of the problems that arise in your classroom. You can come to feel overwhelmed by guilt about your inability to be all things to all people. Crucial to your survival is judicious and frequent use of the resources provided to support classroom teachers and their exceptional students, the focus of much of this book. You also need to think about your advancement as inseparable from the advancement of the collective of educators in your school, your board, and your province. Seeing yourself as part of a collective and learning to collaborate are essential to your effectiveness and to your well-being as an inclusive educator.

# The Place of Inclusion in Canadian Society

In Canada inclusive education is an issue within the context of Canadian society, not just within the context of Canadian schools. In 1982 the Canadian constitution was patriated from Britain. At that time we adopted the *Canadian Charter of Rights and Freedoms*, which has influenced every aspect of our society. The *Charter* guarantees rights for minorities and specifically names persons with disabilities. The *Charter* not only guarantees rights but also specifies responsibilities of the Canadian government, of provincial governments, and of institutions to ensure that these rights are attained and maintained. This means that in Canada inclusion is closely related to equity: inclusion of exceptional persons follows from our commitment to equitable treatment guaranteed in the *Charter*. For example, legislation supplementary to the *Charter* (Bill 62, *Employment Equity Act*, 1986) requires all employers with more than one hundred employees to submit plans for employment equity to the federal government, specifically with regard to women, people with disabilities, visible minorities, and First Nations. At the same time, preschools, universities, community colleges, parks, libraries, shopping facilities, scout troops, and schools are consulting individuals with disabilities, their families, and the groups that speak for them.

## Inclusive Schools

Inclusive schools are a natural part of inclusive society, and equitable treatment of students regardless of (dis)ability is closely related to equitable treatment of students regardless of gender, race, and so on. In Canada, if we choose to teach, we are choosing to teach in inclusive settings.

## Dilemmas in Inclusive Schools

Dilemmas are a constant and pressing feature of teachers' lives (Berlak & Berlak, 1989; Norwich, 2008). Rarely do we get through a day, let alone a week, of inclusive teaching without confronting some kind of a dilemma. Many of these may look, at first analysis, like they are only decisions about teaching methods. However, upon critical examination, they frequently turn out to have implicit ethical dimensions. Do I allow a student's insensitive comment to an exceptional classmate to go unanswered? How much time do I spend preparing modified outcomes and assignments for two students, one who has a physical disability and another who is gifted, when I know I have not spent enough time thinking about the learning outcomes of the core activity? How far can I push my commitment to every student participating in hands-on learning when some can only complete the activities with so much assistance that finishing makes them feel more helpless than empowered? How much modification of assessment is fair, and why is it easier for us and our students to accept these changes for blind students than for students with learning disabilities? The reality is that we live on the horns of complex ethical dilemmas every day of our teaching lives (Brookfield, 1995) and that these dilemmas are only intensified by our commitment in Canada to an inclusive society and inclusive classrooms.

## Action Research: Teachers' Voices on Inclusive Education

Sometimes, there is little classroom research to guide teachers, which is why this Introduction closes with a challenge to teachers to become action researchers and to share their findings. Knowing how students are experiencing learning is fundamental to our doing good work as teachers. Without this knowledge, we may unwittingly exercise our pedagogic skill in ways that confuse or intimidate learners. This insight has been accepted and acted on by a number of educators interested in what they describe as "action research" or "classroom research."

Action research is a way to study your own teaching practice. The intent is to change and improve your practice. Whether you focus on one student or your whole class, the question is, How can I help my students improve the quality of their learning?

The four steps to follow are

1. Identify a concern in your practice.
2. Decide what you will do about this concern.
3. Select the evidence (one or more indicators) that will allow you to make a judgment about what is happening before, during, and after your action research.
4. Think about how you can validate any claims you might make about the success of your action research. Select evidence to show that you have done what you claim to have done.

You can see how action research could be an important vehicle for answering your own questions about what adaptations to your teaching work best for individual exceptional students. Typically, action research is carried out over several weeks or months. Some improvements in teaching practice take longer to accomplish than others and some require more time for you to demonstrate improvement. Teachers usually start with a concern that they can act on, something that is important to them and to their students. Talking about your action research with one or more colleagues (often called "critical friends") is a good idea.

What you do about this concern could be a small change, anything that will be likely to improve the quality of learning for students or even for one individual. Starting small and achieving success is more likely to mean you will continue to use action research to improve your practice. To evaluate whether your actions are making a difference, look for indicators of improvement you can see in what the students do, or in what they learn, or in how they treat one another during discussions in the classroom. If your focus is on the amount an exceptional student participates in class discussions, you could make a check mark each time he or she raises a hand and put a cross over the check mark each time the student speaks. You could ask the child to put a check on a card taped to the student's desk each time he or she speaks in a small group.

In the fourth step, always prepare a written report, even if it is very brief. It should summarize the four steps you have taken. Discuss the report with other teachers and ask for suggestions. Perhaps you and your colleagues will find that you want to support one another in action research as each of you sets out to study your own teaching practice to improve it.

For examples of beginning attempts at action research, you might read some pieces by teacher candidates at Queen's University, published in Featherstone, Munby, and Russell (1997) and in Upitis (2000). The Ontario Action Researcher is published online and contains articles like Terri Lynn Kirkey's "Differentiated Instruction and Enrichment Opportunities" (www.nipissingu.ca/oar/PDFS/V833E.pdf). Kirkey teaches in Hastings and Prince Edward District School Board in Ontario. Highly readable introductions appear in two sources: *You and Your Action Research Project* by Jean McNiff and two colleagues (McNiff, Lomax, & Whitehead, 2004), and *The Reflective Educator's Guide to Classroom Research* (Dana & Yendol-Silva, 2003). These authors remind you that this approach focuses on "I" the researcher changing "my practice" in ways that make a difference to "my students." Many examples help to show the wide range of aspects of professional practice that teachers could choose to improve in action research. Look to the journals and magazines published by provincial teachers' associations and by subject councils (e.g., teachers of mathematics) for examples of teachers' action research. One teacher reported on his experience in improving his practice with his peers to a focus group of the Ontario College of Teachers: "Instead of having some people come in and tell you what to do, it came out that people sitting as a group came to define their own goals." He continued, "I believe that's what changed the way I work" (Grant, 2000, p. 255).

@

**Weblinks**

BRITISH COLUMBIA TEACHER INQUIRER (TEACHER ACTION RESEARCH)
http://bctf.ca/publications/TeacherInquirer.aspx

THE ONTARIO ACTION RESEARCHER: A REFEREED ELECTRONIC JOURNAL
www.nipissingu.ca/oar/index.htm

QUEEN'S UNIVERSITY ACTION RESEARCH HOMEPAGE (MAINTAINED BY DR. TOM RUSSELL)
http://educ.queensu.ca/~ar

MARTIN RYDER'S ACTION RESEARCH PAGE AT THE UNIVERSITY OF COLORADO AT DENVER
http://carbon.cudenver.edu/~mryder/itc/act_res.html

## Further Reading

Hinchey, P. (2008). *Action research primer*. New York: Peter Lang.

Stringer, E.T. (2008) *Action research in education*. Upper Saddle River, NJ: Pearson/Merrill Prentice Hall.

Roberts, D., Bove, C., & van Zee, E. (Eds.). (2007). *Teacher research: Stories of learning and growing*. Arlington, VA: NSTA Press.

McNiff, J., & Whitehead, J. (2006). *Action research for teachers: A practical guide*. London, UK: David Fulton Publishers.

Hannay, L., Wideman, R., & Seller, W. (2008). *Professional learning to reshape teaching*. Toronto: Elementary Teachers' Federation of Ontario.

## Becoming a Teacher

Throughout this book you will hear the voices of exceptional children, their parents, and teachers who are working together to enhance the learning experiences of exceptional students in regular classrooms. I hope that their words will strengthen and inspire you to use all your available resources, including action research, to meet the challenges of inclusive teaching. Finally, I hope this book will help you to become knowledgeable about, and sensitive to, the realities of teaching real kids in a real school.

# Chapter 1
# Educating Exceptional Students: The Canadian Experience

**Gurjit is a bright and articulate girl in grade 3 who was identified as gifted in grade 1.** On the first day of the social studies unit about Canada, Gurjit answered all of Ms. Wang's questions about the provinces. She asked questions the teacher had not thought of, especially about Nunavut, which joined Canada as a separate territory on April 1, 1999. In a bored voice Gurjit asked how long they would have to "do Canada." Gurjit read reference books independently, surfed the internet on her family's computer, and wrote pages while most of her classmates penned a few sentences. Gurjit had already met the unit's outcomes and needed a challenge. The next day, Ms. Wang assigned a province or territory to each group of students. She challenged Gurjit to research the human and physical geography of Nunavut and to work closely with the small group who were focusing on the Northwest Territories. Gurjit found information about Nunavut on the Web, and contributed many ideas to the samll group about life in the Northwest Territories. While the rest of the class prepared booklets about their provinces, Gurjit developed activities for her classmates to complete at a centre on Nunavut, which remained available to the grade 3 class for the next two months.

## Learner Objectives

After you have read this chapter, you will be able to

1. Describe the current state of social inclusion in Canadian society.

2. Describe the current state of inclusive education for exceptional students in Canada.

3. Discuss recent developments in responsive pedagogy across Canada related to universal design for learning (UDL), differentiated instruction (DI), and progress monitoring including response to intervention (RTI).

4. Trace highlights in the development of inclusive education in Canada.

5. Analyze the controversy over inclusive education for exceptional students.

6. Describe briefly various exceptionalities that are identified across Canada.

7. Discuss what it means to differentiate or adapt teaching and classrooms to meet the needs of exceptional learners, and describe the steps of a strategy for adapting teaching to include exceptional learners.

Ben has a learning disability that was identified in grade 9. His grade 9 teachers said he rarely handed in assignments or contributed to class discussions, but when he did speak he had good ideas. Ben was often late for classes and forgot his books. His report card comments included, "Could work harder" and "Ben is disorganized." An assessment showed that Ben's reading comprehension was below grade level. He skipped over words he didn't understand and could not answer interpretive questions. At Ben's request and with the approval of his teachers, Ben transferred from the academic to the applied stream at the beginning of grade 10. The resource teacher, who then began to work with Ben and his teachers, focused on organizational strategies. She showed him how to use an agenda book to keep track of activities, classes, and assignments, and how to break an assignment into parts and set a date for the completion of each part. The resource teacher also taught Ben to use the RAP strategy—**R**ead, **A**sk yourself questions, **P**araphrase—for comprehending one paragraph at a time. She encouraged Ben's teachers to make adaptations, that is, to differentiate their teaching. One teacher used a paired reading strategy, another taught RAP to the entire class, and the chemistry teacher adopted occasional open-book tests. Ben passed all his applied courses in grade 10 but says that the courses were too easy. Now he wants to return to the academic stream.

1. Why are both Gurjit and Ben considered exceptional students?

2. How common do you think it is to teach an exceptional student like Gurjit and Ben in your classroom?

3. What should teachers be expected to do to meet the learning needs of students like Gurjit and Ben?

4. What expectations might Gurjit have after engaging in the enriched experience about Nunavut, while her classmates completed more traditional projects?

5. How do you think Ben's teachers and parents should respond to his request to return to the academic stream?

# Introduction

Gurjit and Ben are two of the more than 600 000 exceptional learners in Canadian schools. As a classroom teacher, you will probably find students like Gurjit and Ben in every class you teach because learning disabilities and giftedness are common exceptionalities. Occasionally you will teach students with less common exceptionalities, perhaps students who are deaf or blind. This book will prepare you to include exceptional students in the life and learning of your classroom. You will find that kids such as Gurjit and Ben are like other students in most ways: first, they are children or adolescents; second, they have exceptionalities.

This chapter introduces you to the context in which we educate exceptional students. The discussion focuses on the current state of inclusion of persons with disabilities and of inclusive education, policies across the country, historical and legal roots, and controversies. We are also concerned with how instructors can best help exceptional students to reach their potential, using what can be described as responsive teaching. The chapter includes brief descriptions of exceptionalities and closes by introducing a strategy for differentiating or adapting teaching to include exceptional learners: ADAPT.

# Exceptional Education in Canada

In Canada **exceptional students** are those pupils who are either gifted or have disabilities. Across the country a number of terms are used interchangeably. Ontario and New Brunswick use *exceptional children*, while Yukon and British Columbia use **students with special needs**. Alberta uses the term *students with special education needs* (Alberta Learning, 2004). Ontario (in the highlights of Regulation 181/98) defines an exceptional student as "a pupil whose behaviour, communication, intellectual, physical or multiple exceptionalities are such that he or she is considered to need placement in a special education program. . . . Students are identified according to the categories and definitions of exceptionalities [which includes gifted students] provided by the Ministry of Education." Some provinces acknowledge that students who are **at risk** due to poverty and other social conditions are more likely to develop special needs. For example, Saskatchewan has developed the School$^{PLUS}$ Initiative, in which schools are mandated to provide "public education in an environment of other human services supports for children and youth" and to promote "learning success and well-being for *every* child and young person" (www.learning.gov.sk.ca/SchoolPLUS).

Exceptional students in Canada are entitled to an adapted or differentiated education program, sometimes called a special education program. **Special education** means "programming and/or services designed to accommodate students within the public school system whose educational needs require interventions different from, or in addition to, those which are needed by most students" (Prince Edward Island Department of Education, Minister's Directive No. MD 2001-08 Special Education). In Nova Scotia, "adaptations are strategies and/or resources to accommodate the learning needs of an individual student" (Nova Scotia Special Education Policy Manual). Many provinces break adaptations into two types: accommodations (changes to *how* a student is taught) and modifications (changes to *what* a student is taught). For example, in Ontario **accommodations** refer to the teaching strategies, supports, and/or services that are required for a student to access the curriculum and demonstrate learning.

**Put into Practice**

Look at the Special Education Policies and Procedures Manual for your province or territory and for your local school district. Many schools also have their own protocols about exceptional students.

**Further Reading**

For teaching about human rights:

Cassidy, W., & Yates, R. (2005). *Once upon a crime: Using stories, simulations, and mock trials to explore justice and citizenship in elementary school.* Calgary: Detselig Enterprises Ltd.

Public Legal Education Association of Saskatchewan. (1997). *Just law: Understanding the law in your life.* Saskatoon: Public Legal Education Association of Saskatchewan. www.plea.org/yas/students/jlshome.htm.

Castle, C. (2002). *For every child: The rights of the child in words and pictures.* New York: Red Fox Books in association with UNICEF.

Kiem, E. (2007). *Protecting the world's children: Impact of the Convention on the Rights of the Child in diverse legal systems.* Cambridge, UK: Cambridge University Press-UNICEF.

Darling, L.F. (2004). Teaching human rights in elementary classrooms: A literary approach. *Canadian Social Studies, 39*(1), accessed at www.quasar.ualberta.ca/css.

**Weblinks**

CANADIAN CHARTER OF RIGHTS AND FREEDOMS
http://laws.justice.gc.ca/en/charter/index.html

Accommodations include alternative formats (e.g., Braille or books on tape), instructional strategies (e.g., use of interpreters, visual cues, cognitive strategy instruction), and changes to assessment (e.g., highlighting the important words in a question being asked in a testing situation). **Modifications** are changes made to the grade-level expectations for a subject or course that meet a student's learning needs. These include changes to outcomes, or what an individual is expected to learn, that draw on outcomes from a different grade level in the curriculum or that increase or decrease the number and complexity of the regular grade-level curriculum expectations. A group of gifted grade 3 students may have modifications that include outcomes from the grade 5 math curriculum. A third type of adaptation, alternative expectations, also appears in the Ontario guidelines (2000a). **Alternative expectations** are related to the development of skills deemed essential to learning in areas not represented in the curriculum policy documents, such as mobility training for blind students and anger management for students with behaviour exceptionalities. You will see examples in upcoming chapters of a grade 5 student learning to use the telephone as part of her language arts program and a secondary school student learning life skills such as making a sandwich.

You will need to become familiar with your provincial and school district documents about exceptional students. To examine Canadian policy on the education of exceptional children, we must look at the policies of all ten provinces and three territories. Since Confederation, each province has had the authority to pass laws about education. However, all laws in Canada must be consistent with the *Constitution Act*, which contains the **Charter of Rights and Freedoms** (Government of Canada, 1982, http://laws.justice.gc.ca/en/charter/index.html). The **equality rights** that apply to education are contained in section 15(1): "Every individual is equal before and under the law and has the right to the equal protection and equal benefit of the law without discrimination and, in particular, without discrimination based on race, national or ethnic origin, colour, religion, sex, age or mental or physical disability."

## Canada: Inclusive Society, Inclusive Schools

Participating in all facets of society, including educational institutions, is a fundamental right of all Canadians. Many developments worldwide contributed to Canada's adoption of the *Charter of Rights and Freedoms* in 1982. For example, all members of the United Nations adopted the Universal Declaration of Human Rights in 1948. Education was one of the fundamental human rights listed in the Declaration; however, there was no mention of people with disabilities. In 1975 the United Nations declared that disabled persons had the same rights as other people (including community living, education, work, voting, etc.) in the Declaration of Rights of Disabled Persons. The *Canadian Human Rights Act* of 1977 stated that no one should be discriminated against for reasons of physical or mental ability. Subsequently, 1981 was proclaimed the International Year of Disabled Persons, causing heightened awareness of disabilities and enhancing the self-advocacy of people with disabilities. That year, the Canadian parliament was debating the terms of the *Charter of Rights and Freedoms*. When people with disabilities were not named in an early draft of the Charter, they protested on Parliament Hill and got their story into the newspaper headlines and *Maclean's* magazine. The result was that when the Charter was passed, Canada became one of the first countries to guarantee rights to people with disabilities in its constitution.

The United Nations continued to champion the rights of persons with disabilities, and in 1993 it adopted the Standard Rules on the Equalization of Opportunities for Persons with Disabilities, targeting eight areas for **equal participation**, including education. "Persons with disabilities are members of society and have the right to remain within their local communities. They should receive the support they need within the ordinary structures of health, education, employment and social services" (United Nations Enable, www.un.org/disabilities).

Then on 13 December 2006 the *Convention on the Rights of Persons with Disabilities* was adopted at the United Nations Headquarters in New York. It was opened for signature on 30 March 2007 and came into force on 3 April 2008, after it had received its twentieth ratification. You

Activists with intellectual disabilities at the People First Conference. In 1981 people who are blind and people with physical disabilities and intellectual disabilities held conferences and rallied on Parliament Hill demanding equality.

can read the text of the Convention at www.un.org/disabilities/default.asp?id=259 and can see that, as of June 2008, it has been translated into seventeen languages. The United Nations *Enable* website describes the Convention as a "paradigm shift" in attitudes and approaches to persons with disabilities because it views them as "subjects" with rights who are capable of claiming those rights and making decisions for their lives based on their free and informed consent as well as being active members of society. The *Enable* website describes this as a movement away from viewing persons with disabilities as "objects" of charity, medical treatment, and social protection. The Convention clarifies how all categories of rights apply to persons with all types of disabilities and identifies areas where adaptations have to be made so persons with disabilities can exercise their rights.

Canada's policy on persons with disabilities emphasizes **inclusion**. In 2006 the Government of Canada released its third comprehensive report on disability in Canada, *Advancing the Inclusion of Persons with Disabilities* (available at www.hrsdc. gc.ca/en/disability_issues/reports/fdr/2006/advancinginclusion.pdf). The information is divided into the major life areas: accessibility and disability supports; health and well-being; skills, learning, and employment; and income. Our roles as teachers are relevant to all of these life areas but most closely aligned with skills and learning indicators. The 2006 Participation and Activity Limitation Survey (PALS) reported by Statistics Canada (2 December 2007, www.statcan.ca/Daily/English/071203/ d071203a.htm) estimated that one in seven Canadians, or 14.3 percent of the population, has a disability. Among children aged 5 to 14, learning disabilities and chronic health conditions were the most common forms of disability, and almost three-quarters of school-aged children with a disability reported having multiple disabilities. The executive summary of the *Advancing Inclusion* report stated: "More than 80 percent of Canadians believe there has been some progress in including people with disabilities in Canadian society over the past decade. Yet only one in ten believes these individuals are fully included today. Canadians feel that people

**What do you think?**

In June 2008 the *Globe and Mail* ran a series of articles on recent efforts to acknowledge and eliminate the stigma associated with mental illness, with considerable focus on depression. As you read this book, search for current newspaper articles on issues related to social inclusion in Canadian society. Discuss with your peers the progress we have made as a country and what we can do in our role as educators to advance inclusion in Canada, so all people are valued participants in our society.

with disabilities should have the opportunity to participate in life to their fullest potential—that this is part of the 'Canadian way' of doing things. Most feel that while the solutions might be expensive, they are necessary and the social benefit is worth it."

However, progress is not as robust as we might like. One only has to pick up a newspaper or magazine (e.g., *Abilities: Canada's Lifestyle Magazine for People with Disabilities*, www.abilities.ca) to see articles and letters to the editor about sites and events that are not yet accessible. According to *Advancing the Inclusion of Persons with Disabilities*, in 2002 employment rates were only 53 percent for people with disabilities compared with 76 percent for people without. Key findings for skills and development include that, of children with disabilities (aged 5 to 14), 95 percent attend school. Most of them go to a regular school. About one in ten working-age adults with disabilities has a university degree, compared with one in five without disabilities. Aboriginal people with disabilities have a lower rate of post-secondary completion than other Canadians with disabilities. Many individuals with disabilities need one or more types of support to participate fully in education. Technical aids and human support are the school supports needed by most students with disabilities. Our aspirations to be inclusive still outstrip our accomplishments. However, schools play a key role in the journey we have embarked on toward inclusion of persons with disabilities in all aspects of Canadian society.

## Where We Are Now: The Current State of Inclusive Education for Exceptional Students

In 1998 a review of the policies and procedures across the country (Friend, Bursuck, & Hutchinson, 1998) showed two dominant themes in the education of exceptional learners: change and inclusion. A current review may suggest that accountability should join inclusive education and evolution as dominant themes, as more provinces focus on standards for special education. At the same time, every jurisdiction is striving for inclusive education, although each employs its own terminology and descriptions.

The increasing focus on Aboriginal education and on appropriate services to meet the educational needs of Aboriginal students is apparent from the report on *Advancing the Inclusion of Persons with Disabilities* (Government of Canada, 2004) and the innovative approach of Saskatchewan's focus on education for a diverse population, the School[PLUS] Initiative (www.learning.gov.sk.ca/SchoolPLUS). And Daphne Crowchief McHugh and two other Aboriginal teachers published *A Handbook for Aboriginal Parents of Children with Special Needs* for the Alberta Department of Education (www.education.gov.ab.ca/k_12/curriculum/AboriginalParentHandbook.pdf). They present the traditional Aboriginal perspective on disabled children—that they are a gift to foster an appreciation of life and are therefore included in all parts of community life. Using the story of a boy named Eagle who is hard of hearing, they take Aboriginal parents through each step of the process in identifying and meeting his needs, clarifying the parents' role at each step. The intent is to enable parents to advocate for their children with disabilities so that they will receive at school the same valued recognition bestowed on them in the traditional Aboriginal perspective.

During the 1990s William Smith of McGill University and his colleagues (e.g., Smith & Foster, 1993; Smith & Lusthaus, 1994) reviewed the platform of rights of exceptional children across Canada—non-discrimination and access—on which other more complex rights are constructed. Non-discrimination and access get exceptional learners inside the schoolhouse door. The changes educators experienced in the first few years of the new century were intended "to move from the goal of access for as many students as possible to success for as many as possible" (Gouvernement du Québec, Ministère de l'Éducation, 2000). Many have argued that success for exceptional students depends on complex rights that include identification of their educational needs and differentiated teaching and services to meet those needs. This is usually accomplished through an **Individual Education Plan (IEP)**, a written plan developed for an exceptional student that describes the adaptations (accommodations and modifications) and services to be provided. These processes are even more complex for Aboriginal students, whether they attend reservation schools, band-controlled schools, or urban schools in Toronto, Regina, or Winnipeg (for examples, see Mattson & Caffrey, 2001; Tsuji, 2000). The Centre of Excellence for Children and Adolescents with Special Needs, led by Julia O'Sullivan of Lakehead University (now at the University of Western Ontario), conducted five years of research on these complex processes in the provision of appropriate inclusive education to Aboriginal students and others with special needs living in rural and northern Canada (e.g., Varga-Toth, 2006).

Inclusive education has been viewed as a specific example of social inclusion and is usually thought of as arising from children's rights (Hanvey, 2003). However, in a series of working papers (www.laidlawfdn.org/cms/page1436.cfm), the Laidlaw Foundation revealed what a challenging concept social inclusion is and identified cornerstones including (a) valued recognition and (b) engagement, as well as (c) proximity, (d) material well-being, and (e) learning and development opportunities. In his working paper for Laidlaw, Michael Bach (2002) of the Canadian Association for Community Living argues that emphasizing only the rights of persons with disabilities entrenches exclusion, while what is needed is for societal institutions to provide valued recognition to those who have been marginalized. While rights are necessary, Bach argues that they are not sufficient to enable the social inclusion of diverse groups, and that we must view social inclusion as solidarity.

It is challenging for us as educators to consider the implications of a solidarity perspective on the policies and procedures that guide our work with exceptional learners. As you think about the expectations our society holds for inclusive education, for students with disabilities and gifted students learning the same content as their typical peers, you may be asking yourself how this can be accomplished effectively. It is clear that more research needs to be conducted in regular classrooms, research that focuses on how to include exceptional students successfully while teaching all the other students. And you will experience dilemmas of practice as you learn your role as an inclusive educator and have to make decisions about how to teach and how to vary aspects of your teaching, such as the pacing.

Three concepts that are receiving increasing attention will help you to ensure "education for all." This phrase serves as the title of a recent report in Ontario that introduces these three concepts to teachers. These concepts are universal design for learning, differentiated instruction, and progress monitoring (with one specific form called responsiveness to intervention).

## What do you think?

Read two of the following Canadian resources and contrast their perspectives on disabilities. Think about why we need a range of perspectives to fully understand the experience of life with a disability and to understand how to ensure valued recognition and social inclusion for individuals with disabilities (one aspect, but not the defining characteristic, of their lives). Talk with your peers about your differing points of view.

Tichkosky, T. (2007). *Reading and writing disability differently*: The textured life of embodiment. Toronto: University of Toronto Press.

Bendall, L. (2007). *Raising a kid with special needs: The complete Canadian guide.* Toronto: Key Porter Books.

Prince, M.J. (2001). *Governing in an integrated fashion: Lessons from the disability domain.* Ottawa: CPRN.

Rioux, M.H., Lindqvist, B., & Carbert, A. (2007). International human rights and intellectual disability. In I. Brown & M. Percy (Eds.), *A comprehensive guide to intellectual and developmental disabilities* (pp. 59–68). Baltimore, MD: Paul H. Brookes Pub.

Universal design for learning (UDL) was inspired by work in architecture on designing buildings, right from the start of the design process, that can be accessed by all people including those with physical disabilities. This eliminates the need for retrofitting when a person with accessibility needs arrives; for example, the building already has ramps and wide doorways to accommodate wheelchairs. As it turns out, wide doorways and ramps are advantageous for many people, not just those with physical disabilities. Following on the architectural model, UDL is an orientation intended to shape teaching to provide all students with access to the curriculum, right from the start of the planning process (Turnbull et al., 2002). Rather than developing a unit and making changes after the fact for exceptional students, English language learners (ELL), or students from diverse cultures, UDL encourages teachers to make a class profile and then plan from the beginning to provide means and pedagogical materials that meet the needs of all students (Ontario Ministry of Education, 2005). UDL methods can be seen as falling into three clusters: (1) demonstration and presentation of new content in various ways, including instructional technology, explicit instruction, and inquiry, which are necessary for all students to learn how to acquire and use new information; (2) engagement, or practice, that takes place in numerous ways, including small groups, co-operative learning, a range of materials and activities, guided practice and independent practice as needed, and feedback and ongoing monitoring; and (3) expression, or ways for students to show what they know, including written work of various lengths, oral presentations, and real-life applications. Choice increases meaningfulness and promotes motivation for learning (King-Sears, 2008).

Differentiated instruction (DI) acknowledges that students differ in interests, learning profile, and level of functioning. While UDL can be seen to operate at the curriculum level, DI helps teachers to make similar student-centred decisions at the student level to address specific skills and difficulties. The principles that guide differentiation include respectful tasks, flexible grouping, and ongoing assessment and adjustment. Usually the aspects that teachers can differentiate are described as content, process, and product (Ontario Ministry of Education, 2005; Tomlinson, 1999). You will learn throughout this book about using strategies like tiered assignments, small-group instruction, learning centres, and varied pacing (King-Sears, 2005, 2007, 2008).

The third concept is continual progress monitoring. Progress monitoring is important for learners of all ages. One specific form of progress monitoring, usually focused on primary students, has received considerable attention recently; it is called responsiveness to intervention (RTI). RTI can be thought of as a way of thinking about how teaching can be operationalized for struggling learners. Children who are struggling after receiving excellent instruction are given a different type of instruction, which is more intense and of longer duration than regular classroom instruction. For example, if some students in a grade 1 class are not learning to read with their peers, they could be taught in a small group of two to five; this often takes place for ten to twenty weeks for forty-five minutes on most days. At the end of this period of special instruction, those who have learned to read return to regular classroom instruction, while those who are still struggling have individualized teaching, more intense than the previous intervention, and perhaps short-term placement in special education (Fuchs & Fuchs, 2007). A Canadian study by Marcia Barnes of the University of Guelph and Lesly Wade-Woolley of Queen's University (2007) suggests that learning disabilities can be decreased by up to 70 percent by a combination of early screening, progress monitoring, and intensive teaching. RTI has emerged quite recently, though many states in the US have already identified it as an appropriate means of identifying learning disabilities. A recent review of provincial documents by Chris Mattatall (2008) of Queen's University found that Ontario, New Brunswick, and Newfoundland and Labrador's documents use more of the language and approach of RTI than the other provinces (Mattatall, June 2008), and a recent review of provincial websites showed that Saskatchewan proposes to adopt RTI. Ontario's *Education for All* (2005) describes UDL, DI, and RTI in a document intended to be read by teachers and administrators.

The next section contains descriptions of policies and procedures for exceptional learners in each province and territory, from west to east.

## The Current State in Each Province and Territory

### BRITISH COLUMBIA (www.bced.gov.bc.ca/specialed)

British Columbia has thorough documents describing policies and IEPs (Special Programs—*Individual Education Planning for Students with Special Needs*) and provides many resource guides (e.g., *Teaching Students with Fetal Alcohol Syndrome*) available at the website www.bced.gov.bc.ca/specialed. The *Policy Document—Special Education* (2006) states: "British Columbia promotes an inclusive education system in which students with special needs are fully participating members of a community of learners. Inclusion describes the principle that all students are entitled to equitable access to learning, achievement and the pursuit of excellence in all aspects of their educational programs." It continues, "The practice of inclusion is not necessarily synonymous with full integration in regular classrooms, and goes beyond placement to include meaningful participation and the promotion of interaction with others."

This document explains that the emphasis on educating students with special needs in neighbourhood school classrooms does not preclude the appropriate use of resource rooms, self-contained classes, community-based training or other specialized settings. The IEP is described as including one or more of the following: learning outcomes that are different from, or in addition to expected learning outcomes set out in the applicable educational program guide; a list of support services; a list of adapted materials, instructional strategies and assessment methods.

### YUKON (www.education.gov.yk.ca/specialprograms)

Yukon's *Handbook for Teachers* (2007–2008) includes a section on Special Programs (pp. 29–31) that states that the role of Special Programs is to support teachers in implementing and developing programs and services for students with special needs. The philosophy is to educate students with special needs in "the least restrictive environment," using program modifications and adaptations as necessary "to accommodate each child's unique needs" (p. 29). Yukon Education, according to the *Handbook,* practises "non-categorical service delivery," and a diagnosis is not required for a student to receive "additional supports." IEPs are written when necessary by classroom teachers, the student's parents, and the school-based team. Learning assistance teachers support classroom teachers in meeting the needs of students with mild academic and behavioural difficulties and in providing additional learning opportunities for gifted learners. The **school-based team**, including the classroom teacher and within-school support staff, coordinates services at the school level.

The team also determines when assistance is required from Special Programs for further consultation or assessment. There are three kinds of shared resource programs to which students with severe needs can be referred: life skills programs (elementary and secondary programs), behavioural intervention programs (secondary students and young offenders), and multi-needs programs (elementary and secondary). Parents can also select home education (p. 32).

## ALBERTA (www.education.gov.ab.ca/k_12/specialneeds)

The policy in Alberta states that regular classrooms in neighbourhood or local schools should be the first placement option considered for special needs students, a decision made through consultation among school staff, the students, and the students' parents or guardians. "The placement of students with special needs in regular school programs is based on a philosophy of equality, sharing, participation, and the worth and dignity of individuals. Most Albertans agree that students with special needs must be full participants in school and society. These students have the right to take part in regular school activities, and when they do so, they have a better chance of developing their full potential" (Alberta Education, 2003). This document, *Educational Placement of Students with Special Needs*, notes that the final decision rests with school boards and that successful placement depends on such factors as adequate teacher training, learning resources, and guidance by administrators. Additionally, the document clarifies that "education program for a student with special needs" means a program based on the results of ongoing assessment and evaluation, and includes an Individualized Program Plan (IPP), a concise plan of action, with specific goals and objectives and recommendations for educational services and interventions, which meet the student's needs, based on diagnostic information. All students with special needs—including those who are gifted and those with severe disabilities, mild disabilities, and health conditions that affect learning—require an IPP. In *Standards for Special Education* (Alberta Education, 2004), "adapted programming" is defined as using the outcomes of the program of studies with adjustments to the instructional process, while "modified programming" has outcomes different from the provincial curriculum.

## NORTHWEST TERRITORIES (www.ece.gov.nt.ca)

The *Ministerial Directive on Inclusive Schooling* (2006) on the website of the Northwest Territories Department of Education, Culture and Employment (www.ece.gov.nt.ca) states that **inclusive schooling** defined by equal access means more than the right of all students to participate in education programs offered in regular instructional settings with their age peers. "It also means the provision of support services as necessitated by the needs of individual students." Inclusive schooling is characterized as collaborative, provided in the home community, building on student strengths, responding to student challenges, and promoting parental involvement. Students follow one of: a regular program (with outcomes for their assigned grade level); a modified education program (with learning outcomes from the NWT curriculum, but not at the student's assigned grade level); or an individual education program (with an IEP showing outcomes "driven by the strengths and challenges of the student" and determined through a collaborative process based on assessment information. Students in regular and modified education programs have accommodations/adaptations documented in a student support plan (SSP). Accountability procedures and the appeal process are described in detail.

Nunavut became a territory on April 1, 1999; what had previously been the eastern two-thirds of the Northwest Territories was recognized as a separate jurisdiction. Given that most of the inhabitants are Inuit, it is not surprising that this territory of 30 000 has developed unique educational policies, just as it has developed a unique system of government that reflects its Inuit culture (see Government of Nunavut, www.gov.nu.ca).

Nunavut has an approach that has been described as "culturally defined inclusive education" (Philpott, 2007, p. 14). Nunavut defines inclusion as "an attitude and a belief . . . a way of life, a way of living and working together, based on the belief that each individual is valued and does belong" (Department of Education, Curriculum and School Service, 2002, p. 10). Inclusion is seen as a support for all students, not just those who could be said to have special needs. The elders have captured this idea in an image, central to their culture, of a drum dance which appears in *Inclusive Education in Nunavut Schools: Student Support Handbook* (2006). The *Handbook* provides another image from Inuit culture for the vision of Tumits, footprints of support, which refers to 75 percent to 80 percent of students having their needs met in the regular classroom, and decreasing percentages needing periodic support described in an Individual Accommodations Plan (20 percent), and more intensive supports (5 to 7 percent) for severe learning disabilities, social/ emotional issues, and/or high needs issues. Student support teachers assist teachers with adapting instruction in each school and one itinerant student support consultant works in each of the three regions. Identification is non-categorical, by level of student need rather than by disability. Separation and streaming by ability or diagnosis are viewed as incompatible with inclusive education and with *Qaujimajatuqangit*, the tradition of Inuit culture embodied in Inuit knowledge, in the consultation process that is the hallmark of decision making, and in the method of passing knowledge from elders to younger generations (Department of Education, Curriculum, and School Service, 2002).

In 2000 Saskatchewan Education (www.sasked.gov.sk.ca) released both the final report of the Special Education Review Committee, *Directions for Diversity*, and the minister of education's response, *Strengthening Supports*. Both documents highlighted the province's commitment to inclusion; for example, the first major recommendation of the review committee was to "adopt, implement, and support the philosophy of inclusive schools" (p. vii), while ensuring "availability of a comprehensive array of support services" (p. vi). Since 2000 Saskatchewan has undergone considerable self-examination and gradual change in its documents, terminology, and approach, as evidenced in the documents available on its website. In 2000 the review committee used the term "students with diverse needs" to refer to students with disabilities and gifted learners. Recognizing that many sources of diversity can place students at risk for school failure, *ACCESS 2005–2006*, a document whose name stands for Assistance, Collaboration, Consultation, Evaluation, and Support Services, described a joint program of the Special Education Unit and the Community Education Unit of the Children's Services and Programs Branch. In 2008 Saskatchewan began a review of the "student services service delivery model," with three guiding directives that reflect current research and the direction in which services across North America are moving: (a) focus on results, not process, (b) embrace a model of prevention and early intervention, and (c) consider children with intensive needs as general education children first. The review documents (Caswell & Hadden, 2008; Saskatchewan Children's Services Branch, 2008) embrace response to intervention and continue to speak of "diversity and intensive supports" together, looking to meet all students' needs through "inclusionary practice, differentiated instruction, parental involvement, assessment, team/collaboration, fostering independence, and assistive technology" (Saskatchewan Children's Services Branch, 2008, p. 4). The personal program plan (PPP) remains for exceptional students.

## MANITOBA (www.edu.gov.mb.ca/ks4/specedu/documents.html)

A document titled *Appropriate Educational Programming: A Handbook for Student Services* was released in Manitoba in 2007. It opens with foundational principles, the first of which is the philosophy of inclusion: "Inclusion is a way of thinking and acting that allows every individual to feel accepted, valued, and safe. An inclusive community consciously evolves to meet the changing needs of its members. Through recognition and support, an inclusive community provides meaningful involvement and equal access to the benefits of citizenship." It continues, "In Manitoba we embrace inclusion. . . ." The *Handbook* lists eleven core values and beliefs, which include, "All students can learn, in different ways and at different rates," and "The Individual Education Plan (IEP) is the basis for decision making for students with exceptional learning needs" (p. 7). This thorough document lists relevant federal and provincial legislation, provincial directives, and regulations, about all aspects of education in Manitoba including the IEP. More specific guidance for preparing and implementing IEPs is available in *Individual Education Planning: A Handbook for Developing and Implementing IEP's, Early to Senior Years* (1998).

In 2003 Manitoba Education and Youth published *Independent Together: Supporting the Multilevel Learning Community* (www.edu.gov.mb.ca/k12/cur/multilevel/index.html) because "many Kindergarten to Grade 8 teachers in Manitoba have two or more grades for two or more years in their classrooms" (p. vii). Differentiated instruction is recommended as an essential strategy for meeting student needs and helping students to become independent learners in this context. The document also focuses on using differentiation to meet the needs of exceptional students as identified in their IEPs while recognizing that on occasion some of their needs may be met in instructional contexts other than the regular classroom (p. 44). A recently released protocol identifies who is responsible for developing and implementing transition plans for students with exceptional learning needs when they require government supports to enter the community, such as vocational rehabilitation or supported living programs (Healthy Child Manitoba, 2008, *Bridging to Adulthood: A Protocol for Transitioning Students with Exceptional Needs from School to Community*).

## ONTARIO (www.edu.gov.on.ca/eng/general/elemsec/speced/speced.html)

Ontario, like many other provinces, has seen massive change in all aspects of education in the years since 2000, including a flurry of resource documents for teaching exceptional children (e.g., *The Individual Education Plan [IEP]: A Resource Guide*, 2004). Children or adolescents who require additional supports beyond those ordinarily received in the school setting and who meet definitions for behaviour or communication disorders or intellectual, physical, or multiple disabilities, or who are gifted may be formally identified as exceptional pupils. The identification is carried out by an **Identification, Placement, and Review Committee (IPRC)**, a committee unique to Ontario. The IPRC is directed by the regulations to consider whether integration of pupils into regular classes with appropriate special education services would meet the students' needs and is consistent with parental preferences. When needs cannot be met in a regular class, a range of placement options is available. IEPs are developed for exceptional students that outline expectations, programs and services, how progress will be reviewed, and—for all exceptional students who are age 14 or older, except gifted students—a transition plan.

Since 2000 Ontario has increased the emphasis on accountability by developing standards for IEPs (Ontario Ministry of Education, 2000a) and for school boards' special education plans (Ontario Ministry of Education, 2000b). In 2004 *The Individual Education Plan (IEP): A Resource Guide* (www.edu.gov.on.ca/eng/general/elemsec/speced/guide/resource/iepresguid.pdf) was developed, containing a thorough description of five phases of the IEP process, from gathering information and setting the direction through developing the IEP, implementing the IEP, and reviewing and updating the IEP. Then in 2005 Ontario released *Education for All*, which focused on differentiating instruction, and using UDL and RTI to informally and quickly identify children who were struggling in their first year of learning to read, and to put tiered interventions into practice before any labels are applied to the children, without the delay and bureaucracy of IEPs and IPRC meetings. This expert panel, chaired by two academics, Lesly Wade-Woolley (of Queen's University) and Marcia Barnes (of University of Guelph), has pushed Ontario into a more innovative, research-based stance toward early identification alongside the traditional approach laid out in the IEP documents for Ontario, which is described in Chapter 2.

Cross-Reference
Chapter 2 describes IEPs, your role in the IEP process, and collaboration with parents.

## QUEBEC (www.meq.gouv.qc.ca/gr-pub/menu-curricu-a.htm#se)

In 2000 Quebec released its policy on special education, *Adapting Our Schools to the Needs of All Students*, which recommends providing services "in the most natural environment for the students," favouring integration into regular classrooms, and offering services as close as possible to students' places of residence (p. 20). "The emphasis [in the new policy] is still on the adaptation of services," and "the obligation to establish an individualized education plan adapted to the needs of each student with special needs is maintained" (p. 11). The policy also emphasizes the prevention of difficulties and immediate and effective intervention, as well as collaboration with partners outside the school system. The goal remains to "move from the goal of access for as many students as possible to success for as many as possible" by adapting educational services, adapting existing educational methods, and offering students options in programs and transition plans that enable their participation in the workplace. The policy document suggests that about 12.4 percent of the total school population have special needs. It describes students with special needs in two major groups: those with handicaps (e.g., motor or sensory impairments or moderate-to-severe intellectual impairment; roughly 1.2 percent) and those with social maladjustments or learning disabilities (about 11.2 percent of the school population).

## NEW BRUNSWICK (www.gnb.ca/0000/anglophone-e.asp)

New Brunswick has a long history of commitment to integration. In 1986 the province introduced legislation that stressed integration of exceptional students and in 1988 released *Working Guidelines on Integration* (NB Department of Education). In

2002 the new *Guidelines and Standards: Educational Planning for Students with Exceptionalities* (NB Department of Education) was published to help ensure a consistent and standardized method for the development and application of Special Education Plans (SEPs). An SEP was described as a plan of services for an exceptional student based on continuous assessment and containing objectives and recommendations for services that meet the student's needs. There was a renewed commitment "to a process of inclusive, quality education. Every effort is made to educate all students through instruction commensurate with their individual needs, in regular classes within neighborhood schools" (2002a, p. 3). And 2004 saw New Brunswick release *Inclusive Education: A Review of Programming and Services in New Brunswick* (NB Department of Education).

The MacKay Report (2007), *Inclusive Education*, was compiled after months of research and consultations with New Brunswickers by Wayne MacKay, a law professor at Dalhousie University who has had a distinguished career as a legal scholar and constitutional and human rights expert. His report included the six themes of (a) the desirability of inclusion, (b) the need for flexibility, (c) the importance of educational teams, (d) the need for diverse and well-trained team members, (e) the lack of agreement on vital terminology, and (f) the importance of challenging all students to reach their potential. He described inclusive education as "an approach not a place" emphasizing accommodating all children in learning so as to maximize their potential and foster their sense of belonging to the school community and to the society. MacKay recommended dropping the term *exceptional* and using a broader term like *students in need of intervention*, of which students with disabilities would be one group. MacKay acknowledged the dilemmas that abound in education, including the legal consideration that equality is context-specific and there is no formula for applying it.

## NOVA SCOTIA (www.ednet.ns.ca/index.php?t=sub_pages&cat=841)

Nova Scotia makes available "fact sheets" on inclusion (www.ednet.ns.ca/pdfdocs/studentsvcs/inclusion.pdf) and enrichment (www.ednet.ns.ca/pdfdocs/studentsvcs/enrichment.pdf) that define each concept, describe the characteristics, and suggest strategies to be used in a school that embraces the concept. Inclusion is described as "an attitude and a value system that promotes the basic right of all students to receive appropriate and quality educational programming and services in the company of their peers." The principles in the *Special Education Policy Manual* (1997), which guided the review of special education and the response of the period 2000 to 2003, include this definition of an inclusive school: "a school where every child is respected as part of the school community, and where each child is encouraged to learn and achieve as much as possible . . . a place where all children could learn and where differences are cherished for the richness they bring" (p. 13). The policy also acknowledges that some students, those with special needs, require Individual Program Plans (IPPs) that contain goals for students to work toward and form the foundation for the evaluation of student outcomes (p. 14). These are students for whom the provincial curriculum outcomes are not applicable or attainable. Each school is expected to establish a program-planning team responsible for ensuring that appropriate programs are provided for students with special needs and are monitored. The role of resource teachers in working with students with special needs and their teachers is outlined in a 2002 resource (*Supporting Student Success:*

*Resource Programming and Services*). In 2006 Nova Scotia released *The Program Planning Process: A Guide for Parents*, which describes the team approach that educators and parents are expected to take and the roles and responsibilities of all members of the team.

## PRINCE EDWARD ISLAND
**(www.gov.pe.ca/educ/index.php3?number=74836&lang=e)**

In 2005 Prince Edward Island Department of Education released two documents that lay out standards and guidelines, one on *Individualized Educational Planning (IEP)* (2005a; www.gov.pe.ca/photos/original/ed_ieplanning.pdf) and one for *Teachers and Support Staff Working Together* (2005b; www.gov.pe.ca/photos/original/ed_tssworktog.pdf). The philosophy of education that each expresses is that "the needs of most students will be met by classroom/subject teachers using regular provincial curriculum" (2005a, p. 1). Then teachers will identify that some students are experiencing learning challenges, and a small number of students will have come to school with a diagnosed condition that means they require special education programming and services. The *Minister's Directive on Special Education*, originally issued in 2001, defines an Individualized Education Plan as "a written record that documents the collaborative process for the development of an individualized plan for a student with special educational needs. . . . The IEP outlines support services and educational program adaptations and/or modifications." Adaptations are accommodations such as changes in format, instructional strategies, and assessment procedures that retain the learning outcomes of the curriculum. If adaptations are not successful and the student continues to experience difficulties, modifications may be deemed appropriate, which change the outcomes of the prescribed curriculum to meet a student's special educational needs. Both documents emphasize that all students are to be educated in inclusive settings. In an inclusive classroom the student should participate at some level in all classroom activities. If the teacher is planning lessons that provide opportunities to incorporate IEP goals, they could call for full participation, partial participation, or parallel participation (2005b).

## NEWFOUNDLAND AND LABRADOR (www.ed.gov.nl.ca/edu/dept/sss.htm)

In Newfoundland and Labrador the departments of Education, Health and Community Services, Justice, and Human Resources, Labour, and Employment have used a coordinated model of services for children and youth with special needs since 1995. It is called the Model for the Coordination of Services to Children and Youth with Special Needs. In 1997 the *Individual Support Services Plan (ISSP) Handbook* was revised. The ISSP is a summary of relevant information about the individual's strengths, needs, and goals, as well as supports and services, identified through collaborative planning. Along with the coordinated model of services, *Pathways to Programming and Graduation* is a framework to guide teachers in tailoring curricula to meet the individual strengths and needs of students. *Pathways* describes five routes through the school curriculum with varying degrees of adaptation of the curriculum as shown in Figure 1.1. A document released in 2002, *Handbook for Profiling the Needs of Children and Youth*, was intended to guide the development of a profile of needs and levels of support required from low through moderate to high. It contains definitions of categories of exceptionality (e.g., gifted, learning disabled) and categories of risk (such as environmental and attendance). In 2007 Newfoundland and Labrador

**Further Reading**

Read three recent educational documents produced in Canada that raise questions about the approach to teaching exceptional learners that has developed here over the past twenty-five years. Discuss your thoughts about the directions for change in inclusive education in Canada.

MacKay, W. (2007). *Inclusive education: A review of programming and services in New Brunswick (Connecting care and challenge: Tapping our human potential)*. Fredericton, NB: NB Department of Education. www.gnb.ca/0000/publications/mackay/mackay-e.asp.

Ontario Ministry of Education. (2005). *Education for All (The report of the expert panel on literacy and numeracy instruction for students with special education needs, kindergarten to grade 6)*. Toronto: Queen's Printer for Ontario.

Philpott, D. (2007). Assessing without labels: Inclusive education in the Canadian context. *Exceptionality Education Canada. 17*(3), 3–34.

## FIGURE 1.1 PATHWAYS TO PROGRAMMING AND GRADUATION IN NEWFOUNDLAND AND LABRADOR

### 1. What is Pathways?

Pathways is a way to describe how we plan educational programs to meet the individual needs of **all** students. We use Pathways to tailor the curriculum so that your child can be successful. When the needs of any student are not met by the provincial curriculum, an Individual Support Services Plan (ISSP) is needed. Pathways is the framework schools use to develop and carry out the educational part of the ISSP.

### 2. What are the Pathways?

**Pathway 1** refers to the provincial curriculum for a course or subject. The majority of students in the province follow Pathway 1 for most subject areas.

**Pathway 2** refers to the provincial curriculum, but the student needs accommodations or support (e.g., different teaching methods, materials, classroom environment, evaluation, or time) to meet the required outcomes for each course/subject.

**Pathway 3** refers to the provincial curriculum being changed to a modified subject/course. The general intent remains the same, but

- some outcomes are changed; and/or
- some outcomes are removed; or
- some outcomes are added.

**Pathway 4** refers to a subject/course that is

- based on the prescribed curriculum, but is changed so that it no longer resembles the prescribed subject/course; or
- is in an area where there is no prescribed course, e.g., organizational skills.

**Pathway 5** refers to a program which is totally different (alternate) from the provincial curriculum; academics are only a small part. The main focus of an alternate curriculum may be daily living skills.

### 3. Can a child be on more than one Pathway?

Yes. For example, a child may need Pathway 3 supports in Mathematics, Pathway 1 in Social Studies, Pathway 2 supports in Language Arts and Physical Education, and Pathway 4 programming in organizational skills.

### 4. Can there be movement between Pathways?

Yes, students can get support in an area of need and if that need changes, they may need programming in a different Pathway.

---

Source: Reprinted with permission of Newfoundland and Labrador Department of Education, from *Pathways to Programming and Graduation: A Brochure for Parents*.

released the controversial ISSP and Pathways Commission Report, called *Focusing on Students*. This report was highly critical of the existing process for identifying and meeting the needs of exceptional students, which requires interdepartmental cooperation even for classroom differentiation of teaching (Level 2). The preface states that the message the Commission received from its hearings with parents and teachers was that "the ISSP and Pathways models resembled a good idea gone awry, a sound concept which has lost its focus" because of excessive "workload and volume of paper" and needs to be streamlined to focus on students, not on paperwork (p. 6).

## Cross-Country Summary

After reviewing the provincial and territorial documents, it is clear that, as Wayne MacKay suggests, our aspirations are moving toward "child-centred schools and school-centred communities" that embrace inclusion for all students, including exceptional students. The means for accomplishing these goals that are beginning to emerge, in recent documents across Canada and in ongoing research, include differentiated instruction and regular progress monitoring—in contexts characterized by diversity, fraught with dilemmas, and taught by regular classroom teachers—complemented by opportunities for more intense instruction in a timely fashion, when needed, in the most effective context. However, educators and researchers are experiencing tension between such nimble, responsive teaching and assessment with their continuous progress monitoring and tiered, preventive interventions beginning as soon as students begin to struggle, on the one hand, and, on the other hand, our traditional, laborious process of school-based team meetings, IEP development, and intensive funding supports based on verified student characteristics (Philpott & Dibbon, 2007). It appears that yet again or still, "Change in exceptional education is everywhere" (Hutchinson, 2007), and yet for many exceptional students and their families, "everything remains the same." Our aspirations are changing and remain beyond our grasp, while the traditional process labours on, and the most recent reviews (MacKay in New Brunswick and the Commission as well as Philpott and Dibbon in Newfoundland) suggest that teachers need better preparation and ongoing support, and schools need more resources and flexibility. The expectations are high, our classrooms and our society are diverse, and inclusion is the driving social value. The dilemmas of legislating differentiation and inclusion alongside identification and labelling require our best problem solving and teamwork informed by research and goodwill. The process in exceptional education, which has always been front-and-centre, now shares the limelight with teaching, prevention, and outcomes for students and their families. As educators in Canada in the early twenty-first century, we embrace these challenges.

## How We Got Here: Recent Highlights in the Development of Inclusive Education in Canada

Over the last few decades inclusive education has evolved rapidly (for a better understanding of this evolution within a broad social context, see Table 1.1). In 1950 there was no obligation for schools to educate students with disabilities. In the 1950s Canadian parents began schools for children with intellectual disabilities (Panitch, 2008; Pletsch, 1997). The Canadian Association for Retarded Children was formed in 1958 and the Learning Disabilities Association of Canada in 1963 (Wong & Hutchinson, 2001). Between 1950 and 1970 parents lobbied hard and many school districts developed segregated programs for exceptional students (Panitch).

By 1970 researchers and parents in North America were beginning to question a special education system that paralleled regular education. In the United States Dunn (1968) published an influential paper asking whether the ends (what was learned) justified the means (separate education for students by category of disability). In 1970 the first of a series of reports—the CELDIC report, *One Million Children* (Roberts & Lazure, 1970)—was released in Canada. Radical for 1970, it recommended integration, the right to free public education, and teaching based on an exceptional child's learning needs rather than on the category of exceptionality. In 1971 the SEECC report, *Standards for Education of Exceptional Children in*

**TABLE 1.1 EVOLUTION TOWARD INCLUSION**

### 1800s: Establishing a Country, Establishing Institutions

| Developments in Canadian Society | Developments in Education |
|---|---|
| 1815–50 The Great Migration brings thousands of new settlers to Upper and Lower Canada | 1830–60 Orphanages open in Halifax, Montreal, Kingston, and Toronto |
| 1850s Railway building joins the colonies together | 1831–86 Schools for blind and deaf children open in Quebec, Ontario, Nova Scotia, and Manitoba |
| 1867 Confederation; education becomes a provincial responsibility | 1893 Children's Aid Societies start in Ontario |

### 1900–50: Change and Growth

| Developments in Canadian Society | Developments in Education |
|---|---|
| 1914–18 First World War, followed by the economic boom of the 1920s and the Great Depression of the 1930s | By the 1920s special education classes are offered in urban elementary schools |
| 1939–45 Second World War increases Canada's international reputation | By 1923 summer courses for teachers of special classes are available |
| 1945 Fifty-one nations first meet to establish the United Nations, which has among its goals the promotion of equality among peoples | 1940s Residential institutions are "home" to many people with disabilities (e.g., Weyburn, SK; Smiths Falls, ON); small groups of parents of children with mental retardation form local associations for mutual support |

### 1950–70: The Impact of the Baby Boom Generation

| Developments in Canadian Society | Developments in Education |
|---|---|
| 1950s Baby boomers and immigrant families cause population increases, cultural diversity, and the construction of suburbs | Formation of the Canadian Association for Retarded Children (1958) and the Canadian Association for Children with Learning Disabilities (1963) |
| Cold War and *Sputnik* lead to huge developments in technology | Parent associations establish schools and developmental centres for the education of retarded children |
| Television brings global events into Canadian homes; youth movement for civil rights and social justice worldwide | Growth of segregated programs for gifted students and students with disabilities |
| 1964 Pearson government funds the Company of Young Canadians to give young activists the opportunity to work toward social change in local programs | Growth of post-secondary education: universities and community colleges |

### 1970s and 1980s: Advocacy and Rights

| Developments in Canadian Society | Developments in Education |
|---|---|
| 1975 United Nations Declaration of the Rights of Disabled Persons | In 1970 *One Million Children* (Roberts & Lazure) advocates the integration of exceptional children and instruction based on individual learning needs; in 1971 *Standards for Education of Exceptional Children in Canada* (Hardy, Minto, Perkins, & Quance) sparks teacher education on exceptional children at Canadian universities |
| 1977 *Canadian Human Rights Act* | 1977 deinstitutionalization became the priority of the Canadian Association for the Mentally Retarded |
| 12 April 1980 Terry Fox begins his Marathon of Hope to promote public awareness of the abilities of persons with disabilities and to raise funds for cancer research | In 1978 Alberta's Supreme Court rules that the Lamont County school board must accommodate the physical and educational needs of Shelley Carrière, a student with cerebral palsy; in 1979 Bill 188 (An Act to Provide for the Rights of Handicapped Persons) was advanced and then withdrawn in Ontario in response to pressure from a coalition of disability groups, who described it as "separate and unequal" |

TABLE 1.1 EVOLUTION TOWARD INCLUSION (continued)

| | |
|---|---|
| 1981 United Nations Year of the Disabled | 1980 Bill 82 in Ontario guarantees the right of all exceptional students to an appropriate education with a new funding model |
| 1981 Demonstrations by Canadians with disabilities on Parliament Hill to demand rights for people with disabilities in the Charter | Early 1980s Provinces develop IEPs; Ontario phases in the IPRC |
| March 21, 1985, Rick Hansen sets out on his "Man in Motion" tour of thirty-four countries to raise money for spinal cord research | Mid-1980s Integration is adopted as the prevailing approach to educating exceptional students |
| 1988 People with mental disabilities receive the right to vote | Late 1980s Educational reviews begin across Canada, including reviews of special education |

**1990s: Inclusion, Reform, and Challenges**

| **Developments in Canadian Society** | **Developments in Education** |
|---|---|
| Cutbacks in government funding to schools, social services, and universities | Parents demand inclusion in regular classroom settings |
| August 1994 First inclusive Commonwealth Games, hosted by Victoria, British Columbia | 10 October 1996, Supreme Court of Canada rules that Emily Eaton receive appropriate education to meet her individual needs in a segregated setting, reversing an earlier decision of a lower court |
| 1997 Release of the Report of the Royal Commission on Aboriginal Peoples | Reviews and changes in exceptional education policies across Canada make inclusion the dominant policy |

**2000–2010: Social Inclusion and Differentiated Classrooms**

| **Developments in Canadian Society** | **Developments in Education** |
|---|---|
| 2002 Release of the Laidlaw Foundation's *Working Papers Series on Social Inclusion* | 2005 Ontario Ministry of Education releases *Education for All*, promoting differentiated instruction |
| 2006 Convention on the Rights of Persons with Disabilities is adopted by the United Nations | 2006 SET-BC, which focuses on technology in classrooms, begins initiative to advance practice in BC based on Universal Design for Learning |
| 2008 Exhibit at the Royal Ontario Museum titled Out from Under: Disability, History, and Things to Remember | Large growth continues in every province in numbers of students identified with autism and Asperger syndrome |
| 2008 Canadian government formally apologizes to Aboriginal peoples for treatment during era of residential schools | Increasing emphasis on curriculum development and on policy frameworks for Aboriginal education, including Manitoba's (2007) *Curriculum Framework of Outcomes for Aboriginal Languages and Culture*, kindergarten to grade 12 |

*Canada*, recommended that universities include courses about exceptional children in teacher education (Hardy, McLeod, Minto, Perkins, & Quance, 1971). Within a few years, such courses were being taught to classroom teachers in many provinces. The National Institute on Mental Retardation in Toronto promoted Wolfensberger's concept of **normalization**—that all persons, regardless of disability, should live and learn in environments as close to normal as possible (Wolfensberger, Nirge, Olshansky, Perske, & Roos, 1972).

During the 1970s a number of influential developments took place in the United States as well. In 1972 the federal courts ordered the Commonwealth of Pennsylvania and the District of Columbia to provide free public education to students with disabilities in the same schools as children without disabilities. In 1975 Congress enacted a federal special education law entitled *Education of All Handicapped Children Act*, better known as Public Law (PL) 94-142. The Act governed how students with disabilities were educated in publicly funded schools. The law required that free appropriate public education be made available to all students with disabilities and required procedural safeguards so that students with disabilities could challenge schools that did not live up to the provisions of the law.

As in the US, cases began to appear in the Canadian courts. Before the end of the decade, in 1978, an Alberta Supreme Court decision ordered the Lamont County school board to widen doors, build a ramp, and educate Shelley Carrière, a student with cerebral palsy, in her community school. In 1980 the *Ontario Education Act* was amended to recognize the rights of students with disabilities to receive an appropriate education at public expense, and to permit parents to appeal the identification of their child as exceptional and the placement of their child.

In 1981, with the imminent possibility of people with disabilities being overlooked in the *Charter of Rights and Freedoms*, people with disabilities and parents of children and adolescents with disabilities advocated vigorously, including protesting on Parliament Hill and taking their case to *Maclean's* magazine (Panitch, 2008). The Charter was passed in 1982 and section 15, which named persons with disabilities as an equity group, came into force in 1985. Since then, several court cases have been heard, mainly disputing a school district's decision to place a student with a severe disability in a segregated special education classroom. In 1991, in a case in Quebec (*Re: David M. and Commission scolaire Saint-Jean-sur-Richelieu*), a 9-year-old boy was found to be the victim of direct and indirect discrimination under the Quebec Charter. The school district was ordered to integrate him into a regular classroom with the necessary adaptations and support (Smith, 1991).

In the 1995 case *Eaton v. Brant County Board of Education*, the Ontario Court of Appeal stated: "unless the parents of a child who has been identified as exceptional by reason of a physical or mental disability consent to the placement of that child in a segregated environment, the school board must provide a placement that is the least exclusionary from the mainstream and still reasonably capable of meeting the child's special needs" (*Eaton v. Brant Board of Education*, 1995, pp. 33–34).

Then in 1996 the Supreme Court of Canada overturned the Ontario Court of Appeal's ruling on this case. While many saw this decision as a major setback for the equity of people with disabilities, Lepofsky (1996, p. 393), in a lengthy analysis, disagreed, noting that the decision was "better seen as a mixed result for disability equality. It contains important principles which will serve disability equity well. However, these principles are followed by some judicial comments which are confused, contradictory and counterproductive." Lepofsky argues that the Supreme Court's approach rested on the foundation that the decision to remove a child from an integrated setting (always the preferred setting) must be governed solely by an individualized, case-specific consideration of what is in the best interests of that child. Such a decision cannot be made simply because of the existence of a disability.

In Canada we have arrived at our commitment to inclusive education through a complex set of circumstances including United Nations proclamations, the repatriation of our constitution during the International Year of the Disabled, protests, innovative legislation and human rights codes, and our idealistic notions of a multicultural, diverse, and equitable society. Canadian heroes and ordinary people with disabilities alike have advocated for themselves and raised public awareness that people with disabilities are "People First." Michael Bach of the Canadian Association for Community Living argued that the provision of rights does not ensure that individual persons will receive the recognition and valuing that ensure social inclusion. He envisions social inclusion as solidarity. "I would argue for a social inclusion agenda that focuses more clearly than it has on [a high] level of recognition—of building a social solidarity that can bring value and recognition across differences of gender, language, communication, culture, age, ability, etc." (2002, p. 10). He urges us to remain committed to doing this while fostering the conditions needed for nurturing and attachment as well as strengthening the protection of rights. When we choose to teach in Canada in the first decade of the twenty-first century, we are choosing to teach in inclusive schools in a society committed to inclusion. Although our reach exceeds our grasp, Canadian classrooms include exceptional learners and we must *embrace* this challenge and *value* all our students.

## FOCUS ON PEOPLE

### Terry Fox

Terry Fox is a Canadian hero. When Canadians were asked to name their heroes in 1999, one of the most frequently chosen individuals was a young man who won Canadians' admiration and raised our awareness of people with disabilities. From Coquitlam, BC, Fox was only 19 years old when he lost his right leg to cancer in 1977. While he was recovering, he dreamed of inspiring others with cancer and raising money to fight the disease.

In April 1980 Fox set out from St. John's, Newfoundland, to run across Canada on a "Marathon of Hope." All summer he ran forty kilometres a day, ignoring the pain, heading for the Pacific Ocean. Newspaper reporters described his run as "lift, hop, lift, hop, lift, hop" because he rocked back and forth between his left leg and his prosthetic right leg. Television cameras reported his daily progress and all of Canada began to watch. Thousands lined the streets as he passed through towns and cities. Money for cancer research poured in. Then in September, after running 5300 kilometres and raising $2 million, Terry Fox stopped running on the north shore of Lake Superior. The cancer had returned; Fox died less than a year later.

Canadians were inspired by Terry Fox and his Marathon of Hope. In the months following the end of his run, they donated $25 million for cancer research. Every fall people all over the world hold marathons in his name to raise funds and, annually, thousands visit the memorial marking the site where he halted his run. Since 1980 athletes with disabilities have become much more prominent in our communities and in the news, but Terry Fox was one of the first and has become a Canadian hero.

Over the past two decades there has been a drive by governments around the world toward inclusion as a model for education. While we have followed one path to inclusive education, other countries have pursued their own routes toward the same goal. Fullwood (1990) provided an Australian perspective on the growing recognition of "social justice and equality 20 years ago," while Forbes (2007) provided a more current view of the challenges to inclusion in Australia. Jenkinson (1997) of England reminded us that inclusion in the community is the important

## What do you think?

For two Canadian accounts of the growth of educational services to students with intellectual disabilities, written about a decade apart, read V.C. Pletsch (1997), *Not Wanted in the Classroom*, London, ON: Althouse Press, and M. Panitch (2008), *Disability, Mothers, and Organization*, New York: Routledge. Why do you think these two personal historical accounts of special education in Canada might be so different?

### Further Reading

Learn more about inclusive education in many parts of the world:

*North America and Europe*— Ferguson, D.L. (2008). International trends in inclusive education: The continuing challenge to teach one and everyone. *European Journal of Special Needs Education, 23*(2), 109–120.

*India*—Kalyanpur, M. (2008). Equality, quality, and quantity: Challenges in inclusive education policy and service provision in India. *International Journal of Inclusive Education, 12*(3), 243–262.

*Australia*—Foreman, P., & Arthur-Kelly, M. (2008). Social justice principles, the law and research, as bases for inclusion. *Australasian Journal of Special Education, 32*(1), 109–124.

*Hong Kong*—Chong Suk Ching, S., Forlin, C., & Lan, A.M. (2007). The influence of inclusive education course on attitude change of pre-service secondary teachers in Hong Kong. *Asia-Pacific Journal of Teacher Education, 35*(2), 161–179.

goal, and recently Dyson and Gallannaugh (2007) provided an update on the impact of national policy on inclusion in that country. In 2006 Lambe and Bones of Northern Ireland described how that country has only recently adopted inclusion, which they attribute to its "complex constitutional history" (p. 512). Kauffman and Hallahan (1995) of the United States wrote a blistering critique of inclusive education, and in 2007 Smith argued that while inclusion may be accepted as the dominant approach in that country, progress in including students with intellectual disabilities has been slow. Gordon Porter (2007) of the New Brunswick Human Rights Commission issued a similar "call to action" to Canadians to make Canadian schools inclusive for all exceptional students, including those with intellectual disabilities, advocating for greater leadership, policy clarity, and resources for more systemic supports.

## "I Don't Agree!" The Controversies over Inclusive Education

Inclusive education is a controversial topic in Canada and in other countries. *Inclusion* is a relatively new term. It has largely replaced **mainstreaming** and **integration**, which were used in the 1970s and 1980s and which referred to moving exceptional students from segregated settings into classrooms in the mainstream. Inclusion, however, suggests that we embrace people with exceptionalities as part of the mainstream of society and all its institutions from birth onward. This is one of the main ways in which inclusion differs from its predecessors. Mainstreaming referred to readying students with disabilities who had been placed in segregated settings for re-entry. They were mainstreamed when they could meet traditional academic expectations with minimal support, or when traditional academic expectations were not relevant. Thus exceptional students were mainstreamed for physical education, health, music, art, assembly, and other parts of the day that were viewed as non-academic. They were often taught academic skills in a separate setting, but research suggested that exceptional students taught in segregated classes did not make more academic progress than exceptional students taught in mainstream settings (e.g., Dunn, 1968). With few exceptions, parents wanted their exceptional children to participate in society, and segregated classes did not provide good models of social participation. If segregated classes did not produce better academic learning, then how could they be justified?

There have always been differing views on inclusion. Interviews with teachers about a decade ago suggested that some who expressed concerns about inclusion wanted to have in the classroom only those students who could keep up with all aspects of the curriculum. Angela Valeo and Gary Bunch (1998) of York University interviewed six experienced elementary school teachers. Modifying curriculum was not a role these teachers saw themselves taking on: "It would be easier if he had someone [other than the classroom teacher] working with him" (p. 13).

In contrast, Paula Stanovich of the University of Toronto reported on a focus group (1999) composed of four classroom teachers, one special education teacher, and one resource teacher, from a grade 7–8 school. The teachers spoke of the benefits of inclusion and of "realities," rather than costs. Benefits included opportunities for students with disabilities to learn appropriate social behaviour and for students without disabilities to develop respect for their exceptional classmates.

"There's a mutual respect now, and they're talking to each other outside of class" (p. 56). The teachers also recognized the motivating effects of inclusion on exceptional students who want to be accepted. They reported that the way they taught had a direct influence on the success of inclusion. For example, they made curriculum adaptations that included using materials of various reading levels; changing the length, time, or complexity of assignments; breaking assignments into smaller parts; and using co-operative groups. They also spoke of supports that would help inclusion, including more time, appropriate teaching materials, assistants in the classroom, and administrative support. These two studies underline some of the controversies about inclusion.

Perhaps these differing perspectives on inclusion can be explained in part by the research of Stanovich and Anne Jordan, the latter also hailing from the University of Toronto. They found that teachers who are effective in inclusive classrooms tend to have principals who believe that all children can and should learn in regular classrooms and that teachers should adapt their modes of instruction rather than expect exceptional children to adapt. In such schools the prevailing norm of the school community supports inclusion. The second important predictor of effective teaching behaviour was teachers' responses to the same questionnaire about beliefs completed by principals. These teachers believed that exceptional children should learn in regular classrooms and teachers should collaborate and do their part to make inclusion work (Stanovich & Jordan, 1998; 2004). Exemplary inclusion teachers focused on helping exceptional learners become independent members of the classroom community and made many adaptations. These adaptations often applied in varying degrees to all students (Jordan & Stanovich, 1998; 2004; McGhie, Underwood, & Jordan, 2007). These studies suggest that when we work in schools that value inclusion, we do a better job of including exceptional students and that our beliefs about these students are closely related to our teaching actions. Thus, as teachers, we must examine our beliefs and assumptions about exceptional learners, because they may explain conflicting views on inclusive education.

Recent studies suggest that regular classroom teachers who are very good at meeting the needs of exceptional students in inclusive classrooms have an important characteristic in common with excellent special education teachers. Stough and Palmer (2003) found that expert special education teachers consistently referred to the needs and strengths of individual students rather than speaking in generalities about the class as a whole. Paterson (2007), who studied junior high school teachers teaching in inclusive classrooms in Australia and Canada, found that they demonstrated a similar knowledge of individual students in addition to their awareness of categorical notions of exceptional learners. First, these teachers believed that it was important to focus on the individuality of all students and to develop a detailed understanding of every student. Second, they acted on these beliefs by demonstrating in-flight thinking about students as individuals while teaching and then by using this thinking to inform appropriate instructional choices to meet individual needs. Again, this research demonstrates the close links among teacher beliefs, knowledge, and inclusive teaching.

## Community and Inclusive Education

There are a number of ways in which community is important to inclusive education. A **community** is a group of people who have shared interests and who mutually pursue the common good. Usually community members share an acceptance of

### What do you think?

There are many journal articles reporting teachers' experiences with and views on teaching a variety of subjects to a range of exceptional learners in many different contexts. Look for a source that deals with a topic that is important to you. Here are two examples to get you started. Read a paper that relates to your experience and share the findings with your peers. Listen to their reports of the papers they have read. What similarities and differences do you see? Scott, L.P., Jellison, J.A., Chappell, E.W., Standridge, A.A. (2007). Talking with music teachers about inclusion: Perceptions, opinions, and experiences. *Journal of Music Therapy*, 44(1), 38–56.
Lohrmann, S., & Boggs, E.M. (2006). Elementary education teachers' beliefs about essential supports needed to successfully include students with intellectual disabilities who engage in challenging behaviors. *Research & Practice for Persons with Severe Disabilities*, 31(2), 157–173.

group standards and a sense of identification with the group (Dewey, 1916; McCaleb, 1995). A community ensures that students are well-known and that they are encouraged by adults who care about them (Strike, 2008). Canadian educators Faye Brownlie and Judith King of British Columbia (2000) demonstrate how schools provide the advantage of a community in that we can move beyond a collection of individuals looking for their rights to a welcoming community that works, learns, and experiences together. As discussed earlier, inclusion involves the acceptance and participation of all, a way of being together rather than a place, and inclusive classrooms ought to be communities. There are many ways that we can act on our belief that community is important. For example, we can conduct classroom meetings, use a sharing chair, teach active listening, provide students with choices, and build mentoring relationships (Obenchain & Abernathy, 2003). Phelps (2003) reports that high school practices that facilitate community, inclusion, and authentic learning include high expectations, teacher commitment to inclusion, intellectually demanding tasks, and making accommodations for assessment.

The principle of inclusion is also directed at the participation of all students in the community beyond the school. One strategy that has been used successfully is looking for naturally occurring events that take place in the community and inviting non-disabled classmates to join students with disabilities in community forays such as purchasing clothing, food for cooking, and restaurant meals. The purchase is always contingent on appropriate tasks, such as identifying the care instructions for a garment or reading a menu (Burcroff, Radogna, & Wright, 2003). Sabatella (2003) describes similar strategies for using community resources to enhance the education of gifted students. Manitoba Education, Citizenship and Youth (2008) has released *Bridging to Adulthood: A Protocol for Transitioning Students with Exceptional Needs from School to Community* (www.edu.gov.mb.ca/k12/docs/policy/transition). And Canada's Community Inclusion Initiative (www.communityinclusion.ca) aims to strengthen community capacities to secure inclusion and citizenship for people with intellectual disabilities and their families. These ideas are developed more fully in Chapters 6, 9, and 10.

## Who Are Exceptional Learners?

**Cross-Reference**
Chapters 3 and 4 provide detailed information about the exceptionalities discussed in this chapter.

Earlier, we defined exceptional learners as both students who are gifted and students with disabilities. There are many definitions of disability. The World Health Organization (WHO) (1980, 1997, 2001; www.who.int/classifications/icf/site/icftemplate.cfm) set out three definitions related to disability that focus on interactions with the environment: impairment, disability, and handicap. Research and Theory Highlights from Educational Psychology explains how the WHO replaced these terms with the neutral terms of body, activities, and participation in the International Classification of Functioning (ICF). While some provinces refer to students with special needs, I have chosen to use *exceptional students* and *exceptionalities*, more neutral terms.

This section contains brief descriptions of exceptionalities. These generic descriptions will not apply to all students with these exceptionalities, and they should be quickly replaced by your description focusing on the most relevant characteristics of an individual learner. Exceptional learners are not their exceptionalities; rather, they are children and adolescents with exceptionalities. That is why we use person-first language (see Table 1.2).

TABLE 1.2  USING PERSON-FIRST LANGUAGE: STUDENTS WITH DISABILITIES

**Terminology Guide Concerning Persons with Disabilities**

| Do not use or say | Do use or say |
| --- | --- |
| The blind; visually impaired | Person who is blind; person with a visual impairment |
| Confined to a wheelchair; wheelchair-bound | Person who uses a wheelchair; wheelchair user |
| Crippled | Person with a disability; person who has a spinal cord injury; etc. |
| The deaf | Person who is deaf (when referring to the entire deaf population and their culture, one can use "the Deaf") |
| The hearing impaired | Person who is hard of hearing |
| Epileptic | Person who has epilepsy |
| Fit | Seizure |
| The handicapped | Person with a disability |
| Insane; mentally diseased | Person with a mental health disability; person who has schizophrenia; person who has depression |
| Mentally retarded | Person with an intellectual disability |
| Normal | Person who is not disabled |
| Physically challenged | Person with a physical disability |

Source: Adapted from Human Resources and Social Development Canada's website, *A Way with Words and Images* (www.hrsdc.gc.ca/en/disability_issues/reports/way_with_words/index.shtml).

# Descriptions of Exceptional Students

### STUDENTS WHO ARE GIFTED OR DEVELOPMENTALLY ADVANCED

Students who are **gifted** show exceptionally high abilities in one or several areas, including specific academic subjects, overall intellect, leadership, creativity, or the arts. Gurjit, described in the opening of this chapter, is gifted; she is eager to learn, sometimes reaches the outcomes for a unit before it has begun, and learns quickly.

### STUDENTS WITH LEARNING DISABILITIES (LD)

Students with **learning disabilities** have dysfunctions in processing information. They may have disabilities in reading (dyslexia), writing, or arithmetic calculations. LD is often defined as a discrepancy between ability and achievement despite average or above-average intelligence, although there is controversy about this means of defining LD. Learning disabilities are not a result of another disabling condition or of socio-economic disadvantage. Ben, described at the beginning of this chapter, has a learning disability with difficulties in reading comprehension and organization.

### STUDENTS WITH ATTENTION DEFICIT HYPERACTIVITY DISORDER (ADHD)

Students with **attention deficit hyperactivity disorder** show a persistent pattern of inattention and impulsiveness that may be accompanied by hyperactivity and that hinders their social, academic, and vocational success. ADHD is usually identified by physicians, and students with this exceptionality may take medications to help them focus their attention and to make them more responsive to interventions.

Weblinks

THE LEARNING DISABILITIES ASSOCIATION OF CANADA (WITH LINKS TO PROVINCIAL ASSOCIATIONS)
www.ldac-taac.ca

ASSOCIATION FOR BRIGHT CHILDREN OF ONTARIO (WITH LINKS TO OTHER PROVINCIAL ASSOCIATIONS OF ABC)
www.abcontario.ca

CHILDREN AND ADULTS WITH ADD (CHADD CANADA, INC.)
www.chaddcanada.org

Cross-Reference
Chapter 3 has information about medications prescribed to students with ADHD. Read about the potential benefits and side effects so you can ask questions about this common practice.

# The World Health Organization's Model of Disability

The World Health Organization (WHO) has attempted to develop a set of terms to be used by researchers, clinicians (especially occupational therapists and physiotherapists), health managers, and persons with disabilities. As an international organization, the WHO has always brought together researchers, clinicians, and health managers from around the world, including Canadians, to debate concepts, terminology, definitions, and classification schemes. Because the WHO models are consensus documents, some describe this as "research by committee." And a frustration frequently expressed by those using the WHO framework is that it is constantly changing.

In 1980 the WHO distributed its original framework of disability—*International Classification of Impairments, Disabilities, and Handicaps* (ICIDH). If we consider the example of an individual who stutters, the individual's **impairment** was the stuttering or disruption in fluent speech production. The **disability** was the difficulty, resulting from the stuttering impairment, that the individual experienced in performing certain tasks. **Handicap** involved the disadvantages experienced by the speaker in fulfilling life goals because of the impairment and resulting disability. This set of distinctions seemed to appeal to researchers, and many used the three terms to distinguish the impairment (loss of or abnormality of body or psychological structure) from its impact on the individual's limitations to functioning (disability) and restrictions on participation (handicap). You can still find references to these three terms in many textbooks and research papers.

However, by 1997 the WHO had moved on to release its second framework, in which *impairment*, *disability*, and *handicap* were replaced by the neutral terms of *body*, *activities*, and *participation* (ICIDH-2, WHO, 1997).

The most recent version is termed the *International Classification of Functioning, Disability and Health*, often referred to as ICF (ICIDH-2, WHO, 2001). Although the overall model remains the same, the new structure combines activities and participation largely because the two concepts were difficult to distinguish in the previous version. This new formulation is perceived to assist with the conceptualization of the functional approach in rehabilitation used by speech therapists and physiotherapists (Worrall, 2002). *Activities* is now defined as "the execution of a task or action by an individual," and *participation* refers to "involvement in a life situation." Two qualifiers, *capacity* and *performance*, measure these dimensions. Contextual factors, both environmental and personal, are also given greater prominence in the latest version.

An extensive coding scheme accompanying the main conceptual framework should clarify the distinction between *activity* and *participation*, but it has not been validated yet.

The figure below shows the relationships among the constructs in the conceptual framework of the ICIDH-2 (WHO, 2001). I suspect that it may take researchers, clinicians, and individuals with disabilities some time to let go of the original terms, which still seem to resonate with our understanding of *disability* and *handicap* in the context of the interaction between a person who functions differently (because of an impairment) and a world designed for others (without that impairment).

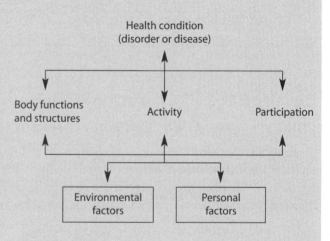

## References

WHO (World Health Organization). (1980). *International classification of impairments, disabilities, and handicaps.* Geneva: WHO.

WHO. (1997). *ICIDH-2: International classification of impairments, activities, and participation—A manual of dimensions of disablement and functioning, beta 1 draft for field trials.* Geneva: WHO.

WHO. (2001). *International classification of functioning, disability, and health: Final draft.* www.who.int/&#8204;icidh

Worrall, L., McCooey, R., Davidson B., Larkins, B., & Hickson, L. The validity of functional assessments of communication and the activity/ participation components of the ICIDH-2: Do they reflect what really happens in life? *Journal of Communication Disorders, 35*, 107–137.

## STUDENTS WITH SPEECH AND LANGUAGE EXCEPTIONALITIES

Students with **speech and language exceptionalities** may have a speech impairment (e.g., lisp or stutter) or an impairment in expressive or receptive language. Students with other disabilities (e.g., autism) may receive services to enhance communication.

## STUDENTS WITH BEHAVIOUR AND EMOTIONAL EXCEPTIONALITIES

Students who show dysfunctional interactions with their environment, including the classroom, home, and community, are described as having **behaviour or emotional exceptionalities**. Some provinces provide examples of characteristic behaviours (e.g., aggressive, extremely withdrawn, depressed, self-destructive, unable to build or maintain relationships with peers and teachers).

**Cross-Reference**
Chapter 9 focuses on promoting social relationships and handling challenging behaviours. It will help you respond to students with behaviour exceptionalities.

## STUDENTS WITH INTELLECTUAL DISABILITIES

Students with **intellectual disabilities** develop cognitive abilities and adaptive behaviours at a much slower rate than do their peers, which results in significant limitations in these areas. Despite these limitations, they can often participate in their communities and neighbourhood schools, and can lead productive adult lives if supported in employment. There are mild and severe levels of intellectual disabilities.

## STUDENTS WITH AN AUTISM SPECTRUM DISORDER (ASD) (AUTISM OR ASPERGER SYNDROME)

The two most common ASDs are autism and Asperger syndrome. Students with **autism** show limited development in communication and social interaction and a severe delay in intellectual, emotional, and behavioural development. Students with **Asperger syndrome** have a severe and sustained impairment in social interaction and develop restricted, repetitive patterns of behaviour, interests, and activities, with no significant delays in language acquisition or cognitive development.

**Further Reading**
For two first-person accounts of life with intellectual disabilities:
Kingsley, J., & Levitz, M. (1994). *Count us in: Growing up with Down syndrome.* New York: Harcourt Brace & Co.
For family members' accounts of life with a child with intellectual disabilities:
Palmer, G. (2005). *Adventures in the mainstream: Coming of age with Down syndrome.* Bethesda, MD: Woodbine House.

## STUDENTS WHO ARE HARD OF HEARING AND STUDENTS WHO ARE DEAF

Students who are **hard of hearing** or **deaf** have partial or complete hearing loss that interferes with the acquisition and maintenance of the auditory skills necessary to develop speech and oral language. They depend on visual sources of information to supplement or replace hearing.

## STUDENTS WITH VISUAL IMPAIRMENTS AND STUDENTS WHO ARE BLIND

Students with **visual impairments** or who are **blind** have partial or complete loss of sight and depend on auditory and tactile sources of information to supplement or replace sight.

**Put into Practice**
Many people who are deaf view themselves as belonging to the Deaf culture and see themselves as different but not disabled. Find resources about Deaf culture and about American Sign Language (ASL), the language of Deaf culture.

## STUDENTS WITH PHYSICAL DISABILITIES

**Physical disabilities** are a range of conditions restricting physical movement or motor abilities as a result of nervous system impairment, musculoskeletal conditions, or chronic medical disorders. I have included descriptions for a number of these because each is slightly different in cause, characteristics, and implications for the classroom.

**Cross-Reference**
Chapter 4 includes information on physical disabilities and chronic health conditions, along with websites about medical aspects and implications for mobility and classroom learning.

Roisin Hartnett, left, was the first blind page to serve in Ontario's legislature.

Weblinks

TOURETTE SYNDROME FOUNDATION OF CANADA
www.tourette.ca

Cross-Reference
Chapters 3 and 4 contain detailed information about all of the exceptionalities introduced in this chapter, focusing on educational implications for you as a classroom teacher.

*Students with Cerebral Palsy.* **Cerebral palsy** is a group of disorders impairing body movement and muscle coordination as a result of an interference in messages between the brain and the body (nervous system impairment).

*Students with Spina Bifida.* **Spina bifida** is a condition developed prenatally that disturbs proper development of the vertebrae or spinal cord and results in varying degrees of damage to the spinal cord and nervous system (nervous system impairment).

*Students with Epilepsy.* **Epilepsy** is a neurological disorder that occasionally produces brief disturbances in normal electrical functions in the brain that lead to sudden, brief seizures. Seizures vary in nature and intensity from person to person. (nervous system impairment).

*Students with Tourette Syndrome.* Students with **Tourette syndrome** have a neurological disorder involving motor tics and uncontrollable vocal sounds or inappropriate words. These are often accompanied by obsessions and hyperactivity (nervous system impairment).

*Students with Traumatic Brain Injury (TBI).* Students with **traumatic brain injury** have sustained damage to their brain tissue as a result of a blow to the head or an accident. Brain injury can cause physical difficulties (such as paralysis) and cognitive problems (including memory loss). The nature of school challenges varies widely, depending on the extent and location of the brain injury (nervous system impairment).

*Students with Fetal Alcohol Syndrome (FAS).* Students with **fetal alcohol syndrome** have physical and physiological abnormalities caused by prenatal exposure to alcohol. Children with FAS have developmental delays and central nervous dysfunction, and show a characteristic pattern of facial features. They experience learning and behavioural challenges in school (nervous system impairment).

*Students with Muscular Dystrophy.* **Muscular dystrophy** is a group of muscle disorders characterized by progressive weakness and wasting away of the voluntary muscles that control body movement (musculoskeletal condition).

*Students with Juvenile Arthritis.* **Juvenile arthritis** is a chronic arthritic condition with continuous inflammation of one or more joints. Students report stiffness and pain, and the eyes can become involved (musculoskeletal condition).

*Students with Diabetes.* Students with **diabetes** have a condition of the pancreas that results in failure to produce a sufficient amount of the hormone insulin required for proper sugar absorption in the body. They may have restrictions on their physical activity at school (health condition).

*Students with Life-Threatening Allergies.* Students with **allergies** have an abnormal reaction to a normal substance (such as peanuts). Those with life-threatening allergies usually carry an EpiPen® to provide an injection and need to be taken to the hospital immediately if they go into anaphylaxis (health condition).

*Students with Asthma.* Students with **asthma** experience obstructed airways that hinder the flow of air into and out of the lungs. An attack—characterized by persistent wheezing, chest tightness, and excess phlegm—can be life threatening and requires that the student be rushed to hospital (health condition).

*Students with Cystic Fibrosis.* **Cystic fibrosis** causes increasingly severe respiratory problems and often involves extreme difficulty in digesting nutrients from food. Students may have to do breathing exercises during school to clear their lungs and passages (health condition).

*Students with HIV or AIDS.* **AIDS** (acquired immune deficiency syndrome) is caused by the virus called **HIV** (human immunodeficiency virus), which attacks the immune system that usually fights infection. When the immune system breaks down, the child loses this protection and can develop serious "opportunistic infections." While treatments can maintain the individual for some time, there is no known cure.

*Students with Cancer or Leukemia.* **Cancer** is characterized by uncontrolled division of cells and the ability of these to spread; **leukemia** is a type of cancer that forms in the bone marrow, causing abnormal white blood cell development. Students may miss periods of school for treatment. Yet they often return to school as soon as possible because school may play a normalizing role in a young life suddenly full of traumatic medical experiences, pain, and fear of the unknown.

# Using the ADAPT Strategy for Adapting Teaching to Include Exceptional Learners

This chapter introduces you to a systematic strategy called **ADAPT**, for adapting or differentiating teaching to include exceptional learners. This strategy is similar to others that serve the same purpose, but it includes considering the perspectives of those influenced by the decision to ADAPT and the consequences for them of the adaptation. This approach is elaborated on throughout the text with many examples, especially in Chapters 3, 4, 7, and 8. This strategy recognizes that both the characteristics of the student (**strengths** *and* **needs**) and the demands of the classroom environment have to be considered when devising adaptations.

The ADAPT strategy for adapting teaching to include exceptional learners has the following five steps:

- Step 1: **A**ccounts of students' strengths and needs
- Step 2: **D**emands of the classroom
- Step 3: **A**daptations
- Step 4: **P**erspectives and consequences
- Step 5: **T**each and assess the match

These five steps constitute a procedure that you can use in both elementary and secondary classrooms with learners who have a variety of exceptionalities.

## Step 1: Accounts of Students' Strengths and Needs

This first step requires that you know each exceptional student well. Start with the student's confidential file—it usually contains the IEP, assessment reports, teachers' anecdotal comments, and relevant medical information. It is your responsibility to be familiar with this file from the first day the student is a member of your class. Your observations will quickly complement the views of others. The IEP includes specific statements of strengths and needs, usually in three general areas: social, emotional, and behavioural; physical; and academic.

Cross-Reference
In Chapter 2 you will find strengths and needs as described in a student's IEP. The IEP will supplement your own observations of a student.

Social, emotional, and behavioural strengths may include carrying on a conversation with peers, turn taking in a group activity, controlling anger, or being highly motivated to improve. You can use a strength such as high motivation to help a student focus on meeting personal goals. Conversely, social, emotional, and behavioural needs could mean that a student requires significant instruction and support because she cries when frustrated by academic tasks or taunts peers.

Physical strengths and weaknesses include motor skills, neurological functioning, and vision. A student may have strong mobility skills in spite of low vision and may be able to move around the school independently; however, her low vision may mean she needs significant instruction or adaptation to read, using a communication aid such as Braille or large print.

Academic strengths and weaknesses include the basic skills of reading, mathematics, etc. They also include strategies for studying and problem solving. Students can demonstrate strengths in completing calculations (with or without a calculator), organizing themselves, and answering questions orally. Student needs can include requiring significant instruction and support to develop beginning reading, comprehend a textbook, or solve word problems in mathematics.

Cross-Reference
Chapter 7 focuses on differentiating teaching and Chapter 8 focuses on adapting assessment.

The IEP is a working document, but it is usually confidential and therefore should not be left where students can access it. Some teachers prepare a brief description of the strengths and needs of each exceptional student and tape it into their agenda. Focus on strengths and needs that are most relevant for your classroom environment and for the way you teach.

## Step 2: Demands of the Classroom

Next, consider the social, emotional, and behavioural demands of your classroom. Do students learn individually or are they working with peers most of the time? A student with attention difficulties may find it hard to focus on and remember the steps in complex assignments without peer support but may also be distracted by learning groups that are never really quiet. How long is the lecture or information-sharing section at the beginning of the class, and is it reasonable to expect a student with behavioural challenges to listen for that amount of time? Do you model positive interactions with and respect for all students?

When you consider physical demands, think about the frequency with which you move the furniture in the classroom. Could changes be dangerous to anyone—especially to a student who is blind or in a wheelchair? Do you rely on an overhead projector, and might some students experience difficulty seeing the projected images from where they sit in the classroom? What are the demands of your physical education classes, and could they endanger a student with asthma?

The academic demands of the classroom are manifested in the instructional materials you use, including textbooks, audiovisual aids, and manipulative devices. Do all of the children in grade 1 have the same basal readers, or do some have readers, others chapter books, and others instruction to learn the sounds in words, followed by reading of highly predictable rhyming books?

The academic demands of the classroom are also shown in your assessment and evaluation methods. Written reports, oral reports, drawings, three-dimensional models, and reports produced on CD-ROM represent different forms of assessment. Do you look for means of assessment that enable exceptional learners to show what they know rather than to show their disabilities?

## Step 3: Adaptations

In this step you compare a student's learning needs to the demands of the classroom and identify potential mismatches and adaptations or ways to differentiate teaching and assessment that will eliminate these mismatches. As we saw earlier, it is almost impossible to develop an account of a student's strengths and needs and to assess the demands of the classroom without thinking about adaptations that would bridge this gulf by taking advantage of the student's strengths. There are a number of ways to make adaptations, as we saw in the examples.

You can ADAPT the fundamental organization and instruction of the classroom. For example, in a secondary history class one group may read speeches made by Canadian politicians during the Second World War and articles that appeared in Canadian newspapers of the same era to study divergent views on conscription. Students who are less competent readers may study political cartoons and view videos of historians discussing the issue of conscription. Both groups could use combinations of visual, oral, and written means to communicate their findings (with the emphasis on written communication varying between 20 and 80 percent).

Bypassing a student's learning need is another way to ADAPT. For example, Chung has not mastered the multiplication tables. In grade 5 his teacher shows the class how to use a calculator efficiently. The teacher reminds Chung to use his calculator and to request a "booster session" if he has forgotten any procedures. Bypassing his weakness in calculations enables Chung to work on the same authentic problems as the rest of the class. A peer editor or computerized spell checker bypasses poor spelling and Braille bypasses lack of vision. Bypass strategies minimize the impact of a disability.

Teaching students basic learning skills is also a way to ADAPT. Chung was taught two basic skills to use a calculator well: how to identify the series of operations required to solve a math problem and how to estimate the answer so he can check that his result is reasonable. Secondary teachers teach basic skills about note taking and test taking. While study skills may be an urgent need for students with LD, there are likely to be others in the class who benefit.

## Step 4: Perspectives and Consequences

Reflect critically on adaptations and consider them from many perspectives. What is your experience of the adaptation? How time consuming is it? Does it change the fundamental nature of the teaching for you? Are you likely to find it satisfying? Your point of view is important because if you are uncomfortable with an adaptation, it is unlikely that you will continue with it. You have limited time and energy, so you want to choose the simplest adaptation that is effective. To get the most return for your effort, choose adaptations whenever you can that are beneficial for many (if not all) students in your class, and choose adaptations that have demonstrated effectiveness. Validated practices are described in textbooks and in professional journals, as well as on websites. For guidelines on evaluating websites, see Figure 1.2 on page 32; for information on pertinent journals, see Figure 1.3 on page 34.

Next, take the perspective of the exceptional student. Is the adaptation age appropriate? Can it be conducted without drawing undue attention to the student? Is the return for effort worthwhile for the student? If you don't consider the student's perspective, you may find yourself putting in great effort, while the student is

Further Reading

For more information on evaluating websites, consult:

Sauers, M.P. (2008). *Reference librarian's guide to mastering internet searching*. London, UK: Facet Publishing.

Adams, T., & Scollard, S. (2005). *Internet effectively: A beginner's guide to the World Wide Web*. Toronto: Pearson Canada.

Barker, J. (2005). *Evaluating Web pages: Techniques to apply and questions to ask*. www.lib.berkeley. edu/TeachingLib/Guides/Internet/ Evaluate.html.

Tillman, H.N. (2003). *Evaluating quality on the net*. www.hopetillman.com/findqual. html.

Kirk, E.E. (1996). *Evaluating information found on the internet*. www.library.jhu.edu/researchhelp/ general/evaluating.

## FIGURE 1.2 QUESTIONS TO ASK WHEN EVALUATING INFORMATION FOUND ON THE INTERNET

**Who is the author?**

- What are the author's credentials on this subject? Does the listed background of this person suggest he or she is qualified to write on this subject? What is the institutional affiliation and address?
- Is the author mentioned in a positive way by a source you trust, or was this document linked to a document you trust?

**Who is the publishing body?**

- Does this entity make sense as the publisher of this information? (Look in the first portion of the URL between *http://* and the first slash [/] after that.)
- If there is a sponsoring organization, is it straightforward about its nature and function? Are there links such as "About us" or "Background" or "Philosophy"?
- Is there a way of verifying the legitimacy of this organization? Is there more than an email address—either a postal address or a phone number?
- Is this organization recognized in the field in which you are studying?
- Has the information undergone peer review or an equivalent process?
- What kind of domain does the page come from? What does the URL tell you? Does it show the website is (a) educational (it names a university or ends in *.edu* in the United States); (b) the product of a government (the URL may include *.gov*); (c) personal (the URL usually includes a name following ~ or may cite users, members, or other people); (d) commercial (the URL ends in *.com*); or (e) posted by an organization, likely nonprofit (the URL ends in *.org*)? Or does the URL end in a country code like *.ca*?

**What is the point of view or bias?**

- Information is rarely neutral. What is the purpose of this internet information?
- Is the intent to sell you something?
- Is the intent to convince you of something, perhaps an extremist point of view?
- What political or religious views might underlie the information provided?
- What links are there to other resources on the topic? Do they represent a range of viewpoints? Do the links work, and are they current?
- Is the information reproduced from another source? Has it been altered, is it complete, and is copyright information provided?

**Are there references to and evidence of knowledge of the discipline?**

- Does the document include a bibliography? What kinds of publications or sites are cited? You should expect documentation to support the claims made in the information.
- Are there links to other pages as sources? Are they to reliable works? Do the links work and are they current?
- Does the author display knowledge of theories, schools of thought, or techniques usually considered appropriate in this discipline?
- If the author's treatment of the subject is controversial, does the author acknowledge this?
- Can the background information that was used be verified?
- Are there indicators of quality information?
- Are there indicators that the information is timely? Does the site contain a copyright date? When was the site last updated?

investing little. Observe and listen to the student to understand his or her point of view, and ADAPT in a way that is respectful of the student.

There are other perspectives to consider. How does the rest of the class view the adaptation? Do they notice; are they concerned, involved, and respectful? Do they feel ignored, or are they bored while you speak slowly to accommodate another student? How do the parents of the exceptional student view your adaptations?

**Do I trust this source?**

- Is it as credible and useful as the print and online sources available through my library?
- Have I stopped to think about the answers to these questions and considered my doubts about this source?
- Could I be the victim of irony, fraud, or falsehood?
- Are my expectations fair; too lenient or too harsh; objective or biased?
- Am I accepting a lower standard than I would in a print source?
- Have I asked hard questions and remained skeptical?

Adapted from sources available on the internet:

Barker, J. (2005). *Evaluating Web pages: Techniques to apply and questions to ask.* www.lib.berkeley.edu/TeachingLib/Guides/Internet/Evaluate.html.

Tillman, H.N. (2003). *Evaluating quality on the net.* www.hopetillman.com/findqual.html.

Kirk, E.E. (1996). Evaluating information found on the internet. www.library.jhu.edu/researchhelp/general/evaluating.

Other parents? Broaden the circle of concern to ask how the community views adapting teaching for exceptional students.

Consider consequences, intended and unintended. What are the consequences for the exceptional student— are participation and learning evident? Are there drawbacks? Pat, who has physical disabilities, may need more time and help to finish seasonal crafts in December. However, too much assistance may make Pat dependent, and the additional time may cause him to fall behind in math. Perhaps completing one craft well is more realistic and rewarding. What are the consequences of the adaptation for others in the class? Do any dilemmas arise? If you provide an open-ended assessment, you may be disappointed when students capable of writing an essay choose to develop a graphic representation of what they learned.

*Activities that enable pairs and small groups to work co-operatively help students to learn cognitive strategies and to improve social skills.*

## Step 5: Teach and Assess the Match

Ask how well the adaptation has matched student strengths and needs to classroom demands. This analysis will help you decide whether to alter the adaptation while it takes place and whether to use the adaptation again. Remember that "things take time"; it is important to persevere and give an adaptation time to be effective. If you have tried everything, you may not have stayed with anything long enough. You can assess the match by observing how engaged the student is, asking how he or she finds the changes, charting the student's marks, analyzing any errors, and talking with the pupil's parents. You will think of many other sources of information to help you decide whether to continue or to rethink an adaptation.

## FIGURE 1.3 READING THE JOURNALS

**Journals about Exceptional Learners**

British Journal of Special Education
Education and Training in Mental Retardation
Exceptional Children
Exceptionality Education Canada
Focus on Autism and Other Developmental Disabilities
Focus on Exceptional Children
Gifted Child Quarterly
Gifted Child Today
International Journal of Disability, Development and Education
Intervention in School and Clinic
Journal of Emotional and Behavioral Disorders
Journal of Learning Disabilities
Journal of Special Education
Learning Disabilities Research and Practice
Learning Disability Quarterly
Remedial and Special Education
Roeper Review
Teaching Exceptional Children

**General Education Journals**

Adolescence
Alberta Journal of Research in Education
Canadian Journal of Education
Canadian Journal of Native Education
Education Canada
Educational Assessment
Educational Leadership
Elementary School Journal
High School Journal
Journal of Reading
McGill Journal of Education
Middle School Journal
Phi Delta Kappan
Psychology in the Schools
Reading Research Quarterly
Reading Teacher
Review of Educational Research
Theory into Practice
Topics in Early Childhood Special Education

## Evaluating Internet Resources

Internet sites are identified throughout this book. I have visited these sites and found them useful; however, websites can change. Site addresses also change, but most Web browsers will automatically forward you to the new link. Each site address was verified shortly before this book went to press; the last date of address verification appears in the reference list. Before beginning to use any new information resource—print, on-line, or Web-based—take a few minutes to examine and evaluate the resource. This is particularly necessary for Web-based resources because they have not undergone the same rigorous process of review by experts in the field as most books and articles. Barker (2005) describes a famous cartoon by Steiner that was published in the *New Yorker* magazine on 5 July 1993. Two dogs are looking at a computer screen, and one says to the other, "On the internet, nobody knows you're a dog." Barker goes on to remind us that there are "some real 'dogs' out there" on the internet amongst all the rich offerings by people exchanging ideas and sharing valuable resources. Figure 1.2 on page 32 contains a brief set of criteria to help you evaluate Web-based resources.

## Reading the Journals to Remain Current

One of the strategies for evaluating internet resources is to return to conventional sources, especially articles in reputable journals, to verify the information. Research journals provide one of the main routes professionals use to remain current in their field. Until internet resources undergo rigorous peer review, they will not take the place of journals. Peer review is the process by which a paper submitted to the editor of a journal is sent to prominent researchers in that field of research, who subject it to a thorough analysis. They consider the research on which it is based, the design and method of the current study, and the analysis and interpretation of the data. Usually reviewers recommend changes that the author must make before the paper is published. Most peer-reviewed journals publish roughly 25 percent of the papers submitted. Figure 1.3 contains a list of peer-reviewed journals about exceptional learners that will help you stay current as a professional educator.

## Summary

Exceptional education refers to the adapted teaching and specialized services that thousands of exceptional students in Canada receive every day. Current practices have developed out of our history, legislation, research, and commitment to an equitable society. The dominant approach currently is inclusive education—with educators currently experiencing expectations that are a hybrid of our focus on IEPs for the past 25 years and recent demands for responsive teaching and assessment that embrace approaches like differentiated instruction and responsiveness to intervention. With these expectations come dilemmas of practice for classroom teachers. Many exceptionalities are recognized across Canada, including students who are gifted and those with learning disabilities, emotional disabilities, or sensory disabilities. As a teacher, you will be expected to differentiate your teaching and adapt your assessment for exceptional learners. The ADAPT strategy will help you meet the needs of exceptional students as you teach, and it will guide you as you learn strategies for the inclusive classroom in the upcoming chapters.

## Key Terms

exceptional students (p. 3)
students with special needs (p. 3)
at risk (p. 3)
special education (p. 3)
accommodations (p. 3)
modifications (p. 4)
alternative expectations (p. 4)
*Charter of Rights and Freedoms* (p. 4)
equality rights (p. 4)
equal participation (p. 5)
inclusion (p. 5)
Individual Education Plan
   (IEP) (p. 7)

universal design for learning
   (UDL) (p. 8)
differentiated instruction (DI) (p. 8)
progress monitoring (p. 8)
school-based team (p. 9)
inclusive schooling (p. 10)
Identification, Placement, and
   Review Committee (IPRC) (p. 13)
normalization (p. 19)
mainstreaming (p. 22)
integration (p. 22)
community (p. 23)
gifted (p. 25)

learning disabilities (p. 25)
attention deficit hyperactivity
   disorder (p. 25)
impairment (p. 26)
disability (p. 26)
handicap (p. 26)
speech and language
   exceptionalities (p. 27)
behaviour or emotional
   exceptionalities (p. 27)
intellectual disabilities (p. 27)
autism (p. 27)
Asperger syndrome (p. 27)

hard of hearing (p. 27)

deaf (p. 27)

visual impairment (p. 27)

blind (p. 27)

physical disabilities (p. 27)

cerebral palsy (p. 28)

spina bifida (p. 28)

epilepsy (p. 28)

Tourette syndrome (p. 28)

traumatic brain injury (p. 28)

fetal alcohol syndrome (p. 28)

muscular dystrophy (p. 28)

juvenile arthritis (p. 28)

diabetes (p. 28)

allergies (p. 28)

asthma (p. 28)

cystic fibrosis (p. 29)

AIDS (p. 29)

HIV (p. 29)

cancer (p. 29)

leukemia (p. 29)

ADAPT (p. 29)

strengths (p. 29)

needs (p. 29)

# Challenges for Reviewing Chapter 1

1. Describe to an acquaintance what social inclusion means in the context of Canadian society and why educators have a particularly important role in relation to this issue.

2. Describe what Canadians mean by inclusive education on the level of policy and on the level of practice, acknowledging that there are differences from province to province and that dilemmas accompany this ambitious approach.

3. Prepare a brochure for the various communities associated with a school with which you are familiar (including families and educators). Your topic is the highlights—as you see them—of the path to inclusive education in Canada.

4. Describe the controversies that have raged over the past 25 years over inclusion in Canadian education, and clarify what schools can do now to be inclusive of all students, not just those with disabilities. Debate with your peers the role of timely, intensive instruction—in contexts other than regular classrooms—in the education of all students, including those with disabilities and those who are gifted. Discuss what you can do as a teacher to ensure that such strategies are not experienced as exclusion by students and their families.

5. Make a list of the various exceptionalities identified across Canada. Then make a personal list of these exceptionalities from the most challenging for you to include to the least challenging. Identify the three that you think are most challenging for you. Given what you know about yourself as a teacher, research these three and develop an approach to teaching that makes you feel more confident about teaching students with these exceptionalities. Compare your list and your strategies with those of your peers. Make a plan for how you can implement this approach in classrooms at the level you teach.

6. Develop an example of using UDL and DI to plan teaching for a class that includes an exceptional learner. Use the ADAPT strategy implicitly or explicitly, and justify the actions it led you to. Compare your ideas with those of your peers. Translate your example into a series of classes that enable this student to succeed. Add more complexity to the classroom by describing groups of students in the class as well as individuals who need differentiated instruction. Then develop a plan for including all these students through the use of UDL and DI. Discuss with your peers how to make the plan feasible for implementation.

# Chapter 2
## The Teacher's Role in an Inclusive Classroom

Joan Hughes telephoned Silver Birch School to make an appointment with her son Andy's grade 2 teacher, Ms. Sauvé. Joan told Ms. Sauvé that Andy's report card—with many ratings of "needs improvement" and "is progressing with close supervision"—seemed poor for a bright young boy who likes to read, gets his friends to take part in plays, and is intensely curious. One comment sounded familiar: "Cannot listen to instructions and complete his work independently. Is easily distracted and has a difficult time organizing his work and his belongings." Joan's older son, who is now in grade 7, had brought home similar report cards and was subsequently identified as having attention deficit disorder. Joan suggested to Ms. Sauvé that Andy be referred to the in-school team. Having an IEP had helped her older son—classroom teachers had adapted teaching and a resource teacher had taught him strategies to focus his attention and complete tasks. Ms. Sauvé was reluctant to make a referral based on a parent's request. As a new teacher, she was not certain if parents could make such referrals, or if teachers had to act on them. Ms. Sauvé kept thinking about the three students who seemed to have more difficulty learning than Andy did. She wondered, "How can I take Andy's case to the in-school team, if I don't take their cases, too?" Ms. Sauvé does not want the principal to think she cannot resolve her own challenges. She is not sure how she would feel about sharing her students with a resource teacher. Ms. Sauvé doesn't know what to do.

**Brenda Piet has a learning disability and an IEP.** It is September and she is hoping to complete grade 11 this year. Her school has instituted Teacher Adviser Groups (TAGs) this fall, and Brenda has asked her teacher adviser, Frank Bogg, to help her make a transition plan. She is worried about what she should do after secondary school. She has always wanted to be an architect, but she has heard recently that the local community college offers a program in architectural technology. She is wondering whether that might be a better option for her. Mr. Bogg has just become a teacher adviser in this new program of TAGs. It is not clear how much he needs to know about all of these career options. He understands that in the future exceptional students will be entitled to a transition plan, but he does not yet know who is responsible for making this plan or for implementing it. There are so many changes taking place in schools, and teachers are expected to take on so many new roles. Mr. Bogg used to feel that he knew what was expected of him. Now he's not so sure.

1. What is a teacher's responsibility when a parent or student asks for a referral to an in-school team, an assessment, or help in developing a transition plan?

2. What steps should Ms. Sauvé and Mr. Bogg take to respond to the requests made of them?

3. Whom should each of these teachers consult to help them decide what to do?

4. As the classroom teacher, what role might Ms. Sauvé expect to play if the in-school team decided to develop an IEP for Andy?

5. What can classroom teachers like Mr. Bogg do to advise students effectively about academic and career planning?

# Introduction

As a classroom teacher, you will know your students well. In an elementary classroom you may be with the same students all day. As a middle or secondary school teacher, you may meet a hundred or more students each day. You will still come to know these students—their interests, their relationships with peers, and their strengths as classroom learners. When you encounter students in difficulty, you may wonder if they should be identified as exceptional students and have IEPs to guide you and other teachers. What is your role in this process? Who do you turn to for advice? How do teachers, parents, and paraeducators work together for the students' good? You are introduced here to the many roles expected of classroom teachers in the implementation of inclusive education. By following a classroom teacher through the steps, this chapter describes the procedure used in most parts of Canada after a teacher recognizes that a student may have exceptional learning needs. The teacher's roles are emphasized in relation to the school-based team that may, after working with a teacher and a student, suggest a fuller assessment. Depending on the assessment findings and the teacher's and the team's success in meeting the student's needs, an IEP could be developed for the student. The teacher also has key responsibilities in informing and supporting the exceptional child's parents, as well as directing the duties of a paraeducator who might be assigned to work with the child, the teacher, or the class.

## The Role of the Classroom Teacher in Identifying Needs of Exceptional Learners

Classroom teachers and parents usually have the most detailed knowledge about the strengths and needs of students with documented or suspected exceptionalities. Many exceptionalities, especially those that occur rarely—low-incidence exceptionalities—are identified early in a child's life. These include developmental disabilities, blindness, deafness, most physical disabilities (e.g., cerebral palsy), and chronic health conditions (e.g., diabetes). Teachers are usually informed about these exceptionalities before the students enrol in their classrooms, read the relevant student files and the IEP, and are responsible for carrying out the recommended adaptations and modifications in the classroom. Observing and listening to these students, talking to previous teachers, listening to parents, and reading about relevant teaching strategies will also help. Classroom teachers are also involved in regular reviews of the IEPs of students with low-incidence exceptionalities.

On the other hand, high-incidence exceptionalities such as learning disabilities, attention deficit disorder, and giftedness are most often identified after students enrol in school. All teachers need to be aware of the characteristics associated with these exceptionalities and of the key teaching strategies. However, secondary teachers frequently find that even students with high-incidence exceptionalities have been identified and have IEPs before they reach grade 9. Usually, the greater challenge for secondary teachers is finding ways to adapt complex curricula and teaching approaches. Thus, while any teacher may be involved in recognizing students' exceptionalities, elementary teachers, especially those working in the primary grades, have a key role in the initial identification of exceptional students. Teachers and parents bring individual students to the attention of other professionals when they suspect that a student needs a school-based intervention beyond

### Weblinks

CULTIVATING ONTARIO'S INCLUSIVE EDUCATION COMMUNITY—SPECIAL NEEDS ONTARIO WINDOW (SNOW)
http://snow.utoronto.ca/index

### Cross-Reference

Chapter 4 contains descriptions of low-incidence exceptionalities and strategies for teaching students who have the various exceptionalities.

## FIGURE 2.1 FIRST STEPS

1. Document the student's characteristics, behaviours, and needs that led to your concern (or to the parent's concern). Also document the student's strengths. Analyze the demands of your classroom. Observe the student in your classroom.
2. Reread the student's file, test results, psychological reports, attendance records, and comments by previous teachers. Consult the protocol for identifying exceptional students.
3. Talk with the resource teacher. Share your observational notes, documentation, and ideas about how to address the student's needs.
4. Ask the resource teacher for suggestions and resources, including community associations. Plan pre-referral interventions. Inform the principal or the student's counsellor. The resource teacher may observe the student in your classroom.
5. Contact the parents to share your concerns and ideas for pre-referral interventions. Listen to the parents. The resource teacher may take part in this meeting. The protocol may recommend that you contact the parents before meeting with the resource teacher.
6. Make pre-referral adaptations or differentiations, keeping brief records of these and the student's responses. Use ADAPT and stay with any adaptation long enough for it to be effective. Reflect on your teaching. Could you be contributing to the student's learning needs? (This step may take from three weeks to three months.)
7. Analyze your records and make recommendations. Focus on the clearest examples of needs and strengths and the most effective adaptations. Look for patterns. Is there a need for further assessment or additional services?

the regular program. You may encounter a student who is reading below grade level and cannot get meaning from a textbook or a student who is restless and cannot focus on classroom tasks. A student's social interactions may be so different from those of the rest of the class that you suspect an emotional or behaviour disability. In the case at the beginning of this chapter, Ms. Sauvé wrote that Andy "cannot listen to instructions and complete his work independently" and that he "is easily distracted and has a difficult time organizing his work and his belongings." She recognized that Andy was not thriving in the classroom, but she was not confident that Andy was experiencing enough difficulty to warrant any action on her part. With experience, she will recognize that the first steps she can take are straightforward and focus on collecting relevant information to help in decision making. These are described in Figure 2.1.

Cross-Reference
For characteristics, identification strategies, and teaching approaches relevant to students with high-incidence exceptionalities, see Chapter 3.

## Making Classroom Adaptations and Keeping Records

Ms. Sauvé described to the teacher assigned as her mentor the meeting she had with Joan Hughes. (Ms. Sauvé's school had a formal mentoring program, but your school may simply encourage you to find a "soulmate" on staff who is willing to talk and help.) Her mentor gave Ms. Sauvé a copy of the school's protocol, which is much like the list in Figure 2.1. Ms. Sauvé began recording the circumstances under which Andy did and did not follow instructions and complete assigned work. She noted when he seemed most distracted. By collecting samples of his work, she came to understand his organizational needs better. Ms. Sauvé also recorded what Andy did well and the times when he did not experience attention difficulties. Three weeks later, Ms. Sauvé showed the resource teacher her notes, which confirmed that most of Andy's inattentive behaviours and inability to follow instructions occurred at three times: during mathematics lessons, late in the day, and when other children were off task. She learned how to cue Andy during oral instructions, especially in mathematics, and how to help him monitor his own behaviour. The resource teacher gave Ms. Sauvé two books to read and observed Andy twice in the classroom. Armed with her own observations and the suggestions of the resource teacher, Ms. Sauvé telephoned Joan Hughes to report what she would be doing to adapt or differentiate the classroom for Andy. They agreed to meet in six weeks.

In many jurisdictions mentoring has been used to link beginning teachers with experienced teachers formally. Joan Richardson (2005) has described the professional learning community that enhances mentoring relationships between experienced and beginning teachers in the Northern Lights School Division in Alberta. Neil Scott (2001) reported on a six-year study of formal mentoring conducted in New Brunswick. Like Ms. Sauvé, many early-career teachers in Canada benefit from formal (or informal) mentoring or induction programs. For example, Ontario has developed the New Teacher Induction Program (NTIP; www.edu.gov.on.ca/eng/teacher/induction.html) and Prince Edward Island the Beginning Teachers Induction Program (www.gov.pe.ca/photos/original/ed_teacherhandb.pdf). If your first school does not have a formal mentoring or induction program, you may want to suggest such a program to your principal or to seek your principal's advice in choosing an informal mentor. If you are an experienced teacher, you may want to volunteer to fill such a role for a new colleague; research suggests that induction programs benefit mentors (e.g., Conway, 2006) as well as enhancing the confidence of beginning teachers (Turley, Powers, & Nakai, 2006).

## Using the ADAPT Strategy

Ms. Sauvé was making **pre-referral interventions** to meet Andy's needs. Consider how the ADAPT strategy discussed in Chapter 1 might help if you were in Ms. Sauvé's place. First, it suggests you begin by providing an **A**ccount of the student's strengths and needs. Andy has many strengths, both social and academic: He likes to read (academic), he has friends in the class (social), he likes to get his friends to take part in plays (social), and he shows an intense curiosity about the world (academic). Andy also needs help focusing so that he can listen to instructions (academic), and he needs to learn to concentrate on his assigned work and complete it more independently (academic). He is easily distracted and needs to learn to ignore other children when they are off task (social). He also needs strategies for organizing his work and belongings (academic). Developing this account of strengths and needs will involve some informal assessment of the student's current knowledge and learning approaches.

Second, the ADAPT strategy suggests that you next describe the **D**emands of your classroom. Ms. Sauvé read the questionnaire (shown in Figure 2.2) given to her by the resource teacher. Afterward, she wrote the following list:

- Most math classes start with a fifteen-minute "lecture" that introduces a new concept or activity. Andy interrupts by talking or I have to interrupt to ask him to sit still.

**Further Reading**

If you wish to know more about mentoring and teacher induction:

Ontario Ministry of Education. (2006). *Partnering for success: A resource handbook for new teachers.* Toronto: Ontario Ministry of Education.

Prince Edward Island Department of Education. (2007). *Beginning teachers induction program handbook.* Charlottetown: PEI Ministry of Education.

Portner, H. (Ed.). (2005). *Teacher mentoring and induction: The state of the art and beyond.* Thousand Oaks, CA: Corwin Press.

Hicks, C., Glosgow, N.A., & McNary, S.J. (2005). *What successful mentors do: 81 research-based strategies for new teacher induction, training and support.* Thousand Oaks, CA: Corwin Press.

*Informal assessment includes asking a child to think aloud while solving a problem.*

## FIGURE 2.2 ASSESSING THE DEMANDS OF YOUR CLASSROOM

Teacher _____  Classroom/Course _____

Student _____

1. For what percentage of class time do students typically listen to lectures or instructions?
2. How many pages of in-class reading do you assign to be done in a typical class?
3. How many pages of out-of-class reading do you assign to be done in a typical evening?
4. List typical classroom activities (e.g., lectures, demonstrations, labs, co-operative learning, independent work, discussion, pairs, videos, etc.).
5. How many hours of homework do you typically assign in a week?
6. Describe the typical assignment and the number of days from assignment given to assignment due.
7. Do you assign projects or long-term assignments? (If so, how much structure or guidance is given?)
8. Do you give a final test at the end of each unit?
9. How are grades assigned?
10. What are your expectations for student behaviour in class?

After answering these questions, star up to three items where you perceive a mismatch between the strengths of the named student and the demands of your classroom or course.

Source: N.L. Hutchinson, *Teaching exceptional children and adolescents: A Canadian case-book*, p. 142. Copyright © 2004 by Prentice Hall. Reprinted by permission.

### What do you think?

Ms. Sauvé knows that Chen can help Andy by reviewing the teacher's instructions with him to ensure that he understands. What are the advantages and disadvantages of this strategy for each boy?

### Put into Practice

Interview a resource teacher from the panel in which you teach (elementary or secondary) about the pre-referral interventions that the teachers on that panel might make if they were in Ms. Sauvé's position.

- I expect students to work in groups, and sometimes the noise is distracting. I often have to ask Andy to move to the quiet table at the back of the room because he "clowns around" when in a group.

- I am growing to dread the last half-hour of the day. During this "catch-up time" I want the children to finish anything not completed and ask about anything they haven't understood. Andy wanders around the classroom and talks to his friends rather than catching up.

The third step in ADAPT is making **A**daptations that help to eliminate the kinds of mismatches seen in Ms. Sauvé's list. After talking with the resource teacher, Ms. Sauvé reduced the introduction to new math concepts and activities from fifteen to ten minutes. The resource teacher hinted that fifteen minutes was perhaps too long for grade 2 students. Ms. Sauvé also told Andy to check with his friend Chen to be sure that he understood what to do after she had given instructions. She also arranged a cue with Andy. When she snapped her fingers, it was a reminder to him to "sit up straight and listen." During group work, Andy had to "work hard" or move himself to the quiet table before Ms. Sauvé asked him to move. Andy was told to consult with Ms. Sauvé at the beginning of catch-up time. She recommended that he sit with a friend who would refuse to chat with him while he was catching up.

Every day, Ms. Sauvé jotted informal observations about Andy on yellow sticky notes. At the end of the day, she copied all of these observations onto one page. Usually she made about five short comments or observations. Below is her summary for one day:

- Had to snap my fingers three times in a ten-minute period while introducing the math activity Halloween Sets. Andy did not understand the activity until I explained it to him one on one.

- Andy moved to the quiet table by himself during math. He stayed quiet for roughly five minutes. Then he argued with the next child who came to the quiet table. Andy completed only half the examples, although he could do the questions. Quiet table only works when Andy is there alone.

- Andy fidgeted through the Halloween story. He didn't remember any characters except the witch. He had great ideas for a play after Chen told him what had happened in the story.
- Andy spent catch-up time discussing the play with two children. No catching up was done.

The fourth step in ADAPT is to consider **P**erspectives and consequences. The fifth step is to **T**each and assess the match. If you were in Ms. Sauvé's place, what would your view be of the pre-referral adaptations already made for Andy and how successful they had been? Ms. Sauvé felt that she had made a considerable effort to change her math teaching for all students. The changes were an improvement, but Andy needed even more effective strategies for staying focused. Andy told her he was trying to work hard, but that he didn't know how. She believed him. Ms. Sauvé was concerned that the consequences of pushing Andy to work harder would be frustration and self-criticism.

By the next parent–teacher meeting, Ms. Sauvé had come to agree with Joan Hughes and the resource teacher that further assessment and services might be a good idea. Although he had tried to follow Ms. Sauvé's cues and to monitor his own attention, Andy continued to distract himself and others. This occurred mainly during mathematics and following a disruption. Andy needed more consistent and intensive intervention to learn **self-monitoring** strategies (to monitor his own behaviour, especially his focus) than Ms. Sauvé could provide within her grade 2 classroom of thirty-one children. Joan Hughes agreed. Ms. Sauvé told the resource teacher and the principal about her observations, documentation, parent meeting, and recommendations. Together, they decided it was time for more collaboration—time for a meeting of the school-based team.

Self-monitoring is a specific instance of **self-regulation**, a key concept in educational psychology. To learn more about self-regulation, see the box entitled Theory and Research Highlights from Educational Psychology: Self-Regulated Learning.

## THEORY AND RESEARCH HIGHLIGHTS FROM

## EDUCATIONAL PSYCHOLOGY

## Self-Regulated Learning

The overall goal of education—for exceptional learners and for their classmates without exceptionalities—is to help children and adolescents become self-regulated learners. Our conceptual and empirical understanding of self-regulation has been advanced by the work of many researchers, including Phil Winne of Simon Fraser University and Nancy Perry of the University of British Columbia (e.g., Winne, 2005; Winne & Perry, 2000). Self-regulated learners have a combination of academic learning skills and self-control that makes learning easier. That is, they have the *skill* and the *will* to learn. Their *skill* or knowledge about learning includes knowing about themselves, so they recognize which subjects they prefer and which tasks they do best, the strategies upon which they can rely, and the contexts in which those strategies apply. They are knowledgeable about the subjects they are learning and about how they can use what they know to learn more. They recognize when a task requires them to rehearse in order to remember straightforward facts and when a task requires them to make a concept map and concentrate on the relationships among complex ideas (Schunk & Zimmerman, 2007). They understand that academic learning is challenging and effortful, and over time they

*continued*

come to use their repertoire of strategies automatically. Their *will to learn*, or motivation, is reflected in their initiative, independence, commitment, and effort. Usually they are able to sustain learning, no matter what distractions or setbacks they encounter. When they complete tasks successfully, they recognize their accomplishments, and this increases their sense of self-efficacy for similar tasks in the future (Klassen, 2007).

Self-regulated learners "proactively direct their behavior or strategies to achieve self-set goals" (Cleary & Zimmerman, 2004, p. 538). Self-regulated learning emphasizes autonomy and control by the individual who "monitors, directs, and regulates actions toward goals of information acquisition, expanding expertise, and self-improvement." Measurement of self-regulated learning has been addressed through quantitative means using surveys, interview schedules, and inventories. Two instruments frequently used to measure self-regulated learning are the Learning and Strategies Study Inventory (LASSI; Weinstein, Schulte, & Palmer, 1987) and the Motivated Strategies for Learning Questionnaire (MSLQ; Pintrich, Smith, Garcia, & McKeachie, 1991). These methodologies have produced correlations showing a strong relationship between self-regulated learning and academic achievement, and have conceptualized self-regulated learning as an aptitude (Winne & Perry, 2000). In contrast, the measurement of self-regulated learning as an event involves recording a change in the behaviours indicative of self-regulated learning. Recently, qualitative methods have been used to expand our understanding of self-regulated learning as an event (Perry, Phillips, & Dowler, 2004; Perry, VandeKamp, Mercer, & Nordby, 2002). These studies have generated rich descriptive data by observing individuals as they engage in self-regulated learning.

Recent research suggests that gifted students demonstrate high self-regulation (Ee, Moore, & Atputhasamy, 2003). On the other hand, many children and adolescents with disabilities need our help to become more self-regulated learners. For example, Robert Klassen (2007) of the University of Alberta reported that children with learning disabilities demonstrated less self-regulation than children without learning disabilities. Deborah Butler of the University of British Columbia has described the characteristics of older students with learning disabilities and ways that teaching can be structured to promote their self-regulated learning (e.g., Butler, 2003). There is also research on the self-regulation of children with language-learning disorders (Bashir & Singer, 2006), intellectual disabilities (e.g., Eisenhower, Baker, & Blacher, 2007), and ADHD (Reid, Trout, & Schartz, 2005).

Throughout this book you will find examples of instructional approaches for teaching self-regulation of attention, learning behaviours, and strategies for learning to write, solve problems, and learn classroom content. Self-regulation involves complex interactions among cognition, metacognition, and motivation. Research in educational psychology and special education is beginning to demonstrate the significance of self-regulation for understanding and enhancing the learning of exceptional students.

## References

Bashir, A.S., & Singer, B.D. (2006). Assisting students in becoming self-regulated writers. In T.A. Ukrainetz (Ed.), *Contextualized language intervention: Scaffolding preK–12 literacy achievement* (pp. 565–598). Greenville, SC: Thinking Publications University.

Butler, D.L. (2003). Structuring instruction to promote self-regulated learning by adolescents and adults with learning disabilities. *Exceptionality, 11*(1), 39–60.

Cleary, T.J., & Zimmerman, B.J. (2004). Self-regulation empowerment program: A school-based program to enhance self-regulated and self-motivated cycles of student learning. *Psychology in the Schools, 41*, 537–550.

Ee, J., Moore, P.J., & Atputhasamy, L. (2003). High-achieving students: Their motivational goals, self-regulation, and achievement and relationships to their teachers' goals and strategy-based instruction. *High Ability Studies, 14*(1), 23–39.

Eisenhower, A.S., Baker, B.L., & Blacher, J. (2007). Early student–teacher relationships of children with and without intellectual disability: Contributions of behavioral, social, and self-regulatory competence. *Journal of School Psychology, 45*, 363–383.

Klassen, R.M. (2007). Using predictions to learn about the self-efficacy of early adolescents with and without learning disabilities. *Contemporary Educational Psychology, 32*, 173–187.

Perry, N.E., Phillips, L., & Dowler, J. (2004). Examining features of tasks and their potential to promote self-regulated learning. *Teachers College Record, 106*, 1854–1878.

Perry, N.E., VandeKamp, K.O., Mercer, L.K., & Nordby, C.J. (2002). Investigating teacher–student interactions that foster self-regulated learning. *Educational Psychologist, 37*, 5–15.

Pintrich, P.R., Smith, D.A.F., Garcia, T., & McKeachie, W.J. (1991). *A manual for the use of the Motivated Strategies for Learning Questionnaire (MSLQ).* (Tech. Rep. No. 91-B-004). Ann Arbor: University of Michigan, School of Education.

Reid, R., Trout, A.L., & Schartz, M. (2005). Self-regulation interventions for children with attention deficit/hyperactivity disorder. *Exceptional Children, 71*, 361–377.

Schunk, D.H., & Zimmerman, B.J. (2007). Influencing children's self-efficacy and self-regulation of reading and writing through modeling. *Reading and Writing Quarterly, 23*, 7–25.

Weinstein, C.E., Schulte, A., & Palmer, D. (1987). *LASSI: Learning and Study Strategies Inventory.* Clearwater, FL: H&H Publishing.

Winne, P.H. (2005). A perspective on state-of-the-art research on self-regulated learning. *Instructional Science, 33*, 559–565.

Winne, P.H., & Perry, N.E. (2000). Measuring self-regulated learning. In M. Boekaerts, P.R. Pintrich, & M. Zeidner (Eds.), *Handbook of self-regulation* (pp. 531–566). San Diego, CA: Academic Press.

# Collaboration: Working with the Resource Teacher and Other Professionals

We saw in Chapter 1 that any school's success in meeting the needs of exceptional students in inclusive classrooms depends on the beliefs and actions of its teachers and administrators (Jordan & Stanovich, 2004). Another critical factor is collaboration. According to Anne Jordan of the University of Toronto and Paula Stanovich of Portland State University, **collaboration** entails teachers and other professionals learning from each other's experiences and working in teams where all members feel that their contributions are valued. Alberta Learning describes collaboration as joint planning, decision making, and problem solving directed toward a common goal (Tungland, 2002). As a classroom teacher, you are central to collaboration—you are the expert on the curriculum, organization, and management of your classroom (Stanovich & Jordan, 2004). However, you do not have to be an expert on every aspect of the exceptional student's needs. Collaboration provides you with a support network and enables you to draw on the expertise and resources of many individuals. You will work closely with fellow educators, including resource teachers, special educators, guidance counsellors, district consultants, and your principal. Other professionals you could find yourself collaborating with include speech therapists, occupational therapists, social workers, and psychologists. The introduction of inter-school electronic networks enables teachers in rural schools to collaborate with colleagues in other communities (Parr & Ward, 2006). Stevens (2006) describes the advantages of inter-school collaboration for isolated schools in Newfoundland. Paraeducators and parents also play important roles in collaboration.

Creating collaborative relationships requires effort on the part of everyone. First, you need team members who hold positive beliefs about inclusion and about working together. Anne Beveridge of Queen's University (see Hutchinson, Freeman & Steiner Bell, 2002) described the beliefs and practices of four elementary teachers who were recognized as outstanding in their inclusion of exceptional learners. All valued and demonstrated excellent collaboration and communication with colleagues, parents, and administrators. Similar findings have emerged about the beliefs and collaborative practices of secondary school teachers who are acknowledged as leaders in inclusive education. Karol Lyn Edwards (see Hutchinson et al., 2002) of Queen's University interviewed secondary school science teachers known for their effective inclusion of students with learning disabilities. These teachers expressed positive beliefs about inclusion and adapted teaching to meet individual needs. Collaboration has also been found to be beneficial for gifted students and the teachers who provide enriched programming for them (Purcell & Leppien, 2004; Kane & Henning, 2004).

Michelle Levac (2004), a resource teacher in Ontario, reported on her interviews with three dyads made up of experienced classroom teachers and resource teachers who demonstrated best practices in their collaborations. Their descriptions of how they worked together focused on building and maintaining strong relationships, growing and developing professionally, and maintaining regular contact. They also reported that the biggest challenge to collaboration was "finding the time." Jennifer Ramsay (2007), a classroom teacher, described, in her master's thesis, the collaboration between a classroom teacher and a paraeducator who each recognized the other's contribution, made time each day to work together, and attributed some of the credit for their successful collaboration to the resource

**Cross-Reference**
Chapter 7 focuses on adapting teaching and Chapter 9 describes best practices for enhancing social relations, including collaborative learning and peer tutoring.

**Put into Practice**
You might be interested in taking on a personal project to improve your ability to work with others. If so, check out Sharon Cramer's unusual book, *The Special Educator's Guide to Collaboration* (published by Corwin Press of Thousand Oaks, CA, in 2006), in which she challenges readers to empower themselves and acquire the motivation, understanding, and skills to analyze and improve collaboration relationships. For a more traditional approach, read M. Friend and L. Cook (2003), *Interactions: Collaboration Skills for School Professionals* (4th ed.), Boston: Allyn & Bacon Pearson.

**What do you think?**

How would you answer the kinds of questions asked of teachers in the interview studies reported here? How do you collaborate with your colleagues to meet the needs of exceptional students? What are your beliefs about including exceptional students in regular classrooms?

Put into Practice

There are a variety of names for problem-solving teams that meet before an IEP is considered for a student. Talk with educators and principals to learn what such a team is called in your school district and how its role is described.

teacher and the principal of the school. They reported that the principal and resource teacher set a positive tone, expected collaboration and inclusion to be effective, and provided the support and resources teachers requested to ensure students' needs were met.

These studies highlight the importance of your role as a classroom teacher in the inclusion of exceptional learners. In her study of successful inclusion Cheryl Duquette of the University of Ottawa wrote, "Perhaps the most important element is the quality and quantity of support for the classroom teacher. The classroom teacher needs to be part of an in-school team that can provide him or her with information, strategies that work and moral support" (1992, p. 151).

# The Classroom Teacher and the School-Based Team

As policies emphasizing inclusive education have been adopted across Canada, more school districts are developing school-based teams or in-school teams to share the responsibility for exceptional students. These teams are usually composed of members of the school staff and parents. Occasionally professionals from the school district or community may be added if they have particular expertise relevant for the child's education that is not available in the school.

## Suggesting a Meeting of the School-Based Team

When should you suggest that the in-school team meet to discuss a student in your class? You and the resource teacher have carried out all of the steps in the pre-referral stage (see Figure 2.1 on page 40), and you feel that the adaptations you have tried in your classroom are not sufficient to meet the student's needs. That is usually a sign that the in-school team should consider the child's case. After Ms. Sauvé's initial meeting with Andy's mother, she collected information about Andy and the demands of her classroom and she tried to eliminate mismatches between the two by adapting her teaching. While Andy engaged in more self-regulated learning, paid more attention, and completed more of his assignments, Ms. Sauvé could see that he would benefit from intensive teaching of these strategies over a period of time. She was not certain how to teach these strategies and recognized that she did not have time for such concentrated work with one student.

Ms. Sauvé worked closely with the resource teacher. A **resource teacher** can have many titles, including learning assistance teacher, tutor, and curriculum resource teacher. Resource teachers support classroom teachers and exceptional students, usually by consulting with teachers and offering some direct services to exceptional students, either in the classroom or the resource room.

If you and the resource teacher believe that the first level of intervention has not been effective, then you will approach the **school-based team**. In many jurisdictions you may be asked to complete a form similar to Figure 2.3 prior to making a referral to the school-based team. This team is a solution-finding group whose purpose is to provide a forum for dialogue by parents, teachers, and other professionals about the needs of students (Prince Edward Island Department of Education, www.gov.pe.ca/photos/original/ed_st_assess_04.pdf). As the classroom teacher or **referring teacher**, you are a key member of the in-school team, along with the principal and the resource teacher. Usually the parents are invited to take part and sometimes the

## FIGURE 2.3 FORM TO BE COMPLETED PRIOR TO MAKING A REFERRAL TO THE SCHOOL-BASED TEAM

Student Name:                                   Student #:

Grade:                                          Date of Birth:

Reason for referral:

Student's strengths and needs:

Brief listing of colleagues consulted:

Brief description of contact with family:

Relevant classroom assessment:

Please check off and list the interventions that have been tried in the classroom:

**Environmental**
- ☐ Preferential seating
- ☐ Proximity to instructor
- ☐ Frequent breaks
- ☐ Alternative workspace
- ☐ Study partner

**Instructional**
- ☐ Intensive individual instruction
- ☐ Intensive small group instruction
- ☐ Graphic organizers
- ☐ Calculator
- ☐ Taped texts
- ☐ Copy of notes
- ☐ Tracking sheets
- ☐ Repeated instructions

**Assessment**
- ☐ Oral assessment
- ☐ Alternative test/ assignment
- ☐ Scribe
- ☐ Shorter assignments
- ☐ Extended time

Additional comments:

Teacher's Signature:                            Date:

student is invited as well. Parental consent is sought for decisions that significantly alter the education of an exceptional student. If a school-based team is meeting about a student to whom a **paraeducator** has been assigned, the paraeducator is normally part of the in-school team. Paraeducators are employed to assist teachers in carrying out the program and care of exceptional students. Teachers of English as a second language and Aboriginal community representatives are often members of the team for students of diverse cultural groups. School-based teams make the best possible use of the resources within a school, and supplement with key professionals from the school district or the community. Other professionals who may be asked to join the school-based team include a district special education consultant, psychologist, nurse, social worker, behaviour specialist, speech and language therapist, occupational or physical therapist, child-care worker, mobility teacher, and sign-language interpreter. Usually in-school teams work better when they are small and focused.

# The Work of the School-Based Team

According to British Columbia's *Manual of Policies, Procedures, and Guidelines*, the school-based team "provides support through extended consultation on possible classroom strategies, and may become a central focus for case management, referrals and resource decisions" (2006, Section C). Usually the team appoints a case coordinator and problem solves informally. As the referring teacher, you will likely be asked to present the student data from the pre-referral interventions. The team brainstorms and suggests additional assessment strategies and additional teaching strategies, including **informal assessment** conducted by you or the resource teacher and, perhaps, formal assessment conducted by the resource teacher, a psychologist, or another professional.

When the team recommends that you and the resource teacher continue with assessment and intervention, then the team continues to monitor and support your actions. In some jurisdictions the team would prepare an IEP at this point. As the referring teacher, you supply the relevant classroom information. Regardless of the decision to pursue an IEP at this time, members will confer with you informally and another meeting of the team will likely take place to assess what has been accomplished. Steps in the school-based team process are shown in Figure 2.4.

The in-school team is the cornerstone of the process of identification, assessment and planning. If the decision of the team is to seek an extended assessment, to access other school district or community-based services, and to seek an IEP, then other **formal assessments** will be conducted. These could include an intelligence test; behaviour observation checklists; vision, hearing, or language assessments; or medical tests. In some school districts there is a long waiting list for assessment services, and parents may choose to pay for assessments administered outside the school system. When results are available, the in-school team, including the parents, meets to consider the recommendations. In most provinces the IEP (or equivalent) would be written at this stage; again, you will likely play a large role in this. In Ontario there is a two-stage process in which an **Identification, Placement, and Review Committee (IPRC)** meets to consider whether the child is exceptional and recommends a placement. This is followed by an IEP, usually written by the teacher and the resource teacher in elementary schools and by the resource teacher with input from the classroom teachers in secondary schools, and participation by the parents or guardians. In Newfoundland and Labrador an **Individual Support Services Plan (ISSP)** is developed in a collaborative process that involves the child, parent(s), school personnel, and personnel from other agencies including the departments of Health, Human Resources and Employment, and Justice. Ask about the procedures in your school, because there are slight variations even within a district.

## THE SCHOOL-BASED TEAM AND THE IEP PROCESS

The IEP process addresses all areas of student need, including adaptations in the regular classroom, supports and services to be provided there, and other services the student may receive. With inclusive education as the predominant approach, services are increasingly offered within the neighbourhood school, and even within the classroom. However, some students still require and receive services outside the neighbourhood school. For example, an IEP may recommend that a violent student attend a board-wide program for anger management and self-control until

## FIGURE 2.4 STEPS IN A SCHOOL-BASED TEAM PROCESS

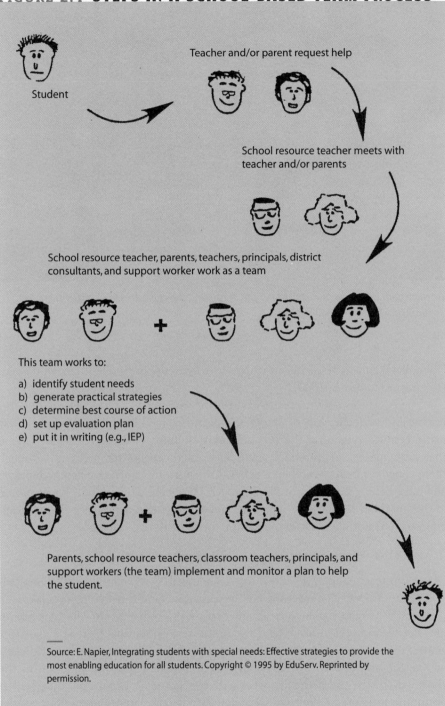

Student

Teacher and/or parent request help

School resource teacher meets with teacher and/or parents

School resource teacher, parents, teachers, principals, district consultants, and support worker work as a team

This team works to:

a) identify student needs
b) generate practical strategies
c) determine best course of action
d) set up evaluation plan
e) put it in writing (e.g., IEP)

Parents, school resource teachers, classroom teachers, principals, and support workers (the team) implement and monitor a plan to help the student.

Source: E. Napier, Integrating students with special needs: Effective strategies to provide the most enabling education for all students. Copyright © 1995 by EduServ. Reprinted by permission.

able to cope with the social demands of the classroom. Sometimes an itinerant teacher or a resource teacher can meet a student's needs best by removing the student from the regular classroom for intensive and direct instruction in Braille, for example (Cooper & Nichols, 2007). This issue is addressed in a discussion paper by Patricia MacCuspie (2002) of the Atlantic Provinces Special Education Authority, and the issue arises in a study by Cay Holbrook of the University of British

*Teachers with experience in collaboration say it is worth the effort. In-school teams share the responsibility for exceptional students.*

Columbia about high-quality instruction for students in Braille literacy programs (Koenig & Holbrook, 2000).

The educators on the school-based team share with the teacher the ongoing responsibility for the student's program when they hold brief, frequent, and informal meetings, even after the IEP has been established. Researchers have found that participating in in-school teams has other benefits for teachers, although these benefits are greatest when teachers have a strong knowledge base to build on and have beliefs aligned with the approach (Brownell et al., 2006). Participation in the in-school team can be a professional development experience that teachers view as contributing to better instruction for exceptional students.

### CLARIFYING YOUR ROLE ON THE IN-SCHOOL TEAM

Classroom teachers play a central role (Pierangelo & Giuliani, 2007). But occasionally, in-school team meetings can be frustrating and threatening for classroom teachers. What can you do to ensure that this does not happen to you? One month into her second year of teaching, Leanne was reassigned from a grade 6 class to a grade 3 class because of increases in enrolment. One of her new students, Mickey, had autism and needed many adaptations and modifications to function in the classroom. By the end of the first week with her new class, Leanne felt that she was beginning to make progress with Mickey. A few days later, the resource teacher told Leanne that Mickey's parents had requested a meeting to discuss his program. Leanne asked the resource teacher, "What should I do to prepare? I've never been to an in-school team meeting." The resource teacher replied that people could hardly expect Leanne to present the case when she had only taught Mickey for two weeks. On the day of the meeting, the vice-principal decided to chair. At the beginning of the meeting, he asked Leanne to present Mickey's history from his arrival at the school up to the current adaptations she was making in her classroom. Leanne had read Mickey's file but had not brought her notes to the team

## FIGURE 2.5 PREPARING FOR AND PARTICIPATING IN AN IN-SCHOOL TEAM MEETING

**Communicate Regularly with Parents**

- Send out a monthly newsletter with space for parents' comments.
- Host a class curriculum night to communicate your curriculum and expectations.
- Make a positive contact with parents of exceptional students before you make a negative contact.
- If you have not met the parents, make telephone contact before an in-school team meeting.
- Respond to parents' notes and telephone calls promptly.

**Look at Each Student as an Individual**

- Read all of the student files before the term starts.
- Make notes on the files, reports, IEPs, and medical information of exceptional students.
- Make written observations of all exceptional students early in the term.
- Meet with the resource teacher, ask questions, secure resources, and learn strategies to adapt teaching; make written notes.
- Collect work samples that demonstrate the student's strengths and needs in your class.

**Prepare for the In-School Team Meeting**

- Ask for and read the information about responsibilities of the members at in-school team meetings.
- Ask the chair of the meeting what will be expected of you.
- Discuss the student's case thoroughly with your best source of information, probably the resource teacher; ask his or her opinion on what you plan to say.
- Prepare to give briefly the student's history in the school as well as in your classroom.
- Bring all of your written notes to the in-school team meeting.
- Bring work samples to show the student's strengths and needs in your classroom.

**During the In-School Team Meeting**

- Approach the meeting in a spirit of goodwill.
- Think about how stressful these meetings can be for parents.
- Listen actively to what others have to say; take notes; do not interrupt.
- Answer questions briefly and honestly without becoming defensive.
- Ask questions if you do not understand; do not agree to commitments you cannot keep.
- Make your presentations brief, clear, and to the point; be positive and realistic in saying what you can do to meet the student's needs.
- Ensure that the meeting is summarized and ends on a positive note; thank the parents and other team members for their participation.
- Clarify when the next meeting is likely to occur and what is expected of you.

meeting. After some initial panic she described Mickey's history from memory, feeling frustrated and defensive. The parents were pleased with the adaptations Leanne described. Everyone else judged the meeting a success, but Leanne felt that she had appeared unprepared and unprofessional. Leanne, Mickey, and the rest of the grade 3 class went on to have a very successful year. However, Leanne still describes this meeting as the worst experience in her professional life. What could she have done before the meeting so that she would have felt prepared? Figure 2.5 contains suggestions for preparing for and participating in an in-school team meeting.

## The Teacher and the Individual Education Plan (IEP)

The Individual Education Plan is the formal document that is used to plan an exceptional student's program and serves as the blueprint for that student's education. In various provinces different terms are used: **Individual Program Plan (IPP)** in Nova Scotia; **Personal Program Plan (PPP)** in Saskatchewan; **Special Education Plan (SEP)** in New Brunswick; and **Individual Support Services Plan (ISSP)** in Newfoundland and Labrador. The Northwest Territories requires a **Student Support Plan (SSP)** if a student has a modified education plan based on outcomes in the NWT curriculum and an IEP if a student has a unique, student-specific plan. Generally, across Canada, whenever significant changes in learning expectations, curriculum, or teaching approaches are made to a student's educational program over the long term, an IEP or an equivalent must be prepared.

## Components of an IEP

The following description of an IEP is based on Ontario's (2004) resource document on IEPs, one of the most comprehensive in the country. An IEP is a written plan. It is a working document that describes the strengths and needs of an individual exceptional student (those that affect the student's ability to learn and to demonstrate learning) and the learning expectations for that individual student. It also includes a description of the accommodations needed to help the student achieve his or her learning expectations, and the special education program and services established to meet that student's needs. It also describes the specific knowledge and skills to be assessed and states who is responsible for ensuring that that the IEP is followed.

Although the specifics included in the documents vary from province to province, wherever you teach in Canada, you will likely find the following seven **components of an IEP**:

1. a description of the student's present level of functioning, including strengths and needs
2. long-term goals
3. short-term goals
4. instructional strategies, accommodations, materials, and services
5. dates for review
6. identification of the case coordinator and participants (including parents) and their responsibilities
7. evaluation or assessment procedures

**Present level of functioning** refers to recent test results, observations of the student, medical and school history, and degree of participation in current classes. If there is sufficient information to plan for and implement programming, no further assessment is necessary. **Long-term goals** may include learning goals within the curriculum, independence goals within the community, and career goals. Setting these goals involves considering parental and student values and priorities as well as what is age-appropriate and realistic. **Short-term goals** are usually steps on the way to the long-term goals, and may be goals for a term or half-term. **Instructional strategies, materials, and services** comprise the adaptations or accommodations to teaching and modifications to curriculum as well as other efforts made to provide an appropriate education for the student. **Related services** include such things as speech therapy, physical therapy, and alternative transportation. **Equipment** includes tape recorders, wheelchairs, computers, and other technological devices. **Evaluation or assessment procedures** refer to how the in-school team will demonstrate accountability by showing that the student is making reasonable progress. If the student is progressing slowly toward the objectives, alternative instructional strategies should be employed before revisions to the goals and objectives are made. Look for assessment strategies that are simple and that occur naturally in the context of learning in the classroom. Anecdotal comments may be more appropriate than letter or mark grades when students experience major modifications to the grade-level curriculum.

**Dates for review** are usually set for the end of the school year in which the IEP is established or renewed. Identification of participants allows parents and educators to consult the members of the team in the future, when they wish to know more about effective strategies and other aspects of the child's program. In most provinces parents have the right to appeal the IEP. As a classroom teacher, your responsibility is to make a good-faith effort to accomplish the short-term goals on the IEP and to keep the in-school team informed of the student's accomplishments.

## Planning to Meet Individual Needs

The IEP demands that you and your colleagues make an individual plan for an exceptional student. However, that does not mean that you must teach the student one on one. In a classic paper written for teachers, Gail Lennon, an Ontario teacher, describes how teachers can meet society's expectations of inclusion and appropriate teaching for exceptional students: "Parents and students want a program which includes the student as part of the class. The measuring stick in teacher decision making should be: *To what extent can the exceptional student learn the content which is being presented to the rest of the class?*" (Lennon, 1995, p. 24).

In a number of provinces including Saskatchewan and Manitoba (for instance, see www.edu.gov.mb.ca/k12/docs/support/multilevel/chap4.pdf), the term differentiated instruction is beginning to appear. However, Ontario makes extensive use of this term in its recent documents (e.g., www.edu.gov.on.ca/eng/studentsuccess/lms/differentiatedInstruction.pdf). This approach is consistent with what Gail Lennon advocates. Haager and Klingner (2005) describe differentiated instruction in inclusive classrooms as ensuring that all students have optimal learning opportunities within the core academic curriculum. They emphasize that assessment and grouping are key to providing differentiated instruction in the classroom. They recommend flexible grouping, that is, learning groups customized to students' individual needs (identified through assessment) and the objectives of the lesson. The composition of such groups would vary on an as-needed basis. Then intensive, focused instruction can be tailored to the needs of the group. This would include instruction above and beyond what the rest of the class requires.

What may need to be changed is the amount of time the student takes to learn the skill. As well, the content may be modified so that certain skills are selected for the exceptional students and others are deleted from his or her program plan. In rare cases the entire content may be replaced by more appropriate learning experiences.

Again, the question to be asked is, *To what extent can the exceptional student learn in the same way as the rest of the class, and how can I differentiate the way I teach, based on the student's unique learning needs?*

Exceptional students sometimes need a different way to demonstrate the learning outcomes they have accomplished. Whenever the same outcome is appropriate, maintain that outcome. When necessary, choose alternative formats or products that enable students to show what they have learned rather than show the impact of their disabilities. Widely used adaptations are more time for tests, speaking into a tape recorder, and using a scribe.

Cross-Reference
In Chapter 10 you can read about strategies for encouraging independent living, including both career education and co-operative education.

## Put into Practice

Obtain a copy of the IEP form used in your school district. Compare it with the IEP for Brenda Piet shown in Figure 2.6.

## Example of an IEP

Brenda Piet, a secondary school student, was introduced at the beginning of the chapter. Her teacher adviser was not certain about his role in developing a transition plan for Brenda, who had been identified as an exceptional student with learning disabilities. Increasingly, provinces (e.g., New Brunswick, Ontario, British Columbia, Alberta, and Nova Scotia) are requiring that a transition plan form part of the IEP for exceptional secondary school students. As Brenda's teacher adviser in the **Teacher Adviser Groups (TAGs)** program, Mr. Bogg may be a member of the in-school team or IEP team for Brenda. However, the **transition plan** to her post-secondary destination forms part of Brenda's IEP, so Mr. Bogg will not have to prepare it alone. Figure 2.6 shows an IEP for Brenda Piet that includes participation in **co-operative education** (that is, learning in the workplace for course credit) as a strategy to respond to her need for increased career maturity.

## Further Reading

About career education and workplace preparation for exceptional adolescents:

Rusch, F.R. (Ed.). (2008). *Beyond high school: Preparing adolescents for tomorrow's challenges* (2nd ed.). Upper Saddle River, NJ: Pearson/Merrill Prentice Hall.

Flexer, R.W., Baer, R., Luft, P., & Simmons, T. (2008). *Transition planning for secondary students with disabilities* (3rd ed.). Upper Saddle River, NJ: Pearson/Merrill Prentice Hall.

Munby, H., Zanibbi, M., Poth, C., Hutchinson, N. L., & Chin, P. (2007). Metacognitive instruction for adolescents in the workplace: A self-questioning strategy. *Education & Training, 49*(1), 8–24.

# The Teacher and the Paraeducator

Most members of the team working with an exceptional student will be qualified professionals—teachers, psychologists, social workers, physical therapists, or speech pathologists. However, there are important team members in inclusive schools who are not usually certified professionals. Your team may include a paraeducator. These non-certified staff members are employed to assist teachers in carrying out the program and to support the personal care, behaviour management, and instruction of exceptional students.

The qualifications required of paraeducators vary from province to province. In many provinces post-secondary institutions provide diploma or certificate programs for paraprofessionals. For example, there are ten-month programs at Keyano College and Grant MacEwan College in Alberta, two-year diploma programs at Sheridan College and Confederation College in Ontario, and a program at North West Regional College in Saskatchewan that can be completed through part-time or full-time study. Generally, post-secondary educational qualifications are set by individual school districts rather than by the provinces. Cobb (2007) describes an approach to ensuring that paraeducators are well prepared to work effectively with all students. Typically, requirements include experience working with exceptional children or adolescents and a certificate from a one- or two-year community college program in a relevant area. The titles given to paraeducators also vary considerably—paraprofessionals, teaching assistants, and educational assistants.

## The Role of the Paraeducator

## Put into Practice

Look for provincial and district policies about paraeducators. Interview a paraeducator about his or her working relationship with teachers and in-school teams.

Sometimes paraeducators are assigned to work full-time or part-time with one or more exceptional students in your classroom, while other times they are assigned to support your work with the entire class while monitoring the progress of the exceptional students and offering them assistance at key moments (Groom & Rose, 2005). You may be wondering who assigns these responsibilities to teacher assistants and how you can know what to expect. Often the IEP includes information about the role of the paraeducator in the program of an exceptional student. The paraeducator could work in one or all of the following places: in the classroom (e.g., supporting completion of assigned work), at a separate workspace in the classroom (e.g., teaching a strategy for organizing an essay), or in a space outside

# FIGURE 2.6  CLEAR LAKE DISTRICT SCHOOL BOARD INDIVIDUAL EDUCATION PLAN YEAR: 2008–2009

**Student:** Brenda Piet    **D.O.B.:** April 23, 1992    **IEP Date:** Oct. 1, 2008

**Parent/Guardian:** Ben and Lois Piet

**Identification:** Learning Disabilities    **Grade:** 11

*Areas of Strength*
Strong math skills
Creative artist, especially line drawing
Motivated to succeed
Participates in sports

*Statement of Needs*
To practise compensatory skills for written expression
To continue to develop organizational skills
To improve reading comprehension
To enhance career awareness

*Current Achievement Level*

Grade 11 in math

Grade 9 in reading comprehension; reading rate slow

*Overview and Goals for the Year*

Adapted program:

Brenda will develop greater independence in application of compensatory strategies for written expression and reading comprehension.

Brenda will choose and carry out a study and time management plan.

Brenda will participate in workplace learning.

| *Response to Statement of Needs* | *Support Personnel* | *Specialized Equipment* |
| --- | --- | --- |
| Curriculum adaptations | Classroom teachers<br>Resource teacher | Laptop computer for assignments<br>Texts on tape & tape player |
| Study skills and study plan | Resource teacher<br>Classroom teachers | Study skills group (weekly)<br>Agenda book entries for tests |
| Workplace experience | Co-op ed teacher<br>Resource teacher | Laptop computer for assignments<br>Agenda book entries for assignments |

*Transition Plan*

Workplace experience in grades 11 and 12. Investigate special needs resources at Clear Lake Community College and Plains University for architecture and architectural technologist programs.

*Year End Review Summary*

Brenda used the laptop for all her classes and assignments. She used taped texts whenever available. She needed assistance all year in setting up and following study plans. She was successful in and pleased with a co-op placement in an architectural firm.

Goals for 2008–2009: continue to develop test strategies and study plans for all tests as preparation for grade 12 examinations and for college or university course demands; continue curriculum adaptations; continue co-operative education.

*Date of Review Meeting: June 10, 2009*

**IEP Team Members:** Mona Simpson (resource teacher), Brian Smith (co-op education teacher), Frank Bogg (TAG teacher), Leila Chan (English teacher)

**Case co-ordinator:** Mona Simpson (informs all other teachers about Brenda's IEP)

**Parent who was consulted in development of IEP (signature):** *Lois Piet*

**Student who was consulted in development of IEP (signature):** *Brenda Piet*

*This student with cerebral palsy is included in a secondary school in Vancouver with the support of a paraeducator. The student does not speak and uses a wheelchair and a computer. His intellectual abilities are unaffected by cerebral palsy.*

the classroom (e.g., administering medication). Hill (2003) made observations in ten regular elementary classrooms in Winnipeg. The paraeducators in the study spent 54 percent of their time on instructional tasks, 26 percent on supervision, 13 percent on assistance to teachers, and 7 percent on other duties. Hill suggested that when paraeducators spend time on activities other than direct instruction, it may help teachers to conduct other important classroom tasks and enhance the independent learning of exceptional students. The principal is responsible for assigning roles in your school to a paraeducator, but usually the principal will consult with you when one of your students is involved, and normally the paraeducator works under your direction or the direction of the school-based team.

The research in Canada suggests that in successful inclusive schools, paraeducators and teachers work as partners (Schnell, 2001; Sundmark, 2003). Jennifer Ramsay, a teacher in Ontario, studied the effective working relationship between an educational assistant and a teacher (2007). She found that they shared beliefs about what was most important for inclusive education, recognized that their roles were distinct, and received direct and indirect support from the principal and the resource teacher. The paraeducator in your classroom can provide continuity for staff, parents, and exceptional learners and can contribute to the planning and delivery of services. As the classroom teacher, you should ensure that the paraeducator has a workstation in the classroom and that the two of you have a shared understanding of his or her role. Include the paraeducator in the discussions of the school-based team and value his or her contributions.

When you learn that you will be teaming with a paraeducator, read the job description and expectations of paraeducators in your province and in your school district. Ask for your own copy of these documents, and reread the IEPs of any exceptional children in your upcoming class for guidelines about the role of the paraeducator in regard to these children.

# Your Role in Working with a Paraeducator

It is important to clarify your role before beginning a partnership with a paraeducator (see Figure 2.7). You may be expected to prepare materials that the paraeducator will use with a student or group of students, provide informal training to the paraeducator about new programs and strategies, and inform this partner about the expectations, routines, and transitions you set for the class. Many classroom teachers have never supervised another team member. Some find it difficult to assign tasks they feel they should do themselves. As you have seen, these dilemmas abound in inclusive classrooms. While there may be a few more dilemmas when you work closely with a paraeducator, you can also share the responsibility and ideas with an enthusiastic partner. Many provinces (e.g., New Brunswick; www.gnb.ca/0000/publications/ss/pamphlett.pdf) and school districts (e.g., Peterborough Victoria Northumberland and Clarington Catholic District School Board; www.pvnccdsb.on.ca) have prepared resource guides to clarify the roles of educational assistants. In studies conducted in Alberta (Schnell, 2001) and Ontario (Ramsay, 2007) reporting on successful teams with a positive approach and attitude, the teacher and the paraeducator met frequently before and after school to discuss happenings in the classroom and in their personal lives, and were engaged teaching partners (Giangreco, 2003).

Sometimes paraeducators may work with the same exceptional child for many years and may know the child or adolescent better than the classroom or subject teacher. The most important thing for you to remember is that paraeducators should always complete their job assignments under the supervision of a qualified

### Further Reading

About working with paraeducators:

French, N.K. (2007). *A paraeducator's resource guide.* Port Chester, NY: National Professional Resources, Inc.

Giangreco, M.F. (2003). Working with paraprofessionals. *Educational Leadership, 61*(2), 50–53.

Peterborough Victoria Northumberland and Clarington Catholic District School Board. (2003). *Educational assistants: Resource guide.* Retrieved 28 October 2007 from www.pvnccdsb.on.ca.

## FIGURE 2.7 ROLE OF CLASSROOM TEACHERS IN WORKING WITH PARAEDUCATORS

Classroom teachers who receive support from paraeducators have the following responsibilities:

- informing paraeducators of classroom procedures and rules, and methods of classroom management
- assigning appropriate responsibilities and tasks to paraeducators, taking into consideration their training, knowledge, and skills as well as student needs
- documenting identified responsibilities and tasks with paraeducators, and providing copies for principals (and special education supervisors, where appropriate)
- providing input regarding the supervision and evaluation of paraeducators
- informing principals when students whom paraeducators support are absent so that the paraeducators' schedules can be changed
- ensuring that time is allocated for paraeducators to meet with teachers regularly
- ensuring communication with paraeducators through communication books, logs, regular meetings for collaborative monitoring, and ongoing discussion
- recommending training and resources to support paraeducators in their roles
- modelling the confidentiality of the student–school relationship
- helping paraeducators to develop skills they need such as observation and data-collection strategies and effective behaviour management strategies
- encouraging high standards of practice
- resolving conflicts with paraeducators at the classroom level first, school level second, and regional school board level third

Sources: Alberta Teachers' Association (2002). *Teachers and teachers' assistants: Roles and responsibilities*; New Brunswick Department of Education (1994). *Teacher assistant guidelines for standards and evaluation*; Nova Scotia Department of Education and Culture (1998). *Teacher assistant guidelines*; Warger, C. (2003). *Supporting paraeducators: A summary of current practices.* ERIC/OOSEP Digest #E 642.

## What do you think?

Recently, contrasting perspectives on our work with parents have emerged. Some researchers have argued that educators must develop a new conceptualization of partnership with the community to promote community-based regeneration. For example, see Confronting failure: Towards a pedagogy of recognition in the *International Journal of Inclusive Education, 1,* 121–141 by Jon Nixon and his colleagues (1997). At the same time, educators have begun to receive advice on how to deal with aggressive parents. For example, see *The difficult parent: An educator's guide to handling aggressive behavior* by Charles Jaksec (Corwin Press, 2005) and *Working with challenging parents of students with special needs* by Jean Cheng Gorman (Corwin Press, 2004). Are these perspectives contradictory or complementary? What do you think?

Weblinks

PARENTBOOKS (A BOOKSTORE)
http://parentbooks.ca

WHAT ADOLESCENTS WITH DISABILITIES WANT IN LIFE (A REPORT BY RESEARCHERS AT MCMASTER UNIVERSITY)
www.canchild.ca/Default.aspx?tabid=136

EXCELLENCE FOR ALL: DEVELOPING PARTNERS IN EDUCATION (A DISCUSSION PAPER ABOUT PARENT INVOLVEMENT, ONTARIO EDUCATION)
www.edu.gov.on.ca/eng/document/nr/05.12/developing.pdf

classroom teacher. Margret Winzer of the University of Lethbridge (2005) wrote about the dilemmas that accompany the employment of paraeducators in classrooms. It is important that paraeducators contribute to the participation of exceptional children in regular classrooms and do not come between the children and their classmates, teachers, or learning tasks (Giangreco, Smith, & Pinckney, 2006). A study conducted in British Columbia (Lamont & Hill, 1991) found that paraeducators thought they should take more responsibility for instructional support and classroom organization than teachers thought was appropriate. To make the partnership work smoothly, establish clear communication and a good working relationship with each paraeducator who will work in your classroom. Sundmark (2003) reported on focus groups and interviews with paraeducators who worked with students with severe behaviour exceptionalities in Alberta. The paraeducators consistently reported that each year the teacher with whom they worked could "make or break" the year. Consider the point of view of this member of the team. Look for his or her unique strengths and then work together, because the two of you are the heart of the in-school team for students who require the support of a paraeducator to learn in an inclusive classroom.

# The Teacher and the Parents

In her account of facilitating inclusion of children with moderate and severe disabilities in a school in Nova Scotia, Carla DiGiorgio (2004) describes how parents have developed an increasing awareness of their own and their children's legal and social rights recently, and are asserting themselves more with school personnel. Being aware of these rights and making an effort to understand and support parents who exercise them is likely to enhance your relations with parents. These families have to meet the challenges that accompany the disability as well as all the normal pressures of family life. Families of children with disabilities spend significant amounts of time interacting with educational professionals. By becoming sensitive to parental needs, you will ensure that your meetings with families go more smoothly.

## Understanding the Parents' Perspective

A recurring theme in this book is the importance of taking others' perspectives. This section focuses on the perspectives of parents of exceptional students. Living with an exceptional child or adolescent creates challenges for a family, with both positive and negative effects. Lily Dyson of the University of Victoria has studied how a child's disability influences parents and siblings (1997, 1998, 2003). Dick Sobsey and his fellow researchers at the University of Alberta have described the experience of transformation in parents of children with disabilities (e.g., Scorgie, Wilgosh, & Sobsey, 2004). Patricia Minnes and her colleagues at Queen's University have reported on how families experience both empowerment (e.g., Nachshen & Minnes, 2005) and higher levels of stress because of the responsibilities of caring for and advocating for exceptional children and because of parental concern about the child's future (e.g., Nachshen, Garcin, & Minnes, 2005).

### CARING FOR EXCEPTIONAL CHILDREN AND ADOLESCENTS

Recent research by Lorraine Wilgosh of the University of Alberta and her colleagues (e.g., Wilgosh & Scorgie, 2006b) suggests that coming to terms with a child with disabilities is not a linear process but rather a recurring one, so that difficult questions that parents deal with at the time of diagnosis reappear at critical junctures and major developmental stages. Parents of children with disabilities in Ontario report challenging transitions from preschool to kindergarten (Janus et al., 2007). Similarly, Naomi Sankar-DeLeeuw (2007) described the perspectives of parents and teachers in Alberta on the transition into kindergarten of gifted children and the importance of teachers listening to parents and differentiating instruction. Many families receive comprehensive early intervention at a child development centre (e.g., Yukon Child Development Centre; www.cdcyukon.com/About.aspx; Read, 2000). Such families may find the programming available in their neighbourhood school less intensive. Sometimes following the identification of a child's disability, parents find that their expectations for accomplishment in school are shattered (Russell, 2005). It may help parents, young exceptional children, and their siblings to read about children with disabilities attending school—in order to teach all members of the family about the nature of the exceptionality, what happens at school, and what exceptional children can accomplish. For examples of such books, see Figure 2.8. Figure 2.9 on page 62 identifies websites that may serve a similar purpose for adolescents with disabilities and their families at the time of transition to high school.

Parental challenges in caring for exceptional children and adolescents vary. Some children require physical and personal care daily and need to be lifted frequently. Others have life-threatening allergies that require parents to be constantly vigilant. Some children look different from their peers, and families may have to provide emotional support to overcome the potentially destructive effects of rejection (Reilly, 2003). Others with behaviour disorders behave differently, even unacceptably, although they look like everyone else (Cronin, 2004). It is important for us, as educators, to listen and understand how the family sees the issues when a child has a disability.

Because learning disabilities are an invisible handicap, parents sometimes delay identification and acceptance of their child's exceptionality (Dyson, 1992b; Mattson & Roll-Petterson, 2007). Parents may not receive the same support as they would if their children had more visible disabilities (Cronin, 2004). Gifted children and adolescents also feel different and can be teased and ridiculed at school. Alisha, who tied for second place in a National Mathematics League test, had only one friend. When asked where she got her support, Alisha answered without hesitation, "My mom" (Wong, 2000, p. R7). A parent who tells you there is no time or energy for a parent–teacher meeting may have good reason to feel tired and discouraged.

## EFFECTS ON FAMILIES

Siblings of children and adolescents with disabilities tend to show more social competence and to display the same level of self-concept and behaviour problems as comparable siblings of children without disabilities (Dyson, 1992a). However, school-age siblings of children with disabilities have stresses and needs (Dyson, 1998) and report cognitive and behavioural strategies for coping with the stress of having siblings with disabilities (Harmer Cox et al., 2003). They need to be informed about their sibling's disability because they are often expected to supply information at school and to act as a caretaker at home. Siblings may need help handling teasing and feelings of embarrassment. However, positive effects have

| | |
|---|---|
| **Allergies** | Harrison, T. (1996). *Aaron's awful allergies.* Toronto, ON: KidsCan Press. |
| | Ureel, J. (2004). *The peanut pickle: A story about peanut allergy.* Livonia, MI: First Page Publication. |
| | Zevy, A. & Tebbutt, S. (1995). *No nuts for me!* Downsview, ON: Tumbleweed Press. |
| | Habkirk, L. (1995). *A preschooler's guide to peanut allergy.* London, ON: Ticketar Co. |
| **Asperger Syndrome** | Hoopman, K. (2001). *Blue bottle mystery: An Asperger adventure.* London, UK: Jessica Kingsley Pub. Ltd. |
| | Murrell, D. (2001). *Tobin learns to make friends!* Arlington, TX: Future Horizions. |
| | Myles, H.M. (2002). *Practical solutions to everyday challenges for children with Asperger syndrome.* Shawnee Mission, KS: Autism Asperger Pub. Co. |
| **Asthma** | Weitzman, E. (1998). *Let's talk about having asthma.* Center City, MN: Hazelden Publishing & Educational Services. |
| | London, J. (1997). *The lion who had asthma.* Morton Grove, IL: Albert Whitman & Company. |
| | Carter, A.R. (1996). *I'm tougher than asthma!* Morton Grove, IL: Albert Whitman & Co. |
| **Attention Deficit/ Hyperactivity Disorder** | Corman, C.L. & Trevino, E. (2003). *Eukee the jumpy jumpy elephant.* New York: Specialty Press. |
| | Carpenter, P., Ford, M., & Horjus, P. (2000). *Sparky's excellent misadventures: My ADD journal by me (Sparky).* Washington, DC: Magination Press. Carpr |
| **Autism** | Lears, L. (2004). *Ian's walk: A story about autism.* Morton Grove, IL: Albert Whitman & Company. |
| | Ogaz, N. (2002). *Buster and the amazing daisy.* Philadelphia, PA: Jessica Kingsley Publishers. |
| | Buron, K.D. (2003). *When my autism gets too big: A relaxation book for children with autism spectrum disorders.* Shawnee Mission, KS: Autism Asperger Publishing Company. |
| **Deaf** | Peterson, J.W. (2001). *I have a sister, my sister is deaf.* Bethany, MO: Fitzgerald Books. |
| | Greenberg, J.E. (1985). *What is the sign for friend?* New York: New York: F. Watts. |
| **Developmental Disabilities** | Glatzer, J., & Dineen, T. (2002). *Taking Down syndrome to school.* Plainview, NY: JayJo Books. |
| | Rickert, J.E., & McGahan, P. (2000). *Russ and the almost perfect day.* Bethesda, MD: Woodbine House Inc. |
| **Learning Disabilties** | Robb, D.B. (2002). *The alphabet war: A story about dyslexia.* Morton Grove, IL: Albert Whitman & Company. |
| | Polacco, P. (1998). *Thank you, Mr. Falker.* New York: Philomel Books. |
| | Dunn, K.B., & Dunn, A.B. (1993). *Trouble with school: A family story about learning disabilities.* Bethesda, MD: Woodbine House Pub. |
| **Physical Disabilities** | MacDiarmid, C. (2003). *Wendy Blair and the assignment.* Toronto: Canadian Council on Rehabilitation and Work. |
| | MacDiarmid, C. (2002). *I'm Wendy Blair, not a chair.* Toronto: Canadian Council on Rehabilitation and Work. |
| | Hellan, J.R. (2000). *Rolling along: The story of Taylor and his wheelchair.* Atlanta, GA: Peachtree Publishers. |
| | Thomas, P. (2002). *Don't call me special: A first look at disability.* Georgetown, ON: Barron's Educational Series. |
| | Rogers, F. (2000). *Let's talk about it: Extraordinary friends.* Minneapolis, MN: Sagebrush Education Resources. |
| | Brownridge, W.R. (1995). *The moccasin goalie.* Victoria, BC: Orca Book Publishers. |
| **Speech Disabilities** | Bryant, J.E. & Dineen, T. (2004). *Taking speech disorders to school.* Plainview, NY: JayJo Books. |
| | Lears, L. (2000). *Ben has something to say: A story about stuttering.* Fremont, CA: Shen's Books. |
| | Stanek, M. (1979). *Growl when you say R.* Morton Grove, IL: Albert Whitman & Co. |

## FOCUS ON FAMILIES

## Letter to Andrew

Families of exceptional children in Calgary published a book entitled *Letters to Our Children*.

Here is the letter to Andrew Ziebell, who was born three weeks prematurely with cerebral palsy that affects all four limbs. Andrew has some hearing and vision loss.

Dear Andrew,

You, my love, turned seven years old on March 3, 1993. In your short lifetime you have had a long, hard road to follow. And that road will not get any easier. Always know, Andrew, that I love you more than anything in the world and I will always be there right beside you, helping your every step, sharing in your dreams, your hopes, your tears and your fears.

You have a circle of friends who love you and love to share in your life. These friends are special in every way because they see you as Andrew, a person first and foremost, and your disability doesn't matter.

The sky was the limit when you entered preschool. Your teachers, Jill, Jo-Anne, and Val took you through two years of learning, socializing, and fun-filled experiences. Your summer program there was just as wonderful because I could see the look of excitement on your face each and every day when you came home from the Leisure Centre. You had a great year at your community school where you moved mountains and acquired lifelong friendships.

In the beginning of 1993, another chapter opened in your life. You entered the world of Scouting. In full uniform you and your brother proudly stand united with all Boy Scouts of Canada. We are all proud to feel your sense of belonging.

Your world is not always full of joy and not all people see your strength, but dwell on your disabilities. The most difficult challenge began in June 1992 when you were not allowed to continue in your community school placement. Not only did this cost you a year of education, but the emotional devastation this inflicted on your brother and sister, who could not understand why you were not allowed to go to school with them, has been very traumatic. We will continue to fight to obtain your right to a fair and equal education in your community school, no matter how long it takes.

What your future holds for you, my son, I cannot say; but what I hope it holds for you is full acceptance into society and a world that is kind and full of love; a circle of friends and independence.

Lovingly,

Your Mom, Dad, Jennifer-Lea, Christopher and last, but not least, your watchful puppy Kelsey

Source: Excerpted from D.E. Badry, J.R. McDonald, & J. LeBlond (Eds.), *Letters to Our Children.* Copyright © 1993 by University of Calgary Press. Reprinted by permission.

also been observed: "Having a brother with a learning disability . . . the kids have gained values well beyond their years that will stay with them forever" (Wilgosh, 1990, p. 307). One mother said of inclusion, "this is how we choose to value our family." The siblings of children with disabilities interviewed by Michelle Pompeo (2004) of the University of Western Ontario reported that their experiences had contributed to their determination to become teachers of and advocates for individuals with disabilities.

### PARENTS' TEACHING AND ADVOCATING FOR EXCEPTIONAL YOUTH

Parents assume the roles of teachers and advocates (Hess, Molina, & Kozleski, 2006; Wilgosh & Scorgie, 2006a). They often spend long hours helping their children with disabilities complete unfinished school work. One parent expressed it this way: "He has me working with him, up reading every night, constantly, even on the weekends" (Hess et al., p. 153). Some exceptional children and adolescents cannot communicate effectively with their parents about school, which causes parents to say, "The biggest part of a perfect school would be a communication part, being able to call that teacher after school and say, 'Hey, what kind of day did my son have?'" (Hess et al., p. 154). A "communication book" for children or an agenda book for adolescents, which the students carry between school and home each day, may

Weblinks

CANADIAN NATIONAL INSTITUTE FOR THE BLIND (CNIB) (FOR HELP WITH ADVOCACY)
www.cnib.ca/library/advocacy/index.htm

NATIONAL EDUCATIONAL ASSOCIATION OF DISABLED STUDENTS (NEADS) (ADVOCATES FOR ACCESS TO COLLEGE AND UNIVERSITY)
www.neads.ca

ADVOCACY RESOURCE CENTRE FOR THE HANDICAPPED (ARCH) (A LEGAL RESOURCE CENTRE IN ONTARIO)
www.archlegalclinic.ca

## FIGURE 2.9  WEBLINKS FOR YOUTH WITH DISABILITIES

**www.focusas.com/Canada.html**
Focus Adolescent Services—A free internet clearinghouse of information and resources on teen and family issues to help and support families with troubled and at-risk teens. Includes hotlines adolescents may call and provides links to many informative websites.

**www.disabilityresources.org**
Disability Resources on the Internet—A comprehensive source including thousands of links, answers to FAQs (frequently asked questions), and publications.

**http://abilityonline.org**
AbilityOnline.org—A Canadian website with great resources and information. Worth the effort to register.

**www.focusas.com/Stress.html**
Focus Adolescent Services: Helping Teenagers with Stress—A listing of potential sources of stress for adolescents and suggestions for how adolescents can help themselves and how adults may be able to help.

**www.rcpsych.ac.uk/college/faculties/childandadolescent/booksforteensadults.aspx**
Royal College of Psychiatrists [in the United Kingdom]: Books for Teens and Adults—A list of books about disabilities written for individuals with disabilities.

remind the students about assignments and may enable parents to see what is expected. Sometimes parents report that their teaching role interferes with their parenting role: "I learned to be a mom first and not turn into a teacher only, but to work teaching into the normal home routines as much as possible" (Wilgosh & Scorgie, 2006a, p. 132). It seems more important for exceptional children and adolescents to have accepting and supportive parents than to have another academic teacher. Teaching is, after all, your role. Many parents also assume the role of **advocate**: "My child's success depends on my ability to advocate for him." You may also hear a parent say, "If you need something, let me know. I will go to bat to get whatever you need. If it's computers for your room . . . whatever you need, I will be there helping" (Hess et al., 2006, p. 154). Advocating can be a transformative, emotional, and satisfying experience for parents (Wilgosh, Scorgie, & Fleming, 2000), and parents' advocacy and involvement in homework may also positively influence the views and accomplishments of exceptional adolescents, according to a study conducted in Quebec (Deslandes, Royer, Potvin, & Leclerc, 1999).

### CONCERN FOR THE FUTURE

Focusing on the future enables individuals and their families to consider what might be and how they can use their energy to make the possible real. Kim Anderson is a Cree/Métis writer, editor, educator, and storyteller from Guelph, Ontario. She has written about why it is especially important for Aboriginal people to engage in "future-oriented stories" (2004, p. 126). She writes, "while telling is a critical part of the healing journey," time must also be spent "envisioning where we want to go in the future" (p. 127).

Depending on the nature and severity of their disabilities, some individuals may not be able to live independently and may face an uncertain future in career and work. The Focus on Community box describes one successful plan that is working for Canadian families. Strategies to prepare students for adulthood include workplace

**Further Reading**

On parents' planning for the future of their children with disabilities:

Pike, K., & Steinemann, P. (1997). *Connections: A Planning Guide for Parents of Sons and Daughters with a Mental Handicap.* Brampton, ON: Brampton Caledon Community Living (available from 34 Church St. West, Brampton, ON L6X 1H3).

The "Special Needs" Planning Group (SNPG). www.specialneedsplanning.ca/tools.html.

learning and co-operative education during secondary school (Hutchinson, Versnel, Chin, & Munby, 2007). Kathleen Manderville (2005) describes a co-operative education program tailored to meet the needs of youth on the Mohawk Tyendinaga reserve near Belleville, Ontario. The case of Brenda Piet illustrates that, increasingly, IEPs contain transition plans that include workplace experience.

## Planned Lifetime Advocacy Network (PLAN)

At some point, parents of children with disabilities recognize that they will not personally be able to provide emotional support and financial security in their children's later years. PLAN is based in Burnaby, BC, and was started by parents of children with disabilities.

PLAN tries to help create a good life for every member, regardless of level of disability, age, or income, by working with parents, friends, and existing social services. At its website, the organization writes:

> PLAN's mission is to help families secure the future for their relative with a disability and to provide you with peace of mind. This means ending isolation and loneliness, creating financial security, enabling everyone to make a contribution, ensuring choice, and creating genuine homes.

> PLAN's vision is simple: we want everyone to have access to a good life. Not surprisingly, a good life for people with disabilities is not very different from a good life for anyone else: friends and family, a place of one's own, financial security, choice, and the ability to make a contribution to society.

> At PLAN we envision a future where people with disabilities:

- Are supported by caring family and friends
- Are encouraged to participate in and contribute to their community
- Have their wishes and choices respected
- Have financial security
- Live in a place of their own choice
- Are protected from abuse and exploitation

(from www.plan.ca/AboutPlan_MissionAndVision.php)

Josh is 14 years old and has severe epilepsy and brain damage. His parents have established a plan that will take care of Josh

*Josh, sitting beside his father, has always been included in all family activities and attends a neighbourhood school. His father wants him to become a member of the community as an adult.*

financially, and Josh has a circle of friends at his neighbourhood school, where he is in grade 8. His family plans to establish a formal network for Josh in his last year of secondary school, a time when adolescents with disabilities and their families can feel abandoned.

A network of support usually consists of four to twelve people who pledge to look out for and remain involved with Josh for the rest of his life. Families pay fees to join and remain members of PLAN. For lifetime members, PLAN promises that a network will ensure that the person with disabilities, regardless of age, is cared for his or her entire life (Picard, 1998).

Source: Based on Picard, A. (1998). When disabled kids grow up. *The Globe and Mail*, August 7, pp. A1, A4.

# Collaborating with Parents

It would be difficult to overstate the importance of parents in the lives of their off-spring. Many teachers recognize that the real experts on a student are usually the parents: "I am his mother and I know him better than anyone" (Wilgosh & Scorgie, 2006a, p. 130). In turn, some parents recognize the pressure that teachers are under and can be a source of support and advocacy for additional resources (Hess et al., 2006; Wilgosh, Nota, Scorgie, & Soresi, 2004). Research suggests that the more extensive the collaboration between schools and families, the more successful children with exceptionalities are likely to be (Carter et al., 2007). Not all parents choose to collaborate with teachers and schools, but parents are more likely to co-operate with educators if the school, program, and teacher make them feel welcome (Rogers, 2007; Stanovich & Jordan, 2004).

What will parents of exceptional students expect of you? Many Canadian parents believe that excellence in teaching leads to school success for children with special needs. The qualities they look for in teachers include patience, approachability, comfort, flexibility, a positive attitude, and adequate training (Wilgosh & Scorgie, 2006a). Parents feel that teacher–parent communication and co-operation are important and that the teacher must accept the child's disability. Parents also want to feel supported (Janus et al., 2007). Bill Lucas and Alistair Smith (2004) have developed a guide to help parents enjoy learning with their young children—a good resource for all parents of children in the primary grades, but especially helpful for those who have exceptional children. For Alberta mothers of exceptional children, inclusion has meant, "[t]he child is a fully participating, valued, and contributing member of a regular classroom of age appropriate peers. The child should feel safe, accepted and encouraged, being given choices and making decisions in a learning environment rich with opportunities" (Wilgosh & Chomicki, 1994, p. 30).

## PARENT–TEACHER CONFERENCES

**Parent–teacher conferences** are one of the most commonly used methods to facilitate productive partnerships between parents and professionals. To ensure strong working relationships with the parents of exceptional students, try to communicate effectively with them at every opportunity. In spite of your busy schedule, you should make calls to these parents yourself, rather than ask the school secretary to do it. Prepare well by being informed about the student and the resources available in the school and community.

## BEFORE PARENT–TEACHER CONFERENCES

If possible, contact the parents of exceptional students prior to the start of term. Introduce yourself and assure the parents that you are concerned about their child and want to work with them to ensure a positive working relationship. Simmons (2002) suggests that successful alliances can be established by adhering to three basic assumptions:

1. Assume goodwill—that the parents, like you, have a deep desire to see the child do well.

2. Assume competence—that parents whose input is welcomed and valued will make constructive suggestions.

3. Assume a shared responsibility—that everyone needs to co-operate and actively participate in making and carrying out plans toward a common goal.

Set up parent–teacher conferences in a way that communicates effectively to your school's community. Be flexible with time, with inviting the child if that is likely to help reach the goals, and with using child-produced invitations as well as formal announcements in newsletters, on the radio, and in local newspapers (in the languages most used in the community). Encourage parents to prepare for the conference.

## DURING PARENT–TEACHER CONFERENCES

The message you want to convey is that there is a team approach between home and school, between students and teachers, and among teachers (Simmons, 2002). Parents report that they find an "us versus them" atmosphere to be a serious impediment to communication (Alper, Schloss, & Schloss, 1995; Wilgosh & Scorgie, 2006a). Create a comfortable atmosphere. Use adult chairs. Parents prefer to receive information about their children informally, in conversational meetings with teachers, so avoid jargon and give examples to show what you mean (Stevens & Tollafield, 2003). While you may want to focus on teaching methods, parents are usually most interested in the outcomes for their children, so be prepared to discuss frankly the goals for the next week, month, and term (Duncan, 2007). You may need to remind parents gently about what the student is accomplishing now and what is reasonable to expect in the upcoming months. Rather than forecasting far into the future, focus on what is feasible in your classroom if everyone makes a concerted and collaborative effort. All of this will be easier if you make a plan and ensure that you have all the information and examples that you need to communicate effectively. If you are not familiar with a disability, read up on it prior to the meeting to ensure you can contribute to the discussion. Then while communicating, invite parents to talk and remember to look at the parents and listen attentively to what they say. After consensus has been reached, make a plan that supports the student in age-appropriate and culturally sensitive ways.

It is not always easy to reach consensus, and researchers suggest that you should be aware of approaches for solving problems if they arise (Kamimura & Ishikuma, 2007; Simmons, 2002). Be honest but tactful. Discuss strengths as well as weaknesses and offer to work with parents to reach solutions. Let the parents know that you like their child. If there are responsibilities to be shared, discuss what you can do, what the parents can do, and what the exceptional student can do. Sometimes it is helpful to include the student in the conference. But don't surprise anyone by doing this without prior discussion with the family members.

Exceptional adolescents are expected to learn **self-advocacy**. Then they can negotiate with their teachers for accommodations consistent with the IEP and with the recommendations of the resource teacher or case manager. Adolescence is a period of development toward autonomy, responsibility, and personally relevant life goals. Participating in parent–teacher conferences may contribute to this development. Remember to prepare students to take part, and prepare their parents for the idea that the adolescent should join the conference. In a recent study in a Halifax school, Versnel (2005) found that grade 6 students learned a strategy for participating in parent–teacher conferences during ten one-hour group strategy lessons. The students used the strategy to advocate with teachers, sports coaches, parents, and classmates, as well as to discuss their classroom needs, and they highly recommended the

> **Cross-Reference**
> Chapter 5 describes many situations that place families at risk—homelessness, unemployment, discrimination, poverty, violence—and might reduce their collaboration with schools.

## Put into Practice

Read about the challenges of creating welcoming parent–teacher conferences in schools with diverse student populations. Then develop a plan for engaging parents who may be reluctant to attend or uncomfortable in meetings with educators. Use the strategy of putting yourself in the parents' place and thinking about what they might find helpful. Resources you could consult include:

Allen, J. (2007). *Creating welcoming schools: A practical guide to home–school partnerships with diverse families.* Newark, DE: International Reading Association.

Copenhaver, J. (2007). *Parent/school and mediator's manual* (revised). Logan, UT: Bureau of Indian Education Dispute Resolution in Special Education through Mediation.

Crozier, G., & Davies, J. (2007). Hard to reach parents or hard to reach schools? *British Educational Research Journal, 33,* 295–313.

program for other youths. Some school districts have found that implementing student-led, teacher-supported conferences, beginning with students in the middle years, has improved communication with parents and improved student learning (for an example, see Goodman, 2008).

## AFTER PARENT–TEACHER CONFERENCES

After a conference, you have several responsibilities. First, write notes to remind yourself of the important points discussed. Second, if you and the parents have made any major decisions, you may want to write a brief note to the parents to confirm what was decided. Third, if you agreed to take any action (such as consulting the resource teacher), carry it out as soon as possible. Provide other educators who work with the child with a brief update on the outcomes. Some schools require that an update be entered in the parent–teacher conference log so the principal and other educators can access it.

It also can be helpful to look at the situation from the parents' perspective when reflecting on the conference. While you may find it challenging to include their child or adolescent in your classroom for one year, remember that the parents have this challenge for their entire lives. While you have an important job—to teach this child and include him or her in your classroom—these parents also have an important job. Theirs is to love and care for this child and to be the child's advocate. This is the basis from which you can expect them to communicate with you. Partnerships are built over time; both you and the parents may have to challenge long-held beliefs and even live through a few mistakes.

There may be families who do not form partnerships with you. Because of situations families face—including homelessness, unemployment, discrimination, poverty, and violence—parents may not engage in collaboration. As educators, we have to respect their decisions and encourage them to attend the next parent–teacher conference.

# Summary

The role of the classroom teacher in the education of exceptional children is increasing. Teachers identify the needs of exceptional students, carry out pre-referral adaptations, and collaborate with school-based teams to facilitate inclusion. Teachers also play a central role in developing IEPs and carrying out these IEPs by ADAPTing or differentiating their teaching, assessment, and classroom organization. Just as Ms. Sauvé recognized her responsibility to refer Andy Hughes to the in-school team, Mr. Bogg came to understand his role in advising Brenda Piet on her transition to college. Strategies for meeting these challenges appear in upcoming chapters. Both parents and paraeducators are partners in the education of exceptional students and can work with you to share the responsibility in these changing times.

# Key Terms

pre-referral interventions (p. 41)
self-monitoring (p. 43)
self-regulation (p. 43)
collaboration (p. 45)
resource teacher (p. 46)
school-based team (p. 46)
referring teacher (p. 46)
paraeducator (p. 47)
informal assessment (p. 48)
formal assessments (p. 48)
Identification, Placement, and
    Review Committee (IPRC) (p. 48)
Individual Support Services Plan
    (ISSP) (p. 48)

Individual Program Plan (IPP)
    (p. 51)
Personal Program Plan (PPP)
    (p. 52)
Special Education Plan (SEP) (p. 52)
Student Support Plan (SSP) (p. 52)
components of an IEP (p. 52)
present level of functioning (p. 52)
long-term goals (p. 52)
short-term goals (p. 52)
instructional strategies, materials,
    and services (p. 52)
related services (p. 52)
equipment (p. 52)

evaluation or assessment
    procedures (p. 52)
dates for review (p. 53)
Teacher Adviser Groups (TAGs)
    (p. 54)
transition plan (p. 54)
co-operative education (p. 54)
advocate (p. 62)
parent–teacher conferences (p. 64)
self-advocacy (p. 65)

# Challenges for Reviewing Chapter 2

1. Why is your role as a classroom teacher so important in identifying the needs of exceptional students, especially students with high-incidence exceptionalities such as learning disabilities?

2. Identify the steps a teacher would take before referring a child to an in-school team.

3. Prepare to assume the role of one of the members of a school-based team (e.g., teacher, parent, resource teacher, principal, special education consultant; see Figure 2.4 on page 49) for a meeting about Andy Hughes whose case was described in the opening of this chapter. List (a) the resources you would use to prepare for the meeting, (b) the contributions you plan to make in the meeting, and (c) the reasons you think these contributions are important. Participate with your peers in a role-play of the school-based team meeting about Andy.

4. Using Figure 2.6 on page 55 as a model, develop an IEP for Andy Hughes. Refer to sources identified in this chapter as well as the information provided in this chapter.

5. Identify three aspects of your role as a classroom teacher working with a paraeducator at the grade level at which you teach.

6. Describe the actions you would take at the beginning of the school year to ensure collaborative working relationships with the parents and guardians of exceptional students in your class or classes. Participate with your classmates in role-playing a parent–teacher meeting for one of the two students described in the cases at the beginning of Chapter 2—Andy Hughes or Brenda Piet.

7. Return to the opening cases of Andy and Brenda and answer the five questions that follow the cases.

# Chapter 3
# Exceptional Students: High-Incidence Exceptionalities

**Urjo is 15 years old and in grade 10.** His teachers describe him as non-compliant and underachieving. Their observations describe a boy who fails to complete assignments in class, refuses to do his homework, has difficulty following instructions, and rarely co-operates with teachers or classmates. Teachers describe him muttering under his breath, folding his arms across his chest, and shouting at peers. However, he excels in art class. While he engages in loud, verbal power struggles with most teachers, Urjo is quiet and engrossed when drawing or painting. The counsellor who interviewed him suggests that Urjo uses power struggles to avoid work he finds boring and pointless and to exert control over others. In an interview Urjo's parents report that he initiates the same battles at home and that his younger brothers are starting to engage in the same behaviours. When teachers pressure Urjo to comply, he bad-mouths them and indulges in negative self-talk. Achievement tests show that Urjo is slightly below grade level in reading, written expression, and mathematics and is easily distracted but does not have a learning disability. His difficulties have been described as a behaviour exceptionality, with a focus on defiant behaviours and disruptions to the classroom.

**Scott is included in a grade 3 class and learns to read in a small group in the resource room.** Scott was born with Down syndrome. His family has always involved him in all their activities and he has always been in regular education programs. After participating in early intervention (from the age of 2 months to 4 years) and attending the neighbourhood preschool, he moved with his classmates to kindergarten. At his teacher's suggestion Scott stayed in kindergarten for a second year. Since then he has moved to the next grade each year. Like many people with Down syndrome, Scott learns much by watching. For the past two years, he has watched and asked Billy, a friend and classmate with ADHD, whenever he didn't know what to do. Scott's parents and teachers know that the gap between Scott's academic achievement and that of his classmates will gradually increase. However, Scott works hard, likes school, and especially likes learning to read. Scott recognizes and sounds out many words, is reading small books with predictable stories, and recognizes the names of all the students in his class for the past year. In math Scott can add and subtract numbers less than 10 and hopes to learn to use his new calculator this year. He loves environmental science, discusses issues such as recycling, watches nature programs on television, and attends the "young naturalists" program in his community. Scott hopes to work in environmental protection when he grows up. His IEP (part of which appears in Figure 3.6 on page 111) lists his exceptionality as mild intellectual disabilities and refers to Scott's lower-than-average intellectual, social, and adaptive functioning.

1. Which of the characteristics of each student are most likely to affect learning and participation in the regular classroom? What learning needs are implied by these characteristics?

2. With such a range of characteristics and learning needs, what do exceptional students like Urjo and Scott who are learning in inclusive classrooms have in common?

3. How frequently is a teacher likely to be teaching a student with each of these exceptionalities?

4. What types of differentiation does each student need in order to be included in the social life and the group learning activities of the classroom?

5. What community resources can a teacher draw on to supplement in-school resources when teaching each of these students?

Cross-Reference
Chapter 4 focuses on descriptions of, and adaptations or differentiations for, students with low-incidence exceptionalities, physical disabilities, and chronic health conditions.

# Introduction

In this chapter you will learn about the characteristics and needs of students with a range of **high-incidence exceptionalities** and about classroom differentiations that help these students to learn. When you read the definitions and characteristics of exceptionalities, try to think of individual exceptional students whom you have met or taught. Definitions enable communication, but they never capture the essence of the individual exceptional learner. Our language must be respectful and professional; for example, don't refer to exceptional children with learning disabilities as "the learning disableds." Keeping two things in mind may help you to use person-first language: (1) exceptional students are children and adolescents *first* and (2) they also have *some* characteristics associated with their exceptionality; think about how you would want teachers to speak if you were the parent of an exceptional student. We usually refer to the student first and describe the student as *having* an exceptionality second. The exception to this general rule, for the exceptionalities described in this chapter, is the expression "children who *are* gifted."

The focus here is on teaching students with each of six high-incidence or frequently occurring exceptionalities. For each exceptionality, the section begins with the words of a child or adolescent, modelled on sources like *The Kids on the Block* book series (Aiello & Shulman, 1991a, b; 1995a, b; 1997a, b) that contain the diaries or personal stories of exceptional individuals. The remainder of each entry follows a pattern: first, the exceptionality is described with information about its incidence or frequency. Then we focus on characteristics and on implications for learning and for differentiating in the classroom. There are examples of teachers differentiating or ADAPTing in elementary and secondary classrooms. The implications for social and adult participation of exceptional learners in employment and community life are explored briefly because these are important in a society committed to inclusion. Throughout the chapter, you will find reminders that exceptional students are most successful when their teachers and parents hold realistic but high expectations for them. The intent of this chapter is to provide information for other parts of the book as well as a resource to which you can return when you encounter exceptional learners in your classroom.

Students with high-incidence exceptionalities are gifted or have learning disabilities, attention deficit hyperactivity disorder, speech or language disabilities, behaviour or emotional exceptionalities, or mild intellectual disabilities. It is usually thought that they make up approximately 75 percent of the exceptional student population in Canadian schools. (This may be a bit misleading because some of these students will also have asthma, allergies, diabetes, and other chronic health conditions described in Chapter 4.) The definitional terms and characteristics for high-incidence exceptionalities are summarized in Table 3.1. These students are often difficult to distinguish from peers without exceptionalities, especially outside school settings. Students with high-incidence exceptionalities frequently show a combination of behavioural, social, and academic needs. Gifted students usually benefit from challenges and opportunities to work with developmentally advanced peers. Other students with high-incidence exceptionalities usually benefit from differentiated teaching and systematic, structured, instructional interventions such as those described in this chapter and throughout the book.

**TABLE 3.1 STUDENTS WITH HIGH-INCIDENCE EXCEPTIONALITIES**

| Exceptionality | Description |
|---|---|
| Gifted or developmentally advanced | Demonstrated or potential abilities show exceptionally high capability in specific disciplines, intellect, or creativity. |
| Learning disabilities | Dysfunctions in processing information. Often defined as a discrepancy between ability and school achievement. Difference in ability/achievement not due to (a) visual, hearing, or motor disability; (b) emotional disturbance; or (c) environmental, cultural, or economic disadvantage. General intellectual functioning within normal range. |
| Attention deficit hyperactivity disorder | Persistent pattern of inattention and impulsiveness that may be accompanied by hyperactivity. |
| Communication exceptionalities | Refers to exceptionalities in speech or language. Speech is disordered when it deviates so far from the speech of other people that it calls attention to itself, interferes with communication, or causes the speaker or listeners distress. Language is disordered when student has impairment in expressive or receptive language. |
| Behaviour and emotional exceptionalities | Dysfunctional interactions between a student and his or her environment, including the classroom, home, and community. Can be seen in inability to build or maintain satisfactory interpersonal relationships with peers and teachers. |
| Mild intellectual disabilities | Lower-than-average intellectual functioning and adaptive behaviour. Knows a great deal about living in the community without supervision; requires some instruction that could be provided under relatively non-intensive conditions. |

## THEORY AND RESEARCH HIGHLIGHTS FROM

## EDUCATIONAL PSYCHOLOGY

## The Concept of Intelligence

Definitions of a number of the high-incidence exceptionalities in this chapter include references to intelligence (e.g., gifted, learning disabilities, intellectual disabilities). However, there is considerable controversy about what is meant by intelligence and how it should be measured and even whether it should be measured. Early theories about intelligence referred to one or more of the following: capacity to learn, total knowledge already learned, and ability to adapt to new situations. In 1986 twenty-four psychologists attended a symposium on intelligence and provided twenty-four distinct views about the nature of intelligence (Sternberg & Detterman, 1986). There was little agreement about the structure of intelligence, whether it was composed of a single, general ability or of many separate, domain-specific abilities (Gustafsson & Undheim, 1996). However, there was more agreement about the importance of higher-order thinking (e.g., abstract reasoning,

decision-making, problem solving) as well as metacognition—that is, thinking about thinking and knowledge of oneself.

An early theorist supporting general ability, Charles Spearman (1927), advocated a general factor, $g$, or general intelligence which he thought combined with specific abilities to enable us to perform mental tasks such as memorization and mental addition. Today, theorists suggest that intelligence has many components which can be viewed as a hierarchy of abilities with general ability at the top (Sternberg, 1998). And researchers like Byrnes and Fox (1998) suggest that general ability is related to maturation and functioning of the frontal lobe of the brain, while other parts of the brain may be responsible for specific abilities.

In contrast, Edward Thurstone (1938) theorized a number of distinct "primary mental abilities" for memory, numerical ability, reasoning, word fluency, etc., and no general intelligence. Guilford

*continued*

(1988) also proposed separate cognitive abilities, and Howard Gardner (1993) has gone so far as to postulate that there are eight or more multiple intelligences: verbal, spatial, logico-mathematical, naturalist, musical, bodily-kinesthetic, interpersonal, and intrapersonal. He contends that intelligence is the ability to solve problems and create products valued by one's culture.

Recent work in cognitive psychology has focused on how we gather and use information to solve problems, which is sometimes called cognitive processing or information processing. Robert Sternberg (1990) developed a triarchic theory of intelligence with three components: analytic or componential intelligence (consisting of abstract thinking abilities, verbal abilities, etc.); creative or experiential intelligence (emphasizing the ability to formulate new ideas and deal with novel situations); and practical or tacit intelligence (meaning the ability to adapt to changing environments). By 2008 Sternberg was describing these three components as the theory of successful intelligence: creative skills in generating novel ideas, analytical skills in discerning whether they are good ideas, and practical skills in implementing the ideas and persuading others of their worth (Sternberg, 2008b). His data suggest that when tests based on the theory of successful intelligence are used to supplement the SAT (admissions tests to American colleges), the prediction of college success is improved and differences in scores among members of diverse ethnic groups are reduced.

The irony is that while these theoretical developments proceed, schools, for the most part, continue to use standardized tests to measure children and adolescents' intelligence in a completely atheoretical way. In 1904 Alfred Binet developed a test with his collaborator, Theophile Simon, intended to measure mental age. By this they meant that a child who passed the tests normally passed by an 8 year old had a mental age of 8, regardless of chronological age. The Stanford-Binet Intelligence Scale has been revised a number of times and, while the concept of mental age has been altered somewhat, no one has developed theoretical underpinnings for the test. The most-used intelligence test in Canada and the United States is the Wechsler Intelligence Test for Children (WISC-III, Sattler, 1992), which was designed to predict school achievement. It is similar to the Stanford-Binet in design and concept, and is also atheoretical. Most intelligence tests are designed so an average score is 100, and 68 percent of the population will earn scores between 85 and 115. Only about 16 percent of the population will receive scores either above 115 or below 85. However, the tests are less reliable as one gets away from the normal range, and yet they are most often used to identify those students with high scores (gifted students) or low scores (students with developmental disabilities), and those with discrepancies between ability or IQ and achievement (students with learning disabilities). Canadian students may be disadvantaged by questions that contain references to US content (such as imperial measures), and the tests are not likely to be valid for students from culturally diverse backgrounds for whom English is a second language.

There have been vigorous debates over whether intelligence is better understood as domain-specific (applicable only to one subject, such as mathematics) or as domain-general (applicable to any field of instruction). Sternberg (2008a) argues for a domain-general understanding of intelligence. There are also debates over whether intelligence is more a matter of nature (born with it, cannot do anything about it) or nurture (can be developed through stimulation and education). Today most psychologists believe both are important (e.g., Weinberg, 2007). Because we, as educators, can do little about nature, we must make every effort to influence nurture—to produce stimulating, caring classrooms in which students take risks and are willing to use and develop their intelligence.

## References

Byrnes, J.P., & Fox, N.A. (1998). The educational relevance of research in cognitive neuroscience. *Educational Psychology Review, 10*, 297–342.

Gardner, H. (1993). *Multiple intelligences: The theory in practice.* New York: Basic Books.

Guilford, J.P. (1988). Some changes in the Structure-of-Intellect model. *Educational and Psychological Measurement, 48*, 1–4.

Gustafsson, J.-E., & Undheim, J.O. (1996). Individual differences in cognitive functioning. In D. Berliner & R. Calfee (Eds.), *Handbook of educational psychology* (pp. 186–242). New York: Macmillan.

Sattler, J.M. (1992). *Assessment of children* (rev. 3rd ed.). San Diego, CA: Jerome M. Sattler, Publisher, Inc.

Spearman, C. (1927). *The abilities of man: Their nature and measurement.* New York: Macmillan.

Sternberg, R.J. (1990). *Metaphors of mind: Conceptions of the nature of intelligence.* New York: Cambridge University Press.

Sternberg, R.J. (1998). Myths, countermyths, and truths about intelligence. In A. Woolfolk (Ed.), *Readings in educational psychology* (2nd ed., pp. 53–60). Boston: Allyn & Bacon.

Sternberg, R.J. (2008a). Applying psychological theories to educational practice. *American Educational Research Journal, 45*, 150–165.

Sternberg, R.J. (2008b). Increasing academic excellence and enhancing diversity are compatible goals. *Educational Policy, 22*, 487–514.

Sternberg, R.J., & Detterman, D.L. (Eds.). (1986). What is intelligence? Contemporary viewpoints on its nature and definition. Norwood, NJ: Ablex.

Thurstone, E.L. (1938). Primary mental abilities. *Psychometric Monographs,* No. 1.

Weinberg, R.A. (2007). Beyond nature–nurture. *Monograph for the Society for Research in Child Development, 72,* 145–149.

# Teaching Students Who Are Gifted or Developmentally Advanced

Teacher: How can I help you stay out of trouble?

Brian: I don't want to be bored. Challenge me. Let me work ahead on things that really interest me.

*Brian is a gifted Aboriginal boy in grade 3. This exchange took place after his teacher had intervened in a scuffle between Brian and a classmate for the third time in a week.*

Teacher: Why did you push Larry?

Brian: When I have nothing to do, he gets to me. He calls me "brainer" and tells me that I'm weird. When I'm busy, I don't notice as much. I need more stuff to do … please.

## Description of Gifted Students

Students who are advanced in one or in many areas of development are described as gifted or talented. They exceed the expectations of teachers and parents in specific areas of development or of the school curriculum. Over the years definitions of giftedness have provoked controversy; for example, see a classic paper by Robert Hoge of Carleton University (1988). In the past gifted students were identified by high scores on intelligence tests and often were assumed to be advanced in all areas. Michael Pyryt of the University of Calgary has conducted research on the role of general intelligence in giftedness (e.g., 2000). However, recent provincial definitions tend to reflect the research of Dan Keating and Dona Matthews (1996; Matthews, 1997; Matthews & Steinhauer, 1998; Matthews et al., 2007) conducted in Ontario schools. They emphasize that gifted learners are **developmentally advanced** in specific **domains**. They have argued that teachers should consider their students' "habits of mind" and also take into account socio-emotional factors (e.g., motivation, engagement) and respect variation in pace and learning characteristics (e.g., curiosity, anxiety, etc.) (Keating, 1996; Keating & Matthews, 1999). Matthews and her colleagues (2007) argue that when children demonstrate advanced subject-specific ability at a particular point in time, teachers need to make significant adaptations to the curriculum so learning opportunities are suitably challenging.

Students are considered gifted when they possess demonstrated or potential abilities that give evidence of exceptionally high capability with respect to intellect, creativity, or the skills associated with specific disciplines. Students who are gifted often demonstrate outstanding abilities in more than one area. They may demonstrate extraordinary intensity of focus in their particular areas of talent or interest. However, they may also have accompanying disabilities and should not be expected to have strengths in all areas of intellectual functioning (BC Special Education Branch, 2006).

## Incidence of Giftedness

Incidence of giftedness is estimated at 2 to 5 percent of school-aged children (Winzer, 2007), although one frequently hears the claim that a student can be gifted in one province and "not gifted" in another province (Lupart et al., 2005). Although some gifted students can be easily identified because they use their abilities and are willing to be recognized for them, some gifted students go unnoticed.

**Further Reading**

On applying Sternberg's concept of successful intelligence to teaching gifted learners:

Sternberg, R.J. (2007). Who are the bright children? The cultural context of being and acting intelligent. *Educational Researcher, 36*(3), 148–155.

Sternberg, R.J., & Grigorenko, E.L. (2004). Successful intelligence in the classroom. *Theory into Practice, 43*(4), 274–280.

Sternberg, R.J., & Grigorenko, E.L. (2003). Teaching for successful intelligence: Principles, procedures, and practices. *Journal for the Education of the Gifted, 27*(2/3), 207–228.

**Weblinks**

COUNCIL FOR EXCEPTIONAL CHILDREN (GIFTED EDUCATION/DUAL EXCEPTIONALITIES)
www.cec.sped.org/Content/NavigationMenu/NewsIssues/TeachingLearningCenter/ExceptionalityArea

GIFTED CANADA
www3.telus.net/giftedcanada

UNIVERSITY OF CALGARY CENTRE FOR GIFTED EDUCATION
www.gifted.ucalgary.ca

Studies suggest that groups at risk for being unidentified include young boys, adolescent girls, students from diverse cultural groups, and students with disabilities (Lupart & Pyryt, 1996; Lupart & Wilgosh, 1998; Pedersen & Kitano, 2006). Judy Lupart of the University of Alberta has studied the career aspirations of adolescent girls who are gifted in science (e.g., Lupart & Cannon, 2000) and the accomplishments of gifted women (Lupart, Barva, & Cannon, 2000). Her studies show that women consider their personal accomplishments, as well as their career accomplishments, to be important. A recent paper suggests that adolescent girls report similar patterns with "mixed emotions" about family and career aspirations (Lupart et al., 2004).

## Characteristics of Students Who Are Gifted

What should you look for to ensure that you recognize students who are gifted? No student will show all of the characteristics described here. Gurjit, who was described in the case study that opened Chapter 1, could meet most, if not all, of the learning outcomes for a social studies unit before it began. Gurjit's questions in class indicated she was bored by the discussion. On challenging tasks, she read and wrote more and at a higher level of complexity than her classmates. Like many gifted students, Gurjit was articulate. Often gifted students' vocabularies are advanced and sophisticated. They may show an unusual degree of curiosity, of ingenuity in seeking answers, and of persistence with tasks they enjoy. The same students may surprise you with their ordinary performance in subjects in which they do not excel.

### COGNITIVE CHARACTERISTICS

In general, students gifted in academic skills and cognitive functioning differ from their classmates in three key ways: (1) the rate at which they learn new knowledge or skills, (2) the depth of their comprehension, and (3) the range of their interests (Maker & Nielson, 1996). Research by Bruce Shore of McGill University (e.g., Shore, 2000; Hannah & Shore, 2008; Martini & Shore, 2008) suggests they often demonstrate enhanced **metacognition** or ability to decide when and where to use their knowledge and skills. Characteristics that suggest advanced cognitive development include

- a large vocabulary and high verbal fluency;
- an excellent retention of new knowledge;
- a facility for learning quickly and easily;
- a demonstrated ability to generalize information;
- a demonstrated ability to make abstractions readily;
- good observational skills; the capacity to identify similarities, differences, and relationships; and
- good organizational and planning skills.

Renzulli's Enrichment Triad Model (MacRae & Lupart, 1991; Reis & Renzulli, 2002; Renzulli, 2005) describes giftedness as an interaction among three primary clusters of characteristics: (1) above-average **cognitive abilities**, as described above, (2) high levels of task commitment, and (3) high levels of creativity. **High task commitment** is found in students who work hard and need little external motivation, especially in areas that interest them. In general, they set their own goals, embrace

*Gifted students are challenged by authentic problem solving in places such as the Toronto Zoo. These students examine specimens in the butterfly meadows, a natural habitat area at the zoo.*

new challenges, and show perseverance. However, high task commitment sometimes results in perfectionism; gifted students may chastise themselves when they make a mistake or misbehave, and may think they should excel at everything (Pyryt, 2007). High levels of **creativity** are demonstrated by students' contributing many ideas, transforming and combining ideas, asking questions, and being insatiably curious about many topics.

## BEHAVIOUR CHARACTERISTICS

The behaviour of gifted students varies. For example, for the past fifteen years, studies have reported inconclusive findings on the relationship between giftedness and self-concept (Bain & Bell, 2004; Hoge & Renzulli, 1993; Swiatek, 2007). Pyryt and Romney of Alberta reviewed the research on social giftedness (2002). Sometimes gifted students are more advanced intellectually than emotionally (Delisle & Galbraith, 2004). These students may also show enhanced concern for justice and advanced awareness of complex ethical, environmental, and societal issues (Hartsell, 2006; von Karolyi, 2006). Foster and Matthews (2006) wrote a paper following the December 2004 tsunami disaster in South and Southeast Asia (revised in 2006), Troubling Times: How Parents and Teachers Can Help Children Understand and Confront Adversity. They suggest that parents and teachers listen

**Further Reading**

Smith, C.M.M. (Ed.). (2006). *Including the gifted and talented: Making inclusion work for the gifted and able learners.* London, UK: Routledge.

Lupart, J.L., Pyryt, M.C., Watson, S.L., & Pierce K. (2005). Gifted education and counseling in Canada. *International Journal for the Advancement of Counseling, 27*(2), 173–190.

Matthews, D.J., & Foster, J.F. (2005). *Being smart about gifted children: A guidebook for parents and educators.* Scottsdale, AZ: Great Potential Press.

Reis, S.M., & Renzulli, J.S. (2002). *The Secondary Triad Model: A practical plan for implementing gifted programs at the junior and senior high school levels.* Heatherton, Australia: Hawker Brownlow Education.

Delisle, J., & Galbraith, J. (2004). *When gifted kids don't have all the answers: How to meet their social and emotional needs.* Minneapolis, MN: Free Spirit Publishing.

Colangelo, N., & Davis, G.A. (2003). *Handbook of gifted education* (3rd ed.). Boston: Allyn & Bacon.

Sternberg, R.J. (Ed.). (2004). *Definitions and conceptions of giftedness.* Thousand Oaks, CA: Corwin Press.

to children's concerns, acknowledge that there are troubles in the world, focus on how problems are being addressed, and help children to set reasonable goals for what they can do about the circumstances (www.sengifted.org/articles_social/FosterMatthews_TroublingTimes.shtml).

## Implications for Learning and Differentiating in the Classroom for Students Who Are Gifted

Interestingly, differentiated education was originally developed to meet the needs of gifted learners (Tomlinson, 1999) and then recognized as appropriate for all learners. So consider differentiation when planning teaching for gifted students. To teach students who are gifted effectively, it also helps to discover what challenges individual students. In areas of the curriculum where a student is not challenged, look for ways to remedy that. Strategies that are often suggested include enabling students to pursue their interests (e.g., Gentry, Peters, & Mann, 2007; Renzulli, Gentry, & Reis, 2003); using tiered assignments as has been discussed throughout this book (Rakow, 2007); introducing technologies, like spreadsheets, to increase the sophistication of student projects (Siegle, 2005); assigning self-directed research projects (Hargrove, 2005); designing thought-provoking multicultural literature units (e.g., Pederson & Kitano, 2006); and developing accelerated programs (Renzulli, 2008). Acceleration refers to placing students based on readiness and potential to succeed rather than on chronological age (Colangelo & Assouline, 2005). Some acceleration strategies involve changing the placement of the student such as moving the student into the next grade for math class only, having the student skip a grade and move to the next grade in all subjects, creating combined classes, giving early entrance to kindergarten or grade one or early graduation from secondary school. Some acceleration strategies involve changing the curriculum while the student stays for all or most of the day with his or her same-age peers; examples include correspondence courses, subject-matter acceleration, curriculum compacting, continuous progress, access to a mentor, self-paced instruction, advanced placement, and the International Baccalaureate program. Reporting on the acceleration practices used across Canada, Kanevsky and McGrimmond (2008) found wide variation; acceleration practices that kept quick learners with age-mates while pursuing content beyond their grade level were supported and implemented to a greater extent than those that involve moving students to settings with older students. In Quebec, however, the opposite was true, and gifted students were more likely to be placed with older students. Some provinces had specific policies, but few reporting school districts in those provinces were aware of or offered options to advanced students that were consistent with the policies. Kavevsky and McGrimmond concluded, "It is clear that policy does not guarantee participation and participation does not depend on policy" (p. 13).

Research suggests that gifted learners need to be with their intellectual peers for at least part of the school day so they are stimulated in areas in which they are advanced (Cross, 2002). However, they also benefit from learning with same-age peers during each school day. Some gifted students prefer to work independently and learn alone (Pyryt, Sandals, & Begoray, 1998). It may be important to honour this preference at some time during each day as well. Students sometimes need help to understand their rights and responsibilities and to make sound choices; teaching self-advocacy will encourage gifted students to become partners in differentiation (Douglas, 2004). Strategies for differentiating the curriculum to meet the needs of gifted students appear in Table 3.2. Figure 3.1 on page 78 is an example of an **open-ended assignment**.

TABLE 3.2 ENRICHMENT STRATEGIES FOR TEACHING GIFTED STUDENTS

| Strategies | Descriptions and Examples |
|---|---|
| Sophistication | Introduce students to the theories and concepts that underlie the content being learned by the class. *Example:* When teaching about child development in a secondary course on psychology, provide gifted students with writings by Piaget and Montessori and encourage them to make systematic observations in a preschool. |
| Novelty | Students explore required curricular content from different and unique perspectives. *Example:* In history, gifted students write from the perspective of the oxen pulling the Red River cart across the Canadian West, or of the child who lived in Montreal while her father was a member of the North West Trading Company. |
| Authentic problem solving | Students apply their knowledge and skills to problems that are significant to their own lives. *Example:* When studying watersheds, gifted students test the water quality of a stream that runs through a park or that collects runoff from a parking lot in their community and prepare a report for town council. |
| Independent studies | Students pursue an area of personal interest or investigate a topic from the curriculum on their own. *Example:* Students select a character from *Hamlet* and prepare a résumé for that character based on their knowledge of the play. |
| Telescoping | Taking advantage of the overlap in curricula of adjacent grades, students do two curricula in a year. *Example:* Students complete grades 7 and 8 science in one year. |
| Compacting | After discerning what the student already knows of the unit, provide assignments so the student can master unfamiliar material. Then provide enrichment activities in the compacted area. *Example:* For a student who has already read and understood many of the events and issues of World War II as they appear in the curriculum, assign readings and written synopses of unfamiliar topics. When these are completed, encourage the student to choose a topic of interest about the role of the war in changing Canadian society, communicate with the War Museum, use the internet, conference with you regularly, and prepare a multimedia presentation on the chosen topic. |
| Ability grouping | Students work with their intellectual peers on a regular, part-time basis, within the classroom or outside the classroom, providing social and emotional support, as well as intellectual stimulation. *Example:* An advanced reading or math work group, perhaps with peers from other classes, for enrichment in one or more subject areas. |
| Mentor programs | Students apply their knowledge and skills in a hands-on, real-life setting under the supervision of an adult in the community. They can pursue special interests, grow in self-confidence, and try out possible career paths. *Example:* A student who has considerable skill as an artist might be partnered with a painter who invites her to visit her studio and share the experience of being a working artist preparing for an upcoming show. |
| Open-ended assignments | Students are given options for completing an assignment and decide how far to take their learning. *Example:* In a kindergarten unit on whales, provide required assignments that must be completed by all students about the habitat and diet of the whales studied; provide optional assignments that require more writing, allow children to create games for whales based on knowledge of whales' particular skills and characteristics, etc. See Figure 3.1 for an example of an open-ended assignment on whales. |
| Tiered assignments | You prepare a range of distinct assignments, from fairly simple to complex, all focusing on key learning outcomes for the lesson or unit. Students may be assigned a particular activity or activities, you may select one activity to be completed by everyone and allow students to choose another, or students may choose the level of assignments they will complete. *Example:* In a secondary drama unit, the tiers for a culminating assignment might include preparing a scene, an act, or a short play while employing two, three, or more actors, and embodying one or more of the themes from a list generated by the class. Each tier can be described separately so students see that they have choices with regard to degrees of complexity. |

# FIGURE 3.1 AN OPEN-ENDED ASSIGNMENT FOR A KINDERGARTEN CLASS CONTAINING GIFTED STUDENTS

**A Whale of a Party!**
Kindergarten Independent Project
Due Date: January 29, 1999

Dear Parents,
The following is an outline of the Independent Project for term two. The format I have set out does not have to be followed strictly, so if you or your child has something to add or change, please feel free to do so. The items that are starred (*) are optional. The written sections may be typed on a computer, but I would encourage student printing wherever possible. Obviously, I would like the students to do as much of the work as possible and to be making the decisions regarding their projects. However, this should be an enjoyable experience, so if they have reached their limit, feel free to give extra help or to cut something out. Stress quality over quantity and the experience/process over the final product. Finally, if you have any questions, don't hesitate to ask me in person or via the homework books.

You are going to throw a party, and all of your friends are whales. Pick two different kinds of whales to invite (three, if you are feeling extra keen) and fill out the following party plan. Plan on having 10 whale guests.

**The Guest List**

(a) What kind of whales did you choose to invite and why? Make sure you invite whales that will get along (i.e., whales that will not eat each other!).
(b) Make a list of their names (e.g., Ollie Orca, Mandy Minke, etc.).
(c) *List the general address you would send an invitation to in January for each type of whale (e.g., Arctic Ocean).

**The Invitation**

Hand in a sample of the invitation you would send out to your guests.
Your invitation should include
(a) A cover design.
(b) The name and type of whale (e.g., Ollie Orca) to whom the invitation is addressed.
(c) *Location of the party (consider the size of your guests, but you can pretend that the whales can be out of the water for your wingding).
(d) Date and time of the party.
(e) RSVP address or telephone number.

**The Party**

(a) Draw me a picture of how you would decorate the party location to make your guests feel at home.
(b) Draw and/or print a menu of the food you will serve your guests.
    On another piece of paper, list the following:
(c) *The kind of music you will listen to at your party (this can be people music—Hilary Duff rocks!)
(d) *Will you ask your guests to do any tricks or play any games at your party (find out if your guests are especially good at something)?
(e) *Will you send your guests home with a party favour? What will it be?

**The Party's Over**

(a) Draw me a picture of what a photograph taken at your party might look like.
(b) *Write a thank-you letter that you think one of your guests might have sent you after the party.

Source: Developed by Jennifer A. Taylor of Kingston, Ontario, 1999, for a kindergarten class that included a number of students who were developmentally advanced in reading and writing. Used by permission.

## Implications for Social and Career Participation of Students Who Are Gifted

**Weblinks**

NATIONAL YOUTH ORCHESTRA OF CANADA (FOR TALENTED YOUTH)
www.nyoc.org

COLONY OF AVALON AT FERRYLAND, NEWFOUNDLAND (CANADIAN ARCHAEOLOGICAL SITE)
www.heritage.nf.ca/avalon

SUPPORTING EMOTIONAL NEEDS OF THE GIFTED (SENG)
www.sengifted.org/articles_social

Surprisingly, gifted adolescents often find it difficult to focus their career aspirations and to make appropriate course selections. This may be because they have so many talents and interests. Allen is a talented musician and a top student in almost every curriculum subject. He has been invited to audition for the Canadian Youth Orchestra (CYO) this spring. If Allen attends CYO, he cannot take part in an archaeological dig for which only eight students have been accepted. Allen says that every cello lesson reinforces his desire to be a professional musician.

However, after spending a day at the dig, he is just as passionate about becoming an archaeologist. Allen's guidance counsellor invites him to a seminar on careers and course choices. After the seminar Allen tells the counsellor he has not realized that there were prerequisite courses for entering a university program in archaeology. Allen also enrols in a co-operative education placement with an archaeologist, for which he will receive a secondary school credit. Research in Ontario (Chin, Munby, Hutchinson, & Steiner-Bell, 2000) reports that many university and community college students have completed co-operative education placements to try out careers they think they want to pursue. For example, one college student described taking a co-op placement in a veterinary clinic to decide whether she wanted to be a veterinarian technologist. Like over 95 percent of the former co-op education students questioned, she recommended co-op education to others (Chin et al., 2000). Gentry and her colleagues (2007) reported that gifted and talented students valued their experiences in a career development program in which teachers sought and built on the students' interests and connected them with adults and with other students who shared their interests.

# Teaching Students with Learning Disabilities

> Frank watched his teacher putting the afternoon schedule on the board. The list included reading, social studies, and journal writing. Did that mean oral reading? Frank had not practised the next story in the book. If the teacher asked him to read, he would die, the other kids would laugh, and.... He tried to think of a way to get out of class before oral reading started. He felt his chest tightening, his stomach flipping, and his palms growing damp. Frank hated to stutter and stumble. He slouched down in his seat and worried. He kept asking himself, "How bad can it be?" But he knew the answer: "Bad!" When you can't read in grade 6, it's bad.

## Description of Students with Learning Disabilities

The words above are those of a grade 6 student with learning disabilities. Students with learning disabilities have dysfunction in **information processing**. They may have disabilities in reading (**dyslexia**), writing (**dysgraphia**), or arithmetic (**dyscalculia**). In the provincial documents the term *learning disabilities* (LD) is usually used to refer to exceptional students with a **discrepancy** between ability (usually measured by an intelligence test) and achievement in one or more of the following areas: reading, writing, language acquisition, mathematics, reasoning, and listening. In most provinces the documents on LD specify that this discrepancy is not primarily the result of a visual, hearing, or motor disability; emotional or behaviour disability; or environmental, cultural, or economic disadvantage. Usually the term LD is used to describe students who have at least average ability and from whom we would ordinarily expect better achievement (Klassen, 2002; Philpott & Cahill, 2008). Much of the research on LD focuses on inefficient cognitive processing and the need for direct teaching.

### CONTROVERSIES

Controversies surround definitions of LD (Fletcher et al., 2007). In two recent papers Robert Klassen of the University of Alberta (2002) and David Philpott and Millie Cahill of Memorial University of Newfoundland (2008) describe the consistencies and inconsistencies in definitions and procedures for identification. The discrepancies across provinces give a larger role to the Learning Disabilities Association of Canada (LDAC). In its definition of learning disabilities published in 2002, LDAC emphasized four aspects: that learning disabilities are neurobiological, genetic, lifelong, and felt in all areas of life, not just education. The Learning Disabilities Association of Ontario (LDAO) (2001) proposed a definition that emphasized impairments in psychological processes related to learning that cause difficulties in skills such as oral language, reading, written language, and mathematics.

According to both these definitions, learning disabilities are caused by genetic, congenital, and/or acquired neurobiological factors that result in impairments in one or more of the psychological processes related to learning. Both these definitions include reference to the "unexpected" aspects of learning disabilities: that individuals' difficulties with learning in specific areas are at odds with their overall ability. This has been called the discrepancy aspect of LD.

Linda Siegel of the University of British Columbia (e.g., 1999) and Keith Stanovich of the University of Toronto (e.g., 2005) have argued against using discrepancy formulas in the way most provinces do. They argue that all students who show disabilities in learning (e.g., in phonological processing in beginning reading) should be identified as having LD. In a recent book that reviews the extensive research on learning disabilities in academic subjects, Jack Fletcher and his colleagues, including Marcia Barnes of the University of Guelph, argue that learning disabilities are based on strengths and weaknesses in academic skills. "For each LD, the primary manifestation of the disability represents specific academic skill deficits (e.g., in word recognition, reading comprehension, reading fluency, mathematics computations/problem solving, and written expression)" (2007, p. 2).

Since 2004 some American states have begun to use response to intervention (RTI) to identify students with learning disabilities. "Models incorporating RTI typically involve identification based in part on mass screening of all students and repeated probe assessments of the same core area, such as reading or math, in students who demonstrate risk characteristics" (Fletcher et al., p. 50). Those who do not benefit adequately from increasingly intense

*Students with learning disabilities often find written work in the classroom challenging.*

instruction can be identified as having LD. Thus one criterion for identifying LD is that a student does not respond to appropriate instruction and high-quality intervention. Although New Brunswick, Ontario, and Saskatchewan have all referred to RTI in at least one of their provincial documents, no province in Canada currently uses RTI to identify LD (Mattatall, 2008). In Philpott and Cahill's study (2008), five provinces or territories reported efforts to move toward using RTI to identify LD. In 2007 a study of the views of American school psychologists showed that they thought all of RTI, cognitive processing, and phonemic awareness should be components of the definition of LD, although over half still endorsed the use of an IQ-achievement discrepancy criterion for identification (Machek & Nelson). It appears that, as in exceptional education generally, the field of LD is undergoing a period of change in fundamental definitions and approaches to assessment and intervention while controversies abound.

Some jurisdictions state that learning disabilities are apparent in both academic and social situations (e.g., Ontario Ministry of Education, 2001b). Researchers debate whether **social skills difficulties** are a **primary disability** or a **secondary disability** that arises from living with a learning disability (Cartledge, 2005). Research findings about social skills are inconsistent. Teachers report that *most* students with LD experience social skills difficulties and peers report that *many* have low **social status**; however, only a *few* children with LD report low social **self-concept**. For reviews see Bryan (1999) or Vaughn, Elbaum, & Boardman (2001); for recent studies, see Walker and Nabuzoka (2007) and Nirit and Ilanit (2008).

### READING DISABILITIES OR DYSLEXIA

Most students with LD experience difficulties learning to read. Recent research strongly supports insufficiently developed phonemic awareness as a characteristic of most children with reading disabilities in the primary grades. **Phonemic awareness** refers to the awareness that words can be segmented into component sounds, identifying sounds in various positions in words, and manipulating sounds in words. Ryder, Tunmer, and Greaney (2008) defined phonemic awareness as "the ability to reflect on and manipulate the phonemic elements of spoken words" (p. 351). Studies by Keith Stanovich of the University of Toronto (e.g., 1996) and John Kirby of Queen's University (e.g., Parrila, Kirby & McQuarrie, 2004) have contributed to this literature. One Canadian study reported that phonemic processing in grade 1 was the best predictor of grade 6 reading (Cunningham & Stanovich, 1997). Recent reviews have shown that phoneme awareness is key to reading an alphabetic system and explicit, systematic instruction in phonemic awareness is necessary for most children and does no harm to those for whom it is redundant (Shankweiler & Fowler, 2004). Snow & Juel (2005) concluded that the development of detailed orthographic patterns is necessary for children to develop automatic word recognition, and that phonemic awareness interventions are effective in helping *most* children with learning disabilities to learn to read (e.g., Ehri et al., 2001 [US National Reading Panel]; Martinussen, Kirby, & Das, 1998; Ryder et al., 2008; Schneider, Ennemoser, Roth, & Kuspert, 1999). Studies by Maryanne Wolf and other researchers suggest that **rapid naming** (sometimes called RAN) also plays a significant role in beginning reading (Johnston & Kirby, 2006; Katzir, Wolf, et al., 2008; Stringer, Toplak, & Stanovich, 2004). This has been called the **double-deficit hypothesis**, referring to deficits in both phonemic awareness and rapid naming.

**Weblinks**

Investigate the report of the National Panel on Reading online or on video:

NATIONAL READING PANEL, 2000
www.nationalreadingpanel.org
www.nationalreadingpanel.org/
Publications/textversionvideo.htm

Cross-Reference
Chapter 7 contains practical strategies to implement phonemic awareness interventions.

Ellery, V. (2005). *Creating strategic readers: Techniques for developing competency, in phonemic awareness, phonics, fluency, vocabulary, and comprehension.* Newark, DE: International Reading Association.
Adams, M.J., Foorman, B.R., Lundberg, I., & Beeler, T. (1998). *Phonemic awareness in young children: A classroom curriculum.* Toronto: Irwin Publishers.
Cunningham, P.M., & Hall, D.P. (2008). *Making words: Second grade: 100 hands-on lessons for phonemic awareness, phonics and spelling.* Boston: Pearson/Allyn & Bacon.

A recent review of sixty-six studies, part of the US National Reading Panel's meta-analysis, showed that systematic instruction in phonics also had a moderate but positive effect on learning to read. The three other research-based components of early reading essential for balanced literacy programs are fluency, vocabulary development, and text comprehension (National Reading Panel, 2000; www.nationalreadingpanel.org). John McNamara of Brock University and Bernice Wong of Simon Fraser University suggest in a recent paper (2003) that students with learning disabilities manifest significant difficulties in memory for everyday information; perhaps this reflects specific deficiencies in central executive functioning, which may not be limited to school subjects like reading and math.

## Incidence of Learning Disabilities

For more than a decade provinces have been reporting that roughly half of exceptional students have learning disabilities, making this the most frequently occurring exceptionality (Friend et al., 1998). Definitional controversies and inconsistent identification procedures influence Canadian estimates, which suggest that 2 to 4 percent of the school-age population has LD. Boys outnumber girls, although the reasons for this are still unclear (Whitley et al., 2007). In some provinces students with ADHD, another 3 to 5 percent, are considered to have LD. Similar data appear on the website of LDAC (www.ldac-taac.ca/InDepth/inDepth-e.asp#teachers).

## Characteristics of Students with LD

Teachers are the most likely people to suspect learning disabilities because the characteristics interfere with classroom learning. However, characteristics vary greatly from student to student.

### COGNITIVE CHARACTERISTICS

Students with LD demonstrate lower-than-expected achievement in one or more areas. You will also see academic strengths on which you can build and for which you can give praise. Frequently these students perform poorly on tasks requiring memory, focused attention, organization, metacognition, and information processing. These characteristics are elaborated in Table 3.3. You may see inaccurate, seemingly careless reproductions of teacher-created notes, with words omitted and organizational details overlooked. These students sometimes process information slowly, do not finish work in class, and appear to manage time poorly. Possibly they cannot start assignments because they don't know how to tackle them (Bennett et al., 2008), so you may be able to develop a strategy to help them begin promptly.

### CHARACTERISTICS: LEARNING TO READ

The subjects in which students with LD have academic needs are most often reading, writing, spelling, and mathematics, although difficulties in these subjects can sometimes affect learning in all areas of the curriculum. Differentiating teaching and adapting assessment in each of these subjects is discussed further in Chapters 7 and 8. In reading, insufficiently developed phonological processing (discussed earlier) is often followed by challenges in **reading comprehension** including missing the main idea, getting events out of sequence, and deducing content that is not there (Cunningham & Stanovich, 1997; Graham & Wong, 1993; Parrila et al.,

Weblinks

LEARNING DISABILITIES ASSOCIATION OF CANADA
www.ldac-taac.ca

DIVISION FOR LEARNING DISABILITIES OF COUNCIL FOR EXCEPTIONAL CHILDREN (CEC)
www.dldcec.org

LD ONLINE (TEACHING LD)
www.ldonline.org

**TABLE 3.3 WHAT ARE CHILDREN AND ADOLESCENTS WITH LEARNING DISABILITIES LIKE?**

Hard question. They are all different. No list of characteristics would describe every student with learning disabilities. Frequently they puzzle us because they strike us as bright kids, but closer inspection reveals real strengths and real weaknesses. Often they are overwhelmed by the volume of work they must do in the classroom, they always seem to be behind, and they can feel frustrated by these things. They do have average or better ability, but achievement lags behind ability.

Let's think about how students with learning disabilities learn. Definitions suggest they have "a disorder in one or more of the basic psychological processes involved in understanding or using language." Language refers to symbols of communication—spoken, written, or even behavioural. "Basic psychological processes" refers to taking in information (listening, reading, observing), making sense of information (relating, remembering, evaluating), and showing (speaking, writing, calculating). Students with LD seem to be less active as learners, to do less meaning-making, to be less strategic.

| Psychological Processes | What We Can Do |
|---|---|
| 1. PERCEPTION: organizing, interpreting what we experience; most impact when perception is critical to learning—early years; may confuse letters when learning to read, more often and longer. | WE CAN: keep pieces of information that are perceptually confusing from being presented together until at least one is learned well; important characteristics of information need to be highlighted. |
| 2. ATTENTION: refers to focusing on information; coming to and maintaining attention; some identified as having attention deficit disorder (ADD) or attention deficit with hyperactivity (ADHD); "in her/his own world"; distracted, in constant motion. | WE CAN: break task into smaller segments; gradually build up; cues can bring attention to key words in explanations; meaning-check for instructions; help identify the important, independently. |
| 3. MEMORY: arranging what they have perceived and attended to; many processes, e.g., problems in working memory (storing and retrieving information); too much so they only take in part of it (e.g., note-taking during a lecture); may not make connections. | WE CAN: help develop strategies for remembering (e.g., minute hand is longer than hour hand, minute is longer word); more practice; remind to find relationships; make it meaningful; teach strategies. |
| 4. METACOGNITION: monitoring and evaluating own learning; identifying most effective way to learn; key to learning from experience, generalizing, and applying; may act impulsively, or without monitoring or planning. | WE CAN: teach self-monitoring; model thinking out loud; ask the student to give reasons, give cues, give feedback, encourage, be clear, teach strategies. |
| 5. ORGANIZATION: come without pencil; lose papers; have difficulty getting good ideas into an essay or assignment; lose track of goal, especially if it is long-term. | WE CAN: teach routines, put checklist on desk or in notebook, break task into steps, put agenda on board, warn about major changes, ask questions to keep putting the onus on the student. |

Source: Hutchinson, N.L. (2004). *Teaching exceptional children and adolescents: A Canadian casebook* (2nd ed.), p. 144. Copyright Prentice Hall. Used by permission.

2004; Roberts et al., 2008). The areas of difficulty seen in adolescents weak in reading comprehension can include word recognition, language comprehension, and executive processes. Those poor in word recognition can be seen struggling to sound out words and seen not recognizing words by sight automatically that their

# FIGURE 3.2 CHARACTERISTICS OF LEARNING DISABILITIES IN YOUNG CHILDREN

**Problems in Reading**

- often lacks awareness of sounds that make up words, does not "attack" a new word but guesses or waits for the teacher to say the word
- loses meaning of sentence before getting to the end; loses sequence of what has been read
- is painful to listen to, finds reading painful and finds creative ways to avoid reading

**Difficulty in Copying**

- copies better from a page beside him than from the board, appears careless
- loses his place frequently and ignores organizational cues

**Difficulty with Alphabet**

- has difficulty remembering sounds of letters and names of letters
- confuses letter names and sounds if learning both at once
- shows poor penmanship with frequent reversals or distorted shapes or sizes of letters (or numbers)

**Strengths**

- often shows strengths in some areas and weaknesses in others, and really benefits from recognition of his strengths
- often expresses ideas better orally than in writing
- often highly motivated by small successes and willing to work very hard to succeed again
- often shows imagination and complex ideas when asked to draw or act out his ideas, but reverts to simpler ideas when writing to avoid errors or embarrassment

Source: Hutchinson, N.L. (2004). *Teaching exceptional children and adolescents: A Canadian casebook* (2nd ed.), p. 60. Copyright Prentice Hall. Used by permission.

peers already know. In language comprehension difficulties we see young people who are not able to speak easily about the background knowledge related to what they are reading because they lack the knowledge, the vocabulary, or the text structures. Their executive processes, both cognitive and metacognitive, may be inefficient and poorly chosen when they are executed. (For a thorough discussion of these issues, see Faggella-Luby & Deshler, 2008.)

The printed or written letters of students with LD can be distorted in size and shape, mirrored or reversed, and barely legible (Berninger et al., 2006; Terepocki, Kruk, & Willows, 2002). Because all students tend to reverse letters until about age 8, reversals are only a problem when they persist past that age. Some students also have difficulty learning to spell (James, 1996; Lennox & Siegel, 1996). The website of the LDAC contains lists of signs of LD for various ages (www.ldac-taac.ca/InDepth/background_signs-e.asp#k-4). The typical characteristics of young children with learning disabilities appear in Figure 3.2.

## CHARACTERISTICS: LEARNING MATH

Researchers suggest that **number sense** may be the mathematical equivalent of phonemic awareness in reading for students with LD (Chard et al., 2008; Jordan et al., 2007). According to Robbie Case (1998; Griffin & Case, 1997), who conducted research at the University of Toronto, number sense refers to children's flexibility with numbers, the sense of what numbers mean, and an ability to look at the world and make mental comparisons about quantities. Recent research has been conducted with students who experience difficulty retrieving basic number facts from long-term memory. It suggests that students with learning disabilities only in mathematics may have weak number sense, while those with learning disabilities in math and reading may be characterized by weak phonological processing (Robinson et al., 2002). Challenges often arise in learning addition facts and multiplication tables, and students may ignore columns in computations and carry or borrow incorrectly, issues addressed in research by Derek Berg of Mount St. Vincent University (Berg, 2006, 2007). Older students with LD often find it challenging to represent mathematical relations in math and science word problems (Montague et al., 2000). Perhaps this is a more complex form of number sense. High school students with LD in math are being hit hard by the increasing graduation requirements, which include algebra in many cases (Witzel et al., 2008). In students unable to grasp algebra, you may see lack of understanding of the use of symbols to replace numbers, and thus students treat algebra as if it were the same as arithmetic. They may memorize procedures when what is needed is to represent word problems (Hutchinson, 1993). They need more concrete methods of representation than are usually available in algebra classrooms (Witzel et al., 2008).

## SOCIAL AND BEHAVIOURAL CHARACTERISTICS

Some students' social and behavioural needs are expressed in task avoidance, social withdrawal, frustration, and **depression**. Nancy Heath of McGill University found that while more children with LD may have depressive symptoms, the relationship between depression and LD is complex (2001; Heath & Ross, 2000). Judy Wiener of the University of Toronto found that students with LD generally have low social status in the eyes of their peers (Kuhne & Wiener, 2000). These findings are supported by recent research (Estell et al., 2008; Walker & Nabuzoka, 2007). A Canadian study by Jess Whitley (2007) of the University of Ottawa shows that teachers rated social skills of students with LD lower than those of their peers and held lower aspirations for these students along with lower views of their work ethic. However, in a series of qualitative studies on social relations of children and adolescents with LD, graduate students at Queen's University reported more positive results. Some students with LD showed well-developed social skills and peer relations (for two case studies, see Lévesque, 1997), while others showed good social skills, peer acceptance, and peer relations in some contexts more than others (Chan, 2000; Stoch, 1999). This series of studies on the social competence of learners with LD was reviewed in Hutchinson, Freeman, and Steiner-Bell (2002). A literature review on the social competence of adolescents with LD, conducted by Hutchinson, Freeman, and Berg (2004), explored the implications for intervention. The authors recommend that interventions embrace the developmental characteristics of adolescents, adopt a contextualist perspective that honours the extent to which adolescents' social competence is context-dependent, and capitalize on adolescents' interests.

Rob Klassen has reported that adolescents with LD tend to overestimate their efficacy for spelling and writing (2007). He has also found that teachers who knew adolescents with LD well thought these adolescents were overconfident about their ability to complete academic tasks successfully (Klassen & Lynch, 2007). Dealing constructively with these data may be challenging for teachers because, as Klassen points out, we want these students to have realistic self-assessments but we don't want to discourage them by insisting on how incompetent they are. As

# Learning Disabilities in Mathematics

During the past twenty years, researchers like Byron Rourke at the University of Windsor and Linda Siegel at the University of British Columbia have found that while reading disability is dominant in children and adolescents with LD, it is not the only kind of disability. Both researchers discovered students with reading disability who have concomitant disability in mathematics. The older the student, the more likely reading disability will be accompanied by learning problems in mathematics.

Learning problems in mathematics are shown in a wide range of errors. These include difficulties with spatial organization, with aligning numbers in columns, and with visual details such as reading mathematical signs. Procedural errors in the steps in mathematical operations are common. Students with LD also tend to experience difficulties with the logic and reasoning that go into understanding mathematical problems and into generalizing from what is known to new problems or problems that appear different.

Rourke and his associates have also shown that there is a group of students with learning disabilities whose problems in mathematics are primarily centred on poor memory. They fail to remember the multiplication tables and the steps in computation. They also are likely to avoid math problems that demand reading.

Recent research suggests different connections between mathematics and memory. Studies by Lee Swanson of the University of California-Riverside, Jeffrey Bisanz of the University of Alberta, and Derek Berg of Mount Saint Vincent University report that mathematical computation is better predicted by verbal working memory than by visual–spatial working memory. Perhaps disabilities in mathematics are influenced by difficulties with both mathematics-specific memory and difficulties with general working memory.

There are many students with learning disabilities in mathematics. However, there is much more research on learning problems in reading and there is much more learning assistance for reading disabilities than for mathematics disabilities. Researchers like Russell Gersten and Nancy Jordan are beginning to develop early identification and interventions for students with mathematics difficulties.

To read more about students with learning disabilities in mathematics, consult any of the following research sources:

Berg, D.H. (2008). Working memory and arithmetic calculation in children: The contributory roles of processing speed, short-term memory, and reading. *Journal of Experimental Child Psychology, 99*(4), 288–308.

Gersten, R., Jordan, N.C., & Flojo, J.R. (2005). Early identification and interventions for students with mathematics difficulties. *Journal of Learning Disabilities, 38*(4), 293–304.

Hutchinson, N.L. (1993). Effects of cognitive strategy instruction on algebra problem solving of adolescents with learning disabilities. *Learning Disability Quarterly, 16*(1), 34–63.

Mabbott, D.J., & Bisanz, J. (2008). Computational skills, working memory, and conceptual knowledge in older children with mathematics learning disabilities. *Journal of Learning Disabilities, 41*(1), 15–28.

Rourke, B.P. (1989). *Nonverbal learning disabilities: The syndrome and the model.* New York: Guilford Press.

Shafrir, U., & Siegel, L.S. (1994). Subtypes of learning disabilities in adolescents and adults. *Journal of Learning Disabilities, 27*, 123–134.

Wilson, K.M., & Swanson, H.L. (2001). Are mathematics disabilities due to a domain-general or a domain-specific working memory deficit? *Journal of Learning Disabilities, 34*, 237–248.

Witzel, B.S., Riccomini, P.J., & Schneider, E. (2008). Implementing CRA with secondary students with learning disabilities in mathematics. *Intervention in School and Clinic, 43*(5), 270–276.

Source: Adapted from Hutchinson, N.L. (2004). *Teaching Exceptional Children and Adolescents: A Canadian Casebook* (2nd ed.), page 160.

teachers, we need to be approachable and encouraging while being realistic and creating classroom contexts in which students with LD can participate with enthusiasm and optimism, socially as well as academically.

## Implications for Learning and Classroom Differentiation: Students with LD

Most students with LD require differentiations in instruction and in the learning environment. They are usually taught in inclusive classrooms and may receive services in resource rooms.

## ESTABLISHING AN INCLUSIVE CLASSROOM

Establishing a safe classroom characterized by understanding and acceptance is the first step. In a study of inclusive secondary science teachers, Karol Lyn Edwards (2000) of Queen's University found that exemplary teachers helped students with LD to participate by using interactive teaching, checking the understanding of individual students, and eliminating bullying. Stough and Palmer (2003) reported that teachers who were expert at teaching exceptional students demonstrated knowledgeable, reflective, and concerned responsiveness to individual students. Long and her colleagues (2008) emphasized the importance of teachers' empathy, approachability, and willingness to differentiate instruction in promoting the confidence and engagement of students with learning disabilities. You can make a huge difference.

## DIFFERENTIATING TEACHING

You can build on an inclusive learning environment by differentiating your instructional techniques to make them more accessible to students with LD (Newfoundland and Labrador Department of Education, 1998). These differentiations include

- providing overviews of lessons in chart form;
- varying the **mode of presentation** (oral, visual, activity-based);
- **cueing** students to listen to, or make notes about, important points;
- relating material to students' lives and using experiential teaching approaches;
- making directions short and reinforcing oral directions with visual cues;
- clarifying definitions and ensuring understanding by having students repeat definitions;
- breaking a large topic or task into manageable parts with individual deadlines;
- using collaborative and co-operative learning approaches;
- offering assistance when it is needed, after students have asked their peers; and
- preparing **study guides** of key words and concepts so students have clear notes from which to study.

Students with LD may find **colour-coded** materials easier to organize and may benefit from manipulative learning materials. They may be able to complete a partially filled-in task. A tape recorder can provide a textbook in an alternative format, enable an older student to tape a complex lecture, and give almost immediate feedback for oral reading practice. It can also serve as a scribe to record an assessment or a composition. Cross-age teaching can help students with LD to learn by either teaching younger children or being befriended by older role models.

## TEACHING STRATEGIES

It is important that you demonstrate how to learn for the benefit of students with LD and allow students with LD time to practise the skills they find difficult. General organizational skills, highlighting main ideas, and note-taking strategies can be taught to the whole class; then provide additional practice for those who need it. For example, introduce agenda books and model how to make entries, and put

**Put into Practice**

Read the following papers and make a plan for what you could do to differentiate your teaching and ensure you are approachable for the students with LD whom you are likely to be teaching. Do everything you can, with the help of your peers, to make these readings relevant for your teaching:

Klassen, R., & Lynch, S.L. (2007). Self-efficacy from the perspective of adolescents with LD and their specialist teachers. *Journal of Learning Disabilities, 40*(6), 494–507.

Faggella-Luby, M.N., & Deshler, D.D. (2008). Reading comprehension in adolescents with LD: What we know; what we need to learn. *Learning Disabilities Research & Practice, 23*(2), 70–78.

Witzel, B.S., Riccomini, P.J., & Schneider, E. (2008). Implementing CRA with secondary students with learning disabilities in Mathematics. *Intervention in School and Clinic, 43*(5), 270–276.

**Further Reading**

On learning disabilities:

Greenbaum, J., & Markel, G. (2001). *Helping adolescents with ADHD and learning disabilities: Ready-to-use tips, techniques, and checklists for school success.* San Francisco: Jossey-Bass.

Wong, B.Y.L. & Donahue, M. (Eds.) (2002). *The Social dimensions of learning disabilities: Essays in honor of Tanis Bryan.* Mahwah, NJ: Erlbaum.

Wong, B.Y.L. (Ed.) (2004). *Learning about learning disabilities* (3rd ed.). Toronto: Academic Press.

Fletcher, J.M., Lyon, G.R., Fuchs, L.S., & Barnes, M.A. (2007). *Learning disabilities: From identification to intervention.* New York: Guilford Press.

Kass, C.E. & Maddux, C.D. (2005). *A human development view of learning disabilities: From theory to practice* (2nd ed.). Springfield, IL: Charles C. Thomas Pub.

a daily agenda on the board. Teach outlining by providing a partial outline of your notes for students to complete, and teach highlighting by having pairs of students decide what main ideas should be highlighted. Model on an overhead before the students begin and debrief with reasons at the end of the lesson. Provide students with opportunities to practise what you teach. In a recent meta-analysis, Swanson and Deshler (2003) reported that eight instructional factors—(1) questioning, (2) sequencing and segmentation, (3) skill modelling, (4) organization and explicit practice, (5) small-group setting, (6) indirect teacher activities (e.g., homework), (7) technology, and (8) scaffolding—captured the majority of successful intervention programs for adolescents with LD. Most important was the organization/explicit factor, which included two important instructional components: advance organization and explicit practice. Remember that you may need to find a way to teach more intensely—to students in a small group where you can be more responsive when an individual does not understand—and if that is not enough, it may be necessary to arrange for yourself or a paraeducator, a volunteer, or an older student to provide individual teaching or practice.

Students with LD are frequently taught **cognitive strategies** for reading comprehension (Baker, Gersten, & Scanlon, 2002; Faggella et al., 2007; Sencibaugh, 2007) and math problem solving (Hutchinson, 1993; Montague, 2008;). Similar strategies are often used to teach social competence. Gumpel (2007) reports on how complex it is to try to change the social skills and social competence of students with LD and other concomitant exceptionalities. Alan Edmunds (1999) of the University of Western Ontario developed a successful individualized approach to learning strategies to provide students with cues. Edmunds suggests that teachers "talk out" the cues with an individual student, key the steps into the computer, and print them out on a credit card–sized space. By laminating the card, punching a hole in one of its corners, and affixing a cable tie, the student can attach the cognitive credit card (CCC) to his or her pencil case.

In a very thorough review of the research on the education of individuals with dyslexia, Shaywitz and her colleagues (2008) describe evidence-based interventions as explicit, intense, systematic and developmentally appropriate. They also describe the three kinds of accommodations that are most important, which we have considered in Chapter 1: those that bypass the reading difficulty by providing information through the auditory mode; those that provide compensatory assistive technologies (access to recorded materials, computers, and print-to-speech software); and those that provide additional time so dysfluent readers can demonstrate their knowledge (on examinations, in particular, based on the students' previous experiences).

For many students with LD in reading, the challenges persist beyond learning to read and are manifested in comprehension difficulties when these students are reading to learn. Faggella-Luby and Deshler (2008) describe what you need to pay attention to in order to achieve optimal outcomes in reading comprehension in the limited instructional time you have. They describe a six-tiered continuum of literacy instruction:

Level 1: Enhance content instruction of critical content for all students.

Level 2: Embed strategy instruction in your large-group teaching.

Level 3: Provide more intense instruction in learning strategies and more time for practice for those who need it.

Level 4: Develop and provide, as a team, intensive basic skill instruction for students with severe deficits.

Level 5: Access therapeutic intervention for students with significant deficits in basic language competencies.

Level 6: Work with your colleagues and the students' families to extend instructional time through strategic before- and after-school tutoring (p. 76).

Because there are similar challenges in teaching mathematics to adolescents with LD, Witzel and his colleagues (2008) have developed a clear process for using their concrete-to-representational-to-abstract (**CRA**) sequence of instruction. This approach takes students through **C**oncrete hands-on instruction with manipulative objects, then through pictorial **R**epresentations of the manipulatives used in the concrete stage, to learning through **A**bstract notation including operational symbols. Witzel et al. (2008) lay out seven steps for you to follow in implementing CRA:

1. Choose the math topic to be taught.
2. Review procedures to solve the problem.
3. Adjust the steps to remove notation or calculation tricks.
4. Match the abstract steps with an appropriate concrete manipulative.
5. Arrange concrete and representational lessons.
6. Teach each concrete, representational, and abstract lesson to student mastery.
7. Help students generalize what they learn through word problems.

There is extensive research under way to develop appropriate tiered interventions that differentiate instruction for students with learning disabilities. Learn to use the journal resources available to you in your community, through your school district, or available from the university where you take courses—so you can keep up with the rapidly changing landscape in the field of LD. You should be able to access journal articles online through an organization or association that subscribes to the journals or through your subscription to organizations like Council for Exceptional Children and International Reading Association.

Put into Practice

Observe a teacher experienced with students with learning disabilities in an inclusive classroom. Focus on how the teacher makes everyone feel like a valued member and differentiates teaching and adapts assessment.

## Implications for Social and Career Participation of Students with Learning Disabilities

There are successful adults with learning disabilities in almost every career, but many other adults with LD experience underemployment (Gerber & Price, 2003; Shaywitz et al., 2008). **Career development** programs have used cognitive strategy approaches to teach employment readiness and career awareness explicitly. Effective Canadian programs of career development for adolescents with LD include *The BreakAway Company: A Career Readiness Program for At-Risk Youth* (Campbell, Serff, & Williams, 1994) and *Pathways* (Hutchinson & Freeman, 1994), which provide teachers with collaborative activities that accommodate heterogeneity. Both of these programs were developed more than ten years ago but are still used in Canadian classrooms. The research my colleagues and I have conducted over the past ten years suggests that adolescents with LD and other disabilities, as well as at-risk youth, benefit from opportunities to both gain workplace experience and learn-by-doing how to negotiate workplace accommodations (Hutchinson et al., 2008a, 2008b). The Learning Disabilities Association of Ontario has developed a resource, *Job-Fit*, with modules that focus on topics such as understanding assessments, setting employment goals, and making decisions about disclosure (www.ldao.ca/resources/ld_employment/job_fit/index.php). Such programs should help reduce the under-employment of adults with LD.

# Teaching Students with Attention Deficit Hyperactivity Disorder (ADHD)

I have Attention Deficit Disorder, which is often called ADD for short ... Dad says that I have eagle eyes; I notice everything. But eagles know when to stop looking around and zoom in on their prey. Me, I just keep noticing more things and miss my catch.

Once when Dad and Emily and I hiked at Birdsong Trail, a thunderstorm sent us rushing back toward the car. Dad tripped over a rock and twisted his knee. His face wrinkled with pain. He asked Emily to go for help, but she was not sure of the way.

"I can find it, Dad!" I interrupted. And I told him the whole route. "Ben, I knew those eagle eyes of yours would come in handy," Dad replied. "You'll find the way just fine. Emily can stay here to keep me company." As I turned to go, Dad called, "Hurry, Ben! I need you." Swift as an eagle, I zoomed off toward the ranger station and got help for Dad. I was the only one who could do it. And that's when I realized it's good to be me.

*Gehret, 1991, p. 11.*

## Description of Students with Attention Deficit Hyperactivity Disorder

Children and adolescents with ADHD are usually described as displaying chronic and serious **inattentiveness, hyperactivity,** and sometimes **impulsivity** (DSM-IV-TR, American Psychiatric Association, 2000). While controversy surrounds the definition (Cooper, 2001; Schlachter, 2008), some characteristics are typical. These children and adolescents have difficulty staying focused on instructions, schoolwork, and chores; are easily distracted and forgetful; and are constantly on the go and into everything. These characteristics occur prior to the age of 7 but might go unobserved that early because young children typically experience few demands for sustained attention. Recently, it has become more common for pre-school children who are unable to focus, pay attention, and sit still to be identified and even to be medicated for ADHD (Wolraich, 2006). At school, students identified with ADHD may be described as having LD when there is no separate category of ADHD. Both British Columbia and Alberta have a category for ADHD and a well-developed resource for teachers (see Weblinks). In contrast, Ontario's recent edition of *What Works? Research into Practice* (Monograph #3, 2007, April) says, "Although ADHD is not named as a specific category of exceptionality, students with ADHD may present characteristics that can be identified in the various categories such as Learning Disability or Behaviour."

## Incidence of Attention Deficit Hyperactivity Disorder

The prevalence of ADHD is estimated at 4 to 12 percent of school-aged students (Alberta Education, 2006), consistent with estimates in the United States of 2 to 18 percent (CDC Mental Health in the United States, 2005). Given the lack of

**Weblinks**

TEACHING STUDENTS WITH ADHD DISORDER: A RESOURCE GUIDE FOR TEACHERS (2007, BC EDUCATION)
www.bced.gov.bc.ca/specialed/adhd

FOCUSING ON SUCCESS: TEACHING STUDENTS WITH ATTENTION DEFICIT/HYPERACTIVITY DISORDER (2006, ALBERTA EDUCATION)
http://education.alberta.ca/search.asp?q=adhd

TEACH ADHD (BY SICK KIDS HOSPITAL, TORONTO)
http://research.aboutkidshealth.ca/teachadhd

CH.A.D.D.—CHILDREN AND ADULTS WITH ATTENTION DEFICIT DISORDERS (CANADIAN SITE)
www.chaddcanada.org

CENTRE FOR ADHD/ADD ADVOCACY, CANADA
www.caddac.ca

ATTENTION DEFICIT RESOURCE NETWORK
www.adrn.org

CANADIAN ADHD RESOURCE ALLIANCE
www.caddra.ca/english/educators.html

agreement on definition, there have been questions about the accuracy of prevalence estimates (e.g., Schlachter, 2008). Boys are three times more likely to be affected than girls, although recent Canadian and American data suggest girls may be at higher risk for more psychological impairment (e.g., anxiety, depression) (Hinshaw et al., 2006; Rucklidge & Tannock, 2001). Cuffe and his colleagues (2005) analyzed data from a national survey in the United States and produced a lower prevalence than most of approximately 4 percent, but they showed that ADHD symptoms vary by ethnicity, gender, age, and other emotional and behavioural difficulties. Research by many investigators, including Rosemary Tannock of the Hospital for Sick Children in Toronto, suggests neurological causes with a genetic basis (Barkley, 2002, *Consensus Statement on ADHD*; MMWR Weekly Report, September 2, 2005; Tannock, 1998), while researchers like Antrop and his colleagues (2006) suggest that children with ADHD have difficulty delaying rewards and choose small immediate rewards over large delayed rewards unless they receive stimulation during the delay. The diagnosis is made by gathering information from the child, parents, and teachers through behavioural checklists, interviews, and observations; physicians and psychologists are considered qualified to make this medical diagnosis (Canadian ADHD Resource Alliance; www.caddra.ca/english/educators.html). Alan Edmunds of the University of Western Ontario (2008) reported on the process of diagnosis and assessment of ADHD across Canada, showing inconsistencies in diagnostic criteria, the need for a multidisciplinary approach, and educators' need for professional development about ADHD, on topics such as student characteristics and ways of differentiating teaching.

## Characteristics of Students with ADHD

The characteristics and learning needs of students with ADHD vary. *The Diagnostic and Statistical Manual of Mental Disorders* (DSM-IV-TR) (American Psychiatric Association, 2000) defines three subtypes of ADHD: Predominantly Inattentive, Predominantly Hyperactive-Impulsive, and Combined Type.

### CHARACTERISTICS OF ADHD, PREDOMINANTLY INATTENTIVE

Students with ADHD, Predominantly Inattentive, display many more characteristics of inattention than hyperactivity-impulsivity. They may ignore details, make careless errors, or have trouble staying on task while working or playing. They do not seem to listen when you speak to them directly; often they do not follow through on instructions and do not complete homework and classroom tasks. Students who are predominantly inattentive may have difficulty organizing their activities, and they may lose or forget things. They dislike or try to avoid becoming involved in work that requires them to concentrate for long periods of time, and may be easily distracted by movement, objects, or noises in the classroom. They may have a tendency to daydream and may rush through tasks.

### CHARACTERISTICS OF ADHD, PREDOMINANTLY HYPERACTIVE-IMPULSIVE

Students with ADHD, Predominantly Hyperactive-Impulsive, display many more characteristics of hyperactivity-impulsivity than inattention. They may fidget and squirm, leave their desks, and run and climb at inappropriate times. They usually find it challenging to play or work quietly, they move constantly, and they talk excessively. Impulsivity characteristics include blurting out answers before you have

**Further Reading**

On teaching students with ADHD:

Lougy, R., DeRuvo, S., & Rosenthal D. (2007). *Teaching young children with ADHD: Successful strategies and practical interventions for PreK-3*. Thousand Oaks, CA: Corwin Press.

Greenbaum, J., & Markel G. (2001). *Helping adolescents with ADHD and learning disabilities: Ready-to-use tips, techniques, and checklists for school success*. San Francisco: Jossey-Bass.

Nadeau, K.G., & Dixon., E.B. (2005). *Learning to slow down and pay attention: A book for kids about ADHD* (3rd ed.). Washington, DC: American Psychological Association.

finished asking a question, not waiting for their turn or not following other class-room rules, and disturbing or interrupting other students. Their impatience can cause them to demonstrate unsafe behaviour and to neglect to consider the consequences of their actions. Transitions within the school day can be particularly challenging.

## CHARACTERISTICS OF ADHD, COMBINED TYPE

Most students with ADHD have the Combined Type. They display many characteristics of both inattention and hyperactivity-impulsivity. The key behaviour patterns you may recognize in your students are (1) not listening when you speak to them directly, (2) having difficulty making and keeping a schedule for assignments and activities, (3) fidgeting, (4) having difficulty paying attention for sustained periods of time, (5) answering questions before they are called on, and (6) being always "on the go."

## QUESTIONING THE PREVAILING CONCEPTION OF ADHD

Some have challenged the validity of the "diagnosis" of ADHD as a condition within the individual, either emphasizing the interaction between the individual and the context (a concept already accepted by the major theorists) or placing full responsibility on the failure of the context to tolerate variation (e.g., Slee, 1998). Challengers have also objected to the emphasis on behavioural manifestations. Barkley's model (1997) suggested that neurologically based problems of response inhibition (sometimes described as impulsivity) led directly to problems in four major executive functions of cognition: working memory, internalized speech, motivational appraisal, and synthesizing past experience relevant to a current situation. In an extensive literature review, Tannock (1998) showed the great strides made during the 1990s toward an integration of findings in cognitive research (e.g., on response inhibition, working memory, and difficulties understanding the passage of time) with neurobiological and genetic research. Her review emphasizes the cognitive rather than the behavioural aspects of ADHD. Tannock's *Monograph for Ontario Literacy and Numeracy Secretariat* (2007) refers to the evidence that ADHD is associated with subtle cognitive differences in the brain and argues that ADHD be reconceptualized as a learning disorder but distinct from recognized LD. Others have concentrated on weighing the evidence for genetic factors contributing to ADHD. For a current review read Thapar et al. (2007). And recent studies have suggested that while children may meet the criteria for mainly hyperactive when they are young, over time many desist from ADHD and even more shift to the combined subtype (e.g., Lahey et al., 2005). Clearly this is a complex phenomenon about which we are still learning.

## CHARACTERISTICS OF SOCIAL INTERACTIONS

ADHD influences all aspects of an individual's life, including social interactions. The classroom is often a problematic environment for students with ADHD because of their impulsivity, distractibility, and overactivity (Alberta Education, 2006; Roberts, White, & McLaughlin, 1997) as well as their cognitive characteristics (Tannock, 2007; Tannock & Martinussen, 2001). These social and emotional characteristics can cause both students and teachers to react negatively when students with ADHD show limited self-confidence, are unable to contribute to a team, misinterpret social cues, have difficulty with anger management, or overreact emotionally. A recent paper reported on the peer relations of 165 children with ADHD, finding that they were less well-liked than their peers without ADHD, had fewer reciprocal friendships, and were disliked to a greater extent by more popular peers (Hoza et al., 2005). You can see that it is important that you treat students with ADHD respectfully and patiently, both to enhance your relationship with them and to make yourself a model for the class so they receive better treatment from their peers. There are a number of programs designed to improve the social problem solving of students with ADHD, some of which are group-facilitated (e.g., Gresham, 2002) and some computer mediated (e.g., Fenstermacher et al., 2006). Chapters 6 and 9 include information about implementing such programs with the assistance of colleagues, special educators, and student services personnel.

## Implications for Learning and for Differentiating in the Classroom: Students with ADHD

Because students with ADHD often have difficulty getting started on assignments and then concentrating on them, help them to begin. Try scheduling frequent, but short and specific, break times (DuPaul & Stoner, 2003). **Checkpoints** for project completion and homework journals for nightly assignments can help many students. Providing students with clear numbered and written as well as verbal instructions will help them complete tasks. Some of the ways that teachers report differentiating instruction for students with ADHD include being flexible for all students, using tailored lists of spelling words, teaching strategies for reading in the content areas, allowing students to dictate to a scribe rather than write a test answer, providing copies of textbook pages so students don't have to copy math questions into their notebooks, permitting students to choose where they want to work, as well as making accommodations that promote attention and that allow movement in the classroom.

Different teachers who were interviewed reported using different approaches to promote acceptance of students with ADHD by their peers; one "hit problems head-on," while another reported using "subtle" means, but all said they modelled patience and acceptance, tried to "ward off" situations, and focused on self-esteem and accepting differences within discussions of course content (e.g., novel study) whenever possible (Nowacek & Mamlin, 2007). These teachers demonstrated awareness of key elements of differentiated instruction: flexibility, choice, creativity in both differentiating the content and how students develop understanding of concepts, and in the ways students demonstrate what they have learned (Anderson, 2007). Resource teachers recommended that classroom teachers use three strategies to make their paper-based teacher-designed materials more accessible to learners with ADHD and other exceptionalities: leave more white space on the page so materials are better spaced, use large fonts on the computer instead of hand-written materials, and make the key information or directions clear to students through bolding, colour-coding, highlighting, or boxes (Rotter, 2004). Remember that such differentiations may help many students in your classroom to learn.

### ADAPTING CLASSROOM ORGANIZATION

There are also strategies for classroom organization that are intended to enhance the learning of students with ADHD, which also may benefit other students.

**Put into Practice**

Develop a set of consequences for a class you have taught or may be teaching in the near future. Describe the characteristics of a student with ADHD who is a member of this class, and consider how the consequences will apply in this case. Consult Chapter 6. Develop a plan for a lesson; describe the cognitive characteristics of a student with ADHD and how you would differentiate instruction to ensure that the student with ADHD would understand and learn. Use resources like these:

Anderson, K.M. (2007). Differentiating instruction to include all students. *Preventing School Failure, 51*(3), 49–54.

Nowacek, E.J., & Mamlin, N. (2007). General education teachers and students with ADHD: What modifications are made? *Preventing School Failure, 51*(3), 28–35.

Rotter, K.M. (2004). Simple techniques to improve teacher-made instructional materials for use by pupils with disabilities. *Preventing School Failure, 48*(2), 38–43.

For example, minimize distracting factors. A **carrel** is a protected space, with wooden or cardboard walls, that blocks out distractions. You may be able to borrow a carrel from your school library or make one from the carton for a large appliance. If you introduce a carrel, be sure to use it yourself, so it is seen as a high-status opportunity, not a punishment. Provide a predictable, structured environment, so students know what you expect of them and what they can expect of you. Communicate explicitly about predictability and structure to ensure that students with ADHD have understood prior to the beginning of a specific activity (DuPaul & Stoner, 2003). When you teach, ADAPT, maintain the students' interest, model by **thinking aloud**, and ensure adequate opportunities for practice. Sometimes teachers remove recess privileges from students with ADHD when the students fail to complete their work, requiring them to "stay in" and finish. However, that increases levels of inappropriate behaviour, restlessness, and distractibility in class for the remainder of the day (Ridgway et al., 2003). Look for other ways to help these and other students complete their assigned work, and enable them to exercise and socialize with their classmates during the recess breaks. Table 3.4 provides specific examples of cognitive characteristics of students with ADHD and actions you can take to meet their needs in the classroom.

## TABLE 3.4 PROMOTING ACADEMIC SUCCESS FOR STUDENTS WITH ADHD

Current treatment approaches have focused on medication and behavioural interventions. However, emerging data on cognitive characteristics have implications for the classroom.

| Cognitive Characteristics | Cognitive Adaptations in the Classroom |
| --- | --- |
| Difficulty understanding words such as *before, after, more than*. | Make language clear at beginning of task. |
| Lack of understanding of passage of time and of temporal events. | Post a list of items to be completed. Strike through items as they are finished. |
| Mismatch of student needs to lesson content and delivery. | Model what is to be done, repeat, and explain instructions, tasks. |
| Difficulty understanding language used in teaching and materials. | Rephrase student's language when that helps others to understand student's meaning. |
| Lack of understanding about taking turns, working co-operatively. | Teach social skills (e.g., use microphone to show children whose turn it is to talk). |
| Difficulty understanding the process expected in practice activities following direct teaching. | Provide as much support as necessary for the student to begin the activity—guided practice. Gradually reduce support and increase self-direction. |
| Difficulty focusing on the needed information to complete tasks. | Reduce demands on working memory by providing external memory aids, mnemonics, graphic reminders, lists of steps, strategies. |
| Lack of self-regulation. | Model strategies that can be used to self-regulate. Teach one strategy thoroughly and then another, helping students to discern when each is useful. Cue strategy use. |

Sources: Tannock, R., & Martinussen, R. (2001). Reconceptualizing ADHD. *Educational Leadership*, 20–25; Mariage, T.V., Englert, C.S., & Garmon, M.A. (2000). The teacher as "more knowledgeable other" in assisting literacy learning with special needs students. *Reading and Writing Quarterly*, 16(4), 299–336.

## RESPONDING TO INAPPROPRIATE BEHAVIOUR

In spite of your best efforts, on occasion you will have to respond to inappropriate behaviour by students with ADHD. The best response is to give inappropriate behaviour as little attention as possible and instead provide positive reinforcement for appropriate behaviour as soon as it occurs (DuPaul & Weyandt, 2006; Roberts et al., 1997). However, a **verbal reprimand** may be necessary when behaviour is getting out of hand. To be effective, reprimands should be immediate, unemotional, brief, and backed up with a time out or loss of privileges. Sometimes you will need to follow up with the consequences developed at the beginning of the year. For a clear description of ways to use consequences effectively in a classroom context, read DuPaul & Weyandt, 2006, *School-Based Intervention for Children with Attention Deficit Hyperactivity Disorder: Effects on Academic, Social, and Behavioural Functioning.*

A **time out** is a type of punishment in which a student is removed from opportunities for reward. In-school teams sometimes develop time-out procedures for children with ADHD. A time out can be carried out in the classroom or in the hall, as long as it is away from the immediate setting that is reinforcing the behaviour. Refer to Chapter 6 for more information on time outs. Roberts et al. (1997) suggest that a one- to five-minute time out will have the same effect as a longer one. A general rule is to assign one minute per two years of age.

## STRATEGIES FOR SELF-MANAGEMENT

Self-management strategies are interventions that are implemented by the student and are designed to increase self-control of behaviour (DuPaul & Weyandt, 2006. **Cognitive-behaviour management (CBM)** programs teach students how to use cognition to control behaviour. Usually you and the student agree on a problem that is getting in the way of learning (e.g., looking around instead of completing assignments). You develop steps for the student to follow, put these on a cue card, and model their use. The student practises using the steps aloud, and gradually covertly, to solve the problem. The student monitors his or her own performance of the steps. Some teachers use a signal to remind the student to begin using the CBM steps. Chapters 6 and 9 contain examples of CBM programs developed for students. These take considerable thought and time in the early stages but are worth the effort when they are effective. The student must know the steps and be able to carry them out individually. At first, the student can be cued, but eventually he or she must initiate the steps independently. Other ways to encourage self-management include giving students with ADHD responsibilities they can handle so they feel they are contributing to the school environment, as well as working with the in-school team to help the student develop better social and academic skills and improve time management and organization.

## MEDICATION

Medication is one of the most controversial issues surrounding ADHD (you might want to view the *W-Five* series shown on CTV, titled "A Convenient Diagnosis"). Many people seem to believe that medication is the answer to ADHD. However, in 1999 a large study compared medication, behaviour therapy, and a combination of both. All groups improved, but medication, when carefully monitored, was more effective than behaviour therapy alone and its effects were similar to combination therapy. The combined approach, however, allowed lower doses of medication and also improved academic performance and family relationships. In addition, it was more helpful for children who also had oppositional defiant disorder or mood disorders such as depression or anxiety (MTA Cooperative Group, 1999). The effects were seen on behaviour in general but did not necessarily translate into changes in learning in the classroom. For a discussion of this issue, see Jensen et al. (2001), Purdie et al. (2002), or Tannock (2007).

Two classes of medication are commonly used to treat children with ADHD: **psychostimulant medications** and **antidepressants**. The amount of the stimulant Ritalin consumed in Canada increased more than fivefold from 1990 to 1997 (Health Canada, 1997, www.hc-sc.gc.ca/dhp-mps/medeff/advers-react-neg/fs-if/methylphenidate_adhd-thada_fs-if-eng.php). On 4 June 2007, the CBC reported that 6.1 percent of children whose parents had divorced were on the medication, compared with 3.1 percent of those in two-parent families (www.cbc.ca/health/story/2007/06/04/adhd-divorce.html?ref=rss). By 1990 nearly 2 percent of the US school-age population received stimulant medications for ADHD (Barkley, 1990), despite concerns about abuse and addiction. There has always been concern about adolescents selling and obtaining these medications illicitly, and the US data suggest this is happening. Monitoring the Future, a US group associated with the National Institute on Drug Abuse, reported that the data for 2007 indicate non-medical use of Ritalin by 2.1 percent of 8th graders, 2.8 percent of 10th graders, and 3.8 percent of 12th graders (www.nida.nih.gov/infofacts/ADHD.html). The most commonly prescribed psychostimulants have been Ritalin (methylphenidate) and Dexedrine (dextroamphetamine) (Sweeney, Forness, Kavale, & Levitt, 1997), since Cylert (pemoline) was taken off the Canadian market because it was suspected of causing liver damage (Health Canada, 1999). Researchers have reported a decrease in classroom performance in some children treated with psychostimulants. They have questioned whether the resultant decrease in behaviour problems or relative gains in attention are worth the loss of learning performance in some children (Forness et al., 1992). The most common side effects of the stimulants are insomnia, decrease in appetite, gastrointestinal problems, irritability, increase in heart rate, and sometimes a worsening of the presenting symptoms. Uncommon side effects are depression, cognitive impairment, growth retardation, and tic disorders (e.g., Tourette syndrome) (Sweeney et al., 1997). However, controlled studies show that psychostimulant medications, generally, when applied in relatively low and moderate doses, are widely regarded as highly effective in reducing the core symptoms of ADHD (Hill & Cameron, 1999). Kewley (1998) argues that with careful monitoring and prompt adjustment of dosage, methylphenidate can be safe as well as effective.

The current best practice in the management of ADHD requires combining a psychosocial approach with medical intervention (Austin, 2003; Cooper, 2001). The recommended psychosocial approach includes cognitive-behaviour management programs for the child, interventions that focus on the family as well as the classroom, and individual psychotherapy for the child if depression occurs. For the medical approach, Cantwell (1996) suggests that 70 percent of children with ADHD respond to one of the stimulants on the first trial and if a number are tried, the likelihood of positive response increases to between 85 and 90 percent.

The other class of medication prescribed frequently for ADHD is antidepressants. Drugs in this class can cause an array of side effects, including cardiac complications, nervousness, insomnia, and seizures in rare cases.

## FIGURE 3.3 QUESTIONS FOR TEACHERS AND PARENTS TO ASK ABOUT MEDICATION FOR CHILDREN WITH ADHD

The most commonly prescribed medications for children and adolescents with ADD are Ritalin (methylphenidate) and Dexedrine (dextroamphetamine). Parents and teachers should be well-informed about these medications and able to answer questions such as these:

1. What is the medication? What information can I read about it?
2. Why is this medication prescribed for this adolescent? What changes should we expect to see at home? At school?
3. What behavioural program or behavioural therapy is being implemented in conjunction with this drug therapy?
4. How long will this medication be prescribed for this adolescent?
5. What are the side effects in the short term? In the long term?
6. What is the dosage? What is the schedule on which the medication will be taken?
7. How often will the adolescent be seen by the prescribing physician for re-evaluation?
8. Should the medication be stopped for a short period of time to see if it is still required? When?
9. Are there foods, beverages, or other substances that should not be consumed when one is taking this medication?
10. What kind of communication is necessary among home, school, and the adolescent to evaluate whether the medication is having the desired effect?
11. What procedures should be followed if the adolescent accidentally ingests an overdose?
12. Who explains all of this to the adolescent and what should the adolescent be told?

### References

Austin, V.L. (2003). Pharmacological interventions for students with ADD. *Intervention in School and Clinic, 38,* 289–296.

Barkley, R.A. (1995). *Taking charge of ADHD: The authoritative guide for parents.* New York: Guilford Press.

Sweeney, D.P., Forness, S.R., Kavale, K.A., & Levitt, J.G. (1997). An update on psychopharmacologic medication: What teachers, clinicians, and parents need to know. *Intervention in School and Clinic, 33*(1), 4–21, 25.

Ziegler Dendy, C.A. (1995). *Teenagers with ADD: A parents' guide.* Bethesda, MD: Woodbine House.

———

Source: Hutchinson, N.L. (2004). *Teaching exceptional children and adolescents: A Canadian casebook.* Toronto: Prentice Hall. Reprinted by permission.

### What do you think?

Read about both sides of the debate on medication and ADHD:

Pro: Silver, L.B. (2003). *Attention-deficit/hyperactivity disorder: A clinical guide to diagnosis and treatment for health and mental health professionals* (2nd ed.). Arlington, VA: American Psychiatric Publishing.

Con: Stein, D.B. (2002). *Ritalin is not the answer action guide: An interactive companion to the bestselling drug-free ADD/ADHD Parenting Program.* Somerset, NJ: John Wiley & Sons.

The book *Scattered Minds* by Gabor Maté (2000), a Vancouver physician who has ADHD, recommends a balanced view. While there are strongly held opinions on both sides of this issue, parents make the decisions about medication and receive prescriptions from physicians. Figure 3.3 contains questions for parents and teachers to ask physicians about medication.

## Implications for Social and Career Participation of Students with ADHD

The account by Ben at the beginning of this section illustrates that people with ADHD have many strengths and plenty of energy. Like people with LD, they may find themselves underemployed as adults unless they have opportunities for hands-on learning and for acquiring career awareness through explicit teaching. In his book *ADD Success Stories*, Hartmann (1995) suggests that adults with ADHD need to choose careers that are particularly suited to their characteristics.

# Teaching Students with Communication Exceptionalities

**Put into Practice**

Seek resources to help you understand the level of language development of children entering grade 1. Look for books. Consider videos such as *Children Learning Language: How Adults Can Help* (1997). Lake Zurich, IL: Learning Seed.

Useful books include:

Silliman, E.R., & Wilkinson, L.C. (Eds.) (2004). *Language and literacy learning in schools.* New York: Guilford Press.

Beaty, J.J. (2009). *50 early childhood literacy strategies.* Upper Saddle River, NJ: Pearson Education.

Griffith, P.L., Beach, S.A., Ruan, J., & Dunn, L. (2008). *Literacy for young children: A guide for early childhood educators.* Thousand Oaks, CA: Corwin Press.

Writing in my journal every day helps me feel better and write better. I used to go to speech therapy every week. Now my therapist comes to school once a month. In between, I practice my sounds with helpers. Today my speech therapist told me that I am really getting better at making my sounds. She recorded me talking and I listened to myself on the tape recorder. I felt proud. I have to talk like that in my class so the other kids will stop saying that I talk like a baby. I am going to ask if I can be in the next play for social studies. So they can see that I talk like them now.

*From the journal of Ruth, a grade 2 student with an articulation speech disorder.*

## Description of Communication Exceptionalities

Generally, communication exceptionalities include disorders of speech (**articulation**, voice, and fluency) and disorders of language (expressive or receptive). The term **speech impairment** is widely used to refer to a disorder that involves the perceptual motor aspects of transmitting oral messages. The Ontario Ministry of Education (2001b) describes language impairment as "an impairment in comprehension and/or use of verbal communication or the written or other symbol systems of communication, which may be associated with neurological, psychological, physical, or sensory factors" (p. A19). Usually **language impairment** is described as involving one or more of the form, content, and function of language in communication and is characterized by language delay. You may see delayed development of expressive language, receptive language, or both.

## Incidence of Communication Exceptionalities

Generally, school districts in Ontario report that 3 to 5 percent of the school population receives intervention for speech disorders (Bennett, Weber, & Dworet, 2008). This is comparable to data from a US sample (Shriberg, Tomblin, & McSweeney, 1999), with 3.8 percent of children continuing to show speech delay at age 6. However, recent funding cutbacks have reduced services for communication exceptionalities across the country. Incidence data for speech and language disorders are uncertain because criteria and levels of service vary widely from district to district and even across schools within a district. Sometimes services are provided by the health-care system, and some parents seek private therapy rather than face waiting lists. Boys with communication disorders outnumber girls by roughly two to one. In 2006 the New Brunswick Department of Education reported that 2.65 percent of students in the province had communication exceptionalities (2006).

## Characteristics of Students with Communication Exceptionalities

Many students with communication disorders experience difficulties with both speech and language, but some students have difficulty in only one of these areas. Many students with other exceptionalities (e.g., autism, learning disabilities, cerebral palsy, intellectual disabilities) have communication disorders as a secondary disability. However, the designation "communication disorders" is most often used

## TABLE 3.5 SPEECH AND LANGUAGE DISORDERS AND THEIR CHARACTERISTICS

| Communication Disorder | Example of Characteristics |
| --- | --- |
| Language delay | For young students, at least six months behind in reaching language milestones; a grade 2 student uses three words rather than full sentences. |
| Receptive language | Student in grade 6 consistently fails to understand an oral instruction, even when given individually. |
| Expressive language | Student in grade 10 begins each sentence four or five times and cannot be understood by peers; refuses to speak in front of class. |
| Aphasia | Student cannot understand speech or produce meaningful sentences. |
| Apraxia | Student cannot sequence muscle movements and thus does not produce meaningful speech. |
| Articulation | Student in grade 2 cannot produce the S sound. This results in teasing by classmates. |
| Dysfluency | Student in grade 12 stutters but persists to express ideas. |
| Voice disorders | Student speaks slowly and softly in a husky voice (does not speak with normal pitch, loudness, duration, or quality); is shy about expressing ideas. |
| Orofacial defects | Student in grade 5 with cleft palate has difficulties with speech and feeding. |
| Dysarthria | Grade 9 student's speech is distorted because of paralysis of speaking muscles. |

when speech or language is the primary exceptionality. There is a wide variety of communication disorders. You may recognize students with communication disorders in your classroom from some of the characteristics listed in Table 3.5. Learners with communication exceptionalities often have less developed vocabularies than their classmates (Beitchman et al., 2008). If you suspect that a young child has a speech or language disorder, talk with the parents. Recommend a thorough evaluation by a speech-language pathologist to determine the child's communication strengths and weaknesses. This professional can provide a plan for meeting the child's needs and can recommend services within the school district and other agencies. In some cases these services are provided by the school district and in other cases by the health department or by a local agency that has been contracted.

## Implications for Learning and Classroom Adaptations: Students with Communication Exceptionalities

Historically, speech and language disorders have been the responsibility of speech and language therapists, and students have been removed from the classroom for short periods of time for therapy. Teachers carried out follow-up exercises in the classroom. In the scenario presented at the opening of this section, Ruth practises with helpers or volunteers between visits to the specialist. Today, many teachers rely on volunteers from the community for individual activities such as articulation practice. Forbes (2008) describes the knowledge that the speech-language therapist and the teacher need in order to collaborate effectively.

You can assist students with communication disorders. Create an accepting atmosphere and never allow classmates to mock or tease. Collaborate with the student, the parents, and the speech and language specialist to obtain suggestions and goals. Be proactive: give students opportunities to answer questions that require brief responses, and teach them to monitor their speech.

Put into Practice

Read the following papers about intensive interventions designed to enhance the communication of students with speech and language exceptionalities and develop a plan for differentiating instruction for such students at a grade level and in a subject that you have experience teaching.

Myers, C. (2007). "Please listen, it's my turn": Instructional approaches, curricula and contexts for supporting communication and increasing access to inclusion. *Journal of Intellectual & Developmental Disability, 32*(4), 263–278.

Adams, C., & Lloyd, J. (2007). The effects of speech and language therapy intervention on children with pragmatic language impairments in mainstream school. *British Journal of Special Education, 34*(4), 226–233.

You can help students who have difficulty responding orally by taking some simple actions. Be a good role model for all students in the class when speaking to students with communication disorders. Speak clearly and a bit slower than normal, pause at appropriate times, and use straightforward language and simple grammatical structures. When responding to a student with a communication disorder, respond to the meaning of the student's speech rather than to how the student speaks. Resist the temptation to interrupt students or to finish their sentences when they stutter or pause. Make eye contact with the speaker, and wait for a few seconds before responding (Reed, 2005; Silliman & Wilkinson, 2004).

Early language development underpins much of academic learning. Thus many children with communication disorders also experience difficulty with academics. Problems with speech sounds can result in underdeveloped phonemic awareness, which is required for learning to read and spell. Receptive language delays are characterized by challenges producing narrative accounts and delays in development of working memory (Dodwell & Bavin, 2008) and can contribute to difficulties in reading comprehension and in understanding specialized terms in mathematics (e.g., *carry*, *regroup*, *minus*, *times*) and other subjects (Stojanovik & Riddell, 2008). Language disabilities can seriously impede content-area learning in upper grades, where lectures and independent reading provide complex conceptual information (see Miller et al., 2008). Research suggests that children with both speech-sound and language disorders are at greater risk for reading, spelling, and language difficulties during elementary and high school (Lewis, Freebairn, & Taylor, 2000), as well as less ready for independence than their peers by the end of the high school years (Conti-Ramsden & Durkin, 2008).

Many provinces include relevant information on their websites to help you teach students with speech and language disabilities. For example, teachers in Yukon can consult www.education.gov.yk.ca/specialprograms/speech.html. The Newfoundland and Labrador Department of Education has developed a handbook, *Programming for Individual Needs: Communication Disorders Handbook* (2000), which defines relevant terms, describes students' needs, and discusses the role of professionals and how communication needs can be met (www.ed.gov.nl.ca/edu/dept/pdf/comm_disorder/TOC.pdf).

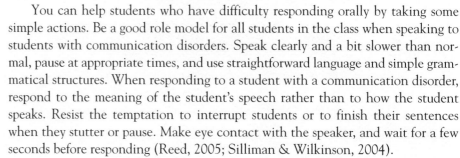

Weblinks

TYKETALK (A PARTNERSHIP OF AGENCIES IN THAMES VALLEY)
http://tyketalk.com

EXPRESSIVE COMMUNICATION HELP ORGANIZATION (ECHO)
www.apraxia.ca

CANADIAN ASSOCIATION OF SPEECH-LANGUAGE PATHOLOGISTS AND AUDIOLOGISTS
www.caslpa.ca

ONTARIO ASSOCIATION OF SPEECH-LANGUAGE PATHOLOGISTS AND AUDIOLOGISTS
www.osla.on.ca

NET CONNECTIONS FOR COMMUNICATION DISORDERS AND SCIENCES (AN INTERNET GUIDE BY JUDITH MAGINNIS KUSTER)
www.mnsu.edu/comdis/kuster2/welcome.html

NEW BRUNSWICK ASSOCIATION OF SPEECH-LANGUAGE PATHOLOGISTS & AUDIOLOGISTS
www.communicationnb.ca

## Implications for Social and Career Participation of Students with Communication Exceptionalities

Being unable to communicate effectively can contribute to social needs. Children with speech and language disorders can feel neglected or even rejected if their peers cease to include them in games and classroom activities. These pressures can be felt acutely during adolescence, when peer acceptance is so highly valued. However, many adults are able to overcome speech disorders if these are their only exceptionalities. Not developing either comprehension or production of language may prevent adults from participating fully in the workplace unless adaptations are provided. For example, recent research suggests that adult employers still hold stereotypes and judge individuals with speech and language disorders, especially language disorders, as less decisive and less reliable than those without language disorders (Allard & Williams, 2008). Studies like this remind us of the potential ramifications of ignoring students' communication exceptionalities.

# Teaching Students with Behaviour and Emotional Exceptionalities

I don't like the work we do here. It is easy and boring. I can figure out the questions and after that I don't feel like doing them, so I don't. Most of the teachers back off when a student yells at them. They don't make me do it then. Other guys leave me alone when they see I can make the teacher afraid. I don't know what good this boring stuff is. I like to draw. I'm awesome at drawing. I should just do drawing all day at school so I can be an artist. I want to draw comic books and stuff like that.

*From Urjo's interview with a counsellor about his experiences at school. Urjo, who is 15 years old, was identified as having a behaviour exceptionality.*

**Further Reading**

If you want to learn more about the nature of language impairments in individuals with autism and Asperger syndrome, you could read the following papers and look for other, similar sources.

Colle, L., Baron-Cohen, S., Wheelwright, S., & van der Lely, H.K.J. (2008). Narrative discourse in adults with high-functioning autism or Asperger syndrome. *Journal of Autism and Developmental Disorders, 38*(1), 28–40.

Whitehouse, A.J.O., Barry, J.G., & Bishop, D.V.M. (2008). Further defining the language impairment of autism: Is there a specific language impairment subtype? *Journal of Communication Disorders, 41*(4), 319–336.

## Description of Students with Behaviour Exceptionalities

Urjo was described at the opening of this chapter as refusing to do his homework, engaging in loud, verbal disagreements with teachers and having been identified as having a behaviour exceptionality, also sometimes called a behaviour disorder. In a classic paper analyzing the definitions used in the provincial special education documents across Canada, Don Dworet of Brock University and Arthur Rathgeber of Nipissing University (1998) demonstrated the range of meanings for the term *behaviour exceptionality*. The guidelines in British Columbia provide the following definitions:

> Students can experience behaviour, social/emotional, or mental health problems that range from mild to serious. Most students with social/emotional difficulties can be supported in school through regular discipline, counselling, and school-based services. A smaller number of students require more intensive support. Students who require behaviour supports are students whose behaviours reflect dysfunctional interactions between the student and one or more elements of the environment, including the classroom, school, family, peers and community. This is commonly referred to as behaviour disorders. Behaviour disorders vary in their severity and effect on learning, interpersonal relations, and personal adjustment (*Special Education Services: A Manual of Policies, Procedures and Guidelines*, 2006).

### MILD AND MODERATE TO SEVERE BEHAVIOUR EXCEPTIONALITIES

Students with mild behaviour exceptionalities usually can be supported in the classroom with the assistance of a resource teacher, counsellor, or other in-school resources. Students with moderate and severe behaviour disorders may require more intensive interventions in addition to classroom adaptations. Students with moderate behaviour disorders demonstrate one or more of

- **aggression** (physical, emotional, or sexual) and/or hyperactivity;
- **negative psychological states** (such as anxiety, depression, stress-related disorders); and
- behaviours related to **social problems** (such as delinquency, substance abuse, neglect).

These students have a disruptive effect on the classroom learning environment, social relations, or personal adjustment. They have demonstrated these behaviours over an extended period of time, in more than one setting, and with more than one person (teachers, peers, parents, siblings). In addition, they have not responded to interventions provided through classroom management strategies (BC Special Education Branch, 2006). Students with more severe behaviour disorders than those just described are likely to require intensive intervention over a period of time from community as well as school personnel.

## Incidence of Behaviour Exceptionalities

Educators treat behaviour exceptionalities as denoting behaviour that varies markedly and chronically from the accepted norm and that interferes with the student's own learning or the learning of others. That is, educators refer to educationally relevant characteristics. In contrast, psychologists and psychiatrists focus on more clinical characteristics. Who makes the identification—educators or clinical personnel—varies, contributing to variation in incidence. Variations in expectations and norms across communities also contribute to difficulties in estimating incidence of behaviour exceptionalities. The British Columbia Special Education Branch recognizes that roughly 2 percent of students in BC schools may have a moderate behaviour disorder (2006). The New Brunswick data (2006) suggest that about 30 percent of exceptional students have some form of behaviour exceptionality, including conduct disorders, emotional disorders, and other behavioural conditions.

## Characteristics of Students with Behaviour Exceptionalities

One thing many students with emotional and behaviour disorders have in common is that they are less satisfied with their quality of life in all domains (general, self, relationships, and environment) than their peers without disabilities (Sacks & Kern, 2008). Because students who experience behaviour exceptionalities make up an extremely heterogeneous population, any list of characteristics must be highly varied in type and intensity. No student would exhibit all of the following characteristics. However, you are likely to observe some of these characteristics in students with mild or moderate behaviour disorders (Smith, et al., 2008):

- aggressive acting-out behaviours
- social deficits, irresponsibility
- inadequate peer relationships
- hyperactivity
- distractibility
- lying and stealing
- academic deficits
- depression
- anxiety

If a student has a moderate behaviour disorder, you are likely to see that the student needs some or all of the following while in the classroom (Reithaug, 1998a):

- **structure**, predictability, and consistency

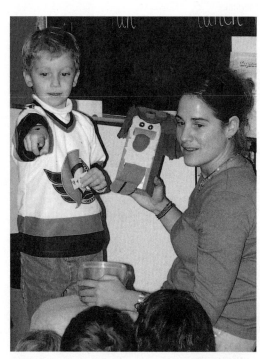

*Help all students to participate constructively. This boy is demonstrating a puppet he has made.*

- immediate, frequent, and specific **feedback** with consequences
- academic success
- responsibility and independence
- positive problem solving
- positive alternatives to current behaviours
- enhanced self-confidence
- positive school-to-home support systems
- evidence that he or she is making changes for the better

**What do you think?**

The characteristics in this list can be seen on occasion in many students. What distinguishes those with behaviour and emotional difficulties from other students?

In addition, most students with behaviour exceptionalities need challenging, respectful, and cognitively engaging activities. Sometimes we think we must lower our expectations or excuse the student from learning; however, as Urjo suggests, boredom often contributes to students' acting out their behaviour disorders in the classroom. Recent research suggests that when students, especially adolescents, experience positive emotions during school, they demonstrate higher levels of engagement (Reschly et al., 2008). The challenge for us as educators is to create a classroom milieu in which students feel valued and have positive experiences. If their needs are not addressed, students with behaviour exceptionalities fail more courses, miss more days of class, and are more likely to drop out of school than students with other exceptionalities (Gunter et al., 2002; Sugai & Horner, 2008).

Studies have shown the impact of peers in the lives of adolescents, even adolescents in middle school. For example, in a recent interview study middle-schoolers reported that they did not take risks in class because they were worrying about their standing in relation to their classmates (Cushman & Rogers, 2008). Questionnaire research with adolescents in dating relationships has found that adolescents who experience aggression in their relationships with their peers are likely to transfer that to relational aggression in their dating relationships (Leadbeater et al., 2008). And when adolescents are psychologically maltreated by their romantic partners, they report more depressive symptoms and more hassles in all spheres of their lives, along with more interpersonal sensitivity and overreaction to day-to-day interpersonal hassles (Gallaty & Zimmer-Gembeck, 2008).

One group of students has recently gained the attention of educators and mental health professionals who work with schools: those who have experienced trauma. They could be dealing with neglect, abuse or violence, experiences of war, illness, injury, or death. These situations can be extremely stressful and lead to emotional distresses that challenge a young person's ability to cope effectively. This type of stress is referred to as traumatic stress. For many children and adolescents, traumatic experiences are accompanied by feelings of intense fear, terror, and helplessness and cause significant psychological and physical distress. This can be exhibited in sleep disturbances, panic, aggression, hypervigilance, or exaggerated startle response (APA, 2000). These ongoing symptoms become maladaptive in the presence of any safety threat and at times may be at the root of emotional and behavioural needs seen in the classroom. You can find suggestions for teachers prepared by a psychologist from University of Waterloo, Donald Meichenbaum (2006), at www.teachsafeschools.org/Resilience.pdf. Malchiodi (2008) describes creative interventions that therapists use with traumatized children, including art, music, drama, and relaxation strategies, and the implications for classroom participation.

## Implications for Learning and Classroom Adaptations: Students with Behaviour Exceptionalities

Students with behaviour exceptionalities, like Urjo, can be a disruptive force in the classroom and affect everyone present. When teacher candidates and experienced teachers tell me that they have reservations about inclusion, most of their negative personal experiences focus on children with behaviour exceptionalities who have been disruptive to the learning of the entire class.

### HELPING STUDENTS TO IMPROVE THEIR BEHAVIOUR

You can help students improve their behaviour in many ways, ranging from preventive measures to direct responses. Figure 3.4 focuses on preventive measures and ways to ensure they are effective for students with behaviour exceptionalities. Focus on People describes a teacher who is effective in teaching students with behaviour exceptionalities.

### DIFFERENTIATING THE CURRICULUM AND STRUCTURING THE CLASSROOM

Differentiate the curriculum and structure the classroom environment to take advantage of "getting off to a good start." Apply your procedures, rules, and consequences consistently and discuss any changes (reasons and implementation) with the class. Research suggests that you should use differentiated teaching for academic instruction with students who have behaviour exceptionalities without waiting for their behaviour problems to be resolved (Gable et al., 2002). In fact, recent studies suggest that, for some students, academic difficulties contribute to students' behavioural problems (Morgan et al., in press). Gable et al. (2002) provide a set of procedures for a three-step planning process: class-wide and school-wide interventions, targeted interventions for subgroups of students at risk, and student-specific interventions for students with identified special needs.

> **Cross-Reference**
> Chapter 6 focuses on preventive classroom organization and classroom management, while Chapter 9 describes proactive ways of ensuring a positive milieu in which students respect and value one another.

## FIGURE 3.4 PREVENTIVE MEASURES AND ADAPTATIONS FOR STUDENTS WITH BEHAVIOUR DISORDERS

Establish on orderly and predictable classroom:

- Inform students of what is expected of them and of the consequences of not meeting your expectations.
- Check to ensure that the student with a behaviour disorder understands both expectations and consequences.

Then establish a positive climate for participating and learning:

- Model behaviour that treats everyone fairly, makes everyone feel included, and challenges but does not threaten.
- Talk with the student with a behaviour disorder about what each of you can do to ensure that he or she feels part of the class.
- Focus on the positive, rather than the negative, by exhibiting your self-confidence and building the self-confidence of your students.
- Encourage the student with a history of behaviour problems to believe that the two of you can work together for a positive experience.
- Recognize positive student attributes; catch students "being good."
- Focus on recognizing the positive attributes of the student with a behaviour disorder at optimal times; be vigilant so you don't miss the times when he or she is co-operating, etc.

The Manitoba Department of Education provides resources to help teachers develop behaviour intervention plans at its Student Services website (www.edu. gov.mb.ca/k12/specedu/bip). These plans help teachers to understand

- what a student is trying to accomplish with problem behaviours,
- what the student needs from his or her teachers so the negative behaviour is not necessary,
- proactive interventions to prevent reoccurrences, and
- reactive interventions to end the incident and minimize the disruption to learning.

Develop a behaviour or learning **contract** with a student with a behaviour disorder that is specific to his or her greatest challenge, and ensure that it is realistic and immediate. Both of you should sign it. Contracts are described in Chapter 6.

Use the resources of the school, the school district, and the community—to secure group intervention for the class—to teach **prosocial behaviours** and to develop co-operation. Some police services offer a VIP program; find a local equivalent and work collaboratively. (The VIP program focuses on Values, Influences, and Peers. It is a joint program of the Ontario Ministry of Education and the Ministry of the Solicitor-General. Topics include peer pressure, responsible citizenship, and interpersonal skills.) Be persistent in securing individual therapy, counselling, and instruction in self-management strategies (whatever is needed for the student with a behaviour exceptionality) consistent with the group intervention. Differentiate your teaching (e.g., Tomlinson, 2001) so that all of your students feel that they are learning; engage your students fully. Two ways to differentiate that are positive for all students and especially helpful for students with behaviour exceptionalities are (a) providing students with choice of activities or at least the order in which activities will unfold, and (b) choosing high-interest activities based on

## Milly Fraser, Grade 4, Alexander Forbes School, Grande Prairie, Alberta

A teacher who catches students being good and much more.

### "Stop, Drop, and Phone" Award

Milly Fraser will drop everything in the middle of the school day and phone parents, even at work, to let them know their child did especially well on a test. Milly Fraser might even suggest that mom or dad make the child a favourite meal as a reward.

### Best Supporting Role

When Nancy Goheen's son, Taylor, was in a church play, Milly Fraser took in a rehearsal—because she couldn't make the performance. On skate night, she showed her support by coming, even though she doesn't skate. And when she heard that a local missionary group was going to help children in Nicaragua, Milly Fraser organized a class bake sale to raise money for school supplies for them. The kids saw their charitable efforts in action when the missionaries returned with a video of the Nicaraguan schoolchildren.

### A Rewarding Experience

Taylor Goheen, a bright but troubled boy, was in danger of becoming the class outcast, but Milly Fraser brought him into the fold by employing savvy behavioural modification techniques that engaged the whole class. She put Taylor on a program where he was marked on his conduct. When he behaved well, he got to choose an enjoyable activity for everyone in the class—not just himself. Fraser also rewarded him, personally, with stickers and other little gifts. "She has given so much to my son," says Nancy Goheen, "that it has totally changed the person he is."

Source: Based on Nixon, D. (2000). Inspiring teachers. *Today's Parent*, September. Today's Parent Online, September 4, 2000 (www.todaysparent.com).

**Put into Practice**

Read two of these resources and develop differentiated instruction and a highly structured classroom approach that you think would address the issues raised in the description of Urjo in the opening case for this chapter. Compare your choice of readings and your plan with the choices and plans of your peers.

BC Special Education Branch (2006). *Teaching students with learning and behavioural differences: A resource guide for teachers.* http://www.bced.gov.bc.ca/specialed/landbdif/toc.htm.

Reithaug, D. (1998). *Orchestrating positive and practical behaviour plans.* Vancouver: Stirling Head Enterprises.

Rockwell, S. (1995). *Back off, cool down, try again: Teaching students how to control aggressive behavior.* Reston, VA: Council for Exceptional Children.

Rogers, B. (Ed.). (2004). *How to manage children's challenging behavior.* London, UK: Paul Chapman Pub.

**Weblinks**

CANADIAN MENTAL HEALTH ASSOCIATION: MY LIFE—"IT'S COOL TO TALK ABOUT IT!" (YOUTH MENTAL HEALTH)
www.cmha.ca/mylife

NATIONAL INSTITUTE FOR MENTAL HEALTH (CHILD AND ADOLESCENT MENTAL HEALTH)
www.nimh.nih.gov/health/topics/child-and-adolescent-mental-health/index.shtml

PRINCE EDWARD ISLAND DEPARTMENT OF EDUCATION STUDENT SERVICES, *MEETING BEHAVIOURAL CHALLENGES*
www.gov.pe.ca/photos/original/ed_mebech.pdf

students' stated preferences, your prior observations, or informal polls of the class (Heacox, 2002; Kern, Bambara, & Fogt, 2002). As Karen Hume of the Durham District School Board (2008) says, "Start where they are."

You can use the ADAPT strategy to differentiate your teaching and ensure that a student with a behaviour exceptionality finds classes meaningful; you may find it helpful to work with a resource teacher, paraeducator, or volunteer to ensure that individual tutoring reinforces your adaptations (see Kamps et al., 2000). Although time-consuming and challenging, these actions can get the student with behaviour exceptionalities "onside" from the first day of term. Many programs that use literature to connect with youth have been effective in helping students with behavioural difficulties to learn about themselves and about others. For example, Regan and Page (2008) describe a program that used the "Circle of Courage Model" (Brendtro et al., 1990). Many schools have initiated positive behavioural interventions and supports (PBIS) (Horner et al., 2001) with three tiers. The program starts with school-wide interventions, sometimes called primary prevention, to ensure all students understand behavioural expectations; secondary prevention, for groups of students with at-risk behaviour, follows; and finally there is specialized intervention for individuals. Cuccaro and Geitner (2007) describe a targeted intervention for a group of grade 5 students who had persistent problems at lunch and recess. They received direct instruction and practice in social skills at lunch every day for two weeks, with positive results. This action research may inspire you to develop a systematic approach to those students who require intensive help learning appropriate behaviour and respectful treatment of peers.

### THE IMPORTANCE OF CLASSROOM PROGRAMS IN PROSOCIAL BEHAVIOUR

You may feel that your efforts as a teacher with these students are insignificant compared with the work of psychologists and psychiatrists. If so, you are underestimating your importance. A 2001 report from the National Institute for Mental Health (*Teens: The Company They Keep*, www.mental-health-matters.com/articles/article.php?artID=225) in the United States highlights the roles of teachers and schools. It suggests that many attempts to "reform" severely delinquent youths have had little positive effect. Typically these programs place delinquent youth together in settings such as group homes where they learn violence from one another. Research suggests that we prevent anti-social behaviour through interventions aimed at peers and other key people in the student's social environment. "The challenge . . . is to alter these adolescent norms [where] . . . an aggressive reputation is positively related to adolescent peer popularity. The primary strategy currently employed to achieve this goal is through the use of classroom and school-based programs in social problem solving, conflict management, violence prevention, and more broad-based curriculum for promoting emotional and social development in the total school population."

## Implications for Social and Career Participation of Students with Behaviour and Emotional Exceptionalities

Students with behaviour and emotional exceptionalities tend to lack advocates (Dworet & Rathgeber, 1998; Smith, 2004). There is no high-profile national organization like the Learning Disabilities Association of Canada that offers workshops to teachers and community support to parents. Perhaps the stigma associated with emotional problems contributes to the lack of advocacy. In June 2008 the *Globe and Mail* ran an extensive series of newspaper articles, online contributions from readers, and question-and-answer opportunities with mental health experts with the aim of reducing the stigma associated with mental health conditions. They reported what the research has shown in recent years: adolescents and young adults are particularly vulnerable to depression, anxiety, schizophrenia, and other mental illnesses. They reported the story of Jesse Bigelow's descent into schizophrenia at the age of 19, struggling with what was real and what was imagined, withdrawing from his friends, growing moody and paranoid, and refusing to accept help (Anderssen, 21 June 2008). Nancy Heath of McGill University provides classroom teachers with an introduction to self-injury in adolescents (www.education.mcgill.ca/heathresearchteam/images/QPAT2005SelfInjury.pdf) because adolescence is when self-injury peaks. (For information for administrators and teachers, see Lieberman, 2004.) These are challenging problems that require the expertise of mental health professionals. In most communities the family, the individual, and you and your school can enlist the support of the local mental health association and other community organizations, depending on the nature of the behaviour exceptionality or the student's mental health needs. Stereotypes abound and make it difficult for these young people to make a successful transition into adult responsibilities and employment. Organizations like the local branch of the Canadian Mental Health Association (www.cmha.ca/bins/index.asp) provide employment support to adolescents and adults with emotional and mental health disorders.

# Teaching Students with Mild Intellectual Disabilities

To Ms. Starr: I want to work in recycling. Because I want to help the environment and I won't need to read too much. I'm not too good at reading or writing, but I am learning this year. I like this class. You and Mr. T. [Mr. Tymchuk, the resource teacher] make me want to learn. You let me try my way. Thank you. That's why I want to be in recycling. The end.

*Dictated to the resource teacher, following a lesson about careers, by Scott, who is in grade 3 and has mild intellectual disabilities.*

## Description of Intellectual Disabilities

The term *intellectual disabilities* is widely used in Canada to replace *mental retardation*, a term unacceptable to most people but still used interchangeably with intellectual disabilities by the American Association on Mental Retardation (AAMR), which is now called the American Association on Intellectual and Developmental Disabilities (AAIDD). "Intellectual disability is characterized by significant limitations both in intellectual functioning and in adaptive behavior as expressed in conceptual, social, and practical **adaptive skills**. This disability originates before age 18" (Schalock et al., 2007, for AAIDD).

This definition rests on five assumptions:

1. Limitations in present functioning must be considered within the context of community environments typical of the individual's age peers and culture.

2. Valid assessment considers cultural and linguistic diversity as well as differences in communication, sensory, motor, and behavioural factors.

Further Reading

About interventions for students with behavioural exceptionalities:

Lane, K.L., Menzies, H.M., Barton-Arwood, S.M., Doukas, G.L., & Munton, S.M. (2005). Designing, implementing, and evaluating social skills interventions for elementary students: Step-by-step procedures based on actual school-based investigations. *Preventing School Failure, 49*(2), 18–26.

Mooney, P., Ryan, J.B., Uhing, B.M., Reid, R., & Epstein, M.H. (2005). A review of self-management interventions targeting academic outcomes for students with emotional and behavioral disorders. *Journal of Behavioral Education, 14*(3), 203–221.

Frederickson, N., & Turner, J. (2003). Utilizing the classroom peer group to address children's social needs: An evaluation of the Circle of Friends intervention approach. *Journal of Special Education, 36*(4), 234–245.

Doll, B., & Cummings, J.A. (Eds.) (2008). *Transforming school mental health services: Population-based approaches to promoting the competency and wellness of children.* Thousand Oaks, CA: Corwin Press.

Doll, B., & Cummings, J.A. (Eds.) (2008). *Transforming school mental health services: Population-based approaches to promoting the competency and wellness of children.* Thousand Oaks, CA: Corwin Press.

Further Reading

On teaching students with emotional and behaviour disorders:

Jensen, M.M. (2005). *Introduction to emotional and behavioral disorders: Recognizing and managing problems in the classroom.* Upper Saddle River, NJ: Pearson Merrill Prentice Hall.

Morris, R.J., & Mathers, N. (Eds). (2008). *Evidence-based interventions for students with learning and behavioral challenges.* New York: Routledge.

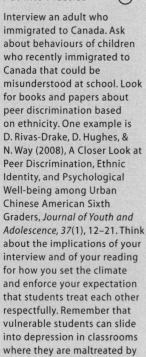

**Put into Practice**

Interview an adult who immigrated to Canada. Ask about behaviours of children who recently immigrated to Canada that could be misunderstood at school. Look for books and papers about peer discrimination based on ethnicity. One example is D. Rivas-Drake, D. Hughes, & N. Way (2008), A Closer Look at Peer Discrimination, Ethnic Identity, and Psychological Well-being among Urban Chinese American Sixth Graders, *Journal of Youth and Adolescence, 37*(1), 12–21. Think about the implications of your interview and of your reading for how you set the climate and enforce your expectation that students treat each other respectfully. Remember that vulnerable students can slide into depression in classrooms where they are maltreated by their peers. Compare notes with your classmates.

**What do you think?**

Visit the websites representing the various perspectives on mild intellectual disabilities. How can teachers become effective advocates for students with intellectual disabilities?

3. Within an individual, limitations often coexist with strengths.

4. An important purpose of describing limitations is to develop a profile of needed supports.

5. With appropriate personalized supports over a sustained period, the life functioning of the person with intellectual disabilities generally will improve.

By intellectual functioning, the AAIDD means a general mental capability that involves the ability to reason, plan, solve problems, think abstractly, comprehend complex ideas, learn quickly, and learn from experience. Generally, **intelligence** is represented by intelligence quotient (IQ) scores obtained from standardized tests given by a trained professional. By adaptive behaviour, the AAIDD means the collection of conceptual, social, and practical skills that people have learned so they can function in their everyday lives. The AAIDD refers to supports as the resources and individual strategies necessary to promote the development, education, interests, and well-being of a person with intellectual disabilities (ID). Supports can be provided by a parent, friend, teacher, psychologist, doctor, or any other appropriate person or agency.

In recent years in educational and community service contexts in Canada, the term *developmental disabilities* has sometimes been used instead of the terms mental retardation or intellectual disabilities (e.g., Ontario Ministry of Community Services; www.mcss.gov.on.ca). However, across North America *developmental disabilities* is generally used to refer to a broad collection of disabilities, attributed to a mental or physical impairment or a combination of the two, that do not necessarily involve intellectual impairment. There are usually limitations in three or more of self-care, receptive and expressive language, learning, mobility, self-direction, capacity for independent living, and economic self-sufficiency; examples include autism, brain injury, cerebral palsy, Down syndrome, fetal alcohol syndrome, and spina bifida (http://ici.umn.edu/relatedresources/definition.html). The Ontario Ministry of Education uses the term *developmental disabilities* to refer to severe intellectual disabilities; these contradictory uses of a term can be very confusing for parents, teachers, and other professionals. If someone uses the term *developmental disabilities*, be sure to ask what characteristics they are referring to.

In Chapters 1 and 2, we considered a range of perspectives on exceptionality. All of these perspectives are represented in the field of intellectual disabilities (ID). A human rights perspective emphasizes what persons with disabilities are entitled to (e.g., Independent Living Canada, www.vilrc.ca/web/guest/home). An educational perspective emphasizes the learning needs of individuals with exceptionalities and of professionals who work with them (e.g., the Ontario Association on Developmental Disabilities, www.oadd.org, and the J.P. Das Developmental Disabilities Centre, www.ualberta.ca/~jpdasddc/INDEX.html). A medical or psychological perspective emphasizes limitations experienced by these individuals (e.g., the Developmental Disabilities Program at University of Western Ontario, www.psychiatry.med.uwo.ca/ddp).

## TWO LEVELS OF INTELLECTUAL DISABILITIES: MILD AND SEVERE

In the past, four categories—mild, moderate, severe, and profound—were used to describe ID, primarily associated with IQ score ranges. Recently, practitioners have begun to use two levels of functioning—mild and severe—to describe individuals with intellectual disabilities, primarily associated with level of adaptive functioning. Mild ID disabilities are discussed in this chapter as a high-incidence exceptionality, while severe intellectual disabilities are discussed in Chapter 4.

## MILD INTELLECTUAL DISABILITIES

"Persons with mild [intellectual disabilities] are those who know a great deal about living in the community without supervision and who require some instruction that could be provided under relatively non-intensive conditions" (Dever, 1990, p. 150). Ontario describes mild ID as characterized by ability to profit educationally within a regular classroom with modifications, slow intellectual development, and potential for academic learning, independent social adjustment, and economic self-support (2001, p. A20). Besides the ongoing debates about terminology, recent research has dispelled the earlier belief that individuals with **Down syndrome** necessarily function at a moderate level of developmental disability. Research shows that many individuals with Down syndrome have mild intellectual disabilities (Rynders & Horrobin, 1990), similar to those of Scott, whose case is highlighted at the opening of this chapter. Figures 3.5 and 3.6 on pages 110 and 111 provide information about Down syndrome and an excerpt from Scott's IEP, respectively.

## Incidence of Mild Intellectual Disabilities

It is estimated that roughly 2 to 3 percent of the general population has mild intellectual disabilities, depending on how the term ID is defined. In a school of four hundred students, this would be about eight to twelve students, but it is important to remember that there is variation from one community to another, with a higher rate associated with psychosocial disadvantage.

## Characteristics of Students with Mild Intellectual Disabilities

### DELAYED DEVELOPMENT: COGNITIVE AND PHYSICAL

Usually, students with mild intellectual disabilities learn to meet the everyday demands of living and develop into self-sufficient adults. However, in school they may have difficulty in attaining the academic skills associated with their grade level and in acquiring skills and knowledge at the same rate as other students.

Students with mild intellectual disabilities pass through the same developmental stages as other students, but at a much slower rate. Delays can be seen in physical, cognitive, language, and social development. In physical development, fine motor coordination may be delayed, affecting cutting, colouring, printing, etc. Cognitive delays affect short-term memory, attention, and ability to generalize and to recognize similarities and differences (e.g., Ven der Molen et al., 2008). Frequently these students are less interested in letters, words, reading, and numbers than their classmates in the early school years. They are likely to find reading comprehension, arithmetic reasoning, and problem solving most difficult, but they may attain lower levels of achievement in all curriculum areas (e.g., Chung & Tam, 2005). Exceptions may be curriculum areas where they can use experiential learning, such as Scott's expertise about recycling and nature acquired by camping and watching television programs.

### Weblinks

MINDYOURMIND.CA
This site says: "mindyourmind.ca is an award winning site for youth by youth. This is a place where you can get info, resources and the tools to help you manage stress, crisis and mental health problems. Share what you live and what you know with your friends. That's what we're about."

Visit this site and think about what makes it unique and why it might be more effective with youth than a site designed by adults. Can you find other similar sites for youth by youth?

### Further Reading

About the challenges for adolescents and their families:

Mojtabai, R., & Olfson, M. (2008). Parental detection of youth's self-harm behavior. *Suicide and Life-Threatening Behavior, 38*(1), 60–73.

Silver, R. (2008, May). Identifying children and adolescents at risk for depression and/or aggression. *Online submission*, ERIC Document Reproduction Service No. ED501283.

Crowell, S.E., Beauchaine, T.P., McCauley, E., Smith, C.J., Vasilev, C.A., & Stevens, A.L. (2008). Parent-child interactions, peripheral serotonin, and self-inflicted injury in adolescents. *Journal of Consulting and Clinical Psychology, 76*(1), 15–21.

Spoth, R., Randall, G.K., & Shin, C. (2008). Increasing school success through partnership-based competency training: Experimental study of long-term outcomes. *School Psychology Quarterly, 23*(1), 70–89.

Weblinks

CANADIAN DOWN SYNDROME SOCIETY
www.cdss.ca

Weblinks

CONNECTING TO THE WHEEL: A CULTURAL
RESOURCE TOOLKIT (ABORIGINAL
FAMILIES AND DOWN SYNDROME)
www.cdss.ca/site/resources/
down_syndrome/
CDSS%20Connecting%20to%20th
e%20Wheel.pdf

FIRST NATIONS CIRCLE OF FRIENDS (FOR
INDIVIDUALS WITH DEVELOPMENTAL
DISABILITIES TO EXPERIENCE THEIR
ABORIGINAL BACKGROUND)
www.pdd.org/Central/firstnations/
aboutus.htm

## FIGURE 3.5 INFORMATION ABOUT DOWN SYNDROME

Down syndrome is a chromosomal arrangement that causes limitations in physical and cognitive development. All persons with Down syndrome have extra genetic material associated with the twenty-first chromosome. One in every eight hundred live births in Canada will be affected by Down syndrome. Though the likelihood of having a child with Down syndrome increases to some degree with the age of the mother, three-quarters of all children with the syndrome are born to mothers under 35.

Recent studies show that, though all children with Down syndrome have some degree of intellectual disability, other factors, such as environment, misinformation, and low expectations, have a considerable impact on their learning potential. Generally, progress will be slow, and certain complex skills may be difficult. Each individual has unique strengths and weaknesses. Learning differences are highly variable and individualistic, like physical characteristics and health concerns.

Physically, children with Down syndrome have low muscle tone and a generalized looseness of the ligaments. There is also a strong susceptibility to hearing and vision difficulties. About one-third of the children will have heart defects.

**Classroom Strategies: Teaching**

- Discuss scheduling and activities before they happen; use wall charts, calendars, photos of a single activity or a single day. These activities reinforce structure and sequencing.
- Allow time to finish a task.
- Help the student to structure play as well as work or the activity may become confusing.
- Break up tasks into small steps; use short blocks of time.
- Avoid the abstract in favour of the concrete and the visual.
- Phrase questions simply and allow response time. Use short sentences.
- Encourage speech by having the student express wants rather than forming simple "yes" or "no" responses.
- Gain attention by using simple commands, e.g., by using eye contact. Be precise.
- Help the child focus on the task—remove items that might distract.
- Expect appropriate behaviour. All students are accountable for their behaviour.
- Co-operate with the parents in integrating learning activities, e.g., shopping, banking, renting a video, travel. Be mutually aware of what the student knows and is learning.
- Be aware of the available computer software specially designed to facilitate reading and communication.

**Classroom Strategies: Social**

- Help the student develop independence; this will both increase self-esteem and improve social relationships.
- Help the student and others understand Down syndrome. Initiate open discussion, considering individual differences and wide variations of abilities. Your own behaviour and acceptance will serve as a model.
- Encourage interaction and involvement with other students through play and classroom activities.

Source: British Columbia Ministry of Education (1996). *Awareness of Chronic Health Conditions: What the Teacher Needs to Know.* Victoria: Queen's Printer for British Columbia. (www.cdss.ca.) Used with permission.

### DELAYED DEVELOPMENT: COMMUNICATION AND SOCIAL ADJUSTMENT

In speech and language development, you may see delay—less-developed expressive and receptive vocabulary. Students may not understand long sentences or complex ideas when they are presented for the first time. Characteristics include articulation disorders, concrete language, and difficulty with advanced grammar rules. Students with ID usually experience challenges in social adjustment, part of adaptive behaviour. They may lack initiative and sometimes display **learned helplessness**. Thus

## FIGURE 3.6 SECOND PAGE OF INDIVIDUAL EDUCATION PLAN (GOALS FOR THE YEAR/ADAPTATIONS)

Student: Scott Boudin          Teacher: Pat Kostas
Exceptionality: Mild intellectual disability (Down syndrome)

**Long-Term Goals for the Year**

1. Reading: Scott will continue to develop phonemic awareness and reading comprehension.
2. Writing: Scott will improve his written expression using full sentences in his journal and curriculum areas.
3. Listening: Scott will improve listening to and following instructions.
4. Speaking: Scott will speak clearly in social and learning situations, asking questions when he does not understand.
5. Math: Scott will improve counting, use of money, addition and subtraction of numbers to 10.
6. Social and environmental studies: Scott will participate in a collaborative learning group.
7. Motor development: Scott will engage in games, increase independence in eating lunch, increase hand–eye coordination.
8. Art and music: Scott will gain experience with various art media.
9. Self-management: Scott will follow lunch routines, join an extracurricular activity.
10. Social: Scott will develop close relationships with several peers and participate in group activities.

**Adaptations**

1. Materials at his level; individualized instruction (resource teacher).
2. Using drawings or pictures from magazines as necessary (support of educational assistant).
3. Using comprehension check (repeating instructions to educational assistant or classroom buddy).
4. Asking educational assistant or classroom buddy about what to say.
5. Using coins, other concrete materials for addition and subtraction.
6. Asking educational assistant or classroom buddy when unsure of what to do.
7. Assistance with eating lunch, using computer (educational assistant).
8. Tasks at level.
9. Adult volunteer to support in eating and cleaning up lunch.
10. Watching and following positive actions of peers (encouraged by educational assistant).

Source: Adapted from Hutchinson, N.L. (2004). *Teaching Exceptional Children and Adolescents: A Canadian Casebook*, p. 30. Copyright Prentice Hall. Used by permission.

they are less socially prepared to pay attention, initiate conversation, and co-operate, and they may appear immature or shy (see Canney & Byrne, 2006). During the adolescent years this can be especially difficult.

### TEACHER REFERRALS

Some students with mild intellectual disabilities will be identified before they start school, for example, those with Down syndrome who have physically distinguishing characteristics. Other students with mild intellectual disabilities may be identified after starting school. Teachers frequently make pre-referral adaptations, consult with resource teachers, and refer these students for assessment (as described in Chapter 2). This exceptionality has been referred to as the **six-hour handicap**, because students who lag behind their peers at school may meet the everyday demands of life outside school. Occasionally school districts describe these students as "slow learners." They often are advised to register in the **applied or basic stream** in secondary schools. When there is no clear evidence of an **organic cause** for delay, the suspected causes include disadvantage—poverty, inadequate nutrition, family instability, and lack of stimulation and opportunity to learn.

## Further Reading

About collaborative and co-operative learning:

Cohen, E.G. (1994). *Designing groupwork: Strategies for the heterogeneous classroom* (2nd ed.). New York: Teachers College, Columbia University.

*Getting results from cooperative learning* (3 video recordings and a facilitator's guide). (2005). Alexandria, VA: Association for Supervision and Curriculum Development (ASCD).

English, R., & Dean, S. (2004). *Show me how to learn: Key strategies and powerful techniques that promote cooperative learning.* Markham, ON: Pembroke Publishers.

Jaques, D., & Salmon, G. (2007). *Learning in groups: A handbook for face-to-face and online environments* (4th ed.). New York: Routledge.

Gillies, R.M., Ashman, A., & Terwel, J. (Eds.). (2007). *The teacher's role in implementing cooperative learning in the classroom.* New York: Springer.

# Implications for Learning and Classroom Adaptations

### DIFFERENTIATING TO SUPPORT COGNITIVE DEVELOPMENT

To promote cognitive development, encourage students with intellectual disabilities to interact with the environment and with other students. Arrange the environment to provide sensory and intellectual stimulation. Structure and consistency will help them function in a world that can seem chaotic (Bennett, Weber, & Dworet, 2008). Set cognitive goals and use action-oriented activities and concrete materials to facilitate their attainment (Smith, Polloway, Patton, & Dowdy, 2003). Other ways to differentiate include colour-coding notebooks, reducing choices, and highlighting key text; these make learning easier because students can focus on the important parts of a lesson (Newfoundland Department of Education, 2005; Bennett et al., 2008). Some ways to differentiate described in the BC resource *Students with Intellectual Disabilities: A Resource Guide for Teachers* (www.bced.gov.bc.ca/specialed/sid) include having the student arrive ten minutes early to go over the day plan; providing support to preview materials before the lesson; preparing a summary of important information with blanks for the student to fill in while listening; and the modification of giving more concrete assignments on a related topic. Many of these differentiations may make learning easier for other students as well. This BC resource guide includes the important reminder that "when making modifications teachers should change only that which is necessary to meet the needs of the student, with a view to fostering inclusion."

Extending deadlines and arranging for peers to create social opportunities can improve the learning environment for students with mild intellectual disabilities. Learn what alternative resources are available, such as parallel textbooks at **lower reading levels**, audiotaped texts, manipulatives that appeal to the senses, and games to practise important concepts. Students with intellectual disabilities will benefit from reteaching, practice, and application of skills and concepts. They often experience particular difficulty in learning mathematics, and you may find that using money and other authentic, concrete manipulative materials is helpful. Cognitive strategy instruction, in combination with worked examples, has also been shown to be effective in teaching mathematics (Chung & Tan, 2005). Cheryl Duquette (2001) of the University of Ottawa also recommends strategies for differentiating to meet the needs of learners with mild ID.

### ADAPTATIONS TO SUPPORT LANGUAGE DEVELOPMENT

To promote language development, simplify the language you use in instructions and relate new ideas to the student's experiences. Provide opportunities for students to use speech and language, without fear of correction or criticism, for a variety of communication purposes. These kinds of activities may also promote social development. Ensure that classmates treat

*Adults with intellectual disabilities in H'Art studio in Kingston, Ontario, feel empowered by producing and selling folk art.*

the student who has mild intellectual disabilities with respect, and create many contexts in which students learn by collaborating and using strengths other than traditional academic knowledge. Canney and Byrne (2006) provide an example of teachers using circle time in primary classrooms, and the BC resource guide on ID has many suggestions for working with adolescents (www.bced.gov.bc.ca/specialed/sid). To adapt assessment procedures for students with mild ID, look for ways to simplify, shorten, and make clearer what you are looking for in an answer. Alternatives may also include oral exams, portfolios, or interviews.

## Implications for Social and Career Participation of Students with Intellectual Disabilities

**Put into Practice**

Read the document *Down Syndrome and You* (www.cdss. ca/site/resources/ down_syndrome/ Down%20Syndrome%20and%2 0You.pdf), written for young people with Down syndrome. Consider how you would use it to help a young person with Down syndrome to gain self-knowledge. How could you use this booklet to help other students understand a classmate with Down syndrome?

During the secondary years the focus usually shifts to functional, vocational, or applied learning, and students may learn in the community and in specialized classes as well as in regular classes. Adolescents and young adults with mild ID benefit from learning through experience in programs like co-operative education and on-the-job training. Hutchinson et al. (2008) reported that Max, an adolescent with mild intellectual disabilities, benefited from a series of workplace experiences with gradually increasing demands for independence and productivity. Other studies suggest that workplaces where young adults with intellectual disabilities are successful provide specific social opportunities for them and have interdependent job designs that foster social interaction (Butterworth, 2000; Eisenman, 2007). John Lord of Kitchener-Waterloo has pioneered peer support approaches to evaluation of employment programs for these young people (Lord & Rush, 2002) and describes the role of social networks in creating "pathways to inclusion" in our communities (Lord & Hutchison, 2007).

Some youth with intellectual disabilities participate in programs in community colleges. Crawford (2005) provides an account of Shafquat Hussain's high school preparation (at Toronto's York Memorial Collegiate) for attending Humber College. H'Art Studio in Kingston, Ontario, has recently developed the H'Art Prep program, described on its website as "a ten-month program for people with intellectual disabilities, 21 years of age and older, who want to learn more about goal setting while pursuing continuing education and post-secondary education experiences, and meaningful volunteer opportunities. Students will explore these topics while enhancing basic literacy, study and social skills in our creative setting. At the end of the program, students will have a skills portfolio. The portfolio is a tool students can use, and add to, to express their interests and goals" (www.kingston.org/hartstudio/HartPrep.htm).

People with mild ID are primarily disadvantaged in formal school settings but thrive in the community, where they can use their life experience and are not required to use literacy skills or grapple with abstract concepts. In my community young adults with mild intellectual disabilities attend community college, deliver mail in a large institution, organize audiovisual equipment in a university department, do cleaning in a small business, and work in food preparation. They have found niches as volunteers or employees in the service sector or in predictable jobs that don't require high levels of problem solving or literacy. However, data suggest that fewer than half of those with ID are involved in work or training after leaving secondary school (Yamaki & Fujiura, 2002).

It is thought that the vast majority of adults with mild ID can obtain and maintain gainful employment (Butterworth, et al., 2000). However, to do this they must develop personal and social behaviours appropriate to the workplace through transition experiences that prepare them for the expectations of employers. And employers must be aware of the contributions they can make as well as their needs for accommodations. A recent survey of adults in Ontario suggests that most respondents believe people with intellectual disabilities would not negatively affect the image of workplaces, but most thought lack of employment training for people with ID was a major obstacle to increased inclusion (Burge, Ouellette-Kuntz, & Lysaght, 2007). To be successful, inclusion must prepare youth with intellectual disabilities for inclusion in the workplace and in the community, and not focus only on their learning within the four walls of the school.

# Summary

Students with high-incidence exceptionalities include students who are gifted or who have learning disabilities, attention deficit hyperactivity disorder, communication exceptionalities, behaviour exceptionalities, or mild intellectual disabilities. They comprise roughly 75 percent of exceptional students. This means that you will be teaching these students frequently. In fact, many educators say that it is unusual, these days, to teach a class that does not contain at least one student with a learning disability or ADHD. These students may be inefficient at making sense of what you are teaching and may require encouragement and learning strategies that help them stay on task and complete assignments.

Gifted students will thrive with assignments that offer choice, challenge them, and enable them to go beyond regular curriculum expectations. Students with speech and language exceptionalities may require opportunities to practise in the classroom what they learn with a specialist, and volunteers may assume this responsibility. Expect to seek the assistance of other team members for students who have behaviour exceptionalities. They can be very challenging and often require individual counselling that you simply cannot provide in a classroom setting. Asking for help when you really need it is a sign of strength, not weakness. Students with mild intellectual disabilities will probably not keep pace with the regular curriculum, and you can expect to see the gap widen over time. However, they benefit greatly from observing their peers in a regular class and are likely to participate in regular classrooms during the elementary years and to be enrolled in streams or programs that emphasize inclusion in the community, more than in regular classrooms, during the secondary years.

It is often difficult to distinguish students with high-incidence exceptionalities from their peers because their exceptionalities are not always obvious, with the exception of students with Down syndrome, who have characteristic facial features. Using the ADAPT strategy, in combination with students' IEPs, will help you to differentiate elements of the classroom so that you can meet individual needs. Most of these students will benefit from a structured, predictable, engaging class with a positive tone, in which everyone is treated with respect by you and taught that that is how they are expected to treat one another.

# Key Terms

high-incidence exceptionalities (p. 70)

developmentally advanced (p. 73)

domains (p. 73)

metacognition (p. 74)

cognitive abilities (p. 74)

high task commitment (p. 74)

creativity (p. 75)

open-ended assignment (p. 76)

information processing (p. 79)

dyslexia (p. 79)

dysgraphia (p. 79)

dyscalculia (p. 79)

discrepancy (p. 79)

social skills difficulties (p. 81)

primary disability (p. 81)

secondary disability (p. 81)

social status (p. 81)

self-concept (p. 81)

phonemic awareness (p. 81)

rapid naming (p. 81)

double deficit hypothesis (p. 81)

reading comprehension (p. 82)

number sense (p. 84)

depression (p. 85)

mode of presentation (p. 87)

cueing (p. 87)

study guides (p. 87)

colour-coded (p. 87)

cognitive strategies (p. 88)

career development (p. 89)

inattentiveness (p. 90)

hyperactivity (p. 90)

impulsivity (p. 90)

checkpoints (p. 93)

carrel (p. 94)

thinking aloud (p. 94)

verbal reprimand (p. 95)

time out (p. 95)

cognitive-behaviour management (CBM) (p. 95)

psychostimulant medications (p. 96)

antidepressants (p. 96)

articulation (p. 98)

speech impairment (p. 98)

language impairment (p. 98)

aggression (p. 101)

negative psychological states (p. 101)

social problems (p. 101)

structure (p. 102)

feedback (p. 103)

contract (p. 105)

prosocial behaviours (p. 105)

adaptive skills (p. 107)

intelligence (p. 108)

Down syndrome (p. 109)

learned helplessness (p. 110)

six-hour handicap (p. 111)

applied or basic stream (p. 111)

organic cause (p. 111)

lower reading levels (p. 112)

# Challenges for Reviewing Chapter 3

1. What does it mean for an exceptionality to be described as high-incidence? What high-incidence exceptionalities do you expect to have to differentiate for in your upcoming year of teaching? Discuss with your peers why it is important to be prepared to differentiate the social aspects of your classroom as well as the academic instruction.

2. Read the brief description of Brian, a gifted student, at the beginning of the section on teaching students who are gifted. How could you differentiate instruction for Brian so that he is fully engaged in what he is learning and ensure that he is less likely to be taunted by his peers and to retaliate?

3. Write a description of a student with learning disabilities who is at a grade level you are likely to teach in the near future. Then describe the greatest challenges you will face in differentiating your teaching so this student learns successfully, and consider the possibility of intensive tiered instruction outside your classroom to complement what you are doing.

4. You are currently a member of the in-school team for a student who has been identified as having ADHD, predominantly inattentive. Prepare to assume the role of one member of the team. Choose your role: classroom teacher, special educator, parent, or principal. Make a reading list for yourself. After you have completed the readings, write a script for your contribution to the first meeting after differentiation of instruction has begun. Role-play the meeting with your peers. Generate a plan for keeping the student attentive and engaged in learning, now that she has experienced some success. Take the perspective that some of the student's characteristics are strengths unique to people with ADHD. How does this change what you say and do in the meeting and in your teaching?

5. Consider the learning needs of Ruth, a student with a communication disorder, described at the beginning of that section of the text. What is important to keep in mind when teaching Ruth when she is 6, 12, and 18? How do the major issues change with her age and how do they remain consistent?

6. Look back at the description of Urjo at the beginning of this chapter. He has been identified as having a behaviour and emotional exceptionality. Develop a chart to show his needs and strengths, and ways in which you can use his strengths to overcome his difficulties. Include intrapersonal, interpersonal, academic, and community aspects of Urjo's education. Think about whose support you might want to enlist for Urjo and for yourself while the two of you work together to improve these aspects of his education and to increase his likelihood of a successful transition to adulthood. If you are an elementary teacher, change Urjo's age to the age of students you teach.

7. Scott is described in an opening case for this chapter. Make a plan for differentiating teaching and the social arrangements of the class for Scott. Use Scott's interest in environmental science to help you engage Scott. Consider how his family might be able to help you to accomplish your goals for Scott. If you teach secondary students, consider Scott at the age of 17.

8. Return to the cases of Urjo and Scott, from the beginning of this chapter. Answer the five questions that follow the cases, and discuss your ideas with your peers. Identify the most surprising thing you have learned in this chapter, the most practical thing, and one thing that intrigues you that you will follow up to answer your own questions about teaching students with high-incidence exceptionalities. What dilemmas about teaching stick in your mind after reading this chapter? What resources could you use or actions could you take that might help you to deal with these dilemmas?

# Chapter 4

# Exceptional Students: Low-Incidence Exceptionalities, Physical Exceptionalities, and Chronic Health Conditions

Pamela is in senior kindergarten at Grove Elementary School. She likes playing with water, making towers of blocks, being near the teacher, and exploring the materials the teacher is demonstrating. The classroom is often busy and noisy. For example, today a visitor is teaching the children to drum on the tomato-juice can drums they made last week. While the others sit in a circle, Pamela is running from one side of the room to the other, waving her arms. She has a short attention span for activities with a social component and becomes agitated when the classroom is too busy or too noisy. Pamela wants to sit on the chair beside the visitor and touch his drum. When she can't have her way, she has a tantrum. She repeats, "I like the big chair, I like the big chair," and "Thump the drum, thump the drum," both lines that she has heard the visitor say to the class. Pamela communicates through **echolalia** (echoing what is said), gestures, and limited functional speech, including, "No," "Help me," and "Get that one." Pamela's IEP states that she has autism.

**Brittany has cystic fibrosis and coughs constantly.** Although she is in grade 7, she is as small as most girls in grade 4. She has just returned to school after being hospitalized for two months. Brittany has told teachers and students in previous classes about how her body produces abnormally thick and sticky secretions that cause problems in her respiratory and digestive systems. This mucus builds up in her lungs and also makes it difficult for her to digest her food. Brittany has always left class willingly to take her medication and receive therapy to clear her airways. Most teachers have found that Brittany needs encouragement to follow her regime of medication and treatment. This year she also needs emotional support to deal with the recent insertion of a feeding tube that will ensure that she continues to grow and has enough energy. Brittany's health condition has an impact on her school life, mainly on her social and emotional well-being.

1. Which of the characteristics of each student are most likely to affect learning? What learning needs are implied by these characteristics?

2. With such a range of learning needs, what do exceptional students like Pamela and Brittany have in common?

3. How frequently is a teacher likely to be teaching a student with each of these exceptionalities?

4. What types of differentiation does each of these students need in order to be included in the social life and the learning activities of the classroom?

5. What community resources can a teacher draw on to supplement in-school resources to teach each of these students?

# Introduction

Cross-Reference
For descriptions of and differentiations for students with high-incidence exceptionalities, see Chapter 3.

In this chapter you will learn about the characteristics, needs, and strengths of students with a number of **low-incidence exceptionalities, physical disabilities**, and **chronic health conditions.** The emphasis is on how you can differentiate instruction in the classroom. Students with many of the exceptionalities described in this chapter are identified soon after birth because their needs are high and their disabilities or conditions are severe. Many jurisdictions have screening programs and preschool intervention programs, like the Yellowknife Early Childhood Intervention program described in the *NWT Disability Framework* (2004). There are also a number of collaborative initiatives—for example, Building Healthy Mi'kmaq Communities in Prince Edward Island, a project that was led by Vianne Timmons of the University of Prince Edward Island, which identified the communities' perceptions of their children's health and education needs. The project was an aid to children with and without exceptionalities.

Many children with low-incidence exceptionalities, identified by doctors or psychologists, start school with a detailed IEP. While reading this chapter, think about children and adolescents you have known with these exceptionalities or other conditions with similar implications for learning. Labels give us a shared language, but it is important that, as teachers, our language is respectful and professional. Labels never capture the essence of the individual's experience of an exceptionality or health condition.

As you read about students in this chapter, consider the parents' perspective. The parents of children with low-incidence exceptionalities tend to be very involved in the lives of their offspring (Wysocki & Gavin, 2006). They may assume the role of **case coordinator** and are often better informed than classroom teachers about particular exceptionalities and conditions. You may teach a child with cystic fibrosis, like Brittany, twice in your career. The parents teach their child with cystic fibrosis every day. I have used person-first language, for example, students with cerebral palsy. This means we refer to the student first and describe the student as *having* an exceptionality second.

Each section on an exceptionality begins with the words of a child or adolescent. Frequently these are based on questions asked by a student (in sources like Miriam Kaufman's 2005 book, *Easy for You to Say*) or on sources such as *The Kids on the Block* book series (Aiello & Shulman, 1991, 1995, 1997). Each entry follows a pattern: the exceptionality is described with information about its incidence or frequency, followed by characteristics, classroom implications, and often implications for career participation. For low-incidence exceptionalities, teachers must seek information on a need-to-know basis. It is almost impossible for you to remember the details of fifteen or more low-incidence conditions. However, the principles of inclusion, adaptation, and differentiation always apply. Information is provided about responding to life-threatening and extremely disruptive conditions—for example, teachers who are knowledgeable about allergic reactions and asthma may save a student's life. Table 4.1 introduces the exceptionalities discussed in this chapter.

| Exceptionality | Description |
| --- | --- |
| **Low-Incidence Exceptionalities** | |
| Severe intellectual disabilities | Severe limitation in both intellectual functioning and adaptive behaviour; focus is on the individual's need for support to function in the community |
| *Autism Spectrum Disorders* | |
| Autism | Impairments in verbal and nonverbal communication and reciprocal social interaction; restricted, repetitive patterns of behaviour; and intellectual disability |
| Asperger syndrome | Severe and sustained impairment in social interaction, and development of restricted, repetitive patterns of behaviour and interests |
| *Sensory Exceptionalities* | |
| Hard of hearing and deaf | Hearing loss that has significantly affected development of speech and/or language and caused students to need adaptations to learn |
| Visual impairments | Blind or partially sighted students who need adaptations to learn through channels other than visual |
| **Physical Disabilities and Chronic Medical Conditions** | |
| *Nervous System Impairment* | |
| Cerebral palsy | Disorders affecting body movement and muscle coordination resulting from damage to brain during pregnancy or first three years |
| Spina bifida | Neural tube defect that occurs during first four weeks of pregnancy causing vertebrae or spinal cord to fail to develop properly |
| Epilepsy | Neurological disorder involving sudden bursts of electrical energy in the brain |
| Tourette syndrome | Neurological disorder characterized by tics |
| Brain injury | Damage to brain tissue that prevents it from functioning properly |
| Fetal alcohol spectrum disorders | Neurological disorders caused by significant prenatal exposure to alcohol |
| *Musculoskeletal Conditions* | |
| Muscular dystrophy | Genetically based muscle disorders that result in progressive muscle weakness |
| Juvenile arthritis | Continuous inflammation of joints in young people under 16 |
| *Chronic Health Impairments* | |
| Diabetes | Condition in which the body does not make enough insulin and has problems absorbing and storing sugars |
| Allergies | Sensitivity or abnormal immune response to normal substance, which can cause anaphylactic shock |
| Asthma | Chronic lung condition, characterized by difficulty breathing, in which airways are obstructed by inflammation, muscle spasms, and excess mucus |
| Cystic fibrosis | Incurable disorder caused by inherited genetic defect, affecting mainly the lungs and the digestive system |
| HIV and AIDS | Human immunodeficiency virus and acquired immune deficiency syndrome, virus-caused illness resulting in the breakdown of the immune system; currently no known cure |
| Cancer and leukemia | Characterized by uncontrolled division of cells and the ability of these to spread; leukemia is a type of cancer that forms in the bone marrow, causing abnormal white blood cell development |

# Teaching Students with Severe Intellectual Disabilities

My dream: My name is Reid. I am 17 and I have developmental delay. Caused by a genetic condition—called Coffin-Lowry syndrome. Some people say I am retarded. I don't like to hear that. I am in a life-skills class at Campbell Collegiate. My favourite part is my work placement. Every morning, I clean the cages and walk the animals for a pet store. I also sweep the floors, and do odd jobs. Sometimes I sell kittens. My boss is my neighbour, Ms. Boychuk. I have known her all my life. That makes it easier. My goal is to live in my own place with my friend Dan. I want to move out like my older brother did. My mom says she hopes that I can do that, but she will miss me. We need people to help us. I use my wheelchair more. But I think we can do it. You will see. That is my dream.

*Generated by Reid Ford and his mother in conversation*

**Weblinks**

J.P. DAS DEVELOPMENTAL DISABILITIES CENTRE
www.ualberta.ca/~jpdasddc/index.html

ONTARIO ASSOCIATION ON DEVELOPMENTAL DISABILITIES
www.oadd.org

NEW BRUNSWICK ASSOCIATION FOR COMMUNITY LIVING (LISTING OF BOOKS AND VIDEOS FOR EDUCATORS AND FAMILIES)
www.nbacl.nb.ca/english/resources/books_videos.asp

## Description of Severe Intellectual Disabilities

**Intellectual disabilities** are conditions originating before the age of 18 that result in significant limitations in intellectual functioning and conceptual, social, and practical adaptive skills (American Psychiatric Association, 2000). Intellectual disability is the currently preferred term for the disability historically referred to as mental retardation. The term *intellectual disability* covers the same population of individuals who were diagnosed previously with mental retardation in number, kind, level, type, and duration of the disability and the need of people with this disability for individualized services and supports (see the website of American Association on Intellectual and Developmental Disabilities, www.aamr.org). Individuals with severe intellectual disabilities have greater limitations in intellectual and adaptive functioning than individuals with mild intellectual disabilities.

Sometimes people use the term **developmental disabilities** or **cognitive disabilities**, while in some countries and contexts people still use the term that dominated the field in the past: *mental retardation*. The adaptive skills in which one would expect to see individuals challenged by the expectations of their environment include communication, home living, community use, health and safety, leisure, self-care, social skills, self-direction, functional academics, and work. The definition of the term by the **American Association on Intellectual and Developmental Disabilities (AAIDD)** includes six major dimensions: (1) intellectual abilities; (2) adaptive behaviour; (3) participation, interaction, and social roles; (4) health; (5) environmental context; and (6) age of onset.

Using Reid as an example may clarify the meaning of these six major dimensions. *Intellectual abilities* include reasoning, planning, solving problems, and thinking abstractly. They are assessed by means of a standardized intelligence test. Reid is clear about his need for supports—Reid and his friend Dan can read environmental print (e.g., the symbol for Coke) and functional signs (like EXIT) but not labels on pill bottles. *Adaptive behaviour* refers to social and practical skills—Reid and Dan need paid assistants to help them with bathing, taking medications, etc. The category of *participation, interaction, and social roles* brings to mind the notion of "adaptive fit" and the individual taking advantage of strengths to take part in the community. Reid has many strengths—he communicates well orally, is a hard worker, knows himself, and uses this self-knowledge to make good decisions.

With excellent support at home, at school, and in the neighbourhood, his life functioning has surpassed early predictions, but he is aware that he will increasingly need his wheelchair for mobility. He wants to be as independent as possible but accepts that he will always need support to participate in his environment. *Physical and mental health* influence functioning and Reid recognizes that his participation depends on staying well. *Environmental context* refers to the school setting, the neighbourhood, and the patterns of culture and society. Reid has learned much about independence and responsibility by reporting to his work placement every morning. Finally, to meet the AAIDD's definition, the *age of onset* must be during the developmental years prior to the age of 18.

## An Intentional, Inclusive Community

Tiffany Dawe was born with severe physical and intellectual disabilities. However, because of an inspiring community effort, Tiffany moved into her own apartment in the Rougemont Intentional Community (Deohaeko), a 105-unit, non-profit housing co-operative in Pickering, Ontario. She lives a full and rewarding life, attending school, shopping (with the aid of paid support workers, family, and friends), visiting friends, and participating in the Rougemont choir.

Ten families of youth with severe disabilities worked for five years to provide safe, affordable, inclusive housing where their children could live as independently as possible. They wanted a co-op and an "intentional community," a combination of residents committed to sharing their lives. The families knew that their offspring were accustomed to living in a neighbourhood, attending school and church, and being part of the community. They did not want to live in group homes. The ten families applied for and obtained joint federal–provincial funding, which the governments will recoup through the Canada Mortgage and Housing Corporation, to build a co-op. The building has 105 units, of which 25 are designed for disabled residents—9 for people in wheelchairs and 16 that accommodate people with either hearing or vision impairment—and spread throughout the building to ensure full integration of those residents.

People who live in the "intentional" community must agree to be helpful, supportive, accepting, and friendly to all the residents of the co-op, including the ten who have severe disabilities. Then a second community was created, called the Deohaeko Support Network, taken from the Iroquois word for "spirit-supporters of life." Each family has created a volunteer support network specifically to meet the needs of the individuals with severe intellectual disabilities.

The intentional community is proving to be a great success. For example, Brenda Gray's family believed she would require

*Friendship from Hilda Hawkes, left, is credited with helping her neighbour, Brenda Gray, need less attendant care. Both are residents of the Rougemont Intentional Community (Deohaeko Support Network) in Pickering, Ontario.*

twenty-four-hour care. However, since moving to the co-op, Brenda has grown socially and increased her independence. Her close friendship with a senior citizen neighbour, Hilda Hawkes, has helped Brenda to be able to stay alone for several hours at a time. Another resident, Rose Connors, explained why she moved to Rougemont: "I really liked the idea of living in this community with people working together to provide security for each other. We all need help at some point in one way or another."

In 1997 the Rougemont Co-op won a Caring Community Award, given by the Ontario Trillium Foundation (www.trilliumfoundation.org).

# Incidence of Severe Intellectual Disabilities

Although there are large discrepancies in estimates, it is believed that in the general population severe intellectual disabilities occur at a rate of about one per one thousand people during the ages of typical school attendance (BC Special Education Branch, 2002). Intellectual disabilities are often the result of conditions described in the sections of this chapter on physical disabilities and health conditions. For example, among the leading causes of intellectual disabilities are fetal alcohol spectrum disorder, cerebral palsy, and spina bifida, as well as Down syndrome, fragile X, and other **chromosomal abnormalities**.

### CONTRADICTORY AND CONTROVERSIAL TRENDS WITH IMPLICATIONS FOR INCIDENCE

Two recent developments could influence the incidence of severe intellectual disabilities. Medical advances save the lives of babies who would have died in the past and are now born with severe intellectual disabilities (Palfrey, Tonniges, Green, & Richmond, 2006). However, **genetic screening** and **amniocentesis** enable parents to prevent the birth of babies with severe intellectual disabilities, although this raises ethical questions about the value we place on members of our society with intellectual disabilities (Hodge, 2004).

## Characteristics of Students with Severe Intellectual Disabilities

The category of severe intellectual disabilities now includes students considered at times in the past to have moderate, severe, or profound disabilities. They span a wide range of abilities, from those who can acquire academic skills to those who will require assistance with **self-care** for their entire lives.

You will usually find in the psychological reports and IEPs that students' strengths and weaknesses have been assessed across four dimensions:

- intellectual or cognitive and adaptive behaviour skills
- psychological, emotional, and social considerations
- physical and health considerations
- environmental considerations

Cognitive characteristics of this group include difficulties focusing attention and getting information into memory; however, long-term memory may be excellent. Language is likely to be delayed, and in the most severe cases verbal language may not develop. Adaptive behaviours refer to coping with the demands of daily living. Psychological characteristics often include frustration and impulsivity. Students with severe intellectual disabilities find social interactions challenging; often they do not know how to make friends, even though they may be loyal and caring. They may withdraw or develop repetitive behaviours that seem bizarre to their peers.

Physical and health considerations may depend on concomitant conditions such as cerebral palsy. Less physical dexterity and coordination than others of the same age are to be expected, and in the most severe cases there may be limited locomotion. *Environmental considerations* refers to such things as requiring a wheelchair that holds the head in a specific position or a **voice synthesizer** to produce speech.

Focus on the strengths and weaknesses in the functional and educational assessments of students with severe intellectual disabilities and on teaching strategies that can make a difference.

**What do you think?**

Does it devalue people in our community with severe intellectual disabilities when parents terminate pregnancies that would result in the birth of infants with severe intellectual disabilities?

## Differentiating Curriculum and Teaching for Students with Severe Intellectual Disabilities

Many of the ways of differentiating instruction discussed in Chapter 3 for students with high-incidence exceptionalities are suitable for some students with severe intellectual disabilities. The curriculum outcomes will be appropriate, but materials or presentation need to be changed. For example, you can make accommodations in the environment by positioning the student where there are the fewest distractions, and the desk may be adapted to suit a wheelchair or a laptop computer. An agenda and list of assignments may be taped to the student's desk. You can highlight key points in the text, break information into steps, and complete the first example with the student. Use concrete examples. You could videotape a lesson so the student can review it at home. Allow extra time to complete tasks and tests. The student may draw or write individual words rather than sentences and paragraphs to communicate his or her understanding.

### MODIFYING CURRICULUM AND DEVELOPING ALTERNATIVE EXPECTATIONS

You may also need to modify the learning outcomes for students with severe developmental disabilities. In this case, you would derive curriculum expectations from those outlined in the curriculum policy document for a lower grade. Accommodations will likely be needed as well. Students with severe intellectual disabilities often require alternative expectations that are not derived from curriculum documents. Your guide for generating alternative outcomes is the goals section of the student's IEP. Consult with other members of the in-school team. Two principles usually guide the development of alternative curriculum for these students (Bates, Cuvo, Miner, & Korabek, 2001). The first is the principle of a **functional curriculum**, in which the goals for a student are based on life skills. At his co-op placement in the pet store, Reid learned to be punctual and how to speak to customers, co-workers, and pets. The second principle is that education should be **community-based** and relate what is learned in school to what occurs in the community. While other students in Reid's high school economics class are learning about the role of the Bank of Canada, Reid benefits from learning to cash a cheque, pay bills at the ATM, and withdraw cash from his account at the neighbourhood bank. Robert Sandieson of the University of Western Ontario (1997) and other researchers (e.g., Xin et al., 2005) report that activities such as using money take considerable practice for youth with severe intellectual disabilities.

There will be great variation from one IEP to the next. Each IEP will include a detailed description of strengths and needs, but the goals of an alternative program usually include

- functional academic skills;
- physical development and personal care;
- communication skills and social interaction skills;
- community living skills; and
- career development, work experience, and transition planning.

Figure 4.1 contains examples of ways to generate modified and alternative curriculum.

## FIGURE 4.1 MODIFIED AND ALTERNATIVE EXPECTATIONS FOR STUDENTS WITH SEVERE INTELLECTUAL DISABILITIES

When developing modified or alternative curriculum for a student, change only that which is necessary to meet the needs of the student, with a view to fostering inclusion.

- Give more concrete assignments on a topic related to that being studied by the class.
- Simplify learning tasks on a similar topic by providing more structure or examples for the student to use as a model.
- Ask easier questions related to the same concept.
- Assign the same materials to be used for a different purpose, for example, addition instead of multiplication.
- Use high-interest/low-vocabulary resources on the same topic. With adolescents, choose age-appropriate topics and avoid texts written for primary students that may cause embarrassment.
- Provide community preparation such as:
  - trips to community locations such as stores;
  - opportunities to apply functional skills in different settings; and
  - job-related experiences such as running a small business.
- Individualize community tasks for each student based on need.

How can you explain to other students why someone like Reid has learning activities that differ from theirs? Younger children sometimes ask about this out of curiosity, whereas older students are likely to raise issues of fairness. If you have set a climate of inclusion in which differences are seen as normal, expected, and valued, you may have fewer questions and the ones you do encounter will probably be easier to answer.

Explain the **principles of fairness** so that your students, no matter how young they are, understand that fairness does not mean sameness. You might use examples of different but fair treatment for exceptionalities not represented in your class. Ask whether it is fair to expect a student with no legs to climb stairs, or whether it is fair to expect a blind student to read a paper-and-pencil test. Most students can see that not everyone needs the elevator or Braille, and in fact most would be disadvantaged by Braille. To ensure equity, use routines for exceptional students that are similar to the routines you use for the rest of the class. Students with severe developmental disabilities should be assigned homework, tests, and projects at the same time as the rest of the class, and theirs should be as challenging for them as the assignments given to the rest of the class are for their classmates.

Recent research suggests that inclusive education, when appropriately funded and supported, is more likely than segregated education to enable students with intellectual disabilities to engage with learning and to participate in independent living in adulthood (e.g., Downing & Peckingham-Hardin, 2007; Shogren et al., 2007). A recent survey in Ontario found that a majority of adults viewed some degree of inclusive education in regular schools as best (Burge et al., in press).

# Teaching Students with Autism Spectrum Disorders

I love buses. I know all the routes. And I can tell you anything about buses in Fredericton—the history, the kinds of buses, how they are serviced. But I wish there were no other people on the buses. The people bug me. When I ride the bus, I always get into trouble because of the people. They make noise and come near me. And I get mad at them. My favourite thing is to ride the bus with my dad while all the people are at work and school. We talk to the driver. Buses are my hobby.

*From the free-writing book of Jason, who is 12 and has Asperger syndrome*

This section focuses on autism and Asperger syndrome. Although autism has been recognized for some time, other disorders that are similar to autism in many ways are now typically collected under a broader term: **autism spectrum disorders (ASDs)**, sometimes referred to as the pervasive developmental disorders (PDD) (Volkmar, 2007, p. ix). All the disorders that are considered ASDs are characterized by varying degrees of impairment in three areas: (1) communication skills, (2) social interactions, and (3) repetitive and stereotyped patterns of behaviour (Volkmar, 2007; *DSM-IV*, American Psychiatric Association, 1994; *ICD-10*, World Health Organization, 1990). The five disorders in the autism spectrum are autism, Asperger syndrome (AS), Rett syndrome, childhood disintegrative disorder, and pervasive developmental disorder not otherwise specified (PDD-NOS). In the following sections autism is discussed first, followed by Asperger syndrome because these are the most prevalent of the disorders in this spectrum. The other three, which occur less frequently, are described here. Rett syndrome usually involves normal development for the first five months to four years, followed by regression and mental retardation, is relatively rare, and is thought to affect perhaps one in fifteen thousand to one in twenty-two thousand females (it appears to occur almost exclusively in females) (Fombonne, 2005). Youngsters with childhood disintegrative disorder (sometimes referred to as Heller's syndrome) develop normally for at least two and up to ten years, followed by significant loss of skills; this disorder is very rare (Volkmar & Lord, 2007). Children who are diagnosed with PDD-NOS display behaviours typical of autism but to a lesser degree and/or with an onset later than three years. Volkmar (2007) suggests this disorder was included in *DSM-IV* to encompass "subthreshold" cases, while Peter Szatmari of McMaster University and his team have been differentiating subgroups of PDD-NOS, including a distinctive group showing fewer stereotyped and repetitive behaviours (e.g., Walker et al., 2004). As these authors caution, clinical identification of PDD-NOS remains challenging.

## Autism: Description and Incidence

One of the cases at the beginning of this chapter describes Pamela, a kindergarten student who has autism. Pamela communicates mainly by echoing the words of others, socializes little with her classmates, and sometimes runs from one side of the room to the other waving her arms. **Autism** affects the functioning of the brain and is believed to be genetic in origin, although diagnosis is based on a child's behaviours and must be evident before the child is three years old. In the past it was commonly estimated that there were four to five persons with autism in every ten thousand births. However, recent estimates have been as high as ten in every ten thousand (Bristol-Power & Spinella, 1999) and thirteen in every ten thousand (Volkmar, 2007). The incidence is higher among males, with the ratio estimated to be three males for every female (Fombonne, 2005).

## Autism: Characteristics

Autism is characterized by

- impairments in verbal and nonverbal communication;
- impairments in reciprocal social interaction;

- impairments in imaginative creativity; and
- restricted, repetitive, and stereotypic patterns of behaviour, interests, and activities (American Psychiatric Association, 2000).

Most people with autism have some level of intellectual disability ranging from mild to severe. Language often shows **perseveration** on one topic or echolalia. It is estimated that roughly 50 percent of those with autism never develop functional speech. It is *not* that students with autism do not want to interact reciprocally with others; rather, they are unable to read and understand social situations. Their lack of imaginative creativity can be seen in their inability to understand or even acknowledge the perspective of others; this has been described as lacking a **theory of mind** (Baron-Cohen, 1995; Wellman et al., 2002). It seems that they are unaware that people have intentions, emotions, etc. Unusual and distinctive behaviours you might observe in students with autism include

- a restricted range of interests and a preoccupation with one specific interest or object;
- an inflexible adherence to non-functional routine;
- stereotypic and repetitive motor mannerisms, such as hand flapping, finger licking, rocking, spinning, walking on tiptoes, spinning objects;
- a preoccupation with parts of objects;
- a fascination with movement, such as the spinning of a fan or wheels on toys;
- an insistence on sameness and resistance to change; and
- unusual responses to sensory stimuli.

A recent study suggests a high rate of tics and Tourette syndrome in children with ASDs (Canitano & Vivanti, 2007), so you may see tics as well as other repetitive behaviours.

**Weblinks**

GENEVA CENTRE FOR AUTISM, TORONTO
www.autism.net

SASKATCHEWAN EDUCATION, TEACHING STUDENTS WITH AUTISM: A GUIDE FOR EDUCATORS
www.sasked.gov.sk.ca/branches/curr/special_ed/sepub.shtml

MANITOBA EDUCATION, CITIZENSHIP AND YOUTH, 2005, SUPPORTING INCLUSIVE SCHOOLS: A HANDBOOK FOR DEVELOPING AND IMPLEMENTING PROGRAMMING FOR STUDENTS WITH AUTISM SPECTRUM DISORDER.
www.edu.gov.mb.ca/ks4/specedu/aut/pdf/acknowledgements.pdf

AUTISM SOCIETY CANADA
www.autismsocietycanada.ca

## THEORY AND RESEARCH HIGHLIGHTS FROM

## EDUCATIONAL PSYCHOLOGY

### Theory of Mind

In attempting to explain the typical characteristics of children with autism spectrum disorders (impaired communication skills; impaired reciprocal social interaction; restricted, repetitive, and stereotypic patterns of behaviour; as well as impaired imaginative creativity), some researchers have developed unifying theories. The best known of these is *theory of mind* (ToM) (Baron-Cohen, 1995; Frith, 2003; Wellman et al., 2002). The other two grand theories of ASD are *executive functioning* (Ozonoff, 1997) and *central coherence* (Frith, 2003).

In locating the basis of autism, Baron-Cohen, Leslie, and Frith (1985) postulated that all people have a cognitive model of the world, or theory of mind, which is the ability to appreciate other people's mental states. However, children with autism look at the world differently. They don't see others' intentions, needs, or beliefs and therefore demonstrate a mind-blindness. They are operating with a deficit in theory of mind.

Theory of mind is a cognitive capacity that represents epistemic mental states such as pretending, thinking, knowing, believing, imagining, dreaming, guessing, deceiving, etc. Theory of mind ties together mental-state concepts (the volitional, perceptual, and epistemic) into an understanding of how mental states and actions are related. Basically, this cognitive capacity is described as the ability to attribute mental states to others and to oneself, to recognize these states, to understand they may differ from one's own, and to predict future behaviour from reading these mental states (Baron-Cohen, 1995; Baron-Cohen et al., 1985).

*continued*

*False belief.* The best-known test of theory of mind is called the false-belief test. It is believed that impairments in false belief lead to impairments in theory of mind, and together may be the basis for some of the impairments characteristic of autism (especially difficulties in socialization, communication, and imagination). The best-known false belief task, the Sally-Ann task, studied by Baron-Cohen et al. (1985), involves a child representing a story of a character's false belief that an object is in one location when it is actually in another. Three groups of children were tested: 4 year olds with normal development, children with autism, and children with Down syndrome. The story of Sally and Ann is enacted individually to children in the three groups. Sally has a marble that she places inside a basket. Sally leaves the room and Ann takes the marble and places it in a box while Sally is away and cannot see that the marble has been moved. The child who is watching this scenario is asked three questions: a memory question, "In the beginning where did Sally put the marble?" (correct answer: basket); a reality question, "Where is the marble now?" (correct answer: box); and a prediction question, "Where will Sally look for her marble?" (correct answer: in the basket where she placed it). Only 20 percent of children with autism attributed a false belief to Sally and predicted that she would look in the basket. The other 80 percent failed to recognize that Sally's mental state had changed and that her previously correct belief that the marble was in the basket was now incorrect. Not understanding a change in mental state and not ascribing false belief implies a lack of theory of mind. In contrast, 85 percent of children with normal development and 86 percent of children with Down syndrome were able to predict correctly where Sally would look, recognizing that she falsely believed the marble was still in the basket (Baron-Cohen, 1995; Surian & Leslie, 1999). Normally developing 4 year olds generally answer the prediction question correctly.

*Communication deficits.* Deficits in communication are evident during the early years of an autistic child. They usually hold back a child's ability to interact socially. When normally developing people talk to one another, they are aware of meanings behind messages and why a specific message was sent. Communication is a co-operative act in which each person attends to message and meaning. In 1997 Lord noted that all behaviours that best discriminate autistic children at the age of two involve communication of affect, i.e., greetings, seeking shared enjoyment of an event (joint attention), and responding to others' indications of pleasure (empathy) (as cited in Robertson, Tanguay, L'Ecuyer, Sims, & Waltrip, 1999).

The research of Charman, Swettenham, Baron-Cohen, Cox, Baird, and Drew (1997) focused on communication deficits of empathy, pretend play, joint attention, and imitation. Their study included ten boys with autism, nine boys with developmental delays, and nineteen normally developing boys. A series of five tasks was given in empathic response, spontaneous play, structural play, joint attention, and imitation. The study in empathy involved the experimenter playing with the child, pretending to hurt himself

with a toy hammer, and displaying facial and vocal expressions of distress. Children with autism were observed to see whether they looked to the experimenter's face, the experimenter's hand, and/or stopped playing with or touching the toy. The child's facial affect was also observed as (a) concerned or upset, (b) indifferent or neutral, or (c) positive. They found that on tasks of empathy, fewer autistic children looked to the experimenter's face and none expressed facial concern in response to another's distress. These data also suggest children with autism lack a theory of mind.

*Reservations.* There is a large issue that avoids explanation by theory of mind. And that is the characteristic of restricted, repetitive, and stereotypic patterns of behaviours, interests, and activities. This remains a huge challenge to researchers and practitioners who see theory of mind explaining the myriad characteristics that make daily life challenging for children and adolescents with autism. Researchers like Prior and Ozonoff (2007, p. 101) suggest that an accumulating body of research raises questions about whether every child with autism lacks a theory of mind and suggests that theory of mind deficits are not specific to autism, and that overall theory of mind may be part of larger problems with executive functions.

## References

Baron-Cohen, S. (1995). *Mindblindness: An essay on autism and theory of mind.* Cambridge, MA: Bradford/MIT Press.

Baron-Cohen, S., Leslie, A.M., & Frith, U. (1985). Does the autistic child have a theory of mind? *Cognition, 21,* 37–46.

Charman, T., Swettenham, J., Baron-Cohen, S., Cox, A., Baird, G., & Drew, A. (1997). Infants with autism: An investigation of empathy, pretend play, joint attention, and imitation. *Developmental Psychology, 33,* 781–789.

Frith, U. (2003). *Autism: Explaining the enigma* (2nd ed.). Malden, MA: Blackwell Pub.

Ozonoff, S. (1997). Causal mechanisms of autism: Unifying perspectives from an information-processing framework. In D.J. Cohen & F.R. Volkmar (Eds.), *Handbook of autism and pervasive developmental disorders* (pp. 868–879). New York: John Wiley & Sons.

Prior, M., & Ozonoff, S. (2007). Psyhological factors in autism. In F.R. Volkmar (Ed.), *Autism and pervasive developmental disorders* (2nd ed., pp. 69–128). New York: Cambridge University Press.

Robertson, J.M., Tanguay, P.E., L'Ecuyer, S., Sims, A., & Waltrip, C. (1999). Domains of social communication handicap in autism spectrum disorder. *Journal of the American Academy of Child and Adolescent Psychiatry, 38,* 738–745.

Surian, L., & Leslie, A.M. (1999). Competence and performance in false belief understanding: A comparison of autistic and normal 3-year-old children. *British Journal of Developmental Psychology, 17,* 141–155.

Wellman, H.M., Baron-Cohen, S., Caswell, R., Gomez, J.C., Swettenham, J., Toye, E., & Lagattuta, K. (2002). Thought-bubbles help children with autism acquire an alternative to a theory of mind. *Autism, 6,* 343–363.

# Autism: Implications for Learning and Classroom Adaptations

The IEPs of students with autism usually include goals in the areas used to identify the exceptionality—communication, social interaction, stereotypic behaviours, and, sometimes, imaginative creativity—as well as in functional skills.

## ENHANCING COMMUNICATION

To enhance communication, it may be necessary to teach the student to listen by facing the speaker, remaining still, and focusing on what is being said. Speak in sentences to the student with autism; if you are not understood, use more concrete words and repeat as necessary. Use visual aids at an appropriate level; objects are the most concrete, followed by photographs, and then line drawings. A digital camera or a Polaroid camera enables you to "catch the student doing good" and record the action. You can make a personalized schedule showing the student completing each activity of the day, or a sequence of photographs of the student carrying out the steps in a complex activity. To encourage oral language expression, accept limited verbal attempts and nonverbal behaviour as communication. Use specific praise. In an unpublished paper, an Ontario teacher, Kelly Goddard (2008), makes a number of recommendations for enhancing the communication of students with autism. I have developed a strategy based on her paper and named the strategy PAMELA, after the child in the opening case study:

**Puppets, games, and music** can be used to increase participation and play.

**Anchoring instruction in visual cues** including such things as pictures of snacks for making a choice, in addition to pictures of multi-step activities and schedules.

**Maintaining joint attention and using symbolic play** through pointing and imitation and pretending one object represents another.

**Echolalia** may provide you with clues to what the student is trying to communicate, so rather than becoming frustrated, listen attentively.

**Learning through video modelling and self-as-model video** can replace simple visual cues.

**Adapting teaching** on the same topic being studied by the class, to the extent possible.

## ENHANCING SOCIAL COGNITION AND BEHAVIOUR

To improve social interaction, social skills, and social cognition, students with autism require explicit teaching and practice. Carol Gray (2002) has developed first-person **social stories** that describe a situation from the perspective of the student and direct the young person to practise the appropriate behaviour. Each page in Gray's booklets—which can be up to five pages long—contains one sentence (or two). There is a directive behaviour on one of the five pages. For an example of a social story, see Figure 4.2. Interventions have been developed using videotape to explicitly teach children with autism that others have intentions and emotions. Karin Steiner-Bell of Queen's University (1998) used narratives of children's happy, sad, and surprising experiences. You may be successful in having a student with autism learn classroom routines by observing others. You can also model for other children how to interact with their classmate with autism.

**Put into Practice**

Read about social stories in the resources listed below and develop a social story for Pamela, the kindergarten student with autism described in the case study opening this chapter. Choose a focus different from that illustrated in Figure 4.2 on page 130.

Smith, C. (2003). *Writing and developing social stories: Practical interventions in autism.* Bicester: Speechmark.

Howley, M., & Arnold, E., (2005). *Revealing the hidden social code: Social stories for people with autistic spectrum disorders.* London and Philadelphia: Jessica Kingsley Publishers.

Scattone, D. (2008). Enhancing the conversation skills of a boy with Asperger's disorder through social stories and video modeling. *Journal of Autism and Developmental Disorders, 38,* 395–400.

Reynhout, G., & Careter, M. (2007). Social story efficacy with a child with autism spectrum disorder and moderate intellectual disability. *Focus on Autism and Other Developmental Disabilities, 22,* 173–182.

Bernad-Ripoll, S. (2007). Using a self-as-model video combined with social stories to help a child with Asperger syndrome understand emotions. *Focus on Autism and Other Developmental Disabilities, 22,* 100–106.

Quilty, K.M. (2007). Teaching paraprofessionals how to write and implement social stories for students with autism spectrum disorders. *Remedial and Special Education, 28,* 182–189.

Ali, S., & Frederickson, N. (2006). Investigating the evidence base of social stories. *Educational Psychology in Practice, 22,* 355–377.

## Further Reading

To learn more about teaching students with autism and Asperger syndrome:

Betts, S., Betts, D., & Gerber-Eckard, L. (2007). *Asperger syndrome in the inclusive classroom: Advice and strategies for teachers.* London: Jessica Kingsley Publishers.

British Columbia, Ministry of Education, Special Programs Branch. (2000). *Teaching students with autism: A resource guide for schools.* Victoria, BC: Ministry of Education, Special Programs Branch.

Kluth, P. (2003). *"You're Going to Love This Kid": Teaching Students with Autism in the Inclusive Classroom.* Baltimore, MD: P.H. Brookes Pub. Co.

Palmen, A., Didden, R., & Arts, M. (2008). Improving question asking in high-functioning adolescents with autism spectrum disorders. *Autism, 12,* 83–98.

Crooke, P.J., Hendrix, R.E., & Rachman, J.Y. (2008). Brief report: Measuring the effectiveness of teaching social thinking to children with Asperger syndrome (AS) and high functioning autism (HFA). *Journal of Developmental Disorders, 38,* 581–591.

## FIGURE 4.2 A SOCIAL STORY FOR PAMELA

A social story describes a social situation and includes social cues and appropriate responses. It is written for a specific situation for an individual student. The story can be used to

- facilitate the inclusion of the student in regular classes;
- introduce changes and new routines;
- explain reasons for the behaviour of others;
- teach situation-specific social skills; and
- assist in teaching new academic skills.

Stories can be read, listened to on audio, or watched on video. The language must be understood by the child. The story should be from the child's perspective, using "I," and should direct the child to perform the appropriate behaviour. Social stories use descriptive sentences (which provide information on the setting and people), directive statements (i.e., positive statements about the desired response for a specific situation), and perspective statements (which describe the possible reactions of others).

Use two to five descriptive statements and one directive statement. Put only one or two sentences on a page. Symbols, drawings, or pictures can be included to support the meaning for the student.

Pamela tends to run and wave her arms while the other children sit on their chairs in a circle. Her teacher has made a social story for Pamela. The first page includes a photograph of the children smiling, sitting in a circle while the teacher reads a story. The second page shows Pamela smiling, sitting on her chair while the teacher holds a book. Page three shows a smiling child sitting on each side of Pamela, one speaking to her and the other offering her a toy. Each day, before the children sit in their circle, the teacher reads the story twice to Pamela and then reads each sentence and waits for her to repeat it. Pamela has a videotape of the story at home that she watches with her mother.

Page 1: Other kids like to hear the teacher.
Page 2: I will sit on my chair when the teacher talks.
Page 3: Everyone likes me when I sit on my chair.

Source: Based on Gray, C. (1993). *The Social Story Book.* Jenison, MI: Jenison Public Schools.

### GENERAL ADAPTATIONS AND MODIFICATIONS

For all teaching, use visual approaches, **reinforcers** that you know work for this student, and task analysis to keep tasks at a level that minimizes frustration. Try to keep the theme of the learning consistent with the lesson for others in the class. For example, if others are writing about highlights of the day in a journal, then try teaching the child with autism to take a photograph from a magazine or a digital or Polaroid photograph that communicates "something fun" that she has done today. She can name the picture or dictate a sentence. Use concrete examples and hands-on activities, and allow as much time as the child requires.

It helps to provide a structured, predictable classroom environment. Make a customized visual daily schedule, and give advance warning of any changes from the usual schedule and of transitions from one activity to another. Minimize auditory stimuli such as noisy fans, reduce distracting visual stimuli around the student's desk, and try to remove textures the student finds aversive to maintain a calm learning environment.

## Asperger Syndrome: Description and Incidence

**Asperger syndrome** is a lifelong developmental condition, characterized by a severe and sustained impairment in social interaction and the development of restricted, repetitive patterns of behaviour, interests, and activities. In contrast to autism, a child with Asperger syndrome is unlikely to experience significant delays in the acquisition of language, adaptive behaviour (other than social interaction), cognitive development, and development of age-appropriate self-help skills, or in curiosity about the environment. Incidence for Asperger syndrome is unclear, with large increases in recent years and wide variation in the reported numbers; however, in a recent publication, Eric Fombonne of McGill University (2007) suggests a rate of four per ten thousand. He also brings together data from many sources to estimate that all disorders on the autism spectrum may have a combined incidence of thirty-six per ten thousand.

## Asperger Syndrome: Characteristics and Teaching Strategies

Students with Asperger syndrome are characterized by a qualitative impairment in social interaction. They are often enthusiastic about relating to others but are challenged by the complexity of the language and approach others in unusual ways. You will observe that these students misinterpret social cues, lack empathy, appear socially awkward, and are unaware of the rules of conversation. They need explicit instruction in social skills. With average or better intelligence, they tend to excel at learning facts but need intensive teaching in reading comprehension, problem solving, organizational skills, and inference making. Frequently, students with Asperger syndrome are **hypersensitive** to sensory stimuli and may engage in unusual behaviour to obtain a particular sensory stimulation. The lighting and sounds in the classroom can be annoying, distracting, and even painful for these students. Flickering and fluorescent lights are particular irritants, while subdued lighting may be calming. Loud, unexpected noises bother some, and the buzz of heaters and of other students' voices can prove problematic; allowing students to be seated away from the noise or to wear earphones to reduce the sound may help. Reducing class noise by putting tennis balls on the chair and desk legs is also a good strategy. Kluth (2004) suggests using music as a tool for instruction and support.

Students with AS may be inattentive, easily distracted, and anxious. Some strategies for teaching students with autism will apply, but consider the student's unique learning characteristics and build on those considerable strengths. Draw on the expertise of the in-school resource team, too. Individuals with AS appreciate having a "safe space" in the classroom or somewhere in the school (Kluth, 2004). Donna Williams, a woman with autism, wrote, "Allowing me privacy and space was the most beneficial thing I ever got" (1992, p. 218).

## Implications for Social and Career Participation of Students with Autism and Students with Asperger Syndrome

Transition planning from secondary school to adult life should continue throughout the high school years. Areas to consider include employment options, post-secondary training or education options, residential options, transportation and medical needs, as well as income support opportunities. Advocacy, recreation, and relationships with family and friends are also important. The **McGill Action Planning System (MAPS)** may prove helpful for promoting these (Forest & Lusthaus, 1987; Steer, 1998). The MAPS process involves gathering key people in the student's life who co-operatively answer such questions as, What is the student's history? What is

**What do you think?**

Recently many people with ASDs have written books about their experiences. Some have put a positive spin on their characteristics, challenging traditional views of disability and sharing insights to help teachers differentiate teaching and assessment. You can read a researcher's view of these accounts:

Paula Kluth (2004). Autism, autobiography, and adaptations. *Teaching Exceptional Children, 36*(4), 42–47.

Here is a list of books on ASDs written by people with autism and Asperger syndrome:

Barron, J., & Barron, S. (1992). *There's a boy in here.* New York: Simon & Schuster.

Grandin, T. (1995). *Thinking in pictures.* New York: Vintage Books.

Jackson, L. (2002). *Freaks, geeks, and Asperger syndrome: A user guide to adolescence.* Philadelphia, PA: Jessica Kingsley.

Williams, D. (1994). *Somebody, somewhere: Breaking free from the world of autism.* New York: Times Books.

What do you think teachers can learn from these first-person accounts of autism and Asperger syndrome?

your dream for the child? What are the student's gifts? What would an ideal day at school be like? Plans for structured friendship or peer programs are usually suggested as part of the MAPS meeting. Work experiences, participation in co-curricular activities, and help with developing hygiene, appropriate dress, and self-management are all necessary during the secondary years for students with autism and for many with Asperger syndrome.

Follow-up studies of adults with ASDs suggest that although individual characteristics like intelligence and language ability are important, external factors including appropriate schooling, effective transition planning, and supported work experience and career development programs are also critical (Howlin, 2007). Two of the follow-up studies conducted in Canada (Szatmari et al., 1989; Venter et al., 1992) emphasized the important role teachers and schools play in the social and career development of individuals with ASDs.

# Teaching Students Who Are Hard of Hearing or Deaf

I am deaf and have always gone to school with kids who can hear. I lip read and learned some Sign last summer at camp. Ever since then I have wanted to go to a school where all the kids are deaf.

*Kauffman, 2005, p. 114*

**Weblinks**

CANADIAN HEARING SOCIETY
www.chs.ca

CANADIAN ASSOCIATION OF THE DEAF
www.cad.ca/en/issues/
definition_of_deaf.asp

CANADIAN ASSOCIATION OF THE DEAF:
VOICE FOR HEARING IMPAIRED CHILDREN
(CANADA)
www.voicefordeafkids.com

## Description and Incidence of Students Who Are Hard of Hearing or Deaf

Students who have a hearing loss that has significantly affected the development of speech and/or language and who require adapted teaching to participate effectively and benefit from instruction are described as being **deaf** or **hard of hearing**. Hearing loss is grouped into four general categories: mild, moderate, severe, and profound or deaf, depending on the dB (decibel) Hearing Level an individual can hear

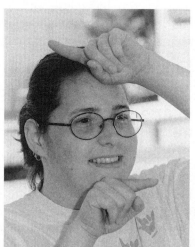

*Young classmates of students who are deaf or hard of hearing are taught sign language by an instructor from the Canadian Hearing Society.*

(Alberta Education, *Special Education Definitions*, 2004/2005). This includes children who have a hearing impairment at birth and those who develop hearing loss later, those with conductive hearing loss (caused by middle ear infection and amenable to treatment), and those with sensory neural hearing loss (resulting from damage to the sensory mechanism or cochlea) (Atlantic Provinces Special Education Authority, 2001b). The Canadian Association of the Deaf (www.cad.ca/en/issues/definition_of_deaf.asp) recognizes a person to be deaf when that person has little or no functional hearing and depends upon visual rather than auditory communication. This organization describes a person with hearing loss as a person whose hearing loss ranges from mild to profound and whose usual means of communication is speech. They consider hearing loss to be both a medical and a sociological term.

Estimates vary, but about one infant in every thousand is born profoundly deaf or is deaf before the age of three (Public Health and Epidemiology Report Ontario, 2000; www.thfc.ca) and about six in one thousand are born with hearing loss (The Hearing Foundation of Canada; www.thfc.ca). In the general population, as many as one in four people may have some form of hearing impairment and one in sixteen an impairment serious enough to affect communication (Canadian Hearing Society Awareness Survey, 2001; www.thfc.ca).

## Characteristics of Students Who Are Hard of Hearing or Deaf

The main characteristics of students with hearing impairments are that they cannot hear well enough to use hearing as a primary channel for learning without significant assistance and that their language development is likely to be influenced.

A complex array of factors influences learning. Two students with similar hearing loss may have completely different experiences before they arrive at school and may communicate in quite different ways. Language development and communication can be affected by

- the age at the onset of the hearing loss, especially whether the student had already developed spoken language at that time;
- the severity of the hearing loss;
- intelligence;
- **hearing status** of the family (a student who is deaf tends to experience higher academic success if the parents are deaf as well); and
- means of communication chosen by the family.

Some young children experience hearing loss when fluid builds up in the middle ear. Characteristics you might see include children failing to respond to their name, asking for directions to be repeated, turning the head to hear, and speaking too loudly or too softly. You might also see a change in behaviour or academic performance or hear the child complain of recurring earaches. Physicians can insert ventilating tubes that drain fluid, reversing the temporary loss of hearing. Teachers of young children who spot these characteristics play an important role in preventing hearing loss and subsequent language delays.

While students who are hard of hearing or deaf tend to fall behind in reading and other language skills, they often meet or exceed expectations in subjects like science and math. As with other exceptionalities, difficulty with a subject does not necessarily imply lack of ability. When fatigued and frustrated by their difficulties in communicating, these students can be disruptive and inattentive.

There are programs across Canada for children who are deaf or hard of hearing. For example, Alberta, British Columbia, Manitoba, Newfoundland and Labrador, and Ontario have residential schools, while all of these provinces as well as Nova Scotia, Nunavut, Quebec, Saskatchewan, and Yukon have local or day programs. Ontario also has a program for deafblind students at W. Ross Macdonald School in Brantford. For a listing of all programs in Canada and descriptions of their programs and services, see *American Annals of the Deaf* (volume 148[2], reference issue, 2003). This resource suggests that in 2002 there were about six hundred students enrolled in schools for the deaf and hard of hearing in Canada (either residential or day students).

## Implications for Learning and Classroom Adaptations for Students with Hearing Loss

The implications for classroom learning and participation are related to the choices parents make for their children in the preschool years. These issues are explored in the Focus on Families box. Table 4.2 describes the options that parents have for communication and education for their children. Be sensitive to parents' concerns about whether they have made the best choice for their child. In inclusive classrooms, you may be teaching children whose parents have chosen auditory-verbal, auditory-oral, cued speech, or total communication. It is less likely that you will teach children who use only **American Sign Language (ASL)**. If children who use ASL are included in your classroom, they will probably be accompanied by an interpreter (for guidance on working with an interpreter, see Atlantic Provinces Special Education Authority, 2001a). There are concerns that deaf children with

## Choosing How to Communicate with a Deaf Child

**FOCUS ON FAMILIES**

One of the most difficult decisions faced by many families of newly diagnosed children who are hard of hearing or deaf is how to communicate with their child. If the parents are deaf and are members of the deaf community, who use **American Sign Language (ASL)**, they will likely choose to initiate their child into their culture and to communicate with their child through ASL. However, if the parents are part of the hearing culture and do not know ASL, they may be apprehensive about being unable to communicate with their child if ASL becomes the child's first language. Ninety percent of parents whose children are deaf or hard of hearing have hearing themselves. These families receive advice and predictions from a variety of professionals. The amount of information is overwhelming, and opposing views are advanced forcefully and convincingly.

There are books to help parents decide on the best approach for their child:

- Schwartz, S. (Ed.) (2007). *Choices in deafness: A parent's guide to communication options*, Third Edition. Bethesda, MD: Woodbine House.

- Marschark, M. (2007). *Raising and educating a deaf child: A comprehensive guide to the choices, controversies, and decisions faced by parents and educators* (2nd ed.). New York: Oxford University Press.

- Luterman, D., & Maxon A. (2006*). When your child is deaf: A guide for parents* (2nd ed). Baltimore, MD: York Press; Austin, TX: Pro-Ed.

- Luterman, D., Kurtyzer-White, E., & Seewald, R. (2006). *The young deaf child*. Austin, TX: Pro-Ed.

There are helpful websites. For example, www.oraldeafed.org provides information for parents about their options that prompts them to consider the merits and drawbacks of the five approaches that appear in Table 4.2.

In Canada parents can consult the Canadian Association of the Deaf (www.cad.ca), which focuses on "protecting and promoting the rights, needs and concerns of deaf Canadians," in particular those who are profoundly deaf and whose preferred mode of communication is sign language. On the other hand, parents might consult Voice for Hearing Impaired Children (www.voicefordeafkids.com), whose mission is "To ensure that all hearing impaired children have the right to develop their ability to listen and speak and have access to services which will enable them to listen and speak." Even greater controversy is sparked by the cochlear implant, an electronic device that bypasses a non-functional inner ear and delivers sound directly to auditory nerves linked to the brain. Data suggest that children with implants can expect to detect conversation and environmental sounds (Atlantic Provinces Special Education Authority, 2001b; Ertmer et al., 2003) but may experience difficulty understanding speech amid noise and performing pitch-based musical tasks (Stohl et al., 2008). Richard Seewald of the University of Western Ontario suggests that matching an implant to the needs of children is challenging (Luterman, Kurtyzer-White, & Seewald, 2006). The deaf community raises issues of invasion of one's person when cochlear implants are chosen. They argue that this decision by parents forces young children to "choose" the hearing society over the Deaf culture, and that those who are deaf can never use spoken language with the facility they can have with ASL. When you teach students who are deaf or hard of hearing in inclusive classrooms, you can expect parents to be coping with all of these dilemmas and more.

**Websites:**

www.oraldeafed.org

www.cad.ca

www.voicefordeafkids.com

## TABLE 4.2 EDUCATIONAL OPTIONS FOR CHILDREN WHO ARE HARD OF HEARING OR DEAF

| Options | How Language Is Taught | School Placement | Additional Information |
|---|---|---|---|
| Auditory-Verbal | Emphasizes use of residual hearing to learn spoken English; amplification | Usually regular class from the beginning | Parents communicate through spoken language; early amplification |
| Unisensory Oral/ Auditory-Oral | Emphasizes use of residual hearing to learn spoken English and use of visual information (speech-reading); amplification and speech-reading | Usually regular class after success is certain | Emphasis on the two approaches varies from program to program; parents communicate through spoken language; early amplification |
| Cued Speech | Uses eight handshapes in four locations near the face to give phonemic cues that assist speech-reading; can be used with all other approaches that include listening; amplification and speech-reading and phonemic cues | Depends on approach with which it is combined | Claims to enhance learning to read; has enabled second language learning |
| Total Communication | Child's environment contains access to full range of communication methods; amplification and speech-reading and sign language (based on English) | Congregated school or class for deaf students; regular class with interpreter | Uses three means of communication simultaneously |
| American Sign Language (ASL) Bilingual/Bicultural | A manual language system that is not based on English grammar/syntax; English is taught as a second language; ASL used extensively in the deaf community | Congregated school or class for deaf students; regular class with interpreter | Emphasis on English varies from program to program; proponents consider ASL natural language for the deaf; sense of belonging to Deaf culture encouraged; young adults sometimes choose this option so they can participate in Deaf culture |

Source: Based on Communications Options Reference Chart, www.ncbegin.org/communication_options/comm_options.shtml.

interpreters may not be receiving all of the information teachers communicate to hearing students (e.g., Langer, 2007). Many students who learn in inclusive classrooms use amplification to help them hear. At first, you may experience difficulty understanding their speech, but teachers usually grow accustomed to their manner of speaking in a few days. Ask a student who is reluctant to speak in front of the class to speak with you individually so you can learn the speech patterns. The spoken language of deaf and hard of hearing children improves as the amplification technology advances (Ackley & Decker, 2006).

### ENHANCING SPEECH-READING

There are many actions you can take to differentiate or adapt your teaching. For students who are **speech-reading**, arrange the classroom so the student can see your face at all times, and get the student's attention before speaking to him or her. Allow the student to move during a lesson. Ensure that you don't turn your back (use an overhead projector instead of the blackboard) and don't put your hands in front of your face. Speak normally and avoid making distracting gestures. Some words, such as *bat*, *pat*, and *mat*, look the same when you pronounce them. Try to put words like this into context, especially during spelling dictation. If other students ask questions, repeat them so the student who is deaf or hard of hearing knows what was asked. Summaries at the end of lessons give all students a second chance to take in information. During group discussions, sit the class in a circle.

You can convey important messages visually as well as orally—for example, many students will benefit from having an agenda and assignments listed on the board. Use visual aids, written summaries, and **manipulatives**. The student with hearing loss will benefit from your **preteaching** any new vocabulary. Pay attention to and try to diffuse the student's frustration. You can plan the day's work so periods of intense concentration are interspersed with less-demanding activities. For more information about including a student who is deaf or hard of hearing, see Figure 4.3.

### SYSTEMS OF AMPLIFICATION

Classrooms often have excessive background noise and reverberation, which interfere with accurate speech perception. Degradation of the speech signal can be reduced for children who are hard of hearing by using **frequency modulation (FM)** devices in the classroom to enhance the speech-to-noise ratio (S/N) of the teacher's voice. There are three types of S/N-enhancing FM devices currently used in classrooms: (a) FM systems linked to personal **hearing aids**, (b) sound field system with speakers placed throughout the classroom, and (c) personal sound field system placed on the student's desk. Carpeted classrooms are best for all these systems; alternatively, place tennis balls over the feet of the desks. **Amplification** makes speech louder, not clearer, and also amplifies background noise. A recent study compared these three kinds of FM devices. Results indicated that the ceiling sound field FM did not provide increased benefit beyond that provided by students' hearing aids alone. Desktop and personal FM systems provided substantial improvements in access to the speech signal and there were indications that listening ease was greater with personal FM systems than with the desktop FM (Anderson, 2003). Expect new devices based on technological advances, and remember to speak clearly, stay still while talking, and allow the student to see your face.

**Weblinks**

HARD OF HEARING AND DEAF STUDENTS: A RESOURCE GUIDE TO SUPPORT CLASSROOM TEACHERS (BC MINISTRY OF EDUCATION)
www.bced.gov.bc.ca/specialed/hearimpair/toc.htm

**Weblinks**

ABLEDATA DEAF AND HARD OF HEARING PRODUCT PAGE
www.abledata.com (search for deaf and hard of hearing general)

CODI: CORNUCOPIA OF DISABILITY INFORMATION—HEARING IMPAIRMENTS
http://codi.buffalo.edu/hearing.htm

## FIGURE 4.3 TIPS FOR TEACHERS OF STUDENTS WHO ARE DEAF OR HARD OF HEARING

Students with hearing loss need to see your face all the time to speech-read and get meaning clues. Your non-verbal communication is crucial. Use your smiles to encourage, invite, and include. Optimum natural lighting is important. Try not to stand in front of lights or windows as they cause your face to go in shadow.

Speaking naturally is the most help to your student with hearing loss. Talking very loudly or over-enunciating does not help your student; in fact it makes it harder for him/her.

- You will need to discuss the best seating arrangement in the room with the student. Consideration must be given to the best place for receiving maximum information within the normal flow of classroom activities.
- Vocabulary lists with definitions of new terms and concepts to be used during the day help the student to develop a personal dictionary of words learned.
- An outline of the class agenda—just three or four points jotted on the board—really helps the student get a sense of purpose, direction, and timing for short term work which fits into the longer range planning.
- Course or grade outline of the topics and kind of work to be done may be useful.
- Provide an outline of a typical school day with the student's own timetable. Include room numbers and a list of people who can assist (e.g., counsellor, school secretary).
- If there is class discussion or group work, it is useful to summarize on the board or have the groups report their work on large paper that can be read as a group.
- Use of overheads, visuals, handouts, and outlines may be helpful.
- Other students in the class may be asked to volunteer as a buddy to take notes and help you watch for the need for more clarification.

———
Source: BC Ministry of Education. www.bced.gov.bc.ca/specialed/hearimpair/tip15.htm. Used by permission.

**Further Reading**

Padden, C.A. & Humphries, T.L. (2005). *Inside Deaf culture.* Cambridge, MS: Harvard University Press.

Garay, S.V. (2003). Listening to the voices of deaf students: Essential transition issues. *Teaching Exceptional Children, 35*(4), 44–48.

Atlantic Provinces Special Education Authority (2001). *Support for students who are deaf or hard of hearing in an inclusive setting.* Halifax: Atlantic Provinces Special Education Authority.

## Implications for Social and Career Participation of Students with Hearing Loss

Social participation is challenging for students with hearing loss or deafness because their exceptionality affects communication. Their system of communication is also influential. As the opening of this section suggests, some adolescents and adults who are deaf or hard of hearing choose to learn ASL and to join the **Deaf community** (Padden & Humphries, 2005), in spite of their parents' earlier choice of oral language. Deaf and hard of hearing adults have a higher rate of underemployment and unemployment than the general population (Capella, 2003). However, one recent study suggests that deaf college graduates have greater career success than those with hearing loss (Punch, Hyde, & Creed, 2004; Schroedel & Geyer, 2000). There are strong lobby groups to assist deaf adults, and career education and co-operative education can help these adolescents learn about themselves and about careers. Garay (2003) provides transition guidelines for teachers of deaf students, which include focusing on career development from grade 6 on, involving adolescents in IEP and transition meetings, and involving the family in transition planning.

# Teaching Children with Vision Disabilities and Blindness

"See you tomorrow, Ms. Fine!" The grade 3 students shouted goodbye to Marie Fine. Marie watched Amber painstakingly packing her books on tape and thick pages of Braille into her backpack. Marie stood nearby in case Amber needed help. However,

Put into Practice

Read *Deaf Education in America: Voices of Children from Inclusion Settings* by Janet Cerney (Washington, DC: Gallaudet University Press). Consider the complex issues surrounding the integration of deaf students into the regular classroom and the steps that can be taken to ensure their success in an inclusion setting. List the three most important things you learned from this book. Compare what you have learned with the learning of your peers. Make brief guidelines that you could use for working with the family, the student, and your colleagues to include a deaf or hard of hearing student in your class.

Amber did the same thing every day; she put everything into her knapsack herself and then asked, "Did I get everything I need to finish my work?" Marie thought about how hard Amber would work at home to complete the day's school tasks. "Good night, Amber! Don't work too hard." As Amber lifted the heavy bag, she answered, "'Night! I'll try not to. But I still have a lot of questions to do in math." Her voice sounded as heavy as her book bag. Amber knew that when you can't see, everything takes longer.

*Adapted from Hutchinson, 2004 (2nd ed.), p. 9*

## Description and Incidence of Students with Visual Impairment

Students with total or partial **visual impairment** who require adapted or differentiated teaching, even with correction, are described as having visual disabilities. For educational purposes, a student with visual impairment is one whose visual acuity is not sufficient "to participate with ease in everyday activities" and whose impairment "can result in a substantial educational disadvantage, unless adaptations are made" in the environment, learning materials, teaching, and assessment (Special Education Technology—British Columbia [SET-BC]; www.setbc.org). The IEP will include the student's need for orientation and mobility skills; efficient use of vision, **Braille** and/or alternative formats such as **taped books**; access to technology; and daily living skills. These are usually the responsibility of a **vision teacher** or paraeducator. Researchers, including Cay Holbrook of University of British Columbia, have described the importance of paraeducators to quality early literacy instruction for children with visual impairments (e.g., Forster & Holbrook, 2005). The IEP will also refer to classroom adaptations that are your responsibility. Estimates of prevalence of visual impairment depend on how the data are collected. In 1987, using data from its records, the Ontario Ministry of Education reported that approximately one in one thousand students was visually impaired and that, of these, 80 percent were print users and 20 percent were potential Braille users. In 2002 the Québec Office des Personnes Handicapées published the results of questionnaire data in which parents reported that 0.8 percent or almost 1 percent of children had visual impairments (eye disorders that had not been corrected with eyeglasses or contact lenses). Recent studies suggest that these estimates may be low. McLeod and McKinnon (2007) found that approximately sixteen students in one thousand were identified as visually impaired in their thorough study of one representative school district. And Gray (2005) reported that the past decade has witnessed a significant increase in the incidence of visual impairment in young children ranging from milder to more severe forms, including total loss of sight.

## Characteristics of Students with Visual Impairments

For two reasons, it is important that you know the characteristics that accompany visual impairment. First, children and adolescents can experience deteriorating vision at any age. Teachers often identify students who need to be assessed. Complaints of blurred print or headaches may signal a need for correction; they can also signal conditions such as brain tumours. Pay attention to the appearance of the eyes (e.g., reddened, encrusted, frequent sties or tears). Listen to student complaints (e.g., headaches, burning eyes after use, nausea, blurred print). Also observe behavioural signs (e.g., the student squints or closes one eye, tilts head extremely,

### Put into Practice

View the video presentation by Dr. Mary Nelle McLennan of the American Printing House for the Blind on organizational strategies, Developing Organizational Skills in Learners with Visual Impairments (2003) at www.setbc.org/setbc/conf/docs/mnmc.html. Discuss the strategies with your peers and develop a plan for implementing these strategies at the grade level you teach. The SET-BC website (www.setbc.org) contains other informative videos that you will find helpful.

rubs eyes, turns head while reading across a page) (Peirangelo & Giuliani, 2007; Weber & Bennett, 2004). Record your observations and encourage the parents to seek a vision assessment.

Second, knowing the characteristics of students with visual exceptionalities will help you understand their actions, postures, and developmental histories. Because they cannot learn social skills through observation, they may need specific instruction in areas such as body language and eye contact (Janssen et al., 2007). Because vision plays a key role in young children's exploration of their environment, students with vision disabilities and blindness have often had a limited range of experiences and restricted movement in their environment. If they do not experience mobility and independence training during the preschool years, this may result in global delays in development (cognitive, motor, social, and emotional) stemming from lack of experience rather than lack of ability (McAllister & Gray, 2007).

## Implications for Learning and Classroom Adaptations for Visual Impairments

Students with visual disabilities and blindness are likely to need adaptations in four areas: presentation of information, classroom environment and organization, learning resources, and assessment.

### ADAPTING PRESENTATION OF INFORMATION

In adapting the presentation of information, you will work closely with a vision teacher, a paraeducator, or a resource teacher. The specific adaptations depend on how the student acquires information—substituting other senses for vision, using partial vision, or both. For students who do not acquire information visually, give directions and notes verbally as well as visually and provide the opportunity to explore three-dimensional models of visual concepts. For example, Jones and her colleagues (2006) describe an effective tactile or haptic instructional technology for teaching cell morphology and function to middle and high school students with visual impairments. For students with partial vision, enlarge print (usually to 130 percent on a photocopier or 18-point font size on your computer) and enhance contrast of written materials. Experiment to see whether coloured acetate (e.g., yellow or pale blue) enhances the contrast or if particular contrasts of paper and print are easiest for the student to read. A peer may serve as a note taker. You can make large-print copies of chalkboard notes and overheads.

You may need to order materials from a provincial resource centre that provides books on tape and adaptive technology. Provincial sources for books on tape and adaptive technology for students who are blind are listed below:

- **Alberta:** www.lrc.education.gov.ab.ca/pro/visual_imp/visual_imp_index.htm
- **Atlantic provinces:** www.apsea.ca
- **British Columbia:** www.prcvi.org
- **Manitoba:** www.edu.gov.mb.ca/k12/blind/index.html
- **Ontario** (W. Ross Macdonald School Resource Services): www.psbnet.ca/webs/wrm/resource%20services.htm
- **Quebec** (Montreal Association for the Blind and MacKay Rehabilitation Centre): www.mab.ca
- **Saskatchewan:** www.sasked.gov.sk.ca/branches/curr/special_ed/docs/guides/blind/teachwithvi.pdf

Further Reading

On students who are deafblind:

McInnes, J.M. (Ed.) (1999). *A guide to planning and support for individuals who are deafblind.* Toronto: University of Toronto Press.

Council for the Advancement of Communication with Deaf People. (2002). *Deafblind awareness curriculum.* London, UK: Council for the Advancement of Communication with Deaf People.

On students who are blind:

MacCuspie, P.A. (1996). *Promoting acceptance of children with disabilities: From tolerance to inclusion.* Halifax: Atlantic Provinces Special Education Authority.

Schaefer, L.M. (2008). *Some kids are blind.* Mankato, MN: Capstone Press.

Hersch, M.A., Johnson, M.A., & Keating, D. (20070. *Assistive technology for the vision-impaired and blind.* New York: Springer.

**Weblinks**

ASSISTIVE TECHNOLOGY FOR PEOPLE WHO ARE BLIND OR VISUALLY IMPAIRED
www.disabilityresources.org/AT-BLIND.html

THE BLIND AND LOW VISION PRODUCT DATABASE
www.abledata.com (search for *blind and low vision general*)

**Weblinks**

TEACHING STUDENTS WITH VISUAL IMPAIRMENTS: A GUIDE FOR THE SUPPORT TEAM (SASKATCHEWAN LEARNING)
www.sasked.gov.sk.ca/branches/curr/special_ed/docs/guides/blind/teachwithvi.pdf

SPECIAL EDUCATION TECHNOLOGY BRITISH COLUMBIA (SET-BC)
www.setbc.org

TEACHING CHILDREN WHO ARE BLIND OR VISUALLY IMPAIRED (NEWFOUNDLAND AND LABRADOR DEPARTMENT OF EDUCATION)
www.ed.gov.nl.ca/edu/pub/vi/VIch6.pdf

SPECIAL NEEDS OPPORTUNITY WINDOWS (SNOW) ADAPTIVE TECHNOLOGY ON-LINE WORKSHOPS FOR EDUCATORS AND PARAEDUCATORS
http://snow.utoronto.ca/index.php

## ADAPTING ORGANIZATION

Organize your classroom and use a seating arrangement so that students with partial vision have the best view possible of chalkboard work and demonstrations. Enclosed (rather than open-concept) classrooms with reduced clutter are better for these students. Ensure that everyone keeps possessions off the floor. To ensure safety, move the furniture as little as possible and always warn the student who cannot easily see any changes. The organization of learning activities can also foster the inclusion of students with visual impairments. Form groups that enable them to practise social and communication skills with empathic peers. Work closely with the vision or resource teacher who may be instructing them in eye contact, body language, facial expression, and alternatives to behaviour patterns such as rocking and eye poking. For more information on including students with visual impairment, see Figure 4.4.

## ADAPTING RESOURCES AND ASSESSMENT

There are many learning resources for students with visual impairments, including large-print books, Braille books, and computer keyboards. Computer technology includes Braillers combined with word processors, programs that convert print to audio output, and **speech-activated** word processors. An IEP usually ensures provincial funding for technology, three-dimensional maps and tape measures, and other learning materials. You may need to plan six months ahead to ensure receipt of Braille textbooks, books on tape, and large-print learning materials before they are needed by the student.

The work and learning of students with vision disabilities and blindness can be evaluated effectively by extending time frames for test taking and homework assignments and by testing students orally. Braille or large-print formats may be necessary, or assessments can be completed on a computer or under supervision in a resource room.

## FIGURE 4.4 TIPS FOR TEACHERS OF STUDENTS WHO ARE VISUALLY IMPAIRED

1. Point out the classroom rules to which the student must adhere.
2. Expect the same quality of work, rather than the same quantity.
3. Don't move furniture in the classroom without warning the student.
4. Reduce glare on boards, desks, etc.
5. Provide multi-sensory experiences, learning by doing, and support without dependence.
6. Stress legibility, not size, as student will tend to print or write in large size, if at all.
7. Remind individual speakers to name themselves (and remind the visually impaired student of who is speaking if individual students forget).
8. Help everyone in the class to provide non-visual feedback to the student with the visual impairment (like saying "well done" instead of smiling or nodding).
9. Encourage peers to be friends, not helpers.
10. Encourage the visually impaired student to share his or her experiences with you, so that you can understand the student's perspective. Help the student to feel like an integral part of the community in the classroom.

Source: Hutchinson, N.L. (2004). *Teaching exceptional children and adolescents: A Canadian casebook* (2nd ed.), p. 13. Copyright Prentice Hall. Used by permission.

## Implications for Social and Career Participation of Students with Visual Impairment

Adults with visual impairments experience higher-than-average rates of unemployment and underemployment. These students need to explore a wide variety of career options while developing a realistic understanding of their potential through a transition plan, adapted career education, job shadowing, and co-operative education (Hutchinson et al., 1999). *Take Charge* (Rabby & Croft, 1990), a career development program, is available in Braille. Nagle (2001) provides suggestions for enhancing the transition to employment and community life for youth with visual impairments.

# Teaching Students with Physical Disabilities and Chronic Medical Conditions

Researchers estimate that at least 15 percent of students experience a serious illness or health condition before the age of 18 (Bethell et al., 2008). Many physical disabilities and chronic medical disorders influence the social participation and learning of children and adolescents at school (Wodrich & Cunningham, 2007). These issues are explored in *Chronic Illness in Children and Adolescents* (Brown, Rickel, & Daly, 2007). These conditions result from genetic, environmental, and unknown causes and may be transient, lifelong, or life threatening. Many students experience unpredictable changes due to deteriorating health, recurring surgery, **remission**, and increasing doses and side effects of medication. Each physical condition can present differently from case to case, and how well families and individuals cope interacts with the physical condition. When you are teaching a student with a physical disability or chronic medical disorder, it will be critical for you to familiarize yourself with characteristics, emergency responses, and teaching strategies on a need-to-know basis.

Physical and chronic health disorders are difficult to categorize. The description depends on whether the focus is on the area of dysfunction, the cause, or the impact. For example, muscular dystrophy can be described as a musculoskeletal impairment, a health disorder, or a motor disability. A student is considered to have a physical disability or chronic medical disorder, based on the need for differentiated teaching or special education services, because of one or more of the following: (1) nervous system impairment, (2) musculoskeletal condition, or (3) chronic health impairment (BC Special Education Branch, 2008).

## Nervous System Impairment

**Nervous system impairment** or **neurological dysfunction** results from damage or dysfunction of the brain or spinal cord that may have occurred before, during, or after birth. The exceptionalities discussed are cerebral palsy, spina bifida, epilepsy, Tourette syndrome, brain injury, and fetal alcohol spectrum disorders.

### CEREBRAL PALSY

> On Wednesday, nobody understood what I wanted. Most days I can point at it or just wheel over in my walker. I've got lots of words inside my head but people don't seem to hear them like I do. Some days, even my mum doesn't know what I mean. Wednesday was a bad day. Nobody understood. My big yellow school bus was on my top

**Further Reading**

DePaepe, P., Garrison-Kane, L., & Doelling, J. (2002). Supporting students with health needs in schools: An overview of selected health conditions. *Focus on Exceptional Children, 35*(1), 1–24.

Lightfoot, J., et al. (2001). Supporting pupils with special health needs in mainstream schools: Policy and practice. *Children and Society, 15,* 57–69.

Brown, R.T., Rickel, A.U., & Daly, B.P. (2007). *Chronic illness in children and adolescents.* Toronto: Hogrefe & Huber.

Clark, C. (2003). *In sickness and in play: Coping with chronic illness.* Piscataway, NJ: Rutgers University Press.

Deutsch, M. (1998). Are you tired again?…I understand: An activities workbook to help children understand and live with a person who has a chronic illness. London, UK: Manson West Corporation.

shelf and I wanted to play with it. Dad handed me the blocks instead. Bbbusss.... That's a hard word to say.

*Yates, 1994, pp. 3–5*

This young girl has **cerebral palsy**. Although she speaks little and cannot walk, she has thoughts to express and can become frustrated. She might enjoy reading or listening to someone read *On Being Sarah*, written by Elizabeth Helfman (Albert Whiman and Co., 1992). Cerebral palsy (CP) describes a group of disorders affecting body movement and muscle coordination resulting from damage to the brain during pregnancy or before age three. This damage interferes with messages in both directions between brain and body. Approximately one in every five hundred to five hundred and fifty people in Canada has CP. There are over fifty thousand Canadians with CP (www.ofcp.on.ca). Many individuals with intellectual disabilities also have cerebral palsy.

The effects vary widely. At its mildest, CP causes awkward movement or hand control. At its most severe, CP may result in almost no muscle control, profoundly affecting movement and speech. Depending on which areas of the brain have been damaged, one or more of the following may occur:

- muscle tightness or spasm
- involuntary movement
- difficulty with gross-motor skills such as walking or running
- difficulty with fine-motor skills such as writing and speaking
- abnormal perception and sensation

*Increasingly, young adults with physical disabilities are completing university and graduate school, like Jenny Clement, who works at ARCH Disability Law Centre in Ontario.*

The brain damage that caused CP may also lead to other conditions, such as seizures, learning disabilities or developmental delay, hearing impairment, or impaired vision. The degree of physical disability experienced by a person with cerebral palsy is not an indication of level of intelligence.

Treat students with cerebral palsy as normally as possible and don't underestimate their ability to learn and participate. They may need more time to complete a task or to respond verbally, and they may need to repeat themselves when misunderstood. Some use voice output communication aids; this can make it challenging for naturally speaking students to take turns in conversation with the student with CP (Clarke & Wilkinson, 2008). Learn to help to position and transfer students who use wheelchairs and how to push wheelchairs by asking the student, a parent, and a physiotherapist. Felt-tipped pens and soft-lead pencils enable the student to exert less pressure when writing. A rubber grip around the shaft may help with holding a pencil. You can help the student set and reach realistic goals in your classroom. For classroom accommodations consult www.bced.gov.bc.ca/specialed/awareness/33.htm and the work of Paul Wright and his colleagues (2004) on adapting physical activity to meet the needs of students with cerebral palsy.

### SPINA BIFIDA

I am going to try out for the swim team this year, even though I may not be chosen. I have been swimming since I was very young because my parents thought I might get hurt in rough team sports. I have always swum by myself, but I really want to be part of a team.

*Excerpt from the diary of a 15-year-old male with spina bifida who wears leg braces and uses crutches*

**Spina bifida** is a neural tube defect that occurs within the first four weeks of pregnancy. The vertebrae or spinal cord fails to develop properly, causing damage to the spinal cord and nervous system. Spina bifida often results in paralysis of the lower limbs as well as loss of bladder control, and is often accompanied by **hydrocephalus**, the accumulation of cerebrospinal fluid surrounding the brain. This fluid can cause brain injury if not treated immediately; usually a **shunt** is installed to drain the fluid for reabsorption. About one in every seven hundred and fifty babies born in Canada has spina bifida, and 80 percent of these have hydrocephalus (http://sbhac.ca/beta). Many individuals with intellectual disabilities also have spina bifida.

You may be asked to watch for signs of headaches, coordination difficulties, vomiting, and seizures—indications of shunt blockage. If the student lacks bladder or bowel control, this can be a barrier to peer acceptance. You can model acceptance and be sensitive to the student's need to leave the classroom unexpectedly. Encourage independence and ensure privacy. Usually a paraeducator assists young students with these functions.

Sitting in a wheelchair makes one vulnerable to sores and skin breakdown. Students need to be positioned properly and moved periodically and may be advised to use prone standers, braces, or crutches for part of the day. Treat changes in position as normal occurrences and assist students without drawing undue attention to them. Be prepared to accommodate extended absences from school that result from skin breakdown, bladder infections, or other medical issues. Encourage students with spina bifida to use computers, audiovisual materials, and calculators, and give them two copies of books: one for school and one for home. By working closely with the family, you can help minimize the impact of spina bifida on school participation. School counsellors can also play an important role in increasing social participation and social acceptance of students with spina bifida (Brislin, 2008).

## EPILEPSY

Last week I had a seizure at school. I have only one or two a year, and this is the first one I've had at this school since I started a year ago. Fortunately, my best friend was in the class and stopped some guy from sticking his pencil in my mouth so I wouldn't "swallow my tongue." She also told the other kids it was no big deal and not to worry. My friend says the teacher fluttered around like she didn't know what to do. Now the teacher is being kind of gooey sweet and sympathetic to me. I think my classmates would forget the whole thing if she would act normal.

*Kaufman, 2005, p. 99*

**Epilepsy** is a neurological disorder involving sudden bursts of electrical energy in the brain. It is characterized by sudden, brief **seizures** that can last from ten seconds to five minutes. If a seizure lasts longer than ten minutes, medical attention may be needed (Epilepsy Toronto; www.epilepsytoronto.org). Roughly 1 percent of the population has epilepsy, and in many cases the causes are unknown. Contributing causes include chemical imbalance and head injury. Many individuals with intellectual disabilities also have epilepsy.

**Put into Practice**

Read the research of Dr. Marcia Barnes of the University of Guelph on students with spina bifida and discuss with your classmates the implications for teaching. For example, Barnes (2004) reports that children with spina bifida who have hydrocephalus have particular difficulty comprehending text even when they can decode or sound the words.

Barnes, M.A., et al. (2004). Meaning construction and integration in children with hydrocephalus. *Brain and Language, 89,* 47–56.

Barnes, M.A., et al. (2006). Arithmetic processing in children with spina bifida: Calculation accuracy, strategy use, and fact retrieval fluency. *Journal of Learning Disabilities, 39,* 174–187.

Lomax-Bream, L.E., Barnes, M.A., Fletcher, J.M., & Swank, P. (2007). Role of early parenting and motor skills on development in children with spina bifida. *Journal of Applied Developmental Psychology, 28,* 250–263.

**Weblinks**

SPINA BIFIDA ASSOCIATION OF AMERICA
www.sbaa.org

SPINA BIFIDA AND HYDROCEPHALUS ASSOCIATION OF CANADA
http://sbhac.ca/beta

**Put into Practice**

Interview an adult with cerebral palsy. View the eleven-minute video *Never Say Never*, available from the Cerebral Palsy Association in Alberta (fax: 403-543-1168). Consult provincial associations for cerebral palsy, such as www.cpalberta.com, or the twenty-nine-minute video *Kids with Courage*, developed at Johns Hopkins University in Baltimore, Maryland (2004) by L. Poole et al.

**What do you think?**

Sex and sexual activity are sensitive issues in both parenting and teaching individuals with disability. Reading on the issue may help you to understand your feelings about it and may help you to be sensitive to the needs of your students, especially adolescents. Relevant Canadian and American sources include:

Kaufman, M., Silverberg, C., & Odette, F. (2007). *The ultimate guide to sex and disability: For all of us who live with disabilities, chronic pain, and illness.* San Francisco, CA: Cleis Press.

Thompson, S.A. (2005). LGBTQ (lesbian, gay, bisexual, transgendered, queer) youth with intellectual disabilities, in J. Sears (Ed.) *Encyclopedia of [Homo] Sexualities, Education and Youth* (pp. 268–272). Toronto: Greenwood Publishing.

Krishnamurthy, K.B., & Osbourne, P. (2007, September). Seizures and teens: Teens, sex, seizures and drugs, what teenage girls and their parents need to know. *Exceptional Parent,* 37(9), 80–81.

Cross-Reference
Chapter 3 contains information about mild intellectual disabilities, while the current chapter contains information about severe intellectual disabilities.

The two main categories of seizures are partial and generalized. **Partial seizures** involve one area of the brain, while **generalized seizures** involve the whole brain. In a partial seizure there may be strange sensations, possibly accompanied by inappropriate movements such as plucking at clothes or books, smacking the lips, or aimless wandering. Complete consciousness is not lost, though confusion usually follows the partial seizure.

Generalized seizures are of two types—simple absence and tonic-clonic. The **simple absence seizure** (formerly known as **petit mal**) occurs in children; they stare or daydream for five to fifteen seconds. There may be small muscle movements in the face, the eyes may roll upward or to one side, and the child may be confused about the seconds "missed." If these seizures are not treated, serious learning problems can result. Teachers most often notice these seizures and urge parents to seek a neurological assessment (Epilepsy Toronto; DePaepe et al., 2002).

The **tonic-clonic** (formerly called **grand mal**) seizure can be frightening when it occurs in the classroom. Sometimes the student gives a sharp cry before falling to the floor, and the muscles stiffen and then begin to jerk rhythmically. There may be loss of bladder control, some breathing difficulty, and saliva may gather at the mouth. In most cases the seizure will not hurt the student and there is no emergency; some school policies require that the student be taken to the hospital. Medical attention is required if the seizure "lasts more than ten minutes or is repeated without full recovery" (Epilepsy Toronto).

A child or adolescent with seizures may experience the world as an unpredictable and scary place. Some young people with epilepsy turn to the internet to chat in peer-to-peer networks and seek information from these peers. A recent study has begun to examine the quality of information exchanged in these peer-to-peer networks (Lorence & Chen, 2007). A parent's or a teacher's concerns regarding safety may lead to overprotecting the child or adolescent. Consequently, an individual may become dependent and feel helpless and unworthy. You may perceive a student with epilepsy as being unmotivated, not realizing that seizures can have a profound cognitive impact. Many individuals with epilepsy feel embarrassed when a seizure occurs in public. Those who are having a difficult time adjusting to their seizures may exhibit acting out behaviours, which could serve to further distance them from their peers. Your day-to-day support for and acceptance of the child or adolescent is critical. A recent study by Wodrich and Cunningham (2007) suggests that, as a classroom teacher, you may need to consult a special educator or school psychologist to help with targeted interventions for students with epilepsy. Many children with epilepsy require daily administration of medication within the school day. Medications often have side effects, which can range from hyperactivity to sleepiness and include clumsiness, difficulty thinking or talking, and rashes, depending on the medication prescribed (DePaepe et al., 2002). In addition, you need to know what to do when a seizure occurs.

Figure 4.5 lists the specific actions to take during a generalized seizure. Familiarize yourself with the student's condition. Students may be excused from activities such as climbing high ropes or operating power tools. Side effects from medications include drowsiness and blurred vision, and repeated seizure activity can contribute to inattentiveness and distractibility.

### TOURETTE SYNDROME

Dear Kellie, Kamilla and Magrau—Hi! My name is Russell. I am nine years old and I have TS. I have tics. They really bother me because they keep me awake at night. I get

## FIGURE 4.5 STRATEGIES FOR HANDLING A GENERALIZED SEIZURE IN THE CLASSROOM

**Before a Seizure**

- Meet with the parents and student at the beginning of the year. Learn the characteristics of the student's seizures.
- Familiarize yourself with the school's policies.
- Discuss with the family how to inform the class that a seizure may occur.
- Keep the area surrounding the student's desk free of objects that could cause harm to the student during a seizure.

**During a Seizure**

- Stay calm, and keep the students calm. Remind them that the seizure is painless. Ask another teacher to remove excited students from the classroom.
- Ease the student to the floor and loosen clothing.
- Try to remove any hard, sharp, or hot objects that might injure the student.
- Place a blanket, coat, or cushion under the student's head to soften the impact of the seizure.
- Place the student on his or her side to allow saliva to flow from the mouth.
- Write down the time the seizure began. If a seizure lasts longer than ten minutes, medical attention may be needed.
- Refrain from restraining the student or placing objects in the student's mouth.
- Refrain from giving the student food or drink.

**After a Seizure**

- Allow the student to rest or sleep and then offer the opportunity to resume classroom activities.
- Be attuned to the student's emotional state, as most but not all students can rejoin classroom activities.
- The student should not leave the school alone if weakness or convulsive behaviour persist.
- Refrain from "fussing over" the student with epilepsy. Foster an attitude of understanding and acceptance. The student with epilepsy needs support from you and peers.

**What do you think?**

Many people with epilepsy feel they are discriminated against. View the website of Epilepsy Toronto (www.epilepsytoronto.org) and of Epilepsy Canada (www.epilepsy.ca) and then discuss with your classmates this charge of unfair treatment.

Further Reading

Sherwood Best, J., et al. (2004). *Teaching individuals with physical or multiple disabilities.* Toronto: Pearson Education Canada.

Downing, J.E. (with invited contributors). (2002). *Including students with severe and multiple disabilities in typical classrooms: Practical strategies for teachers.* Baltimore, MD: Paul H. Brookes.

Haslam, R.H., & Valletutti, P.J. (2004). *Medical problems in the classroom: The teacher's role in diagnosis and management* (4th ed.). Austin, TX: PRO-ED, Inc.

what I call "buggie" when something is frustrating and it makes it hard to work. At school it is sometimes hard to work, I get really hot and my teacher says I can leave the classroom if I want to and get a drink. I don't like it when other kids ask me why I make funny noises. These are some of the tics I have: twirling my hair, arm movements, shrugging my shoulders, sticking my pinky finger in the air and some others. This website is really cool.

—From Russell

*Excerpt from a letter written to Kellie at Kids Korner on the Tourette Syndrome Foundation of Canada website (www.tourette.ca)*

**Tourette syndrome (TS)** is a complex neurological disorder modulated by psychological and social factors. It is characterized by **tics**: involuntary, rapid, sudden muscular movements; uncontrollable vocal sounds; and inappropriate words. Symptoms appear between the ages of 2 and 18 and change over time. Often one type of tic replaces another, and the syndrome is mistaken for a psychological disorder. Stress aggravates TS symptoms; thus, more structure and predictability result in fewer disruptions. Typically, tics decrease with concentration on an absorbing task, so engaging teaching will help students with TS. These children may also have learning disabilities, obsessive-compulsive behaviours, and attentional difficulties. Many individuals with autism also have tics and some have Tourette syndrome (Canitano & Vivanti, 2007).

## Further Reading

Epilepsy can have an impact on the family life of any child, but especially for an adolescent. The publication *Exceptional Parent* has included a series of articles on adolescents and epilepsy. Here are a few of these articles, which will give you a much greater understanding of the lives of adolescents (and children) who live with epilepsy and seizures.

Shafer, P.O., & Schachter, S.C. (2007, November). Seizures and teens: Using technology to develop seizure preparedness. *Exceptional Parent, 37*(11), 64–66.

Sundstrom, D. (2007, April). Seizures and teens: Maximizing health and safety. *Exceptional Parent, 37*(4), 77–79.

Weinstein, S.C. (2007, June). Seizures and teens: The impact of seizures and epilepsy on families. *Exceptional Parent, 37*(6), 61–62.

Shafer, P.O., & Israel, B. (2007, February). Seizures and teens: The practical aspects of managing seizure medications. *Exceptional Parent, 37*(2), 57–59.

## Put into Practice

Watch a video on epilepsy to reduce your discomfort with intervening when a student has a seizure. Make a brief action plan and discuss it with your peers. Epilepsy Toronto has a comprehensive list of videos on its website (www.epilepsytoronto.org/videolist.html). Two that are highly recommended are *Understanding Seizure Disorders*, which is eleven minutes long and includes video clips of various types of seizures; and *Seizure First Aid*, ten minutes long with demonstrations of first aid that should be provided to individuals with different types of seizures.

Controversial issues include incidence. According to the American Psychiatric Association in 1994, this was a relatively rare disorder affecting about one individual per twenty-two hundred. "Recent genetic studies suggest that the figure may be one in two hundred when those with chronic and transient tics are included in the count" (Tourette Syndrome Foundation of Canada, www.tourette.ca). Other controversial topics include whether adolescents with Tourette syndrome have impaired language compared with non-neurologically impaired adolescents (Legg et al., 2005) and whether educational interventions can modify peer attitudes and behaviour toward students with Tourette syndrome (Woods & Brook, 2005). Symptoms definitely appear to be more severe in students with concomitant identifications such as attention deficit disorder.

When teaching a student with Tourette syndrome in a classroom,

- be patient and engage all students fully;
- respond to tics with tolerance, not anger; the student with TS cannot control them;
- encourage the student to leave the room for a short time when tics become distracting;
- provide a quiet place for the student to work or take tests, preferably in the classroom;
- minimize stress by adapting teaching and assignments, using structure, and eliminating chaos; and
- seek assistance for yourself and the student with TS from counsellors, psychologists, and parents.

The Tourette Syndrome Foundation of Canada has developed a resource guide for educators called *Circle of Support* and a handbook, *Understanding Tourette Syndrome: A Handbook for Educators* (2nd edition), both of which are available from the website (www.tourette.ca). *Circle of Support* includes a video or DVD, an interactive workbook, a facilitator's guide, symptom checklists, and a copy of *Understanding Tourette Syndrome*.

### BRAIN INJURY

> How I hated going to school! It was almost a year after my brain injury. I was still relearning to read and write and even to remember. I felt myself getting more and more down. Most of my teachers were helpful, and I had a tutor who helped me write my assignments and read my textbooks. But it was really the counsellor who got me through those "dark periods" until I finished school.
>
> *Mark, reflecting on returning to school after his brain injury (based on Acorn and Offer, 1998)*

Brain injury happens when the brain's tissue is damaged or is not able to function properly. It is sometimes called **acquired brain injury (ABI)**, **head injury**, or **traumatic brain injury**. Many brain injuries are acquired, the result of a blow to the head from a fall, a sports injury, an assault, or a cycling or motor vehicle accident, for example. Cycling and motor vehicle accidents are responsible for most brain injuries to youths. Roughly 56 000 new cases of traumatic brain injury occur each year in Canada, and 9000 result in significant long-term rehabilitation needs (Higenbottam, 1998). There are approximately 27 000 school-aged individuals in Ontario who have sustained a brain injury (Bennett, Good, & Kumpf, 2003).

Students with brain injury experience difficulties remembering, understanding, organizing, and planning that interfere with their ability to function in school.

They often have physical effects such as paralysis and vision and hearing loss and experience socio-emotional challenges. Anti-social behaviour, impulsiveness, confusion, and inappropriate or immature language and behaviour can result (Bullock, Gable, & Mohr, 2005). For a thorough description of the learning characteristics of students with ABI, consult *Educating Educators about ABI: Resource Book* (Bennett, Good, & Kumpf, 2003), the result of a collaborative project led by Sheila Bennett of Brock University. Strategies for teaching these students may appear similar to those used with students who have LD. However, there are important differences between these two exceptionalities and students' needs. Bennett et al. (2003) describe the strategies for students with ABI as redirecting (steering a person away from their preoccupation), restructuring (focusing on the relevant, ignoring the irrelevant or inaccurate), and the "back door approach" (implemented without the person being aware or confronted). Because they know themselves as they were prior to the brain injury, students with ABI may hold onto their pre-trauma academic and career aspirations, although these have become unrealistic. Realistic goals are essential but can be discouraging (Hawley, 2004). Figure 4.6 contains strategies for physical, language, cognitive, and social adaptations in the classroom.

**Further Reading**

Bennett, S., Good, D., & Kumpf, J. (2003). *Educating educators about ABI: Resource book.* St. Catharines, ON: Ontario Brain Injury Association. www.abieducation.com.

Acorn, S., & Offer, P. (Eds.) (1998). *Living with brain injury: A guide for families and caregivers.* Toronto: University of Toronto Press.

Bullock, L.M., Gable, R.A., & Mohr, J.D. (2005). Traumatic brain injury: A challenge for educators. *Preventing School Failure, 49*(4), 6–10.

Hawley, C.A. (2004). Behaviour and school performance after brain injury. *Brain Injury, 18*(7), 645–659.

Jameson, L., & Jameson, B. (2007). *Brain injury survivor's guide: Welcome to our world.* Parker, CO: Outskirts Press, Inc.

## FIGURE 4.6 STRATEGIES FOR TEACHING STUDENTS WITH BRAIN INJURY IN A CLASSROOM SETTING

**Weblinks**

ONTARIO BRAIN INJURY ASSOCIATION
www.obia.on.ca

BRAIN INJURY ASSOCIATION OF NOVA SCOTIA
www3.ns.sympatico.ca/bians1

NEUROSCIENCE FOR KIDS
http://faculty.washington.edu/chudler/neurok.html

### Strategies for Physical Adaptations

- Schedule rest breaks; have a shortened day.
- Schedule more difficult classes early in the day.
- Provide adapted equipment or assistance, including computers and scribes, without drawing undue attention.

### Strategies for Language Adaptations

- Use shorter, simpler sentences, with pictures and gestures to aid comprehension.
- Teach the student to ask for clarification or repetition at a slower rate.
- To aid student communication, use pictures, an alphabet chart, etc.

### Strategies for Cognitive Adaptations

- Remove distractions and limit the amount of information on a page.
- Provide focusing cues and visual cues or a set of steps to follow.
- Adjust the length of assignments to the student's attention span; limit the number of steps.
- Use rehearsal to strengthen memory; have the student practise aloud.
- Use a tape recorder instead of having the student write notes or information about assignments.
- Teach the student to compensate for word-finding problems by describing the size, function, etc., of items that cannot be recalled.
- Praise students with ABI once they begin a task; remind them they are capable of completing the activity.
- Give prior warning for transitions; make transitions clear and structured.
- Role-play appropriate responses and stop inappropriate responses as soon as they begin.

### Strategies for Social Adaptations

- Make asking for assistance a student goal; remind the student to seek assistance.
- Check work after a small amount is begun to reassure the student that he or she can complete the task.
- Emphasize personal progress; discourage comparisons to classmates.
- Arrange for counselling to deal with frustration and aggression.
- Model patience and understanding to the class in your relations with the student.

John [my son] doesn't have an easy time in school. He doesn't have any close friends except for his doggy. You see, John has fetal alcohol syndrome (FAS), a disorder caused by **prenatal exposure to alcohol**. His birth mother's drinking during pregnancy caused John's mild retardation, small stature, unusual facial features, and damage to his central nervous system. He has a hard time learning the rules of life. John needs reminders about how to behave normally around people. I give him verbal cues for everything from how to get ready for school in the morning, to taking care of his dog, to how to behave in public, to how to interact with company, and so on and so on, day after day. His brain just doesn't function like yours and mine.

*www.specialchild.com/archives/dz-011.html*

Prenatal alcohol exposure can lead to significant neurodevelopmental disabilities, now recognized as **fetal alcohol spectrum disorders (FASD)**. This includes both **fetal alcohol syndrome (FAS)**, a lifelong birth defect, and a wider range of enduring learning and behaviour deficits often called **partial fetal alcohol syndrome (PFAS)** and **alcohol-related neurodevelopmental disorder (ARND)**. There is a growing body of research describing the teratogenic effects of alcohol on central nervous system function and physical development, the diversity of children with prenatal alcohol exposure, and the characteristics of these children (Olson et al., 2007). For a description of the features of each disorder in FASD, see Table 4.3. At one time it was believed that only significant prenatal exposure to alcohol could cause FASD; however, recent research suggests that even occasional alcohol consumption during pregnancy can cause damage along the spectrum. For a discussion of myths about FAS, see www.nofas.org.

FASDs are difficult to diagnose. Reasons include the similarity of characteristics to those of other exceptionalities and the resistance of some mothers to the idea that they are responsible for their children's disabilities. A recent study from Quebec reports that with the current state of knowledge, the pooling of all studies

**TABLE 4.3 CRITERIA FOR FETAL ALCOHOL SPECTRUM DISORDERS**

| Disorder | Diagnostic Features |
|---|---|
| Fetal alcohol syndrome (FAS) | Growth deficiency: height or weight < 10th percentile |
| | Cluster of minor facial anomalies: small eye slits, thin upper lip, smooth groove above the upper lip |
| | Central nervous system damage: evidence of structural or functional brain impairment |
| | Reliable evidence of confirmed prenatal alcohol exposure (not required if the cluster of facial anomalies is present) |
| Partial FAS (PFAS) | Some of the characteristic minor facial anomalies |
| | Growth deficiency: height or weight < 10th percentile |
| | Central nervous system damage: evidence of structural or functional brain impairment |
| | Reliable evidence of confirmed prenatal alcohol exposure |
| Alcohol-related neurodevelopmental disorder (ARND) | Central nervous system damage: evidence of structural or functional brain impairment |
| | Reliable evidence of confirmed prenatal alcohol exposure |

makes it possible to estimate that FAS is found in one to four children out of two thousand live births in North America, while the prevalence of FASD (including FAS) is estimated to be nine in one thousand (April, 2005).

A study about a decade ago suggested that teachers in northern Canada are more aware of the presence and needs of students with FASD than teachers in southern Canada (Beddard, 1996), and a recent study of Canadian physicians, conducted by researchers from University of Calgary, suggests that those with a higher proportion of Aboriginal patients appeared to be more attuned to the issues of FASD and to assess risk in a more comprehensive manner (Tough, Clarke, & Cook, 2007). For the perspective of Aboriginal mothers on the tendency to associate FASD with Aboriginal communities, read Amy Salmon's (2007) paper "Adaptation and Decolonization: Unpacking the Role of 'Culturally Appropriate' Knowledge in the Prevention of Fetal Alcohol Syndrome."

Students with FASD can be chatty and charming, and this may initially mask their learning and behaviour difficulties. They usually show impaired rates of learning, poor memory, and difficulty generalizing. They often act impulsively, exhibit short attention spans, and have difficulty staying focused, recognizing and understanding patterns, predicting common sense outcomes, and mastering mathematics and reading. Parents describe examples of fearlessness, lack of social judgment, and lack of internalization of modelled behaviour. Difficulty understanding cause and effect appears to be an integral part of learning and behaviour difficulties for individuals with FASD (Olson et al., 2007). Consistency in behaviour management across home and school usually helps these children and adolescents. Children do not "outgrow" FASD and its serious consequences. They become adolescents and adults who may have difficulties with learning, attention, memory, and problem solving.

Figure 4.7 includes strategies for behaviour management that can be used in both environments, home and school. There is little research to indicate what kinds of interventions are most effective for students with FASD (Burd, 2007; Premji et al., 2006). However, in a case study Carol Johnson and Judy Lapadat (2000) of the University of Northern British Columbia report on the similarities between FASD and LD and on the moderate success they achieved using teaching strategies for students with LD with a student who had been diagnosed with FAS. Figure 4.8 includes strategies for teaching students with FASD.

### Further Reading

Below are listed classic sources about FASD. Notice the use of the term FAE (**fetal alcohol effects**) in addition to FAS (fetal alcohol syndrome). What was meant by the term FAE?

British Columbia, Ministry of Education. (2002). *Teaching students with fetal alcohol syndrome/effects: A resource guide for teachers.* Victoria, BC: Ministry of Education, Special Programs Branch. www.bced.gov.bc.ca/specialed/fas.

Burgess, D.M., & Streissguth, A.P. (1992). Fetal alcohol syndrome and fetal alcohol effects: Principles for educators. *Phi Delta Kappan, 74*(1), 24–30.

Mitchell, K. (2002). *Fetal alcohol syndrome: Practical suggestions and support for families and caregivers.* Washington, DC: National Organization on Fetal Alcohol Syndrome.

Kleinfeld, J., & Westcott, S. (1993). *Fantastic Antone succeeds: Experiences in educating children with fetal alcohol syndrome.* Fairbanks: University of Alaska Press.

Kleinfeld, J. (2000). *Fantastic Antone grows up: Adolescents and adults with fetal alcohol syndrome.* Fairbanks: University of Alaska Press.

## FIGURE 4.7 STRATEGIES FOR CLASSROOM MANAGEMENT OF STUDENTS WITH FASD

- Place the student near the front of the room to help with focus.
- Allow the student to have short breaks when necessary.
- Set limits and follow them consistently.
- Change rewards often to keep interest in rewards high.
- Have pre-established consequences for misbehaviour.
- Review and repeat consequences of behaviours. Ask the student to tell you consequences.
- Do not debate or argue over rules already established. "Just do it."
- Notice and comment when the student is behaving appropriately.
- Avoid threats.
- Redirect behaviour.
- Monitor the student carefully.
- Intervene before behaviour escalates.
- Protect the student from being exploited. These students are naive.

**Put into Practice**

Two recent papers report on teaching approaches that "work" for students with FASD. Laugeson and her colleagues adapted a friendship training program while Coles and her colleagues used computer games to teach safety skills. Read these two papers and discuss the implications for regular classroom teachers with your peers. Make specific recommendations for teachers based on your reading.

Laugeson, E.A., Paley, B., Schonfeld, A.M., Carpenter, E.M., Frankel, F., & O'Connor, M.J. (2007). Adaptation of the children's friendship training program for children with fetal alcohol spectrum disorders. *Child and Family Behavior Therapy, 29*(3), 5769.

Coles, C.D., Strickland, D.C., Padgett, L., & Bellmoff, L. (2007). Games that "work": Using computer games to teach alcohol-affected children about fire and street safety. *Research in Developmental Disabilities, 28*, 518–530.

**Weblinks**

MUSCULAR DYSTROPHY ASSOCIATION OF CANADA
www.muscle.ca or www.mdac.ca

ARTHRITIS CANADA
www.arthritiscanada.com

THE ARTHRITIS SOCIETY
www.arthritis.ca

**Put into Practice**

Obtain a copy of the IEP form used in your school district. Compare it to the IEP for Brenda Piet shown in Figure 2.6 on page 55.

## FIGURE 4.8 STRATEGIES FOR TEACHING STUDENTS WITH FASD

- Use concrete, hands-on learning methods.
- Establish routines and follow them; whenever you vary the routine give the student ample warning.
- Avoid surprises and loud noises.
- Post an agenda, illustrated if the student is preliterate.
- Give short and simple directions.
- Have the student repeat back his or her understanding of directions.
- Whenever you can, use the same directions as in the past.
- Give one task at a time.
- Repeat tasks.
- Provide a calculator and other aids to enable the student to succeed.
- Reduce the auditory and visual distractions in the classroom. Reduce the auditory and visual ReR.
- Put a small number of tasks on a page with white space around them.
- Notice and comment when the student is doing well.
- Work with the family to maintain consistency as much as possible.
- For younger students, use a communication book for daily communication between school and home.
- For older students, work out a regular means of communication that is both effective and age-appropriate.

## Musculoskeletal Conditions

Two **musculoskeletal conditions** that can affect all aspects of a student's life are muscular dystrophy and juvenile arthritis. They have different characteristics, treatments, and educational implications.

### MUSCULAR DYSTROPHY

In March 1999 Jérémie Girard, a young artist in Quebec, painted a work called *Secret* on a pizza box for his art class. His art teacher recognized the merit of the work, as did a neighbour, who suggested that Jérémie have it framed. When the neighbour took the painting to a gallery to be framed for Jérémie, the owner of the gallery offered to promote this new artist. She admired the way he had captured themes of life and death in his painting. Jérémie has muscular dystrophy and was 10 years old when he painted *Secret*. His story appeared on the website of the Muscular Dystrophy Association of Canada (www.mdac.ca or www.muscle.ca).

Muscular dystrophy (MD) refers to a group of genetically based neuromuscular disorders that result in progressive muscle weakness. Muscle tissue is replaced by fatty tissue and connective tissue, which causes the muscles to weaken and eventually waste away, making it difficult to speak, breathe, or move. Roughly twenty-eight thousand people in Canada have MD. Each form of MD is caused by an error in a specific gene associated with muscle function; however, several individuals with the same disorder may experience the disorder and its symptoms quite differently. **Duchenne muscular dystrophy (DMD)** is the most common form of MD and affects approximately one in thirty-three hundred male births (Emery, 2008; Heller, Alberto, Forney, & Schwartzman, 1996). In Duchenne muscular dystrophy marked physical degeneration occurs during the school years, so teachers need to provide adaptations and a supportive school environment.

Symptoms of DMD are first noted between 2 and 5 years of age and include difficulty in rising from the floor and climbing stairs. The calf muscles become prominent. A wheelchair is usually necessary by early adolescence, and breathing is increasingly affected. Recent research confirms that children with DMD had more behavioural concerns and poorer verbal memory spans (Hinton et al., 2004) as well as poorer facial affect recognition (Hinton et al., 2007) than their unaffected siblings, suggesting that the condition (usually described only in physical terms) may be characterized by delayed language and poor social skills, both of which can have wide-ranging consequences for learning in highly social classrooms. Most adolescents with DMD are prone to respiratory infections. Lifespan is shortened, with death typically occurring during the twenties. Other forms of MD include Becker MD and Myotonic MD (Steinart's disease), neither of which is as severe as DMD during the school years.

A physical therapist will be a member of the in-school team and exercise will form part of the treatment, but care must be taken to avoid overactivity and fatigue. Because the disease is progressive, the needs of the student are continually changing—including physical adaptations, adjustment to a wheelchair, exercising to avoid obesity, and coping with the prospect of a reduced lifespan. Emotional support is critical. As a teacher, you may have to cope with the attitudes of people who feel that youths with terminal diseases are a waste of your efforts because they won't live long enough to benefit from differentiated teaching (Talbot, 2002). However, these students are entitled to an education, as are all other students in Canada. For information on all aspects of MD including recent research developments, visit the website of Muscular Dystrophy Canada (www.mdac.ca or www.muscle.ca).

## JUVENILE ARTHRITIS

No one knows for sure what causes juvenile arthritis. Mine was diagnosed when I was eight. I was upset because I played sports, played the piano, and was good at art. My treatment team has helped me to take charge of my life. I play the piano even though I can't practise when my hands are swollen. I continued the sports with the least chance of body contact. Now I am 18. Some days I can't get out of bed, but those days are rare. When my fingers are too swollen to write, my friends at school take turns making carbon copies of their notes for me. With the help of my family, friends, and teachers I do well in school and will go to university next year. You can take charge of your arthritis, too.

*From Helen's speech to children recently diagnosed with juvenile arthritis, at a conference for families*

Juvenile idiopathic arthritis (JIA)—commonly called **juvenile arthritis (JA)**, continuous **inflammation** of one or more joints lasting at least six weeks for which no other cause can be found—is a chronic arthritic condition present before the age of 16. Approximately one in one thousand children under age 16 has JA (Health Canada, 2003; www.phac-aspc.gc.ca/publicat/ac/index.html). This condition can be difficult to detect. Doctors look for signs of joint swelling or loss of mobility that suggest inflamed joints. Students may complain of stiffness or pain, walk with a limp, or have difficulty using an arm or leg. The **immune system** seems to be overactive, inflaming joints as if fighting an infection when none is present. Most children have an up-and-down course for many years; physiotherapy and occupational therapy are essential parts of the treatment program.

**Further Reading**

These sources can help you to develop an insider's perspective on arthritis.

Murphy-Melas, E., & Hartman, A. (2002). *Keeping a secret: A story about juvenile rheumatoid arthritis.* Albuquerque, NM: Health Press, NA.

Miller, D.D.L. (2002). *Taking arthritis to school.* Plainview, NY: JayJo Books.

*I am brave: Children living with arthritis.* www.arthritis.ca/ arthritis%20kids/for%20parents/ publications/default.asp?s=1. (Booklet written by children and adolescents with JA.)

The Arthritis Society (of Canada). (2005). *You, your child, and arthritis.* www.arthritis.ca/arthritis%20kids/ for%20parents/publications/ default.asp?s=1. (Contains a section on adolescents and a section on school.)

For classroom strategies see: www.arthritis.org/ja-school-success.php.

Students with JA will tend to feel stiffness and pain after sitting in one position. They may need to stand in the middle of a class period or move around. Because of low stamina, they may require a shorter day or rest breaks during the day. Medication will probably have to be taken during the school day and often must be taken with food to prevent adverse effects on the gastrointestinal tract. Fever is a symptom of JA and does not indicate an infectious disease. Because eyes can become involved in arthritis, you will need to be alert for any indications of a visual problem and notify the parents.

You may need to make adaptations. The physical education program should take into account decreased stamina and limit strenuous games that put pressure on joints or limbs. Pain can interfere with concentration, so break tasks into shorter segments and check comprehension of the instructions. Students may have a **limited range of motion** in affected limbs and swollen fingers that prevent them from grasping pencils and pens. Writing may be difficult when arthritis affects the student's hands. Timed written tests may need to be changed or extended. Consider other ways to protect hand joints:

- Use foam shells to build up pens and pencils.
- Give the student felt tip pens, which require less effort.
- Computers or other electronic devices can be used for writing assignments.
- Record lectures, copy another student's notes, or give the student copies of teacher overheads.
- Provide extra time for written tests or allow the student to give answers orally.
- Shorten or modify long writing assignments, such as term papers.

Because symptoms vary from day to day, you must be accepting of a wide range of variation in the student's functioning and independence. Encourage as much independence as possible while reassuring the student that support is available (Jenkinson, Hyde, & Ahmad, 2002; www.arthritis.org/ja-school-success.php#5).

Adolescence is a particularly challenging time, but living with arthritis adds to the challenges of separating from family, learning to be independent, and figuring out how to and whether to fit in. Families encourage older children and adolescents to take more responsibility for managing their arthritis—that is, taking medication, monitoring side effects, and following an exercise program. This may mean that you see problems developing at school that the parents do not see, and that you need to discuss these with the adolescent and the family. Be supportive, and remember that your guidance and encouragement may enable the student to adapt so arthritis has little or no impact on his or her life at school, especially if the symptoms are mild to moderate (Erkolahti & Ilonen, 2005).

## Chronic Health Conditions

Usually, students with **chronic health conditions** have been assessed by a qualified medical practitioner who certifies that they require medical procedures, beyond taking medication, while at school to ensure their health and safety. Often they require ongoing monitoring and differentiated instruction because of their limited school attendance for health reasons or because the condition adversely affects their educational performance at school (Gomes & Smith, 2007). The speed and accuracy with which teachers, office staff, and school administrators respond to a student health crisis has far-reaching implications. When you begin working in a

## FIGURE 4.9 STRATEGY TO LEARN ABOUT HOW FAMILIES WOULD LIKE TO INCORPORATE CULTURE INTO INTERVENTIONS

B → ask gently about and listen to **B**eliefs
E
L → ask gently about and listen to **L**ifestyle
I
E
V → ask gently about and listen to **V**alues
E

**Put into Practice**

Read Damiel L. Clay's *Helping Schoolchildren with Chronic Health Conditions: A Practical Guide (Practical Interventions in the Schools)* (2004, Guilford Press). Think about which students in your last teaching experience this information would pertain to. Consider what information you need to locate to ensure the safety of each of these students. How could you learn whether other students in the class have chronic conditions that you don't already know about? Plan the information you would leave for a substitute teacher about the student(s) with chronic health conditions in your class(es). Remember that, as the classroom teacher, it is your responsibility to ensure the safety, health, and continued well-being of individuals in your care.

school, ask to see the Emergency Protocols Manual, question the administrator about an orientation session for new hires, and ask if you can sign up for a CPR and first aid course. Then you will be prepared and confident to respond to school health crises (Gomes & Smith).

Two issues that arise in the education of students with chronic illnesses are the need for culturally competent interventions (Clay, 2007) and the challenges of hospital-to-school transitions (Shaw & McCabe, 2008). Clay (2007) argues that it is critical we consider when and how to incorporate cultural issues into interventions both in medical facilities and in educational contexts for these students. He provides examples such as prayer, rituals to cleanse the body of toxins, and rituals to establish harmony with the earth. He suggests that the best way to understand the cultural issues that may be at play is to gently ask questions of the student and the family and to listen actively to learn what they *believe* might influence their decisions to adhere to the treatment and to choose complementary options like cleansing rituals. Figure 4.9 shows a strategy that you can use, called BELIEVE.

The second issue is the need to facilitate smooth transitions for students with chronic illnesses who have been in the hospital, when they return to school. While healthy students are typically absent from school for about three days per year, students with chronic illness are absent on average for sixteen days a year (Shaw & McCabe, 2008). At one time those with chronic illnesses including cancer or leukemia would have endured an extended stay in hospital, and a short stay at home, followed by a plan for gradual reintroduction to school after they had completed all treatments. Now they may spend only a day or two in hospital at a time, often on repeated occasions, as they receive treatment, and then go home and return immediately to school. Parents may come to school to give medication and monitor progress. However, this scenario puts children in school who are behind in their academic work, enduring treatment, and often dealing with impaired concentration and the side effects of powerful drugs. While school is considered a normalizing influence, parents may have to provide home-schooling on an interim basis if a student refuses to return to school. And teachers are likely to need to differentiate instruction for some time. These students often show an array of social and emotional difficulties, including increased behaviour problems, depression, withdrawal, anxiety, and poor peer relations. By the time they reach adolescence, students with chronic illness may experience suicide ideation and engage in substance abuse. For an extended discussion of these issues consult the work of Steven Shaw of McGill University (e.g., Shaw & McCabe, 2008). Discuss the student's needs with the student and the family, being sure to include the student in all stages of academic planning.

Conditions discussed in this section include diabetes, allergies, asthma, cystic fibrosis, HIV and AIDS, and cancer and leukemia. There are many other chronic health impairments, including congenital and acquired heart disease, gastrointestinal system diseases such as Crohn's disease and ulcerative colitis, as well as hemophilia. In each case you can obtain relevant information from the family, community agencies, websites, and print sources of information, including pamphlets, resource books, and books to be read to children and by adolescents about these conditions.

## DIABETES

> I stayed after school to talk to my homeroom teacher. I told her that I have diabetes. She already knew from my file. I said I don't want the other kids to know I am diabetic until I get to know them better. I told her that I keep juice in my backpack and that if I ask to leave class, it will be because I need sugar or insulin and she should let me go right away. Tomorrow I have to talk with my physical education teacher because I always need to eat after exercising. Today was good—a practice run for tomorrow.

*Phil, describing his first day of high school to his parents*

Further Reading

Wishnietsky, D., & Wishnietsky, D. (2004). *Helping students with diabetes management.* Bloomington, IN: Phi Delta Kappa Educational Foundation.

Brown, P., & Kent, M. (2000). *Guidelines for the care of students with diabetes in the school setting.* Trenton, NJ: New Jersey Dept. of Education.

For those with **diabetes**, the body does not make enough insulin and has problems absorbing and storing sugars. Most children with diabetes receive two **insulin injections** daily. Adolescents give themselves insulin injections and check their blood sugar regularly. Diabetes is controlled somewhat through planned eating, insulin supplementation, and regular physical activity.

There are three types of diabetic emergencies that you could face: low blood sugar, high blood sugar, and ketoacidosis. The symptoms appear similar, but low blood sugar is the more dangerous, so if you are unsure which is occurring, give sugar. The symptoms of **low blood sugar (hypoglycemia)** occur suddenly: cold, clammy, or sweaty skin; trembling; confusion; difficulty speaking; and eventually fainting or unconsciousness. The student may report hunger, headache, dizziness, blurry vision, and abdominal pain. If the student is conscious, give a regular soft drink or juice that contains sugar or two teaspoons of sugar. The amounts may be specified in the student's file. This should be followed by a snack that includes complex carbohydrates and protein (e.g., a nutrient bar). The student may carry such a snack in his or her backpack. The causes include too much insulin, delayed or missed meals, and more exercise than usual without extra food. Contact the parents or a physician, or take the student to hospital. Follow the school's protocol.

**High blood sugar (hyperglycemia)** symptoms show gradually, even over days. Causes include overeating, too little insulin, and stress. You may see thirst, flushed dry skin, nausea, drowsiness, and eventually unconsciousness. Contact the parents or a physician. The student requires insulin to combat hyperglycemia. It may be necessary to take the student to the hospital.

The third condition that you should be aware of is diabetic ketoacidosis, a condition in which blood glucose is highly elevated. This results in the build-up in the blood of ketones, waste products produced when the body burns fat instead of glucose for energy. Ketosis can lead to severe dehydration, loss of consciousness, coma, and even death (Touchette, 2000).

Your school will probably have **diabetes emergency kits** containing juice, raisins, or dextrose. Know the location of these kits and take one on field trips. Most students with diabetes will carry the emergency food or juice they need in their backpack, but if they become weak and confused they may not take out and consume what they need. Explain to younger children the importance of eating their own snacks, without focusing undue attention on the child with diabetes. Speak with the parents about appropriate activity levels. Supervise the student at all times after a reaction and inform the parents. Most students know about their condition and require only support, respect, and information about changes in the routine, especially the timing of snacks and meals.

Diabetes can affect students in the classroom. They need a specific eating schedule. When students are experiencing a high or a low, or the day after they have had high or low blood sugar during the night, they may be weak, tired, irritable, and unable to concentrate. Some students have characteristic high or low periods that cause them to arrive late in the morning. Encourage students with diabetes to speak with you confidentially, develop a sign to be used in class when the student needs to leave quickly (and then follow up within one minute to be sure the student is safe), and talk regularly with parents of younger children so they are comfortable telling you about their child's changing condition. Beware of misconceptions about diabetes (Shaw & McCabe, 2008; Rosenthal-Malek & Greenspan, 1999):

- that the student will inform you of highs or lows—sometimes the student won't be aware;
- that only food affects the level of blood sugar—activity level also influences it;
- that bathroom privileges can wait—a few minutes can put a student into a coma; and
- that all the effects are physical—attention, memory, learning, and processing speed in the classroom may be affected.

In a recent study conducted in Ontario, Kate Walker (2008) interviewed four young women with diabetes, who saw themselves as advocates for people with diabetes. They reported that diabetes influenced every aspect of their lives, including their stamina, choice of friends and social occasions, academic accomplishments, and choice of university program and career. They believed that most of their teachers had no idea how important it is to be understanding and supportive of students with diabetes. Your understanding will make a difference to the well-being and learning of students with diabetes.

## ALLERGIES

On 29 September 2003, Sabrina Shannon resisted her mother's attempts to make her an allergen-free sandwich for her school lunch at Bishop Smith Catholic High School in Pembroke, Ontario. Instead Sabrina insisted on buying French fries, which she had purchased the week before after checking that they were cooked in vegetable oil and not peanut oil. Sabrina's allergy triggers were peanut, dairy products, and soy, all of which put her at risk of anaphylaxis. So Sabrina's mother agreed reluctantly that her thoughtful, careful daughter could purchase her lunch. In class after lunch, Sabrina began to wheeze and headed toward the office saying, "It's my asthma." A teacher raced to Sabrina's locker to get her EpiPen® in case it was her food allergies. Sabrina went into cardiac arrest before the EpiPen® could be administered and before the ambulance arrived. She died one day later. The coroner posited that the allergic trigger was dairy protein and that Sabrina had been exposed to cross-contamination from cheese curds because the tongs had been used to serve poutine as well as fries. Sabrina's mother, Sara, made a promise to her dying daughter that she would do whatever she could to prevent this from happening to any other child. The result of Sara Shannon's campaign with Anaphylaxis Canada was the passage of Sabrina's Law,

**Put into Practice**

Make a contingency plan for when a student has low blood sugar and needs to be rushed to hospital. Consult A. Rosenthal-Malek & J. Greenspan (1999), A student with diabetes is in my class, *Teaching Exceptional Children*, 31(3), 38–43; the New Brunswick Office of the Canadian Diabetes Association, www.diabetes.ca/ Section_Regional/nb.asp; and the Canadian Diabetes Association, www.diabetes.ca.

**Weblinks**

CANADIAN DIABETES ASSOCIATION: KIDS WITH DIABETES IN YOUR CARE
www.diabetes.ca/files/ KidsWithDiabetes_complete.pdf

TEN TIPS FOR TEACHERS
www.diabetes.org/uedocuments/ TenTipsforTeachers.pdf

HELPING THE STUDENT WITH DIABETES SUCCEED: A GUIDE FOR SCHOOL PERSONNEL (AMERICAN DIABETES ASSOCIATION)
www.ndep.nih.gov/diabetes/pubs/ Youth_NDEPSchoolGuide.pdf

**Further Reading**

Engel, J. (2003). *The complete allergy book*. Richmond Hill, ON: Firefly Books.

Gold, M. (Ed.) (2004). *The complete kid's allergy and asthma guide: Allergy and asthma information for children of all ages*. Richmond Hill, ON: Firefly Books.

Thomas, P., & Harker, L. (2008). *First look at: Allergies*. London, UK: Hodder Children's Division.

May, J. (2001). *My house is killing me! The home guide for families with allergies and asthma*. Baltimore, MD: Johns Hopkins University Press.

**Weblinks**

SABRINA'S LAW (ONTARIO)
www.e-laws.gov.on.ca/ Download?dDocName=elaws_ statutes_05s07_e

ALLERGY/ASTHMA INFORMATION ASSOCIATION (AAIA)
www.aaia.ca

which took effect in Ontario on 1 January 2006. Sabrina's Law requires Ontario school boards to have all principals implement anaphylaxis plans that include strategies to reduce exposure to allergens; procedures to communicate to parents, students, and employees about life-threatening allergies; and regular training on dealing with life-threatening allergies for teachers and staff. Principals must also develop an individual plan for each student at risk of anaphylaxis, maintain a file that lists the student's prescriptions and emergency contacts, and ensure that parents supply information about a student's allergies when enrolling the student in school. Other provinces are considering passing similar laws.

*Adapted from Allergic Living (www.allergicliving.com/features.asp?copy_id=17, retrieved April 23, 2008)*

Isabel Grant, a lawyer at the University of British Columbia, has argued persuasively that a child with allergies has the law on his or her side. "Provincial human-rights legislation prohibits discrimination on the basis of disability for services customarily available to the public. It is clear that a life-threatening medical condition that greatly restricts the activities of daily living is a disability" (Grant, 1997, p. A24). She argues that other students' rights are not interfered with because the "rights of others" do not include a right to eat any specific food, even peanut butter, and because all Canadian children have a right to a safe education in the public school system.

An **allergy** is an abnormal immune response to a substance that is tolerated by non-allergic people. It results in individual signs and symptoms that vary in range and severity and that can occur up to seventy-two hours after exposure to the allergen. Allergies can become worse with a single exposure to an allergen. **Anaphylaxis** or **anaphylactic shock** is a sudden, severe allergic reaction that causes breathing difficulties. Death can occur within minutes unless an injection is administered. An estimated 8 percent of children under 3 years and approximately 2 percent of adults have food allergies (Sampson, 1999), while as many as 40 to 50 percent of those with a diagnosed food allergy are at high risk for anaphylaxis (Sheetz et al., 2004).

Allergens, which cause allergic reactions, can enter the body

- if breathed through the nose or mouth—including dust; pollen; moulds; odours from chemicals, markers, perfumes, etc.;
- if ingested through the mouth—including foods such as peanuts, shellfish, and milk; drugs such as aspirin (ASA), penicillin, and other antibiotics;
- by contact with the skin—including powders; lotions; metals such as jean snaps; latex; peanut butter; or
- through insect stings—including the venom of bees and wasps.

Other factors that may aggravate the allergy include weather changes; extremes of heat, cold, and humidity; infections; and second-hand smoke.

For the allergic student reactions often accompany changes in routine, and anaphylactic shock is more likely to take place at school than at home. Before the start of the school year, read the school policy on allergies and meet with the family. Because characteristics of allergic reactions vary, it is important to learn each student's signs and symptoms. The main symptoms are itchy, watery eyes and itchy, runny nose. Other signs include itching elsewhere, eczema, hives, dark circles under the eyes, headache, shortness of breath, wheezing, cough, diarrhea, and stomach cramps. Some teachers watch for what has been called the **allergic salute**—pushing up on a runny nose.

If you read the school policy first and bring it to a meeting with the parents, you can tell them how it compares with their expectations (e.g., some policies name the adults who can administer an injection). Inform the principal and invite others who teach the student to the meeting. The Canadian School Boards Association (1996) has prepared a handbook to help school boards clarify the responsibilities of principals, parents, teachers, and students. Many schools are posting emergency alert forms.

You should know the steps in the individual emergency plan that has been developed for each student with severe allergies and the location of the injector for each student (in the student's fanny pack, in a cupboard, etc.). The general steps in an emergency plan are as follows:

- Administer **epinephrine** immediately (**EpiPen**® or **Ana-Kit**®), following directions on the injector. This can save a life, but note that the injector is only first aid.

- Call 911 or an ambulance, or transport the student to the nearest emergency facility. Warn that there is anaphylaxis. More serious reactions may follow, so a hospital is essential.

- Ensure that you have additional epinephrine available in case it is needed. If breathing difficulties persist, it may be necessary to re-administer it every fifteen minutes until the patient reaches hospital.

- Call the parents or next of kin but only *after* administering the injection immediately. Don't delay by calling the parents first.

Children and adolescents with severe allergies can feel anxious and isolated because they feel "different from everyone else." They usually wear a **MedicAlert**® identification bracelet (www.medicalert.ca) and carry an injector in a fanny pack. Sometimes adolescents leave their "uncool" fanny packs in their lockers or engage in risky behaviours such as eating cafeteria food with their peers (Lightfoot, 1997). You can enhance self-acceptance by respecting feelings, accepting differences, and supporting personal decisions. Try to include the student in all activities, even if this means providing an **allergen-free alternative**.

### ASTHMA

> Ms. Aboul, I need to talk with you. Grade 9 is hard. I'm so far behind. I've missed a lot of classes this year because of my asthma and doctors' appointments. I hate carrying my puffer around at school and trying to avoid stressful situations that make my wheezing worse. Most of all I'm afraid of having a really big attack and not making it to the hospital. I need to talk with you. My homeroom teacher is Mr. Wong.
>
> Meghan Lowie, 9D

*A note left for a guidance counsellor by a student with asthma*

**Asthma** is a chronic lung condition that can develop at any age but is most common in childhood. The most important characteristic is difficulty breathing. The airways are obstructed by inflammation, muscle spasm, and excess mucus. An estimated 2.7 million Canadian adults and children (ages 4 years and over) have asthma, close to 10 percent of the population, and asthma is also an important factor in school absences and hospitalizations in children (Health Canada, *It's Your Health: Asthma*; www.hc-sc.gc.ca/iyh-vsv/diseases-maladies/asthm_e.html). It is usually thought that twice as many boys as girls are affected in childhood, but more girls than boys develop asthma during adolescence.

**Put into Practice**

Learn what to do in an emergency. Consult the Anaphylaxis Reference Kit, which you can order from AAIA (http://aaia.ca/en/products. htm#RE04). Also see Health Canada and the Canadian School Boards Association (2001), *Anaphylaxis: A Handbook for School Boards* (Ottawa: Canadian School Boards Association; (www.cdnsba.org/ newsflash/releases/ Anaphylaxis%20Handbook%20 Eng.pdf).

**Weblinks**

A TEACHER'S GUIDE TO ASTHMA
www.calgaryallergy.ca/Articles/ English/Adobe/ TeachersGuideAsthma.pdf

THE LUNG ASSOCIATION
www.lung.ca

THE LUNG ASSOCIATION: ASTHMA AT SCHOOL
www.lung.ca/diseases-maladies/ asthma-asthme/children-enfants/ school-ecole_e.php

*A young student with asthma administers a "reliever," a drug that offers short-term relief, during the onset of an asthma episode by using what is commonly called a puffer or inhaler.*

The airways respond in an exaggerated way to common irritants (e.g., smoke, smog, scents in markers), allergens (e.g., pollen, foods such as nuts and shellfish), and other triggers (e.g., viral head colds, exercise, cold air). To treat asthma effectively, the individual must know what may trigger an attack and avoid contact with these triggers. Two categories of medication are used for treating asthma. **Preventers** are anti-inflammatory drugs taken regularly to prevent and treat inflammation. **Relievers** are used as rescue medications to relax the muscles of the airways and provide quick relief of breathing problems. They are usually inhaled with a **puffer** or **nebulizer**.

Symptoms of asthma include persistent coughing, **wheezing**, chest tightness, and shortness of breath. Those with asthma are affected to varying degrees, from mild (only during vigorous exercise) to severe (with daily symptoms that cause lifestyle restrictions). In Canada roughly twenty children die annually from asthma. An asthma episode can lead to life-threatening anaphylactic shock. If you can identify the warning signs, you can help prevent an episode. As breathing becomes more difficult, signs of an asthma episode become more evident. Such signs are

- wheezing;
- rapid shallow breathing;
- complaints of chest tightness;
- lips and nails greyish or bluish in colour; and
- contracted and bulging neck muscles, nasal flaring, and mouth breathing.

When you see these signs, start asthma first aid treatment (see Figure 4.10). Time is critical, so you must know what to do before an episode occurs. Your familiarity with the information in the file of a student with asthma could save the student's life. Read the school policy on asthma and advise the principal of your upcoming meeting; then meet with the student and parents before school begins. Learn the student's triggers, warning signs and symptoms, and how the asthma medications (relievers) are administered. Have the parents detail the steps they

## FIGURE 4.10 ASTHMA FIRST AID TREATMENT

In case of breathing difficulty:

- Have the student stop all activity.
- Help the student assume an upright position; sitting with legs crossed and elbows on knees may ease breathing somewhat.
- Stay with the student; talk reassuringly and calmly.
- Have the student take the appropriate medication; it is more detrimental to withhold medication than to give the student medication when it is not needed. This is usually taken by means of an inhaler or nebulizer.
- Notify the proper person, in accordance with school policy. This usually means contacting the parents; if the student's condition does not improve or becomes worse fifteen minutes after giving the medication, call an ambulance.

Source: Based on information provided by The Lung Association at www.lung.ca/asthma.

follow in first aid treatment, and together compare these to the school policy. If the two are not the same, consult your principal. Some schools have a form that parents of students with asthma must complete to describe medications, symptoms, prevention, and first aid.

Always believe students with asthma. Do not make them wait for medication; asthma can be life threatening. If you think a student with asthma is using asthma symptoms to get attention, discuss your concerns with the parents and encourage the student to talk with a counsellor.

Although the physical outcomes associated with this condition have garnered the most attention, the potentially serious academic, social, and psychological ramifications cannot be ignored. Asthmatics miss about ten days of school per year and are frequently wakened during the night by their condition, leaving them tired the next day, which may detract from their school performance. Social problems seem to increase with the seriousness of the condition, and internalizing behaviour disorders, feelings of fatigue and worthlessness, and anxiety have also been reported, as well as difficulties with concentration, memory, and hyperactivity. Some of these effects may arise from the medications. For a thorough account of these issues, see Bray et al. (2008).

Encourage physical activities and remind students to monitor their symptoms. Inform students and parents about potential triggers likely to be introduced into the classroom. Medications may cause behaviour changes in children and adolescents, including poor attention span, lethargy, and irritability (Vail, 2005). Taking medication and having asthmatic episodes at school can make students self-conscious. You can help by arranging for the student to leave unobtrusively when necessary, providing a quiet supervised location in which the student can relax and take medication, and finding someone to remain with your class while you monitor the student with asthma.

### CYSTIC FIBROSIS

Today my mom told me I had no choice, and here I am in the hospital with pneumonia again. I'm sorry I can't be in our class play on Friday. I was really looking forward to that. Mom says I probably got overtired from all the rehearsals, and that might be why I am sick again. But I'm still glad I tried out for the play. I don't want CF to get in the way of having a life. I miss my friends from school. I hope they visit tomorrow.

*From the diary of Brittany, a grade 7 student with CF*

Cystic fibrosis (CF) is incurable, the result of an inherited genetic defect, and causes chronic lung problems and digestive disorders. Approximately one in every twenty-five hundred children in Canada is born with CF (www.ccff.ca). The lungs become covered with sticky mucus that is difficult to remove and promotes infection by bacteria. Most people with CF require frequent hospitalizations and continuous use of antibiotics. (Remember Brittany, whose situation was described in one of the cases that opened this chapter.) They take **enzyme supplements** so they can digest the nutrients in their food. Sometimes a feeding tube is necessary. Life expectancy, which was once only eight years, is now in the mid-thirties, and a lung transplant can extend that. Still, most persons with cystic fibrosis eventually die of lung disease (dePaepe et al., 2002; Korneluk, MacDonald, Cappelli, McGrath, & Heick, 1996).

The student with CF copes with a chronic cough and may need to have therapy during school to remove airway mucus. He or she will probably have an excessive appetite, combined with weight loss, and may need to eat during school hours. Bowel disturbances are common and embarrassing. Repeated bouts of pneumonia mean frequent absences, but communication with the family should ease the process of shifting learning to the hospital room. Cystic fibrosis can have a negative impact on learning. It may mean that a student requires differentiated instruction, because CF has been associated with depressed mood, anxiety, memory and concentration problems, as well as fatigue (dePaepe et al., 2002; Koscik et al., 2004). You might find it helpful to read the Teacher's Guide to CF (www.ccff.ca/pdf/Teachers_Guide.pdf). During adolescence you may witness a rebellion against treatments. Adolescents often need counselling to deal with delayed puberty (Johannesson et al., 1998) and to accept that their life expectancy may be shortened (Chesson, Chisholm, & Zaw, 2004), although recent first-person accounts suggest that many in the current generation of young adults with CF are determined to "beat" cystic fibrosis (e.g., Lipman, 2002, 2003).

Weblinks

CANADIAN CYSTIC FIBROSIS
FOUNDATION (CCFF)
www.ccff.ca

AMERICAN CYSTIC FIBROSIS FOUNDATION
www.cff.org

CYSTIC FIBROSIS WORLDWIDE
www.cfww.org

FOR PERSONAL STORIES (CCFF)
www.ccff.ca/page.asp?id=227

A TEACHER'S GUIDE TO CF
www.ccff.ca/pdf/Teachers_Guide.
pdf

### HIV AND AIDS

> Nobody sits beside me or picks me to work with them. I don't know why. I think it is because I am sick like my Mom. She says that when I am older, she will tell me all about it. It makes school hard because no one likes me. Some people are even afraid of me. But I am used to it now.
>
> *Paul, who is HIV positive, describing his experience in Grade 1 to the school psychologist*

All children today live in a world where **HIV** and **AIDS** are part of life. Human immunodeficiency virus (HIV) can be transmitted through unprotected sexual contact with individuals who have HIV, by sharing needles with infected persons, or through contact with infected blood from mucous membranes or broken skin. The virus can be passed prenatally from an infected mother to a child (DePaepe, 2002), though mother-to-child transmission of HIV has been nearly eliminated in Canada (Public Health Agency of Canada, 2008, www.phac-aspc.gc.ca/aids-sida/info/1_e.html). AIDS is caused by the presence of HIV. HIV makes one susceptible to fatal infections, but children often acquire neurological problems as well, including developmental disabilities, seizures, and behaviour exceptionalities (Hallahan & Kauffman, 2006). Canadian children with HIV and AIDS attend school and teachers are not always aware of their presence. Due to the stigma associated with their condition, many families have great difficulty disclosing to their children's teachers. In the latest data available for children, Health Canada's

Weblinks

CANADIAN AIDS TREATMENT
INFORMATION EXCHANGE (PROVIDES
FACT SHEETS IN MANY LANGUAGES)
www.catie.ca

CANADIAN ABORIGINAL AIDS NETWORK
www.caan.ca

*HIV and AIDS in Canada Surveillance Report* to December 2003 indicated that between 1 November 1985 and 31 December 2003, 678 children under the age of 15 tested positive for HIV. When the report was written, 430 children had AIDS in Canada (Canadian AIDS Society; www.cdnaids.ca/web/backgrnd.nsf/pages/cas-gen-0004). A study by Jillian Roberts of the University of Victoria and Kathleen Cairns of the University of Calgary (1999) reported that parents felt it was very important for them and their children with HIV or AIDS to feel welcome at school and for children to be able to socialize with their peers. Parents reported going to great lengths to teach themselves and their children proper ways of handling blood, to protect themselves and others, should a child be wounded or scraped at school. Teachers should be aware that if reasonable procedures are followed for preventing infections, there is no serious concern regarding transmission of HIV or AIDS in the classroom (Bigge et al., 2001; Huffman et al., 2003). Clark and Schwoyer (1994) described how teachers can ensure the use of precautions and maintain a safe environment, for instance, by keeping latex gloves available and having a first-aid kit in the classroom.

AIDS orphans are a reality in Canada as well as around the world (Evans & Becker, 2008), with over one thousand Canadian children having lost parents to AIDS. Indeed, the number of children affected by HIV and AIDS in Canada is greater than the number infected. The stigma and discrimination that surround these conditions continue to have a large impact on children infected and affected by HIV and AIDS.

## CANCER AND LEUKEMIA

> Kristopher described the positive impact of returning to school after each treatment for leukemia, "I liked everything about returning to school. If you have something you like, and they take it away, and then you go back, you like it a lot." He went on to say, "I really wanted to finish my work at school. I was feeling like I wouldn't pass because I was missing so much work."
>
> *Based on Sullivan et al., 2001*

Childhood **cancer**, particularly **leukemia**, is increasing. Recent data suggest leukemia strikes one in every twenty-five thousand and most often between the ages of 3 and 7. Survival rates for leukemia stand at about 80 percent (Sullivan, 2004). Cancer is relatively uncommon in children. In 2002, of nearly eight million Canadian children and adolescents younger than 20 years of age, an estimated thirteen hundred were diagnosed with cancer. Nevertheless, cancer is the most common disease-related cause of death, second only to intentional and unintentional injuries as the leading cause of death in this age group, excluding the first year of life. In 2002 there were approximately two hundred and fifty childhood deaths attributed to cancer (Public Health Agency of Canada, 2008; www.phac-aspc.gc.ca/ccdpc-cpcmc/program/cccscp-pcslce/facts_e.html). Although survival rates for pediatric cancer and leukemia are much better than in the past, the effects of these chronic illnesses persist, and maintaining a normal lifestyle is essential to positive adaptation (Prevatt et al., 2000). This includes attending school whenever possible because school is a normalizing factor (Sullivan et al., 2001). Effective interactive programs on CD-ROM inform children with leukemia and their parents about what to expect, and findings suggest that well-informed patients and families show increased feelings of control over the individual's health (e.g., Dragone et al., 2002; Van Dongen-Melman et al., 1998). Prevatt and her colleagues (2000) reviewed school reintegration programs and suggest that the educators and peers of

**Put into Practice**

Read widely about AIDS and HIV and about how you can inform students about these health conditions. Then plan a short unit that accomplishes some curriculum goals at the level that you teach and also informs students about AIDS and HIV. For examples, look at Ellen Goldfinch's (2007) course offered at Bishop's College School to young adolescents (appropriate for social studies) and a grade 7 science unit on the biology of HIV (Kesselman et al., 2007).

Keselman, A., Kaufman, D.R., Kramer, S., & Patel, V.L. (2007). Fostering conceptual change and critical reasoning about HIV and AIDS. *Journal of Research in Science Teaching, 44*(6), 844–863.

Watchirs, H. (2008). *AIDS Audit: HIV and Human Rights.* Aldershot, UK: Ashgate Pub. Ltd.

Boler, T., & Archer, D. (2008). *The Politics of Prevention: A Global Crisis in AIDS and Education.* London, UK: Pluto Press.

Visser-Valfrey, M. (2006). *Linking EDUCAIDS with Other On-Going Initiatives: An Overview of Opportunities, an Assessment of Challenges.* Paris: UNESCO.

**Further Reading**

On including children with childhood leukemia and cancer in the classroom:

Sullivan, N.A., Fulmer, D.L., & Zigmond, N. (2001). School: The normalizing factor for children with childhood leukemia. *Preventing School Failure, 46*(1), 4–13.

Prevatt, F.F., Heffer, R.W., & Lowe, P.A. (2000). A review of school reintegration programs for children with cancer. *Journal of School Psychology, 38,* 447–467.

Sullivan, N.A. (2004). *Walking with a shadow: Surviving childhood leukemia.* Portsmouth, NH: Greenwood Publishers.

these students participate in structured programs that answer their questions and make them much better informed, too. Sullivan (2001, 2004) suggests what educators can do to differentiate instruction for students with leukemia and cancer who miss a considerable amount of school, may be vulnerable to communicable diseases circulating in the classroom, and are often both exhausted and changed by their treatments (for example, they may be bald or have an amputation). Sullivan suggests that educators must appreciate the serious nature of the illness and be sensitive, collaborate with the hospital or home schooling teacher, provide opportunities for classmates to maintain contact during absences, and communicate frequently, proactively, and supportively with parents about the student's learning and psychosocial needs at school. Teachers may also find helpful suggestions in sources that provide guidance on including young people with cancer in other activities such as camping (e.g., Winfree et al., 2002).

## Summary

Students with low-incidence exceptionalities comprise only about 15 to 25 percent of all exceptional students. However, the number of students with chronic health conditions like asthma and allergies is growing quickly in Canada. Taken together, the students discussed in this chapter have diverse strengths, challenges, and needs. Many of them can succeed in your classroom. Remember that you will teach only two or three students in your career who have, for example, cystic fibrosis, and you may never be teaching more than a few students at a time who have low-incidence exceptionalities. Many of the strategies you have already learned will be effective in teaching these students, and you should draw on the experience and expertise of parents and in-school team members. While accommodations will usually be adequate, on occasion you may need to modify the curriculum or develop an alternate curriculum, especially for students with severe intellectual disabilities and autism.

In this chapter we focused on differentiating instruction for students with a number of low-incidence exceptionalities, including severe intellectual disabilities, autism, and Asperger syndrome. We considered adaptations for students who are deaf, who are hard of hearing, or who have visual impairments. The range of needs and strengths in students with these low-incidence exceptionalities is huge. Students with physical exceptionalities also benefit from differentiation. We focused on students with nervous system impairment—cerebral palsy, spina bifida, epilepsy, Tourette syndrome, brain injury, and fetal alcohol spectrum disorders—as well as two musculoskeletal conditions (muscular dystrophy and juvenile arthritis). The final area of concentration was chronic health conditions such as diabetes, allergies, asthma, cystic fibrosis, HIV and AIDS, and cancer and leukemia. It is customary to think of the physical and stamina limitations of students with physical and health conditions, as well as the possibility that they will need medication at school. However, meeting the social and emotional needs of these students is also important. Inclusion means more than the physical presence of students with low-incidence exceptionalities in regular classrooms for all or part of the day. Inclusion means making them feel part of the social and academic life of the class and the broader community.

# Key Terms

echolalia (p. 118)

low-incidence exceptionalities (p. 119)

physical disabilities (p. 119)

chronic health conditions (p. 119)

case coordinator (p. 119)

intellectual disability (ID) (p. 121)

American Association on Intellectual and Developmental Disabilities (AAIDD)(p. 121)

developmental disabilities / cognitive disabilities (p. 121)

chromosomal abnormalities (p. 123)

genetic screening (p. 123)

amniocentesis (p. 123)

self-care (p. 123)

voice synthesizer (p. 123)

functional curriculum (p. 124)

community-based (p. 124)

principles of fairness (p. 125)

autism spectrum disorders (ASD) (p. 126)

autism (p. 126)

perseveration (p. 127)

theory of mind (p. 127)

social stories (p. 129)

reinforcers (p. 130)

Asperger syndrome (AS) (p. 130)

hypersensitive (p. 131)

McGill Action Planning System (MAPS) (p. 131)

deaf (p. 132)

hard of hearing (p. 132)

hearing status (p. 133)

American Sign Language (ASL) (p. 134)

speech-reading (p. 136)

manipulatives (p. 136)

preteaching (p. 136)

amplification (p. 136)

hearing aids (p. 136)

frequency modulation (FM) systems (p. 136)

Deaf community (p. 137)

visual impairment (p. 138)

Braille (p. 138)

taped books (p. 138)

vision teacher (p. 138)

speech-activated (p. 140)

remission (p. 141)

nervous system impairment (p. 141)

neurological dysfunction (p. 141)

cerebral palsy (CP) (p. 142)

spina bifida (p. 143)

hydrocephalus (p. 143)

shunt (p. 143)

epilepsy (p. 143)

seizures (p. 143)

partial seizures (p. 144)

generalized seizures (p. 144)

simple absence seizure (petit mal) (p. 144)

tonic-clonic (grand mal) seizure (p. 144)

Tourette syndrome (TS) (p. 145)

tics (p. 145)

acquired brain injury (ABI) / head injury / traumatic brain injury (p. 146)

fetal alcohol spectrum disorders (FASD) (p. 148)

fetal alcohol syndrome (FAS) (p. 148)

partial fetal alcohol syndrome (PFAS) (p. 148)

alcohol-related neurodevelopmental disorder (ARND) (p. 148)

prenatal exposure to alcohol (p. 148)

fetal alcohol effects (FAE) (p. 149)

musculoskeletal conditions (p. 150)

Duchenne muscular dystrophy (DMD) (p. 150)

juvenile arthritis (JA) (p. 151)

inflammation (p. 151)

immune system (p. 151)

limited range of motion (p. 152)

chronic health condition impairment (p. 152)

diabetes (p. 154)

insulin injections (p. 154)

low blood sugar (hypoglycemia) (p. 154)

high blood sugar (hyperglycemia) (p. 154)

diabetes emergency kits (p. 154)

allergy (p. 156)

anaphylaxis/anaphylactic shock (p. 156)

allergic salute (p. 156)

epinephrine (p. 157)

EpiPen® (p. 157)

Ana-Kit® (p. 157)

MedicAlert® (p. 157)

allergen-free alternative (p. 157)

asthma (p. 157)

preventers (p. 158)

relievers (p. 158)

puffer (p. 158)

nebulizer (p. 158)

wheezing (p. 158)

cystic fibrosis (CF) (p. 160)

enzyme supplements (p. 160)

HIV (p. 160)

AIDS (p. 160)

cancer (p. 161)

leukemia (p. 162)

# Challenges for Reviewing Chapter 4

1. What does it mean for an exceptionality to be described as low-incidence? What low-incidence exceptionalities do you expect to have to be informed about during your upcoming year of teaching? Think about which physical and

health conditions you expect to have to understand and differentiate teaching for in your next teaching experience. Discuss with your peers why it is just as important to understand the psychosocial aspects of these exceptionalities and conditions as the physical aspects.

2. Read the brief description of Reid at the beginning of the section on teaching students with severe intellectual disabilities. How could you differentiate instruction for Reid so that he develops both his literacy skills and his workplace skills for the challenges he will meet as an adult trying to live as independently as possible?

3. Write a brief scenario that includes some of the greatest challenges to your teaching and management in a classroom with students with autism spectrum disorders—like Pamela in the opening case, who has autism, and Jason, described at the beginning of the section on ASD, who has Asperger syndrome. Describe how you could differentiate instruction to meet their needs.

4. You are currently a member of the in-school team for a student who is hard of hearing, and last year you fulfilled a similar role for a student who was deaf. Prepare to assume the role of one member of the team. The team includes a classroom teacher, a resource teacher, a principal, and a parent. Use the information in this chapter to develop a systematic approach to differentiating teaching and ensuring social participation of the student who is hard of hearing. Consider how this approach is similar to and different from what was done last year for the student who was deaf. You may want to role-play this scenario with some of your peers, who would each assume the role of a member of the team.

5. Amber, described at the beginning of the section on visual disabilities, is blind. Consider her learning needs. What are some of the most important things to remember when adapting teaching and assessment for Amber?

6. Many physical disabilities were described in this chapter. Develop a chart that includes these exceptionalities (i.e., cerebral palsy, spina bifida, epilepsy, Tourette syndrome, brain injury, fetal alcohol spectrum disorders, muscular dystrophy, juvenile arthritis) and one other you can think of. In the chart compare these exceptionalities on four dimensions, one of which is differentiating teaching. Compare your chart with the charts prepared by your peers. What dimensions are most important to teachers?

7. Consider what is meant by the term *chronic health condition*. Then compare the six chronic conditions described in this chapter, adding one more condition of which you are aware. Why must educators be knowledgeable about these chronic health conditions in order to meet their legal and ethical responsibilities? Provide convincing examples to support your position.

8. Return to the opening case of Brittany, who has cystic fibrosis. Answer the five questions that follow the case, focusing on Brittany. Talk with your peers. Consider the differences in answers given by secondary and elementary teachers. Consider the similarities in the issues raised by secondary and elementary teachers.

# Chapter 5

## Teaching for Diversity: Including Aboriginal Students, Students from Diverse Cultural Backgrounds, and Students Who Are at Risk

### Learner Objectives

After you have read this chapter, you will be able to:

1. Discuss how teachers can address the needs of Aboriginal students.

2. Describe how teachers can address the needs of students from diverse cultural backgrounds and consider what role differentiated instruction might have.

3. Discuss strategies for teaching students who are English language learners (ELL students), including differentiated instruction.

4. Describe how teachers can respond to incidents of inequity in the classroom and foster equitable treatment of all class members.

5. Explain how classroom teachers can differentiate curriculum for students at risk for failure, including students who live in poverty, are homeless, have been abused, or have experienced divorce.

**Ragu is in Dan Borenstein's grade 5 class.** Ragu experienced trauma in his home country before coming to Canada. This is Dan's fifth year of teaching but his first year working in the inner city. Ragu arrived in Canada recently by way of a refugee camp. Most days Ragu wanders the classroom or sits with his head on his arms. He enjoys his English as a second language (ESL) tutorial, where he is beginning to dictate stories to his tutor and read them back. All of Ragu's stories are about violence and killing, except one about games Ragu used to play with his best friend. Ragu told Dan that soldiers attacked them and his friend died. Ragu still has nightmares about it. Until he had to leave school two years ago, Ragu was a quick learner with high grades. Dan tries to communicate his high expectations to Ragu without pressuring him. Dan wonders how long he will have to wait for schoolwork to re-emerge as a priority for Ragu.

**Anita Harper is proud of her Aboriginal heritage.** She is a ceremonial dancer and her mother is a leader in her nation. Anita always spoke openly about her heritage in elementary school and expected to do the same when she entered South River Secondary School two months ago. Now two grade 12 boys taunt Anita after school while she waits for the bus. They call her "squaw" and humiliate her. Anita asks her homeroom teacher, Betty Bird, who is also Aboriginal, for advice. Anita says, "I should be able to work this out myself, but I can't. Teachers don't usually do anything, but you're different. You're like me." Betty Bird knows that only with support will Anita report the racist incidents to the administration. She wishes there were an Aboriginal counsellor at South River for the 120 Aboriginal students in this school of 700. There are so few Aboriginal educators that Betty knows they are fortunate to have three at South River. She will talk with the other two Aboriginal teachers about how they can support Anita and increase their efforts to make South River Secondary more inclusive for Aboriginal students.

1.  How can teachers respond to the situations of Ragu and Anita described in these case studies? What aspects of each situation are most likely to affect learning?

2.  With such a range of characteristics and learning needs, what do students like Ragu and Anita have in common?

3.  How frequently is a teacher likely to be teaching an Aboriginal or refugee student?

4.  What does each of these students need in order to be included in the social and academic life of the classroom and of the school?

5.  What community resources can a teacher access to ensure that each student learns?

# Introduction

This chapter illustrates the conceptual and pragmatic ties between exceptionality and other manifestations of diversity in Canadian society. Equity is the common driving force, and differentiation is the common teaching approach. You will learn about teaching students from Aboriginal cultures and from other cultural backgrounds. Certain issues are unique to the education of Aboriginal students, including the threatened extinction of Aboriginal languages and cultures. You will be challenged to identify your perspectives and question your stereotypes about diversity. Our focus here is also on students who are at risk for school failure for a variety of reasons. Poverty, homelessness, abuse, and other conditions are explored for their impact on learning and participation.

Differentiating teaching for these students is similar to the process explored in earlier chapters. However, fluctuations in students' circumstances and lack of documentation (e.g., no IEP) may mean that you receive less direction. School teams may not include these students in their mandates, although in some provinces funding is directed to the needs of diverse and at-risk students. While the specific causes of the need for sensitive and differentiated teaching vary greatly in the examples throughout this chapter, the process of ADAPTing is consistent, and equity and respect for diversity are central.

# Diversity and Equity in Canadian Society

Communities and schools in Canada are increasing in **diversity**. Sources of this diversity include immigration to Canada and our willingness to receive refugees. For example, there were 436,940 immigrant children and youth (16 and under) in Canada at the time of the 2006 census, and Statistics Canada projects that by 2017 more than 20 percent of the population of Canada will be members of a visible minority (Statistics Canada, 2007a). In addition, more than 200 languages are spoken in Canada, with 20 percent of the population reporting a mother tongue other than English or French, a growth of 18.5 percent since 2001 (Statistics Canada 2007d). Aboriginal families continue to move into urban areas, and the Aboriginal population increased by 45 percent from 1996 to 2006, nearly six times faster than the non-Aboriginal population in that period (Statistics Canada, 2007b). Other sources of the increasing diversity in Canadian schools include the growth of poverty, homelessness, and other social conditions that place Canadian youth at risk for failing to learn in school and for leaving school early, a subject of the research of Michael Ungar of Dalhousie University (e.g., 2005; also Saewyc et al., 2006; Tyler et al., 2007).

In Chapter 1 we discussed the *Charter of Rights and Freedoms*; the equality rights that apply to education cover the rights of all students: "Every individual is equal before and under the law and has a right to the equal protection of and equal benefit of the law without discrimination and, in particular, without discrimination based on race, national or ethnic origin, colour, religion, sex, age, or mental or physical disability" (section 15[1]). This part of the Charter applies to the courts and other institutions including schools.

## The Unique Role of Education, Schools, and Educators

Schools have a unique role in the creation of an inclusive society, for two reasons. First, unlike other institutions, schools are legally responsible for preparing all children and adolescents (including those who have disabilities or are members of minorities) to take meaningful roles as adults in our society. Second, schools have a legislated responsibility to prepare all children and adolescents to participate in an inclusive democracy. This means that you as a teacher are mandated to prepare our youth to accept all individuals (including those who have disabilities or are members of minorities) as fellow citizens.

### TEACHING CHALLENGES

There are many reasons for including in this text a broad discussion of teaching for **equity**. Having an inclusive classroom means creating a learning community in which *all* students feel accepted and safe. The students described in this chapter often benefit from differentiated teaching just as exceptional students do. This serves as a powerful reminder that many of the strategies you learn throughout this book apply to all of your students, not only those with IEPs.

Student needs are complex. A gifted student like Gurjit, described in Chapter 1, can also be a member of a cultural minority. A student with a behaviour disability like Urjo, described in Chapter 3, might be an English language learner (if so, Urjo would be referred to as an ELL student). Children who live in poverty can be at risk because of drug abuse in their family, and so on. To teach students with multiple needs, you will make use of any supports your community can provide—parents, cross-age tutors, volunteers, social workers, public health nurses, police officers, immigration counsellors, translators—in addition to school psychologists, consultants, and resource and ESL teachers. We are challenged to create classrooms that respect diversity and foster learning for *all* students.

Put into Practice

Locate some of the following resources and develop a series of activities to introduce your students to the history of Aboriginal cultures in Canada.

Green, R., with Fernandez, M. (1999), *The encyclopedia of the first peoples of North America.* Toronto: Douglas & McIntyre.

Cardinal, T., Highway, T., Johnston, B., King, T., Maracle, B., Maracle, L., Marchessault, J., Qitsualik, R.A., & Taylor, D.H. (2004). *Our story: Aboriginal voices on Canada's past.* Toronto: Doubleday.

Dickason, O.P. (2006) *A concise history of Canada's First Nations.* Don Mills, ON: Oxford University Press.

# Aboriginal Education

This section begins with a description of the history of **Aboriginal cultures** in Canada and of recent attempts to negotiate education that will help to preserve Aboriginal languages. The focus then moves to strategies for teaching Aboriginal students and for teaching all Canadian students about Aboriginal cultures.

## History of Aboriginal Cultures in Canada

It is impossible to say how many people lived in North America in 1492, but estimates range from one million to eighteen million (Wright, 2003). Archaeological evidence suggests that when Christopher Columbus visited, the Americas were inhabited to their carrying capacities for the ways of life being followed (Dickason, 2002, 2006). There were eleven language families and roughly fifty languages. Several regional economies coexisted. These were hunting-and-gathering cultures in the north and east, partly agricultural economies in the St. Lawrence River valley, buffalo-centred cultures on the plains, and salmon- and whale-based economies on the Pacific west coast. All of these cultures emphasized the group as well as the self (Dickason, 2006). All had delicate relationships with their natural environments until European settlers brought diseases with them. Then the Native populations were decimated by smallpox, and the traditional ways were altered forever. In light of history, the first sentence of the **Report of the Royal Commission on Aboriginal Peoples (RCAP Report)** (1996) sounds conciliatory: "Canada is a test case for a grand notion—the notion that dissimilar peoples can share lands, resources, power and dreams while respecting and sustaining their differences. The story of Canada is the story of many such peoples, trying and failing and trying again to live together in peace and harmony."

In 1991 four Aboriginal and three non-Aboriginal commissioners were appointed to investigate Aboriginal issues and advise the federal government. Canadians had just watched an armed conflict between Aboriginal and non-Aboriginal forces at Kanesatake (Oka). High rates of Aboriginal poverty, disease, and suicide were in the news (Dickason, 2006). The central conclusion of the RCAP Report (1996, http://epe.lac-bac.gc.ca/100/200/301/inac-ainc/royal_comm_aboriginal_peoples-e/biblio92.html) was that the policy of assimilation pursued by Canadian governments for one hundred and fifty years must change. "To bring about this fundamental change, Canadians need to understand that Aboriginal peoples are nations . . . political and cultural groups with values and lifeways distinct from those of other Canadians." An update to the RCAP Report is available at http://dsp-psd.pwgsc.gc.ca/Collection/R32-192-2000E.pdf. This report summarizes the government response (*Gathering Strength: Canada's Aboriginal Action Plan*, 1998) and acknowledges that both the Canadian Human Rights Commission and the United Nations Human Rights Committee have been critical of the government's response to the RCAP Report: "[M]uch more attention still needs to be given to pressing issues. . . ." Figure 5.1 offers some basic facts about Canada's Aboriginal peoples.

@

**Weblinks**

DEPARTMENT OF INDIAN AND NORTHERN AFFAIRS CANADA
www.ainc-inac.gc.ca/index-eng.asp

HIGHLIGHTS OF THE REPORT OF THE ROYAL COMMISSION ON ABORIGINAL PEOPLES
www.ainc-inac.gc.ca/ch/rcap/index_e.html

FIRST NATIONS UNIVERSITY OF CANADA
www.firstnationsuniversity.ca

## Differences Between Issues in Aboriginal Education and Multicultural Education

Aboriginal issues are distinct from multicultural issues. For example, many authors have made the point that Native peoples did not immigrate to a different cultural context thinking that they might have to change their ways to fit into the society of a foreign country (Bell, 2004). Rather, their country became foreign to them with the arrival of other peoples, and they had to deal with forced assimilation. Eber Hampton, of First Nations University of Canada in Saskatchewan, writes about "the world-shattering difference [in perspective] between the conquered and the conqueror" (1995, p. 41). Binding treaties were ignored, spiritual activities were outlawed, and children were forced to attend residential schools (Glavin, 2002; Roberts, 2006). Until 1985 the *Indian Act* listed four ways a Native person could lose his or her Indian status: "A Native woman could lose status by marrying a non-Native

*Larry Pierre of the Okanagan on the occasion of the First Nations Constitutional Conference, 1980, demanding Aboriginal participation in constitutional talks.*

## FIGURE 5.1 ABORIGINAL PEOPLES IN CANADA

**Who are the Aboriginal peoples in Canada?**
They are descendants of the original inhabitants of North America. The Canadian *Constitution Act* (1982) recognizes three separate Aboriginal peoples with unique heritages: Indians, Métis, and Inuit. Aboriginal people make up roughly 4 percent of the Canadian population (976 305 in the 2001 census and 1 172 790 in the 2006 census).

**What is a First Nation?**
This is a term that came into use in the 1970s to replace the word *Indian*, which many people found offensive. No legal definition of *First Nation* exists. There are 609 First Nations in Canada.

**Who are Indians?**
Although many Aboriginal people find the term *Indian* outdated and offensive, the *Constitution Act* (1982) uses this term to describe all Aboriginal people in Canada who are not Métis or Inuit. In the 2006 census 689 025 people identified themselves as North American Indian.

**Who are Métis people?**
They are people of mixed First Nations and European ancestry who identify themselves as Métis people, as distinct from First Nations people, Inuit, or non-Aboriginal people. In the 2006 census 389 785 people identified themselves as Métis.

**Who are Inuit people?**
They are Aboriginal people who live north of the treeline in Nunavut, Northwest Territories, northern Quebec, and Labrador. In the 2006 census 50 480 people identified themselves as Inuit.

**Who are Status, Non-Status, and Treaty Indians?**
A status Indian is a person who is registered under the *Indian Act*, while a non-status Indian is not registered as an Indian under the *Indian Act*. This may be because his or her ancestors were never registered or because he or she lost Indian status under former provisions of the *Indian Act*. A treaty Indian is a status Indian who belongs to a First Nation that signed a treaty with the Crown.

**How many Aboriginal people live on reserves?**
Roughly 60 percent of the Aboriginal people in Canada are status Indians and more than half of all status Indians live on Canada's 2370 reserves. Thus, about 30 percent of Aboriginal Canadians live on reserves.

**How many Aboriginal people live in urban areas?**
About 45 to 50 percent of self-identified Aboriginal people live in cities.

Sources: Based on information from Statistics Canada (www12.statcan.ca/english/census06/data/index.cfm) and the *Report of the Royal Commission on Aboriginal Peoples*.

**Weblinks**

ABORIGINAL EDUCATION CANADA PORTAL
www.aboriginalcanada.gc.ca/acp/site.nsf/en/index.html

THE FIRST PERSPECTIVE, NEWS OF INDIGENOUS PEOPLES OF CANADA
www.firstperspective.ca

WINDSPEAKER, CANADA'S NATIONAL ABORIGINAL NEWS SOURCE
www.ammsa.com/windspeaker

SASKATCHEWAN SAGE, THE ABORIGINAL NEWSPAPER OF SASKATCHEWAN
www.ammsa.com/sage

FIRST NATIONS DRUM: NEWS FROM CANADA'S NATIVE COMMUNITIES
www.firstnationsdrum.com

ALBERTA SWEETGRASS: ALBERTA'S ABORIGINAL NEWS PUBLICATION
www.ammsa.com/sweetgrass

EAGLE FEATHER NEWS
www.eaglefeathernews.com

man . . . by voluntarily enfranchising [voting], enlisting in the armed forces, or receiving a postsecondary degree. Few Native people were willing to trade their status for a degree" (Lickers, 2003, p. 56–57).

## The Importance of Education and Community in Preserving Disappearing Cultures

"The future of our people in Canada and the survival of our cultures, languages, and all that we value are directly linked to the education of our children" (George Erasmus, 1988, cited in the RCAP Report, 1996). The RCAP Report describes the goals of Aboriginal peoples for schools: First, to help children and adolescents learn the skills they need to participate fully in the economy. Second, to help children develop as citizens of Aboriginal nations, with the knowledge of their languages and traditions necessary for cultural continuity.

First Nations people across Canada need to ensure the passing on of **Aboriginal languages** and cultures to future Aboriginal generations. There is a sense of urgency in capturing the knowledge of elders and language speakers in their role as living libraries. "In many areas of Western Canada, Aboriginal languages are in danger of being lost. Unlike other languages, the Aboriginal languages cannot be revitalized or supported in other countries. The source of traditional knowledge and teaching is dying with the Elders. These languages belong in Canada. It is imperative that immediate actions be taken" (Aboriginal Language and Culture Project; www.wncp.ca). Similarly Atlantic Canada's First Nation Help Desk (www.firstnationhelp.com/ali) provides information about actions taken in Quebec as well as in Newfoundland and Labrador, Prince Edward Island, New Brunswick, and Nova Scotia to preserve and increase the use of Aboriginal languages. These initiatives include a talking dictionary (www.firstnationhelp.com/ali/dictionary.php), lessons, posters, and links to many resources. Birch Bark Comics, an illustrated series put together to tell the *Sacred Circles* story, can be accessed from http://prairielibrarian.wordpress.com/2007/09/18/graphic-novels-and-comics-by-aboriginal-peoples.

Initiatives to preserve and increase use of Aboriginal languages are critical. Of the approximately fifty Aboriginal languages spoken at the time of contact, four are extinct (Beothuk, Laurentian, Pentlatch, and Tsetsaut) and fifteen are nearly extinct (Gordon, 2005; www.ethnologue.com/show_country.asp?name=CA). Most others are endangered (Dickason, 2006). Only one in four Aboriginal people speaks an Aboriginal language, but second language learning of Aboriginal languages by young Aboriginal Canadians may offset the declining size of mother tongue populations (Norris, 2007).

The Western and Northern Canadian Protocol: Aboriginal Language and Culture Project (www.edu.gov.mb.ca/ab_languages) supports the implementation of a common curriculum framework for Aboriginal languages for all grades from kindergarten to grade 12. Website addresses of each member of the WNCP appear in the Weblinks sidebar. Each website shows the concrete steps and progress being made to preserve Aboriginal culture and languages in Western Canada.

## Working with the Community

The Assembly of First Nations (http://afn.ca) and the RCAP emphasize that First Nations must assume responsibility for reserve schools. However, almost 70 percent of Aboriginal children attend neighbourhood schools, not reserve schools. Thus neighbourhood schools face challenges in developing community-based programming with Aboriginal parents and communities. The experiences of those engaged in this process suggest that educators must be respectful listeners and the school must empower the community through genuine collaboration. Tracy Friedel (1999) of the University of Alberta studied a parents' council in which Aboriginal parents took an active role. She recommends the participation of Aboriginal community organizations as well as individuals. And the experiences of Bill Murphy and Debbie Pushor (2004) suggest Friedel may be right: they describe how, as Aboriginal parents, they are "involved in most if not all of the parent roles" described in the research, and yet "we are not feeling like partners in our children's schools" (p. 221). Perhaps the difficulties arise from the incompatibility of school

**Weblinks**

ASSEMBLY OF FIRST NATIONS
http://afn.ca

MÉTIS NATIONAL COUNCIL
www.metisnation.ca

CONGRESS OF ABORIGINAL PEOPLES (REPRESENTING OFF-RESERVE INDIAN AND MÉTIS PEOPLE)
www.abo-peoples.org/mainmenu.html

ABORIGINAL CANADA PORTAL
www.aboriginalcanada.gc.ca/acp/site.nsf/en/index.html

**Weblinks**

Websites of all members of the Western and Northern Canadian Protocol (WNCP):

MANITOBA EDUCATION, CITIZENSHIP, AND YOUTH ABORIGINAL EDUCATION AND TRAINING
www.edu.gov.mb.ca/abedu/languages.html

SASKATCHEWAN FIRST NATIONS AND MÉTIS EDUCATION BRANCH
www.sasklearning.gov.sk.ca/branches/fn-me/learning.shtml

ALBERTA EDUCATION ABORIGINAL LANGUAGES PROGRAM
www.education.gov.ab.ca/k_12/curriculum/bySubject/aborigin/default.asp

BRITISH COLUMBIA MINISTRY OF EDUCATION: ABORIGINAL EDUCATION
www.bced.gov.bc.ca/abed

YUKON DEPARTMENT OF EDUCATION: FIRST NATION RESOURCES
www.yesnet.yk.ca/firstnations/index.html

ABORIGINAL LANGUAGE AND CULTURE PROJECT OF THE WNCP
www.wncp.ca

NUNAVUT DEPARTMENT OF EDUCATION
www.gov.nu.ca/education/eng

**Further Reading**

About the maintenance and renewal of Aboriginal languages and culture:

NWT Literacy Council's Languages of the Land, www.nwt.literacy. ca/resources/aborig/land/ language.pdf

Norris, M.J. (2007, Summer). Aboriginal languages in Canada: Emerging trends and perspectives on second language acquisition. *Canadian Social Trends, 83*, 20–28.

Assembly of First Nations (1990). *Towards linguistic justice for First Nations.* Ottawa: Assembly of First Nations, Education Secretariat.

Toulouse, I.B. (2003). Transference of concepts from Ojibwe into English contexts. *Canadian Journal of Native Education, 27*(1), 84–88.

McLeod, Y. (2003). Change makers: Empowering ourselves thro' the education and culture of aboriginal languages: A collaborative team effort. *Canadian Journal of Native Education, 27*(1), 108–126.

Hallett, D., Chandler, M.J., & Lalonde, C.E. (2007). Aboriginal language knowledge and youth suicide. *Cognitive Development, 22*(3), 392–399.

Andrews, T.J., & Olney, J. (2007). Potlatch and powwow: Dynamics of culture through lives lived dancing. *American Indian Culture and Research Journal, 31*(1), 63–108.

Lalonde, C. (2003). Counting the costs of failures of personal and cultural continuity. *Human Development, 46*(2/3), 137–144.

structures and Aboriginal cultural values and practices (Yatt Kanu, 2005, University of Manitoba). To bridge this gap, the Alberta Department of Special Education has published *A Handbook for Aboriginal Parents of Children with Special Needs*, authored by members of the Aboriginal community (Crowchief-McHugh et al., 2000).

In a series of three reports, each including the title *Sharing Our Success*, the Society for the Advancement of Excellence in Education has published case studies of schools producing tangible progress for Aboriginal learners, neighbourhood schools and band schools with a range of 35 percent to 100 percent Aboriginal students. In the patterns drawn from the data, it can be seen that these schools provided culturally relevant learning experiences, affirmed students' pride in their identity, and had a high percentage of Aboriginal staff and quality staff development. Aboriginal language immersion programs were present in many of the schools. These twenty schools were characterized by high expectations, high levels of support for students, and proactive administrative approaches (Bell, 2004; Fulford, 2007a, 2007b).

The University of Northern British Columbia (UNBC) has an institutional mandate to partner with rural and urban Aboriginal communities. Evans, McDonald, and Nyce (1999) recommend mutual autonomy, a respectful approach, and inclusion of Aboriginal individuals and communities. They describe the three parts of the UNBC approach:

- a culturally relevant education and opportunities for students to learn directly from Aboriginal people
- Aboriginal studies infused throughout the curricula for all students
- direct support to Aboriginal students, and a sense of community through the First Nations Centre

## Strategies and Approaches: Putting Community at the Heart

Much has been written about Aboriginal education and the importance of knowing about individual First Nations. It is also generally true that Aboriginal peoples have a holistic perspective and view education, culture, and language as intimately related (e.g., Binda & Calliou, 2001; Castellano, Davis, & Lahache, 2000; Dickason, 2006). Recent curriculum documents provide guidance for strengthening education, culture, and language simultaneously while focusing on community. The next sections elaborate on the three strategies apparent in the UNBC approach.

### CULTURALLY RESPONSIVE CURRICULUM AND OPPORTUNITIES TO LEARN DIRECTLY FROM ABORIGINAL PEOPLE

Many who teach Aboriginal students are neither of Aboriginal heritage nor knowledgeable about Aboriginal cultures. Such teachers must learn to develop a **culturally responsive curriculum**. Ann Pohl (1997), a non-Aboriginal, advises teachers like her to become informed about the local Aboriginal community through reading and by talking with Aboriginal people. A friendship centre or band office can help you contact chiefs, elders, and tribal or band councils. First, focus on the First Nation on whose traditional territory your school is located. "It is a respectful protocol, when working with Aboriginal people, to acknowledge the traditional territory on which you are living and working" (BC Ministry of Education, *Shared Learnings*, 2006, p. 13; www.bced.gov.bc.ca/abed/shared.pdf). *Aboriginal Studies 10: Aboriginal Perspectives, Teacher Resource* (2004) contains a detailed description of how to arrange a visit to an Aboriginal community (p. 424) and how to host an elder in the classroom (p. 428). It also explains how protocols can show respect, contribute to trust, and improve relationships with Aboriginal communities. After learning about local Aboriginal culture, focus on the territories and cultures from which your students and their families originate.

Carol Butler (Butler & Egnatoff, 2002), a teacher in eastern Ontario, describes the process of collaborating with local Aboriginal leaders to develop and teach an arts-based unit on Aboriginal peoples. Mohawk elders, artists, storytellers, and dancers taught in the unit, *Cultural Awareness Through the Arts* (Butler & Swain, 1996). Aboriginal protocol also suggests that you ask permission before telling another culture's sacred tales (see Benton-Benai, 1988).

Teaching materials such as the video series *First Nations: The Circle Unbroken* (Bob et al., 1993; Williams et al., 1998), books (e.g., Roberts, 2006) and websites (e.g., www.innu.ca) will help you to bring Aboriginal voices into the classroom. Harvey McCue of Trent University authored *The Learning Circle: Activities on First Nations in Canada* (2000). The Canada Race Relations Foundation (2002) distributes *Learning About Walking in Beauty: Placing Aboriginal Perspectives in Canadian Classrooms*. Angela Ward (Ward & Bouvier, 2001) of the University of Saskatchewan describes an Aboriginal teacher learning the stories and cultures of many First Nations to help the Aboriginal children in her classroom feel proud of their heritages and feel a connection to her teaching. There were posters to celebrate traditional values (respect yourself, your elders, and the land), children's illustrations of legends, and many books with a connection to Aboriginal life.

"Non-Native teachers who are the most successful [teaching Aboriginal students] are those who are continually learning, who understand and accept Native ways, and who can then transmit values, beliefs, and behavioral norms which are consistent with those of the community" (Gilliland, 1999). In this process, question your taken-for-granted assumptions; you might begin with a CD from the National Film Board, "Qallunaat! Why White People Are Funny," and with the strategies of critical analysis adapted from the guide for *First Nations: The Circle Unbroken* (Williams et al., 1998, p. 8):

- Ask how you know what you know.
- Search for the biases in your socialization and in what you have been told about Aboriginal peoples.
- Consider the competing interests and powers that might have influenced your learning.
- Hunt your assumptions—they may be buried deeply under your positions. Question them.
- Ask whose interests are served by what you have learned about Aboriginal peoples.
- Identify social and political problems. Look for systemic sources of these problems.

You can show respect by adopting teaching approaches consistent with traditional Aboriginal experiential learning. Arlene Stairs (1991), who taught at Queen's University, provides a poignant description of Aboriginal children learning to sew

**What do you think?**

Preview some of the nine videos in the series *First Nations: The Circle Unbroken* (1993, 1998) or the videos in the series *Finding Our Talk* (2001), Episodes 1–13, and *Finding Our Talk II* (2002), Episodes 1–13 (both Montreal: Mushkeg Media Inc.). Do they help you understand the perspectives of Aboriginal peoples? If you are Aboriginal, do these videos represent your perspective?

**Put into Practice**

Develop an annotated bibliography of references for teaching and learning materials on Aboriginal education. To begin, consult:

Van Etten, J. (1996). *Resource reading list: An annotated bibliography of recommended works by and about Native peoples.* Toronto: Canadian Alliance in Solidarity with Native Peoples.

Max, K.E. (2003). *Joining the circle: Working as an ally in Aboriginal education.* Ottawa: National Library of Canada.

Roberts, J. (2006). *First Nations, Inuit, and Métis peoples: Exploring their past, present, and future.* Toronto: Edmond Montgomery Publications. (Teacher's resource available.)

Indian and Northern Affairs Canada (2007). *Share in the celebration! National Aboriginal Day is June 21: Learning and activity guide.* Ottawa: Minister of Public Works and Government Services Canada.

Munro, R. (2005). *Canada's first peoples.* Markham, ON: Fitzhenry and Whiteside. (From *Canada: A People's History*.)

## TABLE 5.1  STRATEGIES FOR ABORIGINAL EDUCATION

| Strategy | Examples |
| --- | --- |
| Engage students in Aboriginal culture through the arts | Invite storytellers, singers, dancers, painters, weavers, and other artists from the Aboriginal community to collaborate |
| Help students to understand Aboriginal perspectives | Provide readings, etc., at the students' developmental level: fiction, reports, films from an Aboriginal point of view |
| | Invite speakers who are comfortable telling their stories and providing their perspectives |
| Use Aboriginal communication and participant structures | The talking circle, where the right to speak is indicated by passing a concrete object such as a feather |
| Explicitly discuss Aboriginal values | Teach environmental education through an Aboriginal perspective, "caring for the earth" |
| Help students to think critically about complex issues such as racism, cultural identity | Deal with sensitive issues and controversial topics in a caring and proactive way |
| | Use video series like *First Nations: The Circle Unbroken* to teach about current issues |

**Put into Practice**

Kainai Board of Education, Métis Nation of Alberta, Northland School Division, & Tribal Chiefs Institute of Treaty Six. (2004). *Aboriginal Studies 10: Aboriginal Perspectives.* Edmonton, AB: Duval House Publishing. (Teacher's resource available.)

Kainai Board of Education, Métis Nation of Alberta, Northland School Division, & Tribal Chiefs Institute of Treaty Six. (2005). *Aboriginal Studies 20: People and Cultural Change.* Edmonton, AB: Duval House Publishing. (Teacher's resource available.)

Kainai Board of Education, Métis Nation of Alberta, Northland School Division, & Tribal Chiefs Institute of Treaty Six. (2005). *Aboriginal Studies 30: Contemporary issues.* Edmonton, AB: Duval House Publishing. (Teacher's resource available.)

The Curriculum Review Team (2005). *Aboriginal peoples & European explorers: An integrated unit for grade 6.* Toronto, ON: Ontario Ministry of Education. http://cup.org/public/units55/AbPeEuEx.pdf.

### What do you think?

Why is it important for teachers to "hunt their assumptions" and cultural stereotypes? Discuss with your peers what makes these undertakings so challenging. Write an action plan for yourself to work toward these professional goals.

garments by watching. This suggests that replacing the verbal with the visual is a good place to begin. **Experiential learning** includes field trips, role-playing, designing, and making. Oral presentations reflect the oral tradition of Aboriginal cultures. Do not assume that Aboriginal students are knowledgeable about the traditions of their people. Aboriginal students appreciate learning directly from **Aboriginal elders** and artists (Butler & Egnatoff, 2002). Table 5.1 presents strategies for Aboriginal education.

### INFUSION OF ABORIGINAL STUDIES THROUGHOUT THE CURRICULUM FOR ALL

The second approach overlaps with and strengthens the first. Learning about Aboriginal cultures, developing respectful teaching, and involving the local Aboriginal community will ensure the **infusion** of Aboriginal studies throughout the curriculum for all students. Many provinces have policies that reflect this approach. For example, the first goal in Alberta Education's (2002) policy framework on First Nations, Métis, and Innu education is to "increase and strengthen knowledge and understanding among all Albertans of First Nations, Métis, and Innu governance, history, treaty, and Aboriginal rights, lands, cultures and languages" (p. 2).

Some recently developed resources can guide schools in this process:

- Manitoba Education, Citizenship and Youth. Aboriginal education, kindergarten to grade 12—Incorporating Aboriginal perspectives: A theme-based curricular approach. www.edu.gov.mb.ca/k12/abedu/perspectives/index.html.
- Toulouse, P.R. (2008, March). *Integrating Aboriginal teaching and values into the classroom* (What Works? Research into Practice). Toronto: Ontario Literacy and Numeracy Secretariat. www.edu.gov.on.ca/eng/literacynumeracy/inspire/research/whatWorks.html.

- B.C. Ministry of Education. (1998). Planning guide and framework for development of Aboriginal learning Resources. www.bced.gov.bc.ca/abed/planguide.
- B.C. Ministry of Education. (1998). *Shared learnings: Integrating B.C. Aboriginal content, K–10.* www.bced.gov.bc.ca/abed/descrip.htm.
- Manitoba Education. (2003). Integrating Aboriginal perspectives into curricula: A resource for curriculum developers, teachers, and administrators. www.edu.gov.mb.ca/k12/docs/policy/abpersp/ab_persp.pdf.
- Coalition for the Advancement of Aboriginal Studies (CAAS). www.edu.yorku.ca/caas.
- Lakehead Public Schools: Aboriginal presence in our schools. www.lakeheadschools.ca/public/aboriginal_ed/AE_Guide_Feb07.pdf

For infusing Aboriginal studies throughout the curriculum, consider *The Learning Circle* in three volumes (activities for ages 4 to 7, 8 to 11, and 12 to 14; www.ainc-inac.gc.ca/ks/12010_e.html). For example, Unit 6 in the volume for students aged 8 to 11 is entitled "First Nations and the Environment." The two objectives are to learn how First Nations viewed their responsibilities to the land and to explore how students' behaviour and actions affect the environment. The activities range from writing poetry through planning sustainable development in an expanding community. Each activity is debriefed to communicate First Nations' perspectives as the Earth's stewards. *Shared Learnings* (www.bced.gov.bc.ca/abed/descrip.htm) is also made up of activities to integrate Aboriginal content into K–10 curricula. One activity, entitled "Using the Internet to Learn about Aboriginal Peoples," challenges secondary students to visit websites to learn about traditional stories, legends, and artwork and to answer questions about Aboriginal people in modern society.

## DIRECT SUPPORT TO ABORIGINAL STUDENTS

The third approach, providing direct services to Aboriginal students, should include much more than the remedial strategies used in the past. Providing opportunities to learn or strengthen **heritage languages** will be vital, as will a sense of community. You can view the *Common Curriculum Framework for Aboriginal Language and Culture Programs, Kindergarten to Grade 12* (Western and Northern Canadian Protocol for Collaboration in Basic Education, 2000) at www.edu.gov.mb.ca/ab_languages.

These are school-based approaches that demand we be knowledgeable about, sensitive to, and respectful of the cultures of individual Aboriginal students. Each of us can do this by learning about our students and their heritages—from them, their parents, and the community.

At UNBC a **sense of community** was fostered through the First Nations Centre, which provides a place where Aboriginal culture is the norm, not on the periphery. Most universities and colleges have such centres, but they are rare within secondary and elementary schools. Counselling, tutoring, and socializing can be provided in such a context. In an elementary classroom, you could create a place where Aboriginal symbols and ways are dominant, perhaps a "circle" for reflection and quiet talk. Secondary schools with Aboriginal counsellors can create a First Nations Centre. Providing Aboriginal counsellors is one of the recommendations of the *Ontario First Nation, Métis, and Inuit Education Policy Framework* (2007) because without them it is not possible to provide culturally responsive contexts for teaching and counselling (Long et al., 2006; Wihak & Merali, 2007).

**Further Reading**

Joe, D. (1999). *Salmon Boy: A legend of the Sechelt people.* Madeira Park, BC: Nightwood Editions. (Teaches respect for the environment. Primary grades.)

Plain, F. (1989). *Eagle Feather: An honour.* Winnipeg: Pemmican Publications. (A story of an Ojibwa boy. Primary grades.)

Thompson, S. (1991). *Cheryl Bibalhats/Cheryl's potlatch.* Vanderhoof, BC: Yinka Dene Language Institute. (Book written in Carrier and English about a Carrier child's naming ceremony and the potlatch in her honour. Primary grades.)

Carvell, M. (2004). *Who will tell my brother?* New York: Hyperion Books. (Story of a boy trying to remove offensive mascots from his school. Junior high and secondary level.)

Monture-Angus, P. (1995). *Thunder in my soul: A Mohawk woman speaks.* Halifax: Fernwood Press. (Autobiography. Grades 10 to 12.)

**Weblinks**

FIRST PEOPLES ON SCHOOLNET
www.fnschools.ca

ABORIGINAL YOUTH NETWORK
www.ayn.ca

INDIAN AND NORTHERN AFFAIRS CANADA, KIDS' STOP
www.ainc-inac.gc.ca/ks/index_e.html

INDIAN AND NORTHERN AFFAIRS CANADA, LEARNING RESOURCES
www.ainc-inac.gc.ca/ks/12000_e.html

CENTER FOR WORLD INDIGENOUS STUDIES
www.cwis.org/index.php

**Weblinks**
**On preparing to teach about Aboriginal culture:**

FOUR DIRECTIONS TEACHINGS (ON THE BLACKFOOT, CREE, OJIBWE, MOHAWK, AND MI'KMAQ BY THE NATIONAL INDIGENOUS LITERACY ASSOCIATION) …
www.fourdirectionsteachings.
com/index.html

… AND TEACHER'S RESOURCE KIT
www.fourdirectionsteachings.
com/resources.html

STATISTICS CANADA LESSON ON DEMOGRAPHICS OF THE ABORIGINAL POPULATION IN CANADA
www12.statcan.ca/english/
census01/teacher%27s_kit/
activity11.cfm

NATIONAL FILM BOARD OF CANADA (NFB) FILMS ON ABORIGINAL PEOPLES
www.nfb.ca/enclasse/doclens/
visau/index.php?mode=
home&language=english

ONLINE ATLAS OF CANADA: ABORIGINAL SOCIETIES OF CANADA—LESSON DESCRIPTION (STATISTICS CANADA)
URL text
http://atlas.nrcan.gc.ca/site/
english/learningresources/
lesson_plans/elementary_school/
nb_es.htm

THE CANADIAN ENCYCLOPEDIA
www.thecandianencyclopedia.com
(Search for Aboriginal culture.)

**Weblinks**

THE INNU NATION
www.innu.ca

VIRTUAL MUSEUM CANADA: TEACHERS' CENTRE
www.virtualmuseum.ca/English/
Teacher/aboriginal_people.html

ABORIGINAL STUDIES CENTRE, TORONTO DISTRICT SCHOOL BOARD
www.tdsb.on.ca/_site/ViewItem.
asp?siteid=185&menuid=
781&pageid=603

# Teaching Students from Culturally Diverse Backgrounds

Canadian classrooms have been increasing in racial, cultural, and linguistic diversity, and this trend is expected to continue. The percentage of Canadians who were visible minorities in the last three census reports was 11.2 percent in 1996 (of the total population of 28 846 761), 13.4 percent in 2001 (30 007 094), and 16.2 percent in 2006 (31 612 897) (Statistics Canada, 2006 Census Trends, www12.statcan.ca/english/census06/data/trends). Almost 20 percent of people in the 2006 census have been or are now landed immigrants, and almost 20 percent report neither English nor French as their mother tongue.

The reasons that students from **culturally diverse backgrounds** can encounter difficulties in school are complex. These students often experience discrimination in society and lack role models because most teachers are from the majority culture. Societal expectations and realities for these students are often contradictory. Although they are told to aim high, low teacher expectations can influence their effort and participation. Schools may use discriminatory assessment practices and textbooks that promote stereotypes and omit culturally important information. This section discusses measures that can begin to rectify discriminatory practices—cultural awareness, high teacher expectations, culturally responsive teaching, co-operative learning, and teachers as role models.

## Being Culturally Aware and Questioning Assumptions

Understanding students who are members of diverse groups involves us in recognizing the nature of their experiences in Canada and of our own. In a book with the poignant title . . . *But Where Are You Really From?*, Hazelle Palmer (1997) describes how this question "keeps us forever foreign, forever immigrants to Canada" (p. vi). Sometimes teachers' cultural insensitivity can contribute to miscommunication, distrust, and negative school experiences. Keren Brethwaite (1996) described a teacher who had not heard a grade 5 girl from the Caribbean read in class. She assessed the student as unable to read and informed the mother at a parent–teacher conference. The mother protested that the girl read fluently at home. "So she brought a Bible to the school, and to the amazement of the teacher, the student read from it fluently. The teacher later recalled that she learned a very important lesson . . . that parent and teacher often see students from different perspectives" (p. 109). Because the student had not shown her reading ability at school, the teacher assumed she could not read—a powerful reminder of the need for **cultural awareness**. In their edited volume *The Great White North? Exploring Whiteness, Privilege, and Identity in Education*, Carr and Lund (2007) bring together a collection of papers that underline the importance of white people understanding not just the racialization of others, but their own whiteness and the privilege that it bestows (e.g., McCaskell, 2007). This is an important issue for teachers because the majority of teachers in Canada are white and thus the culture that pervades Canadian schools is the culture of whiteness.

The implication is that white teachers must know their own whiteness before they can embrace social justice as allies of many of the students they teach and before they can understand the lives of these students. Teachers are responsible for developing an understanding of how their students might approach learning because of their backgrounds. For example, some students don't ask questions of the teacher, an authority figure, and some students don't participate in the classroom until they feel very comfortable. A teacher who came to Canada from Hong Kong when she was a child describes why she rarely answered questions in class: "We were constantly being asked for our opinion and I was never taught [to give my opinion] . . . and I would always fear that question" (Lam, 1996, p. 33). And a student from China said, "I am not brave enough. . . . I wish I had the courage but I don't" (Zhou et al., 2005). If you understand this reticence in a student, you can do more to help him or her feel comfortable.

Not all students from a similar cultural background will have similar characteristics. Jo-Anne Dillabough and her colleagues from the University of British Columbia (2005) interviewed adolescents over the period of a year about their experiences of exclusion in relation to urban schooling and about gaining status in their youth subculture. They describe in depth the experiences of individuals, of both sexes, from a range of ethnic backgrounds including Afro-Caribbean students in their paper titled "Ginas, Thugs, and Gangstas: Young People's Struggles to 'Become Somebody' in Working Class Urban Canada." In contrast, Henry Codjoe (2006) focused on the experiences of black students in an urban context who achieved academic success in spite of adversity and many of the influences described in Dillabough's paper. These students all showed pride in their heritage and knowledge about their cultural backgrounds. Codjoe asserts that "[i]n spite of racism and hostile school environments, black students can also develop successful academic skills," (p. 50), and that we need to be aware of the cultural backgrounds of our students while still regarding them as individuals.

## High Expectations and Respectful Treatment

What does it feel like to be a student from a visible minority? In interviews, black youth told George Dei (2003) of the University of Toronto about three main perceptions of their school experiences: differential treatment by race, inadequate curriculum and teaching approaches, and absence of minority teachers. Students described low teacher expectations and racist incidents: "I mean the way they treat you the way they talk to you it's just different than how they talk to white students" (p. 49). An Asian teacher described a racist experience when she was a student with a teacher who assumed from her appearance that she could not speak English (Lam, 1996, p. 22). Patrick Solomon (1992) of York University found that dominant-group teachers reported differential expectations for students from different racial backgrounds. We have to confront the racism of low expectations and ask hard questions of all students, including minority students (Landsman, 2004). Such expectations can influence teaching approaches and student–teacher relations.

If we teach with low expectations and students are unchallenged, they are unlikely to learn. Enid Lee (1985) of Toronto describes how students sometimes perform accordingly and describe themselves as incapable. Students from some racial backgrounds are more likely to be streamed into less challenging courses (Lewis, 1992) or into particular subject areas but denied opportunities to develop in other important areas. In an articulate letter to his teachers, Kai James suggests, "Like all other students, Black students come to school with expectations that they will

**Further Reading**

About multiculturalism and science teaching:

Grant, C.A., & Sleeter, C.E. (2007). *Turning on learning: Five approaches for multicultural teaching plans for race, class, gender, and disability.* Hoboken, NJ: Wiley Jossey-Bass Education.

Van Eijck, M., & Roth, W.-M. (2007). Keeping the local local: Recalibrating the status of science and traditional ecological knowledge (TEK) in education. *Science Education, 91*(6), 926–947.

Hines, S.M. (2007). *Multicultural science education: Theory, practice, and promise.* New York: Peter Lang Pub.

Krugly-Smolska, E. (1996). Scientific culture, multiculturalism and the science classroom. *Science and Education, 5*(1), 21–29.

Bardwell, G., & Kincaid, E. (2005). A rationale for cultural awareness in the science classroom. *Science Teacher, 72*(3), 32–35.

do well," but teachers believe that "we are more likely to succeed in sports than in academics" (1996, p. 303). Kai asks to be taken seriously as a student (p. 304). Teachers who hold high expectations for their students have been found to spend more time providing a framework for students' learning—better explanations, more challenging questions, and more feedback—and to manage their students' behaviour more positively (Rubie-Davies, 2007). A study conducted in Canada, Australia, and New Zealand reported that principals effective in culturally diverse schools had four common characteristics: (a) holding high expectations for all students and rejecting an "excuse culture"; (b) making a strong commitment to social justice principles, which they embedded in school practices and culture; (c) accepting and accommodating differences, using the diversity of cultures as a school strength; and (d) celebrating individual and group differences through a wide range of cultural and sporting activities (Billot, Goddard, & Cranston, 2007). Figure 5.2 includes a list of strategies for teachers to use in culturally diverse classrooms.

## FIGURE 5.2 STRATEGIES FOR TEACHERS IN CLASSES WITH HIGH DIVERSITY

- Ensure that all students can see themselves in the posters, encouragements, and adornments on your classroom walls.
- Learn about the cultures of all your students from the students and their parents. Be a good listener.
- Incorporate your students' cultures into the learning environment.
- Use non-threatening activities to find out how prepared your students are for the topics that you are about to teach.
- Become aware of the language proficiencies and needs of ELL students. Talk with them individually in a quiet place to help to understand their spoken language. Consult with a language resource teacher or your principal for information.
- Accommodate cultural diversity and ensure you make your teaching meaningful for all your students.
- Read about anti-racist education and actively look for ways to reduce the racism your students experience at school.
- Respond quickly and firmly when you see or hear racist behaviour in the school or the schoolyard.
- Work at understanding how your own stereotypes might interfere with your teaching equitably in a culturally diverse school.
- Examine your topics, materials, and teaching methods for bias.
- Develop activities that truly engage students, and teach them by degrees how to take responsibility for their own engagement with learning. Don't assume they know how to collaborate or co-operate to learn. Teach them how.
- Establish legitimate standards for classroom work, and make the necessary efforts to ensure that all students reach these standards; this may mean making adaptations or accommodations.
- Help all students to relate their lives and issues to classroom learning.
- Model the kind of caring, respectful, and community behaviour that you expect of your students.
- Let your students know when they are meeting your expectations. Positive feedback is essential for enhancing appropriate behaviour and engagement with learning in the classroom.

Source: Hutchinson, N.L. (2004). *Teaching exceptional children and adolescents: A Canadian casebook* (2nd ed.), p. 116. Toronto: Allyn and Bacon. Reprinted with permission of Pearson Education Canada, Inc.

# Culturally Relevant Curriculum and Culturally Responsive Teaching

Minority students in Dei's (2003) interviews expressed concerns about not seeing themselves portrayed in Canadian history or literature. Nancy Hoo Kong (1996) wrote about "the history curriculum that rendered my racial group invisible" (p. 59). Black History Month (February) has offered schools an opportunity to highlight the accomplishments and cultures of black Canadians. In some Canadian schools, May has become South Asian History Month, but what about all the cultures that don't have a special month? And what messages does such an approach send—does it reinforce stereotypes? If we are to truly honour the heritage of our students, we need to address the values, history, current relations, and power relationships that shape a culture, invite representatives from local advocacy groups, and respect the diversity within any group (Menkart, 2003). And this will still not be enough (Scott, 2001; Solomon & Levine-Rasky, 2003). Kai James suggested in his letter, "What we need is a curriculum that all students can relate to and that will motivate us to be the best we can be by introducing us to people like us" (1996, p. 302).

Strategically applying cultural resources in your classroom curriculum is appropriate whether you teach elementary students or specialize in secondary science, and whether you teach predominantly one social group or many distinct social groups of students. All students need to appreciate the role in history of the groups that make up our diverse country. Change of this magnitude calls for inclusive provincial curricula in addition to teachers' making the classroom curriculum culturally diverse. Solomon and Cynthia Levine-Rasky of Queen's University (2003) report an elementary teacher whose views have evolved, saying: "The content of the curricular program should change because the social fabric of the society is full of different cultures and different approaches to life. . . . [T]his should now be an obligation, a part of the curriculum, in order to prepare the kids to really live the challenge of the diversity" (p. 47).

Ratna Ghosh of McGill University and Ali Abdi of the University of Alberta (2004) remind us that non-discrimination involves being colour sensitive and being aware of differences rather than concealing them, including differences in experiences and culture.

**Cultural relevance** may be more straightforward in subjects like social studies and literature. Exemplary curricula in social studies include *Coming to Gum San: The Story of Chinese Canadians* by Shehla Burney (1995) of Queen's University. For language arts consider books like *Lights for Gita* (Gilmore, 1994), a story about Divali, the Hindu festival of lights. Continual under-representation of some cultural groups in science and mathematics, both in schools and in careers, suggests that culturally relevant curricula are necessary in these subjects.

Introducing curricula that reflect the cultural backgrounds of your students requires sensitivity. Andrew Allen (1996) introduced picture books with multicultural characters into his grade 2 classroom in Toronto—with students whose families had immigrated from the Caribbean, East Africa, and South and East Asia. When he used books with bright, colourful illustrations of children engaging in familiar activities, the children's responses were positive. When he used books with pictures that the children thought showed them "with exaggerated features," looking "unhappy," or in unfamiliar scenes, they "acted out" (pp. 162–63). Allen recommends that teachers

- involve students of every age in selecting and critiquing books for the classroom;
- teach students to detect bias in reading materials;
- examine their own biases;
- choose materials that show familiar scenes and people;
- obtain a balance between materials that provide cultural information and those that entertain; and
- be attentive to students' reactions.

**Culturally responsive teaching** is grounded in an understanding of the role of culture and language in learning and involves advocating for and differentiating for the learning of all students (Villegas & Lucas, 2007). When Bondy (2007) studied culturally responsive teachers, she found that they developed respectful, caring, and personal relationships with each student and built a community in the classroom where people could trust one another and laugh as well as learn together. They engaged all their students and used what they had learned from their students about their lives to make what they taught meaningful to the students—with language, expressions, literature, examples, questions, and challenges that the students recognized from their lives and related to. These teachers recognized that definitions of appropriate classroom behaviour were culturally defined and they were well enough informed about their students to understand what this meant. They engaged their students in conversation, listened respectfully, and shared information about themselves, their families, their passions, and their backgrounds.

## Using Co-operative and Collaborative Learning

In *Teaching to Diversity*, Mary Meyers (1993) of Toronto recommends using co-operative learning so that all students develop social, group, and language skills. Fentey Scott (2001) of Lakehead University makes the same recommendation in *Teaching in a Multicultural Setting*. Research demonstrates that co-operative learning improves student attitudes and behaviours toward diversity and boosts self-esteem in elementary and secondary classrooms (Kagan & Kagan, 2000; Aronson & Patnoe, 1997; Slavin 1990; McCafferty, Jacobs, & DaSilva Iddings, 2006). The principles of **co-operative learning** are listed here:

- Tasks are structured so no one can complete the learning task alone.
- Positive interdependence is fostered and developed.
- Students work in teams.
- Students learn language and social skills necessary for co-operation while learning content.

Begin with team-building activities such as brainstorming in triads, interviews in pairs, or assembly-line craft projects (or writing activities) in which each person does one step (or writes one sentence) and passes the project along to the next person. Figure 5.3 provides step-by-step instructions for a number of co-operative learning activities. Chapters 6 and 9 focus on creating a positive classroom climate and helping students to work together.

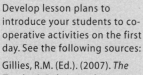

Put into Practice

Develop lesson plans to introduce your students to co-operative activities on the first day. See the following sources:

Gillies, R.M. (Ed.). (2007). *The Teacher's Role in Implementing Learning in the Classroom*. Boston: Springer.

McCafferry, S.G., Jacobs, G.M., & DaSilva Iddings, C. (Eds.). (2006). *Cooperative Learning and Second Language Teaching*. Cambridge, UK: Cambridge University Press.

Jacobs, G.M., Power, M.A., & Wan Inn, L. (2002). *The Teacher's Sourcebook for Co-operative Learning: Practical Techniques, Basic Principles, and Frequently Asked Questions*. Thousand Oaks, CA: Corwin Press.

Vermette, P.J. (1998). *Making Co-operative Learning Work: Student Teams in K–12 Classrooms*. Upper Saddle River, NJ: Allyn and Bacon.

Brownlie, F., Feniak, C., & Schnellert, L. (2006). *Student Diversity: Classroom Strategies to Meet the Learning Needs of All Students*. Markham, ON: Pembroke Pub.

## FIGURE 5.3 CO-OPERATIVE LEARNING STRUCTURES

**Brainstorming**
Can be done in any subject

- to find a solution to school litter, or a story character's dilemma;
- to suggest cause-and-effect relationships (if trees grew dollars instead of leaves. . . .);
- to decide on a class trip or fundraising project.

**Think-Pair-Share**
Everybody gets a say

- Everybody has time to think of his/her own answer.
- Students then pair up and discuss their answers.
- After a signal for silence, students have a chance to share their ideas with the whole group.

**Numbered Heads**
Speak on behalf of the team

- Students number themselves from one to four.
- The teacher then asks a question for discussion, e.g., "What do you think . . . ?" or "Why would . . . ?" Try to frame questions that elicit discussion about current studies.
- Students talk together in their groups to contribute to a team answer.
- After the silent signal is given, the teacher calls out a number. Only those students designated by that number raise their hands to respond.

**Listening Triads**
Everybody is a specialist

- In groups of three, students take on the roles of talker, questioner, or recorder.
- The talker explains or comments on a brief task.
- The questioner prompts and clarifies.
- The recorder takes notes and reports for the group.
- Next time, the students change roles.

**Jigsaw (also called expert groups)**
A four-step structure:

Step 1   Students form a "home" group.
Step 2   Each student is assigned a number, colour, or letter. The topic overview is presented.
Step 3   Students now move to form an "expert group" with other students who have same number or colour, etc. Each "expert group" works on one part of the larger topic.
Step 4   When time is up, the experts regroup with their original home groups. Each expert now teaches the skills or content learned in his/her subtopic to the home group.

- All members contribute something to the topic, so everybody is an expert.
- Team members depend on one another to complete the overall task.
- Each team member must learn skills or content from the others.
- Evaluation depends on both an individual mark and a team effort mark.

Source: Adapted from Meyers, M. (1993). *Teaching to Diversity*. Toronto: Irwin Publishing. Reprinted by permission of Nelson, a division of Thomson Learning: www.thomsonrights.com.

## Teachers as Role Models

Teachers who are members of visible minorities serve as **role models** for students of diverse cultures (see Duquette, 2007; Sterling, 2002; Thiessen et al., 1996). Patrick Solomon (1996) suggests that dominant-group students also benefit from experience with teachers of colour because it helps to modify their stereotypes about

*Teachers can serve as role models for students from minority cultures.*

**Further Reading**

Ontario Ministry of Education and Training. (2008). *Antiracism and ethnocultural equity in school boards.* www.edu.gov.on.ca/eng/document/curricul/antiraci/antire.html.

British Columbia Ministry of Education. (1997). *Multiculturalism and anti-racism education.* www.bced.gov.bc.ca/irp/be810/apcmul.htm.

Joshee, R., & Johnson, L. (Eds.). (2007). *Multicultural education policies in Canada and the United States.* Vancouver: UBC Press.

Ghosh, R., & Abdi, A.A. (2004). *Education and the politics of difference: Canadian perspectives.* Toronto: Canadian Scholars' Press.

Carr, P.R., & Lund, D.E. (Eds.). (2007). *The Great White North? Exploring whiteness, privilege, and identity in education.* Rotterdam, NL: Sense Publishers.

Banks, J.A. (2008). *An introduction to multicultural education.* New York: Pearson, Allyn & Bacon.

Canadian Race Relations Foundation. (2002). *Critical readings: An annotated bibliography on antiracist education.* Toronto: Canadian Race Relations Foundation.

minorities. Stephen Lewis (1992, p. 20) asked the same question that high school students asked of George Dei (2003): "Where are the visible minority teachers?"

This issue is important to every minority group in Canada. Jean-Brenda, interviewed by Dei, said, "I've never had a black teacher. . . . But I think it would really help . . . having someone who's black up there [and] can share some of my experiences" (p. 52). Few minority Canadians choose teaching as a career. June Beynon and Kelleen Toohey (1995) of Simon Fraser University interviewed post-secondary students of Chinese and Punjabi-Sikh heritage. The reasons they gave for not entering the teaching profession included parental influence, lack of proficiency in English, and discrimination. In a book subtitled *The Lives and Careers of Racial Minority Immigrant Teachers* (Thiessen, Bascia, & Goodson, 1996), a teacher of Chinese heritage describes her ease in communicating with Chinese parents. "Chinese parents tend to tell me at the outset that their children are very 'naughty' and express their gratitude towards me for dealing with their naughty children. I, in turn, disagree with them, easing their minds, while at the same time taking advantage of this opening to be honest with them." She continues, "This cultural practice is a required ritual for a successful interview between Chinese parents and their child's teacher" (p. 72). Aboriginal teachers report that members of their community see them as role models, bestowing this status on them even though they don't seek it (Duquette, 2007). And the need for role models was one of the issues raised in the discussions in Toronto in May 2008 about whether to start an Afrocentric alternative school. Jim Grieve, director of education for the Peel District School Board, says of Canadian society and schools, "with this amazing diversity comes a responsibility to reflect the communities" in our teachers (Brown, 2008).

# Teaching ELL Students

Some students from diverse cultures speak **English as a second language (ESL)** and are known as **English language learners (ELL students)**. Some are born in Canada to parents who speak limited English and others arrive in Canada as refugees or immigrants. Roughly 200 000 immigrants arrive in Canada each year; over 80 percent have a first language other than English, and half of those have no English proficiency (Bosetti & Watt, 1995). Canadian schools report that ELL students take between four and six years to match the achievement levels of first-language English students on achievement tests (Cummins, 1981; Klesmer, 1994). Giang Vo (2004) recounts the differences between her experiences as an ELL student in elementary and secondary school. She says: "At first, I just wanted to listen. . . . From day one, there was total inclusion. Since I felt that I was on equal par with everyone else it gave me the confidence to behave like everyone else, and ultimately I tried to speak and learn like everyone else" (p. 7). She is less positive about her secondary school experiences: "Secondary school was a very threatening environment for me. . . . I was picked on at school for being different" (p. 7).

Research shows that ELL students experience many learning difficulties in school. On the Education Quality and Accountability Office (EQAO) of Ontario 2007–2008 grade 3 tests, the average percentage of students achieving at grade level or better (levels 3 and 4) was

- Reading: 45 percent of ELL students; 61 percent of all participating students;
- Writing: 58 percent of ELL students; 66 percent of all participating students;
- Mathematics: 58 percent of ELL students; 68 percent of all participating students (www.eqao.com/pdf_e/08/369e_ProvincialReport_08_web.pdf).

## Teaching Students Who Are Immigrants and Refugees

Each year Canada accepts approximately 225 000 immigrants. Of these, about 20 000 are refugees. There are more than two hundred ethnic groups in Canada (Citizens for Mental Health, www.cmha.ca/citizens/immigrationENG.pdf). Recently, some have begun to question Canada's success at absorbing immigrants, suggesting that recent immigrants are not faring as well as earlier ones, and asking how we can meet the challenges in our schools (e.g., Levin, 2008).

On arrival in a new country, **immigrants** begin a period of adjustment thought to consist of four stages. These stages are (1) arrival and first impressions; (2) culture shock; (3) recovery and optimism; and (4) acculturation (Kim, 1988, 2001). Joining a welcoming classroom may help students feel comfortable at school before they feel comfortable in other contexts; our actions and our non-verbal communication can make a difference. In some cases almost every aspect of our culture, all of which we take for granted, is different from what the student is used to; for example, in some cultures young children kiss one another when they greet, not a practice likely to be welcomed on a Canadian schoolyard. All students need to feel like they belong (Osterman, 2001), a tall order when one has no idea how to interact with peers. A group of researchers at the University of Alberta helped immigrant children to explore their sense of belonging, peer relations, and nonverbal communication with schoolmates, through fotonovela (Emme et al., 2006). Fotonovela combine still photos taken by students and arranged in a narrative

**Weblinks**

CANADIAN MULTICULTURAL EDUCATION FOUNDATION
www.cmef.ca

MULTICULTURALISM (HERITAGE CANADA)
www.pch.gc.ca/progs/multi/index_e.cfm

CANADIAN RACE RELATIONS FOUNDATION
www.crr.ca

CANADIAN EDUCATION TREND REPORT: ANTI-RACISM AND MULTICULTURAL EDUCATION (DESCRIPTION OF SOME CURRENT ACTIVITIES IN CANADA)
www.safehealthyschools.org/whatsnew/racism.htm

MULTICULTURAL EDUCATION INTERNET RESOURCE GUIDE
http://jan.ucc.nau.edu/~jar/Multi.html

CANADIAN ANTI-RACISM EDUCATION AND RESEARCH SOCIETY (CAERS):
www.stopracism.ca/pages/home.php

Hamilton, R., & Moore, D. (2004). *Educational interventions for refugee children: Theoretical perspectives and implementing best practice.* New York: RoutledgeFalmer.

Behnia, B. (2007). An exploratory study of befriending programs with refugees: The perspective of volunteer organizations. *Journal of Immigrant and Refugee Studies, 5*(3), 1–19.

Reynolds, C. (2004). Children of war. *Maclean's, 118*(1), 78–81.

Magro, K. (2006/2007). Overcoming the trauma of war: Literacy challenges of adult learners. *Education Canada, 47*(1), 70–74.

Melzac, S. (2008). *Children in exile: Therapeutic work in the community and the clinic with child survivors of political violence and war.* London, UK: Jessica Kingsley.

sequence with text, often in the form of text balloons (like those that appear in comics). Many factors contribute to adjustment and acculturation. These include whether the family immigrated by choice, the degree of family separation, emotional preparation, and environmental factors like the climate and size of the community (Hamilton & Moore, 2004). Some family characteristics such as English proficiency, socio-economic status, and cultural conflict between home and school are also influential. Additionally, 30 percent of immigrant families with children live in poverty (www.cmha.ca/citizens/immigrationENG.pdf).

Those who arrive as **refugees** may have lived through traumatic experiences including war, violence, oppression, torture, and flight. Those who have experienced torture are at particular risk for mental health problems. Mental health researchers have described typical early stages in the adjustment of refugees to life in a new country. These include relief to be alive, guilt about surviving when others did not, recognition that they may not be able to return home, and stress associated with waiting for their refugee claims to be heard, which can take up to five years (Canadian Task Force on Mental Health Issues Affecting Immigrants and Refugees, 1988; www.cmha.ca/citizens/immigrationENG.pdf).

Canadian teachers describe refugee students as often withdrawn, restless, inattentive, and fearful of noises. Their drawings, like Ragu's in this chapter's opening case, may depict war, violence, bombs, guns, and soldiers. Some show symptoms of post-traumatic stress disorder, including nightmares, disturbed sleep, crying, and depression, and many are still afraid of the government they fled, fearing that someone may be spying on them (Carter & Mok, 1992; Magro, 2006/2007; Yau, 1995). A Canadian study concluded that "the impact of incarceration in a [refugee] camp is dehumanizing" (Kaprielian-Churchill & Churchill, 1994, p. 11). Some refugees have been child soldiers, and "it's hard to imagine what they must be going through trying to adjust to a normal life in the classroom" (Reynolds, 2004, p. 80). Others, like female adolescent refugees from Afghanistan, may never have been to school, making the educational gap between them and their peers very large. All of these students may need psychological support beyond a sensitive and aware teacher, but it is important for us to remember that when they receive support most immigrant and refugee families are resilient and successful in their new lives.

## Welcoming Students

Establish a procedure for welcoming ELL students, immigrants, and refugees and their parents to your classroom. Elementary schools often involve the principal and ESL teacher, while secondary schools may include a counsellor. Whenever possible, an ELL student should be placed in a class where another student speaks the same first language. Many schools hold an informal interview with the student, parents, and an interpreter in the home language (Coelho, 1994). If you sense reluctance to answer particular questions, delay these questions until a later interview. Provide the family with information in a language that they can understand: school information (hours, special days, etc.) and community information (about adult ELL classes, daycare facilities, ethnic associations, and the Red Cross telephone number) (Hamilton & Moore, 2004; Meyers, 1993). You can collect relevant information about the student's linguistic and academic background through the interview and through assessment. Before a new student arrives, try to teach your class and fellow teachers "Hello" in the new student's language. Teach your students about refugees and why they are forced to leave their homes (www.mnadvocates.org/The_Human_Rights_Education_Program.html).

## Teaching Strategies

Many ELL students will be quiet, even silent, in their early days in your classroom. They may be figuring out how to fit in. Remain warm and accepting, even if they are silent for a few months. Observe how the student interacts with someone who understands his or her first language—a friend in the class or a translator. When ELL students understand little of what you are teaching, you can feel unsure about how to begin. The following list highlights what to focus on in the early weeks:

- Make the student feel comfortable; use non-verbal communication to show warmth.
- Seat the student with a classmate who speaks the same language, if possible.
- Seat the student with classmates you know will be welcoming.
- Teach frequently used vocabulary first.
- Use visual aids.
- Speak in short, simple sentences.
- Stress the use of first-language skills.
- Use student translators in teaching content areas.
- If a large number of students speak the same second language, place them in pairs (later singly) into co-operative learning groups so they interact with English speakers.
- Suggest that the new student bring maps, pictures, and articles from his or her home country, but don't push if you see reluctance.

Remember the case of Ragu from the opening of this chapter. He had many memories of his country that he wanted to forget. Be sensitive to this possibility.

## Peer-Mediated Instruction

Research suggests that co-operative **peer-mediated strategies** promote high levels of language and academic learning and social interactions (for a review see Swain et al., 2002, of the University of Toronto). Create pairs and small groups of varied academic abilities and language-proficiency levels. Watanabe and Swain (2007) and Gersten and Baker (2000) describe empirically validated, peer-mediated instruction. You might also look at McKay's (2006) book on using collaborative learning for ELL students within a prescribed curriculum. In such groups the success of one student depends on the help of others. A peer-mediated learning strategy is described in Focus on Research.

## Communicating High Expectations

You can communicate high expectations in many ways. Encourage group rehearsal before selecting individuals to respond to questions. Wait long enough for a response so students can ask peers for help with translation. Provide supportive feedback. Pay attention to, and interact with, all students. Always try to group students heterogeneously for activities. Ensure that your expectations grow and that students have to stretch a bit more on each new assignment. Never provide more assistance than students need.

### Further Reading

Quicho, A.L., & Ulanoff, S.H. (2009). *Differentiated literacy instruction for English language learners.* Boston: Allyn & Bacon.

Travers, P., & Klein, G. (Eds.) (2004). *Equal measures: Ethnic minority and bilingual pupils in secondary schools.* Stoke on Trent, UK: Trentham Books.

McKay, P. (Ed.). (2006). *Planning and teaching creatively within a required curriculum for school-age learners.* Alexandria, VA: Teachers of English to Speakers of Other Languages, Inc.

Adelman Reyes, S., & Vallone, T.L. (2008). *Constructivist strategies for teaching English language learners.* Thousand Oaks, CA: Corwin Press.

Duff, P.A. (2001). Language, literacy, content, and (pop) culture: Challenges for ESL students in mainstream courses. *Canadian Modern Language Review, 58, 103–132.*

### Weblinks

UNHCR, THE UNITED NATIONS REFUGEE AGENCY
www.unhcr.org/cgi-bin/texis/vtx/home

NEW HORIZONS FOR LEARNING: "THE MULTICULTURAL CLASSROOM: TEACHING REFUGEE AND IMMIGRANT CHILDREN"
www.newhorizons.org/strategies/multicultural/adkins_dunn.htm

CANADIAN COUNCIL FOR REFUGEES
www.web.net/~ccr

STRANGERS BECOMING US (TEACHING MATERIALS FOR ELEMENTARY SCHOOLS)
www.classroomconnections.ca/en/sbuelementary.php

STRANGERS BECOMING US (TEACHING MATERIALS FOR SECONDARY)
www.classroomconnections.ca/en/sbusecondary.php

# Classwide Peer Tutoring (CWPT)

### What Is CWPT?

CWPT involves the entire class in tutoring. Students are paired each week. ELL students are initially paired with students who speak their native language with greater English proficiency. Pairs are assigned to one of two teams that compete for the highest point total resulting from daily scheduled tutoring sessions. Students' roles are switched during the daily tutoring session, allowing each child to be both the tutor/teacher and the tutee/student. New content to be learned, teams, and tutoring pairs are changed weekly. Students are trained in the procedures necessary to act as tutors and tutees. In a given session the students know their partner, the material to be covered, how to correct errors, how to award points for correct responses, and how to provide positive feedback. Teachers organize the academic content to be tutored into daily and weekly units and prepare materials to be used in CWPT. Teacher-prepared tests at the end of the week provide feedback to the students. Tutoring occurs simultaneously for all tutor–tutee pairs. This frees the teacher to supervise and monitor students' tutoring sessions.

### What Are the Basic Components?

- weekly competing teams (heterogeneous grouping by cultural group, language, ability)
- highly structured teaching procedure (content material, teams, pairing, error correction, system of rewards)
- daily, contingent, individual tutee point earning and public posting of individual and team scores
- direct practice of functional academic and language skills to mastery

### How Do ELL Students Know What to Do?

Training of ELL students as tutors requires the teacher or a bilingual student to simply and clearly explain the procedure to them individually and, if possible, bilingually. At the beginning of each week, prior to the CWPT session, the new content should be introduced to them by the teacher or a bilingual student, individually or as a group. They should be encouraged to access knowledge and skills they have in their native language to assist them with the new academic content. In addition, the teacher should provide support by thinking aloud, using visual organizers to help students organize and relate information, and by elaborating and clarifying the input of the students.

### What Does the Research Say about CWPT?

CWPT was developed by researchers at the Juniper Gardens Children's Project, University of Kansas (Greenwood et al., 2001; Greenwood et al., 1988). It has been successfully applied to passage reading, reading comprehension, mathematics, vocabulary development, spelling, social studies, and science instruction with culturally and linguistically diverse learners and with regular, special education, and low-achieving students. Studies have been conducted across grades K to 12. The most comprehensive study included more than four hundred low-achieving minority and majority students enrolled in four schools across four years of implementation (grades 1 to 4) and a follow-up of these students in junior high and high schools. Results showed significantly greater gains in spelling, reading, and math for the CWPT students than for students in whole-class instruction. Furthermore, the CWPT students exceeded or approached national norms in all three academic domains, as measured by the Metropolitan Achievement Test (Greenwood et al., 1989). Students and teachers consistently rated all CWPT components highly. Teachers have consistently reported higher levels of peer social interaction during the remainder of the school day and positive self-esteem outcomes as a result of CWPT (Greenwood et al., 1990; Hashimoto et al., 2007; Kamps et al., 2008).

The classroom procedures for CWPT are described in Gersten, R.M., & Jimenez, R.T. (1998). *Promoting/Learning for Culturally and Linguistically Diverse Students*. Scarborough, ON: ITP Nelson Canada. Also see Greenwood 1988, 1989, and 1997 in the References list as well as Hashimoto et al. (2007) and Kamps et al. (2008).

**Cross-Reference**
Chapter 8 focuses on adapting assessment to meet the needs of all students in your classroom.

## Adapting Assessment

Because language plays a large role in most means of assessment, this creates challenges for assessing ELL students equitably. Students may know what you have taught but be unable to verbalize their understanding. If you use essay questions, ELL students have difficulty with the writing demands, and if you use multiple-choice questions, they may have difficulty with the reading demands. In both instances their English language knowledge may prevent them from showing what they know. Try using true/false questions, completion questions, and identification questions in which a series of simple statements can be labelled with the concept they describe (see Reiss, 2008). You can observe ELL students or conference individually, use instructions like "point to," "draw," and "find the page about." A peer may be able to translate, or a translator may be able to tell you the contents of an assignment written in the student's first language. Use performance-based assessment or portfolio assessment and provide models of what is expected. In the early days you can implement a simple system of grades such as: = (meets expectations), + (exceeds expectations), and – (does not meet expectations). Ensure that the student understands your feedback about what was done well and poorly. Generally, ask students how they prefer to learn and consult an ESL teacher when you have questions.

# Other Issues of Equity in the Classroom

## Responding to Incidents in Your Classroom

In classrooms characterized by diversity, you may see incidents of racism, sexism, or bullying. When you set the class rules and procedures, be clear that such behaviours are understood to be unacceptable in your classroom. When students fail to meet your expectations for respectful and equitable treatment, you must act. If you do not have effective procedures for responding to such incidents, you will not have the safe community necessary for inclusive education. Figure 5.4 describes a problem-solving approach for responding to such incidents.

## Proactive Teaching to Minimize Incidents in Your Classroom

It is important that you take action from the first day that sets the tone of community and establishes how students are to treat one another. Model respectful and equitable treatment, and expect to have to teach these ways of behaving and thinking. Students act differently in different situations depending on what is

**Put into Practice**

Read from the following list of resources. Consider how you could help to alleviate the fears of a child or adolescent about terrorism or of a student with a parent deployed in the military. Think about what you could do and then consider the limits to your expertise. Locate a national organization and a community organization that employ professionals with expertise in counselling children and adolescents who fear war or terrorism. Build a list of resources (books, videos, websites, and human resources) that you could share with your colleagues.

Moses, L.F., Aldridge, J., Cellitti, A., & McCorquodale, G. (2003). *Children's fears of war and terrorism: A resource for teachers and parents.* Olney, MD: Association for Childhood Education International.

Ellis, D. (2008). *Off to war: Voices of soldiers' children.* Toronto: Groundwood Books.

Arond, M. (Ed.). (2006). *Feeling safe: Talking to children about war and terrorism.* Darby, PA: Diane Pub. Co.

**FIGURE 5.4  FRAMEWORK FOR ANALYZING EQUITY INCIDENTS IN THE CLASSROOM**

Ask yourself:

1. Is _____ part of what is happening here? (Put in *racism, sexism,* etc.)

2. Who was present and/or involved in the situation? Who must be included in the intervention/response? (All who witnessed must see support given and that the actions are not condoned.)

3. Who does this situation affect? How does it affect them? (Support the victims and teach all who witnessed. Punishment may be required.)

4. Was the behaviour conscious or unconscious? Was malice involved? (Intervention should address intent, carelessness, or both.)

5. What can you achieve with an intervention? (Teach students what is unacceptable or acceptable, and reasons.)

6. What actions must be taken and why? (Immediately support victim, address perpetrator. Over time teach for prevention.)

Equity education means tailoring teaching to challenge inequities and discrimination.

**Cross-Reference**
Chapters 6 and 9 provide strategies for enhancing social relationships in the classroom.

expected of them. That is why you may find a class to be co-operative and eager learners while another teacher may describe them as unmanageable. Many effective, proactive programs are discussed in Chapters 6 and 9. These include *Tribes* (Gibbs, 2001); *Children as Peacemakers* (Fine, Lacey, & Baer, 1995), which describes a program implemented in inner-city Toronto; *Teaching Young Children in Violent Times* (Levin, 2003); and *Counting Them In: Isolated Bilingual Learners in School* (Statham, 2008). Implementing co-operative learning (e.g., Vermette, 1998) may be the most effective proactive approach for secondary school classes (see Coelho, 2003; Edwards, 2000; Gillies, 2007; Gillies & Boyle, 2008; Hutchinson, 1996; Udvari-Solner & Kluth, 2007).

## Issues of Gender Equity

### INEQUITABLE TREATMENT OF MEN AND WOMEN

Sexual harassment is a problem throughout our society but particularly in schools (American Association of University Women, 1993; Joong & Ridler, 2005; Larkin, 1997). Both males and females can be stereotyped and can experience sexual harassment. The researchers in a large study in Ontario concluded that "the young women involved in this project experienced strong feelings of humiliation, fear, and suffering as a result of sexual harassment. They came together to express their helplessness regarding sexual harassment, and their anger that schools had done nothing to effectively prevent or penalize it" (Ontario Secondary School Teacher's Federation, 1995, p. 3). A decade later, Peter Joong and Olive Ridler (2005) of Nipissing University found that both middle and secondary school students and teachers reported experiencing bullying and fights as well as sexual harassment in their schools.

**Sexual harassment** includes put-downs and negative comments made about gender or sexual preference, sexist jokes, and calling someone gay or lesbian. Other examples of sexual harassment include inappropriate staring, bragging about sexual ability, demands for dates or sexual favours, questions or discussions about sexual activities, rating people on a scale, displaying sexually offensive pictures or graffiti, and intimidating behaviour such as blocking a person's way. Anne Lacasse and Morton Mendelson (2006) of McGill University found that 70 percent of Quebec high school students in grades 8 to 11 reported experiencing at least one moderately offensive sexual behaviour (e.g., stared at parts of your body), while over 25 percent experienced at least one severe non-coercive behaviour (e.g., tried to stroke your leg). Behaviours experienced at the hands of a friend were judged less upsetting than those experienced at the hands of other peers. A recent study in Newfoundland (Duffy et al., 2004) suggests that being sexually harassed has psychological consequences for high school students. Students say they don't report incidents because most teachers never do anything about them (Joong & Ridler, 2005). Ensure that you are a teacher who acts. Urge your school and school district to develop, display, and enforce anti-harassment policies.

Curriculum materials have tended to show men and women in stereotyped roles and occupations. You and your students can examine the books you use in your classroom, counting the number of males and females, and identifying the roles in which they are depicted. These activities enable you to teach your students about gender equity issues.

"I was around thirteen when I realized what I was and the more I found out, the more scared I became" (the words of an 18-year-old girl; Baker, 2005). Gay and lesbian youth who are questioning and exploring their sexual identity are also targets of discrimination (D'Augelli, Pilkington, & Hershberger, 2002; Saewyc et al., 2006). **Homophobia** takes the form of taunts, ridicule, and physical assaults. Seeing the way others are treated causes many gay and lesbian youth to hide their sexual orientation. This can cause feelings of alienation, depression, self-abuse, and confusion about sexual identity (Baker, 2005; Williams et al., 2005), putting students at greater risk for poor school performance, criminality, substance abuse, dropping out, and suicide. Misunderstanding and rejection by their families can lead to kids' homelessness. Attempted suicide rates are higher for gay and lesbian students than for their heterosexual peers (sometimes estimated as much as three times higher) (Borowsky, Ireland, & Resnick, 2001). Do not tolerate teasing, bullying, or harassment based on sexual orientation.

*Students who are gay or lesbian are at risk for identity confusion, bullying, and suicide. They need teacher support and safe spaces.*

The rainbow is a symbol understood by gay and lesbian students to indicate support for them. Many school boards offer "Safe Spaces" programs that teach teachers how to communicate that their classrooms are safe spaces for gay and lesbian students and to ensure the safety of their classrooms. If your school district does not have such a program, you might talk with the youth officer in your local police force to learn about community supports. See Figure 5.5 for ways you can support gay and lesbian students. One secondary school teacher said, "I think that teachers and administrators are professionals . . . they have to accept gays and

## FIGURE 5.5 SUPPORTING GAY AND LESBIAN STUDENTS

- Provide safe, non-discriminatory environments in which all students are valued.
- Learn about the social, psychological, and educational needs of gay and lesbian youth.
- Don't assume heterosexuality. Use language that is broad, inclusive, and gender neutral.
- Provide all students with confidential access to materials that address their needs.
- Challenge homophobia, heterosexism, and stereotyping in school and society.
- Help students obtain appropriate services from agencies and professionals who are sensitive and trained to deal with gay, lesbian, and bisexual issues.
- Make it clear that language has power and that abusive language will not be tolerated.
- Offer a range of academic, extracurricular, and mentoring activities for all students.
- Examine the curriculum for bias against gay and lesbian issues and individuals.
- Discuss diversity in families and family structures.
- Enforce your school's policies on sexual harassment, anti-violence, and anti-discrimination.

Source: Adapted from Salend, S.J. (1998). *Effective Mainstreaming: Creating Inclusive Classrooms*, Third Edition. Toronto: Prentice Hall. Used by permission.

lesbians for who they are and treat them with the same respect they treat everybody else" (Baker, 2005). I think our goal as educators is to remove the stigma so it is no longer a slight when students are called gay or lesbian.

Weblinks

THE RAINBOW EDUCATORS' NETWORK
www2.gol.com/users/aidsed/
rainbow

WE ARE FAMILY
www.waf.org/index.php

PARENTS, FAMILIES, AND FRIENDS OF
LESBIANS AND GAYS
http://community.pflag.org/
NETCOMMUNITY/Page.
aspx?pid+194&srcid=-2

# Teaching Students Who Are at Risk from Poverty, Homelessness, Abuse, and Divorce

In this section the characteristics and needs of at-risk students are described. Poverty, homelessness, abuse, and divorce are explored for their impact on learning and classroom participation.

## Teaching Students Who Live in Poverty

In Canada **poverty** has typically referred to insufficient access to the basic goods, services, and opportunities accepted as necessary for a decent standard of living (Ross, Scott, & Smith, 2000; www.ccsd.ca/pubs/2000/fbpov00). We usually associate poverty with lack of income—or too little income—to ensure people's physical well-being. Being poor here usually means having difficulty covering the basic essentials of food, shelter, and clothing. It means having to use food banks each month, and living in overcrowded or substandard housing. And for an increasing number of Canadians, including families with children, it may mean having no roof at all (*Perception*, vol. 29 [1 & 2], pp. 4–6). Canada has no official poverty line; different agencies measure poverty in different ways (deGroot-Maggetti, 2002). Statistics Canada developed a Low Income Cutoff measurement (LICO) that defines a low-income household as one that spends more than about 55 percent of its income on necessities. The Canadian Council on Social Development suggested that almost 25 percent of Canadian households fit this definition. The most recent measure, the Market Basket Measure (MBM), was developed by Human Resources Development Canada in 2002–2003. MBM is calculated by costing a basket of goods and services (including food, clothes, shelter, transportation, and so on) for various types of families in different geographical locations and adjusted for inflation. Using the 2002 MBM gives Canada a poverty rate of 13.7 percent. Both measures suggest that many families in Canada do not have the amount of income that it takes to live and participate as a citizen in Canada.

We have associated poverty with poor academic performance, and data have suggested that students who perform poorly in school have difficulty changing their economic status and that of their children later in life. For example, Hess (1991) wrote that "many [children of poverty in Canada] experience less motivation to learn, delayed cognitive development, lower achievement, less participation in extra-curricular activities, different types of teacher–student interactions . . . an increased risk of illiteracy and higher dropout rates" (p. 1). However, recent research suggests that the relationship between income and achievement is more complex than previously thought. Doug Willms of the University of New Brunswick (2002a, 2002b) defined vulnerable children as those who had an unfavourable cognitive or behavioural outcome and then used the National Longitudinal Study of Children and Youth (NLSCY) data from Statistics Canada to look back to see if they were all from backgrounds of poverty. He estimated about 28.6 percent of Canadian children were vulnerable. Rather than finding that poverty was the main factor related to vulnerability, Willms found vulnerability was only weakly related to family income and other socio-economic factors. Four factors emerged as strong predictors of whether or not a child was vulnerable: the "style" of parenting in the home, the cohesiveness of the family unit, the mental health of the mother, and the extent to which parents engage with their children in learning and play activities.

The Canadian Council on Social Development (2000) reported that about 250 000 Canadians were "working poor," falling below the LICO even though they were employed. Children in low-income families are more likely to experience parental neglect, to witness violence, and to change schools frequently, and these disruptions can show up as behaviour problems at school. Poor children often come to school tired and stressed. They may lack nutritious meals, a quiet place to do homework, basic school supplies, warm clothes in winter, and the footwear needed for gym class. However, the research shows that children in some low-income families will not be vulnerable, so as educators we must be careful not to stereotype our students or their parents.

There are many things we can do to make children less vulnerable at school. Healthy snacks such as apples and granola bars (beware of allergies) and school supplies (e.g., pencils and erasers) can be kept in the classroom for students who need them. Some elementary schools collect winter clothing and teachers invite children to stay after school to choose mittens or a warm hat. Sometimes students may be preoccupied about their families' circumstances. Older students may be expected to work weekends and evenings to support the family or miss school to babysit younger siblings.

The long-held view that poverty causes school difficulties may be questioned today (for controversy on the topic, see Rothstein, 2008), but it is important to remember that while students who live in poverty will not necessarily experience these challenges, they are more likely to be at risk for health problems, inattention, friends who are poor role models, low achievement in math and vocabulary, not participating in organized sports, and dropping out of school without employment. Recent research suggests that social support of parents, neighbourhood services for youth, teachers, and well-behaved peers, along with persistence and understanding of the value of educational attainment, contribute to better social and school outcomes (Mo & Singh, 2008; Molnar et al., 2008; Somers et al., 2008). When teachers and school counsellors create a culture of encouragement and participation where students feel they belong and can express their aspirations, students are more likely to overcome the challenges associated with their life circumstances (Uwah et al., 2008). Research by Michael Ungar of Dalhousie University over the past decade has been directed at understanding **resilience**, what he has called "drifting toward mental health" and "the process of empowerment" (2000). He

Further Reading

Canadian research on resilience:

Kanevesky, L., Corke, M., & Frangkiser, L. (2008). The academic resilience and psychosocial characteristics of inner-city English learners in a museum-based school program. *Education and Urban Society, 40*(4), 452–475.

Kordich Hall, D., & Pearson, J. (2005). Resilience—giving children the skills to bounce back. *Education & Health, 23*(1), 12–15.

McMahon, B.J. (2007). Resilience factors and processes: No longer at risk. *The Alberta Journal of Educational Research, 53*(2), 127–142.

Grover, S. (2005). Advocacy by children as a causal factor in promoting resilience. *Childhood, 12*(4), 527–538.

Hutchinson, N.L., Freeman, J.G., Stoch, S.A., & Chan, J.S. (2004). Academic resilience: A retrospective study of adults with learning difficulties. *Alberta Journal of Education, 50*(1), 5–21.

*Schools continually seek ways to reduce bullying and cyberbullying.*

# The Concept of Resilience in Children and Adolescents

One area of research that has important implications for improving the education of students at risk of academic failure focuses on resilient students, those who succeed in school in spite of adverse conditions. Recently in educational research, both conceptual and empirical papers have helped us to understand why some students may be successful in school while others from the same socially and academically disadvantaged backgrounds and communities are not. Such a framework may help us to design more effective educational interventions that make the most of "alterable" factors that distinguish resilient students from non-resilient students. A number of researchers have reported on these alterable factors; for example, Benard (1993) found that resilient children typically display four personal characteristics: social competence, problem-solving skills, autonomy, and a sense of purpose. McMillan and Reed (1994) describe four other factors that appear to be related to resilience: (a) personable attributes like motivation and goal orientation; (b) positive use of time (including on-task behaviour in the classroom, homework completion, participation in extracurricular activities); (c) family life (such as parental support and high expectations); and (d) positive school and classroom learning environments (including facilities, leadership, caring adults).

There has been much discussion about how resilience should be defined. Some consider it to be both a process of overcoming challenging or threatening circumstances and the outcome of that process (e.g., Garmezy & Masten, 1991). Others focus on the heightened likelihood of success in school and life despite environmental adversities (e.g., Wang, Haertel, & Walberg, 1994). Some researchers emphasize the risk factors (e.g., poverty, drug abuse, sexual activity, single-parent family setting, a sibling who has dropped out of school, a disability), while others ask how many of these risk factors must "pile up" before a successful student can be considered resilient (for a discussion of these issues, see Waxman, Gray, & Padron, 2003).

In studies that have compared resilient and non-resilient secondary students, researchers have found resilient adolescents to report higher satisfaction with school and less interest in gang activity (Reyes & Jason, 1993), and resilient students to report a significantly higher sense of belonging at school (Gonzalez & Padilla, 1997). There have been many studies showing that students' perceptions of their teachers as supportive, caring, and taking a personal interest in them—even one teacher's serving as a caring mentor—are highly related to resilience and academic achievement in the face of adversity. These studies also suggest that teachers of resilient students focus more on the students' achieving through high expectations for learning, homework completion, etc., and provide a high level of support to help students meet these expectations (e.g., Nettles, Mucherach, & Jones, 2000). Resilient students have been observed to spend more time interacting with the teacher for instructional purposes, while non-resilient students spent more time interacting with other students for personal or social reasons (e.g., Padron, Waxman, & Huang, 1999). Other studies have found a higher engagement of students with academic tasks and more authentic instruction (e.g., instructional practices that connect students to meaningful, real-life experiences) in classrooms where at-risk students tend to show resilience (e.g., McClendon, Nettles, & Wigfield, 2000).

While the research on resilience is ongoing and complex and often comes under critical scrutiny, we can draw some implications for practice. There are consistent findings that, as teachers, we should not ignore. The factors that we can affect include learning environment, classroom instruction, and motivational aspects. Classrooms that appear to contribute to resiliency are perceived by students and judged by researchers to be academically challenging and caring. More thorough reviews of the literature suggest that what is needed is flexible teaching but not streaming. It appears that flexible teaching that is differentiated to help students be successful gives the message to students and families that they can do it and we can help them. On the other hand, placement in a non-academic stream and retention in grade give students and families the message that the school—and by implication society—is giving up on them, they are failures, and we are unwilling to help. Based on extensive research with at-risk students and thorough reviews of the literature on resilient students and classrooms, Waxman and his colleagues (e.g., Padron, Waxman, & Rivera, 2002; Waxman, Padron, & Arnold, 2001) describe four explicit practices that can help students to feel in control of their learning, to be highly engaged and satisfied with school, and to show the characteristics associated with resilience:

- cognitively guided instruction
- culturally responsive teaching
- co-operative learning
- instructional conversations

*continued*

All of these teaching approaches have been described throughout this book, where you can find many examples of their use with exceptional students. The research suggests considerable similarities between differentiating teaching for exceptional learners and differentiating teaching for at-risk students.

### References

Benard, B. (1993). Fostering resiliency in kids. *Educational Leadership, 51,* 44–48.

Garmezy, N., & Masten, A.S. (1991). The protective role of competence indicators in children at risk. In E.M. Cummings, A.L. Greene, & K.H. Karraker (Eds.), *Life-span developmental psychology: Perspectives on stress and coping* (pp. 151–174). Mahwah, NJ: Lawrence Erlbaum.

Gonzalez, R., & Padilla, A.M. (1997). The academic resilience of Mexican American high school students. *Hispanic Journal of Behavioral Sciences, 19,* 301–317.

McClendon, C., Nettles, S.M., & Wigfield, A. (2000). Fostering resilience in high school classrooms: A study of the PASS Program (Promoting Achievement in School Through Sport). In M.G. Sanders (Ed.), *Schooling students placed at risk: Research, policy, and practice in the education of poor and minority adolescents* (pp. 289–307). Mahwah, NJ: Lawrence Erlbaum.

McMillan, J.H., & Reed, D.F. (1994). At-risk students and resiliency: Factors contributing to academic success. *The Clearing House, 67,* 137–140.

Nettles, S.M., Mucherach, W., & Jones, D.S. (2000). Understanding resilience: The role of social resources. *Journal of Education for Students Placed at Risk, 5,* 47–60.

Padron, Y.N., Waxman, H.C., & Huang, S.L. (1999). Classroom and instructional learning: Environment differences between resilient and nonresilient elementary students. *Journal of Education for Students Placed at Risk, 4,* 63–81.

Padron, Y.N., Waxman, H.C., & Rivera, H.H. (2002). *Educating Hispanic students: Obstacles and avenues to improved academic achievement* (Educational Practice Report No. 8). Santa Cruz, CA, and Washington, DC: Center for Research on Education, Diversity, and Excellence.

Reyes, O., & Jason, L.A. (1993). Pilot study examining factors associated with academic success for Hispanic high school students. *Journal of Youth and Adolescence, 22,* 57–71.

Wang, M.C., Haertel, G.D., & Walberg, H.J. (1994). Educational resilience in inner cities. In M.C. Wang & E.W. Gordon (Eds.), *Educational resilience in inner-city America: Challenges and prospects* (pp. 45–72). Mahwah, NJ: Lawrence Erlbaum.

Waxman, H.C., Gray, J.P., & Padron, Y.N. (2003). *Review of research on educational resilience* (Research Report No. 11). Santa Cruz, CA: Center for Research on Education, Diversity, and Excellence.

Waxman, H.C., Padron, Y.N., & Arnold, K.A. (2001). Effective instructional practices for students placed at risk of failure. In G.D. Borman, S.C. Stringfield, & R.E. Slavin (Eds.), *Title 1: Compensatory education at the crossroads* (pp. 137–170). Mahwah, NJ: Lawrence Erlbaum.

argues that we need to do our work as communities, schools, and families so that at-risk children and adolescents can exercise personal agency, make choices, and take responsibility with our support (Armstrong et al., 2005; Ungar, 2004). And, among the more culturally pluralistic communities in Canada, we also need to encourage many definitions of successful growth (Ungar, 2006, 2007). **Resilient students** tend to possess attributes like social competence, problem-solving skills, autonomy, and a sense of purpose and future. Families, schools, and communities that protect at-risk children and adolescents tend to be caring and supportive, have positive expectations, show humility, and provide opportunities for participation.

Canada's participation in the **Organisation for Economic Co-operation and Development (OECD)** Programme for International Student Assessment (PISA) has taught us something about our students' academic achievement, and something about our education of children from low income families. First, our OECD results in 2000, when the primary focus was on reading, showed our performance rank was among the top countries in the study. Second, Canada was among the six countries where the performance gap between students from higher socio-economic

## At-Risk Students: Breakfast Club Eases Transition to High School

In British Columbia, Mission Secondary School has developed a Breakfast Club to help moderately at-risk students. The Breakfast Club is designed for younger students, usually in grade 8, who are having difficulty adjusting to secondary school. Students and parents who commit to the program have recognized a need to change their approach to schooling if they wish to avoid failure.

In the Breakfast Club program, small groups of grade 8 students meet three times per week for four weeks, with the aim of improving study skills and setting personal goals. The program operates from 7:00 to 7:45 a.m. To provide motivation, students are provided an opportunity to "job shadow" a potential employer for a day and promised a breakfast at a restaurant upon completion of the program.

The first eight students in the program were failing a total of fifty-eight out of sixty-four courses when they enrolled. At the end of the year the students failed only eighteen courses.

Vice-principal Bill Dickson teaches the program. At 6:50 a.m. on Tuesday, Wednesday, and Thursday mornings the students gather in the main foyer and receive a can of fruit juice. The students and teacher then go to a classroom, armed with juice, student handbooks, and pens. Vic Hollister (from the community) often joins the group.

The students receive instruction on study skills, reading, spelling, math patterns, test taking, memory, and term papers. They keep notes in the back of the handbook and use the handbooks to set up their school day and to ensure that homework is completed.

Mr. Hollister informs the students of job-shadowing opportunities. Often students are released from regular classes for these opportunities. Mr. Hollister or an "employer" provides transportation to the work site. Each student spends an entire day shadowing a person who works at a job that interests the student. Job placements have occurred in horticulture, computer-assisted drafting, electrical engineering, water sprinkler manufacturing, policing, marine biology, medicine, computer programming, cartooning, secretarial work, and others. Dickson, Hollister, and "employers" stress the importance of using school to work toward personal goals.

Upon successful completion, Dickson and Hollister treat the students to a breakfast of their choice. Letters are sent to parents to acknowledge the students' and families' efforts. Students and parents are invited to an evening meeting to provide feedback on the program and help shape its future. Student performance is monitored for the remainder of the year.

Source: Adapted from Dickson, W.W. (1993). Breakfast club eases transition to high school. *The Canadian School Executive, 12*(9), pp. 28–29.

levels and those from lower socio-economic levels was narrow. And, in fact, Saskatchewan had the second smallest gap between the achievement levels of low and high socio-economic status students in the world, second only to Japan (Council of Ministers of Education, Canada [CMEC], *Canadian Report to the 15th Commonwealth Conference of Education Ministers*, 2003). I am not suggesting we rest on our laurels, but rather that we build on what we have already accomplished to eliminate the achievement gap for students who live in poverty.

Education is seen as part of the solution to poverty because good teaching raises achievement for all students. Good teaching includes targeted interventions, high expectations, programs that enhance family–school teamwork, collaborative learning, and effective teams of community professionals as well as educators (Frempong & Willms, 2002; Levin, 1994; Willms, 2002). One intervention that schools say makes a difference is breakfast clubs. Simpson (2001) reported that breakfast clubs improved attendance and punctuality. To start a breakfast club, consult www.humanleague.on.ca/breakfast/faq.htm. (See the Focus on Schools box, which describes a breakfast club in Mission, BC.)

## Homelessness

Some children and adolescents are not only poor but also **homeless**; the loss of the home is usually sudden, unexpected, and traumatic. The family is thrust away from

### Further Reading

Willms, J.D. (ed.) (2002). *Vulnerable children*. Edmonton: University of Alberta Press.

Waxman, H.C., Gray, J.P., Padron, Y.N. (2003). *Review of research on educational resilience: Research report*. Center for Research on Education, Diversity and Excellence, Santa Cruz, CA.

Barone, D.M. (2006). *Narrow the literacy gap: What works in high-poverty schools*. New York: Guilford Press.

its community, friends, and support system. The effects can be devastating (Laird, 2007; Rafferty, 1998; Stronge & Reed-Victor, 2000). Canada's homeless population is somewhere between 200 000 and 300 000, while another 1.7 million people struggle with finding affordable housing (Laird, 2007), and it is estimated that more than 25 percent of Canada's homeless are children. There is increasing concern that homeless children do not attend school regularly (US Department of Education, 2007; Walls, 2003). They move from shelter to shelter and eventually some families move to the street. Obstacles to school attendance include health problems, hunger, a lack of transportation, and a lack of school clothes and supplies (Juianelle & Foscarinis, 2003). When homeless children are at school, you may see socialization and behavioural problems, language delays, and self-esteem problems (Kottler & Kottler, 2006).

Gracenin (1993, 1994) also noted that some homeless children show a behavioural pattern resembling that of abused children—they act out, are distrustful of others, and feel incompetent. Homeless children also confront stigmatization and rejection by classmates and teachers.

Students' academic achievement drops in the face of homelessness (Attles, 1997; National Center for Homeless Education, 2007; Rubin et al., 1996). Teachers can be a powerful force in the lives of homeless students, helping them academically and emotionally (Holloway, 2003; Kottler & Kottler, 2006). Be sensitive and accepting. When a student transfers into your class, be prepared with school supplies and find a subtle and private way to enable the student to choose clothes from a supply collected at the school for such circumstances (Vissing, 2003). Communicate with the previous teacher; when a student transfers to another school, try to contact the next teacher. Refer students to counsellors and differentiate teaching to help students keep up in spite of absences. Do what you can to aid homeless students in making friends and do not tolerate bullying or victimization.

Homeless adolescents have become more common in Canada in the past two decades. Some live a **transient lifestyle**, moving from shelter to shelter. They live in unstable conditions, without adult guidance except perhaps that of a concerned teacher. Others live on the streets and are vulnerable to using and pushing drugs. Sean Kidd of McMaster University has studied the social stigma experienced by homeless youth who live on the street (2007) and the factors that contribute to suicide attempts by homeless youth (2004, 2006). Some make the brave move to return to secondary school only to leave before obtaining credits for their courses (Arnott, 1998). They need encouragement, support, and responsive, differentiated teaching. Often if they can connect with one teacher and one other adolescent, they have enough support to persevere.

## Teaching Students Who Have Experienced Abuse

Reports of **child abuse, neglect,** psychological harm, sexual abuse, and children observing violence have increased (National Clearinghouse on Family Violence, www.phac-aspc.gc.ca/ncfv-cnivf/familyviolence). Contributing factors are thought to be unemployment, poverty, unwanted pregnancy, substance abuse, and history of abuse as a child (Robbins, 2000). Being abused may lead to higher rates of sexual promiscuity, alcohol use, other risky behaviours, and impaired intellectual functioning. Figure 5.6 lists signs that may suggest a student is being abused. If you suspect child abuse or neglect, it is your responsibility to report your concerns to the child welfare agency in your community. When a child tells you about or

**Put into Practice**

Consult resources about youth and homelessness, such as the following, and talk with your peers about what teachers can do to ensure that they connect with homeless students who choose to return to school:

Calos, M. (Producer, Director). (2004). *The fifth estate: No way home* [video recording]. Toronto: Canadian Broadcasting Corporation. (The CBC has a website with further information about homelessness in Toronto and additional links: www.cbc.ca/fifth/main_nowayhome.html.)

Weblinks
For information on poverty in Canada, see:

CANADIAN COUNCIL ON SOCIAL DEVELOPMENT: URBAN POVERTY PROJECT 2007
www.ccsd.ca/pubs/2007/upp

NATIONAL ANTI-POVERTY ORGANIZATION
www.napo-onap.ca

POVERTY REDUCTION IN CANADA: THE FEDERAL ROLE
www.parl.gc.ca/information/library/PRBpubs/prb0722-e.htm

Weblinks
For information on breakfast clubs, see:

THE HUMAN LEAGUE ASSOCIATION
www.humanleague.on.ca/nutrition.htm#breakfast_club

LONGO'S COMMUNITY CARING PROGRAM
www.longos.com/all_about_longos/charity/community_caring_program.asp

QUEBEC BREAKFAST CLUB
www.clubdejeuners.org/index.php?module=CMS&id=33&newlang=eng

discloses abuse, listen calmly. Tell the child that you believe him or her, that you will do your best to find help, and that you cannot keep this a secret because the law says you must report it. Report the disclosure to the child protection services immediately. Consider that there may be emotional and behavioural repercussions and such children may need the support and differentiated teaching usually provided for children with behaviour and emotional exceptionalities. Figure 5.7 on page 198 suggests how you can teach abused students in sensitive and effective ways.

## Teaching Students Who Have Experienced Divorce

In the past forty years the rate of **divorce** in North America has increased. The 2006 Canadian Census reported a divorce rate of 37 percent in Canada (www.pcensus.com). Over this period divorce has been seen as the cause of a range of serious and enduring behavioural and emotional problems (e.g., Amato, 2008; Whitehead, 1998). The effects of divorce on academic achievement have been studied extensively (e.g., Menning, 2006). Jeynes (2002, 2006) reviews this literature

**Put into Practice**

Develop a handout for your peers about another factor that puts students at risk, such as substance abuse, gambling addiction, etc. Here are some readings in various areas to get you started:

Wyatt, T.J., & Peterson, F.L. (2005). Risky business: Exploring adolescent risk-taking behavior (teaching techniques). *Journal of School Health, 75*(6), 229–231.

Ste-Marie, C., Gupta, R., & Derevensky, J.L. (2006). Anxiety and social stress related to adolescent gambling behavior and substance abuse. *Journal of Child and Adolescent Substance Abuse, 15*(4), 55–74.

Walsh, S.P., White, K.M., & Ross, R.M. (2008). Over-connected? A qualitative exploration of the relationship between Australian youth and their mobile phones. *Journal of Adolescence, 31*(1), 77–92.

Gentile, D.A., & Anderson, C.A. (2006). Violent video games: The effects on youth, and public policy implications, in N. Dowd, D.G. Singer, & R.F. Wilson (Eds.). *Handbook of Children, Culture and Violence*, pp. 225–246. Thousands Oaks, CA: Sage.

Roe, S., & Becker, J. (2005). Drug prevention with vulnerable young people: A review. *Drugs: Education, Prevention and Policy, 12*(2), 85–99.

Monti, P.M., Colby, S.M., & O'Leary, T.A. (2001). *Adolescents, alcohol, and substance abuse: Reaching teens through brief interventions*. New York: Guilford Press.

Finn, K.V., & Willert, H.J. (2006). Alcohol and drugs in schools: Teachers' reactions to the problem. *Phi Delta Kappan, 88*(1), 37–40.

### FIGURE 5.6  SIGNS OF ABUSE

Note: These lists need to be used with caution as some of these indicators may reflect problems other than child abuse.

**Signs of Physical Abuse**
If a child is being physically abused, you may see the following **physical indicators**:

- Unexplained bruises, welts, and abrasions; especially on the face, back, buttocks, or thighs; sometimes in the shape of a belt or hairbrush; most often after the child has been absent or after a weekend
- Unexplained burns; from cigarettes on hands, feet, buttocks, back; sometimes in the shape of an iron or electric burner; immersion burns from scalding water
- Unexplained fractures and dislocations; to the skull or facial structure; spiral fractures of the long arm or leg bones
- Inappropriate dress; especially long sleeves or pants in hot weather to cover bruises, burns, etc.
- Unexplained head injuries, including patches of hair pulled out
- Delays in seeking medical attention for any kind of injury

If a child is being physically abused, you may see the following **behavioural indicators**:

- Reports of injury by parents
- Extreme wariness of parents
- Extreme wariness of adults in general
- Wariness of physical contact, especially when initiated by an adult
- Resistance to being touched; pulling away when someone approaches or extends a hand
- Extreme watchfulness
- Fear of going home
- Unexplained prolonged absence; may be kept home while healing
- Unlikely explanations for bruises, burns, etc. or denial of these injuries
- Resistance to undressing to change clothes for physical education
- Poor social relations with peers
- Apprehensiveness when other children cry
- Appearing unhappy, anxious
- Extremes of behaviour from aggressiveness to withdrawal

*continued*

# FIGURE 5.6 SIGNS OF ABUSE (continued)

**Signs of Neglect**

If a child is being neglected, you may see the following **physical indicators**:

- Attending school hungry or fatigued
- Poor hygiene, dirtiness, lice, skin disorders associated with poor hygiene
- Inappropriate dress; exposure symptoms including sunburn, frostbite, frequent colds, pneumonia
- Unattended health problems
- Inadequate supervision or abandonment
- Frequent absence from school

If a child is being neglected, you may see the following **behavioural indicators**:

- Theft
- Begging or stealing food
- Verbal evidence of no caretaker in the home; child's explanations for arriving early, staying late
- Sleeping in class
- Delinquency, alcohol or drug use

**Signs of Emotional Abuse**

If a child is being abused emotionally, you may see the following **physical indicators**:

- Lags in emotional, mental, or physical development
- Extreme lack of confidence or withdrawal
- Inability to concentrate, continual procrastination
- Excessive desire for teacher's attention
- Has-to-win attitude
- Extreme aggressiveness or passivity when playing with other children
- Over-participation in too many activities

If a child is being abused emotionally, you may see the following **behavioural indicators**:

- Conduct disorders; antisocial and destructive behaviour
- Extreme depression, attempted suicide
- Constant apologies, even when not responsible
- Speech disorders, sleep disorders, inhibition of play
- Fear of failure
- Inappropriate adult behaviours, including "bossing" or disciplining others
- Inappropriate childish behaviours, including throwing tantrums, crying, and sulking
- Sucking, biting, rocking
- Fear of failure, giving up, unwilling to try after even small setbacks

Source: Hutchinson, N.L. (2004). *Teaching Exceptional Children and Adolescents: A Canadian Casebook* (pp. 101–102). Toronto: Pearson Education Canada. Used by permission.

---

**Further Reading**

Clarke-Stewart, A., & Bretano, C. (2006). *Divorce: Causes and consequences.* New Haven, CN: Yale University Press.

Department of Justice (2007). *What happens next? Information for kids about separation and divorce.* Ottawa: Department of Justice.

Stinson, K. (2007). *Mom and Dad don't live together anymore.* Toronto: Annick Press.

**Weblinks**

CANADIAN CENTRE ON SUBSTANCE ABUSE
www.ccsa.ca

YUKON EDUCATION POLICY ON SUBSTANCE ABUSE
www.education.gov.yk.ca/pdf/policy_substance_abuse.pdf

KIDS HELP PHONE (HAS INFORMATION FOR TEACHERS ON SUBSTANCE ABUSE)
http://kidshelp.sympatico.ca/beingthereforkids/info-schools/materials_offer.html

REPORT ON SUBSTANCE ABUSE AMONG MANITOBA HIGH SCHOOL STUDENTS
www.afm.mb.ca/Research/documents/HSSU.pdf

---

and concludes that it shows a statistically significant advantage favouring children from intact families. However, many of these studies were conducted within one year of the marital breakup. The risk and resilience framework has been used to frame the long-term adjustment of children of divorce, and the long-term studies suggest that the majority of children from divorced families are well adjusted (Clarke-Stewart & Dunn, 2006; Houseknecht & Hango, 2006). In an interview study Kerry Hartley (2005), a graduate student at Queen's University, interviewed three adolescents who were judged by the staff of their secondary school to be resilient and coping well five years after their parents' divorce. Factors that they perceived contributed to their resilience included a close relationship with the custodial parent (in each case the mother) and in two of the three cases a close relationship with a grandparent. Two of the youths viewed their friends as important in their bouncing back and two emphasized the role of teachers. All agreed

## FIGURE 5.7 TEACHING ABUSED STUDENTS IN SENSITIVE AND EFFECTIVE WAYS

1. **Ensure that the classroom is a safe environment.**
   Exercise enough control to keep the student feeling that the classroom is a safe and pre-dictable place. Minimize chaos. You will want to directly teach positive ways to resolve conflict. Do not tolerate violence of any kind (verbal taunts, gestures, or sexual harassment).

2. **Remember that abused children differ and avoid stereotypes.**
   Children's experiences of abuse differ widely, as do their needs. Factors like frequency, duration, and severity of abuse, as well as identity and role of the abuser (family member or other, such as camp counsellor) are influential. The child's characteristics, thoughts about the experience, and social support are all important. You should pay attention to the child in deciding what the child needs from you and support the child's individual development, no matter the rate. Respect the child's expressed need for privacy, quiet time, or time away from noisy, busy activities.

3. **Change takes time, so be patient.**
   Children may persist with inappropriate behaviours after the abuse has stopped. The problem behaviours may even get worse before they improve. Children who have been "spacing out" to avoid dealing with abuse will require time to drop this once-useful habit. Ask what the counsellor suggests the student do instead of "spacing out," and make the same suggestion. Consistency will be reassuring. Other once-useful responses to abuse may include running away or lying.

4. **Be supportive; the child may be under greater stress than ever.**
   Your reporting may have caused others to punish the child. Other possible consequences include ridicule or being called a liar. Sometimes increased violence takes place in the relationships among family members as they are required to take part in court appearances. Income may drop because a member leaves the family. Separation of the parents or incarceration of a family member are also possible as a direct consequence of your report. The child may be held responsible by the family.

5. **Be compassionate, but also be firm with problematic behaviours.**
   Most of the above suggestions include concrete examples of showing the child compassion, which is very important. It is also critical to be firm and address inappropriate behaviours when they occur. The child is still responsible for his or her actions even though there has been abuse; these actions include internalized and externalized problem behaviours.

6. **Teach the child, expect learning, and promote tangible skills.**
   Use many words of encouragement, support, and informational feedback to create positive experiences at school for the maltreated child. Experiences of maltreatment often cause children to have negative views of themselves. You can contribute to changing these views by helping the child to be able to say, "I am the smart one who is good at math," or "I am the creative one who is good at painting." Hold high expectations for the child and provide high levels of support (and differentiated instruction if it is needed) so the child can reach these expectations. Help the child to recognize small gains, to set realistic proximal goals, and to stay on track learning and moving toward goals.

**Resources**

Horton, C.B., & Cruise, T.K. (2001). *Child abuse and neglect: The school's response*. New York: Guilford Press.

Youngblade, L.M., & Belsky, J. (1990). Social and emotional consequences of child maltreatment. In R.T. Ammerman & M. Hersen, (Eds.), *Children At Risk: An evaluation of factors contributing to child abuse and neglect* (pp. 107–146). New York: Plenum Press.

Source: Hutchinson, N.L. (2004). *Teaching exceptional children and adolescents: A Canadian casebook* (pp. 105–106). Toronto: Pearson Education Canada. Used by permission.

that it is not helpful for teachers to continuously refer to their change in family status or to try to intervene in a formal way; rather they valued informal interactions with caring teachers who had always been supportive and approachable. Perhaps the most important thing teachers can do is ensure they already have this kind of relationship with students, so students know implicitly that they will have support if it is needed. As with other at-risk students, it appears that we need to teach effectively and sensitively, and to engage the student in learning, differentiating teaching when necessary, without drawing excessive attention to their circumstances.

# Summary

This chapter has dealt with many aspects of teaching for diversity. Aboriginal education has become a greater priority in Canada since the 1996 *Report of the Royal Commission on Aboriginal Peoples*. Because of issues like the preservation of almost-extinct languages and cultures, Aboriginal education is distinct from multicultural education. However, students from diverse cultures and students with English as a second language also require differentiated teaching. For all of these students, high expectations, co-operative learning, culturally responsive curricula, and sensitive teaching are appropriate. Other equity issues that arise in classrooms concern gender and students who are gay or lesbian. You can teach proactively to reduce the occurrence of inequitable incidents. We also teach students who are at risk for a range of other reasons, including poverty, homelessness, abuse, and divorce. However, many of these students are resilient and, with the support of a caring teacher and the friendship of a classmate, can overcome what appear to be impossible risks. We are challenged to create classrooms that respect diversity and foster learning for *all* students.

# Key Terms

diversity (p. 167)
equity (p. 168)
Aboriginal cultures (p. 168)
*Report of the Royal Commission on Aboriginal Peoples* (RCAP Report) (p. 169)
Aboriginal languages (p. 171)
culturally responsive curriculum (p. 172)
experiential learning (p. 174)
Aboriginal elders (p. 174)
infusion (p. 174)
heritage languages (p. 175)
sense of community (p. 175)

culturally diverse backgrounds (p. 176)
cultural awareness (p. 176)
cultural relevance (p. 179)
culturally responsive teaching (p. 180)
co-operative learning (p. 180)
role models (p. 181)
English as a second language (ESL) (p. 183)
English language learners (ELL students) (p. 183)
immigrants (p. 183)
refugees (p. 184)

peer-mediated strategies (p. 185)
sexual harassment (p. 188)
homophobia (p. 189)
poverty (p. 190)
resilience (p. 191)
resilient students (p. 193)
Organisation for Economic Co-operation and Development (OECD) (p. 193)
homeless (p. 194)
transient lifestyle (p. 195)
child abuse (p. 195)
neglect (p. 195)
divorce (p. 196)

# Challenges for Reviewing Chapter 5

1.  Consider the case of Anita Harper, described at the beginning of this chapter. Think about the ways in which teachers can create a welcoming classroom climate and differentiate teaching so students like Anita feel safe and are engaged in our classrooms. What are some of the most important things you can do to ensure this at the grade level at which you teach?

2.  Write a brief scenario in which you describe some of the greatest challenges that teachers experience when teaching in schools with high cultural diversity. Remember to include yourself and an examination of your biases and assumptions in your scenario. Describe how you can ensure that all your students feel valued and learn successfully in your classroom. What is the role of differentiated instruction in this classroom? What else is important for you to be mindful of? Chapters 6 and 9 may help you to answer these questions.

3.  You are currently teaching in a school with many ELL students from a wide range of cultural backgrounds. Your principal has shown you the latest document on ELL and it recommends differentiated instruction (DI). You are familiar with DI from your experience including exceptional learners. Describe how you can use DI to meet the needs of your ELL students. And consider how this approach might be different from using DI to include exceptional learners. How might it be similar?

4.  Ragu, who was described in a case at the beginning of this chapter, is in your class. You see that he is taunted and treated unfairly by other students. What will you do to respond to these incidents of inequity? How can you ensure that everyone gets the message that this is unacceptable and begins to act differently? Discuss with your peers what you might do as a school as well as what you are doing individually to change situations like this one.

5.  You have chosen to teach in a neighbourhood where there are many at-risk students, some of whom live in poverty, have been abused, have experienced family breakdown, or are homeless. Some have had all of these experiences. Describe your efforts to differentiate teaching to meet the needs of these students. Describe some of the schoolwide initiatives that have helped. What resources have been particularly helpful and what resources does your school still need? What are the most important lessons you would share with colleagues newly arrived at your school?

6.  Return to the opening cases of Ragu and Anita and answer the five questions that follow the cases. Talk with your peers. Consider the differences in answers given by elementary and secondary teachers. Consider the similarities in the issues raised by elementary and secondary teachers.

# Chapter 6
# Climate, Community, and Classroom Management

## Learner Objectives

After you have read this chapter, you will be able to:

1. Identify and describe the key elements of creating a classroom community.

2. Describe developing an inclusive climate: physical layout and norms for interaction.

3. Identify and describe the major parts of negotiating and enforcing classroom rules and procedures.

4. Describe the major components of managing behaviour in an inclusive classroom and explain how they can be adapted to meet the needs of exceptional students.

Mandy has been at Bayside since September. She is in Ms. Turner's grade 6 class. Ms. Turner tells visitors to her classroom how Mandy invited another student who has few close friends to play basketball in the schoolyard. This act of kindness assumes significance when you know the rest of the story. If you had visited Mandy's grade 5 class at another school the previous June, you might have seen Mandy scream at her teacher, punch another student, or storm out of the classroom. It was terrible for Mandy and for her previous teacher. What has changed? Mandy moved to a small school with a caring and involved principal and to Ms. Turner's classroom. Ms. Turner is described as an exemplary teacher— every year children hope they will be in her class. Pre-service teachers love interning with her. They say, "All the kids treat each other so well. There is never any bullying. She won't have it. Everyone belongs." Mandy says, "I like Ms. Turner. She always says 'good morning' to me and makes me feel important. I don't want her to be disappointed in me. So I try my best. She never lets anyone hurt me and I don't have to hurt anyone back." At her last school, Mandy had been identified as having a behaviour exceptionality. Her principal thought that she needed a fresh start where the students and teachers were unaware of her reputation, with a teacher known for valuing and respecting every student—a teacher like Ms. Turner.

Jacob is in grade 10. He has cerebral palsy and a learning disability. He uses arm crutches to move around the school. To keep his energy up, Jacob has permission to eat healthy snacks in class. Recently he has been bringing chocolate bars and candy to his history class and has become very popular by handing out treats. Mr. Chan knows he will have to tackle this threat to his orderly classroom. Every day when the grade 10 students enter class, they find a "challenge" on their desks and have four minutes to determine, with a partner, which historical figure made the quoted statement. Recently some students have been too busy seeking a treat from Jacob to find solutions to the challenge. Mr. Chan does not approve of bribery, but he has noticed that more students talk with Jacob and invite him to join their groups for collaborative activities. Perhaps talking with the resource teacher who tutors Jacob will help Mr. Chan develop a response to the actions of Jacob and his classmates.

1. Under what circumstances could Mandy and Jacob be considered a challenge to the climate, organization, and management of their inclusive classrooms?

2. How can teachers develop classrooms that feel like communities, where all students are respected?

3. How can teachers discuss their approaches to classroom management with their classes and later refer to these discussions when responding to students who challenge order and learning in the classroom?

4. Whom might teachers like Ms. Turner and Mr. Chan turn to for assistance in teaching students to change their actions in the classroom?

5. How can Mr. Chan enable Jacob to eat a healthy snack when he needs it and to maintain his improved peer relations, while preventing bribery and chaos in the classroom?

# Introduction

Mandy and Jacob are two of the over 600 000 exceptional students in Canadian schools. You know that you can expect to meet exceptional students in almost every class you teach, which means you will meet challenges like those just described. The purpose of this chapter is to introduce you to ways to create positive classroom climate and to negotiation and management as aspects of teaching. The goal is to create a community in which diversity is encouraged and all students feel their contributions are valued.

**Cross-Reference**
Chapter 1 focuses on the general context for inclusion in Canadian society, while Chapter 5 emphasizes diversity arising from sources other than exceptionality. Chapter 9 examines social relations between students and how to enhance the inclusion of diverse students.

# Creating a Community

You know to expect diversity in any Canadian classroom. You will be teaching students with a wide array of exceptionalities and health conditions. Your classes may include Aboriginal students and others with a multiplicity of cultural and ethnic heritages. This diversity reflects our country, and as teachers we must shape an inclusive classroom community in which everyone belongs. Building community is a deliberate process that must be focused on over a period of time. Many provinces have recently renewed their commitment to this process. Examples include the document *Caring and Respectful Schools: Ensuring Student Well-Being* in Saskatchewan (2004), New Brunswick's *Positive Learning Environment Policy* (2002b), and Newfoundland and Labrador's *Safe and Caring Schools Policy* (2006). Prince Edward Island states on its website (www.gov.pe.ca/educ) that "the school should be a centre of learning that presents a welcoming, caring, and safe environment." The three territories—Northwest Territories, Nunavut, and Yukon—have also begun initiatives on enhancing the sense of safety in schools (www. safehealthyschools.org/whatsnew/initiatives.htm). These initiatives are seen to respond to the threat of school violence. Although the juvenile homicide rate has declined since the mid-1990s, the media attention given to school violence and school shootings has made the problem seem large. Only a small percentage of homicides committed by youths in North America take place in or around schools (Henley, 2006). For example, the National Center for Statistics in Education in the US reported fourteen homicides and three suicides of school-age youths (aged 5 to 18) at school from July 2005 to June 2006; that is one death at school per 3.2 million students. It is much more likely that students will be bullied (National Center for Educational Statistics, 2007). Schools and their surrounding neighbourhoods must work together to ensure that, when at school, students experience community, feel safe, and receive the social and emotional support they need.

**Community** involves a sense of belonging, of the group's concern for each individual, of individual responsibility for the good of the group, and of appreciation for shared experiences (Noddings, 1996). This means that classrooms "can become places where teachers and students live together, talk to each other, reason together, and take delight in each other's company" (Noddings, 1991, p. 157). When the Working Forum on Inclusive Schools (1994) documented successful inclusive schools in Canada and the United States, they found these schools were characterized by a common vision; problem-solving teams; parents, teachers, students, and others functioning as partners; time for planning and collaboration; warm relationships; little jargon; and flexible scheduling. These characteristics may help us describe community at the classroom level.

## Put into Practice

Read about creating an inclusive climate. Develop an approach you might use from the first day of school:

Larivee, B. (2008). *Authentic classroom management: Creating a learning community and building reflective practice.* Boston: Allyn & Bacon.

Hensley, M., Powell, W., Lamke, S., & Hartman, S. (2007). *The well-managed classroom: Strategies to create a productive and cooperative social climate in your learning community.* Omaha, NE: Boys Town Press.

Brownlie, F., Feniak, C., & Schnellert, L. (2006). *Student diversity: Classroom strategies to meet the learning needs of all students.* Markham, ON: Pembroke Pub.

## Further Reading

On creating community in the classroom:

Fine, E.S., Lacey, A., & Baer, J. (1995). *Children as peacemakers.* Portsmouth, NH: Heinemann.

Obenchain, K.M., & Abernathy, T.V. (2003). Twenty ways to build community and empower students. *Intervention in School and Clinic, 39*(1), 55–60.

Capuzzi, D., & Gross, D. (Eds.). (2004). *Youth at risk: A prevention resource for counselors, teachers, and parents* (4th ed.). Alexandria, VA: American Counseling Association.

Gill, V. (2007). *The ten students you'll meet in your classroom: Classroom management tips for middle and high school teachers.* Thousand Oaks, CA: Corwin Press.

## Common Vision and Problem-Solving Teams

To help students feel that they have contributed and that they must take responsibility for classroom conduct, teachers can involve them meaningfully in setting classroom rules and the consequences for not following these rules. Don't assume the consequences must be obvious to students; recent research suggests that even gifted students benefit from having the consequences of their actions explained clearly (Kaplan, 2008). Students have many ideas about what classrooms can and should be like and great energy to work toward their own goals (Berry, 2006). Harnessing this energy requires that you provide leadership and a structure for productive student discussion and that you listen and model behaviour that includes everyone. Emphasize the importance of **climate**, that is, the general feeling we create when we treat each other respectfully.

Making groups of students responsible for recommending possible solutions to classroom challenges uses problem-solving teams, teaches students to handle real-world problems, and creates a sense of belonging. In elementary classrooms, this problem solving may be applied, for instance, to devising efficient ways to ensure that all students have computer time or deciding on a realistic timeline and budget for studying pond ecology in the community. In secondary settings, student committees might orchestrate classroom debates or invite community leaders to help stage a simulated election.

## Parents, Teachers, and Students as Partners

Many resources are available on the subject of team building. Some focus on parents and extended families as partners and on culturally responsive parental involvement (e.g., McCaleb, 1995; Goodwin & King, 2002). Remember that all students, even secondary students, are more successful in school when their parents are involved in their education (Jeynes, 2007). Many resources on involving parents recommend sending letters to parents early in the year and meeting to talk about their priorities for their children's learning. Other strategies include inviting a parent to observe his or her child or adolescent who is disrupting the class to devise joint approaches for home and school (Krogness, 1995). Three educators from Toronto suggest student-led parent–teacher conferences and students as peer negotiators or peacemakers (Fine, Lacey, & Baer, 1995). Capuzzi and Gross (2004) have collected strategies for developing and maintaining environments in which adolescents can flourish; again the emphasis is on schools and families working together. Whatever strategies you choose, focus on creating an equitable community (Levin, 2004) with high-quality communication among all partners (Faltis, 2007).

## Time for Collaboration and Joint Planning

Set small amounts of scheduled time aside for your students to learn and practise collaboration and joint planning. Include learning outcomes listed in your curricula, such as effective oral communication, planning and co-operating, and development of self-awareness. Write plans for these times, list them in your term's teaching plans, and be prepared to explain their role in creating community. Ms. Turner, who is discussed in one of the opening cases, spends considerable time with her grade 6 class during the first few weeks of the school year teaching her students what she expects of them and helping them to collaborate and plan together. She is confident that she can easily catch up to the other classes, in the academic realm, in late

September and early October because her students know what she expects and less time is spent on management issues throughout the rest of the school year. Vicki Gill, an award-winning teacher, agrees: "I spend a great deal of time in the first week creating a sense of community, generating excitement for the curriculum, and setting up classroom expectations" (2007). Her two goals for the first week are that every student feels known and that every students understand what will cause a problem in her classroom and how she will react to that problem.

Making the class inviting is part of your work as a teacher.

## Caring Relationships

Recent research documents how teachers begin to create safe and productive environments for diverse student populations on the first day of school through culturally responsive classroom management (CRCM) (Bondy et al., 2007; Weinstein et al., 2004). CRCM is characterized by teachers developing a respectful, caring, and personal relationship with each student in addition to building a learning community with an emotional climate where students can take risks, laugh, and trust one another as well as their teacher. In Bondy's study (2007), each of the three teachers introduced herself to the students on the first day in a way that communicated genuine interest in the students and that shared personal information about herself, her hobbies, and her family. They all engaged their students in activities to get to know one another, and communicated core lessons about the importance of respect and kindness, including this one: "We don't laugh at anyone in here. You can feel very secure in this classroom" (p. 336).

## Clear Language and Flexible Scheduling

You should model clear use of language that is understood by all members of the extended classroom community. Listen to the language of classroom partners and point out when people are referring to the same phenomenon with different names. Communication should be tactful so parents don't feel they are being "talked down to." If you use a classroom website, maintain other means of communication as well for families that do not have computer access. Also use familiar language and referents with your students. The effective teachers studied by Bondy et al. (2007) who demonstrated culturally responsive classroom management used words and expressions that were familiar to the students and were used by their cultural group; these teachers also made references to popular culture—movies, musicians, and television programs that the students were familiar with. They gave straightforward directives that were explicit and used no jargon. One teacher said on the first day of school, "This is how it's going to work this morning. People will come in and I will have to go to the door to welcome them to the class. You will wait quietly. You can work on your favorite worksheet" (p. 344). Although the teachers were warm and funny, there was no question that they meant what they said. Besides thinking about the language you use, consider your use of time. Make schedules as flexible as possible so students can work with volunteers and each other at strategic times. Building community should complement, rather than replace, the mandated curriculum and should enhance collaborative learning.

# Developing an Inclusive Climate

The physical space can be inviting and inclusive for all students, including exceptional students, as well as work efficiently for learning. Classroom norms for interaction and discussion can also contribute to an inclusive climate.

## Making the Physical Space Efficient, Inviting, and Accessible

The social environment you are creating should be supported by a physical arrangement that allows students to talk and collaborate for part of each day or part of each period; it should also allow for learning in a whole-class setting and individually (Charles & Charles, 2004; Hadjioannou, 2007). Arranging the **physical space** to make it inviting as well as accessible and efficient is something you should do before the school year begins and should revisit frequently. Consider furniture (including desks for the students and yourself), audiovisual equipment, visual aids (such as bulletin boards), and any extra items you bring (such as plants). Think proactively about the physical needs of exceptional students for space, adapted desks, computers, and other specialized equipment. Jacob, described in one of the opening case studies of this chapter, can move around comfortably in Mr. Chan's classroom with his arm crutches. The physical space has helped Jacob to feel comfortable and to socialize easily in the classroom, and conveys to Jacob that Mr. Chan cares enough about him to make sure the classroom meets his needs.

### ARRANGING FOR EFFICIENCY AND ACCESSIBILITY

The classroom is a small workspace for thirty or so students and you, for a vast array of learning materials, and for a variety of activities using different structures and parts of the room. There may be exceptional students who need a predictable physical layout because of visual impairments and students who need wide aisles to manoeuvre their wheelchairs. Your goals should be to keep pathways clear to permit orderly movement, keep distractions to a minimum, and make efficient use of the available space. Table 6.1 contains guidelines for arranging the physical features of the classroom.

After your teaching is under way and patterns of use of time and space emerge, make a floor plan showing the size and location of built-in features. Make scale representations of the furniture and consider spaces, pathways, and room for activities. Ask yourself the following questions:

- What learning spaces, for both small and large activities, are available to students?
- Which spaces do students use frequently? Occasionally? Which are never used?
- What are the crowded areas?
- Which spaces are the pathways for movement?
- Which spaces are used for quiet activities? Which for noisy activities?

Use this information to rearrange the room to support all of the learning activities you value and to make access as easy for exceptional students as it is for everyone else.

## TABLE 6.1 GUIDELINES FOR ARRANGING PHYSICAL FEATURES OF THE CLASSROOM

| Features | Guidelines |
|---|---|
| **High traffic areas** | Avoid congestion near doorways, the teacher's desk, pencil sharpeners, and storage areas that are used regularly. |
| | Separate high-traffic areas. |
| | Ensure that you can reach everyone in the room with ease. |
| **Sightlines** | Make certain you can see all of your students easily, so you can monitor their activities and prevent disruptions and distractions. |
| **Teaching materials** | Arrange the teaching materials you use regularly, so you can access them and put them away easily without disrupting your teaching. |
| | Arrange materials that students access frequently in decentralized locations, where they are needed. |
| **Seating arrangements** | Use seating arrangements that allow students to see the chalkboard, overhead projector, video screen, and demonstrations, as well as work with peers collaboratively. |

Source: Adapted from Evertson, C.M., & Emmer, E.T. (2008). *Classroom management for elementary teachers*. Boston: Allyn and Bacon.

## ARRANGING AN INVITING CLASSROOM

Ask yourself what you can do in the physical set-up of the classroom to make each student feel that he or she is a valued member of your classroom. Recent research suggests that students are more likely to be engaged in the classroom and in learning if they think their teachers are positive and sensitive (e.g., Rimm-Kaufman et al., 2005). For ELL students, perhaps you can post a sign in their first language. For a student like Jacob who has a physical disability, it might be a poster that includes someone in a wheelchair or using arm crutches that will communicate a positive message. For students with learning difficulties, feeling that they know exactly what is expected is important, so write an agenda on the board or on chart paper to ensure that all students find the day predictable. For preliterate students use symbols such as a book to show story time. If there is one preliterate student in a literate class, tape a daily schedule in symbols to that student's desk to help avoid embarrassment. Students with behaviour disabilities or ADHD may also benefit from a schedule taped to their desks.

Bulletin boards hold relatively permanent displays. Use inspirational posters and generate interest in an upcoming unit by connecting the topic to current events or popular culture. Post student work or seasonal art. Students can design collaborative displays on curriculum topics or murals about their novel study. Change displays frequently, post classroom rules (discussed in the next section), and ask students for suggestions to enhance bulletin boards. Use colour, but avoid distracting students. Ensure that before the first day of school, you post a welcome message for the students. As one Native student commented, "Last year, I had . . . a history teacher, and I walked into the room and I saw that on his walls were pictures of Native American people. And I think, 'Okay, I'm going to like this guy'" (Pewewardy & Hammer, 2003).

Desktops and tabletops should be clean and the room free of clutter. The appearance of order and organization in the physical environment communicates that you expect students to behave in an organized way. Place relevant materials at a level where a student in a wheelchair can reach them independently—this will communicate that you value independence. Look at the classroom from the

**Put into Practice**

Visit classrooms at your grade level. Observe the physical organization and consider how to ensure that the physical organization supports the classroom community you want to create.

perspective of the students and of a parent who comes to visit, as well as from your own perspective. Ensure that it is inviting.

## Teaching Norms for Classroom Interaction and Learning

Teaching **norms for classroom interaction** and learning is complex. First, be a model of effective communication and respectful interaction in all your dealings with students. You also need to establish norms for discussion and lead discussions effectively.

### MODELLING COMMUNICATION AND LEADING DISCUSSION

You are responsible for making it safe for people to share ideas and for affirming them as part of the community. This means teaching students to engage in give-and-take dialogues. If you are teaching young children, you might consult Diane Levin's book, *Teaching Young Children in Violent Times: Building a Peaceable Classroom* (2003). If you are teaching middle school, see suggestions in *Classroom Management for Middle-Grades Teachers* (Charles & Charles, 2004), and teachers of high school students should consult *Classroom Management for Middle and High School Teachers* (Emmer & Evertson, 2008).

For students of any age, lead **give-and-take dialogues** from the first day to deal with problems that arise. When leading such brainstorming sessions, listen to all ideas, ask students to "tell us more" if their ideas are not clear, write all suggestions briefly on chart paper, and encourage a range of solutions. Don't evaluate during this stage. Model combining suggestions. Stop before everyone tires of the discussion and acknowledge the group's accomplishments in specific terms: "Thanks for listening to one another," etc. Before you leave the topic, suggest what the class will do to complete the task and when this will happen. Make "discussion rules" one of the earliest topics for discussion. Figure 6.1 contains guidelines for leading a successful discussion.

### ESTABLISHING NORMS FOR DISCUSSION

The *Tribes* program is proactive in teaching discussion and community participation (Gibbs, 2001, 2006). The two groupings in *Tribes* are the community circle (all members of the class) and the small groups or tribes that are introduced gradually. For secondary school students, you can refer to whole-class discussion and small-group discussion and use the *Tribes* approach flexibly. During the introductory session introduce the **signal** you will use to get attention. *Tribes* recommends raising your hand, but some teachers flick the lights, play a few notes on the piano, or start rhythmic clapping and invite everyone to join in. Explain that at this signal, everyone stops talking and raises his or her hand, etc. With young students, practise the signal. Tell older students that if they are not successful on the first few occasions, you will practise the signal with them. If there is a paraeducator in your classroom, be sure to include this individual in these introductory activities so the paraeducator knows your expectations and is prepared to act in accord with the classroom approach you are developing.

*Tribes* begins with the whole group or **community circle**. There are over a hundred activities with detailed lesson plans, many of which are appropriate to the

**Weblinks**
Check out these sites designed to inform parents and help them deal with their adolescents. You may find valuable information, and you will certainly be better informed about how parents may be approaching issues of appropriate behaviour in their adolescents, your students. Many of these sites have information on children as well.

CANADIAN PARENTS.COM: TWEENS AND TEENS
www.canadianparents.com/tweens-and-teens

INTERNET ARCHIVE: EDUCATIONAL FILM FROM THE 1950S ON DISCIPLINING ADOLESCENTS
www.archive.org/details/discipline_during_adolescence

ABOUT.COM: PARENTING OF ADOLESCENTS
http://parentingteens.about.com/od/disciplin1

ADOLESCENT DISCIPLINE AND PARENTAL DISAGREEMENT
www.hawaii.edu/medicine/pediatrics/parenting/c40.html

## FIGURE 6.1 LEADING A SUCCESSFUL GIVE-AND-TAKE DISCUSSION

Prepare in advance for the discussion:

- Choose topics in advance and decide how you will introduce them to the children.
- Identify the children's likely key issues and ways of understanding the topic.
- Plan questions that will get children to express their diverse ideas and will stretch their thinking.
- Identify a variety of possible outcomes, so you can guide the children toward them, but also be ready for ideas you never anticipated.

Expect to make constant decisions about such issues as

- what question to ask next and how to ask it;
- how to balance the needs of individual children with the needs of the group;
- how far afield to let comments go before bringing things back to the main topic;
- how to pace the discussion to keep all the children interested and invested;
- when to let "wrong" answers and values you do not want to promote go uncorrected in the service of promoting give and take;
- how to incorporate new ideas and information that extend the children's thinking while acknowledging and accepting what they have to say; and
- when to end the discussion and with what group conclusions.

Offer children a lot of help (especially at the beginning of the year) with

- learning how to participate in give-and-take dialogues;
- feeling safe contributing their ideas;
- staying task-focused in their comments;
- filling in the words and information others need to fully understand what they are saying; and
- applying the ideas they get from the discussions to their everyday actions and experiences.

———

Source: Levin, D.E. (2003). *Teaching young children in violent times: Building a peaceable classroom.* Cambridge, MA: Educators for Social Responsibility. Copyright © 2003 by Educators for Social Responsibility. Used by permission.

community circle. For younger students, you might start with "Five Tribles" (faces ranging from very sad to joyous), in which you ask everyone to report how they feel today. For adolescents, "Bumper Sticker" might be an appropriate introductory activity. One of the earliest discussions should be about what we need in order to feel safe in a group. From this discussion, settle on a maximum of four or five statements. Gibbs (2001, 2006) suggests the four **community agreements**:

- attentive listening;
- appreciation—no put-downs;
- right to pass and right to participate; and
- mutual respect.

Talking circles are described by Paulette Running Wolf and Julie Rickard (2003) and by Cheri Foster Triplett and Anne Hunter (2005). The use of talking circles is an Aboriginal approach to experiential learning that stimulates awareness of and respect for individual differences as well as facilitating group cohesion. It incorporates traditions from various First Nations including the Iroquois Confederacy council meetings. Triplett and Hunter describe how handing a feather around the circle to the student who is going to speak next helps students to listen to one another and ensures that only one person speaks at a time. Anne Hunter, an elementary teacher, says, "I choose to have Talking Circle on Mondays because students are eager to share their weekend stories. Instead of seeing this as a classroom management dilemma, I see it as an opportunity to get to know my students better."

### TEACHING AND PRACTISING CLASSROOM NORMS

The community agreements just described express norms for how students interact in the classroom, distinct from the classroom rules discussed in the next section of this chapter. Attentive listening can be taught and practised with activities in paraphrasing and reflecting the feelings of the speaker. Look at *Tribes*, talking circles, and other similar programs for activities. Students can practise appreciating others by saying something positive about another student's role in the activity—model this yourself. Be specific: "I admire you for [the way you work so patiently with your reading buddy]." Enforce your ban on put-downs vigorously. The **right to pass** means that students have the right to choose the extent to which they will participate in a group activity that requires sharing personal information. Acknowledge a pass by saying, "That is fine," but do not allow students to avoid doing class assignments by saying, "Pass." You can offer a second chance to those who passed. Finally, mutual respect means that everyone's beliefs, values, and needs are honoured. Students' property should be respected, as well as their confidentiality. What is said in community circles, talking circles, and small groups should be treated in confidence and not become the basis for gossip.

The skills for working together need to be taught and practised regularly. You can make these skills explicit. Consider the example of listening. Discuss and come to agreement on what listening *looks like* (e.g., eyes looking, leaning forward), *sounds like* (one person talking at a time, sounds of "good ideas"), and *feels like* (people care, "I'm being heard"). Post the four community agreements in a prominent place. Affirm students when you see them upholding the agreements, and refer to the agreements when you notice infringements.

# Negotiating and Enforcing Classroom Rules and Procedures

Rules and procedures enable the classroom to function smoothly and predictably. After negotiating and teaching rules and procedures, you must monitor students to ensure they are followed. Consistent application of consequences is critical.

## Negotiating Rules

What classroom rules do you intend to establish? Rules help create a sense of order and predictability and enable you to be proactive in preventing difficulties. Teachers who are effective at managing their classrooms engage in community building and communicate the message that they care to each student but also have well-defined rules (e.g., Bondy et al., 2007). Effective classroom **rules** are brief and specific, positively worded, and clearly understood by students. They should be consistent with school rules, so become aware of the school code of conduct before the term begins. Then think about the general rules you hope to enforce for an orderly and predictable classroom. The three effective teachers who used culturally

### What do you think?

Is it sound to allow students to pass when discussing personal feelings or information? How can you ensure that this privilege is not abused? What reading informs your thinking on this issue?

Weblinks

SAFE SCHOOLS AND YOUTH JUSTICE: BRIEFING BOOK ON INNOVATIVE CANADIAN INITIATIVES, ACTIVITIES AND REPORTS (COUNCIL OF MINISTERS OF EDUCATION)
www.safehealthyschools.org/whatsnew/initiatives.htm

THE LEAGUE OF PEACEFUL SCHOOLS
www.leagueofpeacefulschools.sk.ca

SAFE AND CARING SCHOOLS (MANITOBA)
www.edu.gov.mb.ca/k12/safe_schools

responsive classroom management recognized that definitions of appropriate classroom behaviour are culturally defined and developed knowledge of their students' cultural backgrounds so they could use culturally appropriate classroom management strategies (Bondy et al., 2007). That helped each of them to be an authoritative teacher but not authoritarian. They all introduced rules and procedures within the first two hours of school. Even the fifth grade teacher said, "It will probably take about two weeks, so I'm going to keep going over rules and consequences" (p. 338).

Although there is disagreement on this issue, with research supporting both sides (see DiClementi & Handelsman, 2005; Emmer & Evertson, 2008; Lewis & Burman, 2006), I recommend involving the students in the discussion about rules rather than deciding the rules alone. You might ask students to think of reasons for having rules and reasons for dispensing with rules, and ask what kind of class they want to have. Then, ask students to talk in small groups to come up with three rules they think are important. It will help if you provide a general model—short, clear, and positively stated—such as "Respect and be polite to all people." Each group, in turn, states a rule it thinks is important that has not already been stated. Continue eliciting suggestions until no new ones emerge. To prevent key issues being overlooked, you could take a turn. After writing the suggestions on the board, group them into roughly five specific but broad rules and use other student suggestions as examples of the rules. Table 6.2 contains five rules with examples.

As soon as possible, write the rules on a poster and mount it in the classroom. Then you can point to them from the first day of class onward. Student input usually helps enhance classroom climate, build community, develop student understanding of the rationale for rules, and enhance the quality of your relationship with students. The standard to aim for is that there is no difference in student conduct when you leave the classroom briefly. This means that students must be

## TABLE 6.2 CLASSROOM RULES AND EXAMPLES

| Rules | Examples |
|---|---|
| 1. **Be polite and helpful.** | • Wait your turn; say please and thank you.<br>• Ask the teacher for help only after asking your group; offer help in your group.<br>• Behave well for a substitute teacher. |
| 2. **Respect other people's property.** | • Keep the room clean.<br>• Do not borrow without asking.<br>• Return borrowed property. |
| 3. **Listen quietly while others are speaking.** | • During whole-class discussion, raise your hand.<br>• In small groups, speak when the previous person is finished.<br>• Don't call out. |
| 4. **Respect and be polite to all people.** | • Never call anyone a name or bully anyone.<br>• Don't allow anyone to do these things to you or to another person.<br>• Treat the teacher respectfully. |
| 5. **Obey all school rules.** | • Follow rules for the schoolyard, cafeteria, etc.<br>• Remember that all teachers and students are expected to help with enforcement of school rules. |

**Further Reading**

On classroom management:

Emmer, E.T., & Evertson, C.M. (2008). *Classroom management for secondary teachers*, 7th ed. Boston: Allyn and Bacon.

Vitto, J.M. (2003). *Relationship-driven classroom management.* Thousand Oaks, CA: Corwin Press.

Khalsa, S.S. (2007). *Teaching discipline and self-respect: Effective strategies, anecdotes, and lessons for successful classroom management strategies.* Thousand Oaks, CA: Corwin Press.

Jones, V., & Jones, L. (2004). *Comprehensive classroom management: Creating communities of support and solving problems.* Boston: Pearson Education.

enforcing the rules and growing in self-discipline and respect for the rules (Khalsa, 2007). Before discussing the procedures that govern daily routines, I focus on how you can teach rules so they are integral to the life of the classroom.

Many researchers and educators agree that there are three key aspects of teaching rules: demonstration, practice, and feedback (e.g., Marshall, 2005; Martin, Sugarman, & McNamara, 2001). First, describe and then demonstrate the desired behaviours. Be specific. If students may talk to one another in quiet voices while working in small groups, then use a quiet voice when you ask a student to speak quietly. Give feedback about the volume; if it was too loud, repeat the procedure. With adolescents, engage in teaching the rules with sensitivity to their age; perhaps ask each group to teach a rule to the class. Second, rehearsal means asking students to show that they understand. Younger students may need to practise standing up to a bully. Never have a student enact the role of the bully, because that amounts to you teaching someone to be a bully. Rather, ask students to imagine seeing a bully push their friend. Then have them practise asking the bully to stop and helping their friend report the incident to an adult (including asking the adult when they can expect a report on action taken). Again, feedback is important. Develop the habit of giving feedback after students have followed a rule. Make specific comments: "I like the way you were raising your hands in the large group and taking turns talking in your small groups."

If one student violates a rule, take him or her aside and say privately, for instance, "I saw you call John an unpleasant name. Next time that happens, I will call your name, and you will stand beside the door until I discuss this with you. I will not tolerate bullying. We agreed that we would not treat one another that way. Do you understand what I'm saying? Do you need to practise following the rules?" This kind of follow-up is called **enforcing a rule**.

Monitoring is important to ensure that students engage in learning activities and internalize classroom rules and procedures. A discussion of monitoring follows the section on establishing procedures.

## Establishing Procedures

Teachers usually develop classroom procedures for areas of classroom space, seat work and teacher-led activities, transitions into and out of the room, small-group activities, and general procedures. Figure 6.2 contains examples of procedures. **Classroom procedures** are efficient ways of moving everyone through the day or the period that are consistent with your goals for the classroom. Because procedures usually follow from the rules, making this connection will help most students understand them. Teach the most critical procedures first, introduce them as the need arises during the first few days, and introduce only as many in a day as the class can handle. In one of the opening cases Mr. Chan had developed a procedure for getting his grade 10 class straight into academic work—they found a "challenge" on their desks when they entered and had four minutes to determine with a partner which historical figure had made the quoted statement. Many teachers find that procedures that enable a productive and focused opening of class help them to set a positive tone and to be efficient.

## Monitoring Student Actions

**Monitoring** involves being alert and responsive to student action and learning. When you present information to the class, position yourself so you can see every

# FIGURE 6.2 PROCEDURES FOR THE CLASSROOM

**Procedures to Organize Use of the Room**

Teacher's Desk and Storage Areas

- Normally, students remove items only with your permission.

Student Desks and Other Student Storage Areas

- Normally, students remove items from others' desks only with permission.

Storage for Common Materials

- Tell students if and when they may remove texts, paper, rulers, etc.

Drinking Fountain, Pencil Sharpener

- Normally, students use these one at a time, and not during large group presentations.

Centres, Stations, Equipment Areas

- Tell students when they may use these areas, how many at a time, and post instructions for the use of any equipment.

**Transitions into and out of the Room**

Beginning of the School Day

- Establish a routine that you supervise. With young children, it may be a "sharing" time; with older students, it may be a "challenge" that they work on for a few minutes alone, in pairs, or in groups.

Leaving the Classroom

- Younger students leave quietly, in line—and when you give the signal.
- Older students leave quietly and when you give the signal (not just when the bell rings).

Returning to the Classroom

- After a noisy activity allow quiet talking and then request silence before you begin the next activity.
- After a quiet activity provide a challenge to focus students and request silence before you begin the next activity.

Ending the Day or Period

- Review what was learned and look ahead to any homework, upcoming activities; end on a positive note.
- Tidy the room with all students doing their part; use procedures for leaving.

**General Procedures**

Distributing Materials

- Make it efficient; each week assign a student to this task for each group.

Interruptions or Delays

- Teach students that after an announcement on the public address system, they are to return immediately, without comment, to their work.
- If you leave the room, remind students you expect them to act the same as when you are present; leave them working.

Washrooms

- Tell students how many can leave class at a time and whether they need your permission.

Library, Resource Room, School Office, Cafeteria

- Review school rules.

Schoolyard

- Review school rules, prevent bullying, and help students include everyone.

Fire Drills

- Learn school procedures; practise with your class prior to the first drill (October is fire prevention month in Canada).
- Arrange to assist students with physical, visual, hearing, or developmental disabilities.

Classroom Helpers

- Share these privileges systematically; identify helpers (or pairs of helpers) at the beginning of the week.
- Demonstrate how helpers are to fulfill their roles; don't accept shoddy work

---

student's face. Move around the classroom so you come close to all students. Ensure that a student who speech-reads can see your face straight on; you will not be able to move around the classroom while presenting. Scan the whole class; some teachers tend to focus on the middle front rows, but you should be aware of the reactions of students on the periphery. Some teachers use response cards to monitor the responses and understanding of all students—students can write on a response card or hold up a preprinted response card. These can be as simple as yes/no in response to the question, "Are you ready for me to move to the next topic?" or can engage students in creating or selecting a brief answer to a mathematics question, dictated spelling

*Students learn to work collaboratively in small groups, enhancing social skills and social acceptance while meeting learning goals.*

word, etc. Response cards promote high levels of teacher monitoring, active student response, and learning (Randolph, 2007).

If you teach one small group while other groups are working independently, position yourself so you can see all the students and move around the room between working with one group and the next group. When you circulate, look closely to see that the students are completing the assigned work. During this break between your work with groups, ask if anyone has a question that could not be answered by a classmate. If there is a question, tell the students you will give a brief reply. After one minute of responding, name a peer for the student with the question to direct any further questions to. Then call for the next small group to assemble. While you are engaged with a small group, keep monitoring; look up frequently and be alert for disruptions.

When all students are working on independent assignments, circulate and check each individual's progress. Avoid prolonged discussion with one student that interferes with alert monitoring. Remind students that they should ask you for help only after they have tried to obtain the assistance of a peer. If a student requires sustained assistance, the two of you should move to a location from which you can monitor the entire class. If you move to your desk, do not let students congregate there and block your monitoring of the room or distract students seated nearby.

After introducing a new lesson to the whole class, instruct students to take out the appropriate materials. Scan the class to ensure that every desktop has what is needed. Then you may want to have all students try the first example under your direction and to take this example up with the group. Scan the class to see that everyone is writing. Check on exceptional students to ensure that they understand the instructions. Keep checking when students move to the next example. Quietly and individually ask the students experiencing difficulty to join you for reteaching at an area from which you can monitor the rest of the class. To prevent these invitations from being seen as punishment, also ask the advanced students to join you at the reteaching area for challenge activities after they have completed the assigned work. Ensure that all students have opportunities to work with you at this location.

You will find it helpful to monitor student work by collecting assignments frequently, even if you have asked students to check their own work in class. Write brief comments so students see you have read their work, and keep your mark book current. You will see patterns of students who do not attempt assignments, leave assignments incomplete, or complete work only with assistance. When teaching students to do long-term assignments, set quarter-way and halfway **checkpoints**. Devise a checklist for students to complete that shows what they have finished, and write brief, specific, and encouraging feedback on the checklist. It will be necessary to conference with students who need guidance or **scaffolding** (support that can gradually be removed) to ensure that the adapted outcomes of exceptional students are appropriate.

## Applying Consequences Consistently

You know how important it is for teachers to be consistent. **Consistency** and equity should be discussed together to eliminate any misunderstanding on this important matter. Be consistent in your expectations from day to day. Also apply consequences consistently. For example, if you say students must move to the door and await a conversation with you for being disrespectful to a peer, then apply this consequence to all students; don't excuse one student because he begs or suspend another because he annoyed you earlier. Obvious inconsistencies confuse students about what is acceptable behaviour, and students may test you to find the limits.

However, there are occasions when circumstances justify making exceptions. Consider the student who was ill between when the assignment was set and the halfway checkpoint. It makes sense to compare his or her work with the quarter-way checkpoint and ensure that the pupil understands the assignment. Then renegotiate the date for a halfway checkpoint. The student's participation in setting a new timeline increases the likelihood he or she will stay on schedule. Students with IEPs, ELL students, and those at risk for other reasons may need adapted outcomes, differentiated instruction, and more scaffolding. Lead discussions that help students value diversity and understand that fairness does not necessarily mean sameness. Mr. Chan may find it helpful to discuss with his grade 10 class Jacob's need to eat healthy snacks frequently to maintain his energy level, although eating during class is not allowed for those without a medical need to eat. Refreshing students' memories about a rule set at the beginning of term is helpful and reminds us why it is important to set rules together at the start of term. This discussion can serve as a reminder to Jacob that he and his family have agreed that his snacks will be healthy, and that he

Put into Practice

Interview an experienced principal or teacher about how they maintain consistency in applying consequences and still retain the flexibility they need to treat exceptional students equitably. Ask how they talk with students about consistency and flexibility.

must consume them himself and not share them with his classmates. It will also be a reminder to Jacob's classmates that they are contributing to a problem by accepting food from Jacob.

# Managing Behaviour in the Inclusive Classroom

Managing student behaviour contributes to learning in the inclusive classroom. We focus on increasing appropriate behaviour, decreasing undesirable behaviour, and enhancing self-management. This section ends with a short discussion of positive behavioural supports followed by a brief consideration of harsh and inappropriate punishments. If you have the opportunity, you might want to take part in a course or workshop that coaches teachers on how to manage challenging behaviours in the classroom; studies show that teachers show higher levels of positive classroom climate, sensitivity to students, and behaviour management after such coaching (e.g., Raver et al., 2008).

## Increasing Appropriate Behaviour

There are a number of approaches to increasing appropriate behaviour and to helping students to assume responsibility for their actions, including anticipating and preventing inappropriate behaviour and focusing on helping students to be aware of and practise core virtues.

In effective classrooms, teachers and students respect and trust each other and students are engaged in learning. There are many actions you can take to increase students' appropriate behaviour. First, give positive attention to the behaviour you want to maintain or increase. (Lindberg and Swick [2006] call this common sense classroom management.) Provide verbal cues, prompts, and praise to indicate the behaviour you expect. And recognize social and academic achievement and qualities unique to individual students. Two Canadian educators, Barrie Bennett and Peter Smilanich (1994; www.sacsc.ca), describe teachers who are effective and increase students' appropriate behaviour as having **"invisible" classroom management** techniques. The Focus on Schools box describes a program in which teachers clearly concentrate on students' appropriate behaviours, especially respectful behaviour.

Don Jacobs (also known as Four Arrows) suggests that we need to shift our attention to "virtue awareness" when trying to increase positive participation and "decrease negative behaviours that prevent [Aboriginal] children from contributing to healthy and peaceful classroom environments" (2003, p. 2). He argues that we need to weave virtue awareness into all aspects of teaching and demonstrate these virtues in our lives. By core virtues, he means courage, generosity, humility, honesty, fortitude, and patience. The goal is for children to seek inner meaning and to explore their experiences in terms of the core values. He asserts that such understanding would enable all students to be active participants in moral decisions and to take greater responsibility for increasing their virtuous actions.

### CATCH 'EM BEING GOOD

**Catch 'em being good** is a strategy that was developed many years ago and is exemplified in the Focus on Schools box. When a student's behaviour is consistent with

**Weblinks**

SAFE AND CARING SCHOOLS AND COMMUNITIES: BULLYING AND VIOLENCE PREVENTION, CHARACTER EDUCATION, CONFLICT MANAGEMENT, AND RESPECTING DIVERSITY (RESOURCES AND ELABORATIONS OF EARLIER BOOK BY BENNETT AND SMILANICH [1994])
www.sacsc.ca/index.html

LEARNING RESOURCES CENTRE OF THE GOVERNMENT OF ALBERTA
www.lrc.education.gov.ab.ca/pro/default.html

COOL QUOTES FOR TEENS
http://quotations.about.com/cs/inspirationquotes/a/Teens1.htm

BC'S PARTNERSHIP FOR RESPONSIBLE GAMBLING (FOCUS ON YOUTH GAMBLING)
www.bcresponsiblegambling.ca/problem/youth5.html

ADOLESCENT PEER CULTURE: PARENTS' ROLE
www.answers.com/topic/adolescent-peer-culture-parents-role

# The Three Rs Plus Respect Equals Results

The project called Together We Light the Way at Holy Cross Catholic School in Oshawa is an attempt to replicate the remarkable success one principal achieved in a decaying school, South Simcoe Public School, in Oshawa, Ontario, over the past decade. Early in Sandra Dean's tenure at South Simcoe Public School, the students scored the worst out of eighty-nine schools in the Durham District School Board on board-wide tests in reading, writing, and math. But within five years, the school sat among the top performers in the region, just east of Toronto, and won a national award for excellence from the Conference Board of Canada.

Ms. Dean's approach, an attempt to recreate the village environment of her childhood in Trinidad, is hardly revolutionary. If anything, it seems old-fashioned: A teacher at the door, smiling and greeting children by name. Flowers planted in the schoolyard. Neighbourhood businesspeople reading to children. Regular phone calls filled with good news to parents from teachers. And a concerted focus on values such as respect and interdependence, using them as a foundation for better students and more resilient human beings. Students receive a "respect ticket" each time they say or do something that demonstrates good behaviour. A certain number of tickets qualifies them for gifts, the ultimate being a free dinner at Swiss Chalet served by teachers and community leaders such as the police chief.

Nothing in her upper-middle-class background prepared Ms. Dean for South Simcoe Public School, which she joined as principal in February 1991. Her first task was to make the school a "home away from home." If the students were to show respect for themselves and others, they would also have to be respected. Teachers were forbidden to yell at children or use the *S* word: *shut up*. "When a child walks into a room and you like that child, your eyes light up. Then the whole tone and atmosphere is set for learning," Ms. Dean said.

The word *respect* is everywhere at Holy Cross, a lower-middle-class downtown Oshawa school of just 215 students, one-third of them from single-parent homes. On the morning a reporter visited, the school held a "respect assembly" in the gymnasium. Each class presented a song or banner about respect. In the hallway a Respect Tree holds the pictures of every student who collected at least 75 respect tickets. And in the grade 4 classroom, students stand at the front of the class explaining how they earned respect tickets at recess. "I earned a respect ticket for grabbing a ball and giving it to the teacher, instead of just kicking it," a boy said. On the blackboard is the classroom's goal for the week:

"I will walk respectfully in the corridors."

Teaching respect might seem to be the very stock-in-trade of schools, but the truth is it got lost somewhere along the way, Ms. MacInnis, the Holy Cross principal, said. "Has respect always been a part of our curriculum? Truly, we've always expected that it's there, but have we ever taught it?"

When the program started a year ago, she wondered how staff would respond to the challenge of treating students more respectfully. "It's a total shift in philosophy," she said. "Instead of looking for things going wrong, you're looking for ways to support things going right for the child."

Teaching respect starts with acts as small as encouraging a student to push her chair in at the end of the day, Ms. MacInnis said. "You can't minimize the most minimal change in behaviour with some of these children." From such a seemingly small foundation, she says, self-awareness can be built. "They gain a strong sense of self, a respect for themselves, each other, and it extends out into the community. It's no longer a self-centredness. It's a true meaning of who they might be, what their potentials might be."

Grade 7 teacher Andrea Cannon believes the program is working and says praise has played a big part in its success. "A lot of children in this area aren't used to being praised by an adult," she said. "You can see them shine, almost."

(Read about Sandra Dean's program at South Simcoe Public School in her book *Hearts & Minds: A Public School Miracle* [Toronto: Penguin Books Canada, 2000].)

Source: Fine, S. (2000). The three Rs plus respect equals results. *The Globe and Mail*. October 10, p. A9. Used by permission.

expectations, you acknowledge and praise or reward the behaviour. If a student enters the classroom and immediately focuses on the challenge you have placed on her desk, you might say, "Mandy, I like the way you went straight to your desk and started on today's challenge. That's exactly what you are supposed to do." This comment rewards Mandy's behaviour. If she sometimes misbehaves to feel noticed, she receives the message that good behaviour gets your attention. If she sometimes misbehaves to gain control over some aspect of her situation, letting her know that she is positively in control may help to overcome this.

Sometimes students misbehave simply because you have not communicated effectively what is unacceptable and will not be tolerated. You know this is probably the case when you see Mandy behaving well in another class after she has just raised a ruckus in your class. Catching one student being good lets all the others know what you expect and value. However, I have found it more effective to speak privately to adolescents to let them know I appreciate their positive behaviour. For example, Mr. Chan might privately remind Jacob of his expectations on the day after the discussion about not sharing food, and then watch to ensure that he acknowledges privately Jacob's efforts to meet these expectations—eat his own healthy snacks and not pass them around. To compensate for possible negative ramifications to Jacob's popularity, Mr. Chan might want to take steps to ensure that Jacob's other contributions are valued by his peers, and to ensure that Jacob contributes to his group's work. You may also find that it is effective to speak privately to ELL students, so you can discern the extent to which they have understood your comments.

## THE GOOD BEHAVIOUR GAME

Another more formal, if somewhat more controversial, version of the same strategy is the **good behaviour game**. Developed over thirty years ago (Barrish, Saunders, & Wolff, 1969), teachers still find it effective (Babyak, Luze, & Kamps, 2000). Tell students that you will award points to teams within the class for positive behaviours; then describe these behaviours clearly. Points might be awarded for returning materials to their proper places at the end of an activity or for only one person speaking at a time in small-group discussions. Select only a couple of positive behaviours at a time and post them at the front of the classroom to remind all teams. Set a time period during the day when the game will be played. For a secondary school class, it could be the first twenty minutes of the period; usually by then a positive tone has been set. Let the students know every time you see an appropriate behaviour and tally a point. At the end of the day post the points. In a variation, you might set a target for all groups to reach and provide a reward as long as all teams reach the minimum. Choose a reward that is meaningful for students of a particular age and for the particular class. Some teachers use a strategy like this early in the year and then only during the most stressful periods of the school year, such as before winter break.

## REWARD SYSTEMS

In the past, **reward systems** were widely used in special education programs that served students with emotional and behaviour disabilities. They are much less common in today's inclusive classrooms, with their growing emphasis on intrinsic motivation and teaching students to regulate their own behaviour. Point systems have been criticized because they encourage students to gain rewards without teaching them to appreciate the academic and social learning they perform to receive awards. They may discourage teachers from looking for the causes of misbehaviour or learning difficulties (Henley, 2006). Teacher attention and encouragement may be the powerful rewards that have few drawbacks.

In a recent paper Wolford, Heward, and Alber (2001) argue that while teacher praise and attention are powerful influences on student performance, classrooms are busy places. As a consequence, children may have trouble receiving positive attention and teachers tend to offer praise infrequently in the classroom. Alber and

Heward have developed a strategy for teaching exceptional students to "recruit" their teachers' attention in a positive way. They suggest teachers begin by discussing how recruiting can help students to be more successful; for example, you can say to students, "You will get more work done, your grades may improve, and the teacher will be happy you did a good job." Once students understand what is involved, then the teacher should model the steps in recruiting while thinking aloud. The steps are easy to remember using the acronym *CLASS*:

- **C**omplete your work,
- **L**ook it over for mistakes,
- **A**sk yourself if the teacher is available,
- **S**ignal the teacher and ask her or him to look at your work, and
- **S**ay "Thank you" (Alber & Heward, 1997).

Students will need opportunities to practise and to receive feedback on how they are doing. Although some students need individual teaching to learn the strategy, research has shown positive results for students with learning disabilities and with intellectual disabilities in recruiting praise and in student learning. There have also been increases in the amount of praise delivered by teachers. A paraeducator may be able to help a student learn to recruit teacher attention in a positive way.

### ENCOURAGEMENT

Some researchers suggest encouragement is a healthier way for teachers to support and increase appropriate behaviour than praise (e.g., Larivee, 2006). Encouragement refers to giving courage or spurring someone on. Figure 6.3 describes encouragement, which can be provided to all students regardless of how well they are achieving. Encouragement is particularly helpful in alleviating the discouragement that exceptional students can feel when challenged to participate and learn in inclusive classrooms.

## Decreasing Undesirable Behaviour

Your attempts to make everyone feel included and to increase positive behaviour will not be enough for some students. An alternative approach is to focus on decreasing undesirable behaviours. In this approach you act to reduce behaviours you don't want to see and help students replace them with desirable actions. Often we assume that students know what to do and are simply refusing to do it. This is not always the case. Try using the steps of the ADAPT strategy described in Chapter 1 and minimal interventions or low-key responses. When a student exhibits problem behaviour, refer to the classroom rules that were established. Remind the student which rule is being violated. This can be done with a pre-arranged gesture or signal, by using humour (with good judgment), or by verbally confronting the student (but always in private). Try to identify environmental factors that could be altered. Consider changing the student's place in the classroom, or changing the student's task (NEA, 2006). A quick tension- or energy-releasing activity may allow the student to return to work.

### LOW-KEY INTERVENTIONS

Effective teachers appear to respond to misbehaviour at a moment's notice; however, they actually anticipate and act or **pro-act** almost before the behaviour occurs (Carpenter & McKee-Higgins, 1996; Henley, 2006). Such **low-key interventions**

**What do you think?**

How does teaching awareness of core values differ from other approaches to promoting appropriate behaviour? With a peer, discuss how you might teach core values throughout the curriculum, and the benefits and disadvantages of this approach for Aboriginal and non-Aboriginal students.

Cross-Reference
While this chapter focuses primarily on creating an inclusive classroom climate that is well-managed and welcoming for exceptional students, Chapter 9 places much more emphasis on schoolwide approaches. For an example, see Rosenberg, M., & Jackman, L. (2003). Development, implementation, and sustainability of comprehensive school-wide behaviour management systems. *Intervention in School and Clinic, 39*(1), 10–21.

Further Reading
Learn about the root causes of anger and specific methods for responding to anger in the classroom:

Flick, G.L. (2004). *Coping with anger: Complete anger management program, grades 6–12.* Hoboken, NJ: John Wiley & Sons.

Galey, P. (2004). *Keep cool! Strategies for managing anger at school.* Markham, ON: Pembroke Pub.

Leseho, D., & Howard-Rose, D. (2005). *Anger in the classroom: A practical guide.* Calgary: Detsileg Enterprises.

## FIGURE 6.3 PROVIDING ENCOURAGEMENT TO EVERY STUDENT

**Effective Encouragement:**

- Is specific and clear
- Is personal, requiring that we know each of our students
- Is genuine and expressed in a heartfelt way
- Is available to all, not just those who are achieving
- Discourages competition and helps students to focus on their own accomplishments
- Enhances willingness to try and courage to take risks
- Contributes to renewed effort
- Helps students to accept themselves and evaluate their own progress
- Is catching—students tend to pass it on
- Tells students that how they feel about themselves is important
- Helps students to appreciate the successes of others
- Is embedded in trusting relationships and dialogue
- Is part of our experience of community
- Comes from teachers perceived as caring
- Is filled with meaning for the individuals involved
- Helps students to recognize their strengths
- Supports collaboration
- Contributes to internal motivation and values

**Teachers Who Encourage:**

- Expect the best of everyone
- Pay attention, so they know their students and see even their small accomplishments
- Smile to communicate acceptance and caring
- Make eye contact
- Use humour to put students and themselves at ease
- Personalize recognition
- Celebrate with students
- Give credit to others
- Set the example for their students
- Make all members of the class feel valued for what they contribute
- Remember how good it feels to be acknowledged

**The Language of Encouragement:**

- I know you can do this. Let's get started.
- I see that you've thought of a new way to approach this problem. Let's see how well it works.
- I really liked the humour in your short story.
- What did you learn from that mistake?
- You've used many adjectives and it makes your writing interesting to read.
- I see you've decided to work alone instead of with a partner. Tell me at break how that worked for you.
- I can see that you've put a lot of work into this science project.
- How are these two experiences related?
- I like your new haircut.
- I appreciate the way you worked with your group members today.
- You've tried hard. What strategy could you use next time that might be more helpful?
- I know this is a difficult time for you.
- This sort of thing has happened to me, too. I was really hurt.
- I was moved by the way you responded to her feelings.
- I noticed you got right to work and completed the whole assignment.
- You must be proud of the work you did on this.

Resources: Larivee, B. (2002). The potential perils of praise in a democratic interactive classroom. *Action in Teacher Education, 23*(4), 77–88; McIntyre, E., Kyle, D.W., & Moore, G.H. (2006). A primary-grade teacher's guidance toward small-group dialogue. *Reading Research Quarterly, 41,* 36–66; Kouzes, J.M., & Posner, B.Z. (2007). *Encouraging the heart: A leader's guide to rewarding and recognizing others.* Somerset, NJ: John Wiley.

# Motivation and Rewards

*Motivation* is a term educators use frequently. And we may worry about whether rewarding students might make them less motivated. Recent theory and research in educational psychology may help us to understand the issues and to form our own views on this contentious subject.

Motivation is frequently described as intrinsic or extrinsic. *Intrinsic* usually means that a person engaging in a task or behaviour develops internally satisfying consequences during or after his or her actions. Examples of intrinsic rewards include acquisition of knowledge, task completion, and sense of mastery. By *extrinsic*, it is usually meant that a person engages in a task or behaviour to reach satisfying consequences outside himself or herself during or after the actions. Extrinsic rewards include **token systems**, social approval, and tangible objects.

What are the arguments against using extrinsic rewards? Many have argued that children should engage in learning for its own sake. Parents, teachers, and researchers have expressed fear that children who receive external rewards for learning and behaviour will come to depend on and expect these rewards (Greene & Lepper, 1974; Witzel & Mercer, 2003). Extrinsic rewards are easily overused, are ineffective at teaching students how to regulate their behaviour, and may not generalize beyond the classroom. While all of us would prefer students to be intrinsically motivated to learn and manage their own behaviour, we recognize that this is not the case for many students, some of whom are exceptional learners.

What are the arguments in favour of using extrinsic rewards? Teachers are often advised to use extrinsic motivation with young children and exceptional learners, perhaps because these students appear to be dependent on adults for guidance and reassurance (Chapman, 1989). For example, Grolnick and Ryan (1990) found that students with learning disabilities had less internal control for academic work than their classmates without disabilities. In 1994 Cameron and Pierce of the University of Alberta conducted a meta-analysis on one hundred studies involving the use of rewards. They found that, overall, participants receiving tangible rewards reported higher intrinsic motivation than non-rewarded participants. When students received contingent verbal praise, they demonstrated significantly higher motivation (measured by time on task and by attitude) than students who did not receive such praise. These analyses led Cameron and Pierce to conclude that rewards, tangible and verbal, increase positive behaviour and learning while students are being rewarded,

and do not interfere with intrinsic motivation for low-interest activities.

Two aspects of Cameron and Pierce's findings may be key to understanding the role of extrinsic motivation and rewards: first, that extrinsic rewards did not interfere with motivation for *low-interest activities*; and second, that *pairing an external reward with information*, in the form of verbal praise, was most effective.

Why might student interest in the activity be important to understanding rewards and motivation? To answer this question, we turn to a specific theory of motivation called self-determination theory (SDT), developed by Edward Deci and Richard Ryan. They have provided considerable data to show that human beings have three motivational needs in order to be self-determining: competence (feeling effective), autonomy (feeling of acting in accord with one's sense of self), and relatedness (feeling connected to others). SDT postulates a continuum of motivation ranging from amotivation through four degrees of decreasing external motivation to intrinsic motivation. Intrinsic motivation is defined as engagement in a task for the pure joy and inherent satisfaction derived from doing the task (Ryan & Deci, 2000).

They argue that many of the activities people are asked to engage in, including many school activities, are not intrinsically motivating; thus people are not likely to engage in them willingly or fully without some external motivation. They also suggest that to move along the continuum toward intrinsic motivation, people need to experience competence, autonomy, and relatedness. According to SDT, the more that students feel effective at school tasks, feel they have chosen to engage in the tasks, and feel they belong in the classroom, the more likely they are to engage in school tasks for their own sake. And perhaps external rewards have a part in keeping students at uninteresting tasks long enough to develop feelings of competence, autonomy, and relatedness. Therefore, it may be that external rewards enhance motivation for learning that is not inherently interesting. Conversely, a classic study by Greene and Lepper (1974) found that giving preschoolers extrinsic rewards for drawing, an inherently interesting task for these children, led to decreased interest in drawing unless rewards were offered. Deci, Koestner, and Ryan (1999) found the same outcome in a meta-analysis of 128 studies on extrinsic rewards with tasks students found interesting. In summary, the theory and research suggest that rewards may be appropriate for increasing student motivation for tasks that

*continued*

students find uninteresting or very difficult. However, the function of rewards should be to move students toward the development of intrinsic motivation by increasing feelings of competence, autonomy, and relatedness.

Why might pairing an external reward with verbal praise be important? It may be that *how* a reward is delivered matters. Teacher praise can focus students' attention on the value and relevance of the task as well as inform students' self-perceptions of competence, autonomy, and relatedness. This information may be particularly important for exceptional students who look to others for guidance and reassurance. The teacher may in fact be teaching the students how to judge themselves more positively and about the intrinsic interest and value of the activity. Although Deci and Ryan have argued against external rewards, they wrote that "the context within which they are administered has an important influence upon how they are experienced and thus upon how they affect intrinsic motivation" (1992, p. 22). They found that "rewards, when taken as informational rather than controlling, affect a person's autonomy and competence, leading to intrinsic motivation" (Witzel & Mercer, 2003, p. 91). In summary, the relationship between motivation and rewards appears to depend on how rewards are delivered by the teacher.

The research suggests that we should be concerned about using extrinsic rewards to motivate exceptional students to learn and to regulate their own behaviour. It is prudent to avoid overuse, while looking for opportunities to pair informational feedback and praise with rewards, but only for tasks that students do not find intrinsically motivating. Enhancing feelings of competence, autonomy, and belongingness—by teaching well, giving students choices, and creating a positive classroom climate—is likely to contribute to intrinsic motivation.

### References

Cameron, J., & Pierce, W.D. (1994). Reinforcement, reward, and intrinsic motivation: A meta-analysis. *Review of Educational Research, 64,* 363–423.

Chapman, J.W. (1988). Learning disabled children's self-concepts. *Review of Educational Research, 58,* 347–371.

Deci, E.L., Koestner, R., & Ryan, R.M. (1999). A meta-analytic review of experiments examining the effects of extrinsic rewards on intrinsic motivation. *Psychological Bulletin, 125,* 627–668.

Deci, E.L., & Ryan, R.M. (1992). The initiation and regulation of intrinsically motivated learning and achievement. In A. Boggiano & T. Pittman (Eds.), Achievement *and motivation: A social developmental perspective* (pp. 9–36). Cambridge, UK: Cambridge University Press.

Greene, D., & Lepper, M.R. (1974). Effects of extrinsic rewards on children's subsequent intrinsic interest. *Child Development, 45,* 1141–1145.

Grolnick, W.S., & Ryan, R.M. (1990). Self-perceptions, motivations, and adjustments in children with learning disabilities: A multiple group comparison study. *Journal of Learning Disabilities, 23,* 177–184.

Ryan, R.M., & Deci, E.L. (2000). Self-determination theory and the facilitation of intrinsic motivation. *American Psychologist, 55,* 68–78.

Witzel, B.S., & Mercer, C.D. (2003). Using rewards to teach students with disabilities. *Remedial and Special Education, 24,* 88–96.

or minimal actions do not disrupt the flow of the class. They de-escalate rather than raise the stakes, and they communicate to the students that you are "with it" and that they cannot get away with anything. Over time, effective teachers develop a repertoire and match their "proaction" to the action they anticipate. If you overuse a proaction, it loses its effectiveness. Low-key proactions or responses (recommended by Bennett & Smilanich, 1994; www.sacsc.ca/index.html) are explained in Figure 6.4.

You may find it effective to combine these low-key responses. Imagine that one student is speaking to the class and a restless student catches your attention, although you are not certain why. You move silently toward this student, signalling to him or her to be quiet, touching the child lightly and briefly on the shoulder to express calm, and smiling your appreciation when he or she begins to listen again. You did not disturb the flow of the class and prevented a distraction for the others. You can be "artful" in proactively noticing, selecting an effective response, and carrying it out to refocus the student who was venturing into undesirable behaviour. For example, Mr. Chan could stand by Jacob's desk as soon as Jacob entered the classroom and point to direct his attention to the challenge Jacob should attack,

## FIGURE 6.4 LOW-KEY PROACTIVE RESPONSES TO DECREASE UNDESIRABLE BEHAVIOUR

**Proximity:** Move toward a misbehaving student immediately, but not so close that the student feels physically threatened. Usually there is no verbal exchange.

**Touch:** Check your school's policy. A quick, light, non-threatening touch to the shoulder without eye contact or verbal exchange shows that you are aware and care.

**The look:** As soon as attention-seeking begins, quickly and silently communicate to a student that the behaviour is inappropriate. This is not a glare.

**Student's name:** Use this positively to make the student feel included just before misbehaviour or as soon as misbehaviour occurs. Use a kind tone, not a nagging one. Don't overuse.

**Gesture:** Communicate expected behaviour, e.g., forefinger on the mouth to say "shhh" or a shake of the head to say "no." Ensure your meaning is understood by ELL students.

**The pause:** At the beginning of instructions, if a few are not listening, pause obviously. Combine with moving toward them, catching their gazes, and gesturing for quiet.

**Ignore:** Use with caution. Ignoring is best when the student's behaviour does not interfere with teaching or learning. If two students misbehave together, ignoring will be ineffective. Don't show agitation or the students will have won the attention they are seeking.

**Signal to begin/signal for attention:** Signal to get or refocus the attention of the class. Do not continue until you have their attention. Make signal age-appropriate: a flick of the lights, a whistle, rhythmic hand clapping, or a sign you hold up. Bennett and Smilanich (1994) give the example of an elementary school teacher who called out a word ("baseball") and the students gave a choral response ("Blue Jays"); the students chose a new word and response each week.

**Deal with the problem, not the student:** Quietly remove the object the student is tapping on his or her desk, or if two students are fighting over a book, say, "Book, please," and extend your hand. Say it as if you expect them to comply; if they do not, they have escalated the situation beyond a low-key proaction on your part.

**Weblinks**
Check out these sites on anger management. Compare the information to that available in books and articles. Do the different sources provide similar information?

PARENTBOOKS CANADA: ANGER AND STRESS MANAGEMENT
www.parentbooks.ca/ Anger_&_Stress.html

AMERICAN PSYCHOLOGICAL ASSOCIATION: CONTROLLING ANGER— BEFORE IT CONTROLS YOU
www.apa.org/topics/controlanger. html

CANADIAN PSYCHIATRIC ASSOCIATION: SELF-MANAGEMENT
http://publications.cpa-apc.org/ browse/documents/ 329&xwm=true

FLORIDA DEPARTMENT OF EDUCATION: ANGER MANAGEMENT IN SCHOOLS
www.unf.edu/dept/fie/sdfs/notes/ anger.pdf

while giving Jacob a signal to eat his healthy snack himself. Many resources on classroom management provide guidance on how to implement low-key responses (e.g., Henley, 2006; Lindberg & Swick, 2007) and report data on the effectiveness of a proactive, caring approach, especially when it is relationship-driven (Vitto, 2003) and culturally responsive (Bondy et al., 2007).

### TIME OUT: A CONTROVERSIAL STRATEGY

Inappropriate behaviour sometimes requires more than a low-key response. Sometimes a **verbal reprimand** is necessary if a behaviour continues. "If reprimands are to be used, the most effective ones are those that are immediate, unemotional, brief, and backed up with a time-out or loss of privileges" (Roberts et al., 1997, p. 81). A **time out** is the temporary removal of a student from classroom activities because of his or her disruptive behaviour. It is a consequence for inappropriate behaviour that should be planned ahead and used sparingly, as part of a student's IEP or behavioural plan. Before using a time out, an in-school team should explain to the student and parents the serious misbehaviours for which time out will be used and the reasons for this decision. Alberta Learning has developed *Guidelines for Using Timeout in Schools* (2002; http://education.alberta.ca/media/547960/timeout_oct_2002. pdf). The guidelines recommend that time outs be used only when less-restrictive interventions have not been successful, with the exception of unexpected behaviours that jeopardize the safety of other students and of teachers. They also

*Engaging in activities with peers helps to decrease inappropriate behaviour.*

emphasize the need for early or low-key interventions that prevent problem behaviours and minimize the need for using time outs. Recently researchers have shown the effectiveness of alternative strategies for teaching students to quickly and calmly disengage from disruptive behaviours. For an example that uses active response beads and redirects students' attention, see Grskovic and colleagues' (2004) work with students with emotional and behaviour disorders.

### GIVING THE CHOICE TO BEHAVE APPROPRIATELY

Sometimes you want to provide a student or pair of students with a choice to behave appropriately. For example, two students are discussing hockey rather than geography. Say, "You can choose either to work quietly together on the map you are making or to have your seating arrangement changed until the end of this unit." If the two students do not choose to work quietly on the map, then you must follow through and seat them apart. Do not offer any choice that you are unwilling to apply. One of my favourite choices when students play with toys, hair accessories, etc., is, "In your pocket or mine—you choose." These choices are not ultimatums. They are effective in ending problem behaviour without escalating conflict. Often they involve **natural consequences**. Stay calm, speak in a private-conversation voice, and offer to conference with the student. Help the student to feel respected rather than humiliated or overpowered. If possible, thank the student sincerely as soon as the unacceptable behaviour stops (even smile or mouth your thanks). Keep your sense of humour; sometimes it is better to laugh and give a second chance than to prosecute, especially over small infractions.

### HOLDING PATTERN

Sometimes you need to put a student in a **holding pattern**. Some teachers arrange to have a misbehaving student wait in an office, but I find it simpler to have a student stand beside the door in the classroom or, if I think he or she will distract others, immediately outside the door until I come to talk to the pupil. Keep the time brief and ensure the student's safety. If these talks are rare and heartfelt, they are likely to be taken seriously.

## Enhancing Self-Management

The goal of this chapter is that your class conduct themselves the same way whether you are in the classroom or have stepped into the hall. Similarly, you want to help individual students develop self-control or self-management.

### PROBLEM-SOLVING APPROACHES

Some educators develop a **problem-solving approach** that asks a student to answer a set of questions after engaging in unacceptable behaviour. The questions usually ask the students what they think the problem was, what they did to contribute to the problem, how they can make amends, and how they can prevent the problem from recurring. Sometimes the student and the teacher sign the form. What makes

**Cross-Reference**
In Chapters 3 and 4 you read descriptions of many exceptionalities. For which exceptionalities do you think a time out might be suitable? For which personal characteristics might it be a bad match?

**Further Reading**
Consult recent resources on connecting behaviour interventions to IEPs:

Buck, G.H., Polloway, E.A., Kirkpatrick, M.A., Patton, J., & Fad, K.M. (2000). Developing behaviour intervention plans: A sequential approach. *Intervention in School and Clinic, 36*(1), 3–9.

Bateman, B., & Golly, A. (2003). *Why Johnny doesn't behave: Twenty tips for measurable BIPs.* Verona, WI: Attainment Company, Inc.

this an effective strategy is the follow-through, in which the adult and the student decide "who is going to do what" about the situation. If the two can feel that they are on the same side and working together to overcome a common foe—such as an easily lost temper, peers who tease, or restless hands that poke—then the student may work hard to honour the problem-solving solution.

## INFORMAL CONFERENCES

In a sincere offer to help, made in an informal conference, a teacher can often see that an exceptional student wants to change a troublesome behaviour but cannot do it alone. Such conferences can be effective if there is follow-through. Bennett and Smilanich (1994) suggest the following steps for an **informal conference**:

- Greet the student to set a positive tone.
- Define the problem clearly and ensure that you agree before going to the next step.
- Generate solutions together, so you solve the problem mutually.
- Choose the best solution(s) together (and perhaps prioritize the other solutions); agree on what each of you will do to implement the solution; be sure you have a role as well as the student.
- Ensure that you have a shared understanding of the solution(s) to be undertaken.
- End positively by thanking the student.

Improving self-management is not easy for students. Be prepared to provide moral support, encouragement, regular checks on progress, praise when you observe the student being good, and additional informal, positive chats. If the informal conference is no match for the problems that need to be solved, then provide a warning and try a formal contract the next time the problem occurs. Warnings are respectful ways to "raise the stakes" without students feeling attacked, and they remind students that what happens next is a consequence of what they do.

## CONTRACTS

When raising the stakes from informal conferences, contracts can be effective. I found that young students enjoyed contracts and told their classmates about them, while adolescents appreciated private contracts. I informed parents so they would understand my rationale and the student's account of the consequences if the contract were broken. With a young child, a **contract** can be about a matter as straightforward as hanging his or her coat on a hook when the youngster comes into the classroom instead of throwing it on the floor. This reflects the principle of starting with a series of easily and quickly met agreements that provide immediate evidence of success and provide you with a way to give genuine praise (privately or publicly).

After two easy and successful contracts, you can move to your real objective. This might be the student starting the day and getting to her desk without touching another student or having a verbal disagreement. A good start can make quite a difference to how a student conducts himself or herself all day long. You may reap multiple benefits from start-of-day contracts. When they work well, the student avoids getting into "a funk," and you sidestep the problem of that student's

## FIGURE 6.5 BEHAVIOUR CONTRACT

CONTRACT BETWEEN _____ AND _____

(student)       (teacher)

DATE: _____

(may specify period in which contract applies)

_____ AGREES TO _____

(student)       (describe behaviours)

_____

AND _____ AGREES TO _____

(teacher)       (describe behaviours)

_____

CONSEQUENCES: _____

REWARDS: _____

_____

DATES FOR CHECKING PROGRESS: _____

COMPLETION DATE: _____

SIGNATURES: _____ AND _____

(student)       (teacher)

---

disruption of others. As well, you can begin the day by praising the student sincerely instead of reprimanding him or her, and you can build on this success to tackle bigger unacceptable behaviours that sabotage learning throughout the day. I have seen adolescents thrive on contracts when they were private and highly individualized. Word the contract simply (not like a legal document), ensure that it states what both you and the student agree to do, and ensure that it specifies the positive reward and the consequence for failure to live up to the agreement. Figure 6.5 shows a simple form for behaviour contracts.

### SELF-MONITORING

**Self-monitoring** is another strategy for transferring responsibility to the student. It is particularly applicable for students who are off-task and require help focusing attention. Students observe and collect data on their own behaviour (e.g., Peterson et al., 2006). Marking down and keeping track of behaviour can change how frequently the behaviour occurs. Students need an understanding of the behaviour they are to monitor, an easy recording system, and a reward. In the beginning, you should monitor closely and then give increasing responsibility to the student. Explain in advance: "Put a check on your tracking sheet when I say, 'Let's keep track,'" or "Put a check at the end of every page." Dawn Reithaug (1998b), a BC educator, has developed a book of attractive forms and guidelines for making clear behaviour plans. A simple self-monitoring card can be taped to the student's desk; the student makes a check mark at each signal or at the end of each task, etc. After some successful self-monitoring, you could move to checklists taped to the desk or to sticky-note reminders. These strategies work well with young students, but

Put into Practice

Develop a tracking sheet for self-monitoring to be used by a student in grade 3 or a student in grade 10 who is trying to increase his or her focus in your class. Seek models in books and journals.

I have also seen exceptional adolescents inconspicuously use self-monitoring cards taped inside their notebooks to help them focus their attention. For a student with an educational assistant or a paraeducator, this adult may be able to signal the student and prompt the individual steps in a self-monitoring strategy like SNAP. Figure 6.6 outlines SNAP, a cognitive behaviour modification (CBM) strategy with four steps.

Self-management has been used widely in meeting the needs of exceptional students. For example, King-Sears and Carpenter (1997) developed a booklet to teach self-management to elementary school students with intellectual disabilities. Nadia Desbiens and Egide Royer (2003), researchers in Quebec, focused on the social behaviour of elementary school students with behaviour disorders. Mitchem and Young (2001) demonstrated the effectiveness of classwide use of a self-management program in regular classrooms, while Peterson and his colleagues (2006) enabled students in grades 7 and 8 to increase their on-task behaviour and social skills in general education classes.

## Positive Behavioural Supports and Classroom Management

Carr and colleagues (1999) and Heineman, Dunlap, and Kincaid (2005) reviewed the literature pertaining to **positive behavioural supports** (PBS) and interventions. This approach to dealing with problem behaviours focuses on the fixing of poor contexts that have been documented to be the source of the problems. The emphasis is on altering the environment before problem behaviour occurs or teaching appropriate behaviours as a strategy for eliminating the need for problem behaviours to be exhibited. Change should be systemic, build on students' strengths, and improve the quality and predictability of events in school, in the community, and at home. The intent is to make problem behaviours ineffective and to provide students with ways to reach their goals without resorting to inappropriate behaviours. Intensive supports, including functional assessments, are necessary for a small number of students with severe behavioural or cognitive disabilities.

PBS is an assessment-based approach for preventing problems and promoting prosocial behaviour. It is especially well-suited to helping students with behaviour disorders to adapt their behaviour to the regular classroom. In the early implementation, students were taught to ask for a break, or to ask for the teacher's attention in a positive way, with a conventional request. However, the concept has grown and is often implemented at three levels—schoolwide, classroom, and individual student. Essentially one determines the aspects of the environment associated with or contributing to behaviour by documenting circumstances when behaviour occurs and the outcomes that it might enable students to obtain or avoid. Schoolwide programs are intended to establish a safe, positive climate for all students, but they do help students with behavioural exceptionalities in particular because they create predictable school environments. At the classroom level PBS systems are used to create environments where students engage in work and to minimize disruptions. One intervention that you could adopt in your classroom is positive peer reporting, in which peers raise the behaviour of specific students (see Morrison & Jones, 2007). At the individual level PBS provides a problem-solving process for students who do not respond to the first two levels, schoolwide and classroom.

**Further Reading**

Carr, E.G., Horner, R.H., Turnbull, A.P., et al. (2000). *Positive behavior support for people with developmental disabilities: A research synthesis.* Washington, DC: American Association on Mental Retardation.

Koegel, L.K., Koegel, R.L., & Dunlap, G. (Eds.) (1996). *Positive behavioral support: Including people with difficult behavior in the community.* Baltimore: Paul H. Brookes Pub. Co.

Lewis, T.J., & Sugai, G. (1999). Effective behavior support: A systems approach to proactive school-wide management. *Focus on Exceptional Children, 31*(6), 1–24.

**Further Reading**

Recent research on PBS and the questions it raises:

Warren, J.S., et al. (2006). School-wide positive behavior support: Addressing behavior problems that impede student learning. *Educational Psychology Review, 18,* 187–198.

Carr, E.G. (2006). SWPBS: The greatest good for the greatest number, or the needs of the majority trump the needs of the minority? *Research and Practice for Persons with Severe Disabilities, 31,* 54–56.

Lassen, S.R., Steele, M.N., & Sailor, W. (2006). The relationship of school-wide positive behavior support to academic achievement in an urban middle school. *Psychology in the Schools, 43,* 701–712.

Morrison, J.Q., & Jones, K M. (2007). The effects of positive peer reporting as a class-wide positive behavior support. *Journal of Behavioral Education, 16,* 111–124.

## FIGURE 6.6 IMPLEMENTING A COGNITIVE BEHAVIOUR MANAGEMENT PROGRAM

Cognitive behaviour modification (CBM) is a broad term. It describes a number of specific techniques that teach self-control. They all work by increasing a student's awareness of cognitive processes and knowledge of how behaviour affects learning.

CBM interventions require student evaluation of performance rather than teacher evaluation. This means that they are practical for busy teachers and parents.

Self-instruction is one technique that helps students to regulate their own behaviours—social and academic. It uses self-statements to help students recall the steps required to solve a problem—social or academic. Examples of problems include rushing through assigned work, looking around instead of focusing on assigned work, talking out of turn in class, and eating or giving food to others in the classroom. Initially, students say the steps out loud to a teacher or parent and then to a peer or themselves. Gradually they say the steps covertly.

The actions a teacher and student follow include these:

1. They agree on a problem—social or academic—that is getting in the way of learning.

2. The teacher makes a cue card to prompt the student to use the steps of self-instruction.

3. The teacher models using the self-instruction steps to solve a problem like the one impeding the student.

4. The student practises using the self-instruction steps aloud with the teacher to solve the problem.

5. The student practises with a peer and then alone, using the steps to solve the problem.

6. The teacher arranges booster practice regularly to review the strategy with the student. For booster practice, they use verbal rehearsal as well as practising in familiar and new situations.

7. The teacher and the student decide on a signal for the teacher to use to let the student know this is a time to use the steps. Use of the signal is then phased out because the student is supposed to do the monitoring. For the SNAP strategy, snapping fingers may be a good signal.

**Sample Cue Card to Tape to a Student's Desk or Book**

> **SNAP** out of it!
>
> **S**ee my problem.
>
> **N**ame my best plan.
>
> **A**ct on my best plan.
>
> **P**at myself on the back. I solved my problem!

Recently teachers have begun to use a relatively new technique, video self-modelling, to decrease inappropriate behaviour, especially for exceptional adolescents with autism. Two elements are required for children to function as their own models. You need audiovisual technology that allows children to view themselves and the ability to change their behaviour so that they can function or appear to function beyond their present level. Buggey (2007) provides detail on how to capture video footage of students engaging in positive role modelling for themselves and describes some of the dramatic successes that have been obtained. Graetz and her colleagues (2006) describe using video footage of a student with autism engaging in inappropriate behaviours of which he was unaware, followed by self-modelling of appropriate behaviour, again with considerable success. While the method is not universally successful, it shows great promise. Buggey describes using this self-modelling strategy to motivate students with reading disabilities, who were discouraged by their inadequate reading. The teacher videotaped the students reading a practiced text with accuracy and excellent intonation and then, after showing the students their tape, found they made renewed efforts and were more successful in reading.

Source of SNAP strategy: Hutchinson, N.L. (2004). *Teaching exceptional children and adolescents: A Canadian casebook* (2nd ed.). Toronto: Allyn and Bacon. Used by permission of Pearson Education Canada.

Some teachers use daily behaviour report cards to record individual students' behaviour and progress within PBS (see Chafouleas et al., 2005; Chafouleas et al., 2006).

Hieneman et al. (2005) describe who should be involved in the development of PBS at each level, how the supports should be designed, and how to measure desired outcomes (p. 784). This is a complex system, usually implemented by an entire school community. You may want to inquire about the use of PBS in the schools in your district and arrange to visit a school implementing it.

## Harsh Punishments and Inappropriate Punishments

There are harsh punishments, such as suspension and expulsion, and there are inappropriate forms, such as corporal punishment and academic tasks. **Punishment** is usually defined as an unpleasant consequence aimed at reducing the likelihood of inappropriate behaviour. It is expected to work because it causes pain. The research indicates that punishment can control misbehaviour, but by itself it will not teach desirable behaviour (Good & Brophy, 2002). Harsh punishment also alienates students from you and tends to destroy the goodwill you have built up that enables the two of you to be on the same side in helping the student to change.

### SUSPENSIONS AND EXPULSIONS

School policy may dictate that suspensions and even expulsions are used when a student's behaviour is so disruptive that the teacher cannot continue to meet the legal obligations to teach and keep the students safe. These are drastic measures, so try every other possible avenue first. **Suspension** means temporary removal from the classroom (for a day or more), while **expulsion** means permanent removal. For a number of reasons, suspension and expulsion are not effective for teaching students or for changing their behaviour. According to McQueen (1992), these reasons include the following:

- The student misses the content you are teaching.
- The student does not receive assistance from school personnel, including teachers and counsellors.
- Those who want to be out of school are rewarded.
- Some students who have been suspended or expelled come to school to "hang out," and school officials have little authority over them.
- As a general rule, behaviour does not improve as a result of suspensions or expulsions.

The exception to these drawbacks may be in-school suspension: a student is expected to attend school, complete assigned work, spend the day in a suspension room under supervision, and stay away from peers and social interactions. Haley and Watson (2000) developed what they called an in-school literary extension for students who had misbehaved. The researchers focused on helping students use prewriting strategies (or discussion strategies) to reflect on their inappropriate behaviour and discover ways to improve their behaviour. Morris and Howard (2003) described an effective in-school suspension program that involved teaching middle school students organizational skills. Each student completed the work assigned in their regular classroom during the in-school suspension and received counselling

**What do you think?**

Debate with your peers whether *harsh* and *inappropriate* are always apt descriptors for the punishments described in this chapter. Defend the position opposite to what you believe. Why is this exercise a valuable experience for an educator?

Further Reading (and Viewing)

There are many recent multimedia resources to supplement the information in this chapter. View two and discuss them with peers who have viewed other resources.

Kronow, E.L. (2008). *The teacher's guide to success: Teaching effectively in today's classrooms* [multimedia]. Boston: Pearson Allyn & Bacon.

*A practical approach to classroom management and discipline, grades 6–12* [videorecording]. (2007). Bellevue, WA: Bureau of Education and Research.

*Classroom management that works* [videokit]. (2004). Alexandria, VA: ASCD.

*How to promote positive behavior in the classroom* [videorecording]. (2004). Alexandria, VA: Association for Supervision and Curriculum Development. [From the *How to* video series for the classroom teacher, tape 21.]

Put into Practice

There is an extensive literature on using self-management and self-monitoring to enhance the attention, participation, and learning of children and adolescents with a range of exceptionalities. Choose three papers from the following list to read. Develop a simple strategy to help Mandy or Jacob, described in the opening case studies, to be more successful in an inclusive classroom.

Children with LD, speech and language exceptionalities, or emotional and behaviour disabilities:

Hoff, K.E., & Doepke, K.J. (2006). Increasing on-task behavior in the classroom: Extension of self-monitoring strategies. *Psychology in the Schools, 43*, 211–221.

Children with ADHD:

Ardoin, S.P., & Martens, B.K. (2004). Training children to make accurate self-evaluations: Effects on behavior and the quality of self-ratings. *Journal of Behavioral Education, 13*, 1–23.

Reid, R., Trout, A.L., & Schwartz, M. (2005). Self-regulation interventions for children with attention deficit/hyperactivity disorder. *Exceptional Children, 71*, 361–377.

Adolescents with ADHD:

Gureasko-Moore, S., DuPaul, G.J., & White, G.P. (2006). The effects of self-management in general education classrooms on the organizational skills of adolescents with ADHD. *Behavior Modification, 30*, 159–183.

Children and adolescents with emotional and behaviour disorders:

Mooney, P., Ryan, J.B., Uhing, B.M., Reid, R., & Epstein, M.H. (2005). A review of self-management interventions targeting academic outcomes for students with emotional and behavior disorders. *Journal of Behavioral Education, 14*, 203–221.

*Peers and paraprofessionals can help to implement cognitive behaviour modification programs.*

for handling stressful situations and controlling their behaviour in the future. Flanagain (2007) conducted research on students' views of in-school and out-of-school suspensions. The students reported that out-of-school suspensions did not act as a deterrent and tended to antagonize relations of students with teachers and administrators. In-school suspensions were viewed somewhat more positively, although it was important that students received teaching and support for their difficulties during the in-school suspension. Familiarize yourself with your school's policies and ask questions about a school's policies regarding suspension during an employment interview. It is usually easier to teach in a school when you agree with the policies.

### CORPORAL PUNISHMENT AND USING ACADEMIC TASKS AS PUNISHMENT

Because we respect and value our students, we must ensure that we conduct our classes without **corporal punishment** or other cruel and dehumanizing techniques (Weiss, 2005). In Canada it is unacceptable to strike a student or threaten to strike a student. Corporal punishment violates students' rights and is ineffective in changing behaviour (Robinson, et al., 2005). Students report that they perceive the practice of "hushing" the whole class as unfair and in conflict with the behaviour teachers expect of students; whenever teachers blame and punish the whole class for the misdeeds of a few, they endanger the students' trust and respect they have worked so hard to earn (Thornberg, 2006). As well, beware of assigning "lines" or mathematics problems as punishment. The contradictory message sent by assigning **academic tasks as punishment** only makes our job more difficult. However, requiring students to complete work missed due to absence is defensible. Make your classes so well-taught and interesting that students hate to miss anything. The challenge with having exceptional students included in every class is that each of their differentiated programs also has to be so worthwhile that they want to be in class.

# Summary

It is important that classrooms in inclusive schools provide a sense of community so all members feel accepted and valued. Many elements contribute to developing an inclusive classroom climate, including the physical layout and the norms of classroom interaction. Teachers negotiate and enforce classroom rules and procedures to ensure that all students, including exceptional ones, find the classroom predictable and safe. Managing behaviour in an inclusive classroom requires strategies for increasing appropriate behaviour, decreasing unacceptable behaviour, and enhancing self-management.

# Key Terms

community (p. 203)
climate (p. 204)
physical space (p. 206)
norms for classroom interaction
 (p. 208)
give-and-take dialogues (p. 208)
signal (p. 208)
community circle (p. 208)
community agreements (p. 209)
right to pass (p. 210)
rules (p. 210)
enforcing a rule (p. 212)
classroom procedures (p. 212)
monitoring (p. 212)

checkpoints (p. 215)
scaffolding (p. 215)
consistency (p. 215)
"invisible" classroom management
 (p. 216)
catch 'em being good (p. 216)
good behaviour game (p. 218)
reward systems (p. 218)
pro-act (p. 219)
low-key interventions (p. 219)
token systems (p. 221)
verbal reprimand (p. 223)
time out (p. 223)
natural consequences (p. 224)

holding pattern (p. 224)
problem-solving approach (p. 224)
informal conference (p. 225)
contract (p. 225)
self-monitoring (p. 226)
positive behavioural supports
 (p. 227)
punishment (p. 229)
suspension (p. 229)
expulsion (p. 229)
corporal punishment (p. 230)
academic tasks as punishment
 (p. 230)

# Challenges for Reviewing Chapter 6

1. How do teachers go about creating a classroom community in an elementary classroom? In a secondary classroom? Prepare a list of priority tasks you would undertake before the beginning of the school year, during the first day of school, and during the first week of school as either an elementary or secondary teacher. Compare your list with peers who teach in the other panel and identify the common elements on your lists. Identify the priority tasks that differ for the two of you and try to identify whether the differences arise because of the panel in which you teach, because of your individual teaching philosophies, or for other reasons.

2. What does it mean for a classroom to have an inclusive climate? What contribution does the physical layout of a classroom make to an inclusive climate? Compare its importance with the importance of the norms for interaction that you teach to and expect of your students.

3. Prepare a series of lesson plans for negotiating and enforcing classroom rules and procedures. Take into account the age and grade level of the students you teach. Exchange plans with a peer and give each other feedback.

4. Write a brief scenario that includes some of the greatest challenges to your teaching and management in a classroom with a student like Mandy (in the opening case for this chapter), who has a history of losing her temper, punching, and screaming at her classmates. Look back through the chapter and identify the major adaptations you would make in your plan for managing the classroom. Describe how you would establish and maintain a positive relationship with Mandy.

5. You are a member of the in-school team in Jacob's school (Jacob is described in the opening case for this chapter). Prepare to assume the role of one member of the team. The team includes Jacob's history teacher, the resource room teacher in the school, the principal, and two other teachers who have Jacob in their classes this semester. Use the information in this chapter to develop a systematic approach that you recommend for curbing the problems that are emerging—without spoiling Jacob's improving relationship with his classmates. Why do you think that the approach you recommend will be effective? You may want to role-play this scenario with your peers, each of you assuming a role of one of the members of the team.

6. Return to the opening cases of Mandy and Jacob and answer the five questions that follow the cases.

# Chapter 7
# Differentiating Teaching

## Learner Objectives

After you have read this chapter, you will be able to:

1. Describe how to use the ADAPT strategy to analyze and differentiate teaching.

2. Explain how to choose and combine strategies for adapting and differentiating.

3. Discuss the many aspects of teaching that can be differentiated.

4. Describe how to differentiate the teaching of listening, reading, and writing to meet the needs of exceptional learners.

5. Describe differentiating the teaching of mathematics for exceptional learners.

6. Discuss adaptations of teaching in content areas.

7. Describe how to differentiate homework.

**Ms. Ash teaches mathematics at a large inner-city secondary school.** She starts every class with an example of how the day's math can be used—perhaps by engineers to design a heating system. When she teaches new mathematical content, she teaches to the whole class, with the students seated in pairs. First she reviews, pointing out explicitly how recent lessons relate to today's class. Next she hands out a partially completed outline and places the same outline on the overhead projector. She demonstrates, questions, and fills in the overhead transparency while she explains the new content. She stops every few minutes for students to ask questions and complete their outlines. She moves to guided practice by demonstrating an example on the overhead projector while students work in pairs on the same example. Then students complete two or three examples in pairs without Ms. Ash guiding them. She takes up these examples, guides students in practising another if necessary, and then asks students to work together on two or three examples and finally to complete two or three independently. She moves to the round table and invites students who want to review the steps to join her while the rest complete a challenge task in collaborative groups.

Samuel has a learning disability and has always found math difficult. This term, Ms. Ash paired Samuel with a boy who answers his questions with explanations, and Samuel is learning. He likes to go to the round table to hear Ms. Ash explain the concepts and the steps again and to have her correct his work. Ms. Ash has taught him how to use a calculator and encourages him to use it, one of the adaptations listed on his IEP. Now he feels that he is learning to solve problems rather than spending all his time trying to do calculations.

**Hema has an intellectual disability; she has a pacemaker, but it does not restrict her activities.** She is included in a grade 5 class and learns best with visual materials, hands-on activities, and pre-teaching. Hema reads common signs in the neighbourhood, recognizes the written names of family and friends, and reads calendar words. She prints her name on forms or applications, draws simple pictures, and types a couple of sentences on the computer with a model. Her annual goals (on her IEP) include sustaining a conversation; maintaining socially appropriate behaviour; using a telephone; describing events, interactions, etc.; using money; and reading to get information. For the weather unit in Hema's science class, classroom teacher Mr. Carvello along with the resource teacher used the ADAPT strategy. While the other students completed a full-page chart on the weather each day using the class's weather station, Hema recorded only three aspects: she recorded the temperature, drew the cloud cover, and wrote the precipitation. To meet the IEP goals of using the telephone and relaying information, the two teachers designed a learning activity: in the company of a peer, Hema would go to the school office to telephone the regional weather office daily. Eleven peers volunteered to take turns accompanying Hema. Mr. Carvello demonstrated their role to the peer volunteers twice. Hema dialed the number, listened, and repeated what the meteorologist had said. Mr. Carvello printed it neatly and prompted Hema while she practised telling the class. Hema gradually used the telephone more independently, and the peer who had accompanied Hema provided any information she missed in her summary. Hema's daily goal was to give a full account, which she was soon able to do.

**Sally has always struggled with comprehending and interpreting what she reads.** She no longer has an IEP, but she did have one for many years. This year she is in grade 11, and Yolanda Chiang is her language and literature teacher. The class is studying *Romeo and Juliet*. Yesterday Ms. Chiang taught the class elements of Shakespeare's tragedies, and Sally is worried because she knows that she can't yet identify all the elements of a Shakespearean tragedy. Sally is relieved when Ms. Chiang divides the class into three groups. Two groups are given clear instructions, oral and written, and begin to compare the elements of tragedy in *Romeo and Juliet* to the elements of tragedy in *A Doll's House* by Ibsen, a play the class read a month earlier. Each of these two groups is to create a poster using words and drawings, showing the elements in each tragedy, providing examples, and making comparisons. Sally is part of a group of eight students who are working with Ms. Chiang to review the elements of Shakespeare's tragedies as seen in *Romeo and Juliet*. Many of these students have IEPs and others, like Sally, had an IEP for many years. Ms Chiang leads

Sally's group in charting and providing examples of the elements (in words and drawings) from *Romeo and Juliet*. Sally is pleased because she provides an example and suggests how it can be illustrated. After Sally's group is working well and understands the elements in *Romeo and Juliet*, Ms. Chiang moves on to check in with the other two groups. Sally is relieved that Ms. Chiang provides review and makes sure everyone understands each topic before the class moves on to the next topic.

1. How have these three teachers compared the strengths and needs of exceptional students—like Samuel, Hema, and Sally—with classroom demands?

2. What differentiations or adaptations do these teachers make for these exceptional students? How do these adaptations relate to the students' IEPs?

3. How have these teachers considered the perspectives of and consequences for others as well as for Hema, Samuel, and Sally?

4. Are these differentiations beneficial to students other than Sally, Hema, and Samuel? How?

5. How have these teachers ADAPTed teaching without unduly increasing their own workloads?

**Further Reading**

Tomlinson, C.A., & Strickland, A.A. (2005). *Differentiation in practice: A resource guide for differentiating curriculum, grades 9–12.* Alexandria, VA: Association for Supervision and Curriculum Development.

Haager, D., & Klingner, J.K. (2005). *Differentiating instruction in inclusive classrooms.* Boston: Pearson Allyn & Bacon.

Ontario Expert Panel on Literacy and Numeracy. (2005). *Education for all.* Toronto: Queen's Printer for Ontario.

Smith, C.M.M. (Ed.). (2006). *Including the gifted and the talented: Making inclusion work for more gifted and able learners.* London, UK: Routledge.

**Weblinks**

ALBERTA DEPARTMENT OF EDUCATION. DIFFERENTIATED LEARNING FOR ALL: CREATING ACADEMICALLY RESPONSIVE CLASSROOMS
www.education.gov.ab.ca/k_12/special/aisi/pdfs/Differentiated_Learning_For_All.pdf

MANITOBA DEPARTMENT OF EDUCATION. DIFFERENTIATED INSTRUCTION: CURRICULUM DEVELOPMENT AND IMPLEMENTATION
http://www.edu.gov.mb.ca/k12/cur/elements.html

ONTARIO MINISTRY OF EDUCATION: LEADING MATH SUCCESS, GRADES 7–12
www.edu.gov.on.ca/eng/document/reports/numeracy/numeracyreport.pdf

THE ACCESS CENTRE, US OFFICE OF SPECIAL EDUCATION PROGRAMS
www.k8accesscenter.org/index.php

# Introduction

In differentiated classrooms teachers begin where the students are and accept that students differ in important ways. Recently researchers like Diane Haager and Janette Klingner (2005) have demonstrated how teachers can analyze their classroom environment and teaching in relation to students' academic and social needs and make adaptations or, in current terminology, differentiate to ensure success for exceptional students. The terms *differentiate* and *adapt* are used interchangeably in this chapter, as they are in many of the writings of Carol Ann Tomlinson, a well-known proponent of differentiated classrooms (e.g., 2003; Tomlinson & Cunningham Eidson, 2003). Essentially, differentiating instruction means structuring a lesson at multiple levels and in such a way that each student has an opportunity to work at a moderately challenging, developmentally appropriate level. Many provinces across Canada have developed resources to assist teachers in differentiating in their classrooms (e.g., Manitoba; www.edu.gov.mb.ca/k12/cur/elements. html#Differentiated%20Instruction).

This chapter provides explicit examples for using the ADAPT strategy introduced in Chapter 1 to differentiate teaching. These examples represent many exceptionalities and many areas of the elementary and secondary curriculum. Individual teachers find some ways of differentiating more acceptable and feasible than others, and students also find particular adaptations more helpful than others. For example, Ms. Ash finds it easy to model and provide guided practice, followed by independent practice, for the whole class. Samuel finds the partially completed outline helps him follow her teaching. He benefits from using a calculator and from thoughtful pairing of students. Receiving immediate feedback on his completed work motivates Samuel. These accommodations (on the grade level curriculum) help other students as well. Hema is learning about weather at a level consistent with her strengths, prior knowledge, and needs, and meeting goals from her IEP: providing a reliable verbal account and using the telephone. She is also developing better social relationships with her peers. Mr. Carvello is making modifications (using goals from the curriculum for a lower grade) to meet Hema's learning needs without undue effort. In the case of Sally, Ms. Chiang is providing follow-up that is appropriate for all the students in her class. Two-thirds of the students demonstrated in discussion and in their written work yesterday that they understood the elements of Shakespearean tragedies. Ms. Chiang set them to work applying and extending what they had learned while she helped the other third of the class to understand and illustrate the concept, rather than expecting them to apply it. She retaught the concept to these students and helped them to work together to demonstrate their understanding. Sometimes this is called tiering the lesson.

Examples of differentiating for elementary and secondary students in this chapter provide models for ADAPTing literacy instruction, textbook use, and teaching in specific content areas. I hope these examples help you extract patterns for action, ponder the perspectives of those experiencing differentiated teaching, and think about the consequences for all affected by differentiating. Differentiating teaching and assessment is the heart of inclusive education that honours diversity and strives for equity.

# Using the ADAPT Strategy to Analyze and Differentiate Teaching for Individuals and Groups

You need strategies for differentiating teaching that are effective for exceptional students, efficient for you, and become a regular part of your planning and teaching. Curriculum tells teachers what to teach; differentiated instruction helps teachers decide how to teach it to a range of learners by using a number of teaching approaches. You can differentiate one, two, or all three of the following elements: (a) the content (what the students are going to learn), (b) the process (the activities), and (c) the products (the accomplishments following a period of learning) (Tomlinson & Strickland, 2005). Chapter 1 introduced ADAPT. This strategy is similar to many others, but it includes considering the perspectives of many people, including classmates, on the differentiation and on the consequences for them. The characteristics of the student (strengths *and* needs) and the demands of the classroom are important when devising adaptations to build on the student's strengths and either bypass areas of need or help the student strengthen these areas.

**Put into Practice**

View the following multimedia resources and discuss your understanding of differentiated classrooms with your peers:

Curriculum Services Canada. (2006). *Webcasts for educators: Differentiated instruction.* www.curriculum.org/secretariat/march29.html.

Crévola, C. (2006). *Breakthrough: Redesigning classroom instruction to transform learning.* www.curriculum.org/LSA/files/LSAGuideBreakthrough.pdf.

The ADAPT strategy has the following five steps:

- Step 1: **A**ccounts of students' strengths and needs
- Step 2: **D**emands of the classroom
- Step 3: **A**daptations
- Step 4: **P**erspectives and consequences
- Step 5: **T**each and assess the match

These five steps constitute a procedure you can use with all learners, although our focus is on students with exceptionalities and others who may need differentiation, in both elementary and secondary school classrooms.

## Step 1: Accounts of Students' Strengths and Needs

This first step requires that you know your students well. From the first day of school you should be familiar with the content of the confidential file of each exceptional student you teach. Usually the file contains the student's IEP, test reports, comments from previous teachers, and medical information that could be critical to the student's well-being (e.g., indication of allergies, epilepsy, or asthma). The IEP includes specific statements about strengths and needs, usually in three general areas: social, emotional, and behavioural; physical; and academic. Many jurisdictions have protocols to ensure that information is shared among all the professionals, agencies, and government departments involved with a student and his or her family. It is also important to quickly come to know your students as persons with preferences and strengths, which may not always coincide—students are not always best at what

*Talking with your students will help you know their strengths and needs and will enable them to trust you. This boy's father will be out of the country for the next six months.*

**Cross-Reference**
Chapters 6 and 9 focus on ways you can create a classroom community and help all students to feel like they belong in the classroom.

they say they enjoy most. Thus you will need to make the students collaborators with you and help them to understand how you are thinking about the organization of learning in the classroom. As insiders, they can let you know, for instance, when tasks are too difficult or too easy and when activities are engaging. Your effectiveness will increase as the students become better at communicating and collaborating with you and at helping one another and themselves to achieve group and individual goals (Tomlinson, 1999).

Social, emotional, and behavioural strengths include engaging in conversation and responding positively to suggestions. You can use a strength such as engaging in conversation to help the student learn in a collaborative group. On the other hand, social, emotional, and behavioural needs could mean that a student requires significant instruction and support because he or she fights when unsupervised. Physical strengths and needs include motor skills, sight, and hearing. One child may have a strength in printing neatly and quickly, while another may need significant instruction and support to enter assignments into a computer. Academic strengths and needs include the basic skills of reading, writing, mathematics, and learning strategies for test taking and problem solving. Students like Samuel have strengths such as completing calculations with a calculator. Students like Hema have needs such as requiring significant instruction and support to develop beginning reading skills. Sally needs review and more than one opportunity to learn complex ideas like the elements of a Shakespearean tragedy, but it is apparent in her case at the beginning of the chapter that she participates enthusiastically, especially in a small group. It is helpful to prepare a brief description of the strengths and needs of each exceptional student and tape it into your daybook so you see it while planning and teaching. Tomlinson and Cunningham Eidson (2003) use the terms *readiness*, *interest*, and *learning profile* to describe these student characteristics—needs and strengths—that teachers must be familiar with to attend to differences. In all her writings Tomlinson asserts that all tasks should be respectful of each learner.

## Step 2: Demands of the Classroom

Next consider the social, emotional, and behavioural demands of your classroom. Do students learn individually, work with peers, or do they do both? How long is the lecture portion of each lesson? Do you model positive interactions with all students? For physical demands, do you rely on an overhead projector, and can everyone see it clearly? The academic demands are manifested in things like the instructional materials you use (e.g., textbooks, computer programs) and in the instructional approaches. Direct instruction followed by guided and independent practice benefits students with learning disabilities while open-ended assignments challenge gifted students. Academic demands also appear in assessment methods. In Tomlinson's writings on differentiated curriculum, she considers classroom demands under headings such as *focusing on the curriculum essentials* and *connecting assessment and instruction*.

## Step 3: Adaptations

In this step you compare a student's learning needs with the demands of the classroom and identify potential mismatches and differentiations (adaptations) that eliminate them. You can make adaptations—by planning and then carrying them out when teaching—in the fundamental organization and instruction that goes on

**Put into Practice**

Informally ask parents, teachers, and students how they feel about differentiated instruction to meet the learning needs of exceptional students. What "hard questions" might you be asked by students without exceptionalities and their parents?

in the classroom. In making adaptations, you can bypass a mismatch between student and curriculum demands or you can teach through the mismatch. These strategies are discussed in the next section. Tomlinson emphasizes using flexible grouping (like the three teachers in the case studies that open this chapter) and making adaptations through flexible use of space, materials, time, and teacher contact to optimize learning for every student. Look back at the three opening cases for examples.

## Step 4: Perspectives and Consequences

Take time to reflect on each differentiation from many perspectives. What has your experience been with it? If you are uncomfortable with a differentiation, it is unlikely that you will continue to use it. To bolster your self-efficacy, start small and build up to your highest aspirations. Expect glitches. If you accept that setbacks will occur, you will be better prepared to overcome your own disappointment and renew your efforts. To get the most return for your effort, differentiate in ways that are beneficial for many students and that have demonstrated effectiveness. Use observation to learn about the exceptional student's experience of the differentiation. How did the rest of the class view it? How would the parents of the exceptional student view the differentiations you used? And how would the community look on these adaptations? Next consider the consequences, intended and unintended, for the exceptional student—learning, drawbacks—and for others affected by the differentiation. In the case at the beginning of this chapter, Mr. Carvello differentiated instruction for Hema and considered the impact on her peers. He developed a rota of willing volunteers, so many of her classmates learned to interact appropriately with Hema without feeling overly responsible for her progress or missing much instructional time. Tomlinson emphasizes ongoing assessment so you can make adjustments as you teach and encourages teachers to strive to provide the optimal level of challenge for every student. Sally, in the opening case, would have been overwhelmed by the demands placed on two-thirds of the students; however, she felt comfortable and learned through the review and the more concrete task Ms. Chiang provided for the third of her class who still needed to understand the concept.

## Step 5: Teach and Assess the Match

During and following the teaching, assess how well the differentiation overcame the mismatch between student strengths and needs and classroom demands. This analysis will help you decide about altering the differentiation while it takes place and about continuing the differentiation. Persevere and give it time to be effective. You can observe how engaged the student is, ask the student how she finds the changes, chart marks, analyze errors, and talk with parents.

# Choosing and Combining Strategies for Differentiating

Certain types of differentiations are especially effective for thinking about how to teach exceptional students: teaching around the mismatch, remediating or accelerating in hopes of overcoming the mismatch, and teaching through the mismatch. These differentiations can be used individually or in combination.

## Teaching Around the Mismatch

Teaching around the problem is often helpful after teacher and student have been trying concertedly and together for some time. Teaching-around strategies are sometimes called **bypass strategies** (Friend et al., 1998) because they allow students to succeed in the classroom using alternative means. Samuel bypassed his lack of computation skills with a calculator so he could concentrate on solving problems. Like most bypass strategies, it was successful because he was taught to use the calculator proficiently. To teach around a spelling disability, one might allow the student to use a spell checker, and Braille bypasses sight to enable reading. Bypass strategies that enhance independence are usually preferable (e.g., a spell checker rather than a peer editor, although a peer editor may be a step on the way to independent use of a spell checker).

## Remediating or Accelerating to Overcome the Mismatch

A second strategy for overcoming a mismatch is intensive remediation or acceleration. Intensive **remediation** is designed to address basic skills or learning strategies that the student needs and that you believe the student can acquire. A resource teacher may do unison reading with a slow reader in grade 9 to help the student increase reading speed so he can comprehend his textbooks. You could tutor four students who have difficulty printing while the class writes daily journal entries. An example of **acceleration** (used to move academically advanced students into challenging learning) is teaching two adolescents in your geography class to run a statistical program and analyze Statistics Canada data. They are bored by your unit on immigration, well-prepared to take the unit test, and eager to meet this challenge. Some provinces enable high school students to challenge for credit if they believe they have met "all the learning, process, interpersonal, participation objectives or outcomes/requirements of a course" (e.g., New Brunswick; www.gnb.ca/0000/publications/curric/challenge_for_credit.pdf).

## Teaching Through the Mismatch

A third strategy for overcoming a mismatch is teaching through the mismatch. During the planning process you can make differentiations in the fundamental organization and instruction that goes on in the classroom. Try using these four steps (Collicott, 1994):

1. Identify the underlying concepts and learning outcomes of the lesson and differentiate these for exceptional students when necessary. (Why do I teach this?)

2. Identify the methods of presentation and differentiate these for exceptional students when necessary. (How do I teach this?)

3. Identify the means of students' gaining understanding of the concepts or the means of student practice and differentiate these for exceptional students when necessary. (How do students learn this?)

4. Identify the means of student assessment and adapt these for exceptional students when necessary. (How do students show they have learned this?)

In addition to providing examples of differentiated instruction in practice, it is important that you acknowledge what differentiated instruction does *not* mean. It does not mean doing something different for each student in the class. And it does

**Weblinks**

STATISTICS CANADA: LEARNING RESOURCES FOR STUDENTS AND TEACHERS
www.statcan.ca/english/edu/index.htm

STATISTICS CANADA: LESSON PLANS FOR SECONDARY LEVEL MATHEMATICS
www.statcan.ca/english/kits/courses/smath.htm

LESSON PLAN FOR "CANADA'S IMMIGRATION PATTERNS, 1955 TO PRESENT"
www.statcan.ca/english/kits/immig1.htm

**Further Reading**

On using Canadian statistics in the classroom:

*Special Issue of School Libraries in Canada*, 2002, *Vol. 22*, No. 1. (Contains thirty short articles on using statistics to teach in many curriculum areas and to challenge your students.)

not mean disorganized and disorderly student activity, with everyone doing what they like. Differentiated instruction does not mean that you must always use groups, maintain the same groups over time, or isolate students who are experiencing difficulty learning. When using differentiated instruction, you can still engage in whole-class activities with all students taking part in the same activity. Many of these issues are addressed in the Ontario document on differentiating mathematics learning and teaching (Ontario Ministry of Education, 2004, *Ontario leading math success, grades 7–12*; www.edu.gov.on.ca/eng/document/reports/numeracy/numeracyreport.pdf).

Sometimes exceptional students participate fully and sometimes partially. They may complete part of a task or a different task to achieve the same outcome—e.g., drawing instead of writing. Or, as Sally's group did, they work on understanding the ideas fully, while those who already understand move on to making comparisons and extending the ideas taught in the previous class. Many jurisdictions provide teachers with handbooks to guide adapting or differentiating teaching, for example, *The Resource Book for Yukon Teachers* (2004–2005) and *Education for All* (Ontario Expert Panel on Literacy and Numeracy, 2005). The many aspects of the classroom that can be adapted are the focus of the next section.

## Analyzing Teaching: What You Can Adapt

In Chapter 1 we discussed three forms of adaptations: accommodations (specialized teaching and assessment strategies that do not alter the provincial curriculum expectations for the grade); modifications, which refer to changes in grade-level expectations as well as teaching approaches; and alternative expectations, those that are not represented in the curriculum but are appropriate to the student's needs (such as orientation/mobility training or social skills not normally taught in the school context) (Ontario Ministry of Education, 2004). British Columbia has developed a resource for orientation and mobility instruction (www.bced.gov.bc.ca/specialed/docs/fit.pdf), which includes learning outcomes and means of assessment for this alternative programming. At the beginning of this chapter Samuel and Sally received accommodations to the curriculum, and Hema received accommodations and modifications as well as having some alternative expectations, such as learning to use the telephone. When you use the ADAPT strategy to analyze and differentiate teaching, you may be struck by how many ways there are to make changes that meet student needs. For example, you can adapt the substance of your teaching (e.g., outcomes, content, cognitive complexity, authenticity, and interest of the task). Tomlinson (2003) refers frequently to differentiating content. Or you may find that it makes more sense to change the environment (e.g., seating). You may want to enhance student engagement by changing the method of instruction—through activity-based learning or by changing the form of practice. All these aspects of teaching are closely related and are often called differentiating the process (Tomlinson). You can also differentiate what Tomlinson has called the product of learning, which could be a report, debate, poster, brochure, rap song, model, etc. Looking at the components that make up teaching enables us to see myriad ways of differentiating for exceptional students. Adams and Pierce (2003) describe teaching by tiering. They present the content at varying levels of complexity while using the same process for all students. This is what Ms. Chiang did when she grouped students by their current level of understanding of the topic, elements of Shakespeare's tragedies. One tier had two groups (of students ready for

### Cross-Reference
Chapter 1 defined accommodations, modifications, and alternative expectations. Consult your local and provincial documents to see if this distinction is made. What terms are used in your province and in your school district?

### What Do You Think?

Read Paul S. George's paper "A Rationale for Differentiating Instruction in the Regular Classroom," published in *Theory into Practice* (2007, 44(3), pages 185–193). He argues that we differentiate because it is the right thing to do, because it honours diversity and equitable opportunity to learn in heterogeneous classrooms. He makes the case that publicly funded, heterogeneous classrooms are essential for the future of democracy. What do you think of his argument?

extensions) while the other tier had one group (of students like Sally who did not completely understand the elements). For younger students learning science, Adams and Pierce suggest one tier might investigate the kinds of objects a magnet can attract while another tier of students at a more advanced stage of readiness might investigate whether the size of the magnet affects its strength. The Focus on Curriculum Concepts box shows how the concept of universal design for learning (UDL) may inform the way we think about differentiation.

## What Is Universal Design for Learning (UDL)?

The concept of universal design—briefly introduced in Chapter 1—originated in architectural studies, where considerations of physical access led to designs that incorporated assistive technologies and adaptations (e.g., curb cuts and automatic doors). One essential quality of universal design of physical space is that the adaptations allow access to those who have disabilities and also make it easier for everyone to use the space. For example, a ramp allows people to enter a building easily when using a wheelchair or when pushing a cart or a stroller.

Universal design for learning (UDL) uses innovative media technologies to make a curriculum that can respond to individual differences in learning and teaching. UDL means the design of instructional materials and activities that allow the learning goals to be achievable by individuals with wide differences in abilities to see, hear, speak, move, read, write, understand English, attend, organize, engage, and remember. Such a curriculum provides adjustable ways of representing information, expressing ideas, and engaging students in learning. The idea is to make a curriculum accessible to, usable by, and meaningful for people with the widest possible range of functional capabilities. UDL is achieved by means of flexible curricular materials and activities that provide alternatives for students with disparities in abilities and backgrounds. "One central idea of UDL is that as new curricular materials and learning technologies are developed, they should be designed from the beginning to be flexible enough to accommodate the unique learning styles of a wide range of individuals, including children with disabilities" (National Early Childhood Technical Assistance Center; http://nectac.org/topics/atech/udl.asp). Examples of UDL include electronic versions of textbooks and other curricular materials, speaking spell checkers, accessible websites, captioned or narrated videos, talking dialogue boxes, voice recognition, picture menus, and word processors with word prediction. These alternatives should be built into the instructional design and operating systems of educational materials—they should not have to be added later. Using universally designed materials, both print and electronic, teachers only need to teach one flexible curriculum and become familiar with its variations to reach all students.

UDL does not eliminate the need for assistive technology (AT). Students with disabilities will continue to need AT devices, including wheelchairs, communication aids, and visual aids, to interact fully with their environment. However, building accessibility into new technologies and new curricular materials as they are developed will contribute to maximum inclusion of children with disabilities in learning opportunities.

### Three Essential Qualities of Universal Design for Learning

Most authors focus on the three essential qualities of UDL:

1. Curriculum Provides Multiple or Flexible Means of Representation
   - alternative modes of presentation reduce perceptual/learning barriers
   - can adjust to different ways students recognize things
2. Curriculum Provides Multiple or Flexible Means of Expression and Performance
   - students can respond with preferred means of control
   - can accommodate different strategic and motor systems of students
3. Curriculum Provides Multiple or Flexible Means of Engagement
   - students' interests in learning matched with mode of presentation/response
   - can better motivate more students
   - digital format is the most flexible means for presenting curricular materials
   - transformable (easily changed from one medium of presentation to another)
   - transportable (customizable for individual needs)
   - recordable ("learns" and "remembers" user patterns; tracks progress, areas of difficulty)

CAST (Center for Applied Special Technology) has been developing UDL for a number of years. Grace Meo (2008) of CAST describes the **PAL** process developed by CAST: **P**lanning for **A**ll **L**earners. The four steps in the PAL process are

- setting goals,
- analyzing the current status of the curriculum and the classroom,

## Outcomes, Content, Cognitive Complexity, Authenticity, and Interest of Task

Outcomes and these other aspects of teaching are all related to the substance and intent of what is taught. You will remember, from Chapter 1, that when you change the learning outcomes to something radically different from those in the grade-level curriculum that you teach the class, you are setting alternative expectations. This occurs when 14-year-old Adam, who has intellectual disabilities, learns to make a sandwich. He learns this skill with a paraeducator while you and the rest of the class study the geography of your province. However, Sylvia, who is blind, has the geography curriculum accommodated by using raised maps of the province and the guidance of a peer tutor. She may focus on the demographics of the province, which can be accessed on the computer in an auditory form or printed in Braille. Sylvia's outcomes are based on those in the curriculum of the grade level you are teaching. Modifying outcomes for a gifted student may mean including expectations from a higher grade level, for example, conducting a critical analysis of the declining role of landforms in demographic patterns of population and economics. Changes range from minor to massive depending on the students' strengths and needs and on classroom demands, but they will always ensure that the pupil learns.

**Cognitive complexity** refers to the cognitive demands made of the learner. When **authentic tasks** are presented to students, in the form in which they occur in society, students usually find these tasks complex. A class staging a mock municipal election would research how to nominate municipal candidates, hold press conferences, produce brochures, and cast and count votes while learning about the issues. An exceptional student could work toward the goal of improving co-operation with peers (on his or her IEP) by becoming a member of a campaign team. A gifted student might be an ideal candidate to run for mayor. These students are experiencing high cognitive complexity. However, students from other classes who listen to speeches, read newspapers to learn the issues, and cast ballots may be learning

Weblinks

ELECTIONS CANADA
www.elections.ca

HOW TO ORGANIZE AN ELECTION SIMULATION (IN CANADA, AT THE POLLS)
www.elections.ca (Click on Young Voters.)

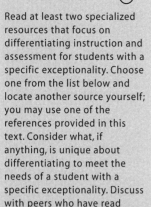

**Put into Practice**

Read at least two specialized resources that focus on differentiating instruction and assessment for students with a specific exceptionality. Choose one from the list below and locate another source yourself; you may use one of the references provided in this text. Consider what, if anything, is unique about differentiating to meet the needs of a student with a specific exceptionality. Discuss with peers who have read different sources.

Gartin, B.C., Murdick, N.L., Imbeau, M., & Perner, D.E. (2002). *How to use differentiated instruction with students with developmental disabilities in the general education classroom.* Arlington, VA: Council for Exceptional Children. (DDD Prism Series, Volume 4; available online through ERIC.)

Bowen, J.M. (2005). Classroom interventions for students with traumatic brain injuries. *Preventing School Failure, 49*(4), 34–41.

Bender, W. (2002). *Differentiated instruction for students with learning disabilities: Best teaching practices for general and special education.* Thousand Oaks, CA: Corwin Press.

Bender, W. (2002). *Differentiated instruction for students with learning disabilities: Best teaching practices for general and special education.* Thousand Oaks, CA: Corwin Press.

about democracy in a concrete way, and not experiencing as much cognitive complexity. Some authentic tasks are valuable because they provide concrete experiences of abstract ideas such as democracy. Research suggests that perhaps gifted students benefit from cognitively complex challenges because they develop deep sensitivities to issues and injustices at an early age (Hartsell, 2006; von Karolyi, 2006). Taking advantage of this may help to hold their interest in the differentiated classroom.

**Interest** comprises an affective interaction between students and tasks. It is often suggested that gifted students should follow their interests (e.g., Rakow, 2007; Renzulli, Gentry, & Reis, 2003). However, interest also plays an important role in engaging students who are not interested in learning for its own sake—often those with learning disabilities, ADHD, and other exceptionalities. In a series of papers John Freeman of Queen's University and his colleagues have argued and shown that, for these students, developing curriculum around interests (in sculpture, trucks, pets, etc.) can produce focused attention and learning (Freeman, 1998; Freeman et al., 2002; McPhail & Freeman, 2005; McPhail et al., 2004). I taught a reading comprehension unit that included all my curriculum goals (identifying the main idea and supporting details, reading captions of figures, etc.) and was based on Saskatchewan's driver handbook. The idea came to me as I watched my students struggle to read the content they needed to pass the test for a learner's driving permit. I capitalized on their interest in learning to drive to improve their reading comprehension, and they all secured the coveted permit. Chapter 6 describes the Theory of Self-Determination (Ryan & Deci, 2000), in the section on motivation and rewards, and how it is often helpful to maintain student interest, when a task is not intrinsically motivating, by increasing student feelings of relatedness, competence, and autonomy. This is another approach to generating an affective interaction between students and tasks.

## Environment, Method of Presentation, Pace, and Quantity

**Environment** has to do with classroom climate and physical layout, both of which are addressed in Chapter 6. High expectations accompanied by high support make for the best learning environments. Increase your support and encouragement by being alert to signs of discouragement and reminding students of their accomplishments. Giving encouragement is another topic discussed in Chapter 6. You can also adapt the environment by changing seating, a useful strategy although rarely intense enough to make big changes in learning. Remove distractions, glare, and clutter to meet the needs of exceptional students. Consider keeping exceptional students near you so they can focus.

You can vary **method of presentation** to the advantage of your whole class. When you present ideas orally, you can use an approach similar to that of Ms. Ash (described in the case study at the beginning of this chapter). She gave students a partially completed outline, modelled how to complete the outline, stopped to allow students to write on their outline, and used methods of direct instruction. Research suggests that most average-achieving students, exceptional students, and English language learners benefit from being directly shown with clear explanations, models, guided practice, independent practice, and feedback in an array of subjects (Hogan & Forsten, 2007; Jones & Leahy, 2006; Olson & Land, 2007; Swanson & Deshler, 2003; Vaughn, Gersten, & Chard, 2000). Videotaped presentations allow all students to learn about atoms, for example, before reading the textbook on the subject. Guest speakers may capture students' interests. Hands-on learning is often necessary for exceptional learners and helpful for other students. When planning a presentation, run down your list of exceptional students and ask what you expect each of them to learn from the presentation. Then ask what you can ADAPT to ensure they learn. This does not mean planning separate lessons; rather, it means making small changes to the lesson while planning it and while teaching it.

**Pace** is the rate of presentation of new information or the rate of introduction of new skills. Often exceptional students need new skills to be introduced in small steps and slowly to ensure mastery, and they need concepts to be introduced slowly with opportunity and time to develop understanding before the next concept. This may mean setting priorities and deleting some concepts or skills for exceptional students. While Ms. Krugly introduced three reading comprehension strategies to her class, the resource teacher taught one comprehension strategy to a group of three exceptional students. Their follow-up activities contained only sequencing exercises. Instead of learning three strategies to a small extent, these three students learned one reading comprehension strategy well and were able to use it when they read. Looking at Hema, who is discussed in one of the chapter-opening cases, she was required to record only three aspects of the daily weather, while the rest of the class completed a full-page chart. Introducing skills slowly is a helpful and easy differentiation—use fewer new spelling words, etc., and expect learning to the same standard as the others in the class. Over time, the volume learned is reduced, and this can have a long-term impact. Be sure to keep parents informed. On the other hand, gifted students may need the pace increased and the expectations raised. Strickland (2007), in a clearly laid-out "action tool" for teachers, describes identifying the unit goals the student has already mastered, and the unit activities for which the student has not shown mastery. With the student, you also have to work out the enrichment or extension activities the student will do while not participating in regular class activities. Strickland provides this example: "Chantal will work on her joint math and language arts project of writing a book for kindergartners about the joys of math" (p. 364), for which criteria should be developed.

## Student Engagement and Activities, Amount of Practice, and Form of Practice

Student **engagement** refers to the extent to which students embrace learning and classroom activities. Students who are disengaged from learning and from the social life of the classroom have little reason to go to school or to co-operate with those around them. It is critical that we engage every student and ensure that every student learns, even if what they learn is not the same as their peers. A danger of poorly implemented inclusion is that students are only physically present in the classroom without being part of the community or engaged in learning. Students must be cognitively active to be engaged (Lutz, Guthrie, & Davis, 2006; Kondor, 2007); if you do not provide choice and make a genuine effort to engage your students, you can expect behaviour problems and alienation (Bowen & Arsenault, 2008; Seidel & Vaughn, 1991). Use three novels of varying levels of difficulty if that means that every student will engage with a book, or place a few students with LD at a listening station with a book on tape and expect them to demonstrate comprehension.

**Further Reading**

On cognitively complex issues, interest, and gifted students:

Hartsell, B. (2006). Teaching toward compassion: Environmental values education for secondary students. *Journal of Secondary Gifted Education, 17,* 265–271.

von Karolyi, C. (2006). Grappling with complex global issues, issue awareness in young highly gifted children: "Do the claims hold up?" *Roeper Review, 28,* 167–174.

Pederson, K.S., & Kitano, M.K. (2006). Designing a multicultural literature unit for gifted learners. *Gifted Child Today, 29*(2), 38–49.

Siegle, D. (2005). Technology: An introduction to using spreadsheets to increase the sophistication of student projects. *Gifted Child Today, 28*(4), 50–55.

Renzulli, J.S., Gentry, M., & Reis, S. (2003). *Enrichment clusters: A practical plan for real-world, student-driven learning.* Mansfield, CT: Creative Learning Press.

**Cross-Reference**
Chapter 6 focuses on classroom climate, community, and management—including strategies for creating an environment in which to ADAPT. It also includes a discussion of how to provide encouragement so that students do not lose heart. Ways to enhance social relations and use co-operative and collaborative learning are elaborated on in Chapter 9.

Further Reading

On differentiation for gifted students:

Smith, K., & Weitz, M. (2003). Problem solving and gifted education: A differentiated fifth-grade fantasy unit. *Gifted Child Today, 26*(3), 56–57.

Van-Tassel-Baska, J., & Stambaugh, T. (2005). Challenges and possibilities for serving gifted learners in the regular classroom. *Theory into Practice, 44*(3), 211–217.

Abell, D.J. (2000). *Differentiation of instruction for disadvantaged gifted students: A systemic change model.* Paper Presented at the Annual Meeting of the Mid-South Educational Research Association (Bowling Green, KY, November 15–17, 2000). ERIC Report ED452651.

Berger, S. (2002, Fall). Surfing the net: Using the web to differentiate. *Understanding Our Gifted, 15*(1), 28–30.

**Additional practice** is often critical to the learning of exceptional students. Brief reviews of key information or skills may help exceptional students' retention. You can use different follow-up activities; for example, the follow-up activity on blue paper may place triads at a centre in the classroom after they have completed the practice examples. The yellow follow-up may require students to independently develop challenge questions, and the green follow-up may place students with you for review and practice. Change the colours so that green is not always the "easiest," change the groups so they don't become the stereotyped "buzzards, bluebirds, and owls," and change the group that receives your attention. Adapting the **form of practice** means accepting oral or written practice or whatever advances the students' learning.

In an Association for Supervision and Curriculum Development (ASCD) "action tool" for teachers, Strickland (2007) describes two tasks that lead students to the same learning goals at the conclusion of a secondary social studies unit. The more complex task asks students, "Using reliable and defensive research, develop a way to show how New World explorers were paradoxes. Include the unit's principles. But also go beyond them." The task that is asked of most students is, "Using the list of resources and list of product options that I have provided, show how two key explorers took chances, experienced success and failure, and brought about both positive and negative change. Provide evidence" (p. 252). If you had students who would struggle with both versions, what could you ask them to do that would be appropriate for them and would still meet the same learning goals as the two tasks already described? Perhaps you could ask these students to focus on one explorer, or direct these students to resources you know they can read or videos they can view on the topic, or plan the assignment with these students so they learn how to plan a culminating activity.

## Scaffolding, Grouping, Collaboration, Independence, and Assessment

**Scaffolding** is the support that may enable a student to do more with the assistance of a peer or the teacher than he or she can do independently. **Zone of proximal development (ZPD)** refers to the learning the student is about to undertake that he or she can already understand with support (Vygotskty, 1986; 1996). Exceptional students often benefit from gradually decreasing scaffolding as they internalize what they first do in social situations. This is why **grouping** is seen as such an important strategy in differentiated classrooms, and collaborative and co-operative learning have appeared as teaching strategies throughout this book. The Atlantic Provinces Special Education Authority has developed a resource, *Support for Students Who Are Deaf or Hard of Hearing in an Inclusive Setting* (www.apsea.ca/download/ssdhh.pdf), on how to assist the student in speech-reading and to scaffold adaptations so the student can follow class presentations and discussions. Every resource on differentiating focuses on flexible grouping. For example, Gregory and Kuzmich (2004, p. 11) encourage teachers to use the TAPS strategy to decide on the size of group:

> **TAPS** for Adjustable Assignments
>
> **T**otal group
>
> **A**lone
>
> **P**airs
>
> **S**mall group

# Differentiating Teaching of Listening, Reading, and Writing

## Building Listening Skills, Storytelling, and the Use of Environmental Print

We sometimes assume that our students know how to listen, but some exceptional students may lack this skill; other students may also benefit from activities that build listening skills. When you teach students to listen, ensure that you have everyone's attention.

The following strategy is effective in elementary classrooms (Evans & Strong, 1996) and can be adapted for secondary school classes in literature and content areas. Create a brief narrative account that you think will interest your students. Remind them of three skills for *paying attention*:

1. Look at the person reading or speaking.
2. Sit still.
3. Keep your hands in your lap.

Then focus on *listening skills* by giving a purpose for listening:

1. With younger students, show three pictures of an event in the story, such as the ending. Ask them to listen so they can choose the correct picture of the ending.
2. With older students, replace the pictures with three brief sentences or passages. Ask them to listen so they can choose the passage with the viewpoint of a particular character, etc.

In a study with older students who experienced difficulty listening, Joffe, Cain, and Maric (2007) demonstrated that teaching them to produce mental images for sentences and stories improved their ability to recount the sentences and stories to which they had listened.

Teach students to recount personal experiences and to listen to each other's accounts. Find another adult to form a pair with you and model telling a brief personal experience while the other adult models active listening and asks a genuine question. Model restating the question and responding. Switch roles. Next have students in pairs follow your model, switching roles. For young children, you could put an older student in charge of small groups. Provide additional practice for those still learning to listen.

Environmental print refers to the common words and symbols of our environment—they represent fast food restaurants, toy companies, carmakers, etc. (Prior & Gerard, 2004). With a bit of practice, children recognize these familiar words in manuscript printing as well as in symbols (Browne, 2007). This is a step toward reading that you can capitalize on with children who acquire literacy slowly and with effort. Environmental print can also be used in teaching mathematics (e.g., Koellner & Wallace, 2007). The following list offers strategies to take advantage of environmental print:

- Encourage cutting and pasting of symbols from magazines until the child can print the words in a personal journal.
- Use manuscript print under the environmental print symbol to promote recognition of the printed form.

**Further Reading**

Evans, D.D., & Strong, C.J. (1996). What's the story: Attending, listening, telling in middle school. *Teaching Exceptional Children, 28*(3), 58–61.

Joffe, V., Cain, K., & Maric, N. (2007). Comprehension problems in children with specific language impairment: Does mental imagery training help? *International Journal of Language and Communication Disorders, 42*, 648–664.

Arnold, K.M., & Hornett, D. (1990). Teaching idioms to children who are deaf. *Teaching Exceptional Children, 22*(4), 14–17.

Smith, C.B. (2003). Skills students use when speaking and listening. ERIC topical bibliography and commentary. ERIC document 480895.

Prior, J., & Gerard, M. (2004). *Environmental print in the classroom: Meaningful connections for learning to read.* Newark, DE: International Reading Association.

- Post printed signs around the classroom on the window, door, desk, etc.
- Post children's names on their desks so the child with developmental disabilities can match names on books to names on desks and distribute books, etc.
- Enlist parents to help their children to use environmental print at home.

## Background to Differentiating Teaching of Reading

In April 2000 the National Reading Panel (NRP) in the United States released its research-based findings on teaching reading (www.nationalreadingpanel.org). Their thorough review of the vast literature on reading led them to focus on five components of teaching reading: **phonemic awareness**, **phonics**, **fluency**, **vocabulary**, and **comprehension**. Phonemic or phonological awareness is the awareness of and sensitivity to the smallest units within words—phonemes or sounds. Phonics stresses sound–symbol relationships, helping learners to match the letters of the alphabet to the already-known speech sounds. Fluency contributes to comprehension and involves children reading out loud with speed, accuracy, and proper expression. Vocabulary focuses on children understanding the meaning of words, and reading comprehension is an active process of understanding that requires an intentional and thoughtful interaction between the reader and the text. A 2003 study (Denton, Foorman, & Mathes) described the characteristics of schools that have been continuously successful in teaching children to read. While they use diverse approaches to reading instruction, all include the five components described above. Walpole and McKenna (2007) provide a clear guide for primary teachers on differentiating reading instruction, in each of the components in the NRP report, with separate chapters for each of the primary grades.

## Adapting to Promote Learning to Read: Phonological Processing and Balanced Reading Programs

The past twenty years saw the so-called **reading wars**—controversies over whole language versus phonics emphases in early reading (Stanovich & Stanovich, 1995). Research indicates that the most critical factor beneath fluent word reading is the ability to recognize letters, spelling patterns, and whole words effortlessly and automatically on sight (Adams, 1990). In his 2000 book *Progress in Understanding Reading: Scientific Foundations and New Frontiers*, Keith Stanovich of the University of Toronto discussed the nature of effective programs for developing word recognition skills and phonemic awareness (early reading) and for developing comprehension (the topics of this and the next section).

Research shows that the best way to develop early reading skills is with explicit instruction and teacher-directed strategy instruction, especially for at-risk children and children with learning disabilities (Stanovich, 1994). Many researchers, like Dale Willows (2002) of the University of Toronto (see the Focus on Schools box on page 252) and Michael Pressley (2002; Pressley et al., 2002), formerly of the University of Western Ontario, suggest balancing explicit instruction of word-recognition skills (e.g., phonemic awareness) with meaningful reading activities (e.g., Collins-Williams & Willows, 1998; Jackett & Willows, 1998). Rachel Heyman (e.g., Heyman et al., 2005) of the University of Western Ontario has also contributed to the research on the issue of balanced literacy. Grenawalt (2004) describes how teachers can use technology to contribute to a balanced reading program.

To teach phonemic awareness, it is important that teachers understand what is involved. Phonemic awareness

- is sensitivity to, and explicit awareness of, individual sounds that make up words;
- demands that children analyze or manipulate the sounds rather than focus on the meaning; and
- includes early skills such as recognizing rhyming, and later skills such as segmenting the sounds in words and synthesizing the sounds in words.

Figures 7.1 and 7.2 demonstrate how to teach phonemic awareness.

## Teaching Phonics

Phonics, knowledge of individual letter names, is combined with phonemic awareness. Albert (1994) suggests that the teaching of phonics should begin with the simple and regular forms and then move to the more complicated irregulars. Teach the more regular consonants like *buh* and *tuh* first, followed by the short vowels that appear in two-thirds of all English words. The *Jolly Phonics* program (Lloyd et al., 1998) is often used to ensure a systematic and engaging introduction of sounds through consonant digraphs (like *sh* in *ship*) and blends (like *bl* in *blends*) followed by long vowels and word patterns. Pattern books, rhymes, songs, and poems can help readers practise letter–sound relationships. At http://reading. indiana.edu/phonics/d8/3directtrial.html you can find *Phonics Online*, which answers teachers' questions and provides instructional modules. On this website direct instruction is recommended for the teaching of phonics. Direct instruction consists of these steps: show, explain, practise, assess, and transfer.

## FIGURE 7.1  TEACHING PHONEMIC AWARENESS

**Instructional Guidelines for Planning Phoneme Awareness Activities**

1. Identify the precise phonemic awareness task on which you wish to focus and select developmentally appropriate activities for engaging children in the task. Activities should be fun and exciting—play with sounds, don't "drill" them.

2. Be sure to use phoneme sounds (represented by / /) and not letter names when doing the activities. Likewise, remember that one sound may be represented by two or more letters. There are only three sounds in the word *cheese:* /ch/–/ee/–/z/. You may want to target specific sounds/words at first and "practise" beforehand until you are comfortable making them.

3. Continuant sounds (e.g., /m/, /s/, /l/) are easier to manipulate and hear than stop consonants (e.g., /t/, /g/, /p/). When introducing continuants, exaggerate by holding on to them: "rrrrrring"; for stop consonants, use iteration (rapid repetition): "/k/–/k/–/k/–/k/–/k/atie."

4. When identifying sounds in different positions, the *initial* position is easiest, followed by the *final* position, with the *medial* position being most difficult (e.g., *top, pot, letter*).

5. When identifying or combining sound sequences, a CV pattern should be used before a VC pattern, followed by a CVC pattern (e.g., *pie, egg, red*).

Note: CV = consonant-vowel; VC = vowel-consonant; CVC = consonant-vowel-consonant.

---

Source: Edelen-Smith, P.J. (1997). How now brown cow: Phoneme awareness activities for collaborative classrooms. *Intervention in Clinic and School, 33*(2), 105. Used by permission.

## FIGURE 7.2 PHONEMIC AWARENESS: AWARENESS OF ONSET AND RIME

Onset and Rime: In families of words (like *lend*, *send*, *tend*), the initial consonant (*l*, *s*, *t*) is the onset, and the following vowel/consonant combination (*end*) is the rime.

**Word Families:**

- Play games and put the resulting words on charts. For example, say /b/ + *it* = *bit*. Ask the children to name other words that sound like *bit*.
- Use literature. For example, *Tog the Dog* (Hawkins & Hawkins, 1986) places various onsets in front of the rime /og/. Many of the books recommended by Yopp could be used to create reference books of families of words. These could be used in making new rhymes. Remember to say the words and draw attention constantly to the sounds.

**Literature:**

Choose books with rhyme patterns (many by Dr. Seuss), with alliteration (e.g., *Aster Aardvark's Alphabet Adventures* by Kellogg, 1987), and with assonance (e.g., *Moses Supposes His Toeses Are Roses* by Patz, 1983). Raffi's tapes contain many songs with these patterns.

**Direct Teaching:**

- Say pairs of words and ask if they sound the same or different (e.g., *run* and *sun* or *hit* and *pan*).
- Say a list of words and ask which is the odd one out (e.g., *kite*, *site*, *pen*, *right*).
- Create card games, songs, and picture collections that provide opportunities for children to say words, attend to their sounds, and decide whether specific sounds are the same or different.

**Simple Phonemic Awareness:**

| Targeted Skill | Example |
| --- | --- |
| Isolated sound recognition | Sammy snake sound says _____. (/s/) |
| Word/syllable/phoneme counting | How many (words/syllables/sounds) do you hear in this (sentence/word)? |
| Sound synthesis | It starts with /l/ and ends with /ight/. Put it together and it says _____. (*light*) |
| What word am I saying? | Put these sounds together to make a word—/f/–/i/–/sh/. |
| Sound-to-word matching | Is there a /k/ in *cat*? What is the first sound you hear in *dog*? |
| Identification of sound positions | Where do you hear the /g/ in *pig*? At the beginning, middle, or end of the word? |
| Sound segmentation | What sounds do you hear in the word *ball*? Say each one. |
| Letter-sound association | What letter goes with the first sound in this word—*book*? |

Source: Edelen-Smith, P.J. (1997). How now brown cow: Phoneme awareness activities for collaborative classrooms. *Intervention in Clinic and School*, 33(2), 106. Used by permission.

## Enhancing Fluency

Fluent readers recognize most words rapidly and accurately and can focus their attention on making sense of the text. Fluency develops through practice reading, especially reading familiar text. The strategy called repeated reading is particularly effective. Practising and then reading to an authentic audience is a good strategy with readers of all ages. Poor readers in grade 6 can read to buddies in kindergarten and grade 1 students can read to their parents and younger siblings. Look for creative ways to enable older readers to practise in comfortable contexts where they feel supported and encounter no teasing. Madden and Sullivan (2008) provide exemplary lessons that help grade 4 to 6 readers achieve well-paced, expressive oral reading within a diverse classroom. At http://content.scholastic.com/browse/article. jsp?id=4367, there are five classic strategies including repeated reading and readers' theatre. For a practical report on the role of enhancing fluency (and four other reading processes) in providing effective instruction for struggling adolescent readers, see www.centeroninstruction.org/files/Practice%20Brief-Struggling%20Readers.pdf or the research report by Roberts, Torgeson, et al. (2008).

## Differentiating Reading to Learn: Using Textbooks by Adapting, Supplementing, and Bypassing

After most students have learned to read, classroom learning activities depend on students' reading to learn. Many exceptional students are inefficient at getting meaning from text, while academically advanced students are proficient, fast readers. In reading to learn, students must comprehend new text, relate new ideas to prior knowledge, and create an elaborate understanding. Inefficient readers often require prompting to attend to their relevant prior knowledge and relate it to their new learning, and they may require assistance with vocabulary and word recognition. Comprehension is purposeful and active, and occurs before, during, and after reading.

You may be able to use scaffolding to help you differentiate reading-to-learn tasks. Scaffolding helps us provide the cueing, questioning, and coaching that "allow students to complete a task before they are able to complete it independently and while they gradually gain control of it" (Pearson, 1998, p. 169). The **scaffolded reading experience (SRE)** is designed for classes with students of varying abilities in reading to learn. It applies the steps of the ADAPT strategy, encouraging teachers to plan by considering (1) the students, (2) the reading selection, and (3) the purpose of the reading. SRE considers three steps in teaching: (1) pre-reading activities, (2) reading activities, and (3) post-reading activities. See Table 7.1 for examples.

Further Reading

On differentiating reading:

*Teaching All Students to Read in Elementary School: A Guide for Principals.* www. centeroninstruction. org/files/Principals%20 Guide%20Elementary.pdf.

Walpole, S., & McKenna, M.C. (2007). *Differentiated reading instruction: Strategies for the primary grades.* New York: Guilford Press.

McCormack, R.L., & Paratore, J.R. (Ed.). (2003). *After early intervention, then what? Teaching struggling readers in grades 3 and beyond.* Newark, DE: International Reading Association.

Tyner, B., & Green, S.E. (2005). *Small-group reading instruction: A differentiated teaching model for intermediate readers, grades 3–8.* Newark, DE: International Reading Association.

Schumm, J.S. (2006). *Reading assessment and instruction for all learners.* New York: Guilford Press.

*Effective Instruction for Adolescent Struggling Readers.* www. centeroninstruction.org/files/ Practice%20Brief- Struggling%20Readers.pdf.

### TABLE 7.1 POSSIBLE COMPONENTS OF A SCAFFOLDED READING EXPERIENCE

| Pre-Reading Activities | During-Reading Activities | Post-Reading Activities |
| --- | --- | --- |
| Relating the Reading to students' lives | Silent reading | Questioning |
| Motivating | Reading to students | Discussion |
| Activating background knowledge | Guided reading | Writing |
| Building text-specific knowledge | Oral reading by students | Drama |
| Pre-teaching vocabulary | Modifying the text | Artistic and nonverbal activities |
| Pre-teaching concepts | | Application and outreach activities |
| Pre-questioning, predicting, and direction setting | | Reteaching |
| Suggesting strategies | | |

Source: Graves, M.F., & Braaten, S. Scaffolded reading experiences: Building bridges to success. *Preventing School Failure, 40*(4), 169–73. Reprinted with permission of the Helen Dwight Reid Education Foundation. Published by Heldref Publications, 1319 Eighteenth St. NW, Washington, DC 20036–1802.

**Put into Practice**

Differentiate or adapt the reading demands of a lesson plan you have prepared, using one of the following sources:

Boling, C.J., & Evans, W.H. (2008). Reading success in the secondary classroom. *Preventing School Failure, 52*(2), 59–66.

Galda, L., & Graves, M. (2006). *Reading and responding in the middle grades: Approaches for all classrooms.* Boston: Pearson Allyn & Bacon.

Ciborowski, J. (1998). *Textbooks and the students who can't read them: A guide to teaching content* (2nd ed.). Cambridge, MA: Brookline.

Graves, M., & Graves, B. (2002). *Scaffolding reading experiences: Designs for student success.* Norwood, MA: Christopher-Gordon Publishers.

Compton-Lilly, C. (2008). Teaching struggling readers: Capitalizing on diversity for effective learning. *Reading Teacher, 61*(8), 668–672.

Graves and Braaten (1996) describe a grade 7 teacher using SRE with a class of twenty-eight (sixteen typical, six better-than-average, and six below-average readers). The text was "The King of Storms" (Flatow, 1985), an expository piece about hurricanes in fifteen hundred words and eight sections,. The **pre-reading activities** for the entire class included a discussion about the movie *Twister*, a video clip of tornadoes, a discussion of destructive weather the students and their families had experienced, a preview of the text by the teacher, and a contrast of hurricanes and tornadoes.

Then the groups participated in differing amounts of scaffolding. The strong readers received written instructions for **post-reading activities** and began silent reading. The average readers began a vocabulary- and concept-building assignment in small groups and then read. The less-skilled readers worked with the teacher on vocabulary and concepts and the teacher read half the article aloud. Then, two groups of three students each received instructions to become experts on a designated section of the article. The teacher served as a resource for all students. The skilled readers contrasted the destruction caused by hurricanes and tornadoes and made a chart to show the path hurricanes usually follow and the countries that can be struck by hurricanes. The average-reader groups wrote a summary of a section of the article and created a visual representation. The two groups of less-skilled readers had the same assignment with more scaffolding prior to and during the activity. A few classes later, each group presented its information, and the teacher corrected any misinformation and closed the unit with highlights and video clips of hurricanes. All students had been challenged to learn content and improve their reading comprehension.

## FOCUS ON SCHOOLS

## Early Reading: A Delicate Balance

It's impossible to escape the sights and sounds of children learning to read at Ridgewood Public School. In Phyllis Trudeau's kindergarten class, the children follow her lead in sounding out—and shaping with their fingers—the letters and sounds of the alphabet. Swaying from side to side to make the letter *T*, the children chant out "tuh, tuh, tuh" to make the sound. In the school library, teacher-librarian Pat Brodie and a group of grade 3 students discuss a Judy Blume novel. The students take turns reading passages, eager to jump in when Ms. Brodie pauses to ask questions about what's happening in the book.

Throughout the school, the tools for learning to read are everywhere. Direct, systematic phonics (to figure out letter–sound relations) is in place from kindergarten. A wide range of books and other print materials are used in the older grades (one of the elements of whole language). Each of the classrooms has a "word wall" for high-frequency words to help build a child's vocabulary.

The letters of the alphabet—and the sounds they make—ring the top of the walls in every room.

This is a school that takes reading very seriously. The results of that commitment show up in steady improvement in reading test scores by the school and the Peel District School Board. The data show students in the kindergarten to grade 5 school who spend their entire time at Ridgewood do better than students who transfer in from other schools. For this school of 650 students, where 58 percent of the population speaks a language other than English, about the only thing missing from the picture is any controversy over reading.

Moving past the "reading wars" of the past decade, Ridgewood is one of a growing number of schools that have adopted a balanced approach to early reading. "There's a movement away from dogma to common sense," observed Professor Dale Willows, a psychology professor at the Ontario Institute for Studies in Education at the University of Toronto and a proponent of "balanced literacy." In addition to her work in coaching classroom teachers on how to put together a balanced literacy program, she has been selected to serve on the National Reading Panel, established last year by the United States Congress to assess the status of research-based knowledge on reading, including the effectiveness of various ways to teach children to read.

The balanced literacy approach at Ridgewood, where Professor Willows has worked with teachers, has many components:

- explicit, systematic phonics so students learn letter–sound combinations that will help decode the words on the page
- teaching of phonemic awareness, through rhymes and other tools, so students go a step beyond the letter–sound combinations (for example, the "S" sound in *sand* is about phonics, but the "and" portion of the word is about phonemic awareness)
- integrated use of the principles of whole language, with students drawing on a wide range of books—sometimes guided by the teacher, sometimes not—to do their own independent writing
- school-based and board-wide testing to identify student weaknesses in spelling, writing, and reading

- informal grouping of students by reading level to offer stimulation to the strong readers and extra help for those in need
- parent contracts for reading, so those at home can support what is happening at school
- daily and weekly book bags, with books selected on the basis of the child's reading ability, that go home with the child
- after-school workshops for teachers and occasional release time during the school year for teachers to confer with each other on strategies to improve the children's reading performance
- dedicated use of scarce school resources to buy test material, books, and other resources to support what the teachers say they need for their reading programs

For Ms. Awde, the grade 1 teacher and a teacher for thirty-three years, the most positive part of the most recent reading trend is the focus on the individual child. In this way, she says, teachers know how to build on strengths and rectify weaknesses.

Source: J. Lewington (1998). *The Globe and Mail*. November 9, pp. C1, C7. Used by permission.

## THEORY AND RESEARCH HIGHLIGHTS FROM

## EDUCATIONAL PSYCHOLOGY

## Phonological Awareness

We have all heard of it, but what is phonological awareness and what role should it play in remediation of students experiencing difficulty in learning to read?

One of the most consistent findings to emerge from research on beginning reading is the relationship between phonological awareness and reading acquisition. Much of the groundbreaking research on this important topic has been carried out in Canada, for example by Keith Stanovich while he was at the University of Toronto, with studies also conducted by Linda Siegel of the University of British Columbia, Rauno Parrila of the University of Alberta, and John Kirby of Queen's University. Converging evidence—that is, the preponderance of evidence—has shown that the phonological domain is causally related to reading acquisition (Stanovich, 2000; Tunmer, 2008).

Phonological awareness has been called phonological processing, phonemic awareness, and phonological sensitivity. It has been

described as the ability to perceive spoken words as a sequence of sounds or the awareness of and access to the sounds of language (Adams, 1990). It is also defined as the ability to think about and consciously manipulate the sounds in words (Cunningham, 1990).

Many learners with reading disabilities experience deficits in the ability to manipulate and use the sounds of language in these ways. The effects are serious and cumulative. In 1994 Stanovich wrote that "children who begin school with little phonological awareness have trouble acquiring alphabetic coding skill and thus have difficulty recognizing words. Reading for meaning is greatly hindered when children are having too much trouble with word recognition" (p. 281). Gradually, not being able to read interferes with learning in other school subjects and can adversely affect many areas of school achievement, something Stanovich called the "Matthew effect" (1986), meaning that the poor get poorer while the rich get richer.

*continued*

You may be asking when we should teach phonological awareness. Research suggests intervention should be made early because these skills are necessary for children to begin learning to read (Adams, 1990). It has been suggested that intervention should start prior to formal reading instruction, as a preventive measure. And some studies suggest that the level of proficiency may need to approach that of skilled readers to be optimally effective (O'Connor et al., 1993). Thus, sooner is better, but one can also recommend beginning as soon as the need is recognized (Ryder, Tunmer, & Greaney, 2008).

In her 1990 book, M.J. Adams suggested five levels of phonological awareness that can be taught prior to formal reading instruction. From easiest to hardest, these are

- rhyme (e.g., nursery rhymes);
- oddity tasks (compare and contrast sounds of words for rhyme or alliteration);
- blending or syllable splitting (e.g., "What word would you have if you put these sounds together: /c/, /a/, /t/?");
- phonological segmentation (e.g., What sounds do you hear in the word *cat*?); and
- phoneme manipulation (e.g., add, delete, or move phonemes).

The most important of these dimensions may be explicitly teaching auditory blending and segmenting prior to formal reading instruction (Ball & Blachman, 1991). Auditory segmenting involves analyzing and breaking speech down into its component parts. Auditory blending, on the other hand, is synthesizing or recombining speech into whole units. Blending may be a bit easier, but segmentation may be the most closely related to early reading acquisition. Data suggest that training in letter sound knowledge along with phonological awareness (especially blending and segmenting) is the best combination to promote reading acquisition (O'Connor et al., 1993).

D.C. Simmons and her colleagues (1994) described five factors that you can include in designing instruction to enhance phonological awareness.

1. Focus initially on the auditory features of words without showing the word in alphabetic symbols. Children can move tokens or clap for each individual sound in words, but don't show the words when first teaching children to combine or segment sounds.

2. Focus initially on explicit, natural segments of language. Then later move to more implicit, complex segments. You can begin by segmenting sentences into words, words into syllables, and syllables into phonemes. Remember that manipulating sounds at the phonemic level is what is important for beginning reading.

3. Focus initially on words and sounds that are easily distinguished; for example, select words with few phonemes and words with vowel–consonant (VC) or consonant–vowel–consonant (CVC) patterns that can easily be stored in working

memory. Proceed to more complex patterns. Also choose words with continuous sounds (*s*, *r*, *m*) rather than stop sounds (*p*, *t*). Later, teach consonant blends found in words like *strap*.

4. Scaffold blending and segmenting through explicit modelling. Provide sufficient time and practice for blending and segmenting to become explicit and obvious to less proficient learners. Model conspicuous strategies often and over time. Also teach when, where, and how to use blending and segmenting in the reading context.

5. After learners are proficient with auditory tasks, integrate letter–sound correspondences. This enables students to move from more contrived tasks to realistic reading, spelling, and writing situations. You can tell the children to "cut up" unfamiliar words into their smallest pieces and see if they know any words that match the combination of sounds in question.

Phonological awareness holds much promise for identifying many of the students who experience difficulty in learning to read. It also offers a means of intervening early to prevent reading disabilities. However, there are students whose reading disabilities may be caused by other factors (such as naming speed; see Georgiou, Parrila, & Kirby, 2006). Also, some students do not respond as well as most to phonological awareness interventions, so it is important to monitor the progress of individual children.

In the past few years researchers, primarily in the United States, have been focusing on response to intervention (RTI), which defines reading disability as the inability of otherwise typically developing children to respond adequately to high-quality instruction because of an impairment in the phonological processing skills required to learn to read (Fletcher et al., 2005). Within the RTI model are procedures for identifying reading disability and for monitoring progress in acquisition of phonemic processing. As well, the model includes a three-tiered approach to intervention moving from group and less intensive to individual and more intensive interventions as children's literacy learning problems persist. Much remains to be both researched and implemented before RTI will be a regular feature in schools in the US or Canada (see Mattatall, 2008). However, as Tunmer (2008) argues, research has made great progress in the past twenty-five years in understanding reading disabilities and interventions.

### References

Adams, M.J. (1990). *Beginning to read: Thinking and learning about print.* Cambridge, MA: MIT Press.

Ball, E.W., & Blachman, B.A. (1991). Does phoneme segmentation training in kindergarten make a difference in early word recognition and developmental spelling? *Reading Research Quarterly, 26,* 49–66.

Bowers, P.G., & Wolf, M. (1993). Theoretical links among naming speed, precise timing mechanisms, and orthographic skill in dyslexia. *Reading and Writing: An Interdisciplinary Journal, 5,* 69–85.

Cunningham, A.E. (1990). Explicit versus implicit instruction in phonemic awareness. *Journal of Experimental Child Psychology, 50,* 429–444.

Fletcher, J.M., Denton, C., & Francis, D. (2005). Validity of alternative approaches for the identification of learning disabilities: Operationalizing unexpected underachievement. *Journal of Learning Disabilities, 38,* 545–552.

Georgiou, J.G., Parrila, R., & Kirby, J.R. (2006). Rapid naming speed components and early reading acquisition. *Scientific Studies of Reading, 10,* 199–220.

Mattatall, C. (2008, June). *Gauging the readiness of Canadian school districts to implement responsiveness to intervention.* Paper presented at the annual meeting of the Canadian Society for the Study of Education, Vancouver, BC.

O'Connor, R.E., Jenkins, J.R., Leicester, N., & Slocum, T.A. (1993). Teaching phonological awareness to young children with learning disabilities. *Exceptional Children, 59,* 532–546.

Ryder, J., Tunmer, W., & Greaney, K. (2008). Explicit instruction in phonemic awareness and phonemically based decoding skills as an intervention strategy for struggling readers in whole language classrooms. *Reading & Writing, 21,* 349–369.

Simmons, D.C., Gunn, B., Smith, S.B., & Kameenui, E.J. (1994). Phonological awareness: Applications of instructional design. *LD Forum, 19*(2), 7–10.

Stanovich, K.E. (1986). Matthew effects in reading: Some consequences of individual differences in the acquisition of literacy. *Reading Research Quarterly, 21,* 360–407.

Stanovich, K.E. (1994). Romance and reality. *Reading Teacher, 47*(4), 280–291.

Stanovich, K.E. (2000). *Progress in understanding reading: Scientific foundations and new frontiers.* New York: Guilford Press.

Tunmer, W.E. (2008). Recent developments in reading intervention research: Introduction to the special issue. *Reading and Writing, 21,* 299–316.

*Newspapers can supplement textbooks in many subjects.*

Textbooks can be supplemented with guest speakers, videos, field trips, television programs, trade books, newspapers, and hands-on activities. Grouping children with similar exceptionalities and assigning these activities to paraeducators are two ways that inclusion teachers can ensure that these activities take place. Provide opportunities for gifted students to challenge one another (Hong et al., 2006). To bypass the textbook, look for alternative texts that cover the same topics. Seek **high-interest, low-vocabulary books** for novel study and general reading.

## Teaching Vocabulary and Comprehension Strategies

For many students it is enough to introduce new vocabulary and connect it to their existing language. However, you may need to do more to ensure that exceptional students acquire new vocabulary. Carnine and his colleagues (1990, 2003) developed an effective and direct way to teach vocabulary with five steps. You might use this adaptation to help students with limited vocabularies at the beginning of a unit, to review at the midpoint, and to reinforce shortly before the assessment at the end of a unit:

1. Choose a range of positive and negative examples to teach the new word or concept. For the concept of leisure, give examples of watching television, camping, playing tennis, etc. Non-examples might include working at a part-time job and running errands for your parents. Use six examples of the concept and at least two non-examples.

2. Use synonyms that the students already know. For *leisure*, you could use the word *play*. State the definition simply and clearly. Leisure is time that is free from work, when you can choose what you want to do.

3. Model or point to positive and negative examples. For the concept of leisure, model telephoning a friend to arrange a game of tennis. Point to pictures of people hiking in the mountains and viewing a painting in a gallery. For non-examples, model going to work and point to pictures of people entering a factory, and so on.

4. Ask a series of yes/no questions to help students discriminate examples from non-examples. Ask how they know whether to say yes or no. Ask the students why they answer no to non-examples by using the definition you have taught.

5. Find out whether students can discriminate this concept from others. Is leisure the same as rest? How might they be different? Explore features that are sometimes present in the concept. For example, leisure is sometimes done alone and sometimes done with friends.

Vocabulary development is important to reading and to understanding content. In mathematics many students need direct teaching of vocabulary (Voytsekhovska, 2008). The research demonstrates that reading comprehension improves when vocabulary is taught explicitly (Beck & McKeown, 1991, 2007; VanDeWeghe, 2007). Klingner and Vaughn (1998) describe using collaborative strategic reading to help all students, including exceptional students, to develop vocabulary and reading comprehension skills. At the following website, you can also find tips for teaching vocabulary: http://people.bu.edu/jpettigr/Artilces_and_Presentations/Vocabulary.htm.

Ruthann Tobin of the University of Victoria and Alison McInnes of the University of Windsor (2008) describe the approaches of two grade 2/3 teachers who successfully differentiated the teaching of reading (vocabulary and comprehension) in grade 2/3 classrooms. The two teachers used slightly different approaches to differentiate their instruction in language arts. Cynthia used guided reading and literacy centres, while Margot opted for book bundles and a menu of work products as a basis for differentiation. This paper by Tobin and McInnes provides two models of teachers differentiating to enhance vocabulary and comprehension in primary classrooms.

In Margot's classroom students were beginning and ending reading tasks at staggered times, so she used an intentional traffic pattern, by checking in first with what she termed reluctant starters and nudging them along by scribing the first

### Further Reading

On resources that are high in interest and easy for exceptional students, reluctant readers, and ELL students to read:

Sullivan, E.T. (2002). *Reaching reluctant young adult readers: A handbook for librarians and teachers.* Lanham, MD: Scarecrow Press.

Libretto, E., & Barr, C. (2002). *High/low handbook: Best books and websites for reluctant teen readers.* Westport, CT: Libraries Unlimited.

Fránquiz, M. (2008). Learning English with high-interest, low-vocabulary literature: Immigrant students in a high school new-arrival center. *English Leadership Quarterly, 30* (3), 5–8.

Blasingame, J. (2007). Books for adolescents. *Journal of Adolescent & Adult Literacy, 50,* 686–686.

Schatmeyer, K. (2007). Hooking struggling readers: Using books they can and want to read. *Illinois Reading Council Journal, 35* (1), 7–13.

High interest books: American pop culture. (2005, February). *Library Media Connection, 23* (5), 83–84.

idea, or echo-reading the first sentences. Margot worked with students on their products, listening to them read from their bundles of books or from their writings, so she could monitor their comprehension. She encouraged rereading of sentences and phrases and revisions of predictions based on text information. Students were encouraged to use graphic features to help them decode unknown words. In summary Margot provided explicit scaffolding and comprehension monitoring along with a range of tasks.

Cynthia's classroom environment was described by the researchers as "rich, inviting and relaxed," with three main components in the language arts block: (a) shared reading and writing instruction, (b) literacy centres, and (c) guided reading groups. Students sat at round tables in groups of six. Cynthia had what she called a rainbow table at the back, where she conducted guided reading, and a carpeted area at the front, where students gathered for shared reading and shared writing activities. In summary Cynthia placed students to work in small groups for a variety of purposes. She matched pupils to texts and pupils to tasks in several ways: by giving them choices, by making choices for them, and by scaffolding instruction.

In a study that demonstrated how teachers can scaffold for engagement in reading instruction with older students, Lutz, Guthrie, and Davis (2006) found that students who received integrated reading and science instruction improved in comprehension and showed high engagement. The approach was most effective when teachers specifically focused on engaging the students in learning. Some of the things teachers did that engaged students included using complex tasks and complex passages, asking students to write based on their understanding, and providing more scaffolding for those with lower achievement in reading in combination with positive expectations and encouragement for all students.

## Enhancing Written Expression and Facilitating Note-Taking

To differentiate the writing of **narrative text**, use a series of scaffolded tasks. For those who write fluently and willingly, use only topic prompts. For students who cannot start with a topic prompt, introduce picture prompts and brainstorming about the pictures. Next time try only topic prompts, reintroducing picture prompts only for those who need them. For students who cannot begin from a picture prompt and brainstorming, add a **story-planning sheet** with the following prompts:

- Setting—where and when the story took place
- Main character—the person or persons around whom the problem or conflict revolves
- Character clues—appearance, actions, dialogue, thoughts of character, comments of others
- Problem—conflicts
- Attempts—how the character tries to solve the problem
- Resolution—how the problem gets solved or does not get solved

Students can complete the prompts briefly on the story-planning sheet while brainstorming with a partner and later independently. Those who don't need a planning sheet can use a checklist of these prompts, with the addition of theme, to check that all essential elements are in their narratives. This approach can be adapted to scaffold student writing of notes from a text, lecture, discussion, or

Put into Practice

Choose a study that reports on successful differentiation for students close to the age group you teach, perhaps Tobin and McInnes (2008) for primary teachers or Lutz et al. (2006) for teachers of older students. Use this study as a model to design a series of lessons, which you could use in your teaching, that are differentiated to meet the needs of learners and highly engaging for them. Compare your lessons to those designed by your peers. Share ideas and continue to read widely on both differentiating teaching and engaging students.

video. The principles are to provide no more scaffolding than students need and to gradually move students from peer and teacher support to independence with self-checking. Keep records of the scaffolding that students use each day so you can prompt for more independence. If you copy each degree of scaffolding onto a different colour of paper, you can encourage students to move from yellow to green, etc., and see at a glance who is using each degree of scaffolding (for ideas see Lutz, Guthrie, & Davis, 2007; Simmons, Dickson, & Chard, 1993; Kameenui & Simmons, 1999).

To differentiate the writing of expository **expository text** or **opinion essays**, you can teach the entire class to use a series of strategies. Then review the steps in the strategy and scaffold the use of the strategy for students with LD and others who find written expression difficult. Place a poster on the wall where it is visible to all students. You can also give students who need it their own copy of the strategy to keep at hand.

Munroe and Troia (2006) suggest using a strategy called DARE for planning the writing of an opinion essay:

> **D**evelop a position statement.
> **A**dd supporting arguments.
> **R**eport and refute counterarguments.
> **E**nd with a strong conclusion.

You can also teach a strategy for prompting students to revise their papers. Many students who have difficulty expressing themselves in writing do not understand that revision is expected; some may even think it is cheating. For revising, you can try introducing the SEARCH strategy (Ellis & Friend, 1991):

> **S**et goals (did I do that?).
> **E**xamine the paper to see if it makes sense.
> **A**sk if you said what you meant.
> **R**eveal picky errors (are my sentences to long or too short, and did I spell all words correctly?).
> **C**opy over neatly.
> **H**ave a last look for errors.

It is often helpful to have students work with a peer and ask each other tough questions about their writing—in a supportive way, of course. Teach students to begin with a positive comment, followed by constructive suggestions for improvement, and to end with a positive summary of what to do next. This should be a conversation in which each student gives feedback to the other and critiques his or her own work. Model how to do this constructively and create pairs carefully, especially pairs involving students with difficulty writing. Try a strategy that goes from small issues to large issues: Words, Sentences, Essay, Counterarguments, SEARCH. Questions students can ask at this stage include:

> Did I use descriptive **W**ords?
> Were my **S**entences varied and clear?
> Was my **E**ssay convincing?
> Have I successfully refuted **C**ounterarguments?
> Did I **SEARCH** thoroughly for all errors?

**What Do You Think?**

Look for a source on teaching students to read and write. Consider the ideas of the author(s) and relate their ideas to what you have learned from experience about the connections between reading and writing in classrooms at the level at which you teach. One source you could consult:

Strickland, D.S., Ganske, K., & Monroe, J.K. (2002). *Supporting struggling readers and writers: Strategies for classroom intervention, 3-6.* Newark, DE: International Reading Association.

Look for other sources to read on the topic, and compare your ideas to the thinking of your peers.

Finally, it may be helpful for students who are reluctant writers to engage in prompted self-regulation. You can encourage students to develop a self-question like, "What are the steps I follow by myself and with my partner?" or "What is the big issue for me to focus on in my writing today?" or a self-instruction like "I need to try hard to do my best today." Look at Harris and Graham (1999) or Munroe and Troia (2006) for ideas about, and evidence for, the effectiveness of this strategy of self-regulation.

# Differentiating Teaching of Mathematics

In mathematics, adaptations reduce the mismatch between the student's strengths and needs and curriculum demands. Number sense is foundational for all mathematical learning, followed by fluency in computation and problem solving. Each aspect may need to be adapted.

## Number Sense

**Number sense** refers to an essential sense of what numbers mean, how to compare numbers, and how to see and count quantities. Most children acquire this conceptual structure informally through interactions with family and peers before kindergarten. Students with good number sense move effortlessly between quantities in the real world and mathematical expressions. They can make up procedures and represent the same quantity in multiple ways, depending on context and purpose. They see that when they have three cars and five trucks, they have more trucks than cars, without executing a precise numerical operation. Children who have not acquired this sense of numbers require formal instruction to do so (Jordan et al., 2007). Number sense may serve the same function for mathematics as phonological awareness serves for beginning reading—it appears to be essential for later competence. There is increasing evidence relating inadequate number sense to learning disabilities (Chard et al., 2008; Geary, 1993; Geary et al., 2000; Gersten & Chard, 1999; Robinson, Menchetti, & Torgeson, 2002).

Robbie Case (1998), who conducted research at the University of Toronto, and Sharon Griffin (Griffin & Case, 1997) developed an instructional program in number sense, called Rightstart, using three representational systems:

1. conventional math symbols: digits and addition, subtraction, and equal signs;
2. a thermometer that shows the number line in a clear vertical direction, so bigger is higher and smaller is lower; and
3. a representational system that looks like the Candyland board game.

Students play games comparing quantities and adding one number to another using the three representational systems, and have frequent opportunities to verbalize their understandings and rationales for the strategies they use to solve problems (see Mascolo, Kanner, & Griffin, 1998). In two recent papers Sharon Griffin provides straightforward accounts of how primary teachers can teach to promote number sense: Teaching Number Sense in *Educational Leadership* (volume 61, issue 5, pp. 39–43) and Building Number Sense with Number Worlds: A Mathematics Program for Young Children in *Early Childhood Research Quarterly* (volume 19, issue 1, pp. 173–180).

Many teachers use a **hundreds chart** to help students explore number sense. N.N. Vacc (1995) modified the hundreds chart to align its vocabulary and format with the vocabulary and methods used when manipulating numbers. It includes the

Further Reading

To learn more about the Right-start program for teaching number sense by Case and Griffin:

Griffin, S.A., Case, R., & Siegler, R.S. (1994). Rightstart. In K. McGilly (Ed.), *Classroom Lessons: Integrating Cognitive Theory and Practice* (pp. 25–50). Cambridge, MA: MIT Press.

Griffin, S.A. (1997). Re-thinking the primary school math curriculum. *Issues in Education, 3*, 1–49.

Mascolo, M.F., Kanner, B.G., & Griffin, S. (1998). Neo-Piagetian systems theory and the education of young children. *Early Child Development and Care, 40* 31–52.

Weblinks

INFORMATION ON NUMBER SENSE AND NUMBER SENSE GAMES
http://cemc2.math.uwaterloo.ca/mathfrog/english/teacher/five/nsn/NSN5.shtml

www.apples4theteacher.com/math.html#numbersensegames

www.gamequarium.com/numbersense.html

www.nzmaths.co.nz/numeracy/Other%20material/Number%20Sense%20Items.pdf

www.tki.org.nz/r/maths/curriculum/statement/p32_35_e.php

www.gecdsb.on.ca/d&g/math/Math%20Menus/gr3nsan.htm

## FIGURE 7.3 REVISED HUNDREDS CHART

| 90 | 80 | 70 | 60 | 50 | 40 | 30 | 20 | 10 | 0 |
|----|----|----|----|----|----|----|----|----|----|
| 91 | 81 | 71 | 61 | 51 | 41 | 31 | 21 | 11 | 1 |
| 92 | 82 | 72 | 62 | 52 | 42 | 32 | 22 | 12 | 2 |
| 93 | 83 | 73 | 63 | 53 | 43 | 33 | 23 | 13 | 3 |
| 94 | 84 | 74 | 64 | 54 | 44 | 34 | 24 | 14 | 4 |
| 95 | 85 | 75 | 65 | 55 | 45 | 35 | 25 | 15 | 5 |
| 96 | 86 | 76 | 66 | 56 | 46 | 36 | 26 | 16 | 6 |
| 97 | 87 | 77 | 67 | 57 | 47 | 37 | 27 | 17 | 7 |
| 98 | 88 | 78 | 68 | 58 | 48 | 38 | 28 | 18 | 8 |
| 99 | 89 | 79 | 69 | 59 | 49 | 39 | 29 | 19 | 9 |

Source: Vacc, N.N. (1995). Gaining number sense through a restructured hundreds chart. *Teaching Exceptional Children, 28*(1), 51. Used by permission.

## What do you think?

Why might this modified hundreds chart help children? Read the following paper and discuss with your peers:

Vacc, N.N. (1995). Gaining number sense through a restructured hundreds chart. *Teaching Exceptional Children,* 28(1), 50–55.

numbers 0 to 99 and progresses from right to left (see Figure 7.3). It places the numerals 0 through 9 in the "ones" column, the numerals 10 through 19 in the "tens" column, and so on. Vacc recommends that teachers use clear, coloured counters so students can see the numeral under the counter and model using a restructured hundreds chart on an overhead transparency. Students manipulate clear, coloured markers on their own hundreds charts to count, match number words and numerals, identify numbers and numerical relationships, and place value. Students can use the chart for numerical patterns, addition, subtraction, multiplication, division, and prime numbers. For example, to teach place value, say, "Cover the number that is 2 'tens' and 4 'ones.' Next cover 5 'tens' and 7 'ones.'"

For numerical patterns say, "Begin with 0, count by 2s, placing a marker on each number counted. Describe the pattern you have made." Next you can add a prediction component for counting by 2s, 3s, etc. This is a systematic way to develop and enhance number sense.

Naylor (2006) provides practical descriptions of five activities for different grade levels using the hundreds chart. The activities are (1) chart tour (grades K–2); (2) mystery number (grades 1–3); (3) missing numbers (grades 1–3); (4) multiple patterns (grades 3–5); and (5) least common multiples (grades 5–8).

## Computation

Often an effect of math learning disabilities is lack of fluency with **computation** and basic number facts. Teaching older students to use a calculator, a bypass strategy, is only justifiable after you have adapted teaching to increase number fact fluency. Recall Samuel in the case study at the beginning of this chapter. Samuel benefited from being taught to use a calculator because the secondary curriculum demands that he carry out basic calculations in the context of problem solving but provides no more opportunities for learning these basic skills. Samuel, his parents, and his teachers had made every effort earlier in his school career and now accepted that a calculator would enable him to use his cognitive capacity to solve problems rather than to make calculations.

When young children are counting the objects in two sets, do not immediately expect them to memorize number facts. Teach them to count on, by naming one number and counting on the other. Model this strategy using fingers, number lines, objects, or the three representational systems suggested by Griffin and Case. For example, for 6 + 3, say, "Six, put your finger on 6 on the number line and put one counter on each of 7, 8, and 9," saying each number as you put the counter on it. Throughout, keep strengthening basic counting skills. Later, teach the child to always start with the larger of the two numbers, remembering that it takes number sense to judge which is larger. This can be called "the trick." Teach the commutative principle by showing that 4 + 5 = 5 + 4. Encourage students to read number problems aloud and verbalize what they are thinking. Garnett (1992) suggests the order in which addition (and multiplication) facts should be learned (see Figure 7.4). As

**Further Reading**

Montague, M., & Jittendra, A.K. (2006). *Teaching mathematics to middle school students with learning difficulties.* Thousand Oaks, CA: Corwin Press.

Martin, H. (2007). *Active learning in the mathematics classroom, grades 5–8* (2nd ed.). Thousand Oaks, CA: Corwin Press.

Stone, R. (2007). *Best practices for teaching mathematics: What award-winning classroom teachers do.* Thousand Oaks, CA: Corwin Press.

## FIGURE 7.4 ALTERNATIVE TEACHING SEQUENCE FOR ADDITION AND MULTIPLICATION FACTS

Addition

Adding 1 or 0 to any number

(1) +1 and +0 principles

(2) Ties        2+2 3+3 4+4 5+5 6+6 7+7 8+8 9+9

(3) Ties +1       2+3 3+4 4+5 5+6 6+7 7+8 8+9

(4) Ties +2       2+4 3+5 4+6 5+7 6+8 7+9

(5) + 10 Principle from 2+10 through 10+10

(6) + 9 Facts from 2+9 through 9+9

Use the linking strategy (n+10) −1

(7) Remaining facts      2+5 2+6 2+7 2+8
                          3+6 3+7 3+8
                          4+7 4+8
                          5+8

Must include major emphasis on the commutative principle (5+6 = 6+5)

Multiplication

(a) × 1 and × 0 Principles

Multiplying any number by 1 or 0

(b) × 2/2 ×

(c) × 3/3 ×

(d) × 9/9 ×

(e) Perfect squares

     (1 × 1, 2 × 2, 3 × 3, 4 × 4, 5 × 5, 6 × 6, 7 × 7, 8 × 8, 9 × 9, 10 × 10)

(f) Remaining facts

     3 × 4      3 × 6      3 × 7      3 × 8
               4 × 6      4 × 7      4 × 8
                          6 × 7      6 × 8
                          7 × 8

Must include major emphasis on the commutative principle (5 × 6 = 6 × 5).

Source: K. Garnett (1992). Developing fluency with basic number facts: Intervention for students with learning disabilities. *Learning Disabilities: Research and Practice, 7,* 210–216. Used by permission.

## Put into Practice

Find an example of strategy instruction for teaching the solving of word problems. Follow the steps to teach a friend or student. Here are four resources:

Montague, M. (2008). Self-regulation strategies to improve mathematical problem solving for students with learning disabilities. *Learning Disability Quarterly, 31*, 37–44.

Xin, Y.P., Jitendra, A.K., & Deatline-Buchman, A. (2005). Effects of mathematical word problem solving instruction on middle school students with learning problems. *Journal of Special Education, 39*, 181–192.

Jitendra, A. (2002). Teaching students math problem solving through graphic representations. *Teaching Exceptional Children, 34*, 34–38.

Owen, R.L., & Fuchs, L.S. (2002). Mathematical problem-solving strategy instruction for third-grade students with learning disabilities. *Remedial and Special Education, 23*, 268–278.

students become more mature in their strategies, teach them to ask, "Do I just know this one?" and use retrieval strategies whenever possible. Press for speed with a few facts at a time, following the order in Figure 7.4. When students are not using retrieval strategies, encourage them to think out loud and discuss the strategies children can use. Technology also offers a means of adapting the teaching of multiplication. For example, Irish (2002) used computer-assisted instruction and a multimedia software program (Memory Math) to teach students with learning disabilities the basic multiplication facts. The software utilizes keyword mnemonics.

## Problem Solving, Representation, Symbol Systems, and Application

Many exceptional students experience difficulty solving problems, a focus of recent curriculum reforms. Number sense and computational fluency are essential for problem solving. It is difficult to bypass number sense, while calculators can be used to bypass lack of computational fluency. Research provides many reasons for using calculators as an adaptation for exceptional students:

- calculators provide all students with practice and success in calculating ratios and solving proportion problems (Mittag & Van Reusen, 1999; Moss & Grover, 2007);
- calculators encourage students to focus on advanced concepts rather than number crunching (Antonijevic, 2007; Gilchrist, 1986; Gilliland, 2002);
- calculators make calculations less tedious for exceptional students (Harvey, Waits, & Demana, 1995; Steele, 2007);
- calculators allow for the use of real data sets (Arnold, 2006; Durham & Dick, 1994); and
- calculator use increases student confidence, enthusiasm, and number sense (Moss & Grover, 2007; Sparrow & Swan, 2001).

Strategies to help students solve problems include using authentic problems, demonstrating concrete examples, providing calculators, and making the reasoning used to represent the problem visible to the student. These strategies are apparent in the following example. Mittag and Van Reusen (1999) taught students about the capture-recapture estimation method used to estimate the population of a fish in a lake. The naturalist takes a sample of fish (120) from a lake, tags them, and releases them. Then, after the tagged sample has had time to mix with the unmarked fish, another sample of 65 is taken and the naturalist finds that only 2 of the 65 fish have tags. The naturalist writes an equation to solve this proportion problem:

$$\frac{\text{number of marked fish in the population}}{\text{total number of fish in the population (N)}} = \frac{\text{number of marked fish in the sample}}{\text{total number of fish in the sample}}$$

$$\frac{120}{N} = \frac{2}{65}$$
$$7800 = 2N$$
$$3900 = N$$

The teacher gave groups of students classroom representations of the fish problem using two kinds of snack food in the shapes of fish (cheddar fish and pretzel fish). Then the students solved other problems in the same form, using samples to predict populations.

I developed a strategy to teach adolescents with learning disabilities to solve algebra word problems (Hutchinson, 1993). In this approach, students learned first to represent and then to solve word problems. The teacher models by thinking out loud using a set of self-questions, students engage in guided practice with an adult or a peer, and then engage in independent practice. I used this approach to teach individuals, pairs, small groups, and finally whole classes (Hutchinson, 1997).

Self-Questions for Representing Algebra Word Problems

1. Have I read and understood each sentence? Are there any words whose meaning I have to ask?
2. Have I got the whole picture, a representation, for this problem?
3. Have I written down my representation on the worksheet (goal; unknown[s]; known[s]; type of problem; equation)?
4. What should I look for in a new problem to see if it is the same kind of problem?

Self-Questions for Solving Algebra Word Problems

1. Have I written an equation?
2. Have I expanded the terms?
3. Have I written out the steps of my solution on the worksheet (collected like terms; isolated unknown[s]; solved for unknown[s]; checked my answer with the goal; highlighted my answer)?
4. What should I look for in a new problem to see if it is the same kind of problem?

Students complete each problem on a structured worksheet designed to match the self-questions. In all seven studies I conducted, students learned to solve the algebra problems they were taught, could solve similar problems six weeks later, and transferred their problem solving to new kinds of problems.

Classroom teachers who differentiate teaching have developed many strategies to help diverse learners succeed in mathematics. For example, Lee and Herner-Patnode (2007) describe how a grade 4 teacher enables students to represent their mathematical understanding. Deb's students keep notebooks in which they use diagrams, graphs, and symbols to define mathematics words in their own ways. She encourages them to connect the vocabulary and meaning to situations that are relevant for them. Creating mathematics-oriented cartoons can provide visual and artistic opportunities for students who struggle with written or verbal strategies (Gay & White, 2002).

These results, taken with the other strategies described in this section, suggest that differentiating the teaching of mathematics can be effective. Remember as well the example of Ms. Ash in the opening case study, who differentiates her math teaching to meet the needs of Samuel, who has a learning disability. In the process she makes learning more effective for all her students. Ms. Ash used a well-researched approach to teaching—advance organizers that make explicit connections between new concepts and previous learning, a structured outline followed by guided practice, and then independent practice (see Steele, 2008, for a description of these and other strategies for helping exceptional students to learn mathematics). Advance organizers can be used effectively in any subject area (Preiss & Gayle, 2006).

# Differentiating Teaching in Content Areas: Science, Social Studies, Visual Arts, Music, Drama, and French

## Differentiating Science Teaching

Differentiating the teaching of science for exceptional students can appear overwhelming. Issues of safety and supervision in the science laboratory (Chin, 1997; Conn, 2001) are intensified by the inclusion of exceptional students. Alberta provides an online newsletter for teachers (www.education.alberta.ca/teachers/resources/connection.aspx). The May 2005 issue contained an update on safety in science classes. Consider, for example, blind students and students with low vision who require an orientation to the location of equipment and supplies and must be paired with a sighted peer; all members of the class must be reminded to return equipment to the same location. The visually impaired student can identify the contribution he or she can make to an activity after reading a Braille description of the activity or listening to an oral description. The student can time phases of an experiment on a Braille watch, make sound observations, or take readings on a Braille or talking thermometer. For students with low vision, a **CCTV** image magnifier can be set up so that experiments can be directly observed, and handouts can be copied at 129 or 156 percent to allow easier reading. For blind students, a listing of the steps of the experiment in Braille and a "blow-by-blow" description by the teacher or a student will be necessary. Because few students have visual impairments, it is unlikely that your school laboratory will be stocked with the materials described here. Another school in your district, the district board office, or a provincial resource centre may have these materials, and you can contact the nearest office of the Canadian National Institute for the Blind (CNIB) (www.cnib.ca). There are many resources available to guide the science teaching of students who have visual impairment, hearing impairment, and physical disabilities (e.g., Riendl & Haworth, 1995; Weisgerber, 1993). Concrete suggestions appear in a recent paper on differentiating science teaching (Fetters, Pickard, & Pyle, 2003). Hema's case study at the opening of this chapter suggests how you might include a student with developmental disabilities in a science unit. Piggott (2002) describes ways to differentiate science teaching for students with disabilities and for students who are gifted, including an example of differentiating the teaching of electrolysis through enrichment and extension (reading extracts from Faraday's notebooks).

Because about half of exceptional students have learning disabilities and because adaptations that help these students tend to be effective for all who read below grade level, consider the reading demands of your science text. The reading expected by science texts has increased over the past few decades. Look for texts with a lower reading level that provide parallel information or a website that is more accessible to students who are poor readers. Other strategies include graphic organizers and study guides that help students pull the main ideas from complex text and see them in order, in a hierarchy, or connected to each other.

Steele (2008) describes many effective strategies for differentiating science teaching for students with learning disabilities. She suggests that teachers adapt their use of lectures and class time to include advance organizers, prompts that draw students' attention to connections, examples from everyday life, and visual displays. She suggests differentiating textbook use by providing chapter notes for students who need them to study, teaching students how the chapters of the science text are organized, and summarizing key concepts before and after students read each chapter. Homework assignments can be differentiated, too, by providing class time for students to begin homework so you can make sure they understand the assignment, breaking large tasks into parts and checking progress on each part. You can differentiate assessment in many ways, as we have already discussed, including encouraging students to organize study time on a regular basis and using class time to model the review and study process.

## Differentiating Social Studies and Literature

**Reciprocal teaching** involves instructing students on teaching one another by taking turns leading discussions in small groups. Usually the teacher models how to lead the discussion and provides scaffolding for the groups as they begin. This teaching approach, developed by Anne Marie Palincsar and Ann Brown (1984; also see Palincsar & Herrenkohl, 2002; Deshler et al., 2007) has been used from kindergarten (Myers, 2006) to high school (Alfassi, 2004). Form groups of four or five students with one or two exceptional students in each group. Choose a different discussion leader for each group on a daily basis, beginning with a confident but patient student who will understand the process and model it well for peers. Students read a selection from their textbook (usually three to four pages). With younger students, you might ask them to stop after each paragraph. Each student receives a worksheet until the class is familiar with reciprocal teaching. Allow students to choose to use the worksheet after you make blank paper available. On the worksheet, ask students to think of three good questions about what they have read. Prompt them to list the subheadings and three main points under each subheading. Then the group goes through the strategies of questioning, summarizing, predicting, and clarifying. For example, for the strategy of questioning, help the discussion leader to use *who, what, where, when,* and *why* questions to elicit the key ideas of the passage. Summarizing involves the leader asking the others to provide a summary of the passage, beginning with the early highlights. After one student has answered, the discussion leader can ask others to add or to correct. Clarifying refers to asking questions "whenever we don't understand something." Encourage students to ask questions by emphasizing that anyone who doesn't understand should ask a question. Suggest that passages often leave readers wondering and that together the group can puzzle these things out. Predicting involves students in considering what comes next. The leader should read out a subheading and ask students to engage in predicting what will appear under this subheading. Discussion of these predictions leads to increased comprehension. A large body of research attests to the effectiveness of reciprocal teaching—for all students, including those with learning disabilities and reluctant readers (Lederer, 2000; Meenakshi et al., 2007; Slater & Horstman, 2002) as well as individuals with intellectual disabilities (van den Bos et al., 2007). Reciprocal teaching has been used in many content areas beyond literature and social studies including science (Herrenkohl, 2006) and math word problems (Van Garderen 2004).

As you know, differentiating teaching in any subject, including social studies, can be as simple as giving students choices in what they read, the tasks they complete, and the products they produce to demonstrate their learning. Kosky and Curtis (2008) integrated the arts into social studies units and found that what

### Weblinks

SCIENCE WORLD
www.scienceworld.bc.ca

TELUS WORLD OF SCIENCE EDMONTON
www.odyssium.com

TELUS WORLD OF SCIENCE CALGARY
www.calgaryscience.ca

SCIENCE NORTH
www.sciencenorth.ca

ONTARIO SCIENCE CENTRE
www.ontariosciencecentre.ca

DISCOVERY CENTRE
www.discoverycentre.ns.ca

PHYSLINK.COM (TEACHING RESOURCES FOR PHYSICS AND ASTRONOMY)
www.physlink.com/Education

*YES MAG:* A CANADIAN MAGAZINE FOR KIDS
www.yesmag.bc.ca

SCIENCE TEACHERS ASSOCIATION OF ONTARIO
www.stao.org

BC SCIENCE TEACHERS' ASSOCIATION
www.bcscta.ca

NATIONAL SCIENCE TEACHERS ASSOCIATION
www.nsta.org

### Further Reading

Ritz, W.C. (2007). *Head start on science: Encouraging a sense of wonder.* Arlington, VA: National Science Teachers' Association.

Moore, S.D., & Bintz, W.P. (2002). From Galileo to Snowflake Bentley: Using literature to teach inquiry in middle school science. *Science Scope, 26*(1), 10–14.

Bloom, J.W. (2006). *Creating a classroom community of young scientists* (2nd ed.). New York: Routledge.

Taber, K.S. (2007). *Science education for gifted learners.* Abingdon, UK: Routledge.

Duschl, R.A., Schweinbruber, H.A., & Shouse, A.N. (2007). *Taking science to school: Learning and teaching science in grades K–8.* Washington, DC: National Academies Press.

Westphal, L.E. (2007). *Differentiating instruction with menus: Science.* Waco, TX: Prufrock Press.

## Further Reading

Chapman, C., & King, R. (2003). *Differentiated instructional strategies for writing in the content areas.* Thousand Oaks, CA: Corwin Press.

Heydon, R. (2003). Literature circles as a differentiated instructional strategy for including ESL students in mainstream classrooms. *Canadian Modern Language Review, 59*(3), 463–475.

Lester, J. (2006). *Differentiating lessons using bloom's taxonomy: Social studies.* Marion, IL: Pieces of Learning.

Zevin, J. (2007). *Social studies for the twenty-first century: Methods and materials for teaching in middle and secondary schools.* New York: Lawrence Erlbaum.

Ogle, D., Klemp, R., & McBride, B. (2007). *Building literacy in social studies: Strategies for improving comprehension and critical thinking.* Alexandria, VA: Association for Supervision & Curriculum Development.

Seefeldt, C., & Galper, A. (2005). *Active experiences for active children: Social studies.* Toronto: Pearson Education Canada.

## Weblinks

NATIONAL INSTITUTE OF ART AND DISABILITIES (SERVES ADULTS WITH DEVELOPMENTAL AND PHYSICAL DISABILITIES)
www.niadart.org

VSA ARTS (FOR PEOPLE WITH DISABILITIES TO LEARN THROUGH, PARTICIPATE IN, AND ENJOY THE ARTS)
www.vsarts.org

*Encourage students to think out loud to you and discuss the strategies they are using.*

students appreciated most was being given choices in what and how they learned. The changes they made increased motivation, especially for students who required differentiated instruction. Meo (2008) provides an example of using universal design for learning (UDL) to plan a differentiated high school social studies curriculum with the goal of supporting all students' understanding of the content. She brings together principles of UDL, the PAL process (planning for all learners—goals, methods, materials, and assessments), and research-based reading comprehension strategies.

**Concept maps** and other explicit structures can help students understand the key relationships between the big ideas in social studies texts (Harniss, Hollenbeck, Crawford, & Carnine, 1994; Sturm & Rankin-Erickson, 2002). Nesbit and Adesope (2006) reviewed the research on concept maps to report that this flexible teaching approach, which can help to differentiate teaching, has been associated with increased knowledge retention not only in social studies, but in almost every area of teaching and learning, from economics to physics and biology. The **problem–solution–effect** is one way to organize expository content. The problems that people or governments encounter might be linked to economic, health, autonomy, or human rights issues; the solutions people generate can be described as inventing, fighting, accommodating, tolerating, etc.; and the effects or outcomes could be new institutions, new problems, or changes in society. In *Her Story, Her Story II,* and *Her Story III,* Susan Merritt (1992, 1995, 1999) tells about Canadian women who were pioneers in their fields. Applying the problem–solution–effect structure to the story of Adelaide Hunter Hoodless (1857–1910) in *Her Story II* takes the form shown in Figure 7.5.

## Differentiating Visual Art

Many view the arts as a great equalizer in education because regardless of language and ability or disability, music, visual art, and drama are accessible to all. They argue that the arts are largely nonverbal and focus on creativity and

## FIGURE 7.5 THE PROBLEM–SOLUTION–EFFECT MODEL FOR READING HISTORY

**Problem**
Unsanitary conditions caused disease and death in Canada in the late nineteenth century. Adelaide Hunter Hoodless's infant son died from drinking contaminated milk.

**Solution**
Adelaide learned everything she could about household management. She began teaching women about nutrition and sanitation. She started the Women's Institute, offering education and companionship for rural women.

**Effect**
Schools started teaching women domestic science. Women's Institutes spread around the world. Adelaide Hoodless changed the lives of women in Canada and beyond.

self-expression, fundamental aspects of being human. Recent studies describe collaborations between ELL teachers and art teachers (e.g., Gregoire & Lupinetti, 2005) and collaborative projects in arts-based literacy (e.g., Cornett, 2006). A visual art program in which students work in small groups or individually on projects at an appropriate level of difficulty can be differentiated for students. In an observational study, Guay (1993) found that teachers who successfully adapted visual art communicated regularly with resource teachers and other specialists, made rules and expectations explicit, and expected students to help one another. They also used clear instructions, repetition when needed by individual students, modelling, and motivational openings to each class. They provided differentiated tasks for students with physical, attentional, and other disabilities that allowed partial or full participation in the activities of the class (Guay, 1995). De Coster and Loots (2004) have developed a framework for art education for blind students that uses both visual and tactile information. Overall, teachers need to keep in mind some of the fundamental principles of differentiating: teach to developmental needs, treat academic struggle as strength, provide multiple pathways to learning, give formative feedback, and, as Wormeli says, "dare to be unconventional" (2006, p. 18)

## Differentiating Music

Music is often seen as a challenging area for exceptional students, especially those who are hard of hearing. Walczyk (1993) describes how students who are deaf and hearing impaired can take part in music in elementary school classes. All children learn to sign the words while singing, and portable electronic keyboards enable children to learn to play keyboard duets. McCord and Watts (2006) describe a number of ways to differentiate the instrumental music curriculum for exceptional students, such as making a videotape so students can see the music and a musician doing the fingering on an instrument like a saxophone at the same time. McCord and Fitzgerald (2006) provide strategies for matching stringed instruments and band instruments to students with disabilities; for example, "Strings are a good choice for children with cystic fibrosis and other physical disabilities that affect breathing" (p. 48). They also provide strategies for music reading such as "Consider highlighting spaces with different colors," and "Simplify parts whenever you can" (p. 50). Lapka (2006) and Mixon (2005) describe including students with

### What do you think?

Some argue that exceptional students do not need or have time to learn music, visual art, French, etc. Construct both sides of this argument, referring to these resources:

Guay, D.M. (1995). The "Sunny Side of the Street": A supportive community for the inclusive art classroom. *Art Education, 48,* 51–56.

Kempe, A. (2004). *Drama education and special needs: A handbook for teachers in mainstream and special schools.* Cheltenham, UK: Nelson Thornes.

Riley, M. (1997). Teaching French in a school for children with moderate learning difficulties. *British Journal of Special Education, 24,* 66–70.

intellectual disabilities in a high school band. Adam Bell (2006), in his master's thesis completed at Queen's University, taught a young man with Down syndrome to express himself through composing and playing music. Bell makes recommendations to teachers for building on his work in inclusive classrooms.

Recently researchers have also focused on differentiating the choral music curriculum for exceptional students and including exceptional students in a choral ensemble (e.g., Harwood, 2006). VanWeelden (2001) recommends planning ahead, writing the rehearsal plan on the board, maintaining consistency, and modifying rehearsal so the routine considers the needs of specific exceptional students. She also advises on promoting quality singing and responding to interruptions. Smith (2006) describes techniques for helping reluctant and exceptional students to sing. She includes two case studies and an extensive resource list in her paper. All these authors believe that the teaching of music can be readily differentiated to include exceptional students.

## Differentiating Drama

Drama includes many means of self-expression, including mime, monologue, tableau, and choral speaking, enabling teachers to negotiate the forms of assignments and self-expression with exceptional students. Adaptations include replacing body movement with facial expression and hand gestures for students in wheelchairs, allowing mime for non-verbal or shy students, and allowing students with learning disabilities to write and perform choral responses rather than monologues. Gifted students can negotiate open-ended assignments. The biggest challenge may be maintaining the attention of easily distracted exceptional students in the relatively unstructured drama classroom. Principles of classroom management and approaches for teaching students with ADHD may prove helpful. You may want to consult Kempe (2004), a recent resource published for teachers in the United Kingdom, or Wilhelm (2006), who illustrates how drama is not only accessible through differentiation but also a motivator that helps to create a learning-to-life connection, especially for young adolescents.

## Differentiating the Teaching of French

"Differentiated instruction is often a necessity in the foreign language classroom, as mixed levels are not uncommon" (Educational website of PBS; www.learner.org/channel/workshops/tfl/glossary.html). In Canadian schools teachers of French often find that they have to differentiate for exceptional students. They report that motivation is a key factor, especially when

- students have language acquisition and literacy difficulties (e.g., learning disabilities);
- the target language has no personal meaning for the student;
- negative socio-political attitudes may be associated with the language; and
- students lack the basics from previous years' French classes.

Some strategies that may reduce the need for adaptations are an assertive behaviour management plan, twenty-minute blocks of time for activities, and a variety of activities to use the four skill areas of reading, writing, speaking, and listening. Riley (1997) provides a practical description of the program developed in one British school to ensure that all students can participate in learning French. Theisen (2002; www.sedl.org/loteced/communique/n06.html) provides many examples of differentiated

### Weblinks

NATIONAL FILM BOARD (NFB) OF CANADA, SHAMELESS: THE ART OF DISABILITY
www.nfb.ca/collection/films/fiche/?id=51620

SOCIETY FOR THE DISABILITIES, ARTS, AND CULTURE
www.s4dac.org/site.html

## FIGURE 7.6 SCAFFOLDING LEARNING AND MOTIVATION IN THE SECONDARY FRENCH CLASS

- Begin the year with a personal inventory sheet that includes students' interests, attitudes, likes, dislikes, parents' names, and telephone numbers; use all of these
- Start with what students know: simple nouns, verbs, adjectives
- Teach the key building blocks: how to conjugate each type of verb, one at a time, with a quiz to follow; in this way, students tend to have three strong quiz results at the start of term, which is motivating for those who have found French difficult in the past

**Pre-Reading, Teaching, and Assessment of a Chapter in the Text**

- Build vocabulary understanding through activities and games
- Explain context of first reading in English or second language so students are prepared to relate new knowledge to prior knowledge
- Discuss the purpose, function, and construction of the grammar introduced in the chapter
- Organize a paired treasure hunt of a grammar concept: pairs of students compete to find all examples of the concept in the reading selection
- Teach the grammar concept formally with cloze exercises or creation of examples
- Give a written/oral assignment that features the grammar concept
- Assess learning through projects, assignments, games, dialogues, listening tests, quizzes, exams

**Differentiations for Students with Disabilities**

- Comprehension checks by the teacher; guidance from peer tutor
- Word cues on tests and quizzes
- Open-text exam with a textbook guide to key topics; guide could be created by students by predicting what will be on the exam

**Differentiations for Developmentally Advanced Students**

- Open-ended projects that allow them to be as creative as they can
- A bonus binder that all students can access when they finish assigned work and earn bonus points by completing challenging puzzles, crosswords, etc.
- Board games in French

**Understanding the Learning Difficulties in French Class of Students with LD**

- They require much support and encouragement
- The hardest part for them is understanding the comprehension questions
- Post a question-word list
- Teach them to use the words from the question in the answer
- Teach them to search for the words that appear in the question in the assigned readings in the text
- For writing, brainstorm sentence starters with the class so no one has a blank sheet

Source: Developed by Nicole Lévesque, Barrie, Ontario. Used by permission.

instruction in the foreign language classroom. Figure 7.6 includes examples of how to increase student motivation, use pre-reading and reading strategies while teaching, and make adaptations for students who are disabled and for gifted students.

# Differentiating Homework

Research continues to show that completing homework is positively related to achievement for students in general (Chang et al., 2007; Trautwein, 2007). Most classroom teachers assign homework, and many report that students with

**Weblinks**
For differentiated instruction in the second language classroom:

FROM THE BLOG OF LUCIE DELABRUERE, A HIGH SCHOOL TEACHER
http://lucie.typepad.com/blog/2006/04/differentiated_.html

COMMUNIQUÉ OF THE LOTE CENTER FOR EDUCATOR DEVELOPMENT IN AUSTIN, TEXAS
www.sedl.org/loteced/communique/n06.pdf

FRENCH IMMERSION IN MANITOBA: A HANDBOOK FOR SCHOOL LEADERS
www.edu.gov.mb.ca/k12/docs/fr_imm_handbook/chap_8.pdf

learning disabilities and other exceptionalities experience difficulties completing homework (Bryan & Burstein, 2004; Salend & Gajria, 1995). These students may have difficulty focusing their attention, especially if they find the assignment difficult, and tend to show poor time management on long-term projects. A special issue of *Reading and Writing Quarterly* (2001, volume 17) focused on remedying the communication problems that make homework problematic (e.g., Polloway, Bursuck, & Epstein, 2001). Bryan and Burstein (2004) make the case that teachers must share the responsibility for the homework problems experienced by exceptional students because they frequently assign the same homework that has been assigned to the rest of the class, which is too difficult or time-consuming and has not been adapted to be appropriate for exceptional students. They also argue that teachers must ensure students properly record assignments and have the necessary materials. Salend and his colleagues (2004) describe the efforts of one teacher to use the internet to improve homework communication and completion.

The following guidelines are relevant for students with and without exceptionalities and can be used to facilitate completion of homework by all students:

- Assign work that students already understand, rather than assigning work they are likely to practise incorrectly. Assigning the latter will mean you will have to reteach.
- Differentiate the amount of work assigned or time for completion as you do for in-class assignments so the homework expectation is realistic.
- Consider the IEPs of exceptional students, and what is most important for them to learn. This may mean a different homework assignment, but it does *not* mean no homework assignment.
- Rather than using homework as a punishment, motivate students to become more independent through imaginative homework assignments; for students who cannot complete the assignment independently, offer the option of working in pairs.
- Comment on homework occasionally so students feel that you value it; give the message that it is worth students' effort to complete homework.
- Discuss the reasons for assigning homework: consolidating classroom learning, increasing independent practice, thinking about and acting on an idea over time (e.g., a long-term project), showing progress to parents (young children reading books at home), etc.
- Use peer tutors, homework co-operative groups, or homework buddies, but develop some form of individual accountability.
- Develop predictable routines for homework early in the year, including a self-monitoring tracking system.
- Assign homework early enough in the period that students can try the assignment and ask for help before they leave if they complete the first few examples.

Recent studies suggest that the families of exceptional students (e.g., Bryan & Burstein, 2004; Mayer & Kelley, 2007) and of students from cultural minorities (e.g., Brock et al., 2007; Sands et al., 2007) can effectively monitor and support their children's completion of homework with some direction from the school, making the benefits of homework accessible to students who need to optimize every opportunity to learn. Teachers can do their part by differentiating

*Loyalist Collegiate in Kingston, Ontario, encouraged students to create a graffiti wall in response to the growth of problematic graffiti throughout the school. Art provides students with an outlet for expressing feelings and ideas and opportunities to develop appreciation as well as skill.*

homework, making tasks meaningful and feasible for each student. For example, practising number facts with immediate feedback can be particularly effective for students with math learning disabilities (Brosvic et al., 2006), and using a personal digital assistant (PDA) can enable a youth with Asperger syndrome to record homework assignments effectively (Myles et al., 2007). And Bryan and Burstein (2004) report that all of reinforcement, graphing, co-operative study teams, homework planners, and real-life assignments, along with parent involvement, have helped students to engage with and learn through homework. Karen Hume of the Durham District School Board, in her book *Start Where They Are*, reminds teachers that while feedback makes homework more effective, teachers can also ask students to self-assess and graph their improvement, lead a class discussion on the homework, and allow students choice in how they communicate their learning so every assignment is not the same (2008, p. 228).

## Adapting Teaching to Integrate Aboriginal Perspectives into Curricula

In its description of the adaptive dimension of curricula, Saskatchewan Education (1992; www.sasklearning.gov.sk.ca/docs/policy/adapt/cc.html#introduction) includes teachers addressing students' cultural needs. *Integrating Aboriginal Perspectives into Curricula* (Manitoba Department of Education, 2003) is intended to "enable teachers to facilitate [all] students' understanding of the Aboriginal perspectives in Manitoba" (p. 2). Although the examples of projects demonstrating the integration of Aboriginal perspectives are drawn from Manitoba schools, they

### Further Reading

On differentiating homework for exceptional students:

Bryan, T., & Burstein, K. (2004). Improving homework completion and academic performance: Lessons from special education. *Theory into Practice, 43*(3), 213–219.

Mayer, K., & Kelley, M.L. (2007). Improving homework in adolescents with attention-deficit/hyperactivity disorder: Self vs. parent monitoring of homework behavior and study skills. *Child and Family Behavior Therapy, 39*(4), 25–42.

Brosvic, G.M., Dihoff, R.E., Epstein, M.L., & Cook, M.L. (2006). Feedback facilitates the acquisition and retention of numerical fact series by elementary school students with mathematics learning disabilities. *Psychological Record, 56,* 35–47.

Myles, B.S., Ferguson, H., & Hagiwara, T. (2007). Using a personal digital assistant to improve the recording of homework assignments by an adolescent with Asperger syndrome. *Focus on Autism and Other Developmental Disabilities, 22,* 96–99.

could serve as models for educators in any part of Canada wanting to adapt teaching by integrating Aboriginal perspectives: an archaeology project; a trip to a fasting camp; a multimedia interactive drama performance workshop on Type 2 diabetes; and the sturgeon classroom project in senior science and math classes. For detailed descriptions, see www.edu.gov.mb.ca/ks4/docs/policy/abpersp/index.html.

## Summary

This chapter has described how teachers can use the ADAPT strategy to analyze and adapt teaching for exceptional learners, choosing from and combining numerous strategies. You can ADAPT many aspects of teaching, including substance (outcomes, content, cognitive complexity, authenticity, and task interest), or you can focus on changing the method of presentation, pace, and quantity for exceptional learners. Depending on the strengths and needs of exceptional students, it may be appropriate to ADAPT student engagement and activities, amount of practice, or the form of practice. Changing any of these aspects of teaching invariably affects other aspects because they are closely linked. Many examples are drawn from practice and research to illustrate adapting the teaching of listening, reading, writing, mathematics, and the content areas. Adapting homework is discussed. While it is necessary to ADAPT aspects of homework assignments, the goal of equity for exceptional students and their peers suggests that, as members of inclusive classrooms, exceptional students should have homework assignments just as their classmates do. Finally, the integration of Aboriginal perspectives into curricula is discussed.

## Key Terms

bypass strategies (p. 240)
remediation (p. 240)
acceleration (p. 240)
cognitive complexity (p. 243)
authentic tasks (p. 243)
interest (p. 244)
environment (p. 244)
method of presentation (p. 244)
pace (p. 245)
engagement (p. 245)
additional practice (p. 245)
form of practice (p. 245)
scaffolding (p. 245)

zone of proximal development
(ZPD) (p. 246)
grouping (p. 246)
phonemic awareness (p. 248)
phonics (p. 248)
fluency (p. 248)
vocabulary (p. 248)
comprehension (p. 248)
reading wars (p. 248)
scaffolded reading experience
(SRE) (p. 251)
pre-reading activities (p. 252)
post-reading activities (p. 252)

high-interest, low-vocabulary
books (p. 255)
narrative text (p. 257)
story-planning sheet (p. 257)
expository text (p. 258)
opinion essays (p. 258)
number sense (p. 259)
hundreds chart (p. 259)
computation (p. 260)
CCTV (p. 264)
reciprocal teaching (p. 265)
concept maps (p. 266)
problem–solution–effect (p. 266)

# Challenges for Reviewing Chapter 7

1. Discuss with your peers how you would like to use the ADAPT strategy to analyze and differentiate teaching. What do you think will be particularly challenging about this process? Particularly rewarding? How can teachers collaborate to enjoy the rewarding aspects and meet the challenges of differentiating teaching?

2. Consider the principles that guide teachers in choosing and combining strategies for differentiating in the classroom. Discuss your ideas with both secondary and elementary teachers. Write a set of steps that you think will help you to differentiate your teaching. Compare them with the steps written by your peers. Why might they be different?

3. List all the aspects of teaching that can be differentiated. Choose one of the opening scenarios of this chapter and see how many of the aspects of teaching in your list can be differentiated to benefit the student in the scenario. How many of these are likely to also benefit other students in the class?

4. Using the opening case of Sally, describe how you would differentiate the teaching of listening, reading, and writing for Sally and other students with similar needs in your classroom. If you teach primary students, create a scenario for Sally in grade 1 and respond to this question for that scenario.

5. Focus on the opening case of Ms. Ash and describe all the ways she differentiates the teaching of math. Create a scenario involving number sense and younger children, and describe how you could differentiate your teaching to benefit your students who are struggling with number sense.

6. Think about a student who might be in one of your classes who is experiencing difficulty in science or social studies, and especially in completing homework in this content area. Describe the thinking process you would engage in to decide how to differentiate both your teaching in this subject and the homework you assign to meet the needs of this student. If you teach secondary students, adjust this question to be relevant for a subject you teach.

7. Return to the opening cases of Ms. Ash, Hema, and Sally and answer the five questions that follow the cases.

# Chapter 8
## Adapting Assessment and Using Assessment to Differentiate Teaching

### Learner Objectives

After you have read this chapter, you will be able to:

1. Describe how to use the ADAPT strategy to analyze and adapt assessment.

2. Describe large-scale assessment in Canada and the adaptations used for exceptional students.

3. Explain how teachers can use classroom assessments to inform differentiated teaching and how rubrics can be used in classroom assessment.

4. Describe adaptations to classroom assessment, including tests, performance assessment, and portfolios.

5. Discuss adaptations and alternatives to report card marks.

**Sasha is in grade 5 and has attention deficit disorder as well as a learning disability in reading.** Sasha's teacher, Mr. Sinclair, has been differentiating teaching with the assistance of the resource teacher, and Sasha feels proud of being able to finish most assignments and understand what is being taught, especially in social studies and science. When Sasha receives his report card in October, he expects it to say he is doing well. He rips it open and sees low grades in every subject. Sasha doesn't understand. He asks the teacher, "Why do you say I'm doing good work and then give me Level 1, the lowest grade? I got 8 out of 10 on my science project." How can Mr. Sinclair explain to Sasha that his science project was only six pages long while those of the other students were eight pages long, and that Sasha was allowed to replace some paragraphs with drawings? These adaptations were consistent with Sasha's IEP, which had provided clear guidance for Mr. Sinclair in differentiating teaching. Unfortunately the IEP contained no information about how to adapt assessment or grades and Mr. Sinclair had worried that Sasha would be crushed by his low marks.

Belle has hearing loss and uses an FM system and speech-reading to learn in the secondary school classroom. She has an IEP that guides her teachers at Pacific Secondary School in differentiating teaching and adapting assessment. Belle's math teacher, Ms. Frost, knows that Belle tires easily and that although she is efficient at speech-reading, it only enables her to catch a fraction of what is said. Belle has math in the last period of the day. Ms. Frost uses a system of frequent oral tests to help students gauge their own learning and prepare for unit tests and term exams. Belle met with Ms. Frost after the first oral test to explain how difficult it was for her to understand the questions and to respond on paper quickly. The two of them reviewed Belle's IEP with the resource teacher. The decision was that Belle would take the tests and do her best, but that the oral quizzes would not contribute to Belle's final grade in the course. The weights of the other assessments—unit tests, homework completion, and term tests—would be increased. Belle felt that this was a fair resolution and was pleased that she could show Ms. Frost that she understood geometry and could use her graphing calculator effectively. However, she worried that other students who disliked the oral quizzes would think it was not fair for her to have different arrangements for calculating her grade.

1. What guidance do teachers need to adapt assessment for students who have disabilities that interfere with meeting the usual assessment expectations?

2. How can teachers match assessment to the differentiated teaching they are providing for exceptional students?

3. How can teachers prevent students like Sasha and Belle from giving up, when effort and improved work are not recognized and rewarded?

4. Why might parents object if schools adapt assignments and then penalize the students after they do well on what they have been asked to do because their tasks have differed from those of their peers?

# Introduction

The subject of this chapter is adapting assessment and using assessment data to differentiate teaching. **Assessment** is data collection. It refers to gathering information of many kinds about a student or a group of students, using a variety of tools and techniques. **Large-scale assessment** refers to nationwide, province-wide, or district-wide efforts to provide information about student achievement, usually by means of paper-and-pencil tests. **Classroom assessment** refers to the day-to-day practices adopted by teachers to describe student learning, often through a variety of means, including portfolios, conferences with students, and other means, as well as paper-and-pencil tests. There is no judgment inherent in assessment. It is the act of describing student performance. **Testing** is one form of assessment, normally using a paper-and-pencil test (either designed by the teacher or commercially available) to gather information that describes a student or group's level of performance. **Evaluation** involves making judgments and decisions, based on the assessment data that have been gathered, about a student or group of students. **Grading** is a symbolic representation of evaluation and **reporting** is the way in which evaluation results are communicated.

## Using the ADAPT Strategy for Assessment

You need strategies for adapting assessment that are effective for exceptional students and efficient for you, and that become a regular part of your planning and teaching. You also need to use assessment data to inform differentiated teaching. Chapter 1 introduced ADAPT and Chapter 7 included examples of using ADAPT for differentiating teaching. The ADAPT strategy is similar to others, but it includes considering the perspectives of many people, including classmates, on the adaptation and on the consequences for them. The characteristics of the student (strengths *and* needs) and the demands of the classroom are important when devising adaptations to use the student's strengths and either to bypass areas of need or to help the student to strengthen these areas.

The ADAPT strategy has the following five steps:

- Step 1: **A**ccounts of students' strengths and needs
- Step 2: **D**emands of the classroom
- Step 3: **A**daptations
- Step 4: **P**erspectives and consequences
- Step 5: **T**each and assess the match

These five steps constitute a procedure for adapting assessment that you can use with learners who have a variety of exceptionalities in both elementary and secondary school classrooms for both large-scale and classroom assessment.

## Large-Scale Assessment and Exceptional Students in Canada

In recent years educators have experienced pressure from governments, parents, and the general public for evidence to show how well schools are preparing Canadian children to compete in the global economy (Bussière, Cartwright, &

Knighton, 2004; Human Resources and Social Development Canada, 2005; Ontario Ministry of Education, 2006). We have already discussed the increasing diversity within communities, as well as the pressure, focused by the 1982 *Charter of Rights and Freedoms,* for institutions such as schools to ensure equity and respect for the rights of individuals regardless of income, social class, disability, race, religion, age, or sex (Ignatieff, 2000; Robertson, 2004). Other social trends that contribute to the pressure on educators to demonstrate their value through assessment results include the changing nature of families and the role they play in the education of youth (Ben Jaafar & Anderson, 2007; Leithwood, 2004). In a monograph on assessment, Lorna Earl of the University of Toronto and Brad Cousins of the University of Ottawa (1995) argue that assessment and evaluation practices are a concrete representation of the values of societies. "What gets measured, how it gets measured, how it is reported and the significance of the decisions that get made give a vivid accounting of what is seen as important" (Earl & Cousins, 1995, p. xi).

Until recently, most schools in Canada were asked to demonstrate accountability by showing that they had conformed to the expected process, in other words that they had implemented new programs and methods of organization (Spencer, 2004). For example, in the education of exceptional students, schools were required to show that they had developed programs, identified exceptional students, and written IEPs for those students. However, in the most recent changes in Ontario, for example, schools have received standards to which IEPs must conform (Ontario Ministry of Education, 2000a). This suggests that demands for accountability are increasingly focusing on whether the process is producing the desired outcomes at the provincial and national levels (Ben Jaafar & Anderson, 2007). In a recent paper Sonia Ben Jaafar (2006b) of the University of Toronto argues that Canada has a unique approach to accountability that reflects our commitment to equitable opportunities to learn and to the Canadian value of social justice (Saul, 2001). One source of evidence she cites is the finding that the beliefs of Canadian school leaders were the key factor determining how they behaved in schools (Ben Jaafar, 2006a), in contrast to data on principals in American schools who aligned their practices with the state policies irrespective of their beliefs (Ladd & Zelli, 2002, 2003). Ben Jaafar calls our unique approach inquiry-based accountability, which means administrators and educators use assessment information to decide "what to do given the local situation and the demands of the broader context" (2006b, p. 69).

## At the National Level

The Council of Ministers of Education, Canada (CMEC), was created in 1967 as a forum for the provincial and territorial ministers of education, although education remains a provincial responsibility. In 1989 CMEC initiated the School Achievement Indicators Program (SAIP), the first attempt by all the ministers of education to reach consensus on a national assessment. The Pan-Canadian Assessment Program (PCAP) replaced SAIP as a cyclical program of pan-Canadian assessments of student achievement in reading, mathematics, and science in 2007. PCAP is designed to complement existing assessments in the provinces and territories, providing data on the achievement levels attained by a random selection of 13-year-old students across the country. Descriptions of the instruments and the reports of the provincial outcomes are available on the CMEC website (www.cmec.ca/pcap/2007/report.en.stm).

**Put into Practice**

Look for articles in local and national newspapers that reflect the recent demands for assessment to show that Canadian schools are delivering excellence. Discuss with your peers the ways that teachers can support one another and can work with families to reduce the feelings of pressure brought on by these demands.

**Further Reading**

Consult the provincial documents that guide IEPs in your jurisdiction to see if standards for IEPs have been released or are under development. Focus on standards related to adapting large-scale and classroom assessment.

Do exceptional students participate in the PCAP assessments? Do they receive accommodations or alternative assessments? Accommodations are changes in testing materials or procedures that enable students to participate in large-scale assessments in a way that assesses abilities rather than disabilities. Alternative assessments evaluate the performance of students unable to participate in large-scale assessments, even with accommodations (e.g., portfolios) (Elliot, & Roach, 2007). *The Handbook for Schools* (CMEC, 2007) urges schools to include as many of the selected students as possible, but to take a balanced approach: "We want all students to have the opportunity to be represented in this assessment. However, we do not want students with special needs to be overly pressured to participate in the assessment if they would be adversely affected or if appropriate accommodations cannot be made for them" (p. 8) (www.eqao.com/pdf_e/07/07P015e.pdf).

We can use a report published by CMEC to gain a sense of the students exempted from these Canada-wide tests. CMEC's (1999) report on the 1994 SAIP reading sample states that only 1.9 percent of selected 13 year olds and 1.5 percent of selected 16 year olds across Canada were declared exempt, which is a very low rate of exemption. Students are entitled to the accommodations usually made for them in the classroom. "For example, students who normally had a scribe to write were permitted a scribe for these assessments. Braille or large-print tests were also provided as needed. Students were given extra time to complete the assessments if they required it in the judgment of the school-based staff" (CMEC, 2003, p. 6). Some of the issues to consider when deciding what accommodations will make a large-scale assessment meaningful for an exceptional student appear in Figure 8.1.

## At the Provincial Level

There is great diversity in provincial large-scale student assessment. However, every jurisdiction has some sort of program in place except Prince Edward Island and Nunavut (Ben Jaafar & Anderson, 2007; De Luca et al., 2005). For some time, Quebec (www.mels.gouv.qc.ca/publications/menu-rapports.htm), Alberta (http://education.alberta.ca/admin/testing.aspx), and British Columbia (www.bced.gov.bc.ca/reporting/exams) have had examinations for students finishing secondary school and have had provincial achievement tests at other grade levels. British Columbia's examinations are administered to all students or to samples of students in selected subjects (www.cmec.ca). Other provinces have more recently developed assessment and provincial indicator programs. Saskatchewan (www.learning.gov.sk.ca/Accountability) and Manitoba (www.edu.gov.mb.ca/k12/assess) have provincially based programs. New Brunswick (www.gnb.ca/0000/anglophone-e.asp#e) piloted assessment programs at grades 4 (literacy) and 6 (science) in 2007, while Nova Scotia (http://plans.ednet.ns.ca/index.shtml) has assessments in grades 3, 6, and 9, and examinations in grade 12. Newfoundland and Labrador (www.ed.gov.nl.ca/edu/pub/crt/crt.htm) has similar assessment programs and also graduating examinations which contribute to grade 12 marks. Ontario has recently implemented tests of mathematics, reading, and writing at grades 3, 6, and 9, and a grade 10 literacy test which must be passed before high school graduation. While the other provinces house the evaluation or assessment office within a department or ministry of education, Ontario has developed an arm's-length organization, Education Quality and Accountability Office (EQAO) (www.eqao.com). Northwest Territories follows Alberta's assessment program; Nunavut is still developing its assessment strategy (Ben Jaafar & Anderson, 2007); Yukon has some territorial

**What do you think?**

If provincial policies require that large-scale assessment generally adopt the adaptations used in classroom assessment, what are the implications for you, the classroom teacher, and for the adaptations you are expected to make daily?

## FIGURE 8.1 ADAPTING LARGE-SCALE ASSESSMENT FOR EXCEPTIONAL STUDENTS: ISSUES TO CONSIDER

**What is the role of the student's IEP?**

- What accommodations for assessment are listed in the student's IEP?
- What accommodations are used for classroom assessment, and are they appropriate for large-scale assessment?
- What accommodations are appropriate for this individual student given the nature of the large-scale test?
- How has the province, school board, school usually approached such accommodations?
- What information is provided by the province or school board about conditions under which an exceptional student is exempted from large-scale assessment?
- Where must the information about accommodations be recorded when the large-scale assessment is submitted?

**When should these adaptations be decided?**

- How much time is needed to consult with the student, the parents, and all educators involved in the decisions?
- How much planning and organizing is required to ensure the accommodations are ready?

**How are accommodations about setting decided?**

- Can the student focus in the presence of thirty classmates?
- Would preferential seating in the classroom be an adequate accommodation?
- Would adaptive equipment be adequate to accommodate the student's needs (e.g., special lighting, pencil grip, keyboarding)?
- Will the student likely distract classmates taking the large-scale assessment?
- Are prompts required to focus the student's attention on the assessment?

**How are accommodations about timing decided?**

- Can the student work continuously for the length of the assessment?
- Should the student have additional time to complete the assessment?
- Should the student be given periodic supervised rest breaks during the assessment?
- Does the student's regular medication affect the time of day when the assessment should be administered to the student?
- Does the student's anxiety about a particular subject area suggest that that assessment should be administered last?

**How are accommodations of presentation decided?**

- Can the student listen to and follow oral instructions?
- Will an interpreter (sign language or oral interpreter) be needed for the student?
- Will a Braille version of the assessment be required?
- Will a large-print version of the assessment be required?
- Will an audio version of the assessment be required?
- Will it be necessary to provide a verbatim reading of the instructions and/or questions? (Interpretation of questions is usually not permitted.)

**How are accommodations to response format decided?**

- Will it be necessary for the student to answer beside the question rather than in a response booklet?
- Will the student require a computer to complete the response booklet?
- Will it be necessary for responses to be audiotaped and transcribed?
- Will other assistive devices or technologies be required (e.g., augmentative communication systems)?
- Will verbatim scribing of responses be necessary?

Sources consulted: Thurlow, M.L., Elliott, J.L., & Ysseldyke, J.E. (2003). *Testing students with disabilities: Practical strategies for complying with district and state requirements* (2nd ed.). Thousand Oaks, CA: Sage; Council of Ministers of Education, Canada. www.cmec.ca/pcap/2007/handbook.en.pdf; Education Quality and Accountability Office, Ontario. https://ozone.scholarsportal.info/bitstream/1873/9691/1/278304.pdf.

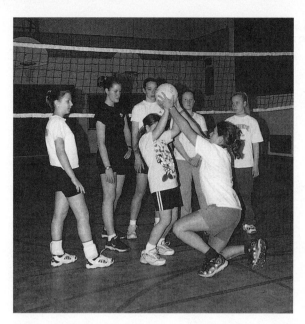

*Students learn together in the classroom and on the volleyball court.*

### What do you think?

In 2004 the Canadian Centre for Policy Alternatives (www.policyalternatives.ca) published *Passing the Test: The False Promise of Standardized Testing* (edited by Marita Moll), questioning the value of standardized testing in Canada. Do you think the issues emphasized in this book apply to exceptional students? For a different perspective, consult the book chapter by Diana Pullin (2005), "When One Size Does Not Fit All: The Special Challenges of Accountability Testing for Students with Disabilities," in *Uses and Misuses of Data for Educational Accountability and Improvement* (edited by J.L. Herman and E.H. Haertel, published by the National Society for the Study of Education).

examinations and also uses some British Columbia assessment tests (Klinger et al., in press).

Some Aboriginal education authorities have been reluctant to require their students to participate in provincial assessment programs, according to the *National Policy Roundtable on Aboriginal Education K–12*, held on 22 February 2005 (www.saee.ca/movingforward/support.html). The website includes a brief summary of the assessment from *Sharing Our Success: Ten Case Studies in Aboriginal Schooling* (Bell, 2005). Two of the ten schools in the study participated in large-scale assessment. There was no discussion on the website of how such tests could be adapted for Aboriginal students, although the concern was expressed that the tests may be culturally inappropriate.

Some Canadian provinces have well-publicized policies on accommodations in large-scale assessments. For example, Alberta's website describes how the province provides accommodations for exceptional students with "special diploma examination writing needs" that are similar to the accommodations routinely provided by the school for examination writing and assignment completion (http://education.alberta.ca/admin/testing/diplomaexams/diplomabulletin.aspx). In Ontario, the policy on accommodations is spelled out in Memorandum no. 127 (13 October 2004) (www.edu.gov.on.ca/extra/eng/ppm/127.html). Educators must make every effort to enable exceptional students to participate in all aspects of the assessment to demonstrate their learning. The recent standards for IEPs in Ontario (Ontario Ministry of Education, 2000) address "exemptions from provincial assessments" and state that only in rare cases will a student be exempted: essentially when, even with accommodations, the student would not be able to provide evidence of learning on the assessment. A statement must appear in the IEP explaining why the assessment is not appropriate for the student and identifying the ministry or EQAO policy under which the exemption is applied.

The necessary accommodations must be made to ensure that students who are receiving special education programs and services and who have an Individual Education Plan (IEP) have a fair and equal opportunity to successfully complete the secondary school literacy test. The memorandum defines accommodations as forms of support and services that enable students with special needs to demonstrate their competencies in the skills being measured by the test. In all jurisdictions the intent is that accommodations change only *the way* in which the tests are administered or *the way* in which the students tested respond to the components of the test. Accommodations are not intended to alter the content of the test or affect the validity or reliability of the test.

## Comparison with the United States

In the United States, much has been written about including exceptional students in state and federal achievement tests. These are often called "high-stakes" tests because they have an impact on whether students proceed to the next grade, or they can contribute substantially to report card grades (e.g., Katsiyannis, Zhang, Ryan, & Jones, 2007). For an overview of the issues in the American context that surround the participation of students with disabilities in district and state testing programs, see Thurlow, Elliott, and Ysseldyke (2003) and Ysseldyke et al. (2004). Since 2000, exceptional students in the United States have been expected to participate in district and statewide assessment, with or without accommodations, or by using alternative assessments. In 2005 the United States Government Accountability Office reported that at least 95 percent of students with disabilities participated in statewide reading assessments in forty-one of the forty-nine states that provided data. In Canada SAIP exemption rates appear to be much lower (generally less than 2 percent) (e.g., CMEC, 1999); however, SAIP and PCAP are not high-stakes tests.

In Canada, in contrast to the United States, we do not offer alternative forms of assessment to students exempted from large-scale assessments. Ysseldyke and his colleagues (e.g., Salvia & Ysseldyke, 2007) recommend that alternative assessments focus on authentic skills and on assessing experience in community and other real-life environments, measure integrated skills across domains, use continuous documentation, and provide descriptions of needed and provided supports. In 2003 Thompson and Thurlow reported that most states used a portfolio or body-of-evidence approach in alternative assessments for students with severe intellectual disabilities. However, there are many challenges associated with this approach (Perner, 2007) including describing it in terms parents can understand (Cortiella, 2007).

In Canada, while it can be said that we have our own approach to large-scale testing (Ben Jaafar, 2006a, 2006b), we have few high-stakes tests. The participation rate of exceptional students in large-scale testing in Canada appears to be high, and accommodations must be provided. In the United States, the source of much of the research we read on large-scale and high-stakes tests, schools are currently in the era of No Child Left Behind (2001), which imposes a rigorous accountability system dominated by high-stakes testing. For example, schools must achieve annual yearly performance goals, include 95 percent or more of students with disabilities in state and district assessment programs, and provide accommodations as well as alternative assessments (Katsiyannis, Zhang, Ryan, & Jones, 2007). Simply put, our contexts are quite different. However, both Canadian and American policy-makers would do well to heed the cautionary tales told by British researchers (e.g., Rustique-Forrester, 2005) about how increased demands for accountability have resulted in increased dropout rates among exceptional and at-risk students, rather than creating incentives for improved student performance. Many have asked whether educators can ensure that high-stakes assessments and other standardized assessments are administered fairly and produce valid results for exceptional students. Some of the questions to ask to ensure fairness and validity appear in Figure 8.2.

## Summary of Exceptional Students and Large-Scale Assessment in Canada

In summary, you can see that no matter where you teach in Canada, your students may be included in a sample for large-scale assessment (Ben Jaafar & Anderson, 2007; De Luca et al., 2005). On the whole, exceptional students who have accommodations in their programs are included in large-scale assessment, and the guidelines suggest they should receive the same accommodations listed in their IEPs that they experience day to day in the classroom. Those students whose goals are considerably different from their peers and whose IEPs recommend alternative

## Further Reading

Locate and read the following Canadian resources on assessment and the dilemmas inherent in both large-scale and classroom assessment in the Canadian context:

DeLuca, C. (in press). Including students with disabilities in large-scale assessment programs. *Exceptionality Education Canada.*

Klinger, D., DeLuca, C., & Miller, T. (2008). The evolving culture of large-scale assessment in Canadian education. *Canadian Journal of Educational Administration and Policy, 76,* available online, www. umanitoba.ca/publications/cjeap/.

Shulha, L., & DeLuca, C. (2005). Accommodating and assessing students with exceptionalities. In R.J. Wilson (Ed.), *Dilemmas in classroom assessment and what to do about them* (pp. 27–37). Winnipeg: Portage and Main Press.

Wilson, R.J. (Ed.). (2005). *Dilemmas in classroom assessment and what to do about them.* Winnipeg: Portage and Main Press.

## What do you think?

Use the ADAPT strategy to recommend accommodations to large-scale testing for one of the students—Sasha or Belle—described in the cases that open this chapter. Which steps of the ADAPT strategy are most relevant for adapting large-scale assessment? Why?

## FIGURE 8.2 ENSURING FAIRNESS AND VALIDITY

To ensure the fairness of standardized assessments and the validity of the results, answer these questions:

1. What test accommodations does the student need to demonstrate his or her knowledge without interference from his or her disability?
2. What test accommodations will not change the skill that the test items are assessing?
3. Has the student been provided with adequate opportunities to learn, practise, and apply the knowledge assessed by the test?
4. Has the student been provided with adequate opportunities to develop the necessary test-taking skills?
5. Has the student received adequate information about the testing process and the ways to express his or her needs during the assessment?
6. What accommodations does the student receive for classroom assessment (these should be identified in the IEP)?

programs (estimated at less than 2 percent of the school population) are likely to be exempt from large-scale assessments. Being familiar with the IEPs of the students you teach will enable you to participate in school-based decisions about the accommodations appropriate for your students on classroom assessments and large-scale assessments (Shriner & Destafano, 2003; Edgemon, Jablonski, & Lloyd, 2006; Wasburn-Moses, 2003).

# Classroom Assessment

## The Many Roles of Classroom Assessment in Teacher Decision-Making

Classroom assessment can help you make decisions in the many roles you play as a teacher—guiding curriculum, reporting students' achievements, and planning and differentiating teaching (Anderson, 2003; Wilson, 1996). All of these tasks are easier when there is consistency among the approaches used in teaching, learning, and assessment (Roach et al., 2008). Assessment helps teachers gauge student learning, decide who has learned, and differentiate teaching so it is responsive to students' needs and interests. Sometimes it is also important to adapt assessment so each student can show what he or she knows, but before adapting assessment, you must prepare all students and parents for the idea that equitable assessment does not mean same assessment.

### MAKING ASSESSMENT CONSISTENT WITH TEACHING

Assessment is most helpful when it is consistent with teaching (Roach et al., 2008). This means assessment should be consistent in content with the learning outcomes of the curriculum, unit, and activity. Thus if you undertake a particular spelling activity so students can spell common words in their daily journal writing, the assessment of that activity should reflect the words you teach and should ask students to produce those words in a context similar to that encountered in writing. Think about how you might adapt assessment. For example, students who have strengths in spelling might be expected to spell words (that were not taught) from the same word families as the taught words, to which these students can reasonably be expected to generalize. Other students who are not strong spellers may use and misspell simpler words in their journal writing and may need to learn these words; thus they may have a list of simpler words to learn and may be assessed on these words. In terms of task content, when the goal has been to help students to improve their editing of their written work, it would make sense to ask students to identify the incorrectly spelled words in a list. Given that written work is usually in sentence format, both the teaching and assessment of identifying incorrectly spelled words should probably be conveyed in sentences rather than lists of words.

Often assessment combines **norm-referenced** data (in which a student's work is compared with the work of other students) and **criterion-referenced** data (in which a student's work is compared with expected outcomes). For more information on norm-referenced and criterion-referenced tests, see the Theory and Research box.

## THEORY AND RESEARCH HIGHLIGHTS FROM

## EDUCATIONAL PSYCHOLOGY

## Norm-Referenced and Criterion-Referenced Test Interpretation

Norm-referenced test interpretation is based on comparisons of a test-taker's performance with the performances of other people in a specified reference population (Frisbie, 2005). Items on norm-referenced tests are designed to ensure a distribution of scores, most often a normal distribution, which means it is not possible for all or even a majority of students to do well. In norm-referenced testing, a sample of people who have taken the test provides norms for interpreting an individual's score. Norms are scores that describe typical levels of performance for the norm group. By comparing an individual's raw score or number of items correct with the norms, we can interpret the individual's score as average, above average, or below average for that group. Sometimes the original sample serves as the comparison group. On large-scale assessment, the individual can be compared with all other grade 6 students in the province. However, the students within the district, school, or class can also serve as the norm group.

Typically norm-referenced tests contain questions that relate to a range of general objectives and are useful for obtaining a measure of overall achievement in an ability (like intelligence or phonemic awareness) or in a subject area (such as mathematics or reading). These tests may not provide helpful, diagnostic information about the learning accomplishments of an individual and are usually used to supplement information gathered by teachers and in-school teams. It is helpful to recognize the limitations of norm-referenced tests. The results are difficult to compare with a specific curriculum and, in fact, may be poorly matched to the curriculum in which you are most interested. They are rarely designed to measure psychomotor or affective objectives, and they tend to encourage competition and comparison of scores.

Criterion-referenced tests are tests that allow users to make score interpretations in relation to a functional performance level or a set standard of performance (Frisbie, 2005). They are sometimes called standards-based assessments. Usually they measure the degree of mastery of very specific objectives and are intended to provide indicators of student attainment of valued learning goals. Student performance may vary greatly, but there is no intent to deliberately spread student scores if all students have attained the goals. Typically one identifies how much students have learned thus far in relation to the goals of a specific curriculum without comparison with the results of other students.

You could set a standard such as four out of five correct for each type of mathematics problem taught in the recent unit as a criterion for students progressing to the next unit. Sometimes a standard of 100 percent is appropriate, for example, when we expect a professional (such as a surgeon) to get it right every time. This is one of the challenges of criterion-referenced assessment—setting the standard in a non-arbitrary fashion. For responding to this challenge, consult Berk (1986). While criterion-referenced tests are useful for assessing psychomotor and affective objectives, they

*continued*

may not prove helpful when ranking candidates or selecting the top few. As a classroom teacher, you should find criterion-referenced tests helpful when grouping students for instruction. Recent authors have argued that standards-based assessment enables more inclusive education; for a compilation of papers expressing this viewpoint, read Goodwin's *Assessment for Equity and Inclusion* (1997).

Self- or individual-referenced comparisons enable us to compare students with themselves and to make claims about their individual progress. For students who have alternative goals these may be very meaningful, especially in reporting their early progress toward goals that do not appear in the provincial curriculum.

Have you ever wondered what your students think about assessment? In a recent study, Dalbert, Scheidewind, and Saalbach (2007) asked secondary students in grades 7 to 12 for their ratings of the fairness of the three kinds of tests just described—norm-referenced, criterion-referenced, and self- or individual-referenced. The three kinds of grading were embedded in vignettes that the students judged. The students rated criterion-referenced as the fairest or most just, and individual-referenced was rated as almost just, while norm-referenced was rated as almost unjust. The authors recommend that when you are unable to use criterion-referenced assessment, you should carefully explain the rationale behind the application of other grading systems. This may be particularly applicable to exceptional students who often recognize that norm-referenced assessment is not really applicable to them.

### References

Berk, R.A. (1986). A consumer's guide to setting performance standards on criterion-referenced tests. *Review of Educational Research*, *56*, 137–172.

Dalbert, C., Schneidewind, U., & Saalbach, A. (2007). Justice judgments concerning grading in school. *Contemporary Educational Psychology*, *32*, 420–433.

Frisbie, D.A. (2005). Measurement 101: Some fundamentals revisited. *Educational Measurement: Issues and Practice, 24*(3), 21–28.

Goodwin, A.L. (Ed.). (1997). *Assessment for equity and inclusion.* New York: Routledge.

In their book *Assessment and Learning: The ICE Approach*, Sue Fostaty-Young and Bob Wilson of Queen's University (2000) emphasize growth, comparing an individual's progress with where that student started, regardless of whether that starting point is ahead of, even with, or behind others in the class. Such **self-referenced** data have long been recommended for assessment of exceptional students (e.g., Deno & Mirkin, 1977); however, Fostaty-Young and Wilson recommend such assessment for all students, making it easier to adopt for exceptional learners. You can give individual students the advice and teaching they need to extend learning, no matter where they are on the continuum, and reduce discouragement, like that expressed by Sasha in the opening case.

In the **ICE model**, the first step is **Ideas**, the building blocks of learning, which include the steps in a process, vocabulary, facts and definitions in a textbook, etc. Most fill-in-the-blanks and multiple-choice questions assess at the level of Ideas. **Connections** are the links or relationships that students make among the Ideas, and the relationships that students establish between new learning and prior learning. In mathematics, students who memorize algorithms are learning Ideas, while those who use their knowledge to solve new problems or apply new learning to solve an old problem are making Connections. Making Connections enables students to combine steps, understand formulas, and explain one phenomenon in terms of another.

The third stage that Fostaty-Young and Wilson describe is Extensions. **Extensions** can be seen in how students internalize learning so that it becomes part of the way they view the world. Extensions are revealed when students use their learning in novel ways, distinct from the initial learning situation, and when they answer the hypothetical question, "So what does this mean for me and how I see things?" The ICE model suggests that assessment should match teaching, in that the level

**TABLE 8.1 EXAMPLES OF QUESTION STARTERS AT THE LEVELS OF IDEAS, CONNECTIONS, AND EXTENSIONS**

| Ideas | Connections | Extensions |
|---|---|---|
| • List the … | • What effect does _____ have on … | • Predict how … |
| • Identify the main … | • Estimate… | • Propose solutions for … |
| • Give examples from the text of … | • What alternative methods … | #• What are the implications of … |
| • Paraphrase … | #• Of what value is … | #• In your opinion … |
| • Who was … | #• Explain the relationship between … | #• What did you learn from … |
| • When did … | #• How is _____ like … | |
| • According to … how is … | #• Compare … | |
| | #• Using an example from your own experience, illustrate … | |

#Examples of questions that are accessible to all students, yet extendable.

——

Source: Fostaty-Young, S.C., & Wilson, R.J. (2000). *Assessment and Learning: The ICE Approach*. Winnipeg: Portage & Main Press (Peguis Publishers). Reprinted with permission.

of assessment should match the level of your outcomes for the students. In classes with diversity it is likely that students will be working at all these levels, and some may be stimulated by your assessment to show that they are beginning to make Connections or establish Extensions that you were not anticipating. Because you are trying to move all your students along this continuum, you will probably use questions from all three levels, although some students may be encouraged to demonstrate their learning at a specific level. Table 8.1 contains examples of question starters you can use at the levels of Ideas, Connections, and Extensions.

## USING ASSESSMENT TO GAUGE STUDENT LEARNING AND TO DIFFERENTIATE TEACHING

You can use classroom assessment to help you differentiate your teaching. Moon (2005) describes the reciprocal relationship between differentiation and assessment in the three phases of planning instruction, guiding instruction, and evaluating instruction. When you are planning instruction, assessment data can help you determine student needs in relation to specific objectives: What does the group generally understand and show interest in? What do individual students understand and show interest in related to these objectives? Answering these questions enables you to start a new instructional unit that begins where the students are and ends at appropriately challenging outcomes. The assessments you use for this purpose could include observations, test results, portfolios, and interviews. You hope to learn where or for whom you might streamline instruction, and where or for whom additional support structures are necessary.

Assessment can guide you when you are in the midst of instruction because you will "constantly gather information to make decisions about when to move on, stop, or change direction" (Lambdin & Forseth, 1996, p. 298). Gathering data while teaching enables you to make in-process decisions about students' levels of mastery as well as their misconceptions, insights, and needs (Moon, 2005). If most are progressing well and a few are not, you will use assessment data to provide scaffolding or adapted teaching for those few. However, if most are not progressing well, you may need to make substantial instructional changes. The same process can be followed for considering students' interest in and engagement with the teaching. Such formative assessment can consist of work samples, paper-and-pencil tests, as well as students' discussions and questions. You could reform student groups, change your pacing, or change the way in which you present materials and content to individuals or to the whole class.

In the third phase, summative assessment tells you about student mastery of the content and may be the preassessment for the next unit of study. This is often reported to the parents as well as to the students. You must discern to what extent each individual has reached the goals, including exceptional students who may have IEP goals, while also assessing the effectiveness of your teaching. You may decide to reteach concepts in this unit, or you may decide that in future units you will supplement the text with audio for some students or ask an individual to write answers in individual words rather than in sentences.

Much has been written recently about the need for constant progress monitoring to improve decision making in schools that are establishing practices within a response to intervention (RTI) model. RTI requires schoolwide screening and frequent progress monitoring of targeted learners who are receiving intensive interventions in small groups or individually. For a description of progress monitoring, see Steckler, Lembke, and Foegen (2008).

Some teachers find that developing rubrics helps with the process of assessment (e.g., Depka, 2007). **Rubrics** are descriptions of learning at different levels of development. Many rubrics can be described as **quantitative rubrics**; that is, they identify students with higher achievement as having greater quantities of valued responses:

- Level 1: Includes some of the main ideas
- Level 2: Includes most of the main ideas
- Level 3: Includes all or almost all of the main ideas

However, quantitative rubrics provide little guidance for teachers in adapting teaching. They imply that inadequacies are inherent in students and fail to focus on the learning that students have accomplished and the challenges or steps that remain.

**Qualitative rubrics** describe the qualities that characterize learning at various levels and provide students with information about the steps they must tackle to improve. Table 8.2 shows the components of a qualitative rubric on written expression. Fostaty-Young and Wilson suggest that when you undertake to develop a rubric, you place examples of student work in front of you and analyze the qualities of the work that you view as "okay," "average," and "wow!" or as Levels 1, 2, and 3. Fostaty-Young and Wilson's qualitative rubrics embrace Ideas, Connections, and Extensions while breaking a learning outcome into elements. Qualitative rubrics tell you what has been demonstrated, not what is missing. You can continue the development of such rubrics, as you read or observe students' work and identify factors that influence your judgments about student work, until you are satisfied that you have an accurate map of the learning you hope to foster. For example, if an exceptional student's work demonstrates that he or she is working at the Ideas level for legibility and visual appeal, you would want to emphasize that the student write words and focus on teaching him or her to leave "white spaces" between the words (see Table 8.2). At the same

Cross-Reference
In Chapters 1 and 7, references were made to response to intervention (RTI) models that are beginning to appear in provincial documents and to be implemented in some school districts and in some provinces in Canada, such as New Brunswick.

**TABLE 8.2 COMPONENTS OF A QUALITATIVE RUBRIC UNDER DEVELOPMENT**

| Elements | Ideas | Connections | Extensions |
|---|---|---|---|
| Legibility and visual appeal | • Forms recognizable letters | • Letters are grouped and spaced to form words | • Words follow in logical sequence |
| | • Initial draft is also the final draft | • Creates a final draft from the original | • Includes illustrations—used where appropriate |
| Planning | • Researches topic | • Sequences ideas | • Considers the readers needs in the planning |
| | • Lists ideas | • Identifies sources | |
| Sentences | • Begins sentences with capital letters | • Sentences are linked in a coherent order | • Uses variety in sentence structure to create effects |
| | • Ends sentences with periods | | |

Source: Fostaty-Young, S.C., & Wilson, R.J. (2000). *Assessment and learning: The ICE approach.* Winnipeg: Portage & Main Press (Peguis Publishers). Reprinted with permission.

time, it might be helpful to encourage the pupil to use illustrations to communicate his or her ideas (see Song et al., 2008, on using cartoons as an alternative learning assessment). For a classmate who is writing full sentences with periods and capitals and who writes only an initial draft, you might focus on planning and sequencing. The student could practise listing ideas and then putting numbers in front of them to improve the order or, if that proves too abstract, he or she could write each idea on a card and then try to sequence them in different orders until the student decides on the best order. A group of academically advanced students who have reached the level of Extensions on legibility and planning might be taught to use variety in sentence structure to create effects like surprise, suspense, or humour. Qualitative rubrics can help you see who has reached each level that you described and guide you in making decisions about differentiating teaching and reteaching to enable students to reach the curriculum outcomes or the goals in their IEPs.

## Preparing Students and Parents for Equitable (but Not Necessarily the Same) Assessment

Sometimes you will be able to set a task for all students and assess their learning with a rubric. On the other hand, while the class writes a history test in forty-five minutes, Jacob (who has learning disabilities) may write the same test in ninety minutes in the resource room. Bonita (who has intellectual disabilities and alternative learning goals) may describe orally to a paraeducator how to travel to the local sites that have historic significance. Two goals on Bonita's IEP are to learn to travel independently by bus and to plan and carry out conversations with adults.

What do you say when students or parents ask you why Jacob gets more time, or why Bonita has an oral test? You can do much to prevent these questions by planning ahead. From the first day with your students, refer to your commitment to meeting individual needs. Describe people as individuals with different strengths. From your first communication with parents, refer to inclusion and differentiation. Explain that exceptional students are included in your classroom because this is

**Put into Practice**

Read "Cartoons, an Alternative Learning Assessment" by Youngjin Song and her colleagues, published in *Science Scope* (January 2008, pages 16–21). Discuss with your peers how to put this alternative assessment strategy into practice in the classes and subjects you teach.

**Put into Practice**

Collect rubrics from the curricula you have taught, the textbooks you are studying, provincial documents from your ministry of education, fellow teachers, and other sources. Compare the quantitative and qualitative rubrics on the basis of thoroughness, guidance for differentiating teaching, and utility to busy teachers.

the policy of the school, school district, and province. Use examples with your students—and at your curriculum night or open house—that make it easy for students and parents to see your point. Blind students are given tests in Braille, just as they are taught in Braille. This does not disadvantage other students because they don't need Braille tests. You can refer to research that demonstrates that students without learning disabilities are not disadvantaged when their learning-disabled classmates are given appropriate accommodations for an assessment. This research is reviewed in the Focus on Research box.

## Research That Supports Extended Time as an Effective and Equitable Accommodation for Students with Learning Disabilities

Research has shown that individuals with learning disabilities (LD) tend to process information more slowly than those without LD (Hayes, Hynd, & Wisenbaker, 1986; Zentall, 1990). This makes extended time on tests appear to be an appropriate adaptation or accommodation. However, many have asked whether this gives students with LD an unfair advantage over their peers without LD (for the controversy, see Phillips, 1994, 1996). Would students who do not have LD also benefit from more time on tests? The answer usually given is that on a power test, where the point is to give adequate time for students to show what they know, this adaptation will not be unfair if the instructor has provided adequate time for the typical students to show what they know. Poorly designed tests may be unfair to all students, and only more unfair to students who process information slowly. However, this argument would be more convincing if there were data to show that students with LD benefit from additional time while those without LD do not.

Centra (1986) compared timed and extended-time scores of students with LD on the Scholastic Aptitude Test (SAT) to determine the effect of extra time on those scores. The scores were drawn from SAT records of 1124 students with LD who took the test under both timed and extended-time conditions. With the unlimited-time test administration, students with LD scored an average of thirty to thirty-eight points higher than they scored on the timed test. This result took into account practice effects and error of measurement. The more the time was increased, the more the scores increased. This suggests that additional time reduced the effects of LD on test scores. However, this study did not answer the question of whether students without LD would be similarly advantaged by more time.

Runyan (1991) also set out to answer the question about the benefit of extended time to university and college students with LD. The scores were reading rate and comprehension scores on the Nelson Denny Reading Test. There were fifty-five students with

LD and fifty-two without LD; groups were controlled for ethnicity, gender, age, and grade-point average. Reading rates were taken at the end of the first minute, and reading comprehension scores were obtained at the end of twenty minutes and upon test completion. The normally achieving students' reading rates were at the sixtieth percentile, whereas the reading rates of the students with LD were at the tenth percentile. The timed comprehension scores of the normally achieving students were higher than the timed comprehension scores of students with LD. However, the students with LD achieved scores on the untimed comprehension test that were not significantly different from students without LD on the timed test. Thus the extra time enabled students with LD to overcome their deficits in processing speed.

Alster (1997) set out to answer the question about the comparable benefits of untimed tests to students with and without LD. There were eighty-eight community college students, forty-four with LD and forty-four without LD; the two groups were matched for age, gender, ethnicity, language background, and math achievement. All were given the ASSET Elementary Algebra Test, which had been divided into two comparable tests, A and B. The two groups took one test in twelve minutes and the other untimed, with twenty-five of each group taking the timed test first. In each of the four groups, thus formed, half took form A first and half took form B first. Under timed conditions, students with LD scored lower than peers without LD, showing that they were disadvantaged by too little time. There was no significant difference between the untimed scores of the two groups, showing that the disadvantage to students with LD was eliminated by the provision of extended time. However, while the scores of students with LD were greatly increased with additional time, the scores of students without LD increased only a small amount (significantly less) with additional time. The students with LD took significantly more time for the untimed test than those without LD. This suggests that the timed test

*continued*

may have provided slightly less than adequate time for students without LD to show all they knew. However, they benefited minimally from extended time while the benefits to students with LD were much greater. If teachers provide adequate time for students without LD, students with LD will benefit fairly from extended time. The average untimed test time for students with LD was double the original twelve minutes of the timed test. This suggests that the current practice of allowing up to double time may be appropriate to enable students with LD to show what they know. A 1998 study by Weaver again showed that students with LD made significant gains on their test scores when provided with additional time, while those without LD did not show similar gains. These results were repeated in a study by Huesman and Frisbie (2000).

A thorough, well-designed study by Lesaux and Pearson with Linda Siegel of the University of British Columbia (2006) again examined the effects of timed and untimed testing conditions on the reading comprehension performance of adults with reading disabilities. Twenty-two adults with LD were compared with forty-two normal readers. Under timed conditions, there were significant differences between the readers with LD and the normally achieving readers. All the readers with LD benefited from more time, while the normally achieving readers performed the same under timed and untimed conditions. Additionally, in the untimed condition, the performance of individuals with a less severe reading disability was not significantly different from that of the average readers. Similar findings were reported for the SAT showing that extended-time conditions for students with LD or ADHD did not present a threat to the validity of the SAT (Lindstrom & Gregg, 2007). Stretch and Osborne (2005) recommended that all students be given sufficient time to perform optimally.

While the results may not be as conclusive as one would like, accumulating evidence clearly shows that individuals with LD process information slowly and are disadvantaged by timed tests. The benefits of extended time on assessment to students with LD are huge. There are no similar advantages to students who do not have LD.

Fairness is a complex concept. Sometimes we treat everyone equally; for example, all children deserve to be treated with respect. Sometimes we make equitable decisions based on merit or need. The child who sings brilliantly plays the lead in the school musical, and the laptop computer is provided to the child who cannot control a pencil to write down classroom work. In a unique study Welch (2000) has investigated students' understanding of fairness. Student perceptions of fairness are influenced by many factors, including age, social and cognitive maturity, culture, and teaching. When students say, "It's not fair," try to reflect their feelings by saying something like, "You don't think it's fair. Write me a note about your feelings and we will discuss your note at recess tomorrow morning." Then follow through. Welch suggests that the act of writing often enhances a student's understanding. The note will help you know what the student means and how to respond. Welch suggests you consider whether this is a request for more of your attention; if so, you need to focus on this student's accomplishments or interests, rather than on justifications of your modifications.

Sometimes young students cannot put themselves into someone else's position, so they don't understand how difficult it is for Vianne, a child with ADHD, to complete an activity. Welch suggests you ask the children who are objecting to Vianne getting stickers if they would like to "work on something that is hard" for them. The other students' unhappiness may also be a message that you are concentrating too much on external rewards with Vianne, and the solution may be to gradually reduce stickers as a reward for everyone.

There are other strategies for dealing with issues of fairness. Adopt a consistent approach (Welch, 2000). With older students, especially, remind them that you cannot discuss another student's work with them, that we are all different, and that the law provides for accommodations and fair treatment. Schools need

Weblinks

FAMILY VILLAGE, A SOURCE OF ONLINE MAGAZINES FOR FAMILIES
www.familyvillage.wisc.edu/bookstore/onlineperiodicals.html

**Cross-Reference**
Chapter 1 contains information about teaching students about the *Charter of Rights and Freedoms* and human rights in Canada.

to adopt consistent schoolwide approaches to accommodations and modifications that are defensible and to teach about the equity issues that have arisen as a result of our *Charter of Rights and Freedoms* and the human rights laws in each province. Ruck and his colleagues at the University of Toronto (1998) have reported that by about the age of 10, children understand that they have rights, and that children's and young adolescents' views of rights are influenced by the perspectives of the adults around them (Peterson-Badali, Morine, Ruck, & Slonin, 2004). Newfoundland and Labrador (1995) developed a K–12 curriculum with classroom learning activities on students' rights and responsibilities (www.ed.gov.nl.ca/edu/dept/sss.htm). The issue of rights is addressed in a paper by Covell and Howe (2001) of the University College of Cape Breton: *Moral Education Through the 3 Rs: Rights, respect, and responsibility.* Such materials might help you to conduct discussion at a level that your students can understand. Finally, remember that the students may be right and you may be providing a crutch, that is, more adaptations than are necessary or fair. Be prepared to review your approach and to reconsider the rate at which you are gradually increasing independence and decreasing scaffolding.

# Differentiating Classroom Assessment

## Adapting Learning Outcomes for Exceptional Students

This chapter contains many examples of adapting learning outcomes for exceptional students. Wormeli (2006) describes tiering assessments for advanced students. He suggests beginning with the on-grade-level task and then raising or lowering the challenge level. He says you can try increasing complexity and challenge by asking students to manipulate information rather than just echoing it, to extend the concept to other areas, to critique something against a set of standards, to identify the big picture connections, or to incorporate more facets (see Wormeli pages 57–58).

In the past, exceptional students spent part of their school day in a resource room, with individualized instruction, teaching, and assessment tailored to their needs (Espin, Deno, & Albayrak-Kaymak, 1998). Now that exceptional students are included in regular classrooms for much more of their school day, you are expected to differentiate your teaching and adapt your assessment for the class as a group, to meet the needs of exceptional learners and other learners as much as possible, but not to individualize all teaching and assessment. The learning outcomes for exceptional students are now guided by the IEP. Thus you need to consider what outcomes are appropriate for an exceptional student when you plan your teaching. These outcomes form the basis for the assessment following teaching for exceptional students, just as they do for students without exceptionalities. If Sasha, in the case study at the beginning of this chapter, is expected to produce less written work but work of a similar quality to his peers, then this outcome needs to be specified clearly. This differentiated outcome can subsequently guide your construction and administration of tests for Sasha as well as your grading for his report card.

**Further Reading**

Wormeli, R. (2006). *Fair isn't always equal: Assessing and grading in the differentiated classroom.* Portland, ME: Stenhouse Publishers.

Ysseldyke, J., & Algozzine, B. (2006). *Effective assessment for students with special needs.* Thousand Oaks, CA: Corwin Press.

Salvia, J., Ysseldyke, J.E., & Bolt, S. (2007). *Assessment in special and inclusive education* (10th ed.). Boston: Houghton Mifflin Co.

*Students learn in many contexts including co-operative education workplaces and while doing community services.*

## Preparing Students for Classroom Tests

What can you do to prepare all students, including exceptional students, for classroom tests? Creating a **study guide** that tells students what to study for the test helps them to prepare more efficiently (e.g., Lifvendahl, 2007). While all students benefit, those who read slowly and who have memory problems can benefit most by focusing on the most important material. Teachers in any subject, including high school math, can create study guides that remove the intimidation of reviewing for tests (Rothery, 2007) or adapt web quests so that all students, including those with learning disabilities, can participate successfully (Skyler et al., 2007). Some teachers use practice tests to prepare their students, especially to inform them about teacher expectations and test format (e.g., Rhone, 2006). Tutoring by a peer, a resource room teacher, or a paraeducator may help. Study buddies or study groups are often acceptable to older students and may also promote social relations (e.g., Fullan & St. Germain, 2006; Sloane, 2007).

You can help students analyze their previous tests for typical errors and then group students to explain to each group how to overcome particular kinds of errors. Demonstrate on an overhead transparency the wrong way to answer and put a large stroke through it. Then demonstrate a correct strategy for tackling that type of question. If you solicit ideas from students, provide explicit feedback about whether they are correct or incorrect. If you are not clear, this kind of session can teach students poor approaches rather than tried-and-true strategies.

Teaching **study skills** and test-taking strategies can be done as small-group or large-group instruction. Provide all students with a passage to study and have them work in pairs. Ask the pair to highlight what is most important in the passage. Then ask each pair to come up with a way to remember two parts they highlighted.

Weblinks
Examine study skills and study guides at the following sites:

UNIVERSITY OF NORTHERN BRITISH COLUMBIA LEARNING SKILLS CENTRE
www.unbc.ca/lsc

TEENS HEALTH: TEST ANXIETY
www.kidshealth.org/teen/ school_jobs/school/test_anxiety. html

TIPS ON GETTING TEENS TO DO THEIR HOMEWORK
http://parentingteens.about. com/cs/homeworkhelp/a/ homeworktips.htm

TORONTO PUBLIC LIBRARY: HOMEWORK HELP FOR TEENS
www.torontopubliclibrary.ca/ spe_ser_teen_index.jsp

SASKATOON PUBLIC LIBRARY: HOMEWORK HELP FOR TEENS
www.saskatoonlibrary.ca/is/ homeworkhelp.html

STUDY GUIDES AND STRATEGIES
www.studygs.net

ELEMENTARY TEACHERS' FEDERATION OF ONTARIO STUDY GUIDES
www.nt.net/~torino/novels3.html

On an overhead transparency, show which sections are most important and explain why. Then ask students to give their plans for how to remember the most important information—systematically go through the sections of the passage you highlighted, asking for memory strategies from students. If they are focusing at the Ideas level, introduce elements of Connections and Extensions to make the content more meaningful. This should enhance their understanding as well as their memory.

Develop **chunking strategies** (ways of grouping information) as well as mnemonics for remembering important lists (Munyofu et al., 2007). A **mnemonic** imposes an order on information to be remembered using poems, rhymes, jingles, funny sayings, or images (e.g., Snair, 2008). To remember the names of the Great Lakes, for instance, you could teach your student the mnemonic *HOMES* for Huron, Ontario, Michigan, Erie, Superior.

Many students find it helpful to make **concept maps** when studying for tests (Gao et al., 2007). Concept maps can be developed individually or collaboratively, and they often prompt students to make Connections and Extensions. After teaching a unit, you might prepare students for a test by showing them a blank concept map with only a few key words filled in. Each student or pair of students completes a concept map. Then you show yours on an overhead and ask students to discuss how their headings and details differ. Distribute copies of your concept map so students have a good model from which to study and to develop concept maps on other topics.

## Adapting Classroom Tests During Test Construction

All students are likely to benefit from tests that are clearly written. However, some test items that will present no difficulties for most students may create problems for exceptional students. When you use classroom tests, expect that exceptional students may find the language and format confusing and may be unable to recall information without an aid. They may require additional time because of slow processing, lack of motor control, or the need to use Braille. They may experience a variety of challenges that result from their reading and writing abilities. Figure 8.3 contains a number of suggestions for adapting a classroom test during its construction.

Some adaptations in Figure 8.3 may help all students and therefore you may incorporate them into the test you distribute to the entire class, or you may make an adapted version for a number of students when you construct the original test. You can mark small changes that only apply to one or two students on the student's copy just before you distribute the test or during the test. If you choose the latter option, take care not to confuse or distract students. Adaptations that can be made on the spot include changing the number of examples required in an answer or highlighting key words in a question. The next section focuses on adaptations made during the administration of tests.

## Adapting Administration of Classroom Tests

What problems would you anticipate might arise during administration when exceptional students are taking classroom tests? For an objective or short-answer test, they could require additional time to finish or fewer questions, oral administration, a scribe, interpretation of a question by you, a calculator for problem solving,

### What do you think?

How might cultural values influence parents and children's views of fairness and adaptations in assessment? How could you learn about these influences and act on them in an effective and sensitive manner?

## FIGURE 8.3 SUGGESTIONS FOR ADAPTING CLASSROOM TESTS DURING CONSTRUCTION

**Suggestions for Adapting Objective Tests**

- Pretape the questions so that a non-reader or poor reader can work from a tape recorder.
- Present questions in a familiar format (the way they were taught).
- Alter the reading level by eliminating difficult words (you could write in an easier word with the same meaning above the difficult word).
- For fill-in questions, provide the possible answers at the bottom of the page.
- Use simple, direct statements in the stem of the question.
- Familiarize students with the format of the test by reviewing samples from previous tests.
- Use both oral and written directions (possibly with an example) for each section of a test.
- Consider an open-book test or allowing the use of a one-page summary.
- Make the print large enough to be read easily.
- Make the visual layout simple and clean.
- Underline, highlight, or bold key words.
- Arrange items in a logical sequence.
- Allow additional time for students who process or write slowly.
- Include or explain the marking scheme.

**Suggestions for Adapting Essay Tests**

- Use simple, direct phrases in the design of your essay questions.
- Underline, highlight, or bold key words in the questions.
- Suggest the number of key points that should be included and give the marking scheme.
- Provide a proofreading checklist.
- Provide an outline organization sheet.
- Alter the reading level by eliminating difficult words (you could write in an easier word with the same meaning above the difficult word).
- Allow additional time for students who process or write slowly.

Source: Adapted from Peel Board of Education (1990). *Looking at Assessment: More Than Just Marks.*

relevant formulas or definitions, and other external memory aids. For an essay test, extended time or fewer required points in answers may be critical for those slow to process information. A quiet, distraction-free environment may be necessary. A means of spell-checking can improve the quality of written work. An open-book test may be appropriate so that you test use of knowledge rather than memory. Allow a student to use a tape recorder only if he or she has previously been taught how to use one in test conditions. Remember that even a well-constructed test will fail to demonstrate the knowledge of exceptional students if it is administered inappropriately.

## Adapting Scoring or Marking of Classroom Tests

Like other adaptations, adapted scoring or marking of classroom tests should be guided by key information in the IEPs about students' needs. You may want to discuss the implications of the IEP for marking with the in-school team. When you mark objective tests or essay tests, students with disabilities in writing, spelling, or memory should not be penalized for spelling or grammatical errors. You could provide these students with an opportunity to edit their own work before you mark their tests, or you could ask them to indicate the places where they think they have made these types of errors. Providing adaptations does not mean that you and the

**Further Reading**

Silva, M., Munk, D.D., & Bursuck, W.D. (2005). Grading adaptations for students with disabilities. *Intervention in School and Clinic, 41*(2), 87–98.

Munk, D.D., & Bursuck, W.D. (2004). Personalized grading plans: A systematic approach to making the grades of included students more accurate and meaningful. *Focus on Exceptional Children, 36*(9), 1–12.

Ring, M.M., & Reetz, L. (2002). Grading students with learning disabilities in inclusive middle schools. *Middle School Journal, 34*(2), 12–18.

Salend, S.J., & Duhaney, L.M.G. (2002). Grading students in inclusive settings. *Teaching Exceptional Children, 34*, 8–15.

students should not make efforts to improve skills in these areas, but don't confuse those efforts with classroom tests that should be a demonstration of learning on reasonable outcomes.

On essay tests, you may review written responses with students individually and allow students with disabilities in writing to elaborate orally on their written responses. You can also adapt the marking scheme for the test. Remember the case study of Belle at the beginning of this chapter. The marking scheme for her mathematics course was adapted because of her hearing loss; the oral quizzes did not count toward her grade. This serves as a model of the kind of reasonable adaptations that can be arranged—for students with disabilities in spelling, you could reduce the credit given on a test for spelling, style, and organization and increase the credit for content. It may be helpful to provide exceptional students with feedback on how they would have scored without and with the adapted scoring, so they can see the effects of the adaptations (a suggestion made in a thoughtful document by the Peel Board of Education, 1990). This kind of information should help individuals with disabilities to enhance their self-awareness and self-advocacy.

Ensure that you know your own perspective on marking classroom tests and then work collaboratively with any others who teach the exceptional students in your class (Christiansen & Vogel, 1998; Hong & Ehrensberger, 2007). Munk and Bursuck (2001) report preliminary findings on teachers' collaborations to develop personalized grading plans for middle school students. All participants—including parents, students, regular classroom teachers, and special educators—found the processes fairer and more effective than previous grading. Munk and Bursuck (2004) describe a systematic approach to grading students in inclusive settings. Remember that to grade classroom tests fairly, you should assess students frequently through a variety of means and make every effort to accurately convey achievement to parents and students. Give useful feedback that helps students to improve and remember that successful classroom tests serve as motivators for students to engage in deep and purposeful learning (Segers, Gijbels, & Thurlings, 2008).

While teachers must recognize their own assumptions and views about adapting assessment, this topic deserves attention at the district level. Figure 8.4 describes a process to help school districts meet this challenge of providing the direction teachers need to implement effective, equitable, adapted assessment.

## Using Adapted Performance Assessments

A **performance assessment** is any assessment activity that "requires a student to perform a task or generate his or her own response" (Black, 2003, p. 42). In studying municipal government, your grade 5 students may read local newspapers, attend a meeting of the municipal council, invite a councillor to visit the classroom, and conduct library research. If you assess what they have learned by asking them to write a letter about a community issue to a local politician, the editor of the community newspaper, or a member of a service group, you will be using performance assessment. In your grade 11 course in career development and co-operative education, teach your students to answer interview questions by having them role-play interviewer and then interviewee. If you assess the students' interview skills while they are conducting an interview with an unfamiliar adult volunteer, then you are using performance assessment.

# FIGURE 8.4 GUIDELINES FOR DEVELOPING EFFECTIVE, EQUITABLE GRADING POLICIES AND PRACTICES

- Establish a district-wide committee, including teachers, family, and community members, to work on policies and practices.
- Review the existing policies and practices of the district.
- Consult stakeholders on their views about grading (parents, educators, community members, students).
- Review the provincial guidelines and policies for grading.
- Develop grading policies that meet the provincial legal requirements and the district's priorities, and that are acceptable to stakeholders (parents, educators, community members, students).
- Develop educational opportunities for all concerned, including students, to learn about the policies and effective practices that have been selected.
- Implement the new policies and practices consistently.
- Review the impact of the new policies and practices regularly and be prepared to fine-tune.

Sources: Adapted from Salend, S.J., & Duhaney, L.M.G. (2002). Grading students in inclusive settings. *Teaching Exceptional Children, 34*, 8–15; Munk, D.D., & Bursuck, W.D. (2001). Preliminary findings on personalized grading plans for middle school students with learning disabilities. *Exceptional Children, 67*, 211–234.

Wiggins (1993; Wiggins & McTighe, 2005) argued strongly that teachers should develop performance assessments that are also **authentic assessments**, close to real-world tasks. Characteristics of authentic assessment are

- performance on engaging and important problems;
- performance on contextualized tasks that represent those expected in the adult world;
- real problems with a number of steps that require more than formulaic solutions; and
- tasks that demand students produce a quality product or performance.

Performance assessments often enable students to show what they know. They do not rely exclusively on reading and writing, as pencil-and-paper tests do, and they need not be subject to the same time constraints. Sasha has ADHD and reading disabilities. He is in the grade 5 class that wrote letters to municipal politicians. Sasha drafted his letter on a computer, read it aloud into a tape recorder, listened to it, and then reorganized the order of the paragraphs. By using a computer with a spell checker and a grammar checker, he was able to correct most of the spelling and grammatical errors and produce a quality product. Because he knows that he speaks better than he writes, Sasha telephoned city hall, made an appointment with the councillor representing his district, and hand-delivered his letter. His teacher was able to assess Sasha taking action in an adult way and demonstrating what he had learned about municipal government. Because of the high level of motivation that accompanied this performance assessment, Sasha made many adaptations himself. The teacher had prepared a rubric against which he assessed each student's performance and product.

Sometimes students with disabilities miss the connections between assessments in school contexts and the real-world contexts to which they apply. That is why Sasha's teacher, Mr. Sinclair, ensured that the letter was written to an adult in the local power structure rather than simply to the teacher. Well-designed performance

Put into Practice

Consult a source on performance assessment, such as one of these:

Hibbard, K.M. (2000). *Performance-based learning and assessment in middle school science*. Larchmont, NY: Eye on Education, Inc.

Berman, S. (2008). *Performance-based learning*. Thousand Oaks, CA: Corwin Press.

Luongo-Orlando, K. (2003). *Authentic assessment: Designing performance-based tasks*. Markham, ON: Pembroke Publishers.

Develop a performance-based task and assessment with an accompanying rubric and make adaptations for an exceptional student (whom you describe in one paragraph).

*For exceptional students, performance assessments can focus on life skills and leisure skills. These students are learning by building an airplane in a program designed to keep at-risk students in school.*

assessments can help students see these connections (Berman, 2008). However, this assessment required that the students in Sasha's class learn how to write a persuasive letter, to provide specific examples that support an argument, to sequence the parts of a letter, etc. They needed plenty of practice before they embarked on the culminating task. At the same time Sasha's teacher recognized that if the process were not engaging, then it would become just another traditional test to exceptional students.

For students on modified programs, you will have to develop modified performance assessments. Bill, a non-verbal adolescent with autism, will have to learn to express his agreement or disagreement to unfamiliar adults if he is to find employment or volunteer work in the community. A modified performance assessment might require him to attend a meeting with the manager of a charity shop who requires a volunteer to sweep the floor, to break up cardboard boxes, and to unpack and sort donations. Bill has to show the manager how he would communicate agreement and disagreement, and that he can perform the tasks she assigns. Because he learns gradually in the real-world context, Bill practises the interview with the paraeducator many times, sweeps the classroom daily, and practises breaking up boxes and sorting a box of housewares and clothing. The paraeducator attends the workplace meeting with Bill and next term will accompany Bill to his two-hour-per-week on-the-job training at the charity shop. Performance assessments have great potential for assessing exceptional students in meaningful ways. For most students you will use performance assessment in combination with the other forms of assessment discussed in this chapter.

## Portfolios as Classroom Assessments for Exceptional Learners

John Anderson (Anderson et al., 2001) and Dan Bachor (Anderson & Bachor, 1998) of the University of Victoria describe a **portfolio** as a collection of student work that represents a sampling of the student's achievements and provides evidence of learning over time. With thoughtful sampling, the portfolio can become an integral part of learning. A portfolio should contain evidence of reflection and self-evaluation that contribute to students' valuing their own work and themselves as learners (British Columbia Ministry of Education, 2004). Recently, much has been written about electronic portfolios (e.g., Glor-Scheib & Telthorster, 2006). The steps involved in portfolio assessment are as follows (adapted from Harper, O'Connor, & Simpson, 1999):

- *collect* in a container that is efficient for your classroom organization;
- *select* purposefully so the contents show students meeting outcomes and learning goals;
- *reflect*—students can write on cover sheets or sticky notes, or teacher and student can summarize a conference together; and

## What do you think?

Read the following paper on researchers' understanding of authentic assessment and performance assessment, and debate with your peers whether the two terms represent the same concept or two distinct concepts.

Frey, B.B., & Schmitt, V.L. (2007). Coming to terms with classroom assessment. *Journal of Advanced Academics*, 18, 402–423.

*Jimmy Kakepetum, 19, shows off the comic he published as part of his studies at Dennis Franklin Cromarty High School in Thunder Bay.*

**What do you think?**

Read two sources on portfolio assessment. Then consult current documents and websites of the ministry of education in your province. What do you think of the use of portfolios in the assessment of learning of exceptional students?

Glor-Scheib, S., & Telthorster, H. (2006). Activate your student IEP team member using technology: How electronic portfolios can bring the student voice to life. *Teaching Exceptional Children Plus,* 2(3), Article 1.

Abrami, P.C., & Barrett, H. (2004). Directions for research and development on electronic portfolios. *Canadian Journal of Learning and Technology,* 31(3), 1–15.

Wade, A., Abrami, P.C., & Sclater, J. (2005). An electronic portfolio to support learning. *Canadian Journal of Learning and Technology,* 31(3), 33–50.

Zubizarreta, J. (2004). *The learning portfolio: Reflective practice for improving student learning.* Bolton, MS: Anker Pub.

Wesson, C.L., & King, R.P. (1996). Portfolio assessment and special education students. *Teaching Exceptional Children,* 28(2), 44–48.

Mahoney, J. (2002). *Power and portfolios: Best practices for high school classrooms.* Portsmouth, NH: Heineman.

■ *inspect*—teacher, student, and parents should consider the accomplishments in light of the outcomes and goals that were set (use this event to close the year or term's portfolio process).

The kinds of content that might go into a portfolio in reading and writing (with adaptations for exceptional students in brackets) include

■ a log of books read with personal reactions to the books (for an exceptional student with limited writing ability, the personal reactions could be captioned drawings);

■ an audio recording of the student reading showing best performance (for a student learning to read, audio recordings made monthly would show progress);

■ representative assignments responding to pre- and post-reading questions (these could change gradually from multiple choice to fill in the blanks to written responses);

■ a scrapbook of representative writing samples (increasing in length and complexity);

■ notes from conferences with the teacher (ranging from a checklist to a paragraph);

■ student-selected best performance in writing of various genres (a limited range of genres); and

■ teacher-developed rubrics that show increasing accomplishments in written expression.

Both elementary and secondary school teachers have adopted this approach to assessment.

Chen and Martin (2000) describe how teachers can use performance assessment and portfolio assessment together in elementary schools, and Siegle (2002) highly recommends that gifted students assemble electronic portfolios. The Focus on Teachers box describes one secondary school business studies teacher who uses portfolio assessment and student-led conferences.

# David Notman: The Effects of Portfolio Assessment and Student-Led Conferences on Ownership, Control, and Learning

David Notman describes himself as "a business teacher with 26 years' experience in the business classroom." He describes his course this way: "The Introduction to Business program is a survey course of business studies, offered at the grade 10 level to 15- and 16-year-old students in their second year of high school." After years of traditional assessment, he asked the question, "What would happen if the students had more ownership of the curriculum; more control of their own assessment? And what would happen if this was done in partnership with parents?"

He writes about ownership: "Ownership begins with the student's contribution to the classroom. The room is decorated with pop cans, cereal boxes, shopping bags, and other examples of interesting packaging. The students are encouraged to contribute to the collection if they can find something that is not already up. They will always point out their contributions to their parents during the student–parent interview. Many students return, even after graduation, to see if their 'stuff' is still there."

In describing his course Notman said: "At the beginning of the semester, each student is required to select a company that he/she will profile throughout the semester. The only requirement is that the companies are traded on a stock exchange; that they are public companies and therefore have open and accessible records to facilitate research. As information is provided in class about business in general (how change affects business, for example) each student connects this information to the business he/she is profiling, and interprets the significance of the information in areas such as investment, expansion of markets, or the new methods of distribution."

Notman does not allow students to work in pairs and no two students can profile the same company. "The student begins to refer to the company as 'my' company. ('My company just sent me some information.') A list is posted in the classroom, matching students with companies, and students are encouraged to share information they find on other companies."

The students experience control through the student-led conference. "At mid-semester the students meet with their parent(s) or guardian(s) in the business classroom after school or in the evening. The student summarizes the curriculum to date and then presents his/her portfolio as a work in progress. The teacher is not present during the presentation but is available to answer questions. The mid-term mark is generated by the student and parent, and is based on both the effort shown up to that point as well as the plans that the student has made to finish the work. As this is a compulsory part of the course evaluation, the parent turnout is almost 100 percent."

The portfolio is the basis for the end-of-term assessment as well. "The final presentation is made one on one between the student and the teacher. The format is up to the student. The student is marked according to a rubric, which he/she has seen and studied throughout the semester. The rubric is based on the ICE model and provides opportunities for students to do well at various stages of the process. Not all students are expected to achieve the same level, but the student is given the opportunity to decide what level they are willing to accept. Passing grades are assigned if the student is working on the Information level, average grades are given for achievement at the Connections level, and honour grades are received by students who work at the Extension level."

Notman's assessment of his change to portfolio assessment and student-led conferences: "Students seem to have been able to do and submit much better work than before. The portfolios contain a thorough presentation of the course material, connected to the real world consistently, and often accompanied by analysis, criticism, suggestions, and other indications that students have gone beyond the course requirements. Their presentations, both to the parents and to me, require that they explain their work in a context; that they connect the course together, then tell about what they know. This experience leads to deeper knowledge than simple memorization. Active learning seems to involve students' taking ownership and control of their learning. I have noticed a marked decrease in the number of behaviour problems. The students say, 'This course is something you do for yourself.' I think [the success] has primarily to do with the amount of ownership and control the students have in directing their learning and assessment."

Source: Extracts from David Notman (2000). Another Way of Coming Downstairs: The Effects of Portfolio Assessment and Student-Led Conferences on Ownership, Control and Learning. Paper presented at the annual meeting of the Ontario Education Research Conference, Toronto. Used with permission.

The kinds of adaptations you may have to make include teaching exceptional students how to select and reflect on portfolio pieces. You may need to provide more guidance in the efficient management and organization of so much information. And you may find that exceptional students cannot function as independently in student–parent conferences; you may wish to be present and participate in such conferences rather than be nearby and monitoring. The applicability of portfolio assessment for exceptional students has been convincingly demonstrated by American states that have pioneered alternative assessments for students who cannot meaningfully complete large-scale assessments. These include such things as a vocational résumé in grade 12, demonstrated promptness, management of a student's own schedule, engagement in hobbies, and working co-operatively with others. Portfolios of student work provide a flexible, individualized approach to capturing the learning outcomes of a heterogeneous group of students (Kleinert, Haig, Kearns, & Kennedy, 2000).

## Adaptations and Alternatives to Report Card Marks

One of the most contentious issues in education is the question of how report card grades can and should be adapted for exceptional students. Assessments must not discriminate against students with disabilities. We do not want our grading practices to serve as disincentives to exceptional students like Sasha, described in one of the chapter-opening case studies. Grades must speak to students, parents, postsecondary institutions, and employers. Teachers must also feel comfortable with the message they send to exceptional students and their classmates. Given that adaptations are a relatively new phenomenon, we still have more questions than answers. What options do you have? Table 8.3 provides examples of grading adaptations. It is important to read the policies for your province, district, and school, so you understand which of these options are acceptable in the school in which you teach.

The first of these options is **changing grading criteria**. Belle's case at the beginning of this chapter demonstrates how you can vary grading weights so students are not disadvantaged by an impossible task—for example, students who are hard of hearing do not have part of their grade determined by their inability to hear during pop quizzes. Modifying curricular expectations must build on the IEP, and then it is critical to assess what is expected for the exceptional student. In effect you are using progress on the IEP objectives as the grading criterion (Silva et al., 2005). If

### Further Reading

Read the following three papers on grading adaptations for exceptional students and discuss with your peers the most important issues that you think arise on this topic. How do the adaptations advanced by each of these papers differ? And how do the processes recommended for arriving at grading adaptations differ?

Munk, D.D., & Bursuck, W.D. (2004). Personalized grading plans: A systematic approach to making the grades of included students more accurate and meaningful? *Focus on Exceptional Children, 36*(9), 1–11.

Silva, M., Munk, D.D., & Bursuck, W.D. (2005). Grading adaptations for students with disabilities. *Intervention in School and Clinic, 41*(2), 87–98.

Salend, S.J. (2005). Report card models that support communication and differentiation of instruction. *Teaching Exceptional Children, 37*(4), 28–34.

## TABLE 8.3 EXAMPLES OF GRADING ADAPTATIONS

| Change Grading Criteria | Change to Letter and Number Grades | Use Alternatives to Letter and Number Grades |
|---|---|---|
| Vary grading weights. | Add written comments. | Use pass–fail grades. |
| Modify curricular expectations. | Add student activity logs. | Use competency checklists. |
| Grade on the basis of improvement. | Add information from portfolios and/or performance-based assessments. | Use contracts and modified syllabi. |

Source: Friend, M., Bursuck, W., & Hutchinson, N.L. (1998). *Including exceptional students: A practical guide for classroom teachers.* Scarborough: Allyn and Bacon Canada, p. 359. Reprinted with permission.

you expect Linda, a student with developmental disabilities, to learn to discuss the historical sites in the community, then assess her on this outcome with a high mark for excellence or a low mark for poor performance. Don't assign her a low grade because she cannot write an essay when this was never expected of Linda or taught to her. **Grading contracts** or **modified course syllabi** *may* enable you to give students credit for attendance, promptness, effort, co-operative behaviour, and improvement (self-referenced assessment) (Munk & Bursuck, 2004). Make the criteria objective and consistent with the IEP, and ensure that the student and parents are aware of the criteria. Sometimes grading on the basis of improvement can motivate students to work hard, attend, and pay attention. This strategy complements the use of qualitative rubrics. You can also grade on students' performance on prioritized content and assignments. Suppose there are two topics in the unit, and you believe the topic on biography is much more important than the work on poetry. You could give an exceptional student 66 percent of the grade on the biography topic and 33 percent on poetry, instead of treating the two topics as if they are of the same value (Silva et al., 2005).

**Changes to letter and number grades** may mean clarifying them with a comment that explains the reading level of the books used in language arts or explaining that Billy is using the grade 3 math text although he is in grade 5. It may be better to make these explanations in a letter stapled to the report card and to also type on the report card that it is valid only if the explanatory letter is attached. This allows the child to show the report to peers without them reading the details of the clarification (a realistic strategy given that children are often under great pressure to allow peers to glance at their reports). Salend (2005) suggests attaching a checklist of classroom-based instructional accommodations and a checklist of classroom-based testing accommodations that the student has received. What you write on the report about the adapted curriculum and the IEP may be limited by policy and by legislation regarding privacy of information. Learn the provincial, district, and school policies well in advance of the first reporting period. A summary of student activities constitutes a **student activity log**. This may be particularly beneficial in reporting progress for students on modified or alternative programs. You may be able to include a summary that describes the key accomplishments shown in the portfolio or performance-based assessments. If this information cannot appear on the report, you can emphasize it in a conference with parents.

There are few **alternatives to the letter and number grades** that dominate North American reporting systems. However, some teachers have used **pass/fail** or **credit/ no credit** designations to show that students have met the minimum requirements for a unit. Be sure to specify objectively what these requirements are and how you arrived at a judgment. Qualitative rubrics can be helpful in this task. Checklists for skills that are taught at the various grades may be available in the curricula or from the resource teacher. These can help you to communicate the skills that students have mastered, are working on, and have not yet begun to acquire. Often students and parents can understand how much progress the student has made and how the skills acquired compare with what is expected of other students by looking at a straightforward checklist or a set of open-ended statements related to curriculum mastery (e.g., recognizes numbers up to 7, or identifies 14 letters of the alphabet). If this information cannot replace a grade, perhaps it can help to explain a grade. Be sure to indicate the skills and knowledge attained compared with those listed in the IEP annual outcomes for the exceptional student.

Whatever forms of grading adaptation you use, you may wish to negotiate them with the student, the parents, and other educators on the in-school team or, at the very least, be prepared to explain them to the student and parents and collaborate with others who teach the exceptional student in question (see Farenga & Joyce, 2000; Silva et al., 2005). You may have to provide a written explanation for the receiving institution when putting together reports for graduating elementary, middle, and secondary school students. Be honest and avoid jargon. Think about how you would want a teacher to report on the progress of your exceptional child (if you were the parent of such a child); hold yourself to the standards you would expect of others.

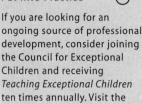

**Put into Practice**

If you are looking for an ongoing source of professional development, consider joining the Council for Exceptional Children and receiving *Teaching Exceptional Children* ten times annually. Visit the website at www.cec.sped.org.

# Summary

This chapter focused on using assessment to inform differentiated instruction, and on a contentious issue in exceptional education: adapting assessment to report fairly the learning of exceptional students. All teaching and assessment of exceptional students should be guided by the annual outcomes listed in their IEPs and by the descriptions of strengths and needs. We reviewed here how to use the ADAPT strategy to analyze assessment. The chapter then described large-scale assessment in Canada and the adaptations used for exceptional students. This was followed by descriptions of how teachers conduct classroom assessment and use it to inform differentiation, and the role of rubrics. There were descriptions of classroom assessment, including tests, performance assessment, and portfolios, and one final topic on adaptations and alternatives to report card marks.

# Key Terms

assessment (p. 276)
large-scale assessment (p. 276)
classroom assessment (p. 276)
testing (p. 276)
evaluation (p. 276)
grading (p. 276)
reporting (p. 276)
norm-referenced (p. 283)
criterion-referenced (p. 283)
self-referenced (p. 283)
ICE model (p. 284)
Ideas (p. 284)

Connections (p. 284)
Extensions (p. 284)
rubrics (p. 286)
quantitative rubrics (p. 286)
qualitative rubrics (p. 286)
study guide (p. 291)
study skills (p. 291)
chunking strategies (p. 292)
mnemonic (p. 292)
concept maps (p. 292)
performance assessment (p. 294)
authentic assessment (p. 295)

portfolio (p. 296)
changing grading criteria (p. 299)
grading contracts (p. 300)
modified course syllabi (p. 300)
changes to letter and number
   grades (p. 300)
student activity log (p. 300)
alternatives to letter and number
   grades (p. 300)
pass/fail (p. 300)
credit/no credit (p. 300)

# Challenges for Reviewing Chapter 8

1.  Discuss with your peers the ways in which you can envision teachers using the ADAPT strategy to analyze and adapt assessment. Why is it not enough to simply differentiate instruction without adapting assessment? What challenges do you foresee, and how can you collaborate with your teaching colleagues to overcome them?

2.  Read the brief descriptions of Sasha and Belle at the beginning of this chapter. Choose one of these students to focus on. This student is in your class and large-scale assessment will be conducted at your grade level this year. Review the relevant sections of this chapter. Describe the thinking process that you will engage in to decide what accommodations will be appropriate for this student, if any, and describe the way you would advocate for the student if accommodations were needed.

3.  Write a brief scenario for a class that includes at least one gifted student and one student with a disability; describe the students briefly. Prepare to discuss this scenario, which focuses on teaching that you are likely to do at your grade level, with your peers. Describe how you would conduct assessment so it would inform differentiated teaching. Think about both tiered teaching and other forms of differentiation. Include a qualitative rubric in your discussion of this scenario. Compare your ideas with those of your peers who teach at different levels. Try to identify aspects of thinking about assessment that were common to you and your peers, regardless of grade level.

4.  Use the scenario you created for question #3. Assume the role of one member of an in-school team for one of the exceptional students in the scenario. Ask a peer to assume one of the other roles on the team. Discuss adaptations to classroom assessment that you would make to ensure assessment was meaningful for all students in the class, including the exceptional student. Include adaptations to tests, performance assessment, and portfolios, when each of these would need to be adapted. Again, discuss with your peers and compare ideas.

5.  Think about a student who might be in one of your classes who needs adaptations to his or her report card marks. Consider a student who might need alternatives to report card marks. What are the characteristics of these students that make these changes to report card marks appropriate? Review the relevant sections of the chapter and discuss your ideas with your peers.

6.  Return to the opening cases of Sasha and Belle and answer the four questions that follow the cases.

# Chapter 9
## Enhancing Social Relations

## Learner Objectives

After you have read this chapter, you will be able to:

1. Discuss the ways in which social development and social acceptance of exceptional learners are central to inclusion.

2. Describe the role of friendship in the development of exceptional individuals.

3. Discuss elementary and secondary schools as social environments, including schoolwide programs and approaches to preventing bullying.

4. Use the ADAPT strategy to analyze the social demands of the classroom and select collaborative and co-operative teaching strategies.

5. Discuss the role of the community in enhancing social relations.

Val started grade 1 in September with the children who had been in her kindergarten class and had attended preschool with her. Val participated in an early intervention program, was always encouraged to explore her environment, and is quite adventuresome once she is familiar with her surroundings. Because Val is blind, she does not play much on the equipment in the playground. Some days she asks the teacher on playground supervision to help her get onto a swing, but at recess she usually invites a class-mate to stand with her under a tree or to sit with her on a bench. One day, Val's teacher reminds the other children to play games at recess that include Val. Peter and Yamun pipe up that they like to play catch and that Val cannot play "because she can't see the ball." Peter says, "It just wouldn't be safe." On the way out to the playground later in the day, Yamun tells the teacher, "It's kind of boring spending recess with Val. She can't do much. And I don't like when she doesn't look at me. Why does she look at my ear when I'm talking to her?"

**Lynn rushes into the resource room with her friend Suparna.** These two grade 11 students are almost inseparable. Lynn and Suparna both have learning disabilities. They participate together on the school cheerleading squad, and when the two aren't together they are talking on the phone. Lynn has severe difficulties with written expression, and she has brought her latest English assignment to the resource room so she can edit it with a peer tutor from grade 12. When I ask Lynn how her day is going, she replies, "Great!" The girls part, promising to meet in the locker room after school. Suparna goes to her history class and Lynn sits down with her peer tutor. Not many people know how severe Lynn's learning disability is—other than her closest friends, her peer tutor, her classroom teachers, and me. As Lynn's resource room teacher and counsellor, I know how hard it is for her to complete her written assignments without "blowing her cover." Lynn leaves class rather than read aloud in front of her peers, works hard with me and with her peer tutor to edit all written work before she submits it, and writes her tests in the resource room where it is quiet and she has extra time. When you ask Lynn why she comes to school, she will tell you, "To be with my friends!"

1. How would you describe the peer relations of Val and Lynn?

2. What should teachers be expected to do to meet the social and friendship needs of students like Val and Lynn?

3. How might the social characteristics and social relations of these students and other exceptional learners affect their learning in inclusive classrooms?

4. What teaching strategies are likely to help exceptional students be part of the social and academic life of the classroom?

5. What school and community resources can a teacher draw on to enhance the social relations of students like Lynn and Val?

# Introduction

The focus of this chapter is the **social relationships** of exceptional learners in inclusive classrooms. Friendships are among the most important of our social relationships. Much has been written about "the complex nature of friendship" and "its likely effects on how we function, how we think about ourselves, and how we deal with life's challenges" (Bukowski & Sippola, 2005). "Friendships provide a safety or comfort zone for self-exploration and the consideration of new roles and goals" (Azmitia, Ittel, & Radmacher, 2005, p. 23). Hartup (2006) argues that within children's social networks, darker relationships coexist with brighter ones, and important developmental outcomes are associated with both. In this chapter we think about our role in fostering the friendships, social acceptance, and full participation that are necessary if inclusion is to be more than a placement (e.g., Hutchinson, Freeman, & Steiner-Bell, 2002; Webster & Carter, 2007). Haring (1991) used the term "social integration" to describe students' full participation in the social interactions of the school community; the term also implies that exceptional children are involved in relationships with typically developing peers that are similar in nature to those formed between typically developing youth.

Recent research informs us of the perspectives of youth with disabilities (e.g., Knox & Hickson, 2001; Steiner Bell, 2005), of gifted youth (e.g., Gross, 2006; Masden, 2005), and of students without disabilities on friendship and on belonging (e.g., McDougall et al., 2004; Hall & Strickett, 2002). Considering the students' points of view may help you to foster the kinds of friendships that are important for emotional well-being, and to respond constructively when children and adolescents pull back from peers who, for example, don't look them in the eye, like Val in the first of the opening case studies. Social interactions are expected to foster learning in many approaches that are used extensively in schools and that are recommended to teachers (co-operative learning, collaborative learning, small groups, activity centres, etc.). You can use the ADAPT strategy to analyze the social demands of your classroom organization and of tasks and compare these demands to student strengths and needs. This chapter provides examples of some of the options for the social structure of learning, with examples drawn from current resources, including many Canadian ones. The role of the community in social development is explored.

## Further Reading

Examples of books and articles available on topics like social relations and friendship:

Ladd, G.W. (2005). *Children's peer relations and social competence.* New Haven, CT: Yale University Press.

Diamond, K.E. (2002). The development of social competence in children with disabilities. In P. Smith & C. Hart (Eds.), *Blackwell handbook of childhood social development* (pp. 570–587). Malden, MA: Blackwell.

Cotterell, J. (2007). *Social networks in youth and adolescence* (2nd ed.). New York: Routledge/Taylor & Francis.

Rillotta, F., & Nettelbeck, T. (2007). Effects of an awareness program on attitudes of students without an intellectual disability towards persons with an intellectual disability. *Journal of Intellectual and Developmental Disability, 32,* 19–27.

Karten, T.J. (2005). *Inclusion strategies that work! Research-based methods for the classroom.* Thousand Oaks, CA: Corwin Press. (Contains teaching ideas for a disability awareness program.)

# The Importance of Social Development and Social Acceptance to Inclusion

Chapter 1 describes how participating in all facets of Canadian society, including educational institutions, is a fundamental right of all Canadians. In 1998 a review of educational policies across the country (Friend, Bursuck, & Hutchinson, 1998) showed two dominant themes in the education of exceptional learners: change and inclusion. Much has been written by Canadians (e.g., Hutchinson, Freeman, & Berg, 2004; Wiener & Tardif, 2004) and others (e.g., Male, 2007; Murray & Greenberg, 2006) about the importance of friendship, **social development**, and acceptance to the inclusion of exceptional students in classrooms. If inclusion means full and valued participation in the life of the classroom, then we need to understand how **social competence** of exceptional students, **social acceptance** by peers, and **friendships** contribute to equity and inclusion. Social competence involves being able to engage

## Cross-Reference

In describing the first two steps in the ADAPT strategy, Chapter 1 emphasizes students' social, emotional, and behavioural strengths and needs as well as the social, emotional, and behavioural demands of the classroom.

in age-appropriate social cognitions and actions (Diamond, 2007; Frostad & Pijl, 2007), while social acceptance refers to the consensual liking or disliking that is directed by the group toward the individual (Ham & Faircloth, 2005; Harter, 2006). Friendships are close relationships characterized by reciprocity and commitment between individuals who see themselves as equals (Hartup, 2006). Using these definitions, consider the snapshots of Val and Lynn that open this chapter—and their social competence, social acceptance, and friendships. In the next two sections, we focus on the perspectives of exceptional students on their peer relations and on the perspectives of their peers on social relations with exceptional students.

## Perspectives of Exceptional Students on Their Peer Relations

What do exceptional students think about their relationships, friendships, and feelings of belonging with their classmates? Do they think these relationships are important to their classroom learning? Only recently have researchers begun to focus on the voices of exceptional students on this issue. While there is great variability in the reports from children and adolescents, the importance of feeling connected with peers, with and without disabilities, seems to be a dominant theme. For example, Tom, an adolescent with Asperger syndrome, described close friendships with four other exceptional adolescents who were members of a social skills group that he attended. He demonstrated a robust understanding of friendship—as developing when individuals share interests, help one another, and care—which showed many similarities to what normally developing 12 year olds think about friendship. He described his best friend: "He helps me figure out things that I really like, if I'm afraid of something, he helps me get over my fear" (Howard, Cohn, & Orsmond, 2006, p. 622). Similarly, adolescents who attended intense programs for gifted and talented youth reported that the greatest benefits were the new friendships formed with peers of similar ability and the feelings of belonging they developed after "being thrown into a social network of interesting peers" (McHugh, 2006, p. 182).

A quantitative study of grade 5 and 6 students with high-incidence disabilities comes to a similar conclusion. Murray and Greenberg (2006) found that students with LD, EBD, or mild intellectual disabilities who had positive peer relations in the classroom were less likely to experience emotional and behavioural problems at school. Students who felt supported by teachers were less likely to experience anxiety at school. All of these studies suggest that students who feel a sense of belongingness or connectedness enjoy school more and are more likely to be engaged in learning in the classroom.

"Friends are what gets me through school I guess you could say. They're always there to support me . . . friends you tell everything and they're always there, so they're very

Two 11-year-old girls with diabetes are best friends. They both enjoy skating and each understands what the other has to deal with—frequent finger-pricking, taking insulin, and a careful diet.

important." These are the words of Lynn, the grade 11 student with LD introduced in the second case study at the beginning of this chapter. Lynn attends the same Canadian secondary school as Matt, a grade 11 student with LD and ADHD. Here is what Matt said, when asked how important friends were to him: "Ah just sometimes I just don't know how to relate to a lot of the people anymore. . . . It's not very important I don't think. . . . Maybe they just don't like me or you know they find me annoying" (Lévesque, 1997).

These two adolescents with LD, who attend inclusive classes in the same school, have very different views of their social relations in these classes. Lynn is a popular cheerleader with close friends, while Matt is socially isolated and cannot find anyone to listen to him talk about his favourite computer game. Buhrmester (1998; Underwood & Buhrmester, 2007) developed a theory of adolescent friendship characterized by four elements of **interpersonal competence**: initiating and sustaining conversation, initiating plans to spend time with friends outside school, disclosing personal thoughts and empathy, and managing conflict effectively. In interviews and observations, Nicole Lévesque (1997) of Queen's University found that Lynn demonstrated these four competencies, while all four posed a challenge for Matt.

Lynn and Matt's social experiences differ radically, yet both cases demonstrate how peer relations can influence thoughts about school and shape psychosocial development. Lynn's close friendships and positive peer relationships enrich her educational experiences and enhance her self-esteem. Her story is an uplifting illustration of how some exceptional students thrive academically, socially, and personally in supportive environments. Matt, on the other hand, stands alone in the halls, cannot carry on a reciprocal conversation, and reports that he had nothing to look forward to when he returned to school after the winter break.

In the past decade a number of studies have given voice to students with physical disabilities who have talked about their relationships with other students in school and about how important teachers were to their social experiences. Lucy, who was in a wheelchair, attended a mainstream secondary school: "On my first day at the school it was scary because I was worried if I was going to make friends or not. But I made friends straight away" (Curtin & Clark, 2005, p. 205). Lucy wanted to be as independent as possible: "I want to do a lot for myself. I don't want [my friends] to push me around from lesson to lesson but maybe just help me with some small easy things, like . . . opening doors for me" (p. 205). Although Lucy made friends in her school, she felt she was accepted in spite of the actions of some of her teachers. Lucy had difficulty writing as fast as her peers and she reported that one of her teachers would continually say, "Come on quickly," and Lucy reported that when she gave a correct answer, this teacher would "bang her head down on the desk . . . she used to make fun of me" (p. 205).

In contrast, Marilyn, another student in a wheelchair, described a teacher who told the class about Marilyn, her disability, and her wheelchair and explained that Marilyn would be a full member of the class. She urged them to make Marilyn feel welcome. In Marilyn's view, "In that class I was included, I was allowed to sit at a desk, and everybody treated me really well." Marilyn suggests, "The key to inclusion is making people without disability comfortable with disability, [but also helping them] accept that they have got a responsibility to help remove the barriers" (Ballard & McDonald, 1999, p. 102). Marilyn's and Lucy's insights point to the need for teachers to understand their role in promoting social relations for all students including exceptional students.

Weblinks

MOVIES ABOUT DISABILITIES (CANADA): LINKS TO A NUMBER OF SITES
www.queensu.ca/equity/disabilities/movies.php

FILMS INVOLVING DISABILITIES (UK): INCLUDES INFORMATION ABOUT OVER 2500 FILMS AND IS DIRECTED TOWARD EDUCATORS
www.disabilityfilms.co.uk/

AMAZON.COM (US), MOVIES ABOUT PEOPLE WITH DISABILITIES: INCLUDES QUOTATIONS FROM CHARACTERS IN THE FILMS
www.amazon.com/Movies-about-People-with-Disabilities/lm/295R795C0Y6NT

Further Reading

*Discover Together: A Disability Awareness Resource* (kit). Department of the Secretary of State of Canada. ($35.00 binder.) (Six units examining different exceptionalities, to raise awareness about the competencies of people with disabilities. Recommended for grades K–8. Adapt the recommendations for developing a (dis)ability awareness program appropriate for a secondary school environment. Consider a film festival.)

Safran, S.P. (2000). Using movies to teach students about disabilities. *Teaching Exceptional Children, 32*(3), 44–47.

Ivory, P. (1997), Disabilities in the media: The movies. *Quest, 4*(4). Retrieved on March 3, 2008 from www.mda.org/publications/Quest/q44movies.html.

## Perspectives of Peers on Social Relations with Exceptional Classmates

The research reports a range of **peer perspectives** on relationships with students with disabilities. The case study of Val reflects findings reported by Pat MacCuspie (1996) of Nova Scotia in an interview study about the inclusion of blind students. Classmates tended to describe their friendships with blind elementary school students as based on helping rather than on shared interests or fun, which were the basis for their relationships with non-disabled friends. Some children described the inconveniences of playing and learning with blind children—blind classmates could not safely play catch or tag, and paired reading was problematic because a Braille reader is slow and pages of Braille are large and awkward. Young children seemed uncomfortable with classmates who did not make eye contact, and some did not understand that blind children could not see at all, but thought they could see less clearly than other people. MacCuspie recommends that teachers be forthright in teaching classmates about the nature of the disability and, for example, explain why a blind child cannot maintain eye contact. Figure 9.1 contains information and resources for planning a **(dis)ability awareness program** for your classroom or school.

Many studies have reported that children and adolescents with disabilities tend to have low social status in regular classrooms (e.g., Hall & Strickett, 2002; Frostad & Pijl, 2007). **Social status** is based on **sociometric rating**, that is, whether classmates would choose these students as best friends, would choose them to play with, etc. Judith Wiener of the University of Toronto and Nancy Heath of McGill University (e.g., Bloom, Heath, et al., 2007; Heath & Wiener, 1996; Weiner & Tardif, 2004) have reported low social status in a number of studies of Canadian children with learning disabilities and emotional and behavioural disorders. Recently, a large study of the social networks of four hundred children from grades 2 through 5 included seventeen focal children with autism or Asperger syndrome. The findings showed that the focal children experienced lower social status, companionship, and reciprocity than their normally developing peers (Chamberlain, Kasari, & Rotheram-Fuller, 2007).

Researchers have attempted to understand what might contribute to the low social status of students with disabilities. For example, a study of high school students in Ontario reported the attitudes of almost two thousand grade 9 students toward their peers with disabilities. The majority of students (61 percent) held positive attitudes; however, 21 percent held attitudes that ranged from slightly below neutral to very negative. Students who reported having a friend or classmate with a disability had more positive attitudes. Dimensions of school culture were related to students' attitudes. When students perceived that the school encouraged learning for all students rather than competition, they viewed peers with disabilities more positively. Positive relationships between teachers and students and positive student relationships were also associated with more positive attitudes (McDougall et al., 2004). Another study, involving eighty children with a range of disabilities, used quantitative and qualitative methods to identify child characteristics that might contribute to low social status. The researchers found that socially accepted children tended to have disabilities that were less likely to affect social problem solving and emotional regulation, whereas children who were socially rejected had disabilities that were more likely to

# FIGURE 9.1 (DIS)ABILITY AWARENESS PROGRAMS

Purposes:  To foster greater understanding of people with disabilities
To increase students' knowledge about specific disabilities
To increase students' sensitivity toward individuals with disabilities

Develop a program that reflects your local school needs. Invite parents of children with disabilities, older students with disabilities, and adults with disabilities to take part in the planning and in the program.

Adults with disabilities may speak about their disabilities, share feelings, demonstrate how their adapted equipment (e.g., motorized wheelchair, hearing aid) works. Some adults are comfortable to eat lunch with a class of students or sit and talk in the schoolyard at recess as well.

Ask students with and without disabilities to be presenters. They can read from books about children with disabilities, show videos, and act as hosts for adult presenters. These students will benefit from a reflective component to their participation and will appreciate recognition as well.

Locate resources (videos, books, pamphlets, and other community resources). Consult the lists in this book, websites, and community organizations.

Take photographs to remember the occasion, invite the local press, and recognize participants in a school assembly.

**Resources to consult:**

**Family Village. Disability Awareness.**
www.familyvillage.wisc.edu/general/disability-awareness.html.

**Center for Disability Information and Referral (Indiana University).**
**Kids' Corner: Have you ever wondered what it's like to have a disability?**
www.iidc.indiana.edu/cedir/kidsweb.

**Easter Seals New Brunswick. Disability Awareness Training CD-ROM.**
http://easterseals.nb.ca/prog_datcd.php.

**DAWN Ontario. Interacting with People with DisAbilities: An Etiquette Hand-book.**
http://dawn.thot.net/Etiquette.html. (Originally developed by the University of Arkansas, 2002.)

Denti, L.G., & Meyers, S. (1997). Successful ability awareness programs: The key is in the planning. *Teaching Exceptional Children, 29*(4), 52–54.

Foley, J.T., Tindall, D., Lieberman, L., & Kim, S.-Y. (2007). How to develop disability awareness using the sport education model. *Journal of Physical Education, Recreation and Dance,* Nov/Dec.

Rillotta, F., & Nettelbeck, T. (2007). Effects of an awareness program on attitudes of students without an intellectual disability towards persons with an intellectual disability. *Journal of Intellectual and Developmental Disability, 32,* 19–27.

Department of the Secretary of State of Canada. *Discover together: A disability awareness resource (kit).* (A teaching kit with six units to raise awareness about the competencies of people with disabilities. Recommended for grades K–8.)

Kirch, S.A., Bargerhuff, M.E., Cowan, H., & Wheatly, M. (2007). Reflections of educators in pursuit of inclusive science. *Journal of Science Teacher Education, 18,* 663–692. (Describes a program for enhancing disability awareness of teachers.)

affect social competence (Odom et al., 2006). These two recent studies suggest that both the characteristics of individual exceptional students and the social contexts we create, as teachers, contribute to the social status of exceptional students in our classrooms.

What can you do as a teacher to contribute positively to the social status of exceptional students in your classroom? Hall and McGregor (2000) reported on the peer relations of three boys with disabilities in an inclusive school in Australia.

**What do you think?**

Why do you think parents of exceptional children might be concerned when classmates see their relationship with the exceptional student as primarily based on helping rather than on reciprocal enjoyment of each other's company? How can teachers encourage children (or adolescents) with and without disabilities to see themselves as equals in their relationships?

Put into Practice

Researchers have reported that some schools tend to be inclusive communities where there are many positive reports of friendships, social relations, and respect among students, including exceptional students. Look for a school that is developing such a reputation and make naturalistic observations of the students, teachers, and administrators in that school. What can you learn from such observations about how to create an inclusive community in your classroom and school?

The school was described as "a school community where all children are viewed as individuals regardless of abilities" (p. 125). The three focal students were Nathan, Mike, and Manuel. Nathan had cerebral palsy, epilepsy, developmental disabilities, and limited verbal communication skills. He used a communication board. Mike had developmental disabilities, hyperactivity, and poor balance. Manuel had Down syndrome. Data were collected at two junctures five years apart (kindergarten and grade 5) by a number of means—this included interviews with peers who chose the boys as playmates in grade 5. One grade 5 classmate suggested that Nathan was "fun to play with," and one said of Mike, "I've been with him since prep and I like him a lot. He's sort of a good friend. I like to help him." Of Manuel, a girl named Erica said, "He's my best friend. We go to each other's house sometimes." These three exceptional students were observed to participate in the same activities as their classmates, to be befriended by girls more than by boys, and to have long-term relationships (since kindergarten) with the children who chose them as playmates. In most cases the children's families were friends in the community and encouraged the children to play together outside school.

In an interview study in a British secondary school known for its inclusive practices, Ainscow, Booth, and Dyson (1999) learned through interviews what the students thought of the school. "Possibly the most significant and frequently mentioned factor relating to [their] positive feelings [was] . . . the school as a source of social encounters" (p. 141). One student said, "It just seems a lot easier to make friends here—it happens in lessons and free time." Students described positive relationships with teachers and opportunities to pursue individual projects. They described the high number of supportive paraeducators present because of the large number of students with disabilities. The researchers reported "relaxed relationships" between males and females, "little or no evidence of racism among the students," and that "students with disabilities are accepted as being just part of the 'normal' school community." They described a blind student who "talked openly about her own disability and referred to the disability of others in a 'taken for granted' tone."

These adolescents defended the practice of including exceptional students. One told the researchers, "I don't see why they shouldn't be in the school because they're just normal, just people same as all of us. They should all have the same chance as anyone else should have" (Ainscow et al., 1999, p. 148). These case studies, which provide the perspectives of students with and without disabilities on their social relations, present a number of implications for teachers and families of exceptional students. These cases suggest that teachers can foster the perception of exceptional students as valued classmates and can teach so that everyone experiences the benefits of being included. You can minimize students' sense that disabilities are foreign and exotic and can help make everyone comfortable with disability, as Marilyn suggested. Providing information and eliminating mystery about the exceptionality can go a long way. Treating exceptional students much as you treat everyone else is also essential. There are implications for parents, too. Long-term friendships appear to provide considerable benefits to exceptional students, as do family connections outside school. Families of exceptional children may need to take an active role in initiating play opportunities with neighbouring families in the early years so that children without disabilities feel comfortable alongside the exceptional child. Figure 9.2 provides suggestions for parents (or teachers) to help children or adolescents with severe disabilities to develop skills for interacting with peers and handling emotions. Chapter 6 provides teachers

## FIGURE 9.2 STRATEGIES FOR PARENTS (AND TEACHERS) TO TEACH SOCIAL SKILLS FOR PEER INTERACTIONS

### Incidental Teaching

This strategy means taking advantage of "teachable moments." During naturally occurring situations, parents (or teachers) remind or show children how to use social skills.

#### Example

Fiona is playing at Maggie's house. Fiona and Maggie reach for the green crayon at the same time. Maggie's mother takes this opportunity to remind Maggie to share, saying, "Maybe you can let Fiona use the green crayon now, and you can use the blue one until she is finished. Then you can use the green crayon. Remember: Fiona is our guest."

### Analyzing an Incident

This strategy involves a parent (or teacher) in guiding a child through an analysis of what went wrong after a child has lost his or her temper or handled a social situation poorly. It usually helps to allow the child to cool down first.

#### Example

Marc was watching a video in the family room with two boys from his class. His father was reading the paper in the next room. When Marc did not understand what was happening in the plot of the movie, he started asking the other boys why the robbers were returning the money. When they didn't explain, Marc asked again and again. The other two boys became annoyed and decided to go home. Marc ejected the video and threw it across the room. Marc was sent to his room to cool down. When he returned to the family room, his father asked him, "What did you do?" "What happened next?" "Was this a good outcome?" "What will you do next time?" Marc's suggestion was to ask the other boys if he could stop the video, ask them to explain what the robbers were doing and why, then turn the video on again as soon as he understood.

### Coaching Emotional Responses

This strategy describes parents (or teachers) leading children through steps to become more emotionally aware. It involves listening and being aware of the emotion, naming the emotion, and planning what to do next time.

#### Example

Vema tells her mother how another girl embarrassed her at school. Her mother asks Vema to explain what the other girl did and how Vema felt. The girl had said she did not want Vema on her softball team because Vema's leg brace made her run too slowly. Vema's mother helped Vema find words to express her feelings. She said, "Oh, Vema, I bet you were embarrassed in front of your friends. I know you don't like your brace to be the centre of attention. Why don't you tell me about it?" Vema described feeling hot and knowing her face was red, and wishing she could fall into the ground. Her mother related a time when she felt like that and explained that this is called embarrassment. She told Vema what she had done in her embarrassing situation and reminded Vema that all people feel embarrassment at times. Vema's mother talked about what was not acceptable—throwing the softball bat or the ball at the girl. Then she and Vema discussed acceptable solutions. Vema laughed. "I won't even embarrass her next time. I will try to remember to suggest what you said—that they have a designated runner for me. Because I can hit the ball. But she's right: I am a slow runner."

Adapted from: Elksnin, L.K., & Elksnin, N. (2001). *Assessment and instruction of social skills.* Mahwah, NJ: Lawrence Erlbaum Associates; Coombs-Richardson, R., & Meisgeier, C.H. (2004). *Connecting with others: Lessons for teaching social and emotional competence.* Champaign IL: Research Press; Vernon, A. (1998). The Passport Program: A journey through emotional, social, cognitive, and self-development. Champaign, IL: Research Press. (3 volumes: grades 1–5, 6–8, 9–12); Northfield, S., & Sherman, A. (2003). Acceptance and community building in schools through increased dialogue and discussion. *Children and Society, 18,* 291–298.

with many ideas for developing a positive classroom climate to foster interaction among all students including exceptional learners. The next section describes the importance of friendship to development and elaborates on why teachers and parents should make the effort to foster such friendships.

# The Role of Friendship in the Development of Exceptional Individuals

Social competence and social acceptance are important for all children and adolescents. Friendship has been called "the most human relationship" (Bukowski & Sippola, 2005, p. 91). Social skills and competencies are acquired in both close friendships and general peer group relationships. Intimacy skills are more likely to develop in friendships, and skills like leadership and feelings of inclusion are more likely to develop in peer relations.

Research suggests that children and adolescents with poor peer adjustment are at greater risk for criminality and dropping out of school (e.g., Bukowski, Rubin, & Parker, 2004). Social skills are also increasingly important to successful participation in the workplace (Conference Board of Canada, 2003; Hutchinson et al., 2007). Researchers have shown that social co-operation also contributes to cognitive development. Vygotsky (1978, p. 163) wrote that "social relations or relations among people . . . underlie all higher functions and their relationships." He argued that all learning is first carried out between the individual and others in the environment and that the individual gradually internalizes what he or she has been doing, saying, and thinking during these social interactions. Speech and dialogue are thought to be important mediators of internalization (Ostad & Sorenson, 2007; Trent, Artiles, & Englert, 1998). Dialogues that lead to developmental change involve finely tuned coordinations between the child and another person, and occur within the "zone of proximal development" between the child's independent problem solving and what the child can do with adult guidance or in collaboration with more capable peers. The most effective partners in these dialogues are thought to be two individuals who differ from one another in expertise, although two novices can contribute to each other's learning of problem solving. Conversation or modelling is necessary for internalization to occur, especially focused on one another's strategies and reasoning (Del Favero et al., 2007; Miller, 2003).

Do children co-operate better with friends than with non-friends? There is evidence that co-operation and friendship are linked in the thinking and behaviour of children and adolescents. For example, children and adolescents co-operate to become and remain friends (Azmitia, Ittel, & Radmacher, 2005; Strough & Cheng, 2000). Children and adolescents want to have their friends as co-operative partners at school, and co-operation increases their liking for one another (Hartup, 1996; Kutnick & Kington, 2005; Strough, Swenson, & Cheng, 2001). Studies conducted during the 1990s suggested that when children do school tasks with friends, they interact more, pay more attention to equity rules, and discuss mutually beneficial outcomes more—they co-operate and collaborate more (e.g., Hartup et al., 1993; Zajac & Hartup, 1997). During the same period, Azmitia and Montgomery (1993) reported that friends learn more, especially when they give differing points of view and try to find the best solution or combine elements of more than one perspective, as long as they remain task-focused. We have heard adolescents working co-operatively say, "Once you've worked in a group, you would never want to just learn alone" (Hutchinson, Freeman, & Quick, 1996). Children's collaboratively written stories are more advanced than individually written stories (Vass, 2002). Furthermore, the benefits of collaborative writing carry over into individual stories (Daiute & Dalton, 1992). When friends (compared with acquaintances) collaborated on writing stories, the dialogue was richer, more detailed, more task-oriented, and the students considered more possibilities for content and vocabulary. However, the immediately resulting stories were not of higher quality (Hartup, Daiute, Zajac, & Sholl, 1995). These findings suggest that children and adolescents benefit from learning co-operatively and that they may benefit even more from learning co-operatively with friends.

Recently, researchers have found that while friendship pairings are generally more successful than acquaintanceship pairings in promoting learning together on creative tasks (MacDonald, Miell, & Mitchell, 2002; Miell and MacDonald, 2000), the issue may be more complex than previously thought. In a large, well-designed study, Kutnick and Kington (2005) reported that girls' friendship pairings performed at the highest levels while boys' friendship pairings performed at the lowest levels. The students were working on science reasoning tasks. Acquaintanceship pairings performed at mid-levels. This finding was consistent across grades 1, 3, and 5 and across three levels of ability (high, medium, and low). Perhaps the friendship pairings of boys did not remain on task, which we know is essential when students are learning together.

Exceptional children who have not learned to socialize, who are not socially accepted in the classroom, or who do not have friends may be disadvantaged cognitively. Why might co-operation between friends be especially well-suited to cognitive development? Think of exceptional students like Matt, who described himself as friendless, or Val, in the opening case study, who did not have anyone to play with at recess. These individuals have few opportunities to improve their interaction skills and become better at learning with their peers.

Children and adolescents who express themselves with individual words or nods rather than rich dialogue—in which children give explanations, consider each other's solutions, and arrive at better outcomes than either could achieve alone—are likely to be disadvantaged in cognitive development and learning. Friends usually show mutual understanding of one another's needs and capacities, and this probably helps them provide responses that are within each other's zone of proximal development, even if each is different in level of development (Berscheid, 1985; Steiner Bell, 2005). The reciprocity or "give and take" that characterizes friendships usually involves sharing and self-disclosure. This may foster open dialogue, willingness to exchange ideas, and constructive feedback. Companions who trust one another are freer to disagree, more readily believe the information they receive, and are more effective at communicating with one another (Azmitia et al., 2005). These characteristics have been observed in friendships of both adolescents and children. All these characteristics are likely to contribute to the social interaction required for cognitive development. Thus, friendships appear to contribute to the social and cognitive development of students.

**Cross-Reference**
Chapter 2 includes a section on paraeducators and their roles in educating students with disabilities in inclusive classrooms. You may remember that the issue was raised of paraeducators sometimes coming between children with disabilities and their classmates. How might that situation contribute to the level of social competence and social acceptance of exceptional students? What can you do as a classroom teacher to ensure that exceptional students benefit from the actions of paraeducators and are not socially disadvantaged?

# Elementary and Secondary Schools as Social Environments

Schools are highly social environments in which students spend the day working and playing with their classmates. Classic studies (e.g., Bryan, 1991; Vaughn, 1991) and recent research (e.g., Northfield & Sherman, 2003; Hutchinson et al., 2004) suggest that it is important to enhance both the social competence of youth with exceptionalities and their social acceptance by peers because neither alone is sufficient.

Social competence and social acceptance require a context where co-operation, community, and peer support thrive. This means that teachers must engage in informal teaching of social competence and acceptance of diversity with the entire class. Such informal teaching takes place in the way you conduct your classroom, express your expectations, and model social acceptance.

## Informal Teaching: Climate and Role Models

Teachers create positive and inclusive climates in their classrooms by showing respect for all members of the class and making all students feel that their presence counts. They interact with all students in ways that communicate caring and acceptance. McIntosh and Vaughn (1993) suggest, specifically, avoiding teasing and sarcasm. Teachers communicate high expectations—that they expect all students to be successful—and provide a high degree of adaptations and support to enable students to reach those high expectations (Urdan & Schoenfelder, 2006). Students learn their manner of treating their fellow students from you. This means that you must provide good models and demand that students behave similarly. When there are difficulties, you can respond by "seizing the moment" and negotiating with the group. When you make your thinking apparent to students, you provide a model of deciding, acting, and explaining that promotes both social competence and social acceptance, without patronizing (Northfield & Sherman, 2004). Recent studies suggest that classrooms that are organized by the teacher as inclusive, caring, pro-social learning communities are more likely to be safe for all students and to enhance the competence of all students—those with and without disabilities (Cefai, 2007; Schmidt & Cagran, 2006).

## Facilitating Friendships

You may feel that it is beyond your responsibilities as a teacher to facilitate friendships among your students. However, facilitating friendships may make the classroom a better place for everyone, including you.

During the early years at school, some children may lack the social skills expected by their classmates. Children who are aggressive or awkward may be ignored by others. A structured and supervised social program can help children practise relationships. In middle childhood, children choose friends on the basis of personality and interests and friendships become increasingly stable. Boys may form gangs, while girls tend to form small intimate groups. Some children can be excluded during the unstructured times of the day, and it helps to provide activities for these students so they can do things with one another. During preadolescence, helping and confiding replace playing and many students need assistance with conversational skills. Using co-operative and collaborative activities throughout these elementary and middle school years gives you an opportunity to teach social skills as part of curriculum activities (Dion, Fuchs, & Fuchs, 2005; Kutnick, Ota, & Berdondini, 2008). For adolescents, friendships are about trust, intimacy, and the sharing of deeply personal thoughts. These close friendships are complemented by membership in larger groups identified by taste in music, clothing styles, and slang expressions.

Research has been conducted and programs have been developed to enhance the friendship and conversational skills of students with many of the exceptionalities described in Chapters 3 and 4. Examples include:

- children with attention deficit hyperactivity disorders (DuPaul & Weyandt, 2006);

Cross-Reference
Chapter 6 contains considerable information on informal teaching of social expectations and social acceptance; it also provides many strategies for creating an inclusive classroom that is a community.

- children and adolescents with autism (Palmen, Didden, & Arts, 2008; Stichter et al., 2007);
- children with Asperger syndrome (Crooke, Hendrix, & Rachman, 2008);
- youth with Williams syndrome (Klein-Tasman, & Albano, 2007);
- children with physical disabilities (Bennett & Hay, 2007; Clarke & Wilkinson, 2008);
- young children with a range of disabilities (Terpstra & Tamura, 2008).

Intensive programs focusing on kids such as those listed above may require the participation of a resource teacher, occupational therapist, or social worker, but many teaching strategies serve as friendship interventions. Provide activities, especially early in the year, to ensure that all students know each other's names. These can involve games, memory challenges, name tags, and name signs on desks. Use literature with friendship themes and integrate friendship into the curriculum whenever possible. This can range from discussions of alliances in history to discussing ways to express emotions. Use modelling, guided practice, and independent practice to teach social skills so students can conduct themselves appropriately in your classroom, in assembly, or on a field trip. Encourage pairs of students who you think might form friendships to learn together. Be vigilant and when you see friendships developing and appropriate social behaviour occurring, provide acknowledgment and support.

For students who have behaviour problems or are lonely, set friendship goals. With young children, meet individually and ask who the student would like to get to know. Goals might include learning the other child's name, sharing a toy or game, or working together at an activity centre. With older students, you may be able to set goals for participation in an extracurricular activity or group. Teach students to handle rejection by considering what they should say if the peer they approach turns them down. Structure social times like recess and lunch periods by forming groups that include isolated students, creating peer buddy programs, or asking socially able students to include a shy child in their conversation. Provide assignments that require pairs of students to visit the community library or another location together as well as work together in class. Use activities with a friend as a reinforcer. Ensure that adult presence does not interfere in fledgling conversations or friendships. Help parents be aware of opportunities for their child to interact with children outside school. To get ideas for friendship interventions, read Searcy (1996) and Turnbull, Pereira, and Blue-Banning (2000). See the boxed feature Theory and Research Highlights from Educational Psychology: The Construct of Friendship.

## Schoolwide Approaches and Teachers' Roles

In Chapter 6 we focused on ways in which you can create a classroom community and a positive climate for learning with your students. The social climate of the school contributes to the social climate of your classroom. Important aspects of the social environment in a school can be influenced by **schoolwide approaches**. For example, your school may have adopted a code of conduct that is to be applied in every part of the school. The most effective violence-reduction programs involve students in many ways (Sugai, Horner, & Gresham, 2002). Some schools adopt schoolwide anti-bullying programs that guide teachers, foster consistency, and ensure a high rate of teacher and peer response to bullying incidents. Research

**Further Reading**

Barrett, W., & Randall, L. (2004). Investigating the circle of friends approach: Adaptations and implications for practice. *Educational Psychology in Practice, 20,* 353–368.

DeRosier, M.E. (2002). *Group interventions and exercises for enhancing children's communication, cooperation, and confidence.* Sarasota, FL: Professional Resources Press.

DeRosier, M.E., & Marcus, S.R. (2005). Building friendships and combating bullying: Effectiveness of the S.S.GRIN at one-year follow-up. *Journal of Clinical Child and Adolescent Psychology, 34,* 140–150.

Laugeson, E.A., Paley, B., Schonfeld, A.M., Carpenter, E.M., Frankl, F., & O'Connoe, M.J. (2007). Adaptation of the Children's Friendship Training Program for children with fetal alcohol spectrum disorders. *Child and Family Behavior Therapy, 29*(3), 57–69.

**Weblinks**
About adolescents and peer relations:

FOCUS ADOLESCENT SERVICES
http://focusas.com/PeerInfluence.html

FRIENDSHIPS—HELPING YOUR CHILD THROUGH EARLY ADOLESCENCE (US DEPARTMENT OF EDUCATION)
www.ed.gov/parents/academic/help/adolescence/part9.html

## The Construct of Friendship

Much has been written about the nature of friendship by philosophers, psychologists, and educators. While it has been called "the most human relationship," there have been calls recently for friendship research to return to its conceptual roots and focus on clarifying the construct and on revealing the dynamics of friendship, positive and negative (Bukowski & Sippola, 2005). Many researchers have suggested that friendship has both a deep structure and a surface structure (Hartup & Stevens, 1997). By deep structure, they mean friendship's essence or meaning—mutuality and reciprocity. The need for enjoyable companionship is filled by friendship; these are the rewarding and pleasurable aspects of friendship. Surface structure refers to the social exchanges within the reciprocal, companionable relationship, but when these exchanges are fraught with difficulty, friendship can create our greatest problems and anxieties (Bukowski, Adams, & Santo, 2006).

Some writers in special education have observed that friendship seems to be harder for exceptional adolescents than for children or adults (Steiner-Bell, 2004). What might make friendship particularly elusive for exceptional adolescents? According to developmental theorists, at every age there are preoccupying concerns to which people must attend. In early childhood, friendships meet the need for equality-based exchange relationships (Brett & Willard, 2002), and adolescence is characterized by concerns with self-clarification, self-validation, and obtaining assistance to cope (Buhrmester & Prager, 1995). These concerns shape the surface structure of friendship and its social exchanges; for example, young children play beside or with one another, often more focused on the play than on themselves. Adolescents "hang out," self-disclose, engage in supportive problem solving, and seek self-defining activities with friends (Buhrmester, 1998). Buhrmester argues that four interpersonal competencies follow from these developmental concerns that are essential for dyadic friendships during the adolescent years:

a) initiating and sustaining conversation;
b) making plans to spend time together;
c) self-disclosing personal thoughts and providing emotional support; and
d) working through conflicts.

Friends are most often of a similar age and preoccupied with similar developmental issues. Friendships provide unique opportunities to wrestle with issues of most concern to both individuals. This may not be the case when exceptional adolescents are cognitively or socially less mature, or more mature, than their non-disabled peers—they may have few common pressing issues. That friends wrestle with common issues suggests that adolescents need at least one supportive peer (who is accepting, understanding, and dependable) to help deal with preoccupying concerns.

Buhrmester (1990) found that for adolescents from 13 to 16 years of age there were strong relations between their reports of close relationships with friends, their interpersonal competence, and their self-reported social adjustment. This is one of many studies of adolescents in the general population that shows that having quality friendships is central to developing social competence.

There appear to be different "cultures" or contexts for male and female relations during adolescence (Tannen, 1990). Interactions between female adolescents focus on building interpersonal connections. This means that adolescent females report more frequent interactions of an intimate and supportive nature with female friends than do males with male friends (Maccoby, 1990). However, recent research shows that females are also more likely to engage in co-rumination, repeatedly focusing on problems and dwelling on negative affect, and this disclosure process has been related to depression in adolescent females (Rose, 2002; Rose, Schwartz, & Carlson, 2005). This suggests that not all close adolescent-female friendships have positive effects.

Interactions between adolescent males focus more on agentic concerns and less on communal ones. They have been described as "side-by-side" interactions because they focus on doing things together, mainly sports and competitive games (Wright, 1982). Their supportive discussions often focus on the accomplishments of sports teams and individuals. Such interactions may meet needs for achievement, recognition, and power. Recent studies show that close male-adolescent friendships can also produce negative effects. Dishion and his colleagues have found that at-risk boys reinforce the deviant behaviours of friends, a process that has been called deviancy training (Dishion, McCord, & Poulin, 1999). The more friends laugh at deviant behaviour, the more it increases over time (Dishion, Nelson, Winter, & Bullock, 2004). In the case of both co-rumination and deviancy training, the interactions between adolescents are friendly and intimate to the outside observer; only an examination of the content of the exchanges and attention to the follow-up shows the dark side of such adolescent friendships.

When we think about how we can structure classrooms, social organizations, and family events to facilitate healthy friendships

*continued*

for children, and especially for adolescents, with exceptionalities, it may be important to consider what developmental needs friendship may address for all the individuals involved and to think about how socializing contexts may differ for adolescents according to gender. In an ethnographic study of three young people with developmental syndromes, Karin Steiner-Bell of Queen's University (2004) described an adolescent boy with Down syndrome whose friendships were based on sports with other males of a similar age with similar disabilities. His family had involved him in school activities, sports teams, and the Special Olympics. He could initiate and sustain conversations and resolve conflicts with same-age peers and with adults in his neighbourhood.

An adolescent male with Asperger syndrome had few adolescent friends and considered his father to be his best friend. He also played computer simulation games with his sisters. His family lived in a remote location and he rarely participated in community activities. He was not strong on any of Buhrmester's four competencies, but he had particular difficulty recognizing and communicating feelings. A young adult woman with Williams syndrome had friends with disabilities and friends without disabilities as well as a boyfriend within the disabled community. She reported finding friendships easier during her adult years—when she was able to meet people outside school who shared her interests in music, art, and book clubs. She showed greater strengths in all four of Buhrmester's competencies than the two adolescent boys.

Case studies like those developed by Steiner-Bell may help us to combine what we know about disabilities with recent work on the psychological construct of friendship to enhance the social relations of exceptional adolescents. We may also learn from the ongoing research program of Barry Schneider of the University of Ottawa, who has begun to focus on interethnic friendships, an important issue in diverse Canadian classrooms (Schneider et al., 2007), and on the role of friendships in transitions (Giovanna, Schneider et al., 2005). He has also systematically reported on the difficulties experienced by exceptional adolescents, for example, those with learning disabilities (Wiener & Schneider, 2002) and those who experience high anxiety (Schneider & Tessier, 2007). While friendship can effect healthy development, it can also contribute to psychopathology (Bukowski et al., 2006), and we must recognize the potential for these darker aspects of friendship in friendship research with exceptional populations (Hartup, 2006).

## References

Brett, B., & Willard, W.W. (2002). The origins of reciprocity and social exchange in friendships. *New Directions for Child and Adolescent Development, 95*, 27–40.

Buhrmester, D. (1990). Intimacy of friendship, interpersonal competence, and adjustment during preadolescence and adolescence. *Child Development, 61*, 1101–1111.

Buhrmester, D. (1998). Need fulfilment, interpersonal competence, and the developmental contexts of early adolescent friendship. In W.M. Bukowski, A.F. Newcomb, & W.W. Hartup (Eds.), *The company they keep: Friendship in childhood and adolescence*, 2nd ed., (pp. 158–185). New York: Cambridge University Press.

Buhrmester, D., & Prager, K. (1995). Patterns and functions of self-disclosure during childhood and adolescence. In K.J. Rotenberg (Ed.), *Disclosure processes in children and adolescents,* (pp. 10–46). New York: Cambridge University Press.

Bukowski, W.M., Adams, R.E., & Santo, J.B. (2006). Recent advances in the study of development, social and personal experience, and psychopathology. *International Journal of Behavioral Development, 30*, 26–30.

Bukowski, W.M., & Sippola, L.K. (2005). Friendship and development: Putting the most human relationship in its place. *New Directions for Child and Adolescent Development, 109*, 91–97.

Dishion, T.J., McCord, J., & Poulin, F. (1999). When interventions harm: Peer groups and problem behavior. *American Psychologist, 54*, 755–764.

Dishion, T.J., Nelson, S.E., & Bullock, B. (2004). Premature adolescent autonomy: Parent disengagement and deviant process in the amplification of problem behavior. *Journal of Adolescence, 27*, 515–530.

Giovanna, T., Schneider, B.H., de Domini, P., Greenman, P.S., & Fonzi, A. (2005). Friendship as a predictor of adjustment following a transition to formal academic instruction and evaluation. *International Journal of Behavioral Development, 29*, 314–322.

Hartup, W.W. (2006). Relationships in early and middle childhood. In A.L. Vangelisti & D. Perlman (Eds.), *The Cambridge handbook of personal relationships* (pp. 177–190). New York: Cambridge University Press.

Hartup, W.W., & Stevens, N. (1997). Friendship and adaptation in the life course. *Psychological Bulletin, 121*, 355–370.

Maccoby, E.E. (1990). Gender and relationships: A developmental account. *American Psychologist, 45*, 513–520.

Rose, A.J. (2002). Co-rumination in the friendships of girls and boys. *Child Development, 73*, 1830–1843.

Rose, A.J., Schwrtz, R.A., & Carlson, W. (2005). *An observational assessment of co-rumination in the friendships of girls and boys*. A paper presented at the Society for Research in Child Development, Atlanta, GA.

Schneider, B.H., Dixon, K., & Udvari, S. (2007). Closeness and competition in the inter-ethnic and co-ethnic friendships of early adolescents in Toronto and Montreal. *Journal of Early Adolescence, 27*, 115–138.

Schneider, B.H., & Tessier, N.G. (2007). Close friendships as understood by socially withdrawn, anxious adolescents. *Child Psychiatry and Human Development, 38*, 339–351.

Steiner-Bell, K. (2004). *Social understanding in the friendships of persons with a developmental syndrome*. Unpublished doctoral thesis, Queen's University, Kingston, Ontario.

Tannen, D. (1990). Gender differences in topical coherence: Creating involvement in best friends' talk. *Discourse Processes, 13*, 73–90.

Wiener, J., & Schneider, B.H. (2002). A multisource exploration of the friendship patterns of children with and without learning disabilities. *Journal of Abnormal Child Psychology, 30*, 127–141.

Wright, P.H. (1982). Men's friendships, women's friendships and the alleged inferiority of the latter. *Sex Roles, 8*, 1–20.

**Weblinks**

Many schools have websites. Visit the websites of Birchwood Intermediate School in PEI and LaSalle Community Comprehensive High School in Quebec. Look at their codes of conduct. Then search for three other schools whose websites include codes of conduct. Think about how these codes of conduct compare to what should appear in such a code. Discuss with your peers.

BIRCHWOOD INTERMEDIATE SCHOOL IN PEI
www.edu.pe.ca/birchwood/code.htm

LASALLE COMMUNITY COMPREHENSIVE HIGH SCHOOL IN QUEBEC
http://lcchs.lbpsb.qc.ca/conduct.htm

**Put into Practice**

Develop a code of conduct for your classroom. Make three lesson plans for introducing the code and two for reviewing it with your class.

suggests this is necessary to make a school safe for all, including the most vulnerable students. If you look at the website for LaSalle Community Comprehensive High School (in Weblinks), you will see that the schoolwide code of conduct extends to how students communicate online and to cyberbullying.

## CODE OF CONDUCT

Many provinces have developed codes of conduct or adopted policies requiring codes of conduct. For example, Ontario has revised its expectations in a set of provincial standards of behaviour and mandatory consequences for student actions that do not comply (www.edu.gov.on.ca/eng/policyfunding/schooladmin.html). It also sets standards for parents, teachers, and other staff members. Nova Scotia Education (2001b) also sets out standards of behaviour in the *School Code of Conduct*. British Columbia provides a resource called *The Building Blocks of Safe, Caring and Orderly Schools* (www.bced.gov.bc.ca/sco/guide/scoguide_app_a.pdf). A **code of conduct** clearly identifies school rules and acceptable student behaviours. The best ones are short and easy to understand, with clearly stated consequences for actions. Many schools involve students and the community in designing and committing to the code (Denton, 2003; Hendrickson et al., 1995). The code should include only rules that will be enforced. Research on school violence emphasizes the need for enforcing the code consistently (Bullock & Gable, 1995; Fenning et al., 2004). It is not only a set of rules for students to follow; it also informs teachers, parents, and others what kind of behaviour is expected of students at a particular school. As we become an increasingly "wired" society, students can exploit technology to deliberately antagonize and intimidate those they see as vulnerable. Those targeted include students who are overweight or small in size, have shown themselves to be sensitive, or have learning disabilities (Willard, 2007). Thus codes of conduct should increasingly be designed to prevent cyberbullying in addition to maintaining school safety in other ways. A copy of the code of conduct should be sent to parents at the start of every school year and distributed to students and staff. Birchwood Intermediate School in Prince Edward Island has its code of conduct on its website (www.edu.pe.ca/birchwood/code.htm). The code consists of five items, the first being, "I will respect myself, and other people's rights, personal space and feelings." The code of conduct for LaSalle Community Comprehensive High School has seven sections covering respect for self, others, property, and safety, as well as punctuality, regular attendance, and preparation for class. It includes the rationale for each item and the possible consequences of noncompliance. Figure 9.3 describes the characteristics usually associated with an effective code of conduct. Recently, researchers have suggested that schools integrate proactive discipline practices into codes of conduct (e.g., Fenning et al., 2004). Fenning and her colleagues argue that the essential components of a proactive discipline code include recognition of the academic needs of many students who violate behaviour codes and of the need to teach the expected behaviours explicitly each school year. They also recommend a description of the positive reward system for expected behaviours in addition to the usual statement of behavioural expectations and, finally, acknowledgment of the roles of key stakeholders.

To make the code of conduct meaningful, you should discuss it with your students, make sure everyone understands its purpose and expectations, and seek agreement from students to follow it. You may appreciate the presence of the principal

## FIGURE 9.3 CHARACTERISTICS OF AN EFFECTIVE CODE OF CONDUCT

A code of conduct should

1.  explain the rules of student behaviour
2.  clearly define roles, rights, and responsibilities of persons involved in the school setting, including teachers, administrators, and support staff, as well as parents and police
3.  describe consequences for misbehaviour
4.  say that striking another person may be considered a criminal act and dealt with as such (especially in secondary school)
5.  say that every student has a right to be safe and secure from threats and harassment, including cyberbullying and cyberthreats
6.  include a policy against crimes of property, racism, sexual harassment, and sexual assault
7.  include proactive discipline practices

or vice-principal in your classroom for at least part of this discussion. For teachers to follow through consistently, there must be a shared understanding. This requires discussion by the staff, agreement on what actions will be taken following common incidents, and agreement on emergency responses to violence and aggression (Mendel, Watson, & MacGregor, 2002; Reinke, Herman, & Tucker, 2006).

While a code of conduct should involve the entire school community, it is only one strategy to improve the social environment of a school. Recent writings in education suggest that principals (and even teachers) must lead by example, ensuring that their actions serve as positive models for students in how we treat one another. Quick and Normore (2004) argue that leadership in any endeavour is a moral task but even more so for educational leaders because "everyone is watching, especially the students" (p. 336). To engage in **moral leadership**, educational leaders must focus their attention on activities that enhance the sense of community within the school, and create rituals and traditions that symbolically represent the values and culture of the school community. This requires educational leaders who are aware of their own values and can translate these into action because integrity demands that we stand for something and exemplify this commitment in our behaviour (Evans, 1996).

There is wide agreement that school codes of conduct should include references to bullying and cyberbullying (see Willard, 2007). However, even in England, where schools are required to have an anti-bullying policy, a recent study suggests that the policies are incomplete and there is little difference between policies from elementary and secondary schools (Smith, Smith, Osborn, & Samara, 2008). Educational leaders and educators who embody moral leadership will develop policies and, importantly, demonstrate behaviour that is free from bullying themselves and intervene if they observe or receive reports of bullying by anyone, anywhere in the school.

## Schoolwide Behaviour Management Systems

Schoolwide behaviour management systems are comprehensive approaches to managing behaviour throughout a school (Colvin, 2007; Nelson, Martella, & Marchand-Martella, 2002). They are process-based models in which collaborative

What do you think?

While many researchers have advocated involving students in all aspects of generating a code of conduct to achieve a safer and more positive school climate, others have argued that codes of conduct marginalize those who do not conform easily and are intended to produce docile citizens and workers. Read the following papers by Paula Denton of the University of Massachusetts and Rebecca Raby of Brock University to decide what you think.

Denton, P. (2003). Shared rule-making in practice: The Jefferson committee at Kingston High School. *American Secondary Education,* 31(3), 66–96.

Raby, R. (2005). Polite, well-dressed and on time: Secondary school conduct codes and the production of docile citizens. *Canadian Review of Sociology and Anthropology,* 42, 71–91.

### Further Reading

Daunic, A. P., et al. (2000). School-wide conflict resolution and peer mediation programs. *Intervention in School and Clinic, 36*(2), 94–100.

Colvin, G. (2007). *Seven steps for developing a proactive schoolwide discipline plan: A guide for principals and leadership teams.* Thousand Oaks, CA: Corwin Press.

### Cross-Reference

Chapter 5 includes a framework for analyzing equity incidents in the classroom that could be used to decide how to intervene to prevent future incidents of bullying and cyberbullying. Chapter 6 focuses on what you can do to create and maintain a positive climate in your classroom. Reviewing Chapter 6 while you are reading Chapter 9 may help you to develop strategies for your class and to work with your colleagues for a schoolwide approach.

teams of teachers, administrators, parents, and students work together to obtain consensus. Rosenberg and Jackman (2003) describe the PAR model:

- **P**revent troubling behaviour;
- **A**ct, or respond, to rule compliance and non-compliance consistently; and
- **R**esolve the issues that underlie troubling behaviour.

The model includes systematic, collaborative work to arrive at a coherent framework which includes a mission statement, a code of conduct or set of rules and expectations, consequences for compliance and non-compliance, crisis management, strategies for resolution (e.g., social skills instruction, peer mediation, etc.), as well as ongoing parent and family involvement and effective instruction and accommodations. Rosenberg and Jackman illustrate how to develop, implement, and evaluate a PAR action plan. Recently a number of descriptive studies have reported on the successful implementation of **schoolwide positive behaviour support (SWPBS)** (Sugai & Horner, 2002) in a wide array of diverse schools, including urban middle schools (Warren et al., 2006), urban elementary schools, and alternative schools (George et al., 2007). SWPBS is a prevention-oriented approach that defines and teaches behaviour expectations, rewards appropriate behaviour, and integrates support for individuals, groups, and the whole school.

### PREVENTING BULLYING

Research suggests that students who are harassed and bullied are more likely to exhibit aggression and anti-social behaviour that might interfere with their participation in social learning activities with peers (Rusby et al., 2005). A recent Canadian study, which used data from the Canadian National Longitudinal Survey of Children and Youth, found that students who reported being bullied at school were more likely to obtain low levels of achievement (Beran, Hughes, & Lupart, 2008). Studies like these contribute to educators' concerns that, for all students, including exceptional students, there are close ties among social acceptance, social development, and learning. Thus, for more than a decade the provinces have been developing and promoting policies like *Keeping Our Schools Safe* (New Brunswick, www.gnb.ca/0000/publications/ss/keepschoolsafe.pdf), *Violence-Free Schools* (Ontario, 1994), and *Anti-Bullying Strategy* (Saskatchewan, 2005b). Manitoba has created checklists that can be used to help students identify concerns about bullying and harassment (e.g., www.edu.gov.mb.ca/k12/specedu/guidance/pdf/Secondary_Student_Checklist.pdf).

Schoolwide programs are thought to be the most effective response to bullying because it is a problem that occurs in the school's social environment as a whole. "**Bullying** is a form of abuse at the hands of peers that can take different forms at different ages" (Craig, Pepler, & Blais, 2007, p. 465). These forms include physical, emotional, verbal, and cyberbullying. "**Cyberbullying** is a form of psychological cruelty perpetrated virtually, and refers to threats, insults, and demeaning messages spread through the internet or by cell phone. Sometimes it takes the form of exclusion when students create a list of users whose messages are blocked from entering their IM (instant messaging) program or from joining online chat rooms. Particularly devastating are chat rooms or "bash boards" that have been set up to receive mean-spirited postings about a classmate (Beale & Hall, 2007). While cyberthreats and cyberbullying usually take place away from school grounds, they have repercussions for our schools and students, and we cannot ignore their

# Anti-Bullying and Anti-Violence Programs

There are many websites available to help you and your school tackle bullying on a schoolwide basis. Most of these Canadian sites also provide links to other international sites.

**London (Ontario) Family Court Clinic:**

www.lfcc.on.ca/bully.htm

This site contains extensive information about bullying for parents and teachers. The highly readable information is an excerpt from the second edition of *A.S.A.P.: A School-based Anti-violence Program* that is available from the London Family Court Clinic. It consists of a video and sixty-five lessons.

**Bully Beware Programs (British Columbia):**

www.bullybeware.com

This site contains information about a video (*Bully Beware*), books (*Take Action Against Bullying* and *How Parents Can Take Action Against Bullying*), and posters that can be used around the school to support the anti-bullying program. There are also tips and news articles from Canadian newspapers and magazines about bullying incidents in our schools and communities.

**Bullying.org (children at Banded Peak School in Bragg Creek, Alberta, and their teacher, William Belsey):**

www.bullying.org

This site was started after the shooting at W.R. Myers High School in Taber, Alberta, when stories emerged that the accused had been bullied. A group of grade 1 to 8 students who met to provide peer support grew into www.bullying.org, which attempts to help young people help each other.

Not only can you and your students learn by visiting this site, but you might be inspired to commit to an online project that would ensure that your students internalize and live the lessons you are learning together.

**Stop Cyberbullying:**

www.cyberbullying.ca

This site was started by the developers of www.bullying.org, Bill Belsey and his students. It contains practical suggestions about combatting cyberbullying, including lobbying the telecommunications industry about the problem.

**PREVnet:**

www.prevnet.ca

This combined research and practice website focuses on promoting relationships and eliminating violence. Based at Queen's University and York University, it involves many of the leading researchers in Canada in the field of bullying and a wide range of organizations and agencies.

**School-Based Violence Prevention Programs:**

www.ucalgary.ca/resolve/violenceprevention/English/index.htm

On this site you can find a resource manual with reviews of a large number of anti-violence and anti-bullying programs, including an analysis of the data on their effectiveness.

**Olweus Bullying Prevention Program:**

www.clemson.edu/olweus

This is the North American website for the most researched anti-bullying program, developed by Dan Olweus of Norway.

potential for destroying students' safety and well-being twenty-four hours a day, in school and out of school (Mason, 2008; Willard, 2007). Bullying begins in elementary school, increases during the middle school years, and usually decreases in secondary school (Beale & Hall, 2007).

Children and adolescents who lack social skills and do not pick up on social cues are among those likely to be victims of any form of bullying. As you know, exceptional students often lack social skills and miss social cues. Two Canadian studies show that children and youth with exceptionalities are at increased risk of being marginalized and are more vulnerable to victimization by peers who have higher status and more social power (Cummings, Pepler, Mishna, & Craig, 2006; Luciano & Savage, 2007). And a recent interview study suggests that, while Canadian teachers recognize and respond to physical bullying, they find it much more difficult to recognize and intervene in cases of indirect bullying (Mishna et al., 2005). Beran (2006) reported, in another Canadian study, that students' and teachers' reports of what constitutes bullying are not highly correlated. These studies remind us how challenging dealing with bullying can be for educators. Your efforts to prevent students in your class from bullying or being bullied will likely be much more effective if your school has a schoolwide anti-bullying program.

All students need to understand that bullying is unacceptable. This means that every class in the school takes part in a consistent program that emphasizes that bullying and cyberbullying and students who bully will be dealt with. All teachers and students need to be alert to recognize bullying. The characteristics of verbal, emotional, and physical bullying as well as cyberbullying should be portrayed around the school, in assemblies, and in classrooms in language that all students can understand. Everyone, adults and children, must have strategies for responding. This means teaching all students, including those exceptional students who use alternative forms of communication, to report incidents that occur to them or others. Protecting children who report bullying will be necessary because children and adolescents must believe there will be no retaliation for reporting. Consistency is necessary, which is why it is preferable for a school to adopt a program and use it widely, making adaptations so presentations and activities are appropriate for various age and ability levels.

Olweus (2003) has conducted extensive research on bullying. His findings show that to minimize bullying, school environments must be characterized by

- warmth, positive interest, and involvement from adults;
- firm limits on unacceptable behaviour;
- consistent application of non-punitive, non-physical sanctions for unacceptable behaviour or violations of rules; and
- adults who act as authorities and positive role models.

Information about the Olweus Bullying Prevention Program is available at www.clemson.edu/olweus. This well-researched program brings together school-level components that include schoolwide rules against bullying, classroom-level components like regular class meetings to reinforce the schoolwide rules, and individual-level components such as interventions with those who are bullied, those who bully, and parents. The program consists of teacher guides, booklets, and videos.

Wendy Craig of Queen's University and Debra Pepler of York University lead the Canadian Initiative for the Prevention of Bullying (http://prevnet.ca). The network has many partners and is known as PREVnet. PREVnet offers toolkits for education, assessment, and intervention. This group of researchers takes the view that bullying is closely related to development and that bullying is about children's and adolescents' relationships. Their recent longitudinal research has found that many of the 10 percent of youths who persistently bully through adolescence have troubled relationships with their parents and friends, and consistently use power and aggression to control and distress others (Pepler & Craig, 2008). Based on their research, they suggest that intervention strategies need to involve the wider community, including parents and other adults, and must help children and adolescents to intervene effectively. They recognize that bullies as well as victims require support and that relationship problems require relationship solutions. PREVnet's website includes tip sheets that parents, teachers, and students can download. To respond effectively to bullying, children must be confident that they have the backing of adults. Canadian research by Debra Peplar of York University (www.arts.yorku.ca/lamarsh) suggests that teachers respond only about 10 percent

## FIGURE 9.4 HELPING STUDENTS RESPOND TO BULLYING

- Help students to recognize when they should seek adult intervention.
- Encourage children and adolescents to come forward and report bullying and cyberbullying early, before the emotional effects become too great. Remind them that by seeking adult help they will help to create an atmosphere where people can feel safe instead of feeling frightened and insecure because they might be bullied.
- Be aware of the signs of bullying and support children and adolescents who experience bullying. Avoidance, including avoiding school, may be a sign that a child is being bullied. Watch for students who experience stomach aches, headaches, and depressive symptoms or who are victims of exclusion, including virtual exclusion.
- Monitor exchanges between more powerful and less powerful students closely. If you don't expect to see a particular pair of students interacting, then ensure that you are aware of the nature of their interactions. Remember that bullying can be physical, verbal, emotional, or virtual. Be vigilant because the longer bullying goes on, the harder it will be to put an end to it.
- Watch for signs of responses to bullying. Girls are more likely to use relationship skills to try to deal with bullying, while boys are more likely to resort to violence or retaliation.
- Provide children and youth who are bullied with effective strategies. Help them to recognize healthy and unhealthy relationships (even friends can engage in bullying). And encourage students to report bullying immediately.
- Help those who are bullied to walk away and try not to show the bully that he or she has succeeded in creating upset or anger. Help students to practise their replies to things that they may be teased or bullied about (unusual name, glasses, hearing aid, etc.) so they can give the impression it doesn't bother them. And encourage students to report bullying immediately.
- Create a positive social climate in which all are valued, teach students your expectations, enforce your expectations for healthy relationships between classmates, help students to develop healthy peer relationships, and respond to bullying and cyberbullying consistently and in accord with the protocol about which students have been informed.

———

Developed after reading: Stones, R. (2005). *Don't pick on me: How to handle bullying* (3rd ed.). Markham, ON: Pembroke Publishers; Craig, W., Pepler, D., & Blais, J. (2007) Responding to bullying: What works? *School Psychology International, 28*, 465–477; Beale, A.V., & Hall, K.R. (2007). Cyberbullying: What school administrators (and parents) can do. *Clearing House, 81*(1), 8–12.

of the time. In addition to consistent teacher response, children need to role-play and practise proactive and prosocial responses to bullying. Figure 9.4 provides teachers with strategies for helping students to respond to bullying. You can use resources like this one (developed after reading Stones, 2005; Craig, Pepler, & Blais, 2007; and Beale & Hall, 2007) to devise student activities for practice. You may also have to coach your students to include all classmates in their activities, and to support victims, report incidents, and take part in role-playing to practise leadership and citizenship (Olweus, 2003). Figure 9.5 introduces a strategy called ABC—TELL NOW, which you can use to help children, and students of all ages with intellectual disabilities, to learn how to report incidents of cyberbullying.

Strong programs to improve the school environment also involve individualized interventions with violent, bullying, and at-risk students (Olweus, 2003). If children in your class are identified as bullies, you may be asked to take part in interventions with a counsellor or resource teacher. This will help you to be consistent with these specialists in your preventive and responsive dealings with bullies. Strong intervention programs involve teachers in ongoing co-operative learning activities that reduce social isolation. They increase adult supervision at key times

### Further Reading

Two recently published papers focus on two different approaches to helping children cope with harassment and bullying. Newman develops a framework for understanding effective and ineffective help seeking by children. Merrell and colleagues review the research on effectiveness of school bullying intervention programs.

Merrell, K.W., Gueldner, B.A., Ross, S.W., & Isava, D.M. (2008). How effective are school bullying intervention programs? A meta-analysis of intervention research. *School Psychology Quarterly, 23(1)*, 26–42.

Newman, R.S. (2008). Adaptive and nonadaptive help seeking with peer harassment: An integrative perspective of coping and self-regulation. *Educational Psychologist, 43*, 1–15.

## FIGURE 9.5 TEACHING STUDENTS A STRATEGY FOR REPORTING CYBERBULLYING

Cyberbullying is an increasing problem in schools in North America and around the world. The first advice usually given to teachers, parents, and other responsible administrators is that students must be encouraged and supported to report any form of bullying, including cyberbullying.

Even children and adolescents who know how to report are reluctant to do so for fear of retaliation. We can respond to those fears by acting on student reports decisively and fairly, speaking individually with the victim immediately and providing emotional support. Then we must move to have the bully receive the appropriate response according to the school's code of conduct. It is more effective to deal with bullies individually, even if a number of them are involved in an incident, because they may find strength in numbers. It is also important to ensure that other students who may have been bystanders see you support the bullied student and deal with the bully.

This strategy, ABC—TELL NOW, is a strategy for teaching students who don't know how to report bullying to recognize what is happening to them and to report it to an adult. It is appropriate to teach children and students with intellectual disabilities, of any age, to use their ABCs to TELL NOW.

Post the strategy in the classroom in large print, review it frequently, and teach older pupils to support children and students with intellectual disabilities in using the strategy.

Sample Poster to Hang in the Classroom

**ABC—TELL NOW**

**A**m I hurt?
**B**y computer or cell phone?
**'C**ause it was mean?

**TELL** an adult **NOW**

such as recess and lunch. Most bullying incidents occur out of the sight of teachers and adult volunteers. Increasing supervision, along with other schoolwide components, contributes to reducing bullying. There are many resources for tackling this important issue in Canadian schools. Reducing bullying through schoolwide efforts contributes to a school in which social relations can grow between exceptional students and their classmates. Other approaches include peer tutoring and co-operative and collaborative teaching in the classroom.

## Using the ADAPT Strategy to Analyze Social Demands in the Classroom: Peer Teaching and Collaborative Learning

You can use the ADAPT strategy to analyze the social demands of classroom organization and tasks and compare these demands with student strengths and needs. There may be opportunities for students to learn from one another through peer teaching, as well as through collaborative and co-operative learning.

### Peer Teaching

**Peer teaching**, which has a long history, can take many forms and goes by a number of names, including peer tutoring, peer-assisted learning, and peer-mediated instruction (for a review of its history, see Topping, 2005). Essentially it involves

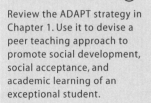

peers as teaching partners. Peers learning together can be especially effective when second-language students translate for one another. In Chapter 5 we read about classwide peer tutoring (e.g., Bowman-Perrott et al., 2007). Reviews of large numbers of studies show that students benefit in many different arrangements of peer teaching (e.g., Stenhoff & Lignugaris/Kraft, 2007). Hughes and Fredrick (2006) describe a program in which middle school students with and without learning disabilities worked in tutoring dyads—after receiving training in tutoring procedures—to teach each other vocabulary in language arts. The students not only learned the vocabulary words but maintained the learned words over time, generalized the words across contexts, and generalized the peer tutoring procedures to tutoring each other spelling. Results showed that the students with LD could function at a level similar to their peers without LD when appropriate instructional strategies were implemented. The students reported that the peer tutoring helped them to remember words and to co-operate while the teachers thought the procedures were easy to implement and engaged the students. Fuchs and Fuchs (2005) provide a summary of their research on pairing high- and low-achieving readers throughout the elementary grades, and show how peer-mediated instruction can enhance students' reading outcomes. However, they remind readers that a small number of children, about 10 percent, did not respond even to their most successful peer-mediated instruction, suggesting the need for more intensive, individualized interventions for a small number of students, as discussed in Chapter 1.

In an example of a classic program designed to enable students with disabilities to take the role of tutor, Blackbourn and Blackbourn (1993) described how an adolescent with moderate developmental disabilities taught a grade 1 non-disabled child. The grade 1 boy needed individual teaching and practice adding and subtracting numbers up to nine with manipulatives. The tutor was skilled in addition and subtraction of up to three-digit numbers and demonstrated a desire to help others. A teacher modelled for the peer teacher how he was to praise the tutee and provided task sheets for the two of them to work on. The grade 1 student improved in mathematics and the tutor became more responsive to learning new and challenging mathematics at his level. Both increased in self-confidence. The grade 1 teacher also began to view older students with disabilities more positively. While an extreme example, this study illustrates findings consistently reported in the reviews of peer teaching; both tutors and tutees benefit, and students with and without disabilities can benefit from tutoring and from being tutored (e.g., Topping, 2005). Overall, reviews have shown that social and self-concept outcomes are positively correlated with academic outcomes (Ginsburg-Block, Rohrbeck, & Fantuzzo, 2006) and that peer tutoring is effective for students with mild disabilities in secondary settings as well as for younger learners (e.g., Stenhoff & Lignugaris/Kraft, 2007).

## Using Co-operative and Collaborative Learning to Meet Academic and Social Goals

Enhancing social development and acceptance requires sufficient opportunities to practise these skills in a supportive environment (Hutchinson, Freeman, & Berg, 2004). You may have heard students say that they prefer to focus on learning and refining social skills within the context of learning "relevant and practical information." All of these perspectives point to integrating social skills enhancement into the ongoing curriculum within the classroom. **Collaborative learning** methods include co-operative learning and problem solving in pairs and groups. These

**Further Reading**

Gillies, R.M. (Ed.). (2007). *The teacher's role in implementing cooperative learning in the classroom.* New York: Springer. (This edited volume provides an overview of the research and underlying theory as well as practical illustrations drawn from the author's research on how teachers can use co-operative and collaborative learning.)

Udvari-Solner, A., & Kluth, P. (2007). *Joyful learning: Active and collaborative learning in inclusive classrooms.* Thousand Oaks, CA: Corwin Press. (Presents techniques for using differentiation, active learning, and collaborative learning at the elementary and secondary levels. Includes reproducible handouts.)

Littleton, K., Miell, D., & Faulkner, D. (Eds.). (2004). *Learning to collaborate, collaborating to learn.* New York: Nova Science Pub. (Focuses on understanding the nature of productive talk and joint work. Identifies the most important aspects of interaction between learners.)

O'Donnell, A.M., Hmelo-Silver, C.E., Erkens, G. (Eds.). (2005). *Collaborative learning, reasoning, and technology.* Mahwah, NJ: Erlbaum. (Presents research on using technology to support learning and reasoning in collaborative contexts.)

Statham, L. (2008). *Counting them in: Isolated bilingual learners in school.* Miami: Stylus Pub. (A current resource that focuses on using a variety of approaches, including co-operative learning, to teach isolated English language learners.)

Coelho, E. (2003). *Adding English: A guide to teaching in multilingual classrooms.* Don Mills, ON: Pippin Pub. Co. (A Canadian resource for meeting the needs of culturally diverse students by an educator known for her writing about collaborative learning.)

*Learning in pairs is good preparation for co-operative and collaborative learning in groups.*

grouping methods usually involve students of varying abilities and skills, that is, heterogeneous groupings rather than homogeneous groupings. The essence of collaboration is the construction of shared meanings for conversations, concepts, and experiences (Palincsar & Herrenkohl, 2002). Collaborative learning methods have been successful in improving academic performance of students of varying ages, grades, subjects, and abilities (see Gillies, 2007; Scheid, 1993). Research has demonstrated a couple of key characteristics of collaborative learning that make it highly effective. Students are more likely to be successful when

1. they are instructed in well-structured, cognitively oriented programs (e.g., Gillies, 2007).
2. they are required as part of their group work to give and receive explanations for answers and ideas suggested in discussion (Ferretti, MacArthur, & Okolo, 2002; Webb & Palincsar, 1996).

During collaborative learning, students tend to reproduce teacher discourse and to meet the expectations communicated by the teacher (Webb, Nemer, & Ing, 2006). This means that if you want students to verbalize their thinking, ask questions, and provide explanations, you must not only structure the activities but also model these ways of thinking and acting and be very clear in communicating these expectations to your students.

Classroom teachers have reported that collaborative learning is effective in meeting the needs of exceptional students included in their classes, and that it works better for some students than for others. The major benefits for exceptional students, teachers reported in a recent study, were improved self-esteem, a safe learning environment, and better classroom success rates and products (Jenkins, Antil, Wayne, & Vadasy, 2003). The primary modification for exceptional students was selecting suitable partners for them. The teachers observed that collaborative learning gave exceptional students greater voice and participation in classroom activities. There are a number of simple techniques you can use, starting on the first day of class, to facilitate collaborative learning and a more interactive classroom.

## Planning for Formal Teaching of Collaboration

Choose a collaborative strategy when you intend to promote positive peer support, social acceptance, and social competence, and especially when the knowledge can be best learned through the contributions of many learners. Figure 9.6 shows the planning decisions that go into designing collaborative learning.

There are many examples of lesson plans for collaborative learning (e.g., Udvari-Solner, & Kluth, 2007; Villa, Nevin, & Thousand, 2007). These sources contain forms for all aspects of the planning and execution of collaborative teaching. There are also excellent models of planning collaborative teaching for classes that include students with special needs (Villa, Nevin, & Thousand, 2007), for techniques ranging from simple to complex.

## FIGURE 9.6 PLANNING DECISIONS IN DESIGNING COLLABORATIVE LEARNING

1. academic goals for the group as a whole and adaptations or modifications of goals for exceptional students

2. social goals for the group and for exceptional students

3. communicating both sets of goals and teaching rather than assuming social skills

4. the type of interaction between students to meet these goals

5. the collaborative learning technique to promote such interaction

6. membership of student groups

7. room arrangement

8. structure of positive interdependence so students get the following messages: We sink or swim together. Do your work; we are counting on you. How can we help each other to do better?

9. student roles to use

10. monitoring student performance

11. guidelines for intervening in poorly functioning groups (as little as possible; with questions rather than answers)

12. individual accountability (during monitoring or in the products)

13. introducing the lesson, fostering collaboration

14. how students obtain closure on the content and feedback, and reflect on the social skills

15. evaluating the learning and reflecting on the process

### TTYPA

A simple method to use during a lecture, film, or reading is called **TTYPA**, or "turn to your partner and . . . ." The teacher stops and tells the students to "Turn to your partner and . . . introduce yourself . . . or describe a time when you. . . . Then switch roles" (Bellanca & Fogarty, 2003). It is useful for making connections between prior learning and a new topic. To ensure that all students understand what to do next, you can use TTYPA for the first partner to describe the instructions and the second partner to describe the first two steps. Such interdependence is easy to achieve and is good preparation for more complex collaborative activities.

### PAIRED PARTNERS: THINK ALOUD

In **Partners Thinking Aloud**, you model thinking aloud and ensure that the students understand what is expected of them (Bellanca & Fogarty, 2003). One student is the problem solver and the other the monitor. The problem solver thinks aloud throughout the task, and the monitor cues the "self-talk" of the solver by asking questions such as, "What is your goal?" "Does this make sense?" "Why?" Then they switch roles. This approach has been adapted by many teachers and researchers to teach exceptional learners:

- Owen and Fuchs (2002) taught math to grade 3 students with learning disabilities;

- Clapper et al. (2002) taught reading comprehension to at-risk secondary school students;

- Klingner et al. (2004) taught reading comprehension in history classrooms;

- Hallenbeck (2002) had adolescent pairs collaborate to learn expository writing; and

**Weblinks**

SASKATOON SCHOOL DIVISION, INSTRUCTIONAL STRATEGIES ONLINE (INCLUDES A SELF-GUIDED TUTORIAL ON CO-OPERATIVE LEARNING)
http://olc.spsd.sk.ca/DE/PD/instr/strats/coop/index.html

THE COOPERATIVE LEARNING NETWORK, SHERIDAN COLLEGE
www-acad.sheridanc.on.ca/scls/coop/cooplrn.htm

PIGS IN SPACE: COOPERATIVE LEARNING LESSON PLANS RELATED TO THE NEW BRUNSWICK CURRICULUM
http://cspace.unb.ca/nbco/pigs/modules

PROJECT CENTRE@2LEARN.CA: COOPERATIVE LEARNING WEB REFERENCES
www.2learn.ca/Projects/Together/KWORDS/cooperaw.html

THE COOPERATIVE LEARNING CENTER AT THE UNIVERSITY OF MINNESOTA
www.co-operation.org

**Further Reading**

Vermette, P.J. (1998). *Making cooperative learning work: Student teams in K–12 classrooms.* Upper Saddle River, NJ: Merrill. (Dated but excellent resource.)

Coelho, E., & Winer, L. (2000). *All sides of the issue: Photocopiable activities for cooperative jigsaw groups* (2nd ed.). Burlingame, CA: Alta Book Center. (Canadian source includes blackline masters.)

Gillies, R.M. (2007). *Cooperative learning: Integrating theory and practice.* Thousand Oaks, CA: Sage. (Contains planning guides and scripts that would be helpful for both in-service and pre-service teachers.)

Jacobs, G.M., Power, M.A., & Loh, W. (2002). *The teacher's sourcebook for cooperative learning: Practical techniques, basic principles, and frequently asked questions.* Thousand Oaks, CA: Corwin Press. (Valuable resource for lesson planning and classroom management.)

- Englert et al. (2001) employed partner writing in a K–2 inclusive classroom;
- Xu et al. (2005) used pairs to increase socialization between ESL students and native speakers of English in grade 2 classrooms.

## CO-OPERATIVE LEARNING

**Co-operative learning** has been used extensively to promote interdependence in classrooms of typical and exceptional students. "Cooperative Learning is a relationship in a group of students that requires positive interdependence (a sense of sink or swim together), individual accountability (each of us has to contribute and learn), interpersonal skills (communication, trust, leadership, decision making, and conflict resolution), face-to-face promotive interaction, and processing (reflecting on how well the team is functioning and how to function even better)" (Johnson & Johnson, www.co-operation.org).

Students work together to accomplish shared goals. They are assigned to small groups and instructed to ensure that all members of the group learn the assignment. Students discuss material, help one another understand it, and encourage one another to work hard. Check individual accountability and learning frequently. You can use this approach for a brief discussion to kick off an activity or in an entire curriculum unit. Johnson and Johnson believe the following five elements are necessary: student interdependence, working face to face, tasks that require everyone's efforts for group success, students knowing how to collaborate, and feedback on social processes in the groups.

You can accept one product from the whole group and give group members a grade based on this product. Assigning roles ensures that everyone participates (for example, the checker ensures that each member understands, the encourager urges members to speak up, the recorder writes down the ideas of the group, the reporter reports to the rest of the class, etc.). Johnson and Johnson (1985) wrote that the elements that promote higher achievement and liking among students include high-quality reasoning strategies, constructive management of conflict over ideas, and feelings of psychological support and acceptance. Recent research shows that co-operative learning strategies that incorporate individual accountability and group rewards are more likely to improve the achievement of students with disabilities (Nyman, McMaster & Fuchs, 2002).

The jigsaw strategy is described in Figure 5.3 on page 181. It is a structured co-operative learning approach.

## Teaching Students to Collaborate

How can you learn to use co-operative learning strategies successfully? In their paper "Learning to Cooperate: A Teacher's Perspective" (2002), Sonnier-York and Stanford describe how one teacher learned to use co-operative learning. They recount the importance of teaching students how to work together (assume nothing!) and making each group member accountable for contributing to completion and quality. They describe how teachers must observe and mediate (but not control students) while making observational notes that can be used to inform instructional decisions. Students need both to see their products completed and published or exhibited and to take part in highly varied co-operative tasks. And, finally, Sonnier-York and Stanford recommend that you evaluate your progress and increasingly integrate co-operative learning across the curriculum. You can use

*Hayden, a young man with autism, walks with his stepfather and his service dog, Printer, who helps to keep him safe by preventing him from running towards water. Printer also helps to break down social barriers and acts as "an ambassador for autism."*

Put into Practice

Read the following article and develop an intervention using direct instruction to improve the social skills of an exceptional student so the student can better participate in collaborative learning:

Johns, B.H., Crowley, P., & Guetzloe, E. (2005). The central role of teaching social skills. *Focus on Exceptional Children, 37*(8), 1–8.

Read the following article and make a plan for supplementing the direct instruction for this student with other strategies (e.g., using children's or adolescent literature to teach social skills and to establish friendships).

Church, K., Gottschalk, C.M., & Leddy, J.N. (2003). 20 ways to … Enhance social and friendship skills. *Intervention in School and Clinic, 38*, 307–310.

ADAPT and observation to decide the behaviours and social skills that students need most. For the most important social skills (such as giving everyone a chance to talk, listening actively, and providing explanations), students need practice. They will probably require effective role models (you can model or use a paired teaching strategy), and you will need to help them persist in the face of deterrents. In her book *Designing Groupwork: Strategies for the Heterogeneous Classroom* (1998), Elizabeth Cohen provides several examples of activities and games to help students acquire group-work skills (also see Cohen et al., 2004).

Begin with simple, short activities that provide frequent occasions for participation. Try participation in pairs through TTYPA, Think-Pair-Share (shown in Figure 5.3 on page 181), and Think Aloud pairs and progress to short co-operative learning activities such as group work on a five-minute mystery. You will learn to form groups and intervene effectively by practising with simple, short collaborative activities.

Researchers describe, in three papers, using collaborative approaches to teach middle school students to understand literature. Blum and his colleagues (2002) used literature circles and found that students with special needs accurately assessed their reading difficulties and perceived an improvement in their reading skills. These students felt that they had learned from their peers. Hindin and her colleagues (2001) used a supported literacy approach to help poor readers participate in high-level conversations and rehearse the reading and thinking processes that good readers use. Fitch and Hulgin (2007) demonstrated the effectiveness of Collaborative Learning Assessment through Dialogue (CLAD), a procedure in which students collaboratively completed multiple choice quizzes using dialogue and critical thinking to reach consensus and received immediate feedback. Students who participated in CLAD made large gains in reading, including reading

Weblinks

HOAGIES' GIFTED EDUCATION PAGE
www.hoagiesgifted.org/play_partner.htm

CHILDREN'S LITERATURE WEB GUIDE
www.acs.ucalgary.ca/~dkbrown/index.html

Consider the challenges when gifted students feel more comfortable with older friends. Look for other websites, books, and articles that focus on enhancing the social relations and friendships of children and adolescents who are gifted.

## Further Reading

Children with autism and Asperger syndrome experience particular challenges because lack of social competence is at the heart of their disability (Chapter 4 contains a section on characteristics of students with autism and Asperger syndrome). The following two papers focus specifically on enhancing the social competence and social acceptance of these students:

Boutot, E.A. (2007). Fitting in: Tips for promoting acceptance and friendships for students with autism spectrum disorders in inclusive classrooms. *Intervention in School and Clinic, 42*, 156–161.

Webb, B.J., Miller, S.P., Pierce, T.B., Strawser, S., & Jones, W.P. (2004). Effects of social skill instruction for high-functioning adolescents with autism spectrum disorders. *Focus on Autism and Other Developmental Disabilities, 19*, 53–62.

## Cross-Reference

Chapter 7 describes differentiating or adapting teaching to meet adapted and modified goals of exceptional students, and Chapter 8 focuses on adapting assessment.

comprehension. These researchers recommend activities that are culturally relevant, interactive, responsive, and collaborative, and that provide a window into students' thinking and extend students' background knowledge.

## Challenges to Collaborative Learning

There are a number of challenges to collaborative learning. We cannot assume that discussion or collaboration among peers is an unproblematic way to help students attain higher-order thinking or greater social competence. We cannot assume that the interactions of children and adolescents are "free of hidden agendas and the sequelae of past interpersonal experiences" (O'Connor, 1996, p. 507). Peers may not always be able to make learning clear and explicit enough for exceptional learners to succeed. Co-operative activities in which all students in a group receive the same grade can result in unfair evaluation outcomes if some students have not contributed, or if some knew all the content before the unit began. Occasionally, a student may become dependent on the more able members of a co-operative group. Exceptional students and gifted students in inclusive classrooms are more likely to experience these drawbacks than are their peers. You may have to provide alternative evaluation criteria for some students and modified or adapted goals and activities for some students with special needs. Johnson and Johnson (2004) describe many methods teachers can use to promote group responsibility and individual accountability when assessing students in groups. For example, they suggest teachers must first recognize the power of groups for assessment purposes, structure effective groups, and make an assessment plan. Then it is possible to use groups to assess individual performances by observing individuals or using individual tests; simply put, students learn it in a group and perform it alone. You can also assess group performances through group products (e.g., case discussions, dramatic or musical productions, and group investigations). In addition, you can structure peer assessment (great for immediate and detailed formative feedback) and self-assessment (which contributes to students' setting their own goals and monitoring their progress toward these goals, our ultimate goal as educators).

To meet these challenges, monitor group interaction. Focus on the needs of exceptional students when creating groups. Gifted students can benefit from being placed in a collaborative group with gifted peers, where they can challenge one another and pursue advanced tasks (Winebrenner, 2007). In areas where they are far ahead of the rest of the class, they may be too impatient to be supportive and good models for the lowest achievers. Use heterogeneous groups as much as possible, but consider the best group composition for meeting the academic and social goals of each lesson. Usually students who are both academically competent (not necessarily gifted), socially competent, and patient make the best partners or group members for exceptional students. Once you know who these students are, you can form groups by putting one of them in each corner of the room and distributing the rest of the class into the four groups (Taylor, 2008).

Secondary school teachers often feel pressure to "cover the curriculum." Many teachers find that the gains in motivation, reasoning, and self-directedness more than compensate for the time required to teach students to work collaboratively (e.g., Bellanca & Fogarty, 2003). In upper years students may be competing for entry to post-secondary education and scholarships. For a variety of reasons, secondary school teachers often find it more challenging to adopt collaborative learning. Some adolescents show a low tolerance for diversity (Cobia & Carney, 2002). Collaborative groups can focus

*Children and adolescents with physical disabilities learn to sail.*

the frustration of group members on students who contribute less than their share when the collaborations are unsuccessful. Cohen, Lotan, and Catanzarite (1990) suggest that groups can be dominated by high-status members who may not pay attention to the contributions of low-status members. Cohen and her colleagues make a number of recommendations for minimizing the impact of status problems:

1. Teach students to listen, take turns, and assume various roles. Emphasize process as much as content, gradually shifting the emphasis to content.

2. Use stimulating materials and activities that are not entirely dependent on reading. These may include diagrams, videos, audio recordings, case studies, and authentic documents.

3. Build on student experience, beyond that typically used in the classroom, with authentic tasks. Bestow status on students who may have had part-time jobs and excel at negotiating resolutions in conflicts, etc. Look for ways to use student expertise (also see Cohen, 1998; Cohen et al., 2004).

4. Collaborate with colleagues, seek professional development, and keep an account of your experiences to share with colleagues.

Although there are considerable challenges, there are also benefits in social development and social acceptance when you use collaborative teaching approaches in the classroom. In addition, look to the community for additional opportunities to enhance social relations of exceptional students.

## The Community and Social Relations

There are two approaches to using the community to enhance social relations. The first is to bring the community into the school, and the second is to take the students into the community. These approaches are often called community-referenced instruction.

Increasingly, communities are playing a role in the development of the social context of schools. Nowhere is this more apparent than in Aboriginal communities. Saskatchewan Learning has put considerable focus on a conceptual framework and policy for community education (*Building Communities of Hope: Effective Practices for Meeting the Diverse Learning Needs of Children and Youth*, 2004). Community education is based on the beliefs that a school is a fundamental part of the community, everyone in the community has a voice in shaping the community's school, and the community culture is a fundamental part of the social and academic life of the school (Decker & Decker, 2000; Decker et al., 2005; Saskatchewan Learning, *Community Education*, 2000b).

While a community school philosophy has been adopted for all public schools in the province, this philosophy is most significant for Aboriginal communities. It has led to growing roles for Aboriginal elders and community workers in schools (Saskatchewan Learning, 2001). In this way Aboriginal students see themselves and their cultural heritage reflected and respected within the school: "All our students benefit from our Elder. Students begin to develop an understanding of the Aboriginal culture. They learn about the spiritual dimension. This is of immense importance in our fight against racism" (Gerry Guillet, former assistant director, Prince Albert Roman Catholic Separate School Division; Saskatchewan Learning, 2001, p. 3). Elders carry on traditional Aboriginal activities and ceremonies in schools and, depending on the people/nation, these include the oral tradition, circles, storytelling, smudging, pipe, and sweat lodge ceremonies. In her description of what elders do, Betty McKenna, an elder at Prince Arthur School in Moose Jaw, says, "Elders . . . should demonstrate the ability to listen and to understand. Elders demonstrate respect for Mother Earth and for others by their practices. Elders conduct themselves in a humble manner" (Saskatchewan Learning, 2001, p. 12).

Community-referenced learning involves using the community as a classroom. This can be conducted informally or through a formal program. If you choose the informal approach, the community newspaper and the newsletters of local associations and organizations may provide you with authentic learning opportunities that are ideal for enhancing social relations. The local friendship centre, swimming pool, or bowling alley may provide an inexpensive venue for children or adolescents to learn together. If it is not feasible for the whole class to take part, look for ways to use paraeducators and volunteers to accompany approximately three pairs of students (perhaps students who work together in peer teaching). There are many summer (and some winter) recreation programs, such as learn-to-sail and learn-to-swim programs, computer camps, and skating at the community rink, that include spaces for exceptional youth. Watch for opportunities that you and your students can access and that you can recommend to families. You can include a few exceptional students in each monthly trip to the symphony or to the local theatre company. Develop activities to be done at the museum in your community (Tam, Nassivera, Rousseau, & Vreeland, 2000). These community integration activities provide you and your students with goals to work toward, special events to share, and evidence of the progress you are making toward inclusion in the community.

Formal **community-referenced learning** includes work experiences, research teams, and service learning. Work experiences are described more fully in Chapter 10. Research teams are heterogeneous groups of students using the community as the place to do research such as conducting interviews, making observations, or exploring artifacts. Kluth (2000) describes a group of three students from a grade 7 home economics class going into the community to shop. For two students, the goals are learning to use mathematics and nutrition skills through comparative shopping to buy the most economical items that contain the fewest grams of fat. For a third student with disabilities, the weekly trip serves as an opportunity to learn to travel by city bus, cross streets, and select and pay for groceries. This example shows how goals can be set around the learning needs of all students and can foster social co-operation and social development using learning-in-community contexts.

# Summary

Social development and social acceptance are critical to inclusion because they refer to exceptional students' ability to take part in the social and academic life of the classroom and to their acceptance by classmates. Both exceptional students and their peers without disabilities have expressed an array of views on inclusion and the social processes that accompany it. Friendship is probably much more important to learning than we have understood in the past, enabling students to gradually internalize the ideas they are challenged with by their peers. Both elementary and secondary schools are social environments, and schoolwide approaches can ensure that schools are inviting and safe for all students. As a teacher, you can analyze social demands and choose a wide range of collaborative and social approaches to learning as well as use the community to enhance social relations.

# Key Terms

social relationships (p. 305)
social development (p. 305)
social competence (p. 305)
social acceptance (p. 305)
friendships (p. 305)
interpersonal competence (p. 307)
peer perspectives (p. 308)
(dis)ability awareness program
     (p. 308)

social status (p. 308)
sociometric rating (p. 308)
schoolwide approaches (p. 315)
code of conduct (p. 318)
moral leadership (p. 319)
schoolwide positive behaviour
     support (SWPBS) (p. 320)
bullying (p. 320)
cyberbullying (p. 320)

peer teaching (p. 324)
collaborative learning
     (p. 325)
TTYPA (p. 327)
Partners Thinking Aloud (p. 327)
co-operative learning (p. 328)
community-referenced learning
     (p. 332)

# Challenges for Reviewing Chapter 9

1. Why are social development and social acceptance of exceptional learners so important to the inclusion of these students? What role can the classroom teacher play—in an elementary school, in a secondary school—in promoting social development and social acceptance of exceptional learners?

2. Identify the role of friendship in the lives of students with and without exceptionalities, and particularly its role in their lives at school. Why is it important for you to be aware of the role of friendship in the development of exceptional individuals?

3. Prepare to assume the role of one of the members of a team that has been assembled in your school to prevent cyberbullying. The team includes three members of the teaching staff, two parents, a guidance counsellor, the president of the student council, and the principal, who will chair the meetings. You want to advocate for a schoolwide approach, but you know that at least one member thinks that approach will take too long to organize, and the needs are immediate. What resources would you use to prepare for the meetings, what points would you make in the meetings, and why do you think these contributions are important? You may want to role-play this scenario with your peers, assuming the roles of the eight members of the team.

4. Create a fuller description of Val, the blind grade 1 student described in the case at the beginning of this chapter, and, using the ADAPT strategy, analyze the social demands of math class and of recess for this student. Select collaborative and co-operative teaching strategies to help deal with each of these situations. Refer to sources identified in this chapter as well as the information provided in this chapter.

5. Lynn, the young woman with leaning disabilities in the opening case, is in your secondary class. Using the ADAPT strategy, analyze the social demands made of Lynn by your typical lesson. Select collaborative and co-operative teaching strategies to help deal with each of the challenges that you identify. Refer to sources identified in this chapter as well as the information provided in this chapter.

6. Describe the actions you would take at the beginning of the school year to ensure that exceptional students in your class benefit from community-referenced learning. Why does inclusion make it necessary for us to think about the role of the community in enhancing social relations?

7. Return to the opening cases of Val and Lynn and answer the five questions that follow the cases.

# Chapter 10
## Enhancing Independent Learning and Independent Living

### Learner Objectives

After you have read this chapter you will be able to:

1. Describe how you can teach strategies to help exceptional students in elementary and secondary schools to become more independent learners (student development).

2. Discuss what can be done to make transitions for exceptional learners as smooth as possible.

3. Describe strategies for enhancing interpersonal development and its contribution to independence.

4. Explain the contribution of career development (including career education and co-operative education) to the development of independence.

5. Discuss community participation and community support approaches to independent living.

**Fran was 16 when she rolled her car and suffered brain damage.** After being in a coma for weeks, she awakened as a different person. The Fran she remembered was an athlete, a dancer, and a student who could write an entire essay the night before it was due and who didn't know the meaning of "can't." While her family, friends, and teachers have struggled to adjust to a Fran who tires easily, can't plan ahead enough to make a sandwich for lunch, and lashes out at those closest to her, Fran has not made the adjustment. Her homeroom teacher describes Fran as a young woman who doesn't know herself. The guidance counsellor who is working with Fran at school keeps reminding her that she won't be studying physical education at university as she had planned. Many adolescents need strategies to improve their self-knowledge and self-advocacy. These strategies are especially important for youth with exceptionalities, and absolutely essential to young people with traumatic brain injury.

Ray is in grade 4 and his next transition will come after grade 5, when he must move from his neighbourhood school, Avon Elementary, to a middle school across town. Ray hates change, unpredictability, and chaos. He has Asperger syndrome. His family started working with the kindergarten teacher eight months before his transition from preschool to Avon Elementary. To get Ray ready for the move from Avon to Brown Middle School, his family and teacher have made a plan to start a full year ahead. In September of grade 5, Ray will start going to Brown for an hour per week, then two hours, with a gradual increase. By the end of grade 5, Ray will know his homeroom teacher and his resource teacher at Brown, the location of both their rooms, as well as how to eat in the cafeteria, how to borrow a book from the library, and how to use a combination lock. This kind of troubleshooting should help Ray to make the transition without the stress and overreaction that can cause him to fight or flee and hide. Ray's IEP for grade 5 focuses as much on preparing him for the transition as on academic learning. Everyone agrees that if the transition is smooth, Ray can begin learning as soon as he arrives at Brown. Without a smooth transition, his first year will probably be disastrous.

1. Why are transitions so critical to many exceptional students? What do the case studies of Fran and Ray have in common?

2. What kinds of strategies can the teachers of Fran and Ray teach them so they can be as independent as possible in their upcoming learning?

3. Describe how schools have become much more focused on the needs of exceptional students for life in the community since the emphasis shifted to inclusion.

4. What strategies do Fran, Ray, and other exceptional students require in order to be aware of their own strengths and needs and to advocate for themselves?

5. How can teachers employ the resources of the community and of others around them to help meet the needs of exceptional students for independent learning strategies and independent living strategies?

# Introduction

Chapter 10 focuses on enhancing the independent learning and independent living of exceptional students. Fran and Ray, who have traumatic brain injury and Asperger syndrome, respectively, are facing transitions and need strategies to help them function independently to meet the demands of school and life. This chapter prepares you for helping your students to be more independent in meeting both kinds of demands.

Throughout this book you have read about young people with exceptionalities and their teachers and parents working together to maximize the young people's opportunities for social and academic participation and for playing a valued role in society. You have reflected on our country's high expectations for inclusion in school and in society. In the recent and ongoing educational reforms across the country (see Chapter 1 for a summary of the rights of exceptional learners) there has been a renewed emphasis on students' developing independence. This emphasis is apparent in the transitions initiative in the PEI *School Administrators Education Handbook* (2003), Ontario's document *Choices into Action* (Ontario Ministry of Education, 1999), and Alberta's *Transition Planning* document (http://education.alberta.ca/media/513294/unlock_7.pdf). Similarly, Objective IV of New Brunswick's long-term *Quality Learning Agenda* (2003) focuses on supporting successful transitions to further learning and training. The focuses and components of these curricula are variously described as guidance, career education, career development, career and personal planning, co-operative education, workplace learning, work-based education, work experience, and so on. Most of these programs have goals that can be described as

- student development (**personal development** or personal independence);
- **interpersonal development** (social responsibility, citizenship, working cooperatively, or responsible interdependence); and
- **career development** (responsible decision-making, employability, successful transitions, independent planning).

This chapter enlarges on the three themes of student development, interpersonal development, and career development for classroom teachers who teach exceptional learners. The emphasis is on two of these themes—student development of strategies for independent learning and career development for independent living—because Chapter 9 focuses on interpersonal development.

# Student Development for Independent Learning

Many people think that development of independence, career development, and the accompanying themes of this chapter are primarily the concerns of secondary school teachers. However, the recently revised provincial curricula emphasize the importance of teaching independence throughout the school years, starting with kindergarten. A **career** is one's progress through life and through the roles appropriate to various ages as well as the process of making a living by means of a particular occupation (Gibson, 2005; Super, 1957). Thus career development involves students' growing understanding of all aspects of changing roles and responsibilities, including adult responsibilities, roles, and the nature and meaning

**Cross-Reference**
How does this chapter relate to the ADAPT strategy in Chapter 1?

**Cross-Reference**
Chapter 4 contains characteristics and strategies specific to students with traumatic brain injury and students with Asperger syndrome.

**Weblinks**

KEVIN'S LEARNING STRATEGIES LINKS AND RESOURCES, CAPE BRETON VICTORIA REGIONAL SCHOOL BOARD
www.cbv.ns.ca/sstudies/links/learn/learn.htm

UNIVERSITY OF KANSAS CENTER FOR RESEARCH ON LEARNING (STRATEGY INSTRUCTION MODEL)
www.ku-crl.org

of work. This understanding encompasses the incredible range of ways in which adults engage independently and interdependently in paid work, volunteer and unpaid work, and other adult roles such as leisure, child rearing, and citizenship. The first theme addressed is enhancing independent learning.

## Strategies for Independent Learning

A large body of research in exceptional education focuses on teaching students learning strategies. The logic is that many learners (often students without exceptionalities) have been observed to develop efficient strategies to learn. They find ways to solve problems, comprehend what they read, write what is expected of them, and so on, even if teachers do not make these strategies explicit. These approaches—to understanding what is expected and finding strategies to meet expectations effectively—remain invisible in many classrooms. Researchers like Bernice Wong of Simon Fraser University, Deb Butler of the University of British Columbia, Ann Brown, Ann Marie Palincsar, and Donald Deshler have spent much of their careers trying to make these learning strategies explicit and to find ways to teach them explicitly to exceptional students.

What are these strategies? Bernice Wong (1996, 2000) of Simon Fraser University describes **learning strategies** as techniques or principles that enable a student to learn to solve problems, read, communicate, organize, and so on independently. According to Donald Deshler and his colleagues at the University of Kansas, "Learning strategy instruction focuses on making the students more active learners by teaching them how to learn and how to use what they have learned to solve problems and be successful" (www.ku-crl.org/sim/strategies.shtml). Learning strategies emphasize the steps necessary to perform a strategy as well as when and why to perform that strategy and how to monitor its use. Often you can teach strategies to your entire class that may benefit many normally achieving students, and additional practise opportunities may be all that is needed in order to help exceptional students to participate better in your class and in life. Sometimes exceptional students need learning strategies that their classmates have already acquired. This means that you may need to use approaches to differentiation described in many chapters in this book—for example, teach a "needs group" at what I call the "round table," a place where students are invited to join the teacher for intense teaching. Or enlist the services of a co-teacher (a resource teacher or a paraeducator) to do this teaching. Perhaps you can model the first session while this co-teacher observes and the co-teacher can conduct the remaining sessions. After years of using the round table approach, both as classroom teacher and as resource teacher, I can vouch for its effectiveness as long as your students always leave the table feeling that they have had your full attention and have learned. Make it a learning privilege—not a punishment—that is used at various times for all students.

## Teaching Strategies

Before you can teach learning strategies, you have to plan for this teaching. The six steps in this planning are as follows:

1. Identify areas in which many students could be working more independently.
2. Specify outcomes you would like to see.
3. List the steps students should follow.

**What do you think?**

Learning strategies were originally designed to meet the needs of students with learning disabilities. In recent years they have been found effective for teaching students with many exceptionalities, and often they are recommended for teaching entire classes. What is it about learning strategies that makes them effective for so many students?

4. Limit the number of steps.

5. Put the strategy steps on cue cards for individual use (students can staple them into their notebooks).

6. Put a poster on the wall for those who need to keep referring to the steps.

**Cross-Reference**
Look for learning strategies in other chapters that might help students learn more independently. Start by examining a cognitive behaviour modification strategy (SNAP; Chapter 6) and a strategy for solving algebra word problems (Chapter 7). What others can you find?

For students to use learning strategies independently, they have to learn to do them accurately and fluently. Many studies have shown the steps that are effective in teaching strategies (e.g., Deshler, Palincsar, et al., 2007; Hutchinson, 1993; Schumaker & Deshler, 2003; Wong, 1996). First, students must see the need for the strategy, so begin by assessing current strategy use and sharing your observations with the students. Also, consider the pre-skills students need for what you are teaching. If many students lack the pre-skills, start by teaching these.

Because learning strategies can help students function independently, they may be motivated to work at them. However, you need to clarify expectations for the strategy, point out benefits, and convince students to "give it a try." You might plan four classes in which you will teach the strategy and then in the fifth class begin a series of activities or a unit in which students will use it. Put up a chart that shows this plan; then students can see that they have four classes in which to master the strategy. This can motivate them to learn as efficiently as they can. Approach it positively; don't threaten.

**Model strategy use** carefully. Exceptional students will probably use the strategy only as well as you do when you model it. Explain carefully, by thinking aloud, your thinking patterns, how you decide when to use the strategy, and how you do each step. For exceptional students you are making the invisible (efficient learning strategies) visible; they may never come up with these strategies on their own. It often helps to demonstrate what *not* to do, but be adamant that these are *not effective strategies*. Stop and discuss with the students why they are not feasible or effective. Then provide additional practice with the steps of the effective strategy.

**Guided practice** or scaffolded practice, in which students are prompted to do each step, enables exceptional students to learn the strategy. Use an overhead or Power-Point to demonstrate or prompt students and stop for a few seconds after each prompt, or have students work in pairs and remind each other of the steps. Throughout the previous nine chapters we've looked at many examples of guided or scaffolded practice. **Independent practice** is necessary for students to be able to use a strategy independently and fluently. If some students still require scaffolded practice after most have learned the strategy, arrange for them to continue to practise with you or with someone else. For a student like Fran, in one of the opening case studies of this chapter, a paraeducator could continue to prompt her for weeks or months. The other students would be working independently, with only a quick booster session at the beginning of each

*Hobbies such as competing in plowing matches can turn into careers. Rebecca Woodman, at 15, competed in the 1998 International Plowing Match.*

**TABLE 10.1  LEARNING STRATEGIES DESCRIBED THROUGHOUT THIS BOOK**

| Learning Strategy | Chapter |
|---|---|
| RAP (Read, Ask questions, Paraphrase) | Chapter 1, case of Ben |
| ADAPT strategy | Chapter 1, introduced; examples throughout |
| Classwide Peer Tutoring (CWPT) | Chapter 5, Focus on Research |
| CLASS (Complete, Look it over, Ask, Signal, Say thanks) | Chapter 6 |
| SNAP (See problem, Name plan, Act on plan, Pat on back) | Chapter 6, Figure 6.6 |
| Scaffolded Reading Experience (SRE) | Chapter 7, Table 7.1 |
| Story Planning | Chapter 7 |
| TAPS (for adjustable assignments; Total group, Alone, Pairs, Small group) | Chapter 7 |
| DARE for planning the writing of an opinion essay | Chapter 7 |
| SEARCH for revising written work | Chapter 7 |
| WSECS (Words, Sentences, Essay, Counterarguments, SEARCH), critiquing written work | Chapter 7 |
| Self-Questions for Representing Algebra Word Problems | Chapter 7 |
| Self-Questions for Solving Algebra Word Problems | Chapter 7 |
| Reciprocal Teaching | Chapter 7 |
| ABC—Tell Now (for Reporting Cyberbullying) | Chapter 9, Figure 9.5 |

**Put into Practice**

Choose an area in which exceptional students you have taught would benefit from a learning strategy. Devise a learning strategy and a plan for teaching it to the whole class and provide extra practice for the exceptional students. Then consider the case of Ray, described at the opening of this chapter. How could you use strategy instruction to help Ray prepare for the transition to junior high school?

week. Give students specific **feedback** about what they are doing correctly and incorrectly, and gradually ask them to assess themselves for efficient strategy use. Self-monitoring is an important aspect of independent strategy use.

You may have to use the ADAPT strategy to differentiate the teaching and practice of learning strategies for some students. This could involve the use of Braille, an interpreter, individual explanations, comprehension checks, etc.

Many effective learning strategies have been designed for elementary and secondary school classrooms. In earlier chapters you have seen strategies for teaching mathematics, spelling, reading, and writing. Table 10.1 lists learning strategies and where they have been discussed in this book. Look back through these discussions, focusing on the examples of learning strategies. Look for strategies that you can use to teach students to learn more independently in your classroom. Also note strategies that can serve as models for developing your own strategies that meet pressing circumstances in your classroom.

Most universities and colleges across Canada have a student learning service that provides learning strategies. Many of these learning strategies are practical for learners from about grade 5 and up. Figure 10.1 shows one of the learning strategies from the website of Queen's University.

## Adapting to Change: Transitions and Student Development

While we most often think of **transition** as referring to the move from secondary school into post-secondary endeavours, there are also considerable challenges associated with the move from preschool to elementary school (Dockett & Perry, 2003; Guralnick, 2001) and from elementary or junior high into secondary school

# FIGURE 10.1 TEN TIPS FOR IMPROVING TIME MANAGEMENT

1. Concentrate on one thing at a time.

2. Plan your day each morning or the night before and set priorities for yourself.

3. Keep paper or a calendar with you to jot down the things you have to do or notes to yourself.

4. Try to avoid wasting time—all time can be useful.

5. Try rewarding yourself when you get things done as you had planned, especially the important ones.

6. Be sure and set deadlines for yourself whenever possible.

7. Stop regretting failures and start learning from your mistakes.

8. Remind yourself, "There is always enough time for the important things." If it is important, you should be able to make time to do it.

9. Examine and revise your life goals on a monthly basis and be sure to include progress toward these goals on a daily basis.

10. Put up reminders in your room about your goals.

Source: Queen's University Health Counselling and Disability Services. 10 tips for improving time management. www.bewell-dowell.org/sos/study_tips-time_management.html.

(Versnel, 2005). As we saw in the case of Ray, issues can also arise in the transition to junior high (or middle school).

Families can perceive a loss of support associated with the move from preschool into elementary school (Lillie & Vakil, 2002; McIntyre et al., 2007). In interviews with three Canadian families, Cheryl Schmid and Nancy Hutchinson (1994) found that this transition was not well coordinated and was jeopardized by poor communication. Two mothers reported on their inability to arrange meetings between the preschool resource teacher and other professionals such as the occupational therapist or speech therapist. Neither of these two mothers had the role she desired in this critical transition. The third mother was about to embark on this vital transition and "planned to compensate for the failure of professionals to consider her a partner in the transition process by continuing to advocate vigorously for Susan [her daughter]" (p. 9).

In a companion study with a preschool resource teacher, Amy, who was considered exemplary, Hutchinson and Schmid (1996) found that this teacher saw herself as an advocate who focused on the needs of individual exceptional children. Another theme in the interviews was her focus on partnerships and transitions. She perceived herself to be responsible for the transition between preschool and elementary school, a crucial juncture that she said many parents found disturbing. Her strategies included

- inviting kindergarten and grade 1 teachers to the preschool to observe an exceptional student, rather than relying on information presented in a case conference;

- recording on videotape the exceptional child at the preschool and giving the video to the parents to take to the kindergarten teacher;

- providing in-service to school staff (especially in rural schools where they had not previously taught a child with a particular exceptionality); and

**Weblinks**

CANLEARN LISTING OF WEBSITES OF COLLEGES AND UNIVERSITIES
http://canlearn.ca

BRANDON UNIVERSITY STUDENT SERVICES (INCLUDING LEARNING SKILLS)
www.brandonu.ca/studentsvc

UNIVERSITY OF VICTORIA SKILLS PROGRAM
www.coun.uvic.ca/learning/study-skills

UNIVERSITY OF TORONTO COUNSELLING AND LEARNING SKILLS SERVICE (CALSS)
www.calss.utoronto.ca

This grade 1 boy ran away from school. When asked why, he said, "School is too hard." Transitions can be tough.

■ recording on videotape a parent of a child with an unusual or severe disability (e.g., a feeding machine) as an expert explaining the child's condition in non-technical terms for the teacher.

In a national study of transition practices in the United States, Paro, Pianta, and Cox (2000) reported that kindergarten teachers implement kindergarten and grade 1 transition practices. A recent replication of that study (LoCasale-Crouch et al., 2008) reported the range of transition practices used by kindergarten teachers receiving students from preschool and preparing students for grade 1. However, transition practices specifically for children with disabilities were rarely used or even mentioned (Lara-Sinisomo et al., 2008; Shirduan & Miller, 2002). Increasing emphasis is being placed on preparing at-risk preschool children for success in school (for an example, see the work of Jennifer LoCasale-Crouch et al., 2007). The strategies used by Amy, the exemplary preschool teacher (Hutchinson & Schmid, 1996), fostered continuity and treated parents as partners. Amy described the transition between preschool and elementary school as "really important because what happens is the child can get lost in the shuffle." We all know that transitions can be stressful. As a kindergarten or grade 1 teacher, you can ensure that you are aware and knowledgeable about your exceptional students before they arrive so that the level of stress is as low as possible for you, the student, and the family.

What about the transition to middle school, junior high, or secondary school? While this is likely to be stressful for parents, chances are that it is extremely stressful for the exceptional student. For many exceptional students, change causes fear (review Chapters 3 and 4 to see how many descriptions of exceptionalities include this characteristic). The actions taken by the family and teacher of Ray, described in one of the case studies at the beginning of this chapter, are designed to minimize the trauma of his upcoming transition. This boy with Asperger syndrome will have gradually learned to meet the most challenging social expectations of his new school before he begins classes there. Because his biggest challenges are the social expectations associated with learning in classrooms, these were made the focus of his IEP for the year during which he was being prepared for the transition. His classroom teacher and resource teacher at Avon Elementary have worked as an effective team with Ray, his parents, and the resource teacher at Brown Middle School. An older boy, Marty, who took an interest in Ray while he was visiting Brown and learning to find his locker, offered to serve as a peer tutor and teach Ray to open his combination lock. Schools with peer tutor programs can often supplement the efforts of teachers to welcome new exceptional students. Marty, who has LD, remembers how difficult his move to Brown was and appreciates the help he received from his peer tutor.

As a classroom teacher, you do not have to develop and execute transition plans alone. Draw on the resources of the in-school team. Joan Versnel (2005) of

Dalhousie University implemented a transition program for sixth graders making the transition to junior high. Students with and without disabilities and their parents reported that the program helped students to participate fully in a transition meeting and to handle the challenges of junior high. Look for resources within the school and the community—the Community Living Association or Spina Bifida Association may be willing to help. The CNIB has mobility specialists to help blind students learn their new environment. Consult local organizations, including Big Brothers, service clubs, church groups, and pensioners' groups who provide volunteers. Remember that your school board may require a police check of these volunteers. The most efficient way to enhance independence during the transitions of exceptional students is to ensure that these goals and strategies are in the student's IEP at least during the final year before they make the transition. Then a whole team, including parents and the student, will be making student independence a priority over the year. Some students use assistive devices and computers to enhance their independence. This is the focus of the next section.

## Using Computers and Assistive Devices to Enhance Learning and Independence

Everyone requires computer skills for independence in today's world, including people with disabilities. For examples, consult an issue of *Abilities* magazine online (www.abilities.ca). Adapted technologies and computers play a significant role in enhancing the independence of exceptional children, adolescents, and adults.

Computing technologies will influence all your students not only in the classroom but also in every aspect of their lives. These technologies are changing our concepts of education, culture, communication, shopping, and work. This means that we are educating students for a future that includes computers in roles we have not yet imagined and for a life of continuous learning. In spite of the *Charter of Rights and Freedoms* (http://laws.justice.gc.ca/en/charter) and the *Employment Equity Act* (http://laws.justice.gc.ca/en/E-5.401/index.html), Canadians with disabilities have much higher rates of unemployment than Canadians without disabilities. According to *Advancing the Inclusion of Persons with Disabilities* (Human Resources Development Canada, 2004), employment rates are only 53 percent for people with disabilities compared with 76 percent for people without. Aboriginal adults with disabilities are almost twice as likely to be out of the workforce as Aboriginal adults without disabilities. Skills in information technology may be more critical to the employment and economic independence of persons with disabilities than to citizens in general because technologies can serve as "equity tools" to provide access for the disabled (Hollingsworth, 1996).

There are many hardware and software tools designed to serve as equity tools to meet the needs of persons with specific disabilities (Ludlow & Foshay, 2002; Mondak, 2000). Their costs and availability have been hotly debated on the listserv that has been in use since the work of the Task Force on Access to Information for Print-Disabled Canadians in the fall of 2000 (www.collectionscanada.gc.ca/accessinfo). A study in the Adaptech Project (http://adaptech.dawsoncollege.qc.ca), conducted by researchers at Dawson College in Montreal, set out to report on access to educational and instructional computer technologies of students with disabilities (Fichten, Asuncion, Jennison, Barile, Fossey, & de Simone, 2000). Most students reported that they used computer technologies. Almost half of the respondents (41 percent) needed adaptations to use a computer effectively, and

**Further Reading**

On Asperger syndrome:

Myles, B., & Simpson, R.L. (2003). *Asperger syndrome: A guide for educators and parents* (2nd ed.). Austin, TX: Pro-Ed.

Kiker Painter, K. (2006). *Social skills groups for children and adolescents with Asperger's syndrome.* London, UK: Jessica Kingsley Ltd.

Betts, S., Betts, D., & Gerber-Eckard, L. (2007). *Asperger syndrome in the inclusive classroom: Advice and strategies for teachers.* London: Jessica Kingsley Publishers.

Bolick, T. (2004). *Asperger syndrome and adolescence: Helping preteens and teens get ready for the real world.* Gloucester, MA: Fair Winds Press.

Sicile-Kira, C. (2006). *Adolescents on the autism spectrum: A parent's guide to the cognitive, social, physical, and transition needs of teenagers with autism spectrum disorders.* New York: The Berkley Publishing Group.

Hewetson, A. (2005). *Laughter and tears: Autism and Asperger syndrome through the years.* London: Jessica Kingsley.

**TABLE 10.2** CANADIAN VENDORS OF ADAPTIVE TECHNOLOGY AND SERVICES

| Company | Web Address |
| --- | --- |
| ALDS Distributing | www.alds.com |
| Aroga Technologies | www.aroga.com |
| Assistive Devices Industry Office (Industry Canada) | www.at-links.gc.ca |
| Aurora Systems | www.aurora-systems.com |
| Braille Jymico | www.braillejymico.com |
| Biolink Computer Research and Development | www.biolink.ca |
| Compusult Limited | www.compusult.nf.ca |
| H.K. EyeCan | www.eyecan.ca |
| Humanware | www.humanware.com/en-canada/home |
| Frontier Computing | www.frontiercomputing.on.ca |
| Madentec Limited | www.madentec.com |
| Neil Squire Society | www.neilsquire.ca |
| Sennheiser Canada | www.sennheiser.com |
| Tash Inc | www.tashinc.com |
| T-Base Communications | www.tbase.com |
| WiVik | www.wivik.com |

**Put into Practice**

Read two of the resources listed below and then talk with your peers who have read different sources. Arrange to visit a community agency that serves individuals with disabilities and their families to learn about the ways in which they are able to provide equity tools such as computer and assistive technology devices.

Specht, J., Howell, G., & Young, G. (2007). Students with special education needs in Canada and their use of assistive technology during the transition to secondary school. *Childhood Education, 83,* 385–396.

Lancioni, G.E., et al. (2008). Enabling two persons with multiple disabilities to access environmental stimuli and ask for social contact through microswitches and a VOCA. *Research in Developmental Disabilities: A Multidisciplinary Journal, 29,* 21–28.

Watson, S., & Johnston, L. (2007). Assistive technology in the inclusive science classroom. *Science Teacher, 74*(3), 34–38.

Parette, H.P., & Peterson-Karlan, G.R. (2007). Facilitating student achievement with assistive technology. *Education and Training in Developmental Disabilities, 42,* 387–397.

many of those who needed adaptations did not have them. Reasons might include the high cost of acquiring and maintaining computers and adaptive technologies, lack of awareness of government programs to absorb or offset the high costs, and our failure as a society to design for access from the outset (Tobias, 2003). Look for the work of Jacqueline Specht of the University of Western Ontario on the use of equity tools and assistive technology in Canadian schools. Table 10.2 contains information about software and hardware that enable the use of assistive technology.

**Assistive technology** is defined as "any item, piece of equipment or product system . . . that is used to increase, maintain, or improve functional capabilities of individuals with disabilities" (Ely, 2004). What kinds of assistive technologies, computer technologies, and equity tools might your students be using? The range is large (Lazzaro, 2001; Specht et al., 2007; www.collectionscanada.ca/obj/p10/f2/eacc-can.pdf). For persons with visual disabilities, speech synthesizers allow access to other software tools. For people with low vision, there are magnification systems. The CNIB lists the following high-tech product categories on its website: Braille displays, Braille embossers, Braille translation software, electronic notetakers, scanning and reading software (OCR and OBR), and screen reading software (www.cnib.ca/en/services/products). Technologies for persons with hearing impairments may incorporate fax and electronic mail as well as visual signals to replace auditory ones. Those with motor impairments may have adapted keyboards, programmable keys, and toggle switches or may wear a headset that tracks head movement and uses a puff and sip switch to replace a mouse.

Assistive technologies enable students with disabilities to access social, communicative, recreational, and academic opportunities. However, assistive technologies are not without problems. Devices are expensive, and sometimes training is unavailable or the device breaks. With the constant changes in technologies, suppliers, and assessment methods, you and your teaching colleagues may be facing questions from parents and students that you cannot answer. Look to your district school board consultants for advice; ask them to recommend provincial experts. For example, in Ontario you can consult Bloorview Kids Rehab (www.bloorviewmacmillan.on.ca) and in Alberta, the Alberta Children's Hospital (www.calgaryhealthregion.ca/ACH). There are books and websites that provide general information about assistive technologies and education (e.g., Ely, 2000; Johns Hopkins University Center for Technology in Education, http://cte.jhu.edu). Most Canadian provinces have funds to support the purchase of assistive technologies for exceptional students.

Figure 10.2 provides a worksheet for parents who think their children might benefit from assistive technologies, available on the website of Temple University (http://disabilities.temple.edu/programs/assistive/atlend/index.htm). Assistive and computer technologies facilitate independence in many ways. They enable people

## FIGURE 10.2 COMPUTERS FOR CHILDREN WITH DISABILITIES: A WORKSHEET FOR PARENTS

If you think your child needs a computer for school or home, use the following worksheet as a tool to help you determine and support your child's needs for computer equipment.

Why do you think your child needs a computer?

I think my child needs a computer because....

Have you identified the educational goals that the computer will help your child achieve?               Yes ___ No___

For example, a computer may help students improve written expression; complete assignments in a reasonable amount of time; assist in electronic research. If the primary purpose of the computer is educational, consider requesting the computer through your local school district.

Have you identified other ways in which a computer will help your child's development?               Yes ___ No ___

For example, a computer may help children to play, socialize, and lengthen attention span.

A computer will help my child....

Has your child had a computer evaluation?               Yes ___ No ___

An evaluation is necessary for determining what type of computer hardware and software are appropriate for your child. An evaluation should also identify any adaptations your child will require in order to access the computer.

An evaluation was provided by _____

The evaluator recommended a computer because....

The evaluator recommended the following equipment, software, or other adaptations for access....

Have you identified when, where, and how often your child will be using the computer?               Yes ___ No ___

The computer may be needed in the classroom, in the library or resource room, or at home.

My child will be using the computer during....

Are the computer hardware, software, and the services necessary to use them included in your child's individualized education plan (IEP)?               Yes ___ No ___

If you anticipate that the computer your child needs will be provided through your local school district, the computer should be written into your child's IEP.

The following hardware, software, and assistive technology service(s) are included in my child's IEP....

Source: Pennsylvania's Initiative on Assistive Technology, Institute on Disabilities, Temple University. Computers for *Children with Disabilities: A Worksheet for Parents*. Prepared under a grant from the National Institute on Disability and Rehabilitation Research, US Department of Education.

## Put into Practice

Visit the websites of the provincial departments of education (web addresses are given in Chapter 1) on pages 9–15. List the kinds of devices that you have learned about and look to see if information about funding to purchase such devices appears on the website of your provincial department of education. Which provinces make this information readily available? Explore the SET-BC website (www.setbc.org), view a video there, and compare notes with your peers who are accessing other resources from this website.

## Put into Practice

Visit a library at a university or college or a public library and familiarize yourself with the assistive devices available there.

## Cross-Reference

Chapter 1 contains a chart (Figure 1.2) on page 32 suggesting how to judge the merit of websites.

## What do you think?

Although individuals with disabilities are entitled to assistive technologies as equity tools, some people feel uncomfortable with this because they think that using assistive devices gives an unfair advantage. What do you think? How could you respond to a parent of a non-disabled student who raises this issue with you?

*Baking is a real-life task which fosters independent living skills; a young man with autism learns to bake with his peers.*

with physical disabilities to engage in self-advocacy by using the internet to access information (Oraveg, 2002) and then to use that knowledge to gain some control over their treatment and care (e.g., see the BC Coalition of People with Disabilities, www.bccpd.bc.ca; The Learning Disabilities Association of Canada www.ldac-taac.ca; Canadian Abilities EnableLink, http://enablelink.org).

## Summary of Student Development

To be independent learners, exceptional students need to develop learning strategies and knowledge and skills for adapting to change. Other important aspects of student development include setting goals, monitoring progress, and using school and community resources effectively and appropriately. The IEPs of exceptional students should include these important aspects of student development. Without as much independence as possible in these aspects of their lives, exceptional students are unlikely to be able to use the curriculum learning that schools usually emphasize. Some provinces (including Alberta, British Columbia, and Ontario) emphasize annual goals for all students from about grade 7 upward. If your school has a process for setting annual goals, ensure that these are aligned with the IEPs for the exceptional students in your classes.

# Fostering Interpersonal Development for Independence

The key components of interpersonal development include students managing themselves, getting along with others, and assuming social responsibility or citizenship. Chapter 6 focused on how you can create a classroom with a positive social climate that makes it easy for students to learn, participate, co-operate, take risks, assume responsibility, and grow interpersonally. In Chapter 9 you learned about enhancing peer relations and about specific strategies for helping students to learn together. However, there are excellent resources for explicitly teaching students so they grow interpersonally and become more independent in this sphere of their lives.

## Strategies for Elementary School Classrooms

For teachers of elementary school students, I recommend *Self-Discipline* by Rob Kerr (1999), a Canadian educator. Daniel Goleman (2005) argues that we need to foster in all children intelligent self-control of emotions and responses. You can create learning activities for your class that teach deliberate strategies for responding to interpersonal challenges. For example, the SAT plan (Kerr, 1999), whose name is short for Sensible Acting and Thinking, advises students to

1. Stop. Relax.
2. Think sensibly . . . just because . . . .
3. Make a plan: Be calm, be strong.
4. Reward yourself.

By using Kerr's (1999) scenarios as models, you can create scenarios that reflect issues currently important to the life of your classroom, school, or community. Don't make them so similar to real incidents that students are embarrassed or see themselves in scenarios.

For example, to teach students to recognize when they overreact, you could change the details of a recent schoolyard incident that you witnessed between the last two students to enter the building. A boy who is known to taunt students waited for a younger child who was slouching toward the school wearing red hand-me-down sneakers from his older sister. The bully taunted him with, "Girls' shoes! You're a loser, wearing girls' shoes." The younger boy punched the aggressor, tore off the sneakers, and threw them into the garbage can beside the door of the school. Figure 5.4 on page 187 contains a strategy to respond to this kind of treatment by bullies (which was an example of "putting down women"). You used this equity strategy but realized that it is also important to teach students how to minimize the impact of being on the receiving end. After disguising the details of the scenario, you can describe it to your students and explain how the young boy overreacted: we overreact if we become more upset than is productive in the context, and/or if we are unfair to others. In their journals, students could reflect on a time they think they may have overreacted. You can ask students to draw a cartoon showing someone of their age overreacting to an unfortunate event. Then teach students that what drives our reaction is what we think or believe. If we think this unfortunate event is the "end of the world," then we tell ourselves it is horrible and engage in negative self-talk that makes us feel worse and worse. If we say to ourselves, "He is a creep. I don't care what he thinks. But I don't like these shoes either. I'm going to talk to my mom about getting a different pair," we are engaging in sensible self-talk and beginning to take action, doing what we can to remedy the situation. Advise students to get control of their self-talk, and to report the incident to an adult or peer negotiator as calmly as they can. Be certain you are not simply encouraging the student to take bullying without responding. In peer

### Further Reading

Lantieri, L., & Goleman, D. (2008). *Building emotional intelligence: Techniques to cultivate inner strength in children.* Louisville, CO: Sounds True, Inc.

Panju, M. (2008). *7 successful strategies to promote emotional intelligence in the classroom.* Harrisburg, PA: Continuum International Publishing Group, Ltd.

Burke, K. (2008). *What to do with the kid who . . . . Developing cooperation, self-discipline, and responsibility in the classroom.* Thousand Oaks, CA: Corwin Press.

### Put into Practice

Develop three scenarios for your students to use to practise the SAT plan. Make the scenarios appropriate to the age of your students and the context in which you teach.

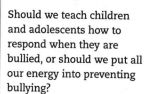

### What do you think?

Should we teach children and adolescents how to respond when they are bullied, or should we put all our energy into preventing bullying?

## FIGURE 10.3 **HAVING COURAGE**

### Further Reading

On Canadian career counselling programs:

Charter, G.A., Persaud, D., Poon-wassie, A., Williams, S., & Zinger, D. (1995). *Career counselling for Aboriginal youth: The journey inward; the journey outward.* Toronto: Guidance Centre.

Campbell, D., Serff, P., & Williams, D. (1994). *The breakaway company.* Toronto: Trifolium. (For at-risk youth.)

Jamieson, M., Paterson, J., Krupa, T., MacEachern, E., & Topping, A. (1993). *Thresholds: Enhancing the career development strategies of young people with physical disabilities.* Ottawa: Canadian Career Development Foundation.

Human Resources and Skills Development Canada. *Essential skills.* www.jobsetc.ca/equalizer/index.jsp.

Conference Board of Canada. *Creating a competency model for diversity and inclusion practitioners.* www.conferenceboard.ca/documents.asp?rnext=2553.

National Life/Work Centre and Human Resources Development Canada. (2005). *Blueprint for life/work designs.* www.lifework.ca/lifework/pr_theblueprint.html.

Canadian Career Development Foundation. (2008). *Career clearinghouse catalogue.* www.ccdf.ca/ccdf2.

Having courage is important to everyone. But acting on our personal values is not always easy. Nor is it always easy to stick up for ourselves or to say "No." We can learn to have courage, to act on our own values, by reminding ourselves to be calm and strong to do the right thing.

### Activity

1. Read Randy's story:

   Randy went out with some friends on Tuesday night. Finally Chip said, "Hey guys, let's go over to the school and throw some rocks through the windows. It'll be a riot." Some of the others laughed. Randy felt uneasy. It wasn't his thing. He believed it was wrong and stupid, yet his friends were important to him. He said to himself, "Be calm, be strong. I have to have some courage here." He looked at Chip, straight in the eye: "Sorry guys, that's a bit stupid. I'm not up for that." Chip became offended: "Are you saying we're stupid, Randy?" "No," Randy replied. "You guys are great, but that idea is a bit stupid. Breaking windows costs my parents and your parents money. Your taxes, my taxes. I'm not up for it. See you guys tomorrow." Randy smiled, turned, and walked away.

2. Have a brief discussion about Randy. What did he tell himself in order to act with courage? Is it harder to be courageous with friends or non-friends?

3. Ask students to work in small groups to plan and present a skit. They should show a character in the skit acting with courage. These characters think out loud to share courageous self-talk.

Make the point that it is often difficult to act with courage, especially with friends. But, in the long run, people respect courageous individuals. Stress too that courageous action comes from courageous self-talk. Ask: What are some courageous self-statements we might use?

### Reflection Journal
Invite students to reflect in their journals on a time when they acted with courage. Have them describe the situation and their courageous self-talk. Ask them how they felt afterwards. Were they proud of themselves?

Source: R. Kerr (1999). *Self-Discipline: Using Portfolios to Help Students Develop Self-Awareness, Manage Emotions and Build Relationships.* Markham, ON: Pembroke Publishers. Used by permission.

negotiator programs children are trained to help resolve conflicts between their peers (e.g., Peace Works PEI, www.isn.net/acph/1.htm). Then continue to teach your students strategies for relaxing, jumping to the right conclusions, laughing about the things that happen, and being "calm and strong" when responding to people who treat them unfairly or rudely (Kerr, 1999). Kerr's activities on building relationships have students role-playing and reflecting on such skills as active listening, win–win plans, and having courage. Figure 10.3 shows Kerr's activity for helping students to learn to have courage and be responsible citizens by refusing to go along with the inappropriate actions of others.

## Strategies for Secondary School Classrooms

Secondary school teachers might want to focus such learning much more on "Solving Problems on the Job" and "Anger Management on the Job." These are the titles of two of the modules in *Pathways* (Hutchinson & Freeman, 1994). The advantage to focusing on the workplace with adolescents is that you can help them look ahead and develop strategies for new challenges that await them, rather than reminding them of failures they have experienced in the school context. These modules include school examples and workplace examples but focus students on preparing for participation in workplace experience within their courses, co-operative learning, part-time jobs, and future careers. "Anger Management on the Job" includes the *CALMER* strategy:

**C**heck that there is a problem.

**A**ssess the nature of the problem.

**L**ist possible alternatives.

**M**ake a decision about the best alternative.

**E**valuate the consequences.

**R**epeat the process, if necessary.

## Summary for Interpersonal Development

Interpersonal development includes children and adolescents learning to take responsibility for the way they interact with others and for their social and civic obligations. It includes students working co-operatively in the classroom and anticipating the collaboration and co-operation that will be required of them in the workplace. These are all essential for independent learning and independent living. Exceptional students sometimes find responsible interdependence challenging because they need practice in reading social cues, speaking up appropriately, and responding to criticism (e.g., Bauminger, Edelsztein, & Morash, 2005; Wagner, Newman, et al., 2007). IEPs should include goals for interpersonal development.

Cross-Reference
Chapter 9 includes suggestions for teaching to enhance interpersonal development, all of which might appear as strategies for implementation on the IEPs of exceptional students.

# Career Development and Career Education for Exceptional Individuals

The third area of learning in the recent guidance and career planning curricula is career development. Clearly related to personal development and interpersonal development, career development contributes to independent learning and especially to independent living. Career development is based on the idea that career aspirations develop gradually over time and require experiences and reflection on those experiences (Cassidy, 2007; Gottfredson, 2002). For exceptional individuals, most would agree that career development begins in childhood and extends through adolescence into the adult years (Cinamon & Gifsh, 2004; Hutchinson et al., 2008; Morningstar, 1997). Super's (Super et al., 1996; Jepsen & Dickson, 2003) lifespan theory of career development indicates that career awareness and exploration begin early in life and continue until the mid-thirties. Super has suggested adolescence should be spent focusing on career exploration rather than preparation for a specific occupation. He has stressed the need for planned exploration, experience, and evaluated trial experience in workplaces to develop career maturity and planfulness. Most career education programs for adolescents with disabilities include three components: self-awareness/career awareness, career exploration, and career experiences.

Recent research on the social cognitive career theory (SCCT) (developed by Lent, Hackett, & Brown, 1999) has been used to understand career development and work-based education (WBE) in minority students (e.g., Gushue, 2006) and in students with disabilities (e.g., Punch, Creed, & Hyde, 2005). This approach to career development assumes that we are agents of and influence our own experiences and development. It focuses on attributes of the individual, contextual factors, and behaviour as well as on how these three aspects interact and influence one

Further Reading

On career development for children:

Watson, M., & McMahon, M. (2005). Children's career development: A research review from a learning perspective. *Journal of Vocational Behavior, 67*(2), 119–132.

Cassidy, R.A. (2007). The benefits of a comprehensive K–12 career deveopment system. *Techniques: Connecting Education and Careers, 82*(4), 44–46.

Stott, K.A., & Jackson, A.P. (2005). Using service learning to achieve middle school comprehensive guidance program goals. *Professional School Counseling, 9*(2), 156–159.

another. Case studies reported by Hutchinson et al. (2008) demonstrated the applicability of SCCT for understanding how youth with disabilities negotiate accommodations in work-based education so they can participate fully and learn by doing. Naomi, who had spastic cerebral palsy, was able to negotiate the removal of barriers that might have interfered with her reaching her goals. She formed links between her interests and her career-related goals. Through her experiences in and reflections on WBE, she formed positive, realistic self-efficacy. Naomi wanted to become a travel agent and to help people with disabilities to travel without barriers. At the end of her final interview, Naomi offered, "Anything worthwhile takes some, takes a bit of risk . . . I think people should go for what they want," adding, "People need to know what they want." Naomi's WBE program facilitated self-awareness/career awareness, career exploration, and career experiences.

## Developing Self-Awareness and Career Awareness

Strategies for self-awareness are important for exceptional learners and should be developed over time so that prior to employment and post-secondary education opportunities, individuals can describe their strengths and needs with confidence and clarity (Hutchinson & Freeman, 1994; Van Reusen & Bos, 1994; Versnel, 2005).

**Self-awareness** refers to knowing oneself, developing a picture of the kind of person one is. For students with disabilities, self-awareness includes understanding the characteristics associated with their disability—their personal strengths and needs. Students need self-awareness about their interests, preferences, abilities, and anything else that defines them. Career is usually thought to refer to both the process of making a living by means of a particular occupation and the broader notion of one's course or progress through life (Super, Savickas, & Super, 1996). Thus career awareness refers to students' understanding of all aspects of adult responsibilities, roles, and the nature and meaning of work. This includes the incredible range of ways in which adults engage in paid work, volunteer and unpaid work, and other pursuits including leisure activities, child rearing, and citizenship.

Counsellors and teachers at secondary and post-secondary levels usually emphasize students' self-knowledge. However, this process can and should start much earlier (Clark, et al., 1991; Gibson, 2005; Lent, Hackett, & Brown, 1999; Stott & Jackson, 2005). Young children can describe their hobbies and interests, what they save their money for, and what they would most like to do on their next vacation. These activities can be carried out in pairs and small groups with drawings and short pieces of writing showing the results of the deliberations. It is difficult to separate self-awareness from career awareness because many activities designed to help students come to know themselves highlight how characteristics, interests, abilities, etc., are related to choices, roles, and careers.

Inviting adults into the classroom to talk about their work can provide lively career education. Prepare questions for children to use as models of what to ask; if you are concerned about inappropriate questions, have a rehearsal session before the first visitor. The school or community librarian can assist by recommending books that match children's professed interests in hobbies and careers. Remember to invite adults who have pursued non-traditional career paths, adults representing the cultural diversity of the neighbourhood, and adults with disabilities. Avoid reinforcing stereotypes and introduce careers that may be unfamiliar to the children. When your school has visitors, arrange for those adults to visit your class. One of

Further Reading

Delisle, D., & Delisle, J. (2007). *Growing good kids: 28 activities to enhance self-awareness, compassion, and leadership.* Minneapolis, MN: Free Spirit Pub.

Hughes, R.S., & Kloeppel, P.C. (1998). *SAIL: Self-awareness in language arts.* Minneapolis, MN: Educational Media Corp.

Huggins, P., Wood-Manion, D.W., Moen, L., & Tyler, E. (1999). *Helping kids find their strengths.* Longmont, CO: Sopris West.

Kincher, J., & Bach, J. (2002). *Psychology for kids: 40 fun tests that help you learn about yourself.* Minneapolis, MN: Free Spirit Pub.

Plue, L., Palmer, W., & Karakokkinos, C. (2000). *Careers today and tomorrow.* Toronto: Irwin Publishing. (Student text and teacher's resource guide.)

my best career and self-awareness units as an elementary teacher included inviting musicians from the Montreal Symphony to speak briefly to my students about themselves and answer the students' questions. The students learned to ask about how the musicians knew that this was the career they wanted, when they learned enough about themselves to know they wanted to be musicians, etc. Then we invited parents, storekeepers, members of our community, the school janitor, and the school principal to visit us. After every session the students made entries in their "Book About Myself," recording what they were learning about themselves through this process. There are many approaches, for example, using literature to enhance children's self-awareness (e.g., Hughes & Kloeppel, 1998); series of activities such as Huggins, Wood-Manion, Moen, and Tyler (1999) and Kincher and Bach (2002); and using service learning (Stott & Jackson, 2005). Remember to turn the emphasis back to the students learning about themselves—increasing self-awareness.

Self-awareness and career awareness are often associated with the developmental tasks of adolescence. Many provinces include courses on career development and co-operative education in the secondary curriculum, which include a component on self-awareness. Kerr (1999) recommends that adolescents develop portfolios to learn about themselves. There are also sources for leading discussion groups made up of adolescents with and without disabilities (e.g., Peterson, 1993) and groups composed entirely of exceptional adolescents (e.g., Dennison, 1997). Many of these ideas are explored in the edited resource by Bakken and Obiakor (2008). The Canadian program *Pathways* (Hutchinson & Freeman, 1994) includes a module called "Knowing About Yourself, Knowing About Careers." Figure 10.4 contains an activity sheet from *Pathways* called "Personal Strengths."

## Career Exploration

**Career exploration**, actions that teach about possible careers and adult roles, can take many forms. Engaging in imaginative play, reading, watching films, playing on teams, and developing hobbies and interests all contribute to career exploration. When parents say that their exceptional children have too much homework and cannot take part in extracurricular activities, you may want to speak up. These after-school pursuits are critical in helping young people to engage in career exploration. You may have known a gifted young woman who chaired the public relations committee in secondary school and began to consider a career in marketing. Or a boy with developmental disabilities who cooked for the school "family days" and asked if he could visit a cafeteria to learn about possible careers in food preparation. Students must reflect on the exploration or experience and relate it to themselves. Questions students can ask include, Did I enjoy doing that and why? How good was I at that? How confident do I feel about doing it again? Why was that so interesting? Is this something that makes me feel "in my element"? If I were to do this every day, how would I feel about it?

You can contribute to career exploration by including discussions of the application of the knowledge you are teaching. When your students study history, you can point out how history is used to create lifelike settings for films and television programs and invite a historian to tell your students what he or she does. When studying design and technology, discuss with students how engineers, technicians, and construction workers on the teams that design and build bridges apply this kind of knowledge. Invite an array of individuals who work with people, including

**What do you think?**

M. Nagler and A. Nagler's (1999) *What's Stopping You: Living Successfully with Disability* (Toronto: Stoddart) is a comprehensive Canadian manual for self-advocacy that focuses more on adults than on adolescents and children. What would you ask the authors if you had an opportunity to meet them?

For a different perspective, read A. Boylan (2008), *Advocacy for Children and Young Adults* (McGraw-Hill Education [Open University Press of the UK]) or C.M. Oliver, J. Dalrymple, and C. Booth's *Developing Advocacy for Children and Young People: Current Issues in Research, Policy and Practice* (Jessica Kingsley Ltd.). Again, what would you ask the authors if you could meet them?

## FIGURE 10.4 PERSONAL STRENGTHS

Name: _____

Partner: _____

Have your partner record your answers to the questions below and list your three greatest strengths.

|  | Yes | Sometimes | No |
|---|---|---|---|
| 1. Do I value other people's opinions? | ___ | ___ | ___ |
| 2. Do I make good decisions? | ___ | ___ | ___ |
| 3. Do I like talking to people? | ___ | ___ | ___ |
| 4. Do I like fixing things? | ___ | ___ | ___ |
| 5. Do I organize my time well? | ___ | ___ | ___ |
| 6. Am I a responsible person? | ___ | ___ | ___ |
| 7. Do I write about my ideas? | ___ | ___ | ___ |
| 8. Do I think for myself? | ___ | ___ | ___ |
| 9. Am I a team player? | ___ | ___ | ___ |
| 10. Do I work hard? | ___ | ___ | ___ |
| 11. Do I try to look my best? | ___ | ___ | ___ |
| 12. Do I finish what I start? | ___ | ___ | ___ |

My three greatest strengths:

1. _____

2. _____

3. _____

Source: Hutchinson, N.L., & Freeman, J.G. (1994). *Pathways: Knowing About Yourself, Knowing About Careers*. Scarborough, ON: Nelson Canada. Used by permission.

occupational therapists, child-care workers, and bus drivers. Remember that chefs and pharmacists are applied chemists. When you focus on the connections between the curriculum and possible careers, you engage your students in career exploration. Encourage students to ask questions, consult books and websites, and learn about the educational qualifications, demands, wages, and dangers of the careers that interest them. Many provinces have extensive websites intended to help adolescents and young adults to secure the information they need to make informed decisions (e.g., SaskNetWork; www.sasknetwork.ca). Provide opportunities for children and adolescents to interview adults in careers that intrigue them. Encourage wide exploration of many possibilities rather than premature narrowing to one or two careers.

Individualized transition plans provide youth with disabilities with systematic opportunities to gradually become aware of their own strengths and weaknesses and to develop career maturity. Using case-study research, Hutchinson and her colleagues (2008) reported on the experiences of two adolescents—one with physical disabilities (Naomi) and one with intellectual disabilities (Max)—negotiating workplace accommodations during co-operative education. In the travel agency where she obtained work experience, Naomi, who has already been introduced in this chapter, negotiated physical accommodations, social and cognitive accommodations, and teaching-and-learning accommodations. She formed links between her interests and her career-related goals, as well as acquiring positive, realistic self-efficacy and outcome expectations. In his placement in a lumber store, Max received the same types of accommodations as Naomi but had only a small role in negotiating them. He also experienced difficulty translating his vague career goals into actions. Also using case-study research, Lindstrom and Benz (2002) reported on the career trajectories of young women with learning disabilities following their graduation from high school. It took many of them a number of years to establish stable, productive careers. In two recent case studies Chris DeLuca, Nancy Hutchinson, and their colleagues at Queen's University (2008) reported on two at-risk youth, Tim and Ashley, who thrived in work-based education (WBE), developed resiliency, and each secured full-time employment within one year of completing a structured WBE program that included work experience designed to facilitate their transitions. Both had been disengaged by regular school programs; Ashley had returned to school after dropping out and Tim had avoided dropping out by choosing WBE.

The Calgary Educational Partnership Foundation (2003) published an excellent resource for secondary school students and their teachers called *Employability Skills Portfolios: Creating My Future* (see www.cepfoundation.com). It is a student document that focuses on career goals, plans, and actions one can take to move toward those goals. It helps students develop a portfolio to record progress and show to employers when applying for employment, to post-secondary programs that require portfolios, or to co-operative educational institutions.

Recently career counsellors have begun to recognize that conventional career counselling may not meet the needs of Aboriginal youth (e.g., Peavy, 1994; 2003) because it is based on a world view not shared by many Aboriginals, and counsellors who lack cultural awareness may not recognize what is important to Aboriginals in career-life planning. In 1994 Anne Charter and her colleagues in Manitoba developed a program, called *Career Counselling for Aboriginal Youth: The Journey Inward; the Journey Outward*, with advice and assistance from four Manitoba First Nations communities. In 2002 Rod McCormick from the University of British Columbia, a member of the Mohawk nation, and two colleagues produced a career-life planning model for First Nations people called Guiding Circles (McCormick, Amundson, & Poehnell, 2002). The background is elaborated in the boxed feature Theory and Research Highlights from Educational Psychology: Career Counselling for Aboriginal Youth.

## Why Career Development Is Critical to the Participation of Youth in the Labour Market

Career development has become a critical issue for at-risk youth and youth with disabilities for a number of reasons. The world faces a growing youth employment crisis. Worldwide, youth are three times as likely to be unemployed as adults (International Labour Office, 2006). Recent international reviews suggest that contributing factors include the disengagement of youth from education as well as a changing labour market that can no longer absorb young workers with minimal qualifications (McGinty & Brader, 2005). Canadian researchers have begun to focus on the relationship of risk factors—including disability, homelessness, and family breakdown—to unemployment and disengagement (e.g., Hutchinson et al., 2008; the cases already described of two at-risk youth, Ashley and Tim). Enabling

# Career Counselling for Aboriginal Youth

In recent years there have been reports of the failure of conventional career counselling to meet the needs of Aboriginal youth (e.g., Herring, 1989; Peavy, 2004). The argument has been that conventional career counselling models are based on a world view not shared by many Aboriginals, and that counsellors who lack cultural awareness fail to recognize what is important to Aboriginals in career-life planning. Offet-Gartner focuses on the core beliefs of First Nations people including the connectedness of the universe (Lightning, 1992) and the necessity of involving family and community members whenever a person seeks any form of help or healing. Another belief is that the Creator bestows unique gifts on every person, and these gifts are "the underlying basis for aptitudes and skill development" (McCormick & Amundson, 1997). Roles and responsibilities, including sharing gifts, are learned through stories, ceremonies, and within the family and the community. Conventional career counselling tends to focus on work to the exclusion of other life responsibilities, and research suggests that First Nations people do not define themselves by their work but put more emphasis on their life responsibilities and on balance among four life functions: mental, physical, emotional, and spiritual (Poonwassie & Charter, 2001). Examples of traditional healing methods for counselling women (Heibron & Guttman, 2000) and students (Wyrstok & Paulson, 2000) and for treating substance abuse (McCormick, 2000) are reported in a special issue of *Canadian Journal of Counselling*, volume 34, issue 1.

In 1994 the Canadian Career Development Foundation supported the development of a career counselling program expressly for First Nations youth, called *Career Counselling for Aboriginal Youth: The Journey Inward; the Journey Outward* (Charter, Persaud, Poonwassie, Williams, & Zinger, 1994). This program, developed in Manitoba, used the concept of a vision quest to integrate Aboriginal values in a unique journey.

Earlier, Norm Amundson of the University of British Columbia had developed a centric model of individual counselling (1987, 1989), which he began to reshape with his colleague, Rod McCormick, a member of the Mohawk nation. Together they produced a *Career-Life Planning Model for First Nations People* (McCormick & Amundson, 1997). They demonstrate how this is a culturally relevant model that considers components critical to First Nations people including connectedness, balance, needs, roles, gifts and aptitudes, and values. These all appear in eight segments in a circular model with the youth at the centre, ringed by

family and then community. Guidelines for practitioners are described in McCormick, Neumann, Amundson, and McLean (1999). After introductory comments (and ceremonies, if desired), the facilitator uses a pattern analysis exercise (Amundson, 1995) to help a youth identify an activity that he or she enjoys, descriptions of feelings, people involved, motivations, etc. The facilitator then seeks input from family and community members present. Metaphors are used to stimulate the development of new insight (Amundson, 1995; Inkson & Amundson, 2002). About two weeks after the initial session, the facilitator sends a copy of the youth's completed Career/Life Planning Guide, a thank you letter, and an invitation to meet again. McCormick and colleagues (1999) include a case study of a youth named Sarah who engaged in this process with family and community members taking part.

In 2003 the Aboriginal Human Resource Council (AHRC) supported a demonstration project for the program that was renamed Guiding Circles (McCormick, Amundson, & Poehnell, 2002). The final report and recommendations appear at www.aboriginalhr.ca/en/programs/guidingcircles. This website includes tip sheets for counsellors, information on how to order the program, and details on the reactions of those involved in the demonstration project. The recent work on Guiding Circles demonstrates the collaboration of researchers—First Nations and non–First Nations—with Aboriginal peoples and organizations. Such collaboration will be necessary to generate effective practices and enable First Nations youth, with and without disabilities, to participate fully in all aspects of Canadian society, including realizing satisfying and productive careers. The Aboriginal Human Resource Council has also developed, in 2008, a set of five modules on *Mastering Aboriginal Inclusion* to help guide organizations toward a culture of Aboriginal inclusion. Each module contains detailed explanation and a wide variety of tutorials, tip sheets, fact sheets, models, templates, guides, and tools (www.aboriginalhr.ca/en/programs/MAI/modules).

## References

Amundson, N.E. (1987). A visual means of organizing career information. *Journal of Employment Counseling*, 24, 2–7.

Amundson, N.E. (1989). A model of individual counseling. *Journal of Employment Counseling*, 26, 132–138.

Amundson, N.E. (1995). Pattern identification exercise. *Clearinghouse*

*continued*

on *Counseling and Student Services* (ERIC Document Reproduction Services N. EDO-CG-95-69).

Charter, A., Persaud, D., Poonwassie, A., Williams, S.W., & Zinger, D. (1994). *Career counselling for aboriginal youth: The journey inward; the journey outward*. Toronto: University of Toronto Press.

Heilbron, C.L., & Guttman, M.A.J. (2000). Traditional healing methods with First Nations women in group counselling. *Canadian Journal of Counselling, 34*, 3–13.

Herring, R.D. (1989). Counseling Native-American children: Implications for elementary school counselors. *Elementary School Guidance and Counseling, 23*, 272–281.

Inkson, K., & Amumdson, N. (2002). Career metaphors and their application in theory and counseling practice. *Journal of Employment Counseling, 39*(3), 98–108.

Lightning, W.C. (1992). Compassionate mind: Implications of a text written by Elder Louis Sunchild. *Canadian Journal of Native Education, 19*, 115–153.

McCormick, R.M. (2000). Aboriginal traditions in the treatment of substance abuse. *Canadian Journal of Counselling, 34*, 25–32.

youth, including those with disabilities, to access the labour market is very important for the well-being of both these individuals and our country.

**Labour market information** provides those working and aspiring to work with details about current and projected demand for labour services and supply of labour services in the economy (www.labourmarketinformation.ca). Thus, youth who might express interest in work that takes advantage of their numerical abilities could learn about the demand for mathematics teachers, actuarial professionals, chartered accountants, mathematics professors, and mathematical engineers. The same kind of information is available about any cluster of ability-related occupations. With the advent of computers and the internet, it is much easier to access labour market information.

Parents, teachers, and employers often assume that career exploration and decision-making are easy for gifted students, who have high academic achievement and many abilities, and can access information easily (Maxwell, 2007). However, research over the past fifteen years suggests that as many as half of academically advanced students experience difficulties and want help with career exploration and decision-making (Emmett & Minor, 1993; Paterson, 2006). Meredith Greene (2006), a former teacher in Nova Scotia, reviewed the psychological and emotional issues that affect career choice for gifted adolescents. Many researchers, including John Stewart (1999) of the University of New Brunswick and Millie Maxwell (2007), have reported that the difficulties experienced by gifted students included indecision, pressure from others, lack of career role models, and lack of meaningfulness or personal challenge in careers. Michael Pyryt (1992; Pyryt & Romney, 2002) of the University of Calgary suggests how counsellors and teachers can help gifted students engage in divergent thinking strategies to combine interests and lifestyle issues into a meaningful occupational choice and use social giftedness in their chosen pursuits.

Kerr and Sodano (2003) and Maxwell (2007) point out some of the specific issues that may differentially affect gifted males, females, and minorities. For example, gifted females often experience uncertainty about their abilities and their interests during the adolescent years, while males are more likely to pursue linear career paths toward high-status careers from adolescence into the early adult years. Many gifted youth from culturally diverse backgrounds have a deep concern for their communities and limit their career interests to careers that would be of

Weblinks

LABOUR MARKET INFORMATION (HUMAN RESOURCES AND SKILLS DEVELOPMENT CANADA)
www.labourmarketinformation.ca

CANADA PROSPECTS
www.canadaprospects.com/
products/cp_nav/home.cfm

LABOUR FORCE SURVEY (LATEST RELEASE), STATISTICS CANADA
www.statcan.ca/english/Subjects/
Labour/LFS/lfs-en.htm

JOBPOSTCANADA.COM
www.jobpostcanada.com/
generalsites.htm

MANITOBA WORKINFONET.CA
http://mb.workinfonet.ca

LEARNING TOOLS (CONFERENCE BOARD OF CANADA)
www.conferenceboard.ca/
education/learning-tools

**Further Reading**

On self-determination and self-advocacy:

McCarthy, D. (2007). Teaching self-advocacy to students with disabilities. *About Campus, 12*(5), 10–16.

Chambers, C.R., Wehmeyer, M.L., et al. (2007). Self-determination: What do we know? Where do we go? *Exceptionality, 15*(1), 3–15.

Bremer, C.D., Kachgal, M., & Schoeller, K. (2003). Self-determination: Supporting successful transition. *Research to Practice Brief, 2*(1). (Available at www.ncset.org.)

National Council on Disability. (2003). *Understanding disabilities in American Indian and Alaska Native communities. Toolkit Guide.* Washington, DC: National Council on Disability. (Available at www.ncd.gov.)

Wood, W.M., Karvonen, M., Test, D.W., Browder, D., & Algozzine, B. (2004). Promoting student self-determination skills in IEP planning. *Teaching Exceptional Children, 36*(3), 8–16.

Pearl, C. (2004). Laying the foundation for self-advocacy: Fourth graders with learning disabilities invite their peers into the resource room. *Teaching Exceptional Children, 36*(3), 44–49.

service there, while grappling with implicit messages from their communities that they may fail to achieve their goals. Whiting (2006) identifies issues specific to black males, and Assouline and her colleagues (2006) focus on the counselling needs of students who are twice exceptional, those who are gifted and also have a disability, while Burney and Cross (2006) identify counselling needs of gifted students who live in poverty in rural settings.

Career exploration is a complex and lengthy process of seeking and reflecting on information and experience, setting goals and monitoring progress toward them, and changing direction and pursuing alternatives. There are many competencies and perspectives that young people need to develop and embrace to progress in career development. Some of these include self-advocacy and self-determination.

## Self-Advocacy

Self-advocacy is essential in every role from student to employee. **Self-advocacy** is important for promoting independent learning and independent living and refers to "an individual's ability to effectively communicate, convey, negotiate or assert his or her own interests, desires, needs, and rights" (Van Reusen & Bos, 1994, p. 466). It also involves making informed decisions and taking responsibility for those decisions. For example, if a student is to explain to a teacher the accommodations he needs in order to submit assignments when his cerebral palsy prevents him from writing with a pencil, he will have to know about his own strengths and needs (Fowler et al., 2007; Nagler & Nagler, 1999). Self-advocacy also contributes to career development. If an employee with a disability is to explain to an employer how her computer will have to be adapted, she must be articulate about her own condition or disability as well as about the demands and routines of the workplace (e.g., Hutchinson et al., 2008). It takes confidence, courage, and determination to be one's own spokesperson. David Test and his colleagues have reviewed the relevant literature (Test, Fowler, Brewer, et al., 2005) and developed a conceptual framework for understanding self-advocacy for students with disabilities (Test, Fowler, Wood, et al., 2005). Their model has four main components: knowledge of self, knowledge of rights, communication, and leadership. Knowledge of self is seen as the first step toward self-advocacy, followed by knowledge of one's rights. Next is communication of what one knows and is entitled to, followed by leadership, which refers to leading oneself and others.

Research has been conducted on self-advocacy for individuals with almost every exceptionality we have discussed. In a program designed to enhance self-advocacy of adolescents with learning disabilities (Van Reusen & Bos, 1990; 1994; Versnel, 2005), adolescents learn strategies to increase their participation in IEP conferences. They learn specific strategies for inventorying their strengths and weaknesses, recording this information on inventory sheets, listening and responding, asking questions, and naming their goals. Lancaster and her colleagues (2002) used an interactive hypermedia program with adolescents with LD for teaching self-advocacy. Similar approaches have been recommended for teaching students who are deaf (Luckner & Muir, 2002), students with visual impairments (Krebs, 2002), individuals with mental illnesses or emotional disabilities (www.nami.org/Content/ContentGroups/Legal/ManagedCare.pdf), and students with physical and cognitive disabilities (Biklen & Schein, 2001; Johnson, 1999; Konrad, Trela, & Test, 2006), as well as gifted students (Robinson, 1996). Other groups have also

## Accessing Information

Marie Laporte-Stark has long been an advocate for access for Canadians with disabilities. While Marie and her husband are blind, their children are sighted. She says that "within the home, access to information was rarely a problem" because this was an environment she could shape. For example, she used a kettle that whistles when water has boiled and labelled microwave controls in Braille. However, the neighbourhood school turned out to be a more challenging environment for accessing important information. While students who were blind had access to Braille textbooks and assignments, Marie could not convince the school that she needed Braille copies of her children's textbooks to help them with their homework. She says, "I found ways around most of these barriers to participation in my children's education." The barrier Marie could not overcome was her need for Braille copies of her children's report cards.

The school suggested that the children read the report cards to their parents or that the parents ask a friend to read the report cards to them. However, Marie knew that she had a right to this critical information in an accessible form. Marie persisted and eventually the family filed a complaint with the Human Rights Commission of their province. After many years of Marie's "advocacy for access," the school district adopted an Alternate Format Policy. Marie says, "This policy means that, today, other parents who are blind can obtain report cards, school materials, and school information in a form they can read independently—just as parents with sight have been doing for decades."

Thinking about school–home interactions from the point of view of the parent may not be easy for us as teachers. However, Marie Laporte-Stark's advocacy reminds us what individuals with disabilities need for full participation in our schools and communities—the same access to information, opportunities, and outcomes as people without disabilities. Principals can authorize that schools fund the provision of information to parents in alternative formats. Blind parents have a right to expect principals and teachers to take these actions.

Source: Based on M. Laporte-Stark (1998). Advocating for access. *Abilities, 37* (Winter), pp. 14–17.

---

emphasized self-advocacy, including persons with traumatic brain injury (www. headinjury.com/advocacy.htm) and Epilepsy Newfoundland and Labrador (http:// epilepsynl.com/membership.html). Self-advocacy is a skill that adults must use frequently to ensure fair treatment in a busy and impersonal world—this is especially so for adults with disabilities. The Focus on Advocacy feature tells the story of one Canadian woman who learned to advocate for herself and her family.

## Self-Determination

Recently researchers and practitioners have begun to focus on a larger construct in preparing youth with disabilities for independence and for playing a valued role: self-determination. **Self-determination** refers to the abilities, motivation, and volition that enable people to define goals for themselves and take and sustain the initiative to reach those goals (Chambers, Wehmeyer et al., 2007; Versnel, 2001, 2005). Self-determination entails choosing, and enacting choices, to control one's life to the maximum extent possible based on knowing and valuing oneself, and in pursuit of one's own needs, interests, and values (Brislin, 2008; Campeau & Wolman, 1993; Malian & Nevin, 2002).

During the 1990s, a number of research groups in the United States developed curricula under the auspices of the Office of Special Education and Rehabilitation Services (OSERS) that were geared primarily to the needs of individuals with developmental disabilities. Wehmeyer (e.g., Chambers, Wehmeyer et al., 2007; Wehmeyer, 1992; Wehmeyer & Palmer, 2003), one of the leaders in this field, emphasized self-determination as enabling one to act as "the primary causal agent in one's life and making choices and decisions regarding one's quality of life" (1992,

**Weblinks**

ONTARIO CO-OPERATIVE EDUCATION
ASSOCIATION
www.ocea.on.ca

NEW BRUNSWICK YOUTH CAREER
CONNECTIONS PROGRAM (FORMERLY
KNOWN AS YOUTH APPRENTICESHIP)
www.youthapprenticeship.ca/
index.php

MANITOBA ABORIGINAL APPRENTICESHIP
TRAINING
www.gov.mb.ca/tce/apprent/
future/aboriginal_apprentice.html

ALBERTA, CAREERS: THE NEXT
GENERATION
www.nextgen.org

p. 305). Each curriculum emphasized the teaching of the skills, behaviours, and dispositions its authors thought necessary for self-determination. These curricula included

- ChoiceMaker Self-Determination Curriculum (Martin & Marshal, 1995)
- Steps to Self-Determination (Field & Hoffman, 1996)
- Take Charge (Powers, Sowers, Turner, Nesbitt, Knowles, & Ellison, 1996)

A review and synthesis of the best practices, curricula, and research on self-advocacy and self-determination is available from the Self-Determination Synthesis project at the University of North Carolina at Charlotte (www.uncc.edu/sdsp/self_advocacy/self_advocacy.asp).

## Career Experiences

*Career experiences* refers to the opportunities adolescents have to try out and experience aspects of the working role that is expected of adults. Some describe this as the reality testing of the understanding developed through career exploration. In Canada the most common forms of career experiences that occur within school programs are co-operative education and work experience. Both the Canadian Labour Force Development Board (1994) and the Advisory Council on Science and Technology (2000) in its report *Stepping Up: Skills and Opportunities in the Knowledge Economy* have recommended co-operative education as a central component of the transition to work. Provincial ministries of education have increased their focus on co-operative education and this emphasis is apparent on their websites (e.g., Ontario: www.uncc.edu/sdsp/self_advocacy/self_advocacy.asp; British Columbia: www.bced.gov.bc.ca/careers/coopinfo.htm; and Nova Scotia: www.ednet.ns.ca/O2).

### CO-OPERATIVE EDUCATION AND WORKPLACE LEARNING

**Co-operative education (co-op)**, in which schools co-operate with employers, involves students in extended periods of time in a workplace (often around one hundred hours over a school term) while enrolled in full-time study. Typically students also engage in classroom orientations to the workplace and in reflective seminars. **Workplace experience** is usually of shorter duration, ranging from a one-day job-shadowing experience to a few half-day visits within the context of a credit course. A review of the co-op education and career education policies across Canada at the end of the 1990s showed that all provinces and territories provide co-op education and/or workplace experiences; however, various organizational approaches are used (Hutchinson et al., 1999). This review also showed that only the co-op education curricula that were revised since 1990 referred directly to the provision of accommodations in co-op education and workplace learning for exceptional students. There were frequent references to the needs of at-risk students.

Research suggests that adolescents with disabilities can benefit from co-op and career education (Hutchinson et al., 2008), as can youth who are at risk for dropping out (DeLuca et al., 2008). These students often learn well in structured, hands-on,

*"I want the same things as other people—to work and to live on my own."*

experiential settings—often much better than in traditional classrooms. In a study of college and university students from four programs, Chin, Munby, Hutchinson, and Steiner-Bell (2000) found that over 95 percent of those who had *and* had not taken co-op education in secondary school recommended it to others. Their reasons for taking co-op education were often combinations of career exploration and career experiences, for example, wanting to try out careers that interested them and use the information to help them decide whether to pursue a particular career. A review of representative curriculum documents from school districts in Ontario (Hutchinson et al., 2001) showed that school districts saw co-op education as a means of helping students make connections between the classroom and the world of work, as well as a means of career exploration and career experiences.

Research conducted in the United States with students with various disabilities suggests that vocational or on-the-job training during the high school years for a particular entry-level job is premature (e.g., Heal & Rusch, 1995; Stuart & Smith, 2002). Morningstar (1997) recommends a balanced program of career development that includes opportunities to develop career maturity and self-determination through meaningful work experiences that are primarily for learning, not simply on-the-job-training. Morningstar describes an ideal program that is much like co-op education as it is practised in Canada. Encourage your exceptional students and their parents to consider co-op education as an integral part of their secondary school years. In our research at Queen's University with adolescents in co-op education, we have learned that co-op stretches adolescents—with and without disabilities—in ways that we had not imagined (Munby et al., 2001; DeLuca et al., 2008).

It is important that career development include opportunities for exceptional students to dream about their futures and become enthusiastic about being valued and taking adult roles, because "the specific nature of a youth's dream is less important than the enthusiasm dreaming generates for goal achievement" (Powers et al., 1996, p. 12). Roets, Goodley, and Van Hove (2007) also encourage us to foster the dreams of individuals with disabilities. Co-operative education enables adolescents to dream, to reality-test their dreams, and to grow into independent adult roles.

# Independent Living

Much has been written in the past decade about independent living, particularly about people with developmental disabilities (e.g., Bakken & Obiakor, 2008; Felce et al., 2008). For some time the emphasis has been on enhancing strategies for community participation, a topic addressed by Zana Marie Lutfiyya and her colleagues of the University of Manitoba (e.g., Schwartz, Mactavish, & Lutfiyya, 2006). Recently researchers and advocates have begun to focus on what is called community support as well. This evolution toward supported participation in the roles, and to meet the goals, chosen by individuals with disabilities could lead to immense changes in social policy in the next decade.

## Strategies for Community Participation

Community participation demands independent living skills and career development. The needs of exceptional adolescents, in particular, may differ from those of their peers (Brolin, 1997). While learning these skills in inclusive classrooms is encouraged, it may also be necessary to increase the intensity of teaching and the opportunities for practice in personal, interpersonal, and career development, just as it may be necessary for academic learning. Many writers have suggested recently that aiming for **community participation** requires community education during the school years and not just classroom education (e.g., Burcroff Radogna, & Wright, 2003; Jenkinson, 1997). Community-based instruction is defined by Wehmeyer (1992; 2002) as involving "teachers and other educational personnel teaching educational objectives in natural environments, such as work sites, shopping malls, and restaurants." For a clear, practical resource on community-based instruction, consult Giangreco and Doyle's (2007) *Quick-Guides to Inclusion: Ideas for Educating Students with Disabilities* (2nd ed.). Learning experiences in the community help youth with disabilities to learn authentic tasks in natural contexts, to develop personally and interpersonally, and to grow to understand career preferences and to develop a work history. These experiences help students to become part of the community culture and workplace culture, alongside other citizens and employees. Throughout this book, there have been many examples of students learning to use the telephone by making authentic phone calls to secure meaningful information, riding the bus to learn to travel independently, and participating in co-operative education or workplace learning. Community-based instruction requires complex arrangements for learning and the co-operation of a number of educators and members of the community. However, this instruction can become the responsibility of the entire team if it is included in the student's annual goals at the IEP meeting. Burcroff et al. (2003) describe how to plan what they call "community forays," and Mechling (2004) provides an example of supplementing forays into the community with computer-based simulations to teach skills like grocery shopping.

## Independence: Community Support

Self-determination is consistent with the recent growth of the movement called community inclusion and an approach to community services based on the concept of support. Knoll and Racino (1994) refer to this as mobilizing the "unique array of supports each individual needs to live in his or her own home and participate in the life of the community" (p. 301). Walker and Cory (2002) speak of shifting from empowered agencies to empowered people. Ferguson and Ferguson (1996) report the personal, cultural, and familial meanings of adulthood as applied to individuals with significant intellectual disabilities and clarify the personal support agent strategy. This reform had its beginnings in grassroots efforts of people with disabilities and their families and service providers who sought to work around the barriers to community membership, true choice, and control or self-determination. Support means working for people with disabilities, meeting their notions of what is supportive to them, and functioning as a community worker (that is, the person who helps make connections, mobilizes resources, plans backup systems, and creates livable communities) (e.g., Oberlink, 2006).

The research on best practices from family support, supported employment, and inclusive education shows that central to each of these is a common focus on support (Ferguson & Olsen, 1989; Muller, Schuler, & Yates, 2008; Walker & Cory, 2002). Organizations providing support have made a commitment to self-determination for individuals with disabilities and empowerment of their organizations. An international think-tank suggested the following eight competencies for professionals whose work involves supporting individuals and empowering organizations (based on Cochran, 1990):

- ability to identify, and commitment to identifying, strengths in people and groups
- respect for diverse perspectives and lifestyles
- capacity to listen and reflect
- ability to put one's own interests aside in the interest of the group
- creativity in helping people become more aware and confident of their abilities
- ability to help an individual or a group assume decision-making responsibility and action
- knowledge of how to access information
- ability to reflect critically on an ongoing process, including one's own role

You may be asking, "What lies ahead?" It is always difficult to predict the future, but we can be fairly confident in predicting change, and if the supported living model gains the endorsement of Canadian citizens, courts, and lawmakers, we could experience great change and increased inclusion on a grand scale.

Weblinks

CANADA ACCESS GRANTS AND CANADA STUDY GRANTS (CANLEARN)
www.canlearn.ca/eng/index.shtml

LISTING OF CANADIAN GRANTS AND SCHOLARSHIPS FOR POST-SECONDARY STUDENTS (CANLEARN SCHOLARSHIP SEARCH)
www.studentawards.com/canlearn

# Summary

Developing independence for learning and for living is an important goal for every exceptional student. Recent curricula have focused on personal development, interpersonal development, and career development. Personal development includes acquiring strategies to be an independent learner, negotiating transitions, and using computers and, if necessary, assistive devices to maximize independence. Interpersonal development refers to a student's ongoing growth in relating to others. Examples include responding with courage and controlling one's anger. Career development includes growth that enables one to assume the various roles associated with maturing and adulthood, including understanding and participating in the world of work. Usually students take part in career exploration and career experience as ways of coming to understand themselves, becoming self-advocates, and being more self-determined. There are a number of approaches to independent living. Which approach is more appropriate to the adult years of an exceptional individual may depend on the nature and severity of the exceptionality, the context within which the individual lives, and the community, which may encourage participation or provide support. There has been a great deal of change in the way exceptional individuals live and learn in the past decade, and we can only expect continued change in the coming years.

# Key Terms

personal development (p. 337)

interpersonal development (p. 337)

career development (p. 337)

career (p. 337)

learning strategies (p. 338)

model strategy use (p. 339)

guided practice (p. 339)

independent practice (p. 339)

feedback (p. 340)

transition (p. 340)

assistive technology (p. 344)

self-awareness (p. 350)

career exploration (p. 351)

labour market information (p. 355)

self-advocacy (p. 356)

self-determination (p. 357)

co-operative education (co-op) (p. 358)

workplace experience (p. 358)

community participation (p. 360)

# Challenges for Reviewing Chapter 10

1.  Why is your role so important, as a classroom teacher, in helping exceptional students (those in elementary as well as those in secondary school) to become more independent learners?

2.  Identify the actions a teacher can take to make transitions for exceptional learners as smooth as possible. Focus on transitions for students in the context in which you teach—elementary or secondary. Think of all the kinds of transitions you can, and identify what you can do.

3.  Prepare to assume the role of the classroom teacher of an exceptional student on a school-based team (or the role of a parent, principal, or resource teacher) for a meeting about Fran or Ray, described in the opening cases of this chapter. List (a) the resources you would use to prepare for a discussion about enhancing this student's personal development, (b) the resources you would use to prepare for a discussion about enhancing this student's interpersonal development, (c) the contributions you would make in the meeting on the discussion about each of these topics, and (d) how the actions you suggest could enhance the student's independence. Participate with your peers in the role-play of the school-based team meeting about this student.

4.  Describe the actions you would take when teaching a class that includes either Fran or Ray to ensure that all students' career development is enhanced. Then describe the way you would accommodate the needs of Ray or Fran and the resources that you would help this student access to ensure career development is differentiated and appropriate to the student's needs. How would such actions contribute to student independence?

5.  Consider the student Reid, described in Chapter 4 in the section on students with severe intellectual disabilities (page 121). Describe how community participation and community support approaches could enable Reid to achieve his dream of living apart from his family with his friend, Dan. Consider the issue from the perspectives of Reid, his mother, and the community.

6.  Return to the opening case of Fran and Ray and answer the questions that follow the cases.

# Conclusion

## Thriving as a Teacher

> My first day of teaching finally arrived and I embarked on a completely foreign adventure. . . . I was scared, excited, and (in hindsight) idealistic. The truth is I continue to operate with this mixed bag of emotions, but underneath it all, I love it!
>
> Christa Armstrong (1997, p. 67)

You may be wondering, after reading about all the challenges involved in including exceptional students in your classroom, whether a teaching career is really for you. This is a good question to ask. Every day somewhere in Canada a teacher or teacher-in-training asks this question. However, remember that people learning to be stockbrokers, physicians, and electricians also ask themselves whether they have chosen the right career. I believe that it can be a good thing—for these individuals and for these careers—that people ask hard questions about the choices they have made. As you will see, this question can also signal that teachers have some problem solving ahead of them if they are to thrive in their work.

## Succeeding as a Beginning Teacher

You will have already noticed that this conclusion is not about exceptional children and adolescents. This chapter is about you. It is about how you can thrive as a teacher. The word *thriving* conjures up accomplishment, satisfaction, and prosperity. Teachers enter the profession with high expectations, a vision of the future, and a mission to educate children and adolescents. Years of research, including studies by Alan King (e.g., King, Warren, & Peart, 1988) of Queen's University, suggest that effective and rewarding teaching is most apt to be accomplished by optimistic and self-confident teachers. Studies that focused on teachers who were successful in their beginning years found that they seemed to be particularly high in self-confidence and energy levels. All these teachers had a number of characteristics in common, including a deep commitment to teaching, genuine caring for students, and the goals to become better teachers and to learn more (Cochran-Smith, 2006; McEwan, 2002). Other research has found that beginning teachers needed both a positive outlook and the support of their colleagues and administrators to succeed (Center for Comprehensive School Reform and Improvement, 2007; Gratch, 1998).

Teachers who have a greater belief in their ability to teach have been found to be more likely to (a) try different ways of teaching, (b) be businesslike by being organized in their teaching and fair and firm in their dealings with students, and (c) be enthusiastic about teaching. Those who believed strongly that students benefit from school experiences were also high in confidence and enthusiasm about teaching

## FIGURE C-1  SURVIVAL SKILLS FOR THE FIRST-YEAR TEACHER

- Find a mentor—a department head or an experienced teacher—who can offer another perspective on the daily dilemmas you face.
- Find a friend—a new teacher like yourself—so you can support one another and talk out your problems and potential solutions.
- Meet resource teachers and guidance staff—as soon as you arrive at your school, learn about the available resources.
- Don't be afraid to borrow resources—replenish the department files or your colleagues' files with your own creations.
- Make a sick-day plan—include lesson plans, the required materials, class seating plan, attendance list, and instructions, just in case.
- Keep lines of communication open with parents.
- Maintain a page for each student—document telephone calls made to parents, calls received, conversations with resource personnel, behaviour observation notes, etc.
- Maintain (or ask designated students to maintain) a logbook of each day's lesson and copies of extra handouts so that absent students can be responsible for finding and catching up on missed work.
- Before you start teaching, set your policy on washroom breaks, late assignments, attendance, truancy, lates, your behaviour plan, methods for getting the students' attention, etc. Discuss these with a mentor so that your policies are consistent with the school's code of behaviour, and adapt them as required as the year progresses.
- Remember that you need time to develop all the creative activities that make your classes exciting and rewarding to teach. Develop a manageable number each week (e.g., one or two), borrow when necessary, and accept that some ideas will have to wait until the next time you teach this unit.
- Take off Friday night and at least one full day on the weekend to recharge for the next week.

———

Source: Prepared by N. Lévesque, a classroom teacher in Barrie, Ontario. Used by permission.

(Burnette, Peters-Johnson, 2004; Nieto, 2003). The picture that emerges suggests that some personal characteristics, such as commitment, self-confidence, and a positive outlook, may contribute to thriving in teaching. These are things over which you have some control. As well, some aspects of the teaching environment, such as colleague and administrator support as well as opportunities to contribute to school decision making (Liu, 2007), over which you exert less control, may also be critical, especially in the early years. Figure C-1 was prepared by an early-career teacher at the conclusion of her first year teaching secondary school French and English.

Teachers cite many rewarding aspects of their work that contribute to their positive outlook. In an Ontario study teachers reported that the three most satisfying aspects of teaching involved their relationships with their students. These were (a) experiencing good rapport and relationships with young people; (b) recognizing that students are suddenly understanding or enjoying their lessons; and (c) seeing student success, achievement, and satisfaction. These rewards of teaching reflect the reasons that many teachers give for choosing their profession: "I enjoy children" and "I love history and really want to pass my love of learning on to others." The next most frequently mentioned reward was interacting with and receiving support from colleagues (King et al., 1988). The same themes persist in recent interview studies of teachers (e.g., Moore Johnson & The Project on the Next Generation of Teachers, 2004).

I encourage you to consider what you need to thrive as an educator. When you listen to experienced teachers who thrive on teaching, what do you hear?

The following are all excerpts from interviews with Canadian teachers (King & Peart, 1992)—people who love teaching and strive to be members of a vibrant community by working closely with colleagues, joining associations, taking on new challenges, and taking care of themselves.

> The most helpful thing is when I go and visit teachers in my field. I think teachers should be encouraged to visit teachers.
>
> *Male teacher, 49 years old, grades 7–12, Alberta (p. 35)*

> It helps to have a supportive family … to go home and talk about things other than teaching.
>
> *Female teacher, twenty-four years of experience, grade 3, Manitoba (p. 126)*

> I fish, I take pictures. I think that one of the keys to being able to last in teaching for a long period of time is to deal with stress. I think you have to have other types of interest outside the school.
>
> *Male teacher, seventeen years of experience, grades 9–12, science/mathematics/health/ computer science, Manitoba (p. 126)*

> [I deal with stress by] being proactive and improving the system on the level that I can work at. Being part of the solution. To actively seek new challenges—I am teaching chemistry this year for the first time in my career. There is also my work with staff committee—helping empower teachers.
>
> *Male teacher, twenty-six years of experience, grades 10–12, geology/chemistry, British Columbia (p. 126)*

> I think it is important that I not necessarily make money at it, but that I keep my musical skills up. So I perform as much as I can without interfering with the rest of my job; I play in a big band and in the symphony orchestra.
>
> *Male teacher, four years of experience, grades 9–12, music, British Columbia (p. 143)*

> [I deal with stress by] having a relaxing period and getting lots of sleep .... [T]hat is one thing I have to do; if I don't get enough sleep, I am a basket case.
>
> *Female teacher, four years of experience, grades 9–12/OAC, music, Ontario (p. 126)*

# Being a Change Agent

Like many other professions, teaching in the current era is caught in the throes of massive and continual change. Some teachers find themselves looking back rather than looking ahead and fighting a rearguard action to maintain the profession as they have known it. Michael Fullan (2001; Levin & Fullan, 2008) of the University of Toronto describes how change has been introduced into Canadian schools without regard for the impact it has on teachers' daily lives. Almost all change, even when we embrace the innovation, results in feelings of loss and grief (Browning, 2008; Marris, 1986). Change also makes teachers feel incompetent (or less competent than when they were doing what they knew well) and creates confusion and conflict. Unless each of these issues is matched with an appropriate response, change is unlikely to succeed (Hargreaves, 2004; Levin & Fullan, 2008), even when we want to improve our practice.

## FIGURE C-2  TIPS FOR CHANGE AGENTS

- If what you desire in the way of change is not immediately forthcoming, take your time.
- Do the best you can, don't stop trying, and don't be afraid to make mistakes. Mistakes are human.
- Remember to take one step at a time and to build in success.
- Recognize and build on your strengths.
- The initial stages of any significant change involve anxiety and uncertainty and/or involve taking a risk.
- Support is crucial.
- Change involves learning new skills through practice and feedback.
- The most significant breakthrough occurs when you understand how the new way will make things better for you.

Source: Patterson, D. (1996). Becoming a change agent in your elementary classroom. In J. Andrews (ed.), *Teaching students with diverse needs: Elementary classrooms*. Scarborough: ITP Nelson Canada, pp. 31–32. Reprinted with permission.

"Teachers vastly underestimate their power to change things" (Sarason, 1993, p. 6). In a perceptive analysis of what it takes to be a change agent, Donna Patterson (1996) of the University of Regina suggests that teachers focus on self-care, political astuteness, planning, effective conflict resolution, and humour. With these strengths, Patterson demonstrates how teachers can become agents of change in their own classrooms, lead by example, and earn the respect of their colleagues for their ideas. Patterson closes with sage advice for teachers working to make their classrooms inclusive (see Figure C-2). Collegial relationships and a culture that encourages teachers to learn together empower them to become agents of change together (Dearman & Alber, 2005; Lovett & Gilmore, 2003; Valverde, 2008).

## Handling Stress

Most teachers thrive on the challenges of the profession. However, for others, the rewards of personal satisfaction and sense of accomplishment do not last. Many of these teachers choose to leave the profession and most often cite stress or burnout as the reason. In the past few decades the helping professions in many countries have experienced this loss of talented and capable members. Over twenty years ago Bryan Hiebert of the University of Calgary summarized the research on teacher stress in Canada (Hiebert, 1985). Canadian teachers reported a variety of stressors but referred most often to work overload (or pace of work) and student discipline problems or challenges in interacting with students whose lives were complex. Across all the studies, representing all parts of the country, the problems usually seemed to involve some form of personal interaction or time-management concerns. A recent study by Jennifer Lawson (2008) of the University of Manitoba focused on women administrators in high-poverty community schools, and the two issues raised in Hiebert's report persist—the pace of the demands and the challenges and complexities of the lives of children and their families, in this case, in high-poverty communities. Since Hiebert's report in 1985 the pressures on Canadian classroom teachers have, if anything, increased with the growing diversity in Canadian classrooms, including the inclusion of exceptional students in regular classrooms (Dei, 2003;

Edmunds, 1998; Fullan, 2001; Hutchinson, 2007). As we have seen, inclusion and increasing diversity can involve many of the factors that contribute to teaching being rewarding (e.g., satisfaction in seeing students "get it," collaboration with colleagues) or being stressful (increased workload, discipline problems, lack of administrative support) (Dearman & Alber, 2005; Grayson, Alvarez, 2008).

Hiebert (1985) also reported that the studies showed that Canadian teachers did not have a large repertoire of strategies aimed specifically at coping with stress. Cochran-Smith (2006) argued that teachers who stay in the profession deal effectively with the pressures because they love teaching, love their students, see teaching as hope and possibility because they feel they make a difference for their students, and continue to be passionate about their own learning as well as others' learning. These characteristics were apparent in Lawson's (2008) interviews with women leaders in schools in high-poverty communities. What is stress, and how can you, as a beginning teacher, cope well with this challenge? Much has been written about stress and burnout in educators, and many definitions have been used. One of the most widely cited perspectives on teacher burnout describes three dimensions—emotional exhaustion (which may underlie the other two), depersonalization, and feelings of low personal accomplishment. While we may not find it easy to define stress or burnout, we can probably all think of examples from our personal experiences as a teacher. Listen to Maria describe to her support group what she found when she returned to her grade 5 class after recess on the afternoon of October 19:

> I am soooo frustrated. I was late getting to my room yesterday because I had separated four students who were fighting on the playground. I felt my blood pressure soar when I yelled at them, avoided taking any random punches, and led them to the principal's office—only to find the office empty. I couldn't leave them alone, on the verge of tearing each other apart, could I? So I worried about the fights that might be breaking out in my class. And fretted that someone might pick on Josh, who has childhood rheumatoid arthritis and is frail and vulnerable. After what seemed like an eternity, the principal's secretary came strolling down the hall. When I asked her where the principal was, she laughed and pointed toward my room. How could I have forgotten? He was in my room waiting to observe me teaching.
>
> In the excitement, it had slipped my mind completely. All I could think of then was, "What an idiot he will think I am! I knew I should have asked someone to switch recess duty with me. Why did no one volunteer? They knew I had an observation." By then I was angry with the whole staff! I was so nervous that my hands were wet, my throat was dry, and my mind was blank. I always feel inadequate when I am evaluated. Especially when it is the first evaluation—I can't seem to stay calm, even though I have taught for five years. I asked myself, "What was the lesson I planned to teach?" I had to look in my daybook to jog my memory; the lesson involved a complex explanation, hands-on practice, and follow-up written practice in adding fractions. Why did I not choose something simpler? I must have been trying to show off and impress him with my up-to-date methods. I fumbled my way through the explanation, forgot to do the hands-on activity, and had to explain the written activity about a thousand times. To almost every student individually. By the time my principal left, my stomach was almost sick. I dread receiving the evaluation. Even I think I should be fired.

Maria went on to explain to the members of her group that she had moved to this downtown school in September when her partner was transferred to the city from a small town. She found that the teachers were not as friendly as in her previous school and the children fought all the time in the schoolyard, "like gang warfare."

Maria's husband was rarely home because he was learning a new job, and her preschool children hated the new daycare, begging every morning to go to Sue's, the home of their previous child minder. To finish her story, Maria added with emphasis, "I'm so stressed!"

Few of us would disagree with Maria's assessment of the situation. This sounds like a case of many threats that together exceed Maria's coping strategies. However, there was reason to be optimistic. To begin to take control of the situation, Maria had called the number on a poster the first day it was tacked on the bulletin board in the staff room. The poster said

Feel stressed? Need support?

New group starting September 30 at Eastside Teachers' Centre.

Call today!

That is how Maria came to be telling eight strangers about her most frustrating day at work.

## Focusing on Your Well-Being

Recently, researchers have studied the stress of large numbers of teachers in Britain and North America. They suggest that stress is triggered and sustained by the cognitive processes we choose to use when we perceive a threat, is affected by the emotions we experience, and affects our health (Gold & Roth, 1993; Grayson & Alvarez, 2008; Vandenberghe & Huberman, 1999; Wood & McCarthy, 2002). This means that stress affects all our being. We make decisions about how we will cope with a threat; when our coping mechanisms are successful, distress is minimized and we may even feel a positive type of stress (eustress). However, when our coping mechanisms are not adequate, we experience negative emotions and feel threatened, and our immune system is affected, which may result in illness. While this all sounds menacing, there are many suggestions to assist teachers in handling their stressors and in learning new coping mechanisms (Nagel & Brown, 2003; Wood & McCarthy, 2002; see Figure C-3).

### FIGURE C-3 STEPS FOR TEACHERS IN COPING WITH STRESS

1. Identify and acknowledge the causes of stress in your life.
   (a) Professional causes of stress
   (b) Personal causes of stress
2. Identify your feelings and your emotional reactions to these feelings.
3. Become aware of the unmet needs behind your feelings.
   (a) Emotional-physical needs
   (b) Psycho-social needs
   (c) Personal-intellectual needs
4. Learn stress-reduction strategies.
   (a) Identify what you can and cannot change.
   (b) Change your beliefs and actions in situations you can control.
   (c) Choose your reaction to situations you cannot control (you can control your reaction).
   (d) Use assertive communication to say no in a constructive way.
   (e) Use relaxation techniques.
   (f) Take charge of your physical health through nutrition, sleep, and exercise.
   (g) Seek social support.

In the *Professional Health* program (Gold & Roth, 2004), problem solving is the focus and personal and professional needs are the content. Teachers are urged to go beyond stress management and focus on their underlying problems and needs. While we all need skills to survive the immediate challenges, we may also need psychological support to grow over the long term and to develop professional health. Otherwise, we could be continuously engaged in stress management when what we need is to gain self-control. Maria found that her teacher support group helped her become aware of the factors that were causing difficulties and getting in the way of her teaching. Through the activities of the group, she recognized her feelings, her stressors, and her own abilities to deal with them in effective ways. She realized how much she wanted to be respected by all her students, and how much she had needed to belong to a group of teachers whom she could talk to for support. Gold and Roth report that teachers begin to withdraw after they feel isolated from their colleagues. Visit other teachers' classrooms, arrange exchanges, join the local association of science teachers, or find a support group like the one Maria found.

Teachers are sometimes surprised to learn that they need to keep mentally active to deal with stress. While teaching offers the promise of intellectual stimulation, it is easy for us to become buried in paperwork and spend the evenings marking, rather than reading about innovative teaching approaches or attending stimulating cultural events. However, discovering new ideas and learning innovative techniques contribute to our personal-intellectual needs. For example, Gold and Roth (2004) encourage teachers to embrace intellectual challenges so they can thrive at work: enrol in professional development or graduate courses, take out a subscription to a concert series, or learn to weave. Rena Upitis, dean of education at Queen's University from 1995 to 2000, always advised teacher candidates and colleagues to learn something new every school year. In recent years her personal projects have included learning to skate, weave, and weld. Upitis argues that not only is this intellectually stimulating but it also allows teachers to become novices and renew empathy for their students who are not experts in everything that is taught in the classroom.

## The Last Word

This book has examined the many facets of teaching and including exceptional children in our classrooms—so they may take their places in Canadian society. In the Conclusion, we have briefly looked at and discussed some teachers who thrive on challenge, change children's lives, and are never forgotten. This is the kind of teacher many of us aspire to be—a teacher who touches the lives of children or adolescents and who leaves a mark. When I read the *The Globe and Mail* obituary reprinted in Figure C-4, I wished I had known Benny Sheardown, and I decided to give him the last word.

# FIGURE C-4 LIFE STORY: HELPED HUNDREDS OF YOUNGSTERS

Benny Sheardown: Father, husband, guidance counsellor, athlete. Born in Whitehorse in 1944. Died of cancer in Calgary aged 55. Cathy Sheardown wasn't surprised by the number of people who paid tribute to her late husband Ben. It was the tenor of it all that caught her off-guard.

More than 1,000 people attended the guidance counsellor's memorial service in Whitehorse, and Ms. Sheardown could easily decorate a huge wall with cards and letters from admirers and friends from all over the Yukon and well beyond its borders. "They feel that he was really there when nobody else could be or cared to be. He felt everybody deserved a second, third and fourth chance depending on the story," said Ms. Sheardown.

Benjamin Clarke Sheardown was born in the Yukon, spent his life there and affected the lives of many, especially young people to whom he devoted so much time. After graduating from the University of Alaska in Fairbanks, the father of two returned to the Yukon and became a gym teacher in 1972. Later on, as a guidance counsellor, he heard more than a few stories of broken homes and suicidal youth.

"He affected a ton of people in different ways, never, ever taking the credit and letting [the kids] almost believe it was their idea," said Ms. Sheardown.

After his death, local newspapers ran letters to the editor from as far away as Mexico City, from people who credited him with shaping their lives, and, in some cases, saving their lives. "I'm getting numerous cards in the mail that start out, 'You don't know me but . . .' and they're telling me, 'If it wasn't for Mr. Sheardown I would never have become who I am or never been able to do what I've done, I certainly wouldn't have gone through school,'" said Ms. Sheardown.

Last year, Mr. Sheardown was inducted into the Yukon Sports Hall of Fame. It was an award he almost refused to accept, thinking it was out of pity for a man with a terminal illness. But after talking to family and friends, he concluded that the award was as much a tribute to those who helped him accomplish great things in his lifetime as it was to him. A planned sports multi-plex in Whitehorse might even be named after him. He always pursued a healthy lifestyle. He played hockey (helping the Yukon to win gold in the Arctic Winter Games in 1972) and basket-ball. He also took part in running, biking, swimming and Nordic skiing. In winter, he was often seen riding his bike or taking his dog Tacumsa on long walks through downtown trails. On the front of his memorial-service pamphlet, he's photographed with Tacumsa in the shadow of a hilltop called the King's Throne near Kathleen Lake, a pristine area on the cusp of Kluane National Park. He's wearing mismatched cross-country skis and, according to a childhood friend, couldn't care less.

Jim Perry knew Mr. Sheardown from the age of 10, when he moved to Whitehorse from Ireland. "He took me under his wing. He reached out to this little immigrant boy and we became lifelong friends," said Mr. Perry, who made the trip from Abbotsford, BC, to Whitehorse to speak at the memorial service. "This memorial was a true indication of the kind of support and the number of lives he touched. Ben left a huge footprint on many hearts." Mr. Perry said he always lived life fully and brought the best out of other people.

Source: Carlucci, M. (1999). Life story: Helped hundreds of youngsters. *The Globe and Mail*, August 3, p. A17. Reprinted with permission.

# Glossary

## A

**Aboriginal cultures** Aboriginal peoples are nations, that is, political and cultural groups with values and lifeways distinct from those of other Canadians.

**Aboriginal elders** The senior members of an Aboriginal community who are respected and looked to for wisdom.

**Aboriginal languages** There were twelve language families and roughly fifty languages when the Europeans arrived in Canada; only about fifteen of those are currently in vigorous use.

**academic tasks as punishment** The practice of assigning students additional homework or lines to write as a punishment.

**acceleration** An approach for educating gifted students that allows them to move through the curriculum in an area of strength at an accelerated pace or to work at the next grade level.

**accommodations** Changes to how a student is taught, including such things as teaching strategies, supports, and alternate formats, when the outcomes are consistent with the student's grade placement.

**acquired brain injury (ABI)** See *traumatic brain injury (TBI)*.

**ADAPT** A systematic strategy for adapting teaching to include exceptional learners consisting of five steps: **A**ccounts of students' strengths and needs; **D**emands of the classroom; **A**daptations; **P**erspectives and consequences; **T**each and assess the match.

**adapted program** An exceptional student's program that retains the learning outcomes of the prescribed curriculum but provides adaptations so the student can participate, including alternate formats, instructional strategies, and assessment procedures.

**adaptive skills** Areas of participation in the life of the community in which individuals with development disabilities may be delayed: communication, home living, community use, health and safety, leisure, self-care, social skills, self-direction, functional academics, work.

**additional practice** Providing more opportunities for exceptional learners to practise what has been taught and to develop full understanding of ideas, procedures, etc.

**advocate** A person who represents or champions the cause of another.

**aggression** Bold, direct action that is intended to hurt someone else or take property; unprovoked attack.

**AIDS (Acquired Immune Deficiency Syndrome)** A disease in which there is severe loss of cellular immunity.

**allergen-free alternative** Refers to the practice of creating an alternative activity or snack that is safe for students with allergies so they can participate in class activities and excursions.

**allergic salute** Children pushing up on a runny nose; a symptom of allergies.

**allergy** An abnormal reaction to a normal substance (e.g., peanuts).

**alternative expectations** Related to the development of skills deemed essential to learning in areas not represented in the curriculum policy documents.

**American Association on Mental Retardation (AAMR)** Promotes progressive policies, sound research, effective practices, and universal human rights for people with intellectual and developmental disabilities.

**American Sign Language (ASL)** A manual language system that has its own rule-governed syntactic system.

**amniocentesis** A test of the fluid surrounding a fetus to check for many kinds of abnormalities.

**amplification** The process of enhancing sound, usually through the use of hearing aids or FM (frequency modulation) systems.

**ANA-KIT®** Brand name of an easily administered form of adrenalin often carried by children who have allergies and suffer anaphylactic reactions.

**anaphylactic shock** See *anaphylaxis*.

**anaphylaxis** A sudden, severe allergic reaction that causes breathing difficulties; death can occur within minutes unless an injection is administered.

**antidepressants** Medications for managing attention deficit/ hyperactivity disorder.

**applied stream** A secondary school program intended to prepare adolescents for entering the workforce rather than for formal post-secondary education.

**articulation** Word and sound production.

**Asperger syndrome** Severe and sustained impairment in social interaction with restricted, repetitive patterns of behaviour, interests, and activities, with no significant delays in language acquisition or cognitive development.

**assessment** Data collection, gathering information of many kinds about a student or a group of students, using a variety of tools and techniques.

**assistive technology** An item, piece of equipment, or product system that is used to maintain or improve the functional capabilities of individuals with disabilities.

**asthma** Obstructed airways that hinder the flow of air in and out of the lungs; an attack is characterized by persistent wheezing, tightness in the chest, and excess phlegm, and can be life threatening.

**at risk** More likely to develop special needs due to poverty and other social conditions, including sexual and physical abuse, exposure to drugs, etc.

**attention deficit/hyperactivity disorder (AD/HD)** A persistent pattern of inattention and impulsiveness that may be accompanied by hyperactivity and that hinders social, academic, and vocational expectations.

**authentic assessment** Assessment on tasks that are engaging, contextualized, and represent those expected in the adult world.

**authentic tasks** Learning activities close to real-world tasks, usually involving problems that are engaging, contextualized, and represent those expected in the adult world.

**autism** Limited development in communication and social interaction, and a severe delay in intellectual, emotional, and behavioural development.

**Autism Spectrum Disorders (ASDs)** All of the disorders that are considered ASDs are characterized by varying degrees of impairment in three areas: communication skills, social interactions, and repetitive and stereotyped patterns of behaviour. The five disorders in the autism spectrum are autism, Asperger syndrome (AS), Rett syndrome, childhood disintegrative disorder, and pervasive developmental disorder not otherwise specified (PDD-NOS).

# B

**base groups** See *home groups*.

**basic stream** See *applied stream*.

**behaviour ratings** Scales on which student behaviour is evaluated for frequency and intensity of symptoms.

**behavioural or emotional exceptionalities** Usually characterized by dysfunctional relationships at home and/or school and at least one of aggression, negative psychological states, and social problems.

**blind** Characterized by loss of sight and use of auditory and tactile sources of information to replace sight.

**Braille** A system of raised dots that can be read by touch by persons who are blind.

**bullying** A pattern of actions that involves an imbalance of power, a victim who is upset, and a bully who is cool and in control and who shows a lack of compassion; can take many forms, including physical, emotional, and verbal.

**bypass strategies** Teaching and learning approaches that allow students to gain access to, practise, or demonstrate learning of the curriculum in alternative ways.

# C

**cancer** A malignant tumour or growth of body cells.

**career** Progress through life and through the roles appropriate to various ages as well as the process of making a living by means of a particular occupation.

**career development** Growing understanding of changing roles and responsibilities, including adult responsibilities, roles, and the nature and meaning of work.

**career exploration** Actions undertaken deliberately or for their own sake that teach about possible careers and adult roles.

**carrel** A private space for working, which can be a booth made out of wood or from a cardboard crate that once held a large appliance.

**case coordinator** Person responsible for ensuring that the various services required by an exceptional student are coordinated; sometimes parents assume this role.

**catch 'em being good** A strategy developed many years ago in which teachers monitor students and acknowledge and reward behaviour that is consistent with expectations.

**CCTV** Closed-circuit television system consisting of a digital camera and display so that anything placed in front of the camera is magnified on the display to allow visually impaired people to see things that are far away—such as a demonstration at the front of a classroom—or read a book or look at a photograph.

**cerebral palsy (CP)** A group of disorders impairing body movement and muscle coordination as a result of an interference in messages between the brain and the body.

**changing grading criteria** Varying grading weights so exceptional students are not disadvantaged by an impossible task; for example, students who are hard of hearing do not have part of their grade determined by their inability to hear during pop quizzes.

***Charter of Rights and Freedoms*** Legislation that protects the rights of all Canadians and, in particular, Canadians who are members of minority groups, including people with disabilities.

**checkpoints** Checklists for students to complete at quarter- and halfway points of long-term assignments to show progress and receive feedback.

**child abuse** Physical abuse (use of force on a child's body), emotional abuse (persistent attacks on a child's sense of self), sexual abuse (any sexual exploitation) by an adult or another child, or neglect of a child by parent or caregiver.

**chromosomal abnormalities** Chromosomes contain genes with the chemical codes that direct cell function; aberrant chromosomes are those with abnormal numbers or structures.

**chronic health condition** A qualified medical practitioner has certified that a student requires medical procedures, excluding administration of medication only, to ensure the health and safety of the student while in school or requires ongoing special education interventions due to the student's limited school attendance or because the condition adversely affects the student's educational performance.

**chronic health impairment** See *chronic health condition*.

**chronic medical disorder** See *chronic health condition*.

**chunking strategies** Ways of grouping information; used for remembering important lists.

**classroom assessment** Day-to-day practices adopted by teachers to describe student learning through portfolios, conferences with students, paper and pencil tests, etc.

**classroom procedures** Efficient ways of moving all members of a class through the day or the period that are consistent with the teacher's goals and follow from the rules (e.g., transitions and distribution of materials).

**climate** The general feeling created in a classroom; positive classroom climate usually is thought to develop when people treat each other with respect.

**code of conduct** Brief guidelines that clearly identify school rules and acceptable student behaviours and contain consequences.

**cognitive abilities** Processes and knowledge, including vocabulary, verbal fluency, retention, generalizing, making abstractions, organizing, and planning.

**cognitive-behaviour management (CBM)** Programs that teach students how to use cognition to control their own behaviour by using self-talk and self-instruction.

**cognitive complexity** The cognitive demands made of the learner by teaching and learning in the classroom.

**cognitive strategies** Plans and processes designed to accomplish learning or solve problems.

**collaboration** Teachers and other professionals learning from each other's experiences and working in teams where all members feel that their contributions are valued.

**collaborative learning** Teaching approaches that include co-operative learning and problem solving in pairs and groups and that usually involve student groups of varying abilities and skills, that is, heterogeneous groupings.

**colour-coded** A cueing system to enhance the organizational skills of exceptional students by consistently using colours for particular kinds of information.

**community** A group of people who have shared interests and who mutually pursue the common good.

**community agreements** Four guidelines for students to use in developing a sense of community in the classroom: attentive

listening, appreciation/no put-downs, the right to pass when given an opportunity to speak, and mutual respect (*Tribes*, Gibbs, 2001).

**community-based** Education that focuses on relating what is learned in school to what occurs in the community; often learning takes place in the community as well as in the school.

**community circle** The gathering of all students in a class in a large circle where each student is given an opportunity to present himself or herself in a structured way and to reflect on what is happening in his or her world (*Tribes*, Gibbs, 2001).

**community-referenced learning** Refers to using the community as a classroom. This can be conducted informally or through a formal program.

**components of an IEP** The seven sections that usually comprise an IEP are present level of functioning, long-term goals, short-term goals, instructional strategies and materials, dates for review, identification of participants (including parents) and their responsibilities, and evaluation procedures.

**comprehension** Reading comprehension is an active process of understanding that requires an intentional and thoughtful interaction between the reader and the text.

**computation** Mathematical skill and understanding in using the four basic operations to combine numbers.

**concept maps** Graphic organizers that show relationships among concepts as well as essential characteristics of the concepts.

**Connections** In the ICE model of learning and assessment, the links or relationships that students make among the Ideas, and to the relationships that students establish between new learning and prior learning.

**consistency** In classroom management, maintaining the same expectations from day to day and applying the same consequences when students fail to meet expectations while honouring adaptations for exceptional students.

**contract** A behaviour management technique involving a written agreement that states what the teacher and the student agree to do, and specifies the positive rewards and the consequences for failing to live up to the agreement.

**co-operative education (co-op)** Involves students in extended periods of time in a workplace (often around one hundred hours over a school term) while enrolled in full-time study as well as in classroom orientations to the workplace and reflective seminars.

**co-operative learning** A teaching approach that involves students in learning with peers in small groups, taking roles, and working interdependently.

**corporal punishment** Punishing a student for misbehaving by striking the student or threatening to strike the student.

**creativity** Demonstrated by students' contributing ideas, transforming and combining ideas, asking questions, and being curious.

**credit/no credit** See *pass/fail.*

**criterion-referenced** Data in which a student's work is compared to expected outcomes.

**Crohn's disease** A chronic inflammatory disease of the intestines.

**cueing** A method of directing students' attention to specific aspects of the learning environment.

**cultural awareness** Sensitivity when one makes the effort to become aware and respectful of the beliefs, values, and lives of members of other cultural groups.

**cultural relevance** Refers to curriculum that represents the cultures and experiences of the students being taught and makes them feel they are at the centre of the society rather than on its margins.

**culturally diverse backgrounds** Used to refer to students who are not from the majority Anglo-European culture.

**culturally responsive teaching** Teaching in which students see themselves and their cultural group represented in a respectful way that shows their role in Canadian society, history, etc.

**Cyberbullying** A form of psychological cruelty perpetrated virtually. Refers to threats, insults, and demeaning messages spread through the internet or by cell phone.

**cystic fibrosis (CF)** Increasingly severe respiratory problems and extreme difficulty in digesting nutrients from food.

## D

**dates for review** On an IEP, these are usually set for the end of the school year in which the IEP is established or renewed.

**deaf** Characterized by hearing loss that interferes with the acquisition and maintenance of the auditory skills necessary to develop speech and oral language and causes one to use visual sources of information to replace hearing.

**Deaf community** Many deaf adults describe themselves as a cultural minority and use the term *deaf* to designate cultural group membership; the common language is American Sign Language (ASL).

**depression** A pervasive mood of unhappiness accompanied by long-term difficulties in sleeping, feelings of worthlessness, and inability to experience pleasure.

**developmental or cognitive disabilities** The development of cognitive abilities and adaptive behaviours at a much slower rate than normal, which results in significant limitations in these areas at mild and severe levels.

**developmentally advanced** See *gifted.*

**diabetes** A condition in which the pancreas fails to produce a sufficient amount of the hormone insulin for proper sugar absorption in the body, which may place restrictions on physical activity.

**diabetes emergency kits** A ration package containing juice, raisins, or dextrose, often carried by an individual with diabetes and sometimes kept in a central location in a school to be used by students with diabetes in an emergency.

**Differentiated instruction (DI)** Acknowledges that students differ in interests, learning profile, and level of functioning.

**disability** Defined by the World Health Organization as the nature and extent of limitations to function (e.g., performing the activities required to read) resulting from impairment.

**(dis)ability awareness programs** Programs developed to foster greater understanding of people with disabilities, to increase students' knowledge about specific disabilities, and to increase students' sensitivity toward individuals with disabilities.

**discipline code** See *code of conduct.*

**discrepancy** A controversial method of identifying a learning disability by establishing a difference between ability (usually measured by an intelligence test) and achievement in one or more of the following areas: reading, writing, language acquisition, mathematics, reasoning, or listening.

**diversity** Variation in culture, ability, and values that characterizes modern Canadian society.

**divorce** The process of radically changing family relationships that follows marital breakup.

**domains** Areas, such as overall intellect, leadership, creativity, or the arts, where gifted students excel.

**double-deficit hypothesis** Refers to deficits in both phonemic awareness and rapid naming.

**Down syndrome** A genetic defect causing limitations in physical and cognitive development; physically, children with Down syndrome have low muscle tone and a generalized looseness of the ligaments.

**Duchenne muscular dystrophy (DMD)** A musculoskeletal condition with marked physical degeneration that occurs during the school years.

**dyscalculia** Learning disabilities in arithmetic, especially calculations.

**dysgraphia** Learning disabilities in writing.

**dyslexia** Learning disabilities in reading.

## E

**echolalia** Speech that is an immediate imitation of that of some other speaker.

**enforcing a rule** In teaching classroom rules, enforcement usually follows demonstration and practice and refers to the follow-up and feedback provided by teachers to commend students when they follow the rules and to ensure that consequences are applied when students fail to follow the rules.

**engagement** The extent to which students embrace learning and throw themselves into the activities of the classroom.

**English as a second language (ESL)** Students who have learned a language other than English as their first language and must acquire English as a second language, often in the context of school; programs designed to teach English to these students.

**English language learners (ELL students)** Students from diverse cultures who speak English as a second language.

**enlarged print** The practice of increasing the print size for students with vision impairment, usually to 130 percent on a photocopier or 18-point font on a computer.

**environment** Context of learning, composed of both classroom climate and physical layout.

**enzyme supplements** Medication taken by a person with cystic fibrosis before a meal or snack to replace pancreatic enzymes that the body does not produce and that are essential to digestion.

**epilepsy** A neurological disorder that occasionally produces brief disturbances in normal electrical functions of the brain that lead to sudden, brief seizures that vary in nature and intensity from person to person.

**epinephrine** Adrenalin; administered in the event of an anaphylactic allergic reaction; can be life saving.

**EPIPEN®** Brand name of an easily administered form of adrenalin often carried by children who have allergies and anaphylactic reactions.

**equal participation** The United Nations' (1993) *Standard Rules on the Equalization of Opportunities for Persons with Disabilities* targeted eight areas for equal participation in the local community, including education, health, employment, and social services.

**equality rights** In Canada, the equality rights that apply to education are contained in section 15(1) of the Charter: "Every individual is equal before and under the law and has a right to the equal protection and equal benefit of the law without discrimination based on race, national or ethnic origin, colour, religion, sex, age, or mental or physical disability."

**equipment** On an IEP, this usually includes tape recorders, wheelchairs, computers, and other technological devices used by an exceptional student to enhance learning.

**equity** Equity education means tailoring teaching to challenge inequities and discrimination.

**evaluation or assessment procedures** Making decisions based on the assessment data that have been gathered about a student or group of students; on an IEP, this refers to procedures the in-school team will use to demonstrate accountability by showing that the student is making reasonable progress.

**exceptional students** Learners who are gifted as well as students with disabilities; used interchangeably with terms like *students with special needs* to describe students in need of special education programs.

**experiential learning** Learning by doing includes field trips, role-playing, designing and making, and other forms of learning by doing.

**expulsion** Permanent removal of a student from the classroom as a consequence of the student behaving inappropriately, violating the code of conduct, etc.

**Extensions** In the ICE model of learning and assessment, the ways that students internalize learning so it becomes part of their perspective; revealed when students use their learning in novel ways.

# F

**feedback** Specific information for students about what they are doing correctly and incorrectly.

**fetal alcohol effects (FAE)** Describes individuals with a documented history of prenatal alcohol exposure and the presence of some, but not all, of the other diagnostic criteria for fetal alcohol syndrome (FAS).

**fetal alcohol syndrome (FAS)** Physical and physiological abnormalities due to prenatal exposure to alcohol causing delays in development, central nervous dysfunction, and a characteristic pattern of facial features, and learning problems.

**fluency** Contributes to comprehension and refers to children reading out loud with speed, accuracy, and proper expression.

**form of practice** Allowing students to engage in oral or written practice or another form of practice that advances their learning; can be ADAPTed for exceptional students.

**formal assessment** Assessment using standardized tests; these could include an intelligence test, behaviour observation checklists, vision, hearing or language assessments, and medical tests.

**formal groups** In collaborative learning, groupings of students assembled, with attention to group composition, to work together for a period of time, for example, throughout a unit.

**frequency modulation (FM) systems** With a classroom FM system, the carrier wave is transmitted through the air by frequency modulation from a teacher-worn microphone to a student-worn FM receiver; students with hearing impairments can hear the teacher clearly from any location in the classroom.

**friendships** Close relationships characterized by reciprocity, that is, give and take, and by commitment between individuals who see themselves as equals.

**functional curriculum** Outcomes for a student are based on life skills such as shopping, banking, and cooking.

# G

**generalized seizures** Epileptic seizures that involve the whole brain.

**genetic screening** Identification of the risk of a couple having a child with a condition caused by chromosomal abnormalities.

**gifted** Exceptionally high abilities in one or several areas, including specific academic subjects, overall intellect, leadership, creativity, or the arts.

**give-and-take dialogues** Problem-solving discussions in which all students feel they can advance ideas, be heard, comment on others' ideas, and feel that the classroom is a safe place.

**good behaviour game** A strategy for reducing disruptive behaviour and promoting positive behaviour in the classroom in which students work on teams to earn points for appropriate behaviour toward a reward.

**grading** Symbolic representation of evaluation or judgments based on assessment data, often in the form of letter grades, percentages, or performance levels.

**grading contract** An agreement between teacher and student on the basis for awarding a grade; may include giving exceptional students credit for attendance, promptness, effort, and co-operative behaviour.

**grouping** The practice of deliberately placing students in learning or working groups; used extensively in co-operative and collaborative learning approaches.

**guided practice** Scaffolded practice in which students are prompted to use each step of a strategy; enables exceptional students to learn the strategy.

# H

**handicap** Defined by the World Health Organization as the nature and extent of restrictions on participation (e.g., being employed) that result from impairment and disability.

**harassment** Communication in any form (e.g., verbal or physical abuse, jokes, slurs, graffiti) that expresses negative attitudes, beliefs, or actions toward an individual or group with the intention of hurting that person or group.

**hard of hearing** Partial hearing loss that interferes with the acquisition and maintenance of the auditory skills necessary to develop speech and oral language; use visual sources of information to supplement or replace hearing.

**head injury** See *traumatic brain injury (TBI)*.

**hearing aids** Systems that amplify all sounds, worn in the ear.

**hearing status** Description of one's ability to hear; used to describe the parents of children who are deaf.

**heart disease** In children, most often refers to a congenital defect; these range widely in severity and outcome from few symptoms to totally incapacitating.

**hemophilia** A hereditary bleeding disorder in which there is a deficiency of a blood clotting factor.

**heritage language** The language of one's ancestors; heritage language programs help children learn and maintain their parents' first language.

**high blood sugar (hyperglycemia)** An abnormally high amount of sugar in the bloodstream; usually associated with diabetes.

**high-incidence exceptionalities** Frequently occurring exceptionalities, including giftedness, learning disabilities, attention deficit/hyperactivity disorder, communication exceptionalities, behaviour exceptionalities, and mild developmental disabilities.

**high-interest low-vocabulary books** Written materials designed to interest and engage students while using simple vocabulary and uncomplicated sentence structures.

**high task commitment** Found in students who work hard and need little external motivation, especially in areas that interest them.

**HIV/AIDS** AIDS (Acquired Immune Deficiency Syndrome) is caused by HIV (Human Immunodeficiency Virus), a virus that attacks the immune system which usually fights infection.

**holding pattern** A strategy teachers use when they have a misbehaving student wait (in the office, at the side of the classroom, immediately outside the door) until the teacher is available to meet and talk with the student.

**home groups** In collaborative learning, these groupings of students serve as small, long-term support groups; may be the groups of peers who sit together at the beginning of each class.

**homeless** Those who have experienced the loss of their home are often thrust away from community, friends, and support systems and living in hostels or on the street.

**homophobia** Discrimination against people who are gay or lesbian that often takes the form of taunts, ridicule, and physical assaults.

**hundreds chart** A chart containing the numbers from 1 to 100 or 0 to 99 in rows and columns; used to help students learn the meaning of place value and relationships among numbers.

**hydrocephalus** A condition characterized by an excessive accumulation of cerebrospinal fluid in the brain due to an obstruction of its flow.

**hyperactivity** Characterized by fidgeting, squirming, moving constantly, talking excessively, and finding it challenging to play or work quietly.

**hypersensitivity** The tendency to be extremely sensitive to sensory stimuli such as touch and to engage in unusual behaviour to obtain a particular sensory stimulation.

# I

**ICE model** Characterizes learning and assessment as consisting of Ideas, Connections among those Ideas, and Extensions of those Ideas and Connections.

**Ideas** In the ICE model of learning and assessment, the building blocks of learning include such things as the steps in a process, vocabulary, and facts and definitions in the textbook; most fill-in-the-blank and multiple-choice questions assess at the level of Ideas.

**Identification, Placement, and Review Committee (IPRC)** In Ontario, this committee, consisting of the teacher, special educators, administrators, and parents, meets to consider whether a child is exceptional and recommends a placement prior to the IEP meeting.

**immigrant** A person who has come to Canada as a permanent resident from a foreign country.

**immune system** The mechanism that enables a body to resist infections, toxins, etc., owing to the presence of specific antibodies or sensitized white blood cells.

**impairment** Defined by the World Health Organization as a loss or abnormality of body structure or of a physiological or psychological function (e.g., loss of vision).

**impulsivity** Characteristics include blurting out answers before the teacher has finished asking a question, not waiting for one's turn, and interrupting other students.

**inattentiveness** Characterized by ignoring details, making careless errors, having trouble concentrating and staying on task while working or playing.

**inclusion** The social value and policy that persons with disabilities are entitled to full participation in all aspects of Canadian society, including education.

**inclusive schooling** The value system that holds that all students are entitled to equitable access to learning, achievement, and the pursuit of excellence in all aspects of their education; incorporates basic values that promote participation, friendship, and interaction.

**increase students' appropriate behaviour** Giving positive attention to the student behaviour one wants to maintain or increase; praising students publicly or privately and providing specific feedback.

**independent practice** Students practising on their own; choosing, using, and monitoring strategies.

**Individual Education Plan (IEP)** A written plan developed for an exceptional student that describes the adaptations, modifications, and services to be provided.

**Individual Program Plan (IPP)** The form that an IEP takes in some provinces (e.g., Alberta).

**Individual Support Services Plan (ISSP)** The form that an IEP takes in Newfoundland and Labrador where a number of government departments collaborate to provide integrated services.

**inflammation** A localized physical condition with heat, swelling, and pain.

**informal assessment** Testing carried out by the classroom teacher or the resource teacher that provides information about an exceptional student's current level of functioning.

**informal conference** A behaviour management technique in which a teacher and student meet to define the problem clearly, generate solutions together, and agree on what each will do to implement the solution.

**informal groups** In collaborative learning, groupings of students put together for a short period of time to complete a particular activity.

**information processing** The human mind's activity of taking in, storing, and using information.

**infusion** A process of integrating a theme throughout the curriculum such as teaching about Aboriginal culture in various areas of the curriculum rather than exclusively in a course on native studies.

**instructional strategies, materials, and services** A section of the IEP that usually describes the adaptations to teaching and modifications to curriculum as well as other efforts made to provide an appropriate education for an exceptional student.

**insulin injections** Shots, often self-administered, of the pancreatic secretion that transports glucose from the bloodstream to the cells.

**integration** A term used in the 1970s and 1980s that referred to moving exceptional students from segregated settings into classrooms in the mainstream, with the emphasis on physical integration or placement rather than on learning or participating.

**intellectual disabilities/cognitive disabilities** Have to do with an individual's functioning within the community and that person's severe limitations in both intelligence and adaptive skills.

**intelligence** Ability or abilities to acquire and use knowledge for solving problems and adapting to the world.

**interest** An affective interaction between students and tasks.

**interpersonal competence** The abilities needed for friendships, including initiating and sustaining conversation, initiating plans to spend time with friends outside of school, disclosing personal thoughts and empathy, and managing conflict effectively.

**interpersonal development** The development in students of social responsibility, citizenship, working co-operatively, and responsible interdependence.

**"invisible" classroom management** Techniques used by teachers to increase students' appropriate behaviour so that they rarely have to draw attention to inappropriate behaviour.

## J

**jigsaw strategy** A collaborative learning approach in which students leave home groups to study in expert groups and later teach what they have learned to their home groups.

**juvenile arthritis (JA)** A chronic arthritic condition with continuous inflammation of one or more joints, stiffness, pain, and possible involvement of the eyes.

## L

**labour market information** Details about current and projected demand for labour services and about supply of labour services in the economy.

**language impairment** Language is disordered when a student has impairment in expressive or receptive language.

**large-scale assessment** Nationwide, province-wide, or district-wide efforts to provide information about student achievement, usually by means of paper and pencil tests.

**learned helplessness** The expectation, based on previous experiences with a lack of control, that all one's efforts will lead to failure.

**learning disabilities (LD)** Dysfunctions in processing information that may occur in reading (dyslexia), writing, or arithmetic calculations; often defined as a discrepancy between ability and achievement despite average or above-average intelligence.

**learning strategies** Techniques or principles that enable a student to learn to solve problems, read, communicate, and organize independently.

**leukemia** A type of cancer that forms in the bone marrow, causing abnormal white blood cell development.

**limited range of motion** An inability to move affected limbs and grasp a pencil with swollen fingers that is seen in children with juvenile arthritis, for example.

**long-term goals** A section of the IEP that usually includes learning goals within the curriculum, independence goals within the community, and career goals for a period of at least a year.

**low blood sugar (hypoglycemia)** The condition in which there is an abnormally low amount of sugar in the bloodstream; a complication of diabetes.

**lower reading level materials** Text materials that parallel the required or recommended text but are written at a lower reading level and are more accessible to those reading below grade level.

**low-incidence exceptionalities** Any of the less common exceptionalities, including severe developmental disabilities, hearing impairment, visual impairments, autism, and Asperger syndrome.

**low-key interventions** Minimal actions taken by teachers to respond to minor misbehaviours so that the teachers' actions do not disrupt the flow of the class and to de-escalate rather than raise the stakes.

## M

**mainstreaming** A term used in the 1970s and 1980s that referred to moving exceptional students from segregated settings into classrooms in the mainstream when they could meet traditional academic expectations or when those expectations were not relevant.

**manipulatives** Learning materials children can handle to aid learning, such as counters when adding in arithmetic.

**McGill Action Planning System (MAPS)** A process of gathering key people in the life of a student with a disability to co-operatively support the individual and plan structured friendships.

**MedicAlert®** An identification bracelet worn by individuals with medical conditions that can help you make fast decisions in an emergency.

**metacognition** Knowledge about our own thinking.

**method of presentation** The means used to communicate information to students, including oral, visual, video-recorded demonstration, live demonstration, and hands-on techniques.

**mild developmental disabilities** Delays in physical, cognitive, language, and social development while passing through the same developmental stages as others, but at a much slower rate; reading comprehension, arithmetic reasoning, and problem solving are likely to be most affected, but there may be lower levels of achievement in all curriculum areas.

**mnemonics** Impose an order on information to be remembered using poems, rhymes, jingles, funny sayings, or images. For example, to remember the names, in order, of the five largest cities in Canada, use Teachers Make Very Odd Exams, for Toronto, Montreal, Vancouver, Ottawa, and Edmonton.

**mode of presentation** See *method of presentation*.

**model strategy use** Explain carefully, by thinking aloud, your thinking patterns, how to decide when to use a strategy, and how to do each step.

**modifications** Changes made to the content of the learning expectations, making them substantially different from the prescribed curriculum for the student's grade placement, and specifically selected to meet the exceptional student's needs in accordance with the IEP.

**modified course syllabus** A document, perhaps produced by the IEP team, that states specific learning expectations, grading criteria, and other changes made in a course for an exceptional student.

**monitoring** The process of the teacher being alert and responsive to student action as part of classroom management.

**multicultural education** Creating a classroom in which students' cultures are acknowledged and valued and that reflects the diversity of Canadian society.

**muscular dystrophy (MD)** A group of muscle disorders characterized by progressive weakness and wasting away of the voluntary muscles that control body movement.

**musculoskeletal conditions** Chronic health conditions that affect the muscles and the skeleton and that can affect all aspects of a student's life (e.g., muscular dystrophy and juvenile arthritis).

# N

**narrative text** Written expression that is intended to tell a story.

**natural consequences** Punishment in which a student suffers the logical outcome of a misbehaviour (e.g., a student removing pencil marks from a desk after writing on the desk).

**nebulizer** An aerosol machine that connects to a mask that fits over the mouth and nose to administer medication to persons with asthma.

**needs** Areas in which an exceptional student has relatively weak abilities and skills that need to be developed or bypassed in his or her education by drawing on or compensating with areas of relative strength; schools often focus on academic, social/emotional, and behavioural needs in preparing a student's IEP.

**negative psychological states** Often seen in students with behavioural and emotional exceptionalities; include anxiety, depression, and stress-related disorders.

**neglect** Omission on the part of parent or caregiver to provide a child with the basic necessities such as food, clothing, shelter, adequate supervision, or medical care.

**neighbourhood schools** A policy of educating exceptional students in regular classrooms in neighbourhood or local schools or at least making these the first placement option considered, in consultation with families.

**nervous system impairment** Results of damage or dysfunction of the brain or spinal cord that may have occurred before, during, or after birth; examples of exceptionalities are cerebral palsy, spina bifida, epilepsy, Tourette syndrome, brain injury, and fetal alcohol syndrome.

**neurological dysfunction** See *nervous system impairment*.

**normalization** The concept that all persons, regardless of disability, should live and learn in environments as close to normal as possible.

**norm-referenced** Data in which a student's work is compared to the work of other students who are comparable in age or grade.

**norms for classroom interaction** Expectations and rules about how students will initiate interactions with and respond to one another: effective communication and respectful interaction in conversation and discussion.

**number sense** Essential sense of what numbers mean, how to compare numbers, and how to see and count quantities in the world around us.

# O

**open-ended assignment** Students are given options for completing an assignment and decide how far to take their learning.

**organic cause** Physical or physiological basis for a disability.

**outcomes** Learning that is expected of students, often expressed as short-term and long-term goals.

# P

**pace** The rate of presentation of new information or rate of introduction of new skills.

**paraeducator** A non-certified staff member employed to assist certified teachers in carrying out the educational program and care of exceptional students; sometimes called *teacher's assistant* or *educational assistant*.

**parent–teacher conferences** Formal meetings of parents and teachers at regular intervals during the school year and more frequent informal discussions that can build a productive partnership.

**partial seizures** Epileptic seizures that involve one area of the brain; there may be strange sensations, possibly accompanied by inappropriate movements such as plucking at clothes or books, smacking the lips, or aimless wandering but without complete consciousness being lost.

**Partners Thinking Aloud** A collaborative learning activity in which students work in pairs, alternating roles of teacher and learner with the learner thinking aloud and the teacher offering prompts and feedback; can be used for guided practice.

**pass/fail** A designation to show that students have or have not met the minimum requirements for a unit; based on objective specification of requirements, and aided by the use of qualitative rubrics and checklists.

**peer-mediated strategies** Classroom instructional approaches in which the pattern of interaction is among students with the teacher serving as facilitator.

**peer perspectives** The views of classmates on their relationships with children and adolescents with disabilities, in the literature on social relationships of exceptional children.

**peer teaching** See *peer tutoring*.

**peer tutoring** A teaching approach that involves peers as teaching partners.

**performance assessment** Assessment that provides opportunities for students to demonstrate directly their ability to combine and use their knowledge, skills, and habits of mind.

**perseveration** Repeating an activity.

**personal development** See *student development*.

**Personal Program Plan (PPP)** The form that the IEP takes in some provinces (e.g., Saskatchewan).

**phonemic awareness** Sensitivity to and explicit awareness of individual sounds that make up words, which demands that children analyze or manipulate the sounds (includes early skills such as recognizing rhyming and later skills such as segmenting the sounds in words and synthesizing the sounds in words).

**phonics** Stresses sound–symbol relationships, helping learners to match the letters of the alphabet to the already known speech sounds.

**physical disabilities** A range of conditions restricting physical movement or motor abilities as a result of nervous system impairment, musculoskeletal conditions, or chronic medical disorders.

**physical space** The physical layout and areas of a classroom that can make it inviting, accessible, and efficient (including arrangement of furniture, audiovisual equipment, visual aids, etc.).

**positive behavioural supports** An approach to dealing with problem behaviours that focuses on the remediation of deficient contexts documented to be the source of the problems, with the emphasis on altering the environment before a problem behaviour occurs or teaching appropriate behaviours as a strategy for eliminating the need for problem behaviours to be exhibited.

**portfolio** A collection of the student's work in an area showing growth, self-reflection, and achievement.

**post-reading activities** Activities following individual, paired, or group reading of an assigned piece of text; usually include application of what has been read and a review of learning by the teacher.

**poverty** Insufficient access to the basic goods, services, and opportunities accepted as necessary for a decent standard of living in Canada, as defined by the Canadian Council on Social Development and Statistics Canada.

**prenatal exposure to alcohol** Maternal use of alcohol during pregnancy.

**pre-reading activities** Activities that occur prior to individual, paired, or group reading of an assigned piece of text and usually include an introduction to the topic and the vocabulary and a preview of the text by the teacher.

**pre-referral intervention** Actions taken by a teacher, possibly with the aid of a resource teacher, after the teacher has voiced concerns about a student and before the student has been referred for formal assessment.

**present level of functioning** A section of the IEP that includes recent test results, observations of the student, medical and school history, and degree of participation in current classes.

**preteaching** The technique of preparing exceptional students, frequently used with students who are deaf or hard of hearing, by teaching them the vocabulary and concepts prior to introducing new material to the entire class.

**preventers** Anti-inflammatory drugs taken regularly to prevent and treat inflammation in persons with asthma.

**primary disability** A term that refers to the disability that is the source of an individual's challenges. See *secondary disability*.

**principles of fairness** Fairness does not necessarily mean sameness; this can be a difficult concept for young children to understand and for adolescents to accept.

**pro-act** The actions of teachers effective at classroom management who appear to respond to misbehaviour at a moment's notice; they actually anticipate and act almost before the behaviour occurs (Bennett & Smilanich, 1994).

**problem–solution–effect** A text structure used to organize expository content that emphasizes that the problems encountered might be linked to issues, and that the solutions people generate can have broad effects such as new institutions, new problems, or changes in society.

**problem-solving approach** A behaviour management technique in which the teacher asks students questions about what they think the problem was, what they did to contribute to the problem, how they can make amends, and how they can prevent the problem from recurring, and then the teacher follows up.

**prosocial behaviours** Behaviours that exemplify the relations of an individual's emotional needs to the social environment.

**psychostimulant medications** Drugs used to treat AD/HD, most commonly Ritalin and Dexedrine, which may have side effects.

**puffer** A small device that delivers medication in a pre-measured amount to persons with asthma; sometimes called an inhaler.

**punishment** A response or consequence aimed at decreasing the likelihood of an inappropriate behaviour.

# Q

**qualitative rubrics** Descriptions of learning that characterize learning at various levels and provide students with information about the next steps they must tackle in order to improve.

**quantitative rubrics** Descriptions of learning that identify that students with higher achievement have greater quantities of valued responses such as some of the main ideas, most of the main ideas, or all of the main ideas.

# R

**reading comprehension** Reading skill involving understanding the meaning of what has been read.

**reading wars** Controversies over the whole language versus phonics emphases in teaching early reading (see Stanovich & Stanovich, 1995).

**reciprocal teaching** A teaching approach that involves enabling students to teach one another by taking turns leading discussion in small groups; usually the teacher models how to lead the discussion and provides scaffolding for the groups as they begin.

**referring teacher** A classroom teacher who recognizes that a student may need an adapted or modified program, implements pre-referral interventions, and then refers the student to the in-school team for problem solving and possibly an individual assessment and an IEP.

**refugee** A person who has left his or her home country and seeks refuge in Canada from war, persecution, or a natural disaster.

**reinforcers** Consequences that cause a behaviour to increase.

**related services** On the IEP of an exceptional student, this usually refers to services such as speech therapy, physical therapy, and alternate transportation.

**relievers** Rescue medications to relax the muscles of the airways and provide quick relief of breathing problems for persons with asthma.

**remediation** Intensive instruction, to address basic skills in an area in which a student has needs, that can be carried out with an individual or a small group in the classroom or in a resource room.

**remission** Temporary disappearance of the symptoms of a health condition or disease.

**reporting** The way in which evaluation results are communicated, including individual student report cards, which can be computer generated or written by teachers.

*Report of the Royal Commission on Aboriginal Peoples* **(RCAP)** In 1991, four Aboriginal and three non-Aboriginal commissioners were appointed to investigate Aboriginal issues and advise the federal government; one of their major recommendations was to end assimilation of Aboriginal peoples.

**resilient students** Students who have risk factors but do not manifest risk outcomes tend to possess four attributes: social competence, problem-solving skills, autonomy, and a sense of purpose and future.

**resource teacher** A special educator who supports teachers and exceptional students, usually by consulting with teachers and offering some direct services to exceptional students, either in the classroom or in the resource room; can have many titles, including learning assistance teacher, learning program teacher, tutor, and curriculum resource teacher.

**reward systems** Teachers give students as a group or as individuals tokens or points in a systematic way for appropriate behaviour or work.

**right to pass** Students having the right to choose the extent to which they will participate in a group activity that requires sharing personal information; teachers acknowledge a pass by saying, "That is fine," and offer a second chance for those who passed (used in community circle; *Tribes*, Gibbs, 2001).

**role models** Adults who show youths how to assume the roles expected in adulthood.

**rubrics** Descriptions of learning at different levels of development; can be quantitative or qualitative descriptions.

**rules** Expressions of what can and cannot be done in the classroom that are brief and specific, positively worded, and clearly understood by students.

# S

**Scaffolded Reading Experience (SRE)** Designed for classes with students of varying abilities in reading, it involves teachers in ADAPTing the three steps of pre-reading, reading, and post-reading activities by providing varying degrees of support so all students can learn.

**scaffolding** Support for learning and problem solving; can be clues, reminders, encouragement, breaking the problem into parts, or anything that enables a student to grow in independence as a learner.

**school-based team** A team of teachers, specialists, and administrators that problem solves about students experiencing academic or behaviour difficulties and decides whether students should be individually assessed for an IEP.

**schoolwide approach** A program that is adopted, implemented, and enforced throughout a school; for example, a code of conduct or anti-bullying policy that is applied in every part of the school.

**schoolwide positive behaviour support (SWPBS)** A prevention-oriented approach that defines and teaches behaviour expectations, rewards appropriate behaviour, and integrates support for individuals, groups, and the whole school.

**secondary disability** Exceptionality that results from living with a primary disability in another aspect of one's life; for example, social skills difficulties that arise from being rejected as a result of having a disability. See *primary disability*.

**seizures** Brief bursts of electrical activity in the brain.

**self-advocacy** An individual's ability to effectively communicate, convey, negotiate, or assert his or her own interests, desires, needs, and rights.

**self-awareness** Knowing about oneself; developing a picture of the kind of person one is.

**self-care** The personal care activities that maintain hygiene and health.

**self-concept** Our perceptions about ourselves.

**self-determination** The abilities, motivation, and volition that enable people to define goals for themselves and to take and sustain the initiative to reach those goals.

**self-monitoring** A strategy in which students are taught to check whether they have performed targeted behaviours.

**self-referenced** Data that compare a student's progress to where that student started from, regardless of whether that starting point is ahead of, even with, or behind others in the class; often the most appropriate form of data for students on modified programs.

**self-regulation** Learners proactively monitoring, directing, and regulating their behaviour to achieve self-set goals of acquiring knowledge and expanding expertise, with the emphasis on autonomy and control by the individual.

**sense of community** A feeling of belonging; for example, for Aboriginal students this can be created in a place where Aboriginal is the norm, not the minority, such as a First Nations Centre in a university.

**severe developmental disabilities** Includes those previously considered to have moderate, severe, or profound disabilities, spanning a range of abilities from those who can acquire academic skills to those who require assistance with self-care.

**sexual harassment** Includes put-downs and negative comments made about gender or sexual preference, sexist jokes, and calling someone gay or lesbian.

**short-term goals** A section of the IEP that usually includes learning outcomes that are steps on the way to long-term goals, and may be goals for a term or half-term.

**shunt** A mechanism installed to drain the fluid that builds up with hydrocephalus, for reabsorption in individuals with spina bifida.

**signal** The means used by teachers to obtain and maintain the attention of students, including flicking the lights, raising a hand, rhythmic clapping or speaking, or even blowing a whistle in the gymnasium; usually taught to classes at the beginning of term.

**simple absence seizure (petit mal)** This generalized seizure occurs in children; they stare or daydream for 5 to 15 seconds and there may be small muscle movements in the face, the eyes may roll up or to one side, and the child may be confused about the seconds "missed."

**six-hour handicap** A description of students who lag behind their peers at school but meet the everyday demands of living.

**social acceptance** The response and evaluation by peers of students' social behaviours, including approving of their behaviours, considering them to be members of the group, and including them in social and learning activities.

**social competence** See *social development*.

**social development** The ability to implement developmentally appropriate social behaviours that enhance one's interpersonal relationships without causing harm to anyone.

**social problems** Risk factors often experienced by students with emotional and behavioural exceptionalities, including delinquency, substance abuse, and neglect.

**social relationships** Friendships, peer relations, and romantic relationships that change with development; for example, by middle childhood, children choose friends on the basis of personality and interests and friendships become increasingly stable.

**social skills difficulties** A controversial aspect of learning disabilities, not present in all students with LD; for example, teachers report that *most* students with LD experience social skills difficulties and peers report that *many* have low social status; however, only a *few* children with LD report low social self-concept.

**social status** A rating of a child's or adolescent's popularity with their classmates, that is, how well they are liked.

**social stories** Describe a situation from the perspective of a student, direct the student to do the appropriate behaviour, and are in the first person; developed by Gray (2002) for children with autism.

**sociometric rating** A system of collecting data by asking children to indicate which classmates they would choose as best friends, to play with, etc., and which they would not choose; enables researchers to develop ratings of popularity or social status for individual students.

**special education** Programs or services designed to accommodate students whose educational needs cannot adequately be met through the use of regular curriculum and services only.

**Special Education Plan (SEP)** The term used in New Brunswick for an IEP.

**spectrum of autistic disorders** Refers to the range of characteristics and degrees of severity displayed by individuals with autism.

**speech-activated** Describes equipment that responds to the human voice, usually computer equipment used by individuals with visual impairments.

**speech and language exceptionalities** Problems encountered in the oral production of language and/or impairment in the use or comprehension of spoken language that interfere with communication.

**speech impairment** Speech is disordered when it deviates so far from the speech of other people that it calls attention to itself, interferes with communication, or causes the speaker or listeners distress.

**speech-reading** The skill of understanding speech by watching the lips and face; sometimes called lip-reading.

**spina bifida** A condition developed prenatally that disturbs proper development of the vertebrae or spinal cord and results in varying degrees of damage to the spinal cord and nervous system.

**stigma** A negative stereotype.

**story-planning sheet** Scaffolding to help students create narrative text that includes prompts such as the following: setting, main character, character clues, problem, attempts to solve the problem, and resolution.

**strengths** Areas in which an exceptional student has relatively strong abilities and skills on which to draw in compensating or learning in areas of relative weakness; schools often focus on academic, social/emotional, and behavioural strengths in preparing a student's IEP.

**structure** Predictability and organization in learning activities that enables exceptional students to feel safe and focus on learning.

**student activity log** A summary of student activities that may be particularly beneficial in reporting progress for students on modified programs because it can include a summary of key accomplishments shown in the portfolio or performance-based assessments.

**student development** The development in students of independence.

**student responsibility** Making students share the responsibility for a safe school environment by creating a group of school leaders who directly involve students in setting a positive social tone for the school.

**Student Support Plan (SSP)** Required by the Northwest Territories if a student has a modified education plan based on outcomes in the NWT curriculum.

**students with special needs** See *exceptional students*.

**study guides** Learning aids that tell students what to study for a test and can enable them to be more efficient in their preparation; they include outlines, abstracts, and questions that emphasize important information in texts.

**study skills** The actions students take to prepare for tests that usually involve reviewing notes and texts.

**suspension** Temporary removal of a student from the classroom (for a day or more) as a consequence of the student behaving inappropriately, violating the code of conduct, etc.

# T

**taped books** A technique of reading books onto audiotape so they can be used by persons who are print-disabled, usually people who are blind or have learning disabilities in the area of reading (dyslexia).

**task commitment** The degree to which students set their own goals, embrace challenges, and show perseverance.

**Teacher Adviser Groups (TAGs)** Formal groups of students who meet with a teacher at regular intervals to plan the students' programs and receive advice about study skills, course selections, and career planning.

**testing** A form of assessment, normally using a paper and pencil test (either designed by the teacher or commercially available) to gather information that describes a student's or a group's level of performance.

**theory of mind** The notion that others think, feel, and know; Baron-Cohen (1995) hypothesized that people with autism do not have a theory of mind.

**thinking aloud** Teachers or peers can make the invisible visible by verbalizing their thoughts and showing students how to use a strategy, solve a problem, etc.

**think-pair-share** A collaborative activity in which the teacher poses a problem, students think and jot down their thoughts, pair with a classmate to discuss the question, and a few students share the thoughts of their pair with the class.

**tics** Involuntary, rapid, sudden muscular movements; uncontrollable vocal sounds; and inappropriate words (seen in Tourette syndrome).

**time out** Punishment in which a student is removed from opportunities for reward as a consequence for inappropriate behaviour.

**token economy** See *token reinforcement*.

**token reinforcement** Often called a "token economy," a system in which a teacher and a student select a specific appropriate target behaviour for which the student earns points or tokens that are collected and then traded in for some kind of reward once the agreed-upon amount has been earned.

**tonic-clonic (grand mal) seizure** In this generalized seizure, the individual sometimes gives a sharp cry before falling to the floor, the muscles stiffen, then begin to jerk rhythmically, and there may be loss of bladder control, some breathing difficulty, and saliva may gather at the mouth.

**Tourette syndrome** A neurological disorder involving motor tics and uncontrollable vocal sounds or inappropriate words that are often accompanied by obsessions and hyperactivity.

**transient lifestyle** A way of living adopted by homeless people who move from shelter to shelter; often seen in adolescents who have left home.

**transition** Changing from one stage of life to another; often used to refer to the transition to work that follows formal education.

**transition plan** A formal, written plan that some provinces require, for students with an IEP, to ensure that preparation for post-secondary endeavours begins early in the high school years.

**traumatic brain injury (TBI)** Damage to brain tissue as a result of a blow to the head or an accident that can cause physical difficulties (e.g., paralysis) and cognitive problems (e.g., memory loss).

**TTYPA** A collaborative learning activity in which a teacher stops and tells the students to "turn to your partner and ... introduce yourself ... or describe a time when you ..." Then the students switch roles.

## U

**universal design for learning** The design of instructional materials and activities that allows the learning goals to be achievable by individuals with wide differences in their abilities to see, hear, speak, move, etc. by means of flexible curricular materials and activities designed to include alternatives for students with diversity in abilities and backgrounds.

## V

**verbal reprimand** Punishment in which a student is reminded of the classroom rules; the most effective reprimands are immediate, unemotional, brief, and backed up with a time out or loss of privileges.

**vision teacher** A special educator who teaches or tutors students who are blind or have impaired vision.

**visual impairment** Disability characterized by partial or complete loss of sight and use of auditory and tactile sources of information to supplement or replace sight.

**vocabulary** The kind and level of language used in oral and written expression to communicate meaning to students; can also refer to the kind and level of language used in oral and written expression by students.

**voice synthesizer** Converts information typed or scanned into a computer into speech.

## W

**wheezing** Breathing with an audible chesty, whistling sound; a symptom of an asthma episode.

**workplace experience** Involves students for brief periods of time in a workplace (ranging from one-day job-shadowing experiences to a few half-day visits) within the context of a credit course.

## Z

**zone of proximal development (ZPD)** Distance between a child's development as shown in independent problem solving and the level of potential development as determined through problem solving with adult guidance or collaboration with more capable peers; from the work of Vygotsky.

# References

Ackley, R.S., & Decker, T.N. (2006). Audiological advancement and the acquisition of spoken language in deaf children. In P.E. Spencer & M. Marschark (Eds.), *Advances in spoken language development of deaf and hard-of-hearing children*. Oxford: Oxford University Press.

Adams, C.M., & Pierce, R.L. (2003). Teaching by tiering. *Science and Children*, 30–34.

Adams, M.J. (1990). *Beginning to read: Thinking and learning about print*. Cambridge, MA: MIT Press.

Advisory Council on Science and Technology (2000). *Stepping up: Skills and opportunities in the knowledge economy* (Report of the expert panel on skills). Ottawa: Government of Canada. [http://acst-ccst.gc.ca/skills/finalrep_html/title_e.html]. (November 14, 2008).

Aiello, B., & Shulman, J. (1991a). *Business is looking up*. Minneapolis, MD: Twenty-First Century.

Aiello, B., & Shulman, J. (1991b). *It's your turn at bat*. Minneapolis, MD: Twenty-First Century.

Aiello, B., & Shulman, J. (1995a). *A portrait of me*. Minneapolis, MD: Twenty-First Century.

Aiello, B., & Shulman, J. (1995b). *Trick or treat or trouble*. Minneapolis, MD: Twenty-First Century.

Aiello, B., & Shulman, J. (1997a). *Friends for life*. Minneapolis, MD: Twenty-First Century.

Aiello, B., & Shulman, J. (1997b). *Secrets aren't (always) for keeps*. Minneapolis, MD: Twenty-First Century.

Ainscow, M., Booth, T., & Dyson, A. (1999). Inclusion and exclusion in schools: Listening to some hidden voices. In K. Ballard (Ed.), *Inclusive education: International voices on disability and justice* (pp. 139–151). London, UK: Falmer Press.

Alber, S.R., & Heward, W.L. (1997). Recruit it or lose it: Teaching students to recruit contingent teacher attention. *Intervention in School and Clinic, 5*, 275–282.

Albert, E. (1994). *Phonics for learning how to read*. (ERIC Reproduction Document No. ED370078).

Alberta Education. (n.d.) *Transition planning*. Edmonton: Alberta Education.

Alberta Education. (2003). *Educational placement of students with special needs*. Edmonton: Alberta Education.

Alberta Education. (2004). *Standards for special education*. Edmonton: Alberta Learning.

Alberta Education. (2004/2005). *Special education definitions*. Edmonton: Alberta Education.

Alberta Education. (2006). *Focusing on success: Teaching students with attention deficit/hyperactivity disorder*. Edmonton: Alberta Education. [www.education.alberta.ca/search.asp?q=adhd]. (November 8, 2008).

Alberta Learning (2002). *First Nations, Métis and Inuit education policy framework: A progress report*. Edmonton: Alberta Learning.

Alberta Learning (2002). *Guidelines for using time-out in schools*. Alberta: Special Programs Branch.

Alfassi, M. (2004). Reading to learn: Effects of combined strategy instruction on high school students. *Journal of Educational Research, 9*(4), 171–184.

Ali, S., & Frederickson, N. (2006). Investigating the evidence base of social stories. *Educational Psychology in Practice, 22*, 355–377.

Allard, E.R., & Williams, D.F. (2008). Listeners' perceptions of speech and language disorders. *Journal of Communication Disorders, 41*(2), 108–123.

Allen, A.M.A. (1996). "I don't want to read this": Students' responses to illustrations of Black characters. In K.S. Brethwaite & C.E. James (Eds.), *Educating African Canadians* (pp. 147–166). Toronto: James Lorimer & Co.

Alper, S.K., Schloss, P., & Schloss, C. (1995). Families of children with disabilities in elementary and middle school: Advocacy models and strategies. *Exceptional Children, 62*, 261–270.

Amato, P.R., & Cheadle, J.E. (2008). Parental divorce, marital conflict and children's behavior problems: A comparison of adopted and biological children. *Social Forces, 86*(3), 1139–1161.

American Association of University Women (1993). *Hostile hallways: The AAUW survey on sexual harassment in America's schools*. Washington, DC: American Association of University Women.

American Psychiatric Association (APA) (200/2004). *Diagnostic and statistical manual of mental disorders* (4th ed., DSM-IV-TR). Washington, DC: APA.

Anderson, J.O., Bachor, D., & Baer, M. (2001, April). *Using portfolio assessment to study classroom assessment practice*. Paper presented at the annual meeting of the American Educational Research Association, Seattle, WA.

Anderson, J.O., & Bachor, D.G. (1998). A Canadian perspective on portfolio use in student assessment. *Assessment in Education, 5*, 353–379.

Anderson, K. (2004). Speaking from the heart: Everyday storytelling and adult learning. *Canadian Journal of Native Education, 28*, 123–129.

Anderson, K.L., & Goldstein, H. (2004). Speech perception benefits of FM and infrared devices to children with hearing aids in a typical classroom. *Language, Speech, and Hearing Services in Schools, 35*(2), 169–184.

Anderson, K.M. (2007). Differentiating instruction to include all students. *Preventing School Failure, 51*(3), 49–54.

Anderson, L.W. (2003). *Classroom assessment: Enhancing the quality of teacher decision making*. Mahwah, NJ: L. Erlbaum Associates.

Anderssen, E. The son who vanished . . . *The Globe and Mail*, June 21, 2008 (in the series, Breakdown: Canada's mental health crisis).

Antonijevic, R. (2007). *Usage of computers and calculators and students' achievement: results from TIMSS 2003*. Online Submission, ERIC ED497737.

Antrop, I., Stock, P., Verte, S., Wiersema, J.R., Baeyens, D., & Roeyers, H. (2006). ADHD and delay aversion: The influence of non-temporal stimulation on choice for delayed rewards. *Journal of Child Psychology and Psychiatry, 47*(11), 1152–1158.

Armstrong, M.I., Birnie-Lefcovitch, S., & Ungar, M.T. (2005). Pathways between social support, family well being, quality of parenting, and child resilience: What we know. *Journal of Child and Family Studies, 14*(2), 269–281.

Arnold, S. (2006). Investigating functions using real-world data. *Australian Senior Mathematics Journal, 20*(1), 44–47.

Arnott, K. (1998, Winter). No address, no education: Keeping homeless children in school. *Education Today, 10*(1), 16–17.

Aronson, E., & Patnoe, S. (1997). *The jigsaw classroom: Building cooperation in the classroom* (2nd ed.). New York: Longman.

Assembly of First Nations. [http://afn.ca]. (September 15, 2005).

Assouline, S.G., Nicpon, M.F., & Huber, D.H. (2006). The impact of vulnerabilities and strengths on the academic experiences of twice-exceptional students: A message to school counselors. *Professional School Counseling, 10*(1), 14–24.

Atlantic Provinces Special Education Authority (2001a). *Resource booklet on educational interpreting*. Halifax: Atlantic Provinces Special Education Authority. [www.apsea.ca/download/rbei.pdf]. (November 14, 2008).

Atlantic Provinces Special Education Authority (2001b). *Support for students who are deaf or hard of hearing in an inclusive setting: A guide for administrators and teachers*. Halifax: Atlantic Provinces Special Education Authority. [www.apsea.ca/download/ssdhh.pdf]. (November 14, 2008).

Attles, H. (1997). *The effects of homelessness on the academic achievement of children*. New York: Garland.

Austin, V.L. (2003). Pharmacological interventions for students with ADD. *Intervention in School and Clinic, 38*, 289–296.

Azmitia, M., Ittel, A., & Radmacher, K. (2005). Narratives of friendship and self in adolescence. In N. Way & J.V. Hamm (Eds.), The experience of close friendships in adolescence. *New Directions for Child and Adolescent Development, 107* (pp. 23–39). San Francisco: Jossey-Bass.

Azmitia, M., & Montgomery, R. (1993). Friendship, transactive dialogues, and the development of scientific reasoning. *Social Development, 2*, 202–221.

Babyak, A.E., Luze, G.J., & Kamps, D.M. (2000). The good student game: Behavior management for diverse classrooms. *Intervention in School and Clinic, 35*, 216–223.

Bach, M. (2002). *Social inclusion as solidarity: Rethinking the child rights agenda*. Toronto: Laidlaw Foundation Working Paper Series.

Bain, S.K., & Bell, S.M. (2004). Social self-concept, social attributions, and peer relationships in fourth, fifth, and sixth graders who are gifted compared to high achievers. *Gifted Child Quarterly, 48(3)*, 167–178.

Baker, J.M. (2005). *How homophobia hurts children: Nurturing diversity at home, at school, and in the community*. Florence, KY: Routledge.

Baker, S., Gersten, R., & Scanlon, D. (2002). Procedural facilitators and cognitive strategies: Tools for unraveling the mysteries of comprehension and the writing process, and for providing meaningful access to the general curriculum. *Learning Disabilities Research & Practice, 17*, 65–77.

Bakken, J.P., & Obiakor, F. (2008). *Transition planning for students with disabilities: What educators and service providers can do*. Springfield, IL: Charles C. Thomas Pub.

Ballard, K., & McDonald, T. (1999). Disability inclusion and exclusion: Some insider accounts and interpretations. In K. Ballard (Ed.), *Inclusive education: International voices on disability and justice* (pp. 97–115). London, UK: Falmer Press.

Barker, J. (2005). *Evaluating Web pages: Techniques to apply and questions to ask*. [http://www.lib.berkeley.edu/TeachingLib/Guides/Internet/Evaluate.html]. (November 14, 2008).

Barkley, R. (1990). *Attention-deficit hyperactivity disorder: A handbook for diagnosis and treatment*. New York: Guilford Press.

Barkley, R. (1997). *AD/HD and the nature of self-control*. New York: Guilford Press.

Barkley, R., et al. (2002). Consensus statement on ADHD. *European Child & Adolescent Psychiatry, 11*, 96–99.

Barnes, M., & Wade-Woolley, L. (2007). Where there's a will there are ways to close the achievement gap for children with learning difficulties. *Orbit Magazine, 37(1)*, 9–13.

Baron-Cohen, S. (1995). *Mindblindness*. Cambridge, MA: MIT Press.

Barrish, H.H., Saunders, M., & Wolf, M.M. (1969). Good behavior game: Effects of individual contingencies for group consequences on disruptive behavior in a classroom. *Journal of Applied Behavior Analysis, 2*, 119–124.

Bates, P.E., Cuvo, T., Miner, C.A., & Korabek, C.A. (2001). Simulated and community-based instruction involving persons with mild and moderate mental retardation. *Research in Developmental Disabilities, 22*, 95–115.

Bauminger, N., & Kimhi-Kind, I. (2008). Social information-processing, security of attachment, and emotion regulation in children with learning disabilities. *Journal of Learning Disabilities, 41(4)*, 315–332.

Bauminger, N., Schorr Edelsztein, H., & Morash, J. ( 2005). Social information processing and emotional understanding in children with LD. *Journal of Learning Disabilities, 38*, 45–61.

Beale, A.V., & Hall, K.R. (2007). Cyberbullying: What school administrators (and parents) can do. *Clearing House, 81(1)*, 8–12.

Beck, I.L., & McKeown, M.G. (2007). Increasing young low-income children's oral vocabulary repertoires through rich and focused instruction. *Elementary School Journal, 107*, 251–273.

Beddard, J.M. (1996). *Fetal alcohol syndrome: Educators' knowledge and needs*. Unpublished master's project, Queen's University, Kingston, ON.

Beitchman et al. (2008). Models and determinants of vocabulary growth from kindergarten to adulthood. *Journal of Child Psychology and Psychiatry, 49(6)*, 626–634.

Bell, A.P. (2006). *The heart of the matter: Composing music with an adolescent with special needs*. Unpublished MEd thesis, Queen's University, Kingston, ON.

Bell, D. (2004). *Sharing our success: Ten case studies in Aboriginal schooling*. Kelowna, BC: Society for the Advancement of Excellence in Education.

Bell, D., Rose, S., Anderson, K., Fortin, T., Spencer, K., Simard, L., & Ottoman, J. (2005). *Sharing our success: Ten case studies in Aboriginal schooling*. Kelowna, BC: Society for the Advancement of Excellence in Education.

Bellanca, J., & Fogarty, R. (2003). *Blueprints for achievement in the cooperative classroom*. Thousand Oaks, CA: Corwin Press.

Ben Jaafar, S. (2006a). *Educational accountability: Differences in policy and practice*. Paper presented at the International Congress for School Effectiveness and Improvement annual conference, Ft Lauderdale, Florida.

Ben Jaafar, S. (2006b). From performance-based to inquiry-based accountability. *Brock Education, 16*, 62–77.

Ben Jaafar, S., & Anderson, S. (2007). Policy trends and tensions in accountability for educational management and services in Canada. *Alberta Journal of Educational Research, 53(2)*, 207–228.

Bennett, B., & Smilanich, P. (1994). *Classroom management: A thinking and caring approach*. Toronto: Bookation. [www.sacsc.ca]. (November 14, 2008).

Bennett, K.S., & Hay, D.A. (2007). The role of family in the development of social skills in children with physical disabilities. *International Journal of Disability, Development and Education, 54*, 381–397.

Bennett, S., Good, D., & & Kumpf, J. (2003). *Educating educators about ABI: Resource book*. St. Catharines, ON: Ontario Brain Injury Association.

Bennett, S., Weber, K., & Dworet, D. (2008). *Special education in Ontario schools* (6th ed.). St David's, ON: Highland Press.

Benton-Benai, E. (1988). *The Mishomis book: The voice of the Ojibway*. Saint Paul, MN: Red School House.

Berg, D.H. (2006). *Role of processing speed and working memory in children's mental addition*. Unpublished doctoral thesis, Queen's University, Kingston, Ontario, Canada.

Berg, D.H. (2008). Working memory and arithmetic calculation in children: The contributory roles of processing speed, short-term memory, and reading. *Journal of Experimental Child Psychology, 99(4)*, 288–308.

Berlak, A., & Berlak, H. (1989). *Dilemmas of schooling: Teaching and social change* (2nd ed.). New York: Routledge.

Beran, T.N. (2006). A construct validity study of bullying. *Alberta Journal of Educational Research, 52*, 241–250.

Beran, T.N., Hughes, G., & Lupart, J. (2008). A model of achievement and bullying: Analyses of the Canadian National Longitudinal Survey of Children and Youth data. *Educational Research, 50*, 25–39.

Berman, S. (2008). *Performance-based learning: Aligning experiential tasks and assessment to increase learning.* Thousand Oaks, CA: Corwin Press.

Berninger, V.W., et al. (2006). Tier 1 and tier 2 early intervention for handwriting and composing. *Journal of School Psychology, 44*(1), 3–30.

Berry, R.A.W. (2006). Inclusion, power and community: Teachers and students interpret the language of community in an inclusion classroom. *American Educational Research Journal, 43*, 489–529.

Berscheid, E. (1985). Interpersonal attraction. In G. Lindzey & E. Aronson (Eds.), *Handbook of social psychology* (3rd ed., Vol. 2, pp. 413–484). New York: Random House.

Bethell, C.D., Read, D., Blumberg, S.J., & Newacheck, P.W. (2008). What is the prevalence of children with special health care needs? Toward an understanding of variations in findings and methods across three national surveys. *Maternal and Child Health Journal, 12*, 1–14.

Beynon, J., & Toohey, K. (1995). Access and aspirations: Careers in teaching as seen by Canadian university students of Chinese and Punjabi-Sikh ancestry. *Alberta Journal of Educational Research, 41*, 435–461.

Bigge, J.L., Best, S.J., & Heller, K.W. (2001). *Teaching individuals with physical, health, or multiple disabilities* (4th ed.). Upper Saddle River, NJ: Merrill/Prentice Hall.

Biklen, D., & Schein, P.L. (2001). Public and professional constructions of mental retardation: Glen Ridge and the missing narrative of disability rights. *Mental Retardation, 39*, 436–451.

Billot, J., Goddard, J.T., & Cranston, N. (2007). How principals manage ethnocultural diversity: Learnings from three countries. *International Studies in Educational Administration, 35*(2), 3–19.

Binda, K.P., & Calliou, S., (2001). *Aboriginal education in Canada: A study in decolonization.* Mississauga, ON: Canadian Educators' Press.

Black, S. (2003). Research: Show what you know. *American School Board Journal, 190*(2), 42–44.

Blackbourn, V.A., & Blackbourn, J.M. (1993). An adolescent with moderate mental disabilities tutors a 1st grade, nondisabled child. *Teaching Exceptional Children, 25*(4), 56–57.

Bloom, E.L., Karagiannakis, A., Toste, J.R., Heath, N.L., & Konstantinopoulos, E. (2007). Severity of academic achievement and social skills deficits. *Canadian Journal of Education, 30*, 911–930.

Blum, H.T., Lipsett, L.R., & Yocom, D.J. (2002). Literature circles: A tool for self-determination in one middle school inclusive classroom. *Remedial and Special Education, 23*, 99–108.

Bob, G., Marcuse, G., Nyce, D., & Williams, L. (1993). *First Nations: The circle unbroken: The teacher's guide (videos 1–4).* Montreal: National Film Board of Canada.

Bondy, E., Ross, D.D., Gallingane, C., & Hambacher, E. (2007). Creating environments of success and resilience: Culturally responsive classroom management and more. *Urban Education, 42*, 326–348.

Borowsky, I.W., Ireland, M., & Resnick, M.D. (2001). Adolescent suicide attempts: Risk and protectors. *Pediatrics, 107*(3), 485–493.

Bosetti, L., & Watt, D. (1995). Structural marginalization in educational policy: The case of English as a second language. *Exceptionality Education Canada, 5*(1), 24–41.

Bowman-Perrott, L.J., Greenwood, C.R., & Tapia, Y. (2007). The efficacy of CWPT used in secondary alternative school classrooms with small teacher/pupil ratios and students with emotional and behavioral disorders. *Education and Treatment of Children, 30*, 65–87.

Bowen, G.M., & Arsenault, N. (2008). It's all about choice. *Science Teacher, 75*(2), 34–37.

Bray, M.A., Kehle, T.J., Grigerick, S.E., Loftus, S., & Nicholson, H. (2008). Children with asthma: Assessment and treatment in school settings. *Psychology in the Schools, 45*, 63–73.

Brendtro, L., Brokenleg, M., VanBockern, & Bluebird, G. (1990). *Reclaiming youth at risk: Our hope for the future.* Bloomington, IN: Solution Tree.

Brethwaite, K.S. (1996). Keeping watch over our children: The role of African Canadian parents on the education team. In K.S. Brethwaite & C.E. James (Eds.), *Educating African Canadians* (pp. 107–130). Toronto: James Lorimer & Co.

Brislin, D.C. (2008). Reaching for independence: Counseling implications for youth with spina bifida. *Journal of Counseling and Development, 86*, 34–38.

Bristol-Power, M.M., & Spinella, G. (1999). Research on screening and diagnosis in autism: A work in progress. *Journal of Autism and Developmental Disorders, 29*, 435–438.

British Columbia Ministry of Education (2004). *Aboriginal studies 10: Aboriginal perspectives (teacher resource).* Victoria: Queen's Printer for British Columbia.

British Columbia Ministry of Education (2004). *Provincial student assessment program.* Victoria: Queen's Printer for British Columbia.

British Columbia Ministry of Education. (2006). Shared learnings. [http://www.bced.gov.bc.ca/abed/shared.pdf]. (November 15, 2008).

British Columbia Special Education Branch (2006, rev. ed.). *Special education services: A manual of policies, procedures, and guidelines.* Victoria: Queen's Printer for British Columbia. [www.bced.gov.bc.ca/specialed/ppandg/]. (February 28, 2008).

British Columbia Special Education Branch (2006). *Special education policy framework for British Columbia.* Victoria: Queen's Printer for British Columbia.

British Columbia Special Education Branch (2006). *Special programs: Individual education planning for students with special needs.* Victoria: Queen's Printer for British Columbia.

British Columbia Special Education Branch (2006). *Teaching students with fetal alcohol syndrome/effects.* Victoria: British Columbia Special Education Branch.

British Columbia Special Education Branch. (2006). *Teaching students with learning and behavioural differences: A resource guide for teachers.* [http://www.bced.gov.bc.ca/specialed/landbdif/toc.htm]. (November 15, 2008).

British Columbia Special Education Branch. (2008). *Special education services: A manual of policies, procedures, and guidelines.* Victoria: Queen's Printer for British Columbia [http://www.bced.gov.bc.ca/specialed/ppandg/toc.html]. (November 15, 2008).

Brock, C.H., Lapp, D., Flood, J., Fisher, D., & Keomghee, T.H. (2007). Does homework matter? An investigation of teacher perceptions about homework practices for children from nondominant backgrounds. *Urban Education, 42*, 349–372.

Brolin, D. (1997). *Life-centered career education: A competency-based approach.* Arlington, VA: Council for Exceptional Children.

Brosvic, G.M., Dihoff, R.E., Epstein, M.L., & Cook, M.L. (2006). Feedback facilitates the acquisition and retention of numerical fact series by elementary school students with mathematics learning disabilities. *Psychological Record, 56*, 35–47.

Brown, L. (2008). Serving students in culturally clustered schools. *The Toronto Star*, May 20, 2008.

Brown, R.T., Rickel, A.U., & Daly, B.P. (2007). *Chronic illness in children and adolescents.* Toronto: Hogrefe & Huber Publications.

Browne, A. (2007). *Teaching and learning communication, language and literacy*. Thousand Oaks, CA: Sage/Paul Chapman Pub.

Brownell, M.T., Adams, A., Sindelar, P., Waldron, N., & Vanhover, S. (2006). Learning from collaboration: The role of teacher qualities. *Exceptional Children, 72*, 169–185.

Browning, F.C. (2008). Synchronizing loss with life over a life span: A dynamic perspective. *Adultspan: Theory Research and Practice, 7*(1), 26–31.

Brownlie, F., & King, J. (2000). *Learning in safe schools: Creating classrooms where all students belong.* Markham, ON: Pembroke Publishers.

Bryan, T. (1991). Social problems and learning disabilities. In B.Y.L. Wong (Ed.), *Learning about learning disabilities* (pp. 195–229). San Diego, CA: Academic.

Bryan, T. (1999). Reflections on a research career. *Exceptional Children, 65*, 438–447.

Bryan, T., & Burstein, K. (2004). Improving homework completion and academic performance: Lessons from special education. *Theory Into Practice, 43*(3), 213–219.

Buggey, T. (2007). A picture is worth: Video self-modeling applications at school and at home. *Journal of Positive Behavior Interventions, 9*, 151–158.

Buhrmester, D. (1998). Need fulfillment, interpersonal competence, and the developmental contexts of early adolescent friendship. In W.M. Bukowski, A.F. Newcomb, & W.W. Hartup (Eds.), *The company they keep: Friendship in childhood and adolescence* (pp. 158–185). New York: Cambridge University Press.

Bukowski, W.M., Rubin, K.H., & Parker, J.G. (2004). Social competence: Childhood and adolescence. In N.J. Smelser, & P.B. Baltes (Eds). *International encyclopedia of the social and behavioral sciences* (pp. 14258–14264). Elsevier: St. Louis, MO.

Bukowski, W.M., & Sippola, L.K. (2005). Friendship and development: Putting the most human relationship in its place. *New Directions for Child and Adolescent Development, 109*, 91–97.

Bullock, L.M., & Gable, R.A. (1995). *Perspectives on school aggression and violence: Highlights from the working forum on children and youth who have aggressive and violent behaviors.* Reston, VA: Council for Exceptional Children.

Bullock, L.M., Gable, R.A., & Mohr, J.D. (2005). Traumatic brain injury: A challenge for educators. *Preventing School Failure, 49*(4), 6–10.

Burcroff, T.L., Radogna, D.M., & Wright, E.H. (2003). Community forays: Addressing students' functional skills in inclusive settings. *Teaching Exceptional Children, 35*(5), 52–57.

Burd, L.J. (2007). Interventions in FASD: We must do better. *Child: Care, Health and Development, 33*, 398–400.

Burge, P., Ouelette-Kuntz, H., Box, H., & Hutchinson, N. (in press). A quarter century of inclusive education for children with intellectual disabilities in Ontario: Public perceptions. *Canadian Journal of Educational Administration and Policy.*

Burge, P., Ouellette-Kuntz, H., & Lysaght, R. (2007). Public views on employment of people with intellectual disabilities. *Journal of Vocational Rehabilitation, 26*(1), 29–37.

Burnette, J., & Peters-Johnson, C. (2004). *Thriving as a special educator: Balancing your practices and ideals.* Arlington, VA: Council for Exceptional Children.

Burney, S. (1995). *Coming to Gum San: The story of Chinese Canadians.* Toronto: D.C. Heath Canada Ltd. & Multicultural History Society of Ontario.

Burney, V.H., & Cross, T.L. (2006). Impoverished students with academic promise in rural settings: 10 lessons from Project Aspire. *Gifted Child Today, 29*(2), 14–21.

Bussière, P., Cartwright, F., & Knighton, T. (2004). *Measuring up: Canadian results for the OECD PISA study: The performance of Canada's youth in mathematics, reading, science and problem solving: 2003 first findings for Canadians aged 15.* Ottawa, ON: Minster of Industry. [http://www.pisa.gc.ca/81-590-xie2004001.pdf]. (November 15, 2008).

Butler, C.M., & Egnatoff, W.J. (2002). Cultural awareness through the arts. *Education Canada, 42*(2), 40–42.

Butler, C.M., & Swain, M. (1996). *Cultural awareness through the arts.* Unpublished manuscript, Lennox and Addington County Board of Education, Ontario.

Butterworth, J., Hagner, D., Helm, D.T., & Whelley, T.A. (2000). Workplace culture, social interactions, and supports for transition-age young adults. *Mental Retardation, 38*, 342–353.

Calgary Educational Partnership Foundation (2003). *Employability skills portfolio: Creating my future (Student Booklet)* (3rd ed.). Scarborough, ON: Nelson Thomson Learning.

Campbell, D.S., Serff, P., & Williams, D. (1994). *BreakAway company.* Toronto: Trifolium Publishing.

Canadian Council on Social Development. (2000). *Immigrant youth in Canada.* Ottawa: Canadian Council on Social Development.

Canadian Labour Force Development Board (1994). *Putting the pieces together, toward a coherent transition system for Canada's labour force: Report.* Ottawa: Canadian Labour Force Development Board.

Canadian Race Relations Foundation; Coalition for the Advancement of Aboriginal Studies (2002). *Learning about "Walking in Beauty": Placing aboriginal perspectives in Canadian classrooms.* Toronto: Canadian Race Relations Foundation.

Canadian School Boards Association (2001). *Anaphylaxis: A handbook for school boards.* Ottawa: Health Canada.

Canitano, R., & Vivanti, G. (2007). Tics and Tourette syndrome in autism spectrum disorders. *Autism, 11*, 19–28.

Canney, C., & Byrne, A. (2006). Evaluating circle time as a support to social skills development: Reflections on a journey in school-based research. *British Journal of Special Education, 33*(1), 19–24.

Cantwell, D.P. (1996). Attention deficit disorder: A review of the past 10 years. *Journal of the American Academy of Child and Adolescent Psychiatry, 34*, 1262–1271.

Capella, M. (2003). Comparing employment outcomes of vocational rehabilitation consumers with hearing loss to other consumers and the general labor force. *Rehabilitation Counseling Bulletin, 47*, 24–33.

Capuzzi, D. & Gross, D. (Eds.) (2004). *Youth at risk: A prevention resource for counselors, teachers, and parents* (4th ed.). Alexandria, VA: American Counseling Association.

Carnine, D., Silbert, J., & Kameenui, E. (1990). *Direct instruction reading.* Columbus, OH: Merrill.

Carnine, D.W., Kameenui, E.J., Silbert, J., & Tarver, S.G. (2003). *Direct instruction reading* (4th ed.). Rutherford, NJ: Prentice Hall.

Carpenter, S.L., & McGee-Higgins, E. (1996). Behavioral management in inclusive classrooms. *Remedial and Special Education, 17*, 195–203.

Carr, E.G. (2006). SWPBS: The greatest good for the greatest number, or the needs of the majority trump the needs of the minority? *Research and Practice for Persons with Severe Disabilities, 31*, 54–56.

Carr, E.G., et al. (1999). *Positive behavior support for people with developmental disabilities: A research synthesis.* Washington, DC: American Association on Mental Retardation.

Carr, P.R., & Lund, D.E. (Eds.). (2007). *The great white north? Exploring whiteness, privilege, and identity in education.* Rotterdam, the Netherlands: Sense Publishers.

Carter, B., & Mok, W.Y. (1992). *Newcomer children: Rights, needs, and adjustment.* Ottawa: Employment and Immigration Canada.

Carter, E., Clark, N., Cushing, L., & Kennedy, C. (2007). Moving from elementary to middle school: A smooth transition for students with severe disabilities. In K. Frieberg (Ed.), *Educating exceptional children* (18th ed.) (pp. 187–192). Dubuque, IA: McGrew Hill.

Cartledge, G. (2005). Learning disabilities and social skills: Reflections. *Learning Disability Quarterly, 28*(2), 179–181.

Case, R. (1998). *A psychological model of number sense and its development.* Paper presented at the annual meeting of the American Educational Research Association, San Diego, CA.

Cassidy, R.A. (2007). The benefits of a comprehensive K-12 career development system. *Techniques: Connecting Education and Careers, 82*(4), 44–46.

Castellano, M.B., Davis, L., & Lahache, L. (2000). *Aboriginal education: Fulfilling the promise.* Vancouver: UBC Press.

Caswell, E., & Hadden, C. (2008, June). *Saskatchewan Ministry of Education Impact assessment profile discovery sessions* (PowerPoint Presentation). [http://www.education.gov.sk.ca/]. (November 7, 2008).

Cefai, C. (2007). Resilience for all: A study of classrooms as protective contexts. *Emotional and Behavioral Difficulties, 12*, 119–134.

Center for Comprehensive School Reform and Improvement. (2007, December). *Improving teacher retention with supportive workplace conditions: Newsletter.* Washington, DC: Center for Comprehensive School Reform and Improvement.

CDC (Centers for Disease Control and Prevention) (2005). Mental health in the United States: Prevalence of diagnosis and medication treatments for Attention-Deficit /Hyperactivity Disorder, United States, 2003. *Morbidity and Mortality Weekly Report, 54*(34), 842–847.

Chafouleas, S.M., McDougal, J.L., Riley-Tillman, T.C., Panahon, C.J., & Hilt, A.M. (2005). What do daily behavior report cards (DBRCs) measure? An initial comparison of DBRCs with direct observation for off-task behavior. *Psychology in the Schools, 42*, 669–676.

Chafouleas, S.M., Riley-Tillman, T.C., & Sassu, K.A. (2006). Acceptability and reported use of daily behavior report cards among teachers. *Journal of Positive Behavior Interventions, 8*, 174–182.

Chamberlain, B., Kasari, C., & Rotheram-Fuller, E. (2007). Involvement or isolation? The social networks of children with autism in regular classrooms. *Journal of Autism and Developmental Disorders, 37*, 230–242.

Chambers, C.R., Wehmeyer, M.L., Saito, Y., Lida, K.M., Lee, Y., & Singh, V. (2007). Self-determination: What do we know? Where do we go? *Exceptionality, 15*(1), 3–15.

Chan, J.S. (2000). *The social skills of two elementary students with learning disabilities: A participant observational study across seven school contexts.* Unpublished master's thesis, Queen's University, Kingston, ON.

Chang, M., Singh, K., & Mo, Y. (2007). Science engagement and science achievement: Longitudinal models using NELS data. *Educational Research and Evaluation, 13*, 349–371.

Chard, D.J., Baker, S.K., Clarke, B., Jungjohann, K., Davis, K., & Smolkowski, K. (2008). Preventing ealy mathematics difficulties: The feasibility of a rigorous kindergarten mathematics curriculum. *Learning Disability Quarterly, 31*, 11–20.

Charles, C.M., & Charles, M.G. (2004). *Classroom management for middle-grade teachers.* Boston: Pearson Allyn & Bacon.

Charter, A., Persaud, D., Poonwassie, A., Williams, S.W., & Zinger, D. (1994). *Career counselling for Aboriginal youth: The journey inward; the journey outward.* Toronto: University of Toronto Press.

Chen, Y.F., & Martin, M.A. (2000). Using performance assessment and portfolio assessment together in the elementary classroom. *Reading Improvement, 37*, 32–38.

Chesson, R., Chisholm, D., & Zaw, W. (2004). Counseling children with chronic physical illness. *Patient Education and Counseling, 55*, 331–338.

Chin, P., & Members of the STAO Safety Committee (1997). Teaching science safely in the ESL classroom. *Crucible, 27*(1), 24–25.

Chin, P., Munby, H., Hutchinson, N.L., & Steiner-Bell, K. (2000). Meeting academic goals: Post-secondary students' intentions for participating in high school co-operative education programs. *Journal of Vocational Educational Research, 25*, 126–154.

Christiansen, J., & Vogel, J.R. (1998). A decision model for grading students with disabilities. *Teaching Exceptional Children, 31*(2), 30–35.

Chung, K.K., & Tam, Y.H. (2005). Effects of cognitive-based instruction on mathematical problem solving by learners with mild intellectual disabilities. *Journal of Intellectual and Developmental Disability, 30*(4), 207–216.

Cinamon, R., & Gifsh, L. (2004). Conceptions of work among adolescents and young adults with mental retardation. *Career Development Quarterly, 52*, 212–224.

Citizens for Mental Health. (2003). *Immigrant & Refugee Mental Health.* [www.cmha.ca/citizens/immigrationENG.pdf]. (July 11, 2008).

Clapper, A., Bremer, C., & Kachgal, M. (2002). *Never too late: Approaches to reading instruction for secondary school students with disabilities.* Minneapolis, MN: National Center on Secondary Education and Transition. (ERIC Document Reproduction Service No. ED 466913).

Clark, G., Carlson, B.C., Fisher, S., Cook, I.D., & D'Alonzo, B.J. (1991). Career development for students with disabilities in elementary schools: A position statement of the Division of Career Development. *Career Development for Exceptional Individuals, 14*, 109–120.

Clark, J., & Schwoyer, C. (1994). Lessons from controversy in applying universal precautions for HIV/AIDS. *Journal of School Health, 64*, 266–267.

Clarke, M., & Wilkinson, R. (2008). Interactions between children with cerebral palsy and their peers 2: Understanding initiated VOCA-mediated turns. *Augmentative and Alternative Communication, 24*, 3–15.

Clarke-Stewart, A., & Dunn, J. (Eds.). (2006). *Families count: Effects on child and adolescent development.* Cambridge: Cambridge University Press.

Clay, D.L. (2007). Culturally competent interventions in schools for children with physical health problems. *Psychology in the Schools, 44*, 389–396.

CMEC (Council of Ministers of Education Canada). (2007). *PCAP-13 Reading, Mathematics, and Science Assessment, Handbook for Schools.* Ottawa: CMEC.

Cobb, C. (2007). Training paraprofessionals to effectively work with all students. *The Reading Teacher, 60*, 686–689.

Cobia, D.C., & Carney, J.S. (2002). Creating a culture of tolerance in schools: Everyday actions to prevent hate-motivated violent incidents. *Journal of School Violence, 1*, 87–103.

Cochran, M. (1990). The transforming role. *Networking Bulletin: Empowerment & Family Support, 1*(3), 25.

Cochran-Smith, M. (2006). *Stayers, leavers, and dreamers: Why people teach and why they stay: The Barbara Biber Lecture.* New York: Bank Street College of Education.

Codjoe, H. (2006). The role of an affirmed black cultural identity and heritage in the academic achievement of African-Canadian students. *Intercultural Education, 17*(1), 33–54.

Coelho, E. (1993). *Learning together in the multicultural classroom.* Markham, ON: Pippin Pub.

Coelho, E. (2004). *Adding English: A guide to teaching in multilingual classrooms.* Toronto: Pippin Pub.

Cohen, E. (1998). *Designing groupwork: Strategies for the heterogeneous classroom* (2nd ed.). New York: Teachers College Press.

Cohen, E., Brody, C.M., & Sapon-Shevin, M. (2004). *Teaching cooperative learning: The challenge for teacher education*. Albany, NY: State University of New York Press.

Cohen, E., Lotan, R., & Catanzarite, L. (1990). Treating status problems in the cooperative classroom. In S. Sharan (Ed.), *Cooperative learning: Theory and research* (pp. 203–229). New York: Praeger.

Colangelo, N., & Assouline, S.G. (2005). Accelerating gifted children. *Principal, 84*(5), 62.

Coles, C.D., Strickland, D.C., Padgett, L., & Bellmoff L., (2006). Games that "work": Using computer games to teach alcohol-affected children about fire and street safety. *Research in Developmental Disabilities, 28*, 518–530.

Collicott, J. (1994, Winter). Multi-level instruction: A guide for teachers. *Keeping in Touch* (Quarterly Newsletter of CEC Canada).

Collins-Williams, M.A., & Willows, D. (1998, December). *A longitudinal study of the effects of inservice teacher education on primary students' literacy success*. Paper presented at the National Reading Conference, Austin, TX.

Colvin, G. (2007). *Seven steps for developing a proactive schoolwide discipline plan: A guide for principals and leadership teams*. Thousand Oaks, CA: Corwin Press.

Conference Board of Canada (2003). *Innovation skills profile*. Ottawa, ON: Conference Board of Canada.

Conn, K. (2001). Supporting special students. *Science Teacher, 68*(3), 32–35.

Conti-Ramsden, G., & Durkin, K. (2008). Language and independence in adolescents with and without a history of specific language impairment (SLI). *Journal of Speech, Language and Hearing Research, 51*(1), 70–83.

Conway, C.M. (2006). Navigating through induction: How a mentor can help. *Music Education Journal, 92*, 56–60.

Cooper, H.L., & Nichols, S.K. (2007). Technology and early braille literacy: Using the Mountbatten Pro Brailler in primary-grade classrooms. *Journal of Visual Impairment and Blindness, 101*, 22–31.

Cooper, P. (2001). Understanding AD/HD: A brief critical review of literature. *Children & Society, 15*, 387–395.

Cornett, C.E. (2006). Center stage: Arts-based read-alouds. *The Reading Teacher, 60*, 234–240.

Cortiella, C. (2007). *Learning opportunities for your child through alternate assessments: Alternate assessments based on modified academic achievement standards*. National Center on Educational Outcomes, University of Minnesota.

Council of Ministers of Education of Canada (2003). *2002 Report on reading and writing assessment: School achievement indicators program*. Toronto: Council of Ministers of Education Canada.

Council of Ministers of Education, Canada (CMEC). (2003, October). *Access, inclusion and achievement: Closing the gap*, Canadian Report to the 15th Commonwealth Conference of Education Ministers, Edinburgh, Scotland.

Council of Ministers of Education of Canada (2005). *School assessment indicators program*. [http://www.cmec.ca/pcap/indexe.stm]. (November 15, 2008).

Covell, K. & Howe, R.B. (2001). Moral education through the 3 Rs: Rights, respect, and responsibility. *Journal of Moral Education, 30*(1), 29–41.

Craig, W., Pepler, D., & Blais, J. (2007). Responding to bullying: What works? *School Psychology International, 28*, 465–477.

Crawford, T. (2005, June 10). Lost in transition. *Toronto Star*.

Cronin, A.F. (2004). Mothering a child with hidden impairments. *American Journal of Occupational Therapy, 58*, 83–92.

Crooke, P.J., Hendrix, R.E., & Rachman, J.Y. (2008). Brief report: Measuring the effectiveness of teaching social thinking to children with Asperger syndrome (AS) and high functioning autism (HFA). *Journal of Autism and Developmental Disorders, 38*, 581–591.

Cross. T.L. (2002). Competing with the myths about the social and emotional development of gifted students. *Gifted Child Today, 25*(3), 44–45 & 65.

Crowchief-McHugh, D., Yellowhorne-Breaker, K., Weasel Fat-White, F. (2000). *A handbook for Aboriginal parents of children with special needs*. Edmonton: Special Education Branch, Alberta Department of Education.

Cuccaro, C., & Geitner, G. (2007). Lunch and recess: The "eye of the storm": Using targeted interventions for students with behavioral problems. *TEACHING Exceptional Children Plus, 3*(4). [http://escholarship.bc.edu/education/tecplus/vol3/iss4/art2]. (June 10, 2008).

Cuffe, S., Moore, C.G., & McKeown, R.E. (2005). Prevalence and correlates of ADHD symptoms in the National Health Interview Survey. *Journal of Attention Disorders, 9*(2), 392–401.

Cummings, J.G., Pepler, D.J., Mishna, F., & Craig, W. (2006). Bullying and victimization among students with exceptionalities. *Exceptionality Education Canada, 16*, 193–222.

Cummins, J. (1981). *Bilingualism and minority language children*. Toronto, ON: Ontario Institute for Studies in Education.

Cunningham, A.E., & Stanovich, K.E. (1997). Early reading acquisition and its relation to reading experience and ability 10 years later. *Developmental Psychology, 33*, 934–945.

Curtin, M., & Clark, G. (2005). Listening to young people with physical disabilities' experiences of education. *International Journal of Disability, Development and Education, 52*, 195–214.

Cushman, K., & Rogers, L. (2008). Middle school students talk about social forces in the classroom. *Middle School Journal, 39*(3), 14–24.

Daiute, C., & Dalton, B. (1992). *Collaboration between children learning to write: Can novices be masters?* (ERIC Document Reproduction Service No. ED 354522).

Dana, N.F., & Yendol-Silva, D. (2003). *The reflective educator's guide to classroom research: Learning to teach and teaching to learn through practitioner inquiry*. Thousand Oaks, CA: Corwin Press.

D'Augelli, A.R., Pilkington, N.W., & Hershberger, S.L. (2002). Incidence and mental health impact of sexual orientation victimization of lesbian, gay, and bisexual youths in high school. *School Psychology Quarterly, 17*, 148–167.

Dearman, C.C., & Alber, S.R. (2005). The changing face of education: Teachers cope with challenges through collaboration and reflective study. *Reading Teacher, 58*, 634–640.

Decker, L.E., & Decker, V.A. (2000). *Engaging families and communities: Pathways to educational success*. Fairfax, VA: National Community Education Association.

Decker, L.E., Decker, V.A., Townsend, T., & Neal, L.L. (2005). Community education: Global perspectives for developing comprehensive integrated human and community services. *World Leisure Journal, 47*(2), 23–30.

De Coster, K., & Loots, G. (2004). Somewhere in between touch and vision: Art education for blind individuals. *The International Journal of Art & Design Education, 23*, 326–334.

deGroot-Maggetti, G. (2002). *A measure of poverty in Canada: A guide to debate about poverty lines*. [http://action.web.ca/home/cpj/attach/A_measure_of_poverty.pdf]. (July 14, 2008).

Dei, G.J.S. (2003). *Anti-racism education: Theory and practice*. Black Point, NS: Fernwood.

Del Favero, L., Boscolo, P., Vidotto, G., & Vincentini, M. (2007). Classroom discussion and individual problem-solving in the teaching of history: Do different instructional approaches affect interest in different ways? *Learning and Instruction, 17*, 635–657.

Delisle, J.R., & Galbraith, J. (2004). *When gifted kids don't have all the answers: How to meet their social and emotional needs.* Minneapolis, MN: Free Spirit Publishing.

DeLuca, C., Hutchinson, N.L., deLugt, J.S., Beyer, W., Thornton, A., Versnel, J., Chin, P., & Munby, H. (2008, submitted). Learning in the workplace: Fostering resilience in disengaged youth. Submitted to *Work: A Journal of Prevention, Assessment & Rehabilitation.*

DeLuca, C., Klinger, D., Brunette, J., & Miller, T. (2005). *Emerging assessment cultures in Canadian education: The provincial perspectives.* Paper presented at annual conference of the Canadian Society for the Study of Education, London, ON.

Dennison, S.T. (1997). *Creating positive support groups for at-risk children.* Torrance, CA: Jalmar Press.

Deno, S.L., & Mirkin, P.K. (1977). *Data-based program modification: A manual.* Reston, VA: Council for Exceptional Children.

Denton, C.A., Foreman, B.R., & Mathes, P.O. (2003). Schools that beat the odds: Implications for reading instruction. *Remedial and Special Education, 24,* 258–261.

Denton, P. (2003). Shared rule-making in practice: The Jefferson committee at Kingston High School. *American Secondary Education, 31*(3), 66–96.

DePaepe, P., Garrison-Kane, L., & Doelling, J. (2002). Supporting students with health needs in schools: An overview of selected health conditions. *Focus on Exceptional Children, 35*(1), 1–24.

Depka, E. (2007). *Designing assessment for mathematics.* Thousand Oaks, CA: Corwin Press.

Desbiens, N., & Royer, E. (2003). Peer groups and behavior problems: A study of school-based intervention for children with EBD. *Emotional and Behavioral Difficulties, 8,* 120–139.

Deshler, D., Palincsar, A.S., Biancarosa, G., & Nair, M. (2007). *Informed choices for struggling adolescent readers: A research-based guide to instructional programs and practices.* Newark, DE: International Reading Association.

Deslandes, R., Royer, E., Potvin, P., & Leclerc, D. (1999). Patterns of home and school partnership or general and special education students at the secondary level. *Exceptional Children, 66,* 496–506.

Dever, R.B. (1990). Defining mental retardation from an instructional perspective. *Mental Retardation, 28,* 147–153.

Dewey, J. (1916). *Democracy and education: An introduction to the philosophy of education.* New York: Macmillan.

Diamond, K.E. (2007). The development of social competence in children with disabilities. In P. Smith & C. Hart (Eds.), *Blackwell handbook of childhood social development* (pp. 570–587). Malden, MA: Blackwell.

Dickason, O.P. (2002). *Canada's First Nations: A history of founding peoples from earliest times* (3rd ed.). Don Mills, ON: Oxford University Press.

Dickason, O.P. (2006) *A concise history of Canada's First Nations.* Don Mills, ON: Oxford University Press.

DiClementi, J.D., & Handelsman, M.M. (2005). Empowering students: Class-generated course rules. *Teaching of Psychology, 32,* 18–21.

DiGiorgio, C. (2004). A learning experience: Case study of an integrated resource teacher. *Westminster Studies in Education, 27,* 189–205.

Dillabough, J.A., Wang, E., & Kennelly, J. (2005). Ginas, thugs, and gangstas: Young people's struggles to "become somebody" in working class urban Canada. *Journal of Curriculum Theorizing, 21*(2), 83–108.

Dion, E., Fuchs, D., & Fuchs, L. (2005). Differential effects of peer-assisted learning strategies on students' social preference and friend-ship making. *Behavioral Disorders, 30,* 421–429.

Dockett, S. & Perry, B. (2003). The transition to school: What's important? *Educational Leadership, 60,* 30–33.

Dodwell, K., & Bavin, E.L. (2008). Children with specific language impairment: An investigation of their narratives and memory. *International Journal of Language and Communication Disorders, 43*(2), 201–218.

Downing, J.E., & Pickingham-Hardin, K.D. (2007). Inclusive education: What makes it a good education for students with moderate to severe disabilities? *Research & Practice for Persons with Severe Disabilities, 32,* 16–30.

Dragone, M.A., et al. (2002). Development and evaluation of an interactive CD-ROM for children with leukemia and their families. *Patient Education and Counseling, 46,* 297–307.

Duffy, J., Wareham, S., & Walsh, M. (2004). Psychological consequences for high school students of having been sexually harassed. *Sex roles, 50*(11/12), 811–821.

Duncan, P.A. (2007). Pet peeves about parents: Turning problems into partnership. *Educational Digest, 73*(2), 53–57.

Dunn, L. (1968). Special education for the mildly retarded: Is much of it justifiable? *Exceptional Children, 35,* 5–22.

DuPaul, G.J., & Stoner, G.D. (2003). *ADHD in the schools: Assessment and intervention.* New York: Guilford Press.

DuPaul, G.J., & Weyandt, L.L. (2006). School-based intervention for children with attention deficit hyperactivity disorder: Effects on academic, social, and behavioral functioning. *International Journal of Disability, Development and Education, 53,* 161–176.

Duquette, C. (1992). Integrating mildly and moderately handicapped children: What goes on in a successful school? *Exceptionality Education Canada, 2*(1&2), 139–153.

Duquette, C. (2001). *Students at risk: Solutions to classroom challenges.* Markham, ON: Pembroke Publishers.

Duquette, C. (2007). Becoming a role model: Experiences of Native student teachers. *Alberta Journal of Educational Research, 53*(4), 387–400.

Durham, P.H., & Dick, T.P. (1994). Research on graphing calculators. *Mathematics Teacher, 87,* 440–445.

Dworet, D., & Rathgeber, A. (1998). Confusion reigns: Definitions of behaviour exceptionalities in Canada. *Exceptionality Education Canada, 8*(1), 3–19.

Dyson, A., & Gallannaugh, F. (2007). National policy and the development of inclusive school practices: A case study. *Cambridge Journal of Education, 37*(4), 473–488.

Dyson, L. (1992a). Adjustment of siblings of handicapped children: A comparison. In M.C. Roberts & J.L. Wallander (Eds.), *Family issues in pediatric psychology* (pp. 165–179). Hillsdale, NJ: Erlbaum.

Dyson, L. (1992b). Siblings of children with learning disabilities. In Z. Stoneman & P.W. Berman (Eds.), *The effects of mental retardation, disability, and illness on sibling relationships: Research issues and challenges* (pp. 235–252). Baltimore: Paul H. Brookes.

Dyson, L. (1997). Fathers and mothers of school-age children with developmental disabilities: Parental stress, family functioning, and social support. *American Journal on Mental Retardation, 102,* 267–279.

Dyson, L. (1998). A support program for siblings of children with disabilities: What siblings learn and what they like. *Psychology in the Schools, 35,* 57–65.

Dyson, L.L. (2003). Children with learning disabilities within the family context. *Learning Disabilities Research and Practice, 18,* 1–9.

Earl, L., & Cousins, J.B. (1995). *Classroom assessment: Changing the face, facing the change.* Toronto: Ontario Public School Teachers Federation.

*Eaton v. Brant (County) Board of Education.* (1995). 22 O.R. (3d) 1 O.C.A.

Edgemon, E.A., Jablonski, B.R., & Lloyd, J.W. (2006). Large-scale assessments: A teacher's guide to making decisions about accommodations. *Teaching Exceptional Children, 38*(3), 6–11.

Edmunds, A. (1998). Classroom teachers are not prepared for the inclusive classroom. *Exceptionality Education Canada, 8*(2), 27–40.

Edmunds, A. (2008). *ADHD assessment and diagnosis in Canada: An inconsistent but fixable process.* Paper presented at the annual meeting of the Canadian Society for the study of Education, Vancouver, BC.

Edmunds, A. (1999). Acquiring learning strategies. *Teaching Exceptional Children, 31*(4), 69–73.

Education Quality and Accountability Office (Ontario). [www.eqao.com]. (October 25, 2005).

Edwards, K.L. (2000). *"They can be successful too!" Inclusive practices of secondary school science teachers.* Unpublished master's thesis, Faculty of Education, Queen's University, Kingston, ON.

Ehri, L.C., Nunes, S.R., Stahl, S.A., & Willows, D.M. (2001). Systematic phonics instruction helps students to learn to read. *Review of Educational Research, 71*, 393–447.

Eisenman, L.T. (2007). Social networks and careers of young adults with intellectual disabilities. *Intellectual and Developmental Disabilities, 453*(3), 199–208.

Elliot, S.N., & Roach, A.T. (2007). Alternate assessment of students with significant disabilities: Alternative approaches, common technical challenges. *Applied Measurement in Education, 20*(3), 301–333.

Ellis, E.S., & Friend, P. (1991). Adolescents with learning disabilities. In B.Y.L. Wong (Ed.), *Learning about learning disabilities* (pp. 505–561). San Diego, CA: Academic Press.

Ely, S. (2004). *What is assistive technology? A basic guide for individuals with disabilities and their families (Revised).* Bloomington, IN: Indiana Institute on Disability and Communication, Indiana University.

Emery, A. (2008). *Muscular dystrophy.* Toronto: Oxford University Press.

Emme, M.J., Kirova, A., Kamau, O., & Kosanovich, S. (2006). Ensemble research: A means for immigrant children to explore peer relationships through photonovela. *Alberta Journal of Educational Research, 52*(3), 160–181.

Emmer, E.T., & Evertson, C.M. (2008). *Classroom management for middle and high school teachers.* Boston: Allyn & Bacon.

Emmett, J.D., & Minor, C.W. (1993). Career decision-making factors in gifted young adults. *The Career Development Quarterly, 41*, 350–366.

Englert, C.S., Berry, R., & Dunsmore, K. (2001). A case study of the apprenticeship process: Another perspective on the apprentice and the scaffolding metaphor. *Journal of Learning Disabilities, 34*, 152–171.

Erkolahti, R., & Ilonen, T. (2005). Academic achievement and the self-image of adolescents with diabetes mellitus type-1 and rheumatoid arthritis. *Journal of Youth and Adolescence, 34*, 199–205.

Ertmer, D.J., Strong, L., & Sadagopan, N. (2003). Beginning to communicate after cochlear implantation: Oral language development in a young child. *Journal of Speech, Language, and Hearing Research, 46*, 328–340.

Espin, C.A., Deno, S.L., & Albayrak-Kaymak, D. (1998). Individualized education programs in resource and inclusive settings: How "individualized" are they? *Journal of Special Education, 32*, 164–174.

Estell, D.B., Jones, M.H., Pearl, R., Van Acker, R., Farmer, T.W., & Rodkin, P.C. (2008). Peer groups, popularity, and social preference: Trajectories of social functioning among students with and without learning disabilities. *Journal of Learning Disabilities, 41*(1), 5–14.

Evans, D.D., & Strong, C.J. (1996). What's the story? Attending, listening, telling in middle school. *Teaching Exceptional Children, 28*(3), 58–61.

Evans, M., McDonald, J., & Nyce, N. (1999). Acting across boundaries in Aboriginal curriculum development: Examples from northern British Columbia. *Canadian Journal of Native Education, 23*, 190–205.

Evans, R. 1996. *The human side of school change: Reform, resistance, and the real-life problems of innovation.* San Francisco, Calif.: Jossey-Bass.

Evans, R., & Becker, S. (2008). *Children caring for parents with HIV/AIDS: Global issues and policy responses.* Bristol, UK: Policy Press.

Evertson, C.M., & Emmer, E.T. (2008). *Classroom management for elementary teachers.* Boston: Allyn & Bacon.

Faggella-Luby, M.N., & Deshler, D.D. (2008). Reading comprehension in adolescents with LD: What we know; what we need to learn. *Learning Disabilities Research & Practice, 23*(2), 70–78.

Faltis, C.J. (2007). *Joinfostering: Teaching and learning in multi culture education.* Oxford, UK: Pearson.

Farenga, S., & Joyce, B. (2000). Preparing for parents' questions. *Science Scope, 23*(6), 12–14.

Featherstone, D., Munby, H., & Russell, T. (Eds.) (1997). *Finding a voice while learning to teach.* London, UK: Falmer Press.

Felce, D., Perry, J., Romeo, R., Robertson, J., Meek, A., Emerson, E., & Knapp, M. (2008). Outcomes and costs of community living: Semi-independent living and fully staffed group homes. *American Journal on Mental Retardation, 113*(2), 87–101.

Fenning, P., Theodos, J., & Benner, C. (2004). Integrating proactive discipline practices into codes of conduct. *Journal of School Violence, 31*, 45–61.

Fenstermacher, K., Olympia, D., & Sheridan, S.M. (2006). Effectiveness of a computer-facilitated interactive social skills training program for boys with attention deficit hyperactivity disorder. *School Psychology Quarterly, 21*(2), 197–224.

Ferguson, P.M., & Ferguson, D. (1996). Communicating adulthood: The meanings of independent living for people with significant cognitive disabilities and their families. *Topics in Language Disorders, 16*, 52–67.

Ferguson, P.M., & Olsen, D. (1989). *Supported community life: Connecting policy to practice in disability research.* Eugene, OR: Specialized Training Program.

Ferretti, R.P., MacArthur, C.D., & Okolo, C. (2002). Teaching effectively about historical things. *Teaching Exceptional Children, 34*(6), 66–69.

Fetters, M., Pickard, D.M., & Pyle, E. (2003). Making science accessible: Strategies to meet the needs of a diverse student population. *Science Scope, 26*(5), 26–29.

Fichten, C., Asuncion, J., Barile, M., Fossey, M., & de Simone, C. (2000). Access to educational and instructional computer technologies for post-secondary students with disabilities: Lessons from three empirical studies. *Journal of Educational Media, 25*, 179–201.

Field, S., & Hoffman, A. (1996). *Steps to self-determination.* Austin, TX: Pro-Ed.

Fine, E.S., Lacey, A., & Baer, J. (1995). *Children as peacemakers.* Portsmouth, NH: Heineman.

Fitch, E.F., & Hulgin, K.M. (2008). Achieving inclusion through CLAD: Collaborative learning assessment through dialogue. *International Journal of Inclusive Education, 12*(4), 423–439.

Flanagain, W.C. (2007). *A survey: The negative aspects of in and out of school suspensions and alternatives that promote academic achievement.* (ERIC Document Reproduction Service No. ED 499538).

Flatow, I. (1985). The king of storms. In M.W. Aulls & M.F. Graves (Eds.), *In another world* (pp. 57–63). New York: Scholastic.

Fletcher, J.M., Lyon, G.R., Fuchs, L.S., & Barnes, M.A. (2007). *Learning disabilities: From identification to intervention.* New York: Guilford Press.

Fogarty, R. (1995). *Designs for cooperative interactions* (2nd ed.). Palatine, IL: Skylight Publishing.

Fombonne, E. (2007). Epidemiological surveys of pervasive developmental disorders. In F.R. Volkmar (Ed.), *Diagnosis and definition of autism and other pervasive developmental disorders* (pp. 33–68). Cambridge, UK: Cambridge University Press.

Forbes, J. (2007). Towards inclusion: An Australian perspective. *Support for Learning, 22*(2), 66–71.

Forbes, J. (2008). Knowledge transformations: Examining the knowledge needed in teacher and speech and language therapist co-work. *Educational Review, 60*(2), 141–154.

Forest, M., & Lusthaus, E. (1987). The kaleidoscope: Challenge to the cascade. In M. Forest (Ed.), *More education/integration* (pp. 1–16). Downsview, ON: G. Allen Roeher Institute.

Forness, S.R., Swanson, J.M., Cantwell, D.P., Guthrie, D., & Sena, R. (1992). Response to stimulant medication across six measures of school-related performance in children with ADHD and disruptive behavior. *Behavioral Disorders, 18*, 42–53.

Forster, E.M., & Holbrook, M.C. (2005). Implications of paraprofessional support for students with visual impairments. *RE:view: Rehabilitation Education for Blindness and Visual Impairment, 36*, 155–170.

Fostaty Young, S.F., & Wilson, R.J. (2000). *Assessment and learning: The ICE approach*. Winnipeg: Portage & Main Press (Peguis Publishers).

Foster, J., & Matthews, D. (2006). *Troubling times: How parents and teachers can help children understand and confront adversity*. [www.sengifted.org/articles_social/FosterMatthews_TroublingTimes.shtml]. (November 2, 2008).

Fowler, C.H., Konrad, M., Walker, A.R., Test, D.W., & Wood, W.M. (2007). Self-determination interventions' effects on the academic performance of students with developmental disabilities. *Education and Training in Developmental Disabilities, 42*(3), 270–285.

Freeman, J.G. (1998). *Interest and special education: The role of interest in teaching children with learning disabilities*. Unpublished doctoral dissertation, University of Michigan.

Freeman, J.G., McPhail, J.C., & Berndt, J.A. (2002). Sixth graders' views of activities that do and do not help them learn. *Elementary School Journal, 102*, 335–347.

Frempong, G., & Willms, J.D. (2002). Can school quality compensate for socioeconomic disadvantage? In J.D. Willms (Ed.), *Vulnerable children* (pp. 277–303). Edmonton, AB: University of Alberta Press.

Friedel, T.L. (1999). The role of Aboriginal parents in public education: Barriers to change in an urban setting. *Canadian Journal of Native Education, 23*, 139–158.

Friend, M., Bursuck, W., & Hutchinson, N.L. (1998). *Including exceptional students: A practical guide for classroom teachers, Canadian edition*. Scarborough, ON: Allyn & Bacon.

Frostad, P., & Pijl, S.J. (2007). Does being friendly help in making friends? The relation between the social position and social skills of pupils with special needs in mainstream education. *European Journal of Special Needs Education, 22*, 15–30.

Fuchs, D., & Fuchs, L.S. (2005). Peer-assisted learning strategies: Promoting word recognition, fluency, sand reading comprehension in young children. *Journal of Special Education, 39*, 34–44.

Fuchs, L.S., & Fuchs, D. (2007). A model for implementing responsiveness to intervention. *Teaching Exceptional Children, 39*(5), 14–20.

Fulford, G. (2007a). *Sharing our success: More case studies in Aboriginal schooling*. Kelowna, BC: Society for the Advancement of Excellence in Education.

Fulford, G. (2007b). *Sharing our success: More case studies in Aboriginal schooling: Band-operated schools*. Kelowna, BC: Society for the Advancement of Excellence in Education.

Fullan, M. (2001). *The new meaning of educational change* (3rd ed.). New York: Teachers College Press.

Fullan, M. & St. Germain, C. (2006). *Learning places: A field guide for improving the context of schooling*. Thousand Oaks, CA: Corwin Press.

Fullwood, D. (1990). *Chances and choices: Making integration work*. Sydney, AU: Paul H. Brookes.

Gable, R.A., Hendrickson, J.M, Tonelsom, S.W., & Acker, R.V. (2002). Integrating academic and non-academic instruction for students with emotional/behavioral disorders. *Education and Treatment of Children, 25*, 459–475.

Gallaty, K., & Zimmer-Gembeck, M.J. (2008). The daily social and emotional worlds of adolescents who are psychologically maltreated by their romantic partners. *Journal of Youth and Adolescence, 37*(3), 310–323.

Gao, H., Shen, E., Losh, S., & Turner, J. (2007). A review of studies on collaborative concept mapping: What have we learned about the technique and what is next. *Journal of Interactive Learning Research, 18*, 479–492.

Garay, S.V. (2003). Listening to the voices of deaf students: Essential transition issues. *Teaching Exceptional Children, 35*(4), 44–48.

Garnett, K. (1992). Developing fluency with basic number facts: Intervention for students with learning disabilities. *Learning Disabilities: Research and Practice, 7*, 210–216.

Gay, A.S., & White, S.H. (2002). Teaching vocabulary to communicate mathematically. *Middle School Journal, 34*(2), 33–38.

Geary, D.C. (1993). Mathematical disabilities: Cognitive, neuropsychological, and genetic components. *Psychological Bulletin, 114*, 345–362.

Geary, D.C., Harmson, C.O., & Hoard, M.K. (2000). Numerical and arithmetical cognition: A longitudinal study of processing and concept deficits in children with learning disability. *Journal of Experimental Child Psychology, 77*, 236–263.

Gehret, J. (1991). *Eagle eyes: A child's guide to paying attention*. Fairport, NY: Verbal Images Press.

Gentry, M., Peters, S.J., & Mann, R.L. (2007). Differences between general and talented students' perceptions of their career and technical education experiences compared to their traditional high school experiences. *Journal of Advanced Academics, 18*(3), 372–401.

George, M.P., White, G.P., & Schlaffer, J.J. (2007). Implementing school-wide behavior change: Lessons from the field. *Psychology in the Schools, 44*, 41–51.

Gerber, P.J., & Price, L.A. (2003). Persons with learning disabilities in the workplace: What we know so far in the Americans with Disabilities Act era. *Learning Disabilities Research & Practice, 18*, 132–136.

Gersten, R., & Baker, S. (2000). What we know about effective instructional practices for English-language learners. *Exceptional Children, 66*, 454–70.

Gersten, R., & Chard, D. (1999). Number sense: Rethinking arithmetic instruction for students with mathematical disabilities. *The Journal of Special Education, 33*, 18–28.

Ghosh, R., & Abdi, A.A. (2004). *Education and the politics of difference: Canadian perspectives*. Toronto: Canadian Scholars' Press.

Giangreco, M.F. (2003). Working with paraprofessionals. *Educational Leadership, 61*(2), 50–53.

Giangreco, M.F., & Doyle, J. (2007). *Quick guides to inclusion: Ideas for educating exceptional students*. Baltimore, MD: P.H. Brookes.

Giangreco, M.F., Smith, C.S., & Pinckney, E. (2006). Addressing the paraprofessional dilemma in an inclusive school: A program description. *Research and Practice for Persons with Severe Disabilities, 31*, 215–229.

Gibbs, J. (2001). *Tribes: A new way of learning and being together*. Windsor, CA: CenterSource Systems.

Gibbs, J. (2006). *Reaching all by creating tribes learning communities*. Windsor, CA: Center Source.

Gibson, G.M. (2005). The use of genograms in career counseling with elementary, middle, and high school students. *Career Development Quarterly, 53*, 353–362.

Gilchrist, W. (1986). Teaching statistics to the rest of humanity. *Proceedings of the Second International Conference on Teaching Statistics* (pp. 494–497). Victoria, BC: University of Victoria.

Gill, V. (2007). *The ten students you'll meet in your classroom: Classroom management tips for middle and high school teachers.* Thousand Oaks, CA: Corwin Press.

Gillies, R.M., Ashman, A., & Terwel, J. (Eds.). (2007). *The teacher's role in implementing cooperative learning in the classroom.* New York: Springer.

Gillies, R.M., & Boyle, M. (2008). Teachers' discourse during cooperative learning and their perceptions of this pedagogical practice. *Teaching and Teacher Education, 24,* 1333–1348.

Gilliland, K. (2002). Calculators in the classroom. *Mathematics Teaching in the Middle School, 8,* 150–151.

Gilmore, R. (1994). *Lights for Gita.* Toronto: Second Story Press.

Ginsburg-Block, M.D., Rohrbeck, C.A., & Fantuzzo, J.W. (2006). A meta-analytic review of social, self-concept, and behavioral outcomes of peer-assisted learning. *Journal of Educational Psychology, 98,* 732–749.

Glavin, T. (2002). *Amongst God's own: The enduring legacy of St. Mary's racism.* Vancouver: New Star Books.

Glor-Scheib, S., & Tel thorster, H. (2006). Activate your student IEP team ember using technology: How electronic portfolios can bring the student voice to life. *Teaching Exceptional Children Plus, 2*(3), Article 1.

Goddard, K. (2008). *Improving oral language skills in children with autism.* Unpublished paper, Queen's University.

Gold, Y., & Roth, R.A. (1993). *Teachers managing stress and preventing burnout: The professional health solution.* London: Falmer Press.

Goldfinch, E. (2007). The forum on AIDS: An exercise in research and statesmanship. *Library Media Connection, 26*(3), 44–46.

Goleman, D. (2005). *Emotional intelligence* (2nd ed.). New York: Bantam Books.

Gomes & Smith (2007, March/April). Responding to school health crises. *Leadership,* 28–29, 46.

Good, T., & Brophy, J. (2002). *Looking in classrooms* (9th ed.). New York: Harper & Row.

Goodman, A. (2008). Student-led, teacher-supported conference: Improving communication across an urban school district. *Middle School Journal, 39*(3), 48–54.

Goodwin, A.K., & King, S.H. (2002). *Culturally responsive parental involvement.* New York: AACTE Publications.

Gottfredson, G.D. (2002). Interests, aspirations, self-estimates, and the self-directed search. *Journal of Career Assessment, 10*(2), 200–208.

Gouvernement du Québec Ministère de l'Éducation (2000). *Adapting our schools to the needs of all students: Draft policy on special education.* Québec: Dépôt Legal, Bibliotèque Nationale du Québec.

Government of Canada (1982). *The Charter of Rights and Freedoms.* Ottawa: Minister of Supply and Services. [http://laws.justice.gc.ca/en/const/annex_e.html#I]. (November 15, 2008).

Government of Canada (1998). *Gathering strength: Canada's Aboriginal action plan.* [http://dsp-psd.pwgsc.gc.ca/Collection/R32-192-2000E.pdf]. (November 15, 2008).

Government of Canada (2002/2004/2006). *Advancing the inclusion of persons with disabilities.* [http://www.hrsdc.gc.ca/en/disability_issues/reports/fdr/2006/index.shtml]. (November 15, 2008).

Gracenin, D. (1993). Culture clash in San Francisco: Reconnecting youth who are homeless with education. *Intervention in School and Clinic, 29*(1), 41–46.

Gracenin, D. (1994). Reaching and teaching the homeless. *Education Digest, 59*(6), 37–39.

Graetz, J.E., Mastropieri, M.A., & Scruggs, T.E. (2006). Using video self-modeling to decrease inappropriate behavior. *Teaching Exceptional Children, 38*(5), 43–48.

Graham, L., & Wong, B. (1993). Two modes of teaching a question-answering strategy for enhancing reading comprehension. *Journal of Learning Disabilities, 26,* 270–279.

Grant, I. (1997, November 26). Life, liberty and peanut butter. *Globe and Mail,* p. A24.

Grant, L.R. (2000). A framework for professional learning and the Ontario College of Teachers. In R. Upitis (Ed.), *Who will teach? A case study of teacher education reform* (pp. 245–258). San Francisco: Caddo Gap Press.

Gratch, A. (1998). *Growing teaching professionals: Lessons taught by first year teachers.* Paper presented at the annual conference on Qualitative Research in Education, Athens, GA.

Graves, M.F., & Braaten, S. (1996). Scaffolded reading experiences: Bridges to success. *Preventing School Failure, 40,* 169–173.

Gray, C. (2002). *My social story book.* London: Jessica Kingsley Publishers.

Gray, C. (2005). Training and the early years professional: Understanding visual impairment. International *Journal of Early Years Education, 13,* 1–12.

Grayson, J.L., & Alvarez, H.K. (2008). School climate factors relating to teacher burnout: A mediator model. *Teaching and Teacher Education, 24*(5), 1349–1363.

Greene, M.J. (2006). Helping build lives: Career and life development of gifted and talented students. *Professional School Counseling, 10*(1), 34–42.

Gregoire, M.A., & Lupinetti, J. (2005). Support diversity through the arts. *Kappa Delta Pi Record, 41*(4), 159–163.

Gregory, G.H., & Kuzmich, L. (2004). *Data driven differentiation in the standards-based classroom.* Thousand Oaks, CA: Corwin Press.

Grenawalt, V. (2004). Going beyond the debate: Using technology and instruction for a balanced reading program. *Teacher Librarian, 32*(2), 12–16.

Gresham, F.M. (2002). Teaching social skills to high risk children and youth: Preventive and remedial strategies. In M.R. Schinn, H.M. Walker, & G. Stoner (Eds.), *Interventions for academic and behavior problems II: Preventative and remedial approaches.* (2nd ed., pp. 403–432). Washington, DC: National Association of School Psychologists.

Griffin, S. (2004a). Building number sense with Number Worlds: A mathematics program for young children. *Early Childhood Research Quarterly, 19*(1), 173–180.

Griffin, S. (2004b). Teaching number sense. *Educational Leadership, 61*(5), 39–43.

Griffin, S., & Case, R. (1997). Re-thinking the primary school math curriculum: An approach based on cognitive science. *Issues in Education, 3,* 1–49.

Groom, B., & Rose, R. (2005). Supporting the inclusion of pupils with social, emotional and behavioural difficulties in the primary school: The role of teaching assistants. *Journal of Research in Special Education Needs, 5,* 20–30.

Gross, M.U.M. (2006). Exceptionally gifted children: Long-term outcomes of academic acceleration and non-acceleration. *Journal for the Education of the Gifted, 29,* 404–429.

Grskovic, J.A., Hall, A.M., Montgomery, D.J., Vargas, A.U., Zentall, S.S., & Belfiore, P.J. (2004). Reducing time-out assignments for students with emotional/behavioral disorders in a self-contained classroom. *Journal of Behavioral Education, 13,* 25–36.

Guay, D.M. (1993). Cross-site analysis of teaching practices: Visual art education with students experiencing disabilities. *Studies in Art Education, 34,* 233–243.

Guay, D.M. (1995). The "Sunny Side of the Street": A supportive community for the inclusive art classroom. *Art Education, 48,* 51–56.

Gumpel, T.P. (2007). Are social competence difficulties caused by performance or acquisition deficits? The importance of self-regulatory mechanisms. *Psychology in the Schools, 44*(4), 351–372.

Gunter, P.L., Coutinho, M.J., & Cade, T. (2002). Classroom factors linked with academic gains among students with emotional and behavioral problems. *Preventing School Failure, 46,* 126–132.

Guralnick, M.J. (Ed.) (2001). *Early childhood inclusion: Focus on change.* Baltimore, MD: Brookes Publishing.

Gushue, G.V. (2006). The relationship of ethnic identity, career decision-making self-efficacy and outcome expectations among Latino/a high school students. *Journal of Vocational Behavior, 68*(1), 85–95.

Haager, D., & Klingner, J. (2005). *Differentiating instruction in inclusive classrooms: The special educator's guide.* Boston: Pearson Education.

Hadjioannou, X. (2007). Bringing the background to the foreground: What do classroom environments that support authentic discussion look like? *American Educational Research Journal, 44,* 370–399.

Haley, A.N., & Watson, D.C. (2000). In-school literacy extension: Beyond in-school suspension. *Journal of Adolescent and Adult Literacy, 43,* 654–661.

Hall, L.J., & McGregor, J.A. (2000). A follow-up study of the peer relationships of children with disabilities in an inclusive school. *Journal of Special Education, 34,* 114–126.

Hall, L.J., & Strickett, T. (2002). Peer relationships of preadolescent students with disabilities who attend a separate school. *Education and Training in Mental Retardation and Developmental Disabilities, 37,* 399–409.

Hallenbeck, M.J. (2002). Taking charge: Adolescents with learning disabilities assume responsibility for their own writing. *Learning Disability Quarterly, 25,* 227–246.

Hamilton, R., & Moore, D. (2004). Education of refugee children: Documenting and implementing change. In R. Hamilton & D. Moore (Eds.), *Educational interventions for refugee children* (pp. 106–116). London: Routledge Falmer.

Hamm, J.V., & Faircloth, B.S. (2005). The role of friendship in adolescents' sense of school belonging. In N. Way & J.V. Hamm (Eds.), The experience of close friendships in adolescence. *New Directions for Child and Adolescent Development, 107* (pp. 61–78). San Francisco: Jossey-Bass.

Hampton, E. (1995). Towards a redefinition of Indian education. In M. Battiste & J. Barman (1995) (Eds.), *First Nations education in Canada: The circle unfolds* (pp. 5–46). Vancouver: UBC Press.

Hannah, C.L., & Shore, B.M. (2008). Twice-exceptional students' use of metacognitive skills on a comprehension monitoring task. *Gifted Child Quarterly, 52*(1), 3–18.

Hanvey, L. (2003). *Social inclusion research in Canada: Children and youth.* Ottawa, ON: Canadian Council on Social Development. [www.ccsd.ca/events/inclusion/papers/hanvey.pdf]. (November 15, 2008).

Hardy, M.I., McLeod, J., Minto, H., Perkins, S.A., & Quance, W.R. (1971). *Standards for education of exceptional children in Canada: The SEECC Report.* Toronto: Leonard Crainford.

Hargreaves, A. (2004). Inclusive and exclusive educational change: Emotional responses of teachers and implications for leadership. *School Leadership and Management, 24,* 287–309.

Hargrove, K. (2005). What makes a "good" teacher "great" in the classroom? *Gifted Child Today, 28*(1), 30–31.

Haring, T.G. (1991). Social relationships. In L.H. Meyer, C.A. Peck, & L. Brown (Eds.), *Critical issues in the lives of people with severe disabilities* (pp. 195–217). Baltimore: Paul H. Brookes.

Harmer Cox, A., Marshall, E.S., Mandleco, B., & Olsen, S.F. (2003). Coping responses to daily life stressors of children who have a sibling with a disability. *Journal of Family Nursing, 9,* 397–413.

Harniss, M.K., Hollenbeck, K., Crawford, A., & Carnine, D. (1994). Content organization and instructional design issues in the development of history texts. *Learning Disability Quarterly, 17,* 235–248.

Harper, M., O'Connor, K., & Simpson, M. (1999). *Quality assessment: Fitting the pieces together.* Toronto: Ontario Secondary School Teachers Federation.

Harris, K.R., & Graham, S. (1999). Programmatic intervention research: Illustrations from the evolution of self-regulated strategy development. *Learning Disability Quarterly, 22,* 251–262.

Harter, S. (2006). Where do we go from here? In M.H. Kernis (Ed.), *Self-esteem issues and answers: A sourcebook of current perspectives* (pp. 430–438). New York: Psychology Press.

Hartley, K. (2005). *Adolescents' self-identified reasons for their academic and social success following parental divorce.* Unpublished master's thesis, Queen's University, Kingston, Ontario.

Hartmann, T. (1995). *ADD success stories: A guide to fulfillment for families with attention deficit disorder.* Grass Valley, CA: Underwood Books.

Hartsell, B. (2006). Teaching toward compassion: Environmental values education for secondary students. *Journal of Secondary Gifted Education, 17,* 265–271.

Hartup, W.W. (1993). Adolescents and their friends. In B. Laursen (Ed.), *Close friendships in adolescence* (Vol. 60, pp. 3–22). San Francisco: Jossey-Bass.

Hartup, W.W. (1996). The company they keep: Friendships and their developmental significance. *Child Development, 67,* 1–13.

Hartup, W.W. (2006). Relationships in early and middle childhood. In A.L. Vangelisti & D. Perlman (Eds.), *The Cambridge handbook of personal relationships* (pp. 177–190). New York: Cambridge University Press.

Hartup, W.W., Daiute, C., Zajac, R., & Sholl, W. (1995). *Collaboration in creative writing by friends and nonfriends.* Unpublished manuscript, Harvard University.

Harvey, J.G., Waits, B.K., & Demana, F. (1995). The influence of technology on the teaching and learning of algebra. *Journal of Mathematical Behavior, 14,* 75–109.

Hawley, C.A. (2004). Behaviour and school performance after brain injury. *Brain Injury, 18,* 645–659.

Haywood, J. (2006). You can't be in my choir if you can't stand up: One journey towards inclusion. *Music Education Research, 8*(3), 407–416.

Heacox, D. (2002). *Differentiating instruction in the regular classroom: How to reach and teach all learners, grades 3–12.* Minneapolis, MN: Free Spirit Publishing.

Heal, L.W., & Rusch, F.R. (1995). Predicting employment for students who leave special education high school programs. *Exceptional Children, 61,* 472–487.

Health Canada (1999). *Advisory: Liver complications result in withdrawal of attention deficit hyperactivity disorder drug Cylert.* [ http://www.hc-sc.gc.ca/dhp-mps/medeff/bulletin/carn-bcei_v10n1-eng.php#PEMOLINE_CYLERT]. (November 15, 2008).

Healthy Child Manitoba. (2008). *Bridging to adulthood: A protocol for transitioning students with exceptional needs from school to community.* Winnipeg: Healthy Child Manitoba [www.gov.mb.ca/healthychild]

Heath, N.L. (2001). Exploring the relationship between learning disabilities and depression: Methodological, pubertal status, gender, and subtyping issues. *Thalamus: Journal of the International Academy for Research in Learning Disabilities*, 19, 2–10.

Heath, N.L. (2008). Introduction to self-injury in adolescents for classroom teachers. Retrieved November 2, 2008 at http://www.education.mcgill.ca/heathresearchteam/images/QPAT2005SelfInjury.pdf

Heath, N.L., & Ross, S. (2000). The prevalence and expression of depressive symptomatology in children with and without learning disabilities. *Learning Disability Quarterly*, 23, 24–36.

Heath, N.L., & Weiner, J. (1996). Depression and nonacademic self-perceptions in children with and without learning disabilities. *Learning Disability Quarterly*, 19, 34–44.

Helfman, E. (1992). *On being Sarah*. Morton Grove, IL: Albert Whitman and Company.

Heller, K.W., Alberto, P.A., Forney, P.E., & Schwartzman, M.N. (1996). *Understanding physical, sensory, and health impairments*. Brooks/Cole: Boston.

Hendrickson, et al. (1995). Creating community: A promising concept for preventing and eliminating aggressive and violent behaviors. In L.M. Bullock & R.A. Gable (Eds.), *Perspectives on school aggression and violence: Highlights from the working forum on children and youth who have aggressive and violent behaviors* (pp. 45–48). Reston, VA: Council for Exceptional Children.

Henley, M. (2006). *Classroom management: A proactive approach*. Upper Saddle River, NJ: Pearson Merrill Prentice Hall.

Herrenkohl, L.R. (2006). Intellectual role taking: Supporting discussion in heterogeneous elementary science classes. *Theory into Practice*, 45(1), 47–54.

Hess, M. (1991). *Children, schools, and poverty*. Ottawa: Canadian Teachers' Federation.

Hess, R.S., Molina, A.M., & Kozleski, E.B. (2006). Until somebody hears me: Parent voice and advocacy in special education decision making. *British Journal of Special Education*, 33, 148–157.

Hiebert, B. (1985). *Stress and teachers: The Canadian scene*. Toronto: Canadian Education Association.

Hieneman, M., Dunlap, G., & Kincaid, D. (2005). Positive support strategies for students with behavioral disorders in general education settings. *Psychology in the Schools*, 42, 779–794.

Higenbottam, J. (1998). What is a brain injury? In S. Acorn & P. Offer (Eds.), *Living with brain injury* (pp. 7–19). Toronto: University of Toronto Press.

Hill, C. (2003). The role of instructional assistants: Are they influencing inclusive practices? *Alberta Journal of Educational Research*, 49, 1–4.

Hill, P., & Cameron, M. (1999). Recognizing hyperactivity: A guide for the cautious clinician. *Child Psychology and Psychiatry Review*, 4, 50–60.

Hindin, A., Cobb Morocco, C., & Mata Anguila, C. (2001). "This book lives in our school": Teaching middle school students to understand literature. *Remedial and Special Education*, 22, 204–213.

Hinshaw, S.P., Owens, E.B., Sami, N., & Fargeon, S. (2006). Prospective follow-up of girls with Attention-Deficit/Hyperactivity Disorder into adolescence: Evidence for continuing cross-domain impairment. *Journal of Consulting and Clinical Psychology*, 74(3), 489–499.

Hinton, V.J., De Vivo, D.C., Fee, R., Goldstein, E., & Stern, Y. (2004). Investigation of poor academic achievement in children with Duchenne muscular dystrophy. *Learning Disabilities Research and Practice*, 19, 146–154.

Hinton, V.J., Fee, R., De Vivo, D.C., & Goldstein, E. (2007). Poor facial affect recognition among boys with Duchenne muscular dystrophy. *Journal of Autism and Developmental Disorders*, 37, 1925–1933.

Hodge, J.G. (2004). Ethical issues concerning genetic testing and screening in public health. *American Journal of Medical Genetics Part C: Seminars in Medical Genetics*, 125C(1), 66–70.

Hogan, B., & Forsten, C. (2007). *8-step model drawing: Singapore's best problem-solving math strategies*. Peterborough, NH: Crystal Springs Books.

Hoge, R.D. (1988). Issues in the definition and measurement of the giftedness construct. *Educational Researcher*, 27(7), 12–16.

Hoge, R.D., & Renzulli, J.S. (1993). Exploring the link between giftedness and self-concept. *Review of Educational Research*, 63, 449–465.

Hollingsworth, M.G. (1996). Computers in secondary education: Practices today, preparing for tomorrow. In J. Andrews (Ed.), *Teaching students with diverse needs: Secondary classrooms* (pp. 243–274). Scarborough, ON: Nelson Canada.

Holloway, J.H., (2003). Addressing the needs of homeless students. *Educational Leadership*, 60(4), 89–90.

Hong, B., & Ehrensberger, W. (2007). Assessing the mathematical skills of students with disabilities. *Preventing School Failure*, 52(1), 41–47.

Hong, E., Greene, M.T., & Higgins, K. (2006). Instructional practices of teachers in general education and gifted resource rooms. *Gifted Child Quarterly*, 50(2), 91–103.

Hoo Kong, N.A. (1996). Confronting a history of exclusion: A personal reflection. In K.S. Brethwaite & C.E. James (Eds.), *Educating African Canadians* (pp. 58–68). Toronto: James Lorimer & Co.

Houseknecht, S.K., & Hango, D.W. (2006). The impact of marital conflict and disruption on children's health. *Youth & Society*, 38(1), 58–89.

Howard, B., Cohn, E., & Orsmond, G.I. (2006). Understanding and negotiating friendships: Perspectives from an adolescent with Asperger syndrome. *Autism*, 10, 619–627.

Howlin, P. (2007). The outcome in adult life for people with ASD. In F.R. Volkmar (Ed.), *Diagnosis and definition of autism and other pervasive developmental disorders* (pp. 269–306). Cambridge, UK: Cambridge University Press.

Hoza, B., et al. (2005). What aspects of peer relationships are impaired in children with attention-deficit/hyperactivity disorder? *Journal of Consulting and Clinical Psychology*, 73(3), 411–423.

Huffman, D.M., Fontaine, K.L., & Proice, B.K. (2003). *Health problems in the classroom 6–12: An A–Z reference guide for educators*. Thousand Oaks, CA: Corwin.

Huggins, P., Wood-Manion, D.W., Moen, L., & Tyler. E. (1999). *Helping kids find their strengths*. Longmont, CO: Sopris West.

Hughes, R.S., & Kloeppel, P.C. (1998). *Self-awareness in language arts (SAIL)*. Minneapolis, MN: Educational Media.

Hughes, T.A., & Fredrick, L.D. (2006). Teaching vocabulary with students with learning disabilities using classwide-peer tutoring and constant time delay. *Journal of Behavioral Education*, 15, 1–23.

Human Resources and Social Development Canada, 2005. *Literacy in Canada*. [http://www.hrsdc.gc.ca/eng/hip/lld/nls/Resources/10_fact.shtml]. (November 15, 2008).

Hume, K. (2008). *Start where they are: Differentiating for success with the young adolescent*. Toronto: Pearson Education Canada.

Hutchinson, N.L. (1993). Effects of cognitive strategy instruction on algebra problem solving of adolescents with learning disabilities. *Learning Disability Quarterly*, 16, 34–63.

Hutchinson, N.L. (1996). Promoting social development and social acceptance in secondary school classrooms. In J. Andrews (Ed.), *Teaching students with diverse needs* (pp. 152–201). Scarborough, ON: ITP Nelson Canada.

Hutchinson, N.L. (1997). Creating an inclusive classroom with young adolescents in an urban school. *Exceptionality Education Canada*, 6(3&4), 51–67.

Hutchinson, N.L. (2007). *Inclusion of exceptional learners in Canadian schools: A practical handbook for teachers* (2nd ed.). Toronto: Pearson Prentice Hall.

Hutchinson, N.L., Chin, P., Munby, H., Mills de Espana, W., Young, J., Edwards, K.L. (1999). How inclusive is co-operative education in Canada? Getting the story and the numbers. *Exceptionality Education Canada, 8*(3), 15–43.

Hutchinson, N.L., & Freeman, J.G. (1994). *Pathways.* Scarborough, ON: ITP Nelson Canada.

Hutchinson, N.L., Freeman, J.G., & Berg, D.H. (2004). Social competence of adolescents with learning disabilities: Interventions and issues. In B.Y.L. Wong (Ed.), *Learning about learning disabilities* (pp. 415–448, 3rd ed.). New York: Academic Press.

Hutchinson, N.L., Freeman, J.G., & Quick, V.E. (1996). Group counseling intervention for solving problems on the job. *Journal of Employment Counseling, 33*(1), 2–19.

Hutchinson, N.L., Freeman, J.G., & Steiner Bell, K. (2002). Children and adolescents with learning disabilities: Case studies of social relations in inclusive classrooms. In B.Y.L. Wong & M. Donahue (Eds.), *The social dimensions of learning disabilities* (pp. 189–214). Mahwah, NJ: Lawrence Erlbaum Associates.

Hutchinson, N.L., Munby, H., Chin, P., Edwards, K.L., Steiner-Bell, K., Chapman, C., Ho, K., & Mills de España, W. (2001). The intended curriculum in co-operative education in Ontario secondary schools: An analysis of school district documents. *Journal of Vocational Educational Research, 26,* 103–140.

Hutchinson, N.L., & Schmid, C. (1996). Perceptions of a resource teacher about programs for preschoolers with special needs and their families. *Canadian Journal of Research in Early Childhood Education, 5*(1), 73–82.

Hutchinson, N.L., Versnel, J., Chin, P., & Munby, H. (2008). Negotiating accommodations so that work-based education facilitates career development for youth with disabilities. *Work: A Journal of Prevention, Assessment & Rehabilitation, 30,* 123–136.

Ignatieff, M. (2000). *The rights revolution.* Toronto: House of Anansi Press.

International Labour Office. (2006). *Global employment trends for youth.* Geneva, Switzerland: International Labour Office.

Irish, C. (2002). Using peg- and keyword mnemonics and computer-assisted instruction to enhance basic multiplication performance in elementary students with learning and cognitive disabilities. *Journal of Special Education Technology, 17,* 29–40

Jackett, E., & Willows, D. (1998, December). *Development of story schemata in the written compositions of primary students: A longitudinal study of the balanced and flexible literacy diet.* Paper presented at the National Reading Conference, Austin, TX.

Jacobs, D. (2003). *Shifting attention from "discipline problems" to "virtue awareness" in American Indian and Alaska Native education.* ERIC Digest (ERIC Document Reproduction Service No. ED 480732).

James, J. (1996). *Phonological processing in early reading and invented spelling.* Unpublished master's thesis, Queen's University, Kingston, ON.

James, K. (1996). Dear high school teacher. In K. Brethwaite & C.E. James (Eds.), *Educating African Canadians* (pp. 302–304). Toronto: James Lorimer & Co.

Janssen, M.J., Riksen-Walreven, J.M., VanDijk, J.P.M., Ruijssenaars, W., & Vlaskamp, C. (2007). Team interaction coaching with educators of adolescents whoa re deaf-blind: Applying the diagnostic intervention model. *Journal of Visual Impairment and Blindness, 101,* 677–689.

Janus, M., Lefort, J., Cameron, R., & Kopechanski, L. (2007). Starting kindergarten: Transition issues for children with special needs. *Canadian Journal of Education, 30,* 628–647.

Jenkins, J.C., Antil, L.R., Wayne, S.R., & Vadasy, P.F. (2003). How cooperative learning works for special education and remedial students. *Exceptional Children, 69,* 279–292.

Jenkinson, J., Hyde, T., & Ahmad, S. (2002). *Occupational therapy approaches for secondary special needs: Practical classroom strategies.* Independence, KY: Taylor & Francis.

Jenkinson, J.C. (1997). *Mainstream or special? Educating students with disabilities.* London: Routledge.

Jensen, P.S. (2001). ADHD comorbidity and treatment outcomes in the MTA. *Journal of the American Academy of Child and Adolescent Psychiatry, 40*(2), 134–136.

Jepsen, D.A., & Dickson, G.L. (2003). Continuity in life-span career development: Career exploitation as a precursor to career establishment. *Career Development Quarterly, 51,* 217–233.

Jeynes, W. (2002). *Divorce, family structure, and the academic success of children.* New York: Haworth Press.

Jeynes, W. (2006). The impact of parental remarriage on children: A meta-analysis. *Marriage and Family Review, 40*(4), 75–102.

Jeynes, W.H. (2007). The relationship between parental involvement and urban secondary school student academic achievement. *Urban Education, 42,* 82–110.

Joffe, V.L., Cain, K., & Maric, N. (2007). Comprehension problems in children with specific language impairment: Does mental imagery training help? *International Journal of Language and Communication Disorders, 42,* 648–664.

Johannesson, M., Carlson, M., Brucefors, A.B., & Hjelte, L. (1998). Cystic fibrosis through a female perspective: Psychosocial issues and information concerning puberty and motherhood. *Patient Education and Counseling, 34,* 115–123.

Johns Hopkins University Center for Technology in Education. [http://cte.jhu.edu]. (October 31, 2005).

Johnson, C.L., & Lapadat, J. (2000). Parallels between learning disabilities and fetal alcohol syndrome/effect: No need to reinvent the wheel. *Exceptionality Education Canada, 10*(3), 65–81.

Johnson, D.W., & Johnson, R.T. (1985). The internal dynamics of co-operative learning groups. In R. Slavin et al. (Eds.), *Learning to cooperate, cooperating to learn* (pp. 103–124). New York: Plenum Press.

Johnson, D.W., & Johnson, R.T. (2004). *Assessing students in groups: Promoting group responsibility and individual accountability.* Thousand Oaks, CA: Corwin Press.

Johnson, J.R. (1999). Leadership and self-determinants. *Focus on Autism and Other Developmental Disabilities, 14*(1), 4–16.

Johnston, T., & Kirby, J.R. (2006). The contribution of naming speed to the simple view of reading. *Reading and Writing: An interdisciplinary Journal, 19*(4), 339–361.

Jones, J., & Leahy, S. (2006). Developing strategic readers. *Science and Children, 44*(3), 30–34.

Jones, M.G., Minogue, J., Oppewal, T., Cook, M.P., & Broadwell, B. (2006). Visualizing without vision at the microscale: Students with visual impairments explore cells with touch. *Journal of Science Education and Technology, 15,* 345–351.

Joong, P., & Ridler, O. (2005). School violence: Perception and reality. *Education Canada, 45*(4), 61–63.

Jordan, A., & Stanovich, P. (1998). *Exemplary teaching in inclusive classrooms.* Paper presented at the annual meeting of the American Educational Research Association, San Diego, CA.

Jordan, A., & Stanovich, P. (2004). The beliefs and practices of Canadian teachers about including students with special education needs in their regular elementary classrooms. *Exceptionality Education Canada, 14*(2&3), 25–46.

Jordan, N.C., Kaplan, D., Locuniak, M.N., & Ramineni, C. (2007). Predicting first-grade math achievement from developmental number sense trajectories. *Learning Disabilities Research and Practice, 22*, 36–46.

Juianelle, P.F., & Foscarinis, M. (2003). Responding to the school mobility of children and youth experiencing homelessness: The McKinney-Vento Act and beyond. *Journal of Negro Education, 72*(1), 39–54.

Kagan, L., & Kagan, S. (2000). *Cooperative learning: Course workbook.* San Clemente, CA: Kagan Cooperative Learning.

Kainai Board of Education, Metis Nation of Alberta, Northland School Division, & Tribal Chiefs Institute of Treaty Six (2004). *Aboriginal Studies 10: Aboriginal perspectives, teacher resource.* Edmonton, AB: Duval House Publishing.

Kameenui, E.J., & Simmons, D.C. (1999) *Toward successful inclusion of students with disabilities: The architecture of instruction: An overview of materials adaptations.* Reston, VA: Council of Exceptional Children.

Kamimura, E., & Ishikuma, T. (2007). Teachers' process of building rapport in parent-teacher conferences: Analysis of teachers' speech based on a grounded theory approach. *Japanese Journal of Educational Psychology, 55*, 560–572.

Kane, J., & Henning, J.E. (2004). A case study of the collaboration in mathematics between a fourth–grade teacher and a talented and gifted coordinator. *Journal for the Education of the Gifted, 27*, 243–266.

Kanevsky, L., & McGrimmond, L. (2008, June). *A survey of acceleration practices in Canada.* Paper presented at the annual meeting of the Canadian Society for the Study of Education, Vancouver, BC.

Kanu, Y. (2005). Teachers' perceptions of the integration of Aboriginal culture into the high school curriculum. *Alberta Journal of Educational Research, 51*(1), 50–68.

Kaplan, S.N. (2008). Curriculum consequence: If you learn this, then . . . *Gifted Child Today, 31*, 41–42.

Kaprielian-Churchill, I., & Churchill, S. (1994). *The pulse of the world: Refugees in our schools.* Toronto: OISE Press.

Karten, T.J. (2005). *Inclusion strategies that work! Research-based methods for the classroom.* Thousand Oaks, CA: Corwin Press.

Katsiyannis, A., Zhang, D., Ryan, J.B., & Jones, J. (2007). High-stakes testing and students with disabilities: Challenges and promises. *Journal of Disability Policy Studies, 18*, 160–167.

Katzir, T., Young-Suk, K., Wolf, M., Morris., R., & Lovett, M. (2008). The varieties of pathways to dysfluent reading. *Journal of Learning Disabilities, 41*(1), 47–66.

Kauffman, J.M., & Hallahan, D.P. (Eds.) (1995). *The illusion of full inclusion: A comprehensive critique of a current special education bandwagon.* Austin, TX: Pro-ed.

Kaufman, M. (2005). *Easy for you to say: Questions and answers for teens' living with chronic illness or disability* (2nd ed.). Buffalo, NY: Firefly.

Keating, D.P. (1996). Habits of mind for a learning society: Educating for human development. In D.R. Olson & N. Torrance, (Eds.), *Handbook of education and human development: New models of learning, teaching, and schooling* (pp. 461–481). Oxford: Blackwell.

Keating, D.P., & Matthews, D.J. (1999). What we are learning about how children learn and what this means for teachers. *Education Canada, 39*(1), 35.

Kempe, A. (2004). *Drama education and special needs: A handbook for teachers in mainstream and special schools.* Cheltenham, UK: Nelson Thornes.

Kern, L., Bambara, L., & Fogt, J. (2002). Class-wide curricular modification to improve the behaviour of students with emotional or behavioural disorders. *Behavioural Disorders, 27*, 317–326.

Kerr, B., & Sodano, S. (2003). Career assessment with intellectually gifted students. *Journal of Career Assessment, 11*, 168–186.

Kerr, R. (1999). *Self-discipline: Using portfolios to help students develop self awareness and manage emotions and build relationships.* Markham, ON: Pembroke.

Keselman, A., Kaufman, D.R., Kramer, S., & Patel, V.L. (2007). Fostering conceptual change and critical reasoning about HIV and AIDS. *Journal of Research in Science Teaching, 44*, 844–863.

Kewley, G. (1998). Medical aspects of assessment and treatment of children with ADHD. In P. Cooper & K. Ideus (Eds.), *ADHD: Educational, medical, and cultural issues* (pp. 136–172). East Sutton, UK: Association of Workers for Children with EBD.

Khalsa, S.S. (2007). *Teaching discipline and self-respect: Effective strategies, anecdotes, and lessons for successful classroom management.* Thousand Oaks, CA: Corwin Press.

Kidd, S. (2004). "The walls were closing in and we were trapped": A qualitative analysis of street youth suicide. *Youth and Society, 36*, 30–55.

Kidd, S. (2006). ". . . and that stairwell felt like a trap": Factors precipitating suicidality among homeless youth. *Youth & Society, 37*, 393–422.

Kidd, S. (2007). Youth homelessness and social stigma. *Journal of Youth and Adolescence, 36*(3), 291–299.

Kim, Y.Y. (2001). *Becoming intercultural: An integrative theory of communication and cross-cultural adaptation.* Thousand Oaks: Sage.

Kincher, J., & Bach, J. (2002). *Psychology for kids: 40 fun tests that help you learn about yourself.* Minneapolis, MN: Free Spirit.

King, A.J.C., & Peart, M. (1992). *Teachers in Canada: Their work and quality of life.* Kingston, ON: Canadian Teachers' Federation and Queen's University Social Program Evaluation Group.

King, A.J.C., Warren, W., & Peart, M. (1988). *The teaching experience.* Toronto: Ontario Secondary School Teachers' Federation.

King-Sears, M.E. (2001). Institutionalizing peer-mediated instruction and interventions in schools: Beyond "train and hope." *Remedial and Special Education, 22*, 89–101.

King-Sears, M.E. (2005). Scheduling for reading and writing small-group instruction using learning center designs. *Reading and Writing Quarterly, 21*(4), 401–405.

King-Sears, M.E. (2007). Designing and delivering learning center instruction. *Intervention in School and Clinic, 42*(3), 137–147.

King-Sears, M.E. (2008). Facts and fallacies: Differentiation and the general education curriculum for students with special education needs. *Support for Learning, 23*(2), 55–62.

King-Sears, M.E., & Carpenter, S.L. (1997). Teaching self-management to elementary students with developmental disabilities. *Innovations: American Association on Mental Retardation, Research to Practice Series, 11.*

Kirkey, T.L. (2005). Differentiated instruction and enrichment opportunities: An action research report. *Ontario Action Researcher, 8*(3). [ww.nipissingu.ca/oar/PDFS/V833E.pdf]. (November 8, 2008).

Klassen, R.M. (2002). The changing landscape of learning disabilities in Canada: Definitions and practice from 1989-2000. *School Psychology International, 23*, 199–219.

Klassen, R. (2007). Using predictions to learn about the self-efficacy of early adolescents with and without learning disabilities. *Contemporary Educational Psychology, 32*(2), 173–187.

Klassen, R., & Lynch, S.L. (2007). Self-efficacy from the perspective of adolescents with LD and their specialist teachers. *Journal of Learning Disabilities, 40*(6), 494–507.

Kleinert, H.L., Haig, J., Kearns, J.F., & Kennedy, S. (2000). Alternate assessments: Lessons learned and roads to be taken. *Exceptional Children, 67*, 51–66.

Klein-Tasman, B.P., & Albano, A.M. (2007). Intensive, short-term cognitive-behavioral treatment of OCD-like behavior with a young adult with Williams syndrome. *Clinical Case Studies*, 6, 483–492.

Klesmer, H. (1994). *ESL achievement project: Development of English as a second language achievement criteria as a function of age and length of residence in Canada*. North York, ON: North York Board of Education.

Klingner, J.K., & Vaughn, S. (1998). Using collaborative strategic reading. *Teaching Exceptional Children, 30*, 32–37.

Klingner, J., Vaughn, S., Arguelles, M.E., Hughes, M.T., & Leftwich, S.A. (2004). Collaborative strategic reading: "real world" lessons from classroom teachers. *Remedial and Special Education, 25*, 291–302.

Kluth, P. (2000). Community-referenced learning and the inclusive classroom. *Remedial and Special Education, 21*, 19–26.

Kluth, P. (2004). Autism, autobiography, and adaptations. *Teaching Exceptional Children, 36*(4), 42–47.

Knoll, J.A., & Racino, J.A. (1994). Field in search of a home: The need for support personnel to develop a distinct identity. In V.J. Bradley, J.W. Ashbaugh, & B.C. Blaney (Eds.), *Creating individual supports for people with developmental disabilities: A mandate for change at many levels* (pp. 299–323). Baltimore, MD: Brookes.

Knox, M., & Hickson, F. (2001). The meanings of close friendship: The views of people with intellectual disabilities. *Journal of Applied Research in Intellectual Disabilities, 14*, 276–291.

Koellner, K., & Wallace, F. (2007). Alternative uses for junk mail: How environmental print supports mathematics literacy. *Mathematics Teaching in the Middle School, 12*, 326–332.

Koenig, A.J., & Holbrook, C. (2000). Ensuring high-quality instruction for students in braille literacy programs. *Journal of Visual Impairment and Blindness, 94*, 677–694.

Kondor, C.A.H. (2007). *One size may not fit all, but the right teaching strategies might: The effects of differentiated instruction on the motivation of talented and gifted students*. Online Submission, ERIC Document ED497701.

Konrad, M., Trela, K., & Test, D.W. (2006). Using IEP goals and objectives to teach paragraph writing to high school students with physical and cognitive disabilities. *Education and Training in Developmental Disabilities, 41*(2), 111–124.

Korneluk, Y.G., MacDonald, N.E., Cappelli, M., McGrath, P., & Heich, C.E. (1996). *CF and you: A guide for adolescents*. Ottawa: Carleton University Press.

Koscik, R.L., et al. (2004). Cognitive function of children with cystic fibrosis: Deleterious effect of early malnutrition. *Pediatrics, 113*, 15549–1558.

Kosky, C., & Curtis, R. (2008). An action research exploration integrating student choice and arts activities in a sixth grade social studies classroom. *Journal of Social Studies Research, 32*(1), 22–27.

Kottler, J.A., & Kottler, E. (2006). *Counseling skills for teachers*. Thousand Oaks, CA: Corwin Press.

Krebs, C.L. (2002). Self-advocacy skills: A portfolio approach. *RE:view, 33*, 160–163.

Krogness, M.M. (1995). *Just teach me, Mrs. K.: Talking, reading, and writing with resistant adolescent learners*. Portsmouth, NH: Heineman.

Kuhne, M., & Wiener, J. (2000). Stability of social status of children with and without learning disabilities. *Learning Disability Quarterly, 23*, 64–75.

Kutnick, P., & Kington, A. (2005). Children's friendships and learning in school: Cognitive enhancement through social interaction? *British Journal of Educational Psychology, 75*, 521–538.

Kutnick, P., Ota, C., & Berdondini, L. (2008). Improving the effects of group working in classrooms with young school-aged children: Facilitating attainment, interaction and classroom activity. *Learning and Instruction, 18*, 83–95.

Lacasse, A., & Mendelson, M. (2006). The perceived intent of potentially offensive sexual behaviors among adolescents. *Journal of Research on Adolescence, 16*(2), 229–238.

Ladd, H.F., & Zelli, A. (2002). School-based accountability in North Carolina. *Educational Administration Quarterly, 38*(4), 494–529.

Ladd, H.F., & Zelli, A. (2003). School-based accountability in North Carolina: The responses of school principals. *Educational Administration Quarterly, 38*, 494–529.

Lahey, B.B., Pelham, W.E., Loney, J., Lee, S.S., & Willcutt, E. (2005). Instability of the DSM-IV subtypes of ADHD from preschool through elementary school. *Archives of General Psychiatry, 62*(8), 896–902.

Laird, G. (2007). *Shelter: Homelessness in a growth economy*. Calgary, AB: Sheldon Chumir Foundation for Ethics in Leadership.

Lam, C.S.M. (1996). The green teacher. In D. Thiessen, N. Bascia, & I. Goodson (Eds.), *Making a difference about difference: The lives and careers of racial minority immigrant teachers* (pp. 15–50). Toronto: Garamond Press.

Lambdin, D.V., & Forseth, C. (1996). Seamless assessment/instruction = good teaching. *Teaching Children Mathematics, 2*(1), 294–298.

Lambe, J., & Bones, R. (2006). Student teachers' attitudes to inclusion: Implications for initial teacher education in Northern Ireland. *International Journal of Inclusive Education, 10*(6), 511–527.

Lamont, I.L., & Hill, J.L. (1991). Roles and responsibilities of paraprofessionals in the regular elementary classroom. *B.C. Journal of Special Education, 15*(1), 1–24.

Lancaster, P.E., Schumaker, J.B., & Deshler, D.D. (2002). The development and validation of an interactive, hypermedia program for teaching a self-advocacy strategy to students with disabilities. *Learning Disability Quarterly, 25*, 277–302.

Landsman, J. (2008). Confronting the racism of low expectations. *International Journal of Leadership in Education, 11*(2), 169–189.

Langer, E.C. (2007). *Classroom discourse and interpreted education: What is conveyed to deaf elementary school students*. Unpublished doctoral dissertation, University of Colorado at Boulder.

Lapka, C. (2006). Students with disabilities in a high school band: "We can do it!". *Music Educators Journal, 92*(4), 54–59.

Lara-Cinisomo, S., Fuligni, A.S., Ritchie, S., Howes, C. Karoly, L. (2008). Getting ready for school: An examination of early childhood educators' belief systems. *Early Childhood Education Journal, 35*(4), 343–349.

Larivee, B. (2006). *Authentic classroom management: Creating a learning community and building reflective practice* (2nd ed.). Boston: Pearson Allyn & Bacon.

Larkin, J. (1997). *Sexual harassment: High school girls speak out*. Toronto: Second Story Press.

Laugeson, E.A., Paley, B., Scholfeld, A.M., Carpenter, E.M., Frankel, F., & O'Connor, M.J. (2007). Adaptation of the children's friendship training program for children with fetal alcohol spectrum disorders. *Child and Family Behavior Therapy, 29*(3), 57–69.

Lawson, J. (2008). Women leaders in high-poverty community schools: Work-related stress and family impact. *Canadian Journal of Education, 31*(1), 55–77.

Lazzaro, J.J. (2001). *Adaptive technologies for learning and work environments*. Chicago: American Library Association.

Leadbeater, B.J., Banister, E.M., Ellis, W.E., & Yeung, R. (2008). Victimization and relational aggression in adolescent romantic relationships. *Journal of Youth and Adolescence, 37*(3), 359–372.

Lederer, J.M. (2000). Reciprocal teaching of social studies in inclusive elementary classrooms. *Journal of Learning Disabilities, 33*, 91–106.

Lee, E. (1985). *Letters to Marcia: A teacher's guide to anti-racist education*. Toronto: Cross-Cultural Communication Centre.

Lee, H.J., & Herner-Patnode, L.M. (2007). Teaching mathematics vocabulary to diverse groups. *Intervention in School & Clinic, 43*(2), 121–126.

Legg, C., Penn, C., Temlett, J., & Sonnenberg, B. (2005). Language skills of adolescents with Tourette syndrome. *Clinical Linguistics and Phonetics, 19*, 15–33.

Leithwood, K. (2004). *Educational accountability: Issues and alternatives* (Briefing paper for the Saskatchewan School Trustees' Association). Toronto: OISE Press.

Lennon, G. (1995, March/Aril). Inclusion: Adapting the curriculum. *FWTAO Newsletter*, 22–26.

Lennox, C., & Siegel, L.S. (1996). The development of phonological rules and visual strategies in average and poor spellers. *Journal of Experimental Child Psychology, 62*, 60–83.

Lent, R.W., Hackett, G., & Brown, S.D. (1999). A social cognitive view of school-to-work transition. *Career Development Quarterly, 47*, 297–311.

Lepofsky, M.D. (1996). A report card on the *Charter's* guarantee of equality to persons with disabilities after 10 years—what progress? What prospects? *National Journal of Constitutional Law, 7*, 263–431.

Levac, M. (2004). How exemplary dyads describe their practice of collaborative consultation: An interview study. *Exceptionality Education Canada, 14*(2&3), 115–14.

Lévesque, N.L. (1997). *Perceptions of friendships and peer groups: The school experiences of two adolescents with learning disabilities*. Unpublished master's thesis, Queen's University, Kingston, ON.

Levin, B. (1994). Strategies for working with children from low income families. *Canadian School Executive, 14*(2), 23–25.

Levin, B. (2008). How much diversity in our schools? *Phi Delta Kappan, 89*(5), 394–395.

Levin, B., & Fullan, M. (2008). Learning about system renewal. *Educational Management Administration and Leadership, 36*(2), 289–303.

Levin, D.E. (2004). *Teaching young children in violent times: Building a peaceable classroom*. Cambridge, MA: Educators for Social Responsibility.

Lewis, B.A., Freebairn, L.A., & Taylor, H.G. (2000). Follow-up of children with early expressive phonology disorders. *Journal of Learning Disabilities, 33*, 433–444.

Lewis, R., & Burman, E. (2006). Providing for student voice in classroom management: Teachers' views. *International Journal of Inclusive Education, 1*, 1–17.

Lewis, S. (1992). *Report on race relations*. Toronto: Government of Ontario.

Lickers, E., (2003). Healing the spirit. *Canadian Journal of Native Education 27*(1). 55–60.

Lieberman, R. (2004). Understanding and responding to students who self-mutilate. *Principal Leadership (High School Ed.), 4*(7), 10–13.

Lifvendahl, S. (2007). Pursuing rigor at the middle level. *Principal Leadership, 8*(1), 30–33.

Lillie, T., & Vakil, S. (2002). Transitions in early childhood for students with disabilities: Law and best practice. *Early Childhood Special Education, 30*, 53–58.

Lindberg, J.A., & Swick, A.M. (2006). *Common-sense classroom management for elementary school teachers* (2nd ed.). Thousand Oaks, CA: Corwin Press.

Lindstrom, L.E., & Benz, M.R. (2002). Phases of career development: Case studies of young women with learning disabilities. *Exceptional Children, 69*, 67–83.

Lipman, A. (2002). *Alive at 25: How I'm beating cystic fibrosis*. Athens, GA: Longstreet Press.

Lipman, E. (2003). Andy versus cystic fibrosis. *Exceptional Parent, 33*(11), 3–31.

Liu, X.S. (2007). The effect of teacher influence at school on first-year teacher attrition. *Educational Research and Evaluation, 13*(1), 1–16.

Lloyd, S. (2006). *Jolly phonics sound stories*. London: Jolly Learning Ltd.

Lloyd, S., Wernham, S., Jolly, C., & Stephen, L. (1998). *Jolly phonics*. Chigwell, UK: Jolly Learning.

LoCasale-Crouch, J., Konold, T., Pianta, R., Howes, C., Burchinal, M., Bryant, D., Clifford, R., Early, D., & Barbarin, O. (2007). Observed classroom quality profiles in state-funded pre-kindergarten programs and associations with teacher, program, and classroom characteristics. *Early Childhood Research Quarterly; 22*(1), 3–17.

LoCasale-Crouch, J., Mashburn, A.J., Downer, J.T., & Pianta, R.C. (2008). Pre-kindergarten teachers' use of transition practices and children's adjustment to kindergarten. *Early Childhood Research Quarterly, 23*(1), 124–139.

Long, C., Downs, C.A., Gillette, B., Kills in Sight, L., & Iron-Cloud Konen, E. (2006). Assessing cultural life skills of American Indian youth. *Child Youth Care Forum, 35*, 289–304.

Long, L., MacBlain, S., & MacBlain, M. (2008). Supporting students with dyslexia at the secondary level: An emotional model of literacy. *Journal of Adolescent and Adult Literacy, 51*(2), 124–134.

Lord, J., & Hutchison, P. (2007). *Pathways to inclusion: Building a new story with people and communities*. Concord, ON: Captus Press.

Lord, J., & Rush, B. (2002). A peer support approach to evaluation: Assessing supported employment programs for people with developmental disabilities. *Canadian Journal of Program Evaluation, 17*, 25–41.

Lorence, D., & Chen, Li. (2007). A study of peer-to-peer information in a domain of uncertainty: The case of epilepsy. *Health Informatics Journal, 13*, 303–316.

Lovett, S., & Gilmore, A. (2003). Teachers' learning journeys: The quality learning circle as a model of professional development. *School Effectiveness and School Improvement, 14*, 189–211.

Lucas, B., & Smith, A. (2004). *Help your child to succeed: The essential guide for parents*. Markham, ON: Pembroke Publishers.

Luciano, S., & Savage, R.S. (2007). Bullying risk in children with learning difficulties in inclusive educational settings. *Canadian Journal of School Psychology, 22*, 14–31.

Luckner, J.L., & Muir, S. (2002). Suggestions for helping students who are deaf succeed in general education settings. *Communication Disorders Quarterly, 24*, 23–30.

Ludlow, B.L., & Foshay, J.D. (2002). Book and software review. *Journal of Special Education Technology, 18*, 50–52.

Lupart, J.L., Barva, C., & Cannon, M.E. (2000). *What happens when girls, gifted in science, grow up?* Paper presented at the CCWEST Conference for the Advancement of Women in Engineering, Science, and Technology, St John's, NF.

Lupart, J.L., Cannon, E., & Telfer, J. (2004). Gender differences in academic achievement, interests, values and life-role expectations. *High Ability Studies, 15*(1), 25–42.

Lupart, J.L., & Pyryt, M. (1996). Identifying the hidden gifted. *Journal for the Education of the Gifted, 20*(1), 7–16.

Lupart, J.L., Pyryt, M.C., Watson, S.L., & Pierce, K. (2005). Gifted education and counselling in Canada. *International Journal for the Advancement of Counselling, 27*(2), 173–190.

Lupart, J.L., & Wilgosh, L. (1998). Undoing underachievement and promoting societal advancement for women and girls. *Gifted Education International, 13*, 159–169.

Luterman, D., Kurtyzer-White, E., & Seewald, R. (2006). *The young deaf child*. Austin, TX: Pro-Ed.

Lutz, S.L., Guthrie, J.T., & Davis, M.H. (2006). Scaffolding for engagement in elementary school reading instruction. *Journal of Educational Research, 100*, 3–20.

MacCuspie, P.A. (1996). *Promoting acceptance of children with disabilities: From tolerance to inclusion.* Halifax: Atlantic Provinces Special Education Authority.

MacDonald, A.R., Miell, D., & Mitchell, L. (2002). An investigation of children's musical collaborations: The effect of friendship and age. *Psychology of Music, 30*, 148–163.

Machek, G.R., & Nelson, J.M. (2007). How should reading disabilities be operationalized? A survey of practicing school psychologists. *Learning Disabilities Research and Practice, 22*(2), 147–157.

MacKay, W. (2007). *Inclusive education: A review of programming and services in New Brunswick (Connecting care and challenge: Tapping our human potential).* Fredericton, NB: NB Department of Education.

MacRae, L., & Lupart, J.L. (1991). Issues in identifying gifted students: How Renzulli's model stacks up. *Roeper Review, 14*(2), 53–58.

Madden, M., & Sullivan, J. (2008). *Teaching fluency beyond the primary grades: Strategy lessons to meet the specific needs of upper-grade readers.* New York: Scholastic, Inc.

Magro, K. (2006/2007). Overcoming the trauma of war: Literacy challenges of adult learners. *Education Canada, 47*(1), 70–74.

Malchiodi, C.A. (2008). *Creative interventions with traumatized children.* New York: Guilford Press.

Male, D.B. (2007). The friendships and peer relationships of children and young people who experience difficulties in learning. In L. Florian (Ed.), *The Sage handbook of special education.* London, UK: Sage.

Malian, I., & Nevin, A. (2002). A review of self-determination literature: Implications for practitioners. *Remedial and Special Education, 23*, 68–74.

Manderville, K. (2005). *Co-operative education: Respectful learning negotiation in an Aboriginal context.* Unpublished M.Ed. thesis, Faculty of Education, Queen's University.

Manitoba Education and Training. (1998). *Individual education planning: A handbook for developing and implementing IEP's, early to senior years.* Winnipeg, MB: Manitoba Education and Training.

Manitoba Education, Citizenship, and Youth. (2003). *Independent together: Supporting the multilevel learning community.* [http://www. edu. gov.mb.ca/k12/cur/multilevel/index.html]. (November 15, 2008).

Manitoba Education, Citizenship, and Youth. (2007). *Appropriate educational planning: A handbook for student services.* Winnipeg, MB: Manitoba Education, Citizenship, and Youth.

Manitoba Education, Citizenship and Youth. (2008). *A protocol for transitioning students with exceptional needs from school to community.* Winnipeg, MB: Manitoba Education, Citizenship and Youth. [http://www.edu.gov.mb.ca/k12/docs/policy/transition/]. (November 15, 2008).

Manitoba Healthy Child. (2008). *Bridging to adulthood: A protocol for transitioning students with exceptional needs from school to community.* Winnipeg, MB: Healthy Child Manitoba.

Marris, P. (1986). *Loss and change.* London: Routledge and Kegan Paul.

Marshall, M. (2005). Discipline without stress, punishments, or rewards. *The Clearing House, 79*(1), 51–54.

Martin, J., Sugarman, J., & McNamara, J. (2001). *Models of classroom management: Principles, applications and critical perspectives* (3rd ed.). Calgary: Detselig Enterprises.

Martin, J.E., & Marshal, L.H. (1995). *ChoiceMaker.* Longmont, CO: Sopris West.

Martini, R., & Shore, B.M. (2008). Pointing to parallels in ability-related differences in the use of metacognition in academic and psychomotor tasks. *Learning and Individual Differences, 18*(2), 237–247.

Martinussen, R., Kirby, J.R., & Das, J.P. (1998). Instruction in successive and phonological processing to improve reading acquisition skills of at-risk kindergarten children. *Developmental Disabilities Bulletin, 26*(2), 19–39.

Masden, C.A. (2005). *Social-perspective coordination in gifted early adolescent friendships.* Unpublished doctoral dissertation, McGill University, Quebec, Canada.

Mason, K.L. (2008). Cyberbullying: A preliminary assessment for school personnel. *Psychology in the schools, 45*, 323–348.

Maté, G. (2000). *Scattered minds: A new look at the origins and healing of attention deficit disorder.* Toronto: Knopf Canada.

Mattatall, C. (2008, June). *Gauging the readiness of Canadian school districts to implement responsiveness to intervention.* Paper presented at the annual meeting of the Canadian Society for the Study of Education, Vancouver, BC.

Matthews, D.J. (1997). Diversity in domains of development: Research findings and their implications for gifted identification and programming. *Roeper Review, 19*, 172–177.

Matthews, D.J., Foster, J., Gladstone, D., Schieck, J., & Meiners, J. (2007). Supporting professionalism, diversity, and context within a collaborative approach to gifted education. *Journal of Educational & Psychological Consultation, 17*(4), 315–345.

Matthews, D.J., & Steinhauer, N. (1998). Giftedness, girls, others, and equity: Theory-based practical strategies for the regular classroom. *Exceptionality Education Canada, 8*(2), 41–56.

Mattson, E.H., & Roll-Petterson, L. (2007). Segregated groups or inclusive education? An interview study with students experiencing failure in reading and writing. *Scandinavian Journal of Educational Research, 51*, 239–252.

Maxwell, M. (2007). Career counseling is personal counseling: A constructivist approach to nurturing the development of gifted female adolescents. *Career Development Quarterly, 55*(3), 206–224.

Mayer, K., & Kelley, M.L. (2007). Improving homework in adolescents with attention-deficit/hyperactivity disorder: Self vs. parent monitoring of homework behavior and study skills. *Child and Family Behavior Therapy, 39*(4), 25–42.

McAllister, R., & Gray, C. (2007). Low vision: Mobility and independence training for the early years child. *Early Child Development and Care, 177*, 839–852.

McCafferty, S.G., Jacobs, G.M., & DaSilva Iddings, C. (Eds.). (2006). *Cooperative learning and second language teaching.* Cambridge: Cambridge University Press.

McCaleb, S.P. (1995). *Building communities of learners: Collaboration among teachers, students, families, and community.* Mahwah, NJ: Lawrence Erlbaum.

McCaskell, T. (2007). Before I was White, I was Presbyterian. In P.R. Carr & D.E. Lund (Eds.), *The great white north? Exploring whiteness, privilege, and identity in education* (pp. 33–41). Rotterdam, Netherlands: Sense Publishers.

McCord, K., & Fitzgerald, M. (2006). Children with disabilities playing musical instruments: With the right adaptations and help from teachers and parents, students with disabilities can play musical instruments. *Music Educators Journal, 92*(4), 46–52.

McCord, K., & Watts, M.H. (2006). Collaboration and access for our children: Music educators and special educators together: When music educators and special educators work together, all students are likely to benefit. *Music Educators Journal, 92*(4), 26–31.

McCormick, R.M., Amundsen, N.E., & Poehnell, G. (2002). *Guiding circles: An Aboriginal guide to finding career paths.* Saskatoon: Aboriginal Human Resources Development Council of Canada.

McCue, H.A. (2000). *The learning circle: Classroom activities on First Nations in Canada*. Ottawa: Indian and Northern Affairs Canada.

McDougall, J., DeWit, D.J., King, G., Miller, L., & Killip, S. (2004). High school-aged youths' attitudes toward their peers with disabilities: The role of school and student interpersonal factors. *International Journal of Disability, Development and Education, 51,* 287–313.

McEwan, E.K. (2002). *10 traits of highly effective teachers*. Thousand Oaks, CA: Corwin Press.

McGhie,-Richmond, D., Underwood, K., & Jordan, A. (2007). Developing effective instructional strategies for teaching in inclusive classrooms. *Exceptionality Education Canada, 17*(1), 27–52.

McGinty, S., & Brader, A. (2005). *Educational disengagement: A review of international, Australian and state policy responses*. In A. Pandian, M.K. Kabilan, & S. Kaur (Eds.), Teachers, practices, and supportive cultures (pp. 25–35). Serdang: Universiti Putra Malaysia Press. [http://www.andybrader.com/downloads/educationaldisengagement.pdf] (November 2, 2008).

McHugh, M.W. (2006). Governor's schools: Fostering the social and emotional well-being of gifted and talented students. *Journal of Secondary Gifted Education, 17*(3), 50–58.

McIntosh, R., & Vaughn, S. (1993). So you want to teach social skills to your students: Some pointers from the research. *Exceptionality Education Canada, 3*(1&2), 39–59.

McIntyre, L.L., Eckert, T.L., Fiese, B.H., DiGennaro, F.D., & Wildenger, L.K. (2007). Transition to kindergarten: Family experiences and involvement. *Early Childhood Education Journal, 35*(1), 83–88.

McKay, P. (Ed.) (2006). *Planning and teaching creatively within a required curriculum for school-age learners*. Alexandria, VA: Teachers of English to Speakers of Other Languages.

McLeod, S., & McKinnon, D.H. (2007). Prevalence of communication disorders compared with other learning needs in 14,500 primary and secondary students. *International Journal of Language and Communication Disorders, 42,* 37–59.

McNamara, J.K., & Wong, B.Y.L. (2003), Memory for everyday information in students with learning disabilities. *Journal of Learning Disabilities, 36,* 394–406.

McNiff, J., Lomax, P., & Whitehead, J. (2004). *You and your action research project* (2nd ed.). London, UK: Routledge.

McPhail, J.C., & Freeman, J.G. (2005). Beyond prejudice: Thinking toward genuine inclusion. *Learning Disabilities Research and Practice, 20,* 254–267.

McPhail, J.C., Pierson, J.M., Goodman, J., & Noffke, J.B. (2004). Creating partnerships for complex learning: The dynamics of an interest-based apprenticeship in the art of sculpture. *Curriculum Inquiry, 34,* 463–493.

McQueen, T. (1992). *Essentials of classroom management and discipline*. New York: HarperCollins.

Mechling, L.C. (2004). Effects of multimedia, computer-based instruction on grocery shopping fluency. *Journal of Special Education Technology, 19*(1), 23–34.

Meenakshi, G., Jitendra, A.K., Sood, S., Sacks, G. (2007). Improving comprehension of expository text in students with LD: A research synthesis. *Journal of Learning Disabilities, 40,* 210–225.

Meichenbaum, D. (2006). *Resilience*. [www.teachsafeschools.org/Resilience.pdf] (November 2, 2008).

Mendel, C.M., Watson, R.L., & MacGregor, C.J. (2002). *A study of leadership behaviors of elementary principals compared with school climate*. (ERIC Document Reproduction Service No. ED 471556).

Menkart, D.J. (1999) Deepening the meaning of heritage months. *Educational Leadership, 56*(7), 19–21.

Menning, C.L. (2006). Nonresident fathering and school failure. *Journal of Family Issues, 27*(10), 1356–1382.

Meo, G. (2008). Curriculum planning for all learners: Applying universal deign for learning (UDL) to a high school reading comprehension plan. *Preventing School Failure, 52*(2), 21–30.

Merritt, S.E. (1992). *Her story: Women from Canada's past*. St. Catharine's, ON: Vanwell Pub.

Merritt, S.E. (1995). *Her story II: Women from Canada's past*. St. Catharine's, ON: Vanwell Pub.

Merritt, S.E. (1999). *Her story III: Women from Canada's past*. St. Catharine's, ON: Vanwell Pub.

Meyers, M. (1993). *Teaching to diversity: Teaching and learning in the multi-ethnic classroom*. Toronto: Irwin Publishers.

Miell, D., & MacDonald, A.R. (2000). Children's creative collaborations: The importance of friendship when working together on a music composition. *Social Development, 9,* 348–369.

Miller, C., Leonard, L., & Finneran, D. (2008). Grammaticality judgments in adolescents with and without language impairment. *International Journal of Language and Communication Disorders, 43*(3), 346–360.

Miller, S.M. (2003). How literature discussion shapes thinking: ZPDs for teaching/learning habits of the heart and mind. In B. Gindis & A. Kozulin (Eds.), *Vygotsky's educational theory in cultural context* (pp. 289–316). New York: Cambridge University Press.

Mishna, F., Scarcello, I., Pepler, D., & Wiener, J. (2005). Teachers' understanding of bullying. *Canadian Journal of Education, 28,* 718–738.

Mitchem, K.J., & Young, K.R. (2001). Adapting self-management programs for classwide use: Acceptability, feasibility, and effectiveness. *Remedial and Special Education, 22,* 75–88.

Mittag, K.C., & Van Reusen, A.K. (1999). One fish, two fish, pretzel fish: Learning estimation and other advanced mathematics concepts in an inclusive class. *Teaching Exceptional Children, 31*(6), 66–72.

Mixon, K. (2005). Including exceptional students in your instrumental music program. *Teaching Music, 13*(3), 30–34.

Mo, Y., & Singh, K. (2008). Parents' relationships and involvement: Effects on students' school engagement and performance. *Research in Middle Level Education Online, 31*(10), 1–11.

Molnar, B.E., Cerda, M., Roberts, A.L., & Buka, S.L. (2008). Effects of neighborhood resources on aggressive and delinquent behaviors among urban youths. *American Journal of Public Health, 98*(6), 1086–1093.

Mondak, P. (2000). The *Americans with Disabilities Act* and information technology access. *Focus on Autism and Other Developmental Disabilities, 15*(1), 43–51.

Monroe, B.W., & Troia, G.A. (2006). Teaching writing strategies to middle school students with disabilities. *Journal of Educational Research, 100,* 21–33.

Montague, M. (2008). Self-regulation strategies to improve mathematical problem solving for students with learning disabilities. *Learning Disability Quarterly, 31*(1), 37–44.

Montague, M., & Applegate, B. (2000). Middle school students' perceptions, persistence, and performance in mathematical problem solving. *Learning Disability Quarterly, 23*(3), 215–228.

Montague, M., Warger, C., & Morgan, T.M. (2000). Solve it! Strategy instruction to improve mathematics problem solving. *Learning Disabilities Research & Practice, 15,* 110–116.

Moon, T.R. (2005). The role of assessment in differentiation. *Theory Into Practice, 44*(3), 226–233.

Moore Johnson, S., and the Project on the Next Generation of Teachers. (2004). *Finders and keepers: Helping new teachers survive and thrive in our schools*. San Francisco: Jossey-Bass.

Morgan, P.L., Farkas, G., Tufis, P.S., & Sperling, R.S. (in press). Are reading and behavioral problems risk factors for each other? *Journal of Learning Disabilities*.

Morningstar, M.E. (1997). Critical issues in career development and employment preparation for adolescents with disabilities. *Remedial and Special Education, 18*, 307–320.

Morris, R.C., & Howard, A.C. (2003). Designing an effective in-school suspension program. *Clearing House, 76*, 156–159.

Morrison, J.Q., & Jones, K.M. (2007). The effects of positive peer reporting as a class-wide positive behavior support. *Journal of Behavior Education, 16*, 111–124.

Moss, L.J., & Grover, B.W. (2007). Not just for computation: Basic calculators can advance the process standards. *Mathematics Teaching in the Middle School, 12*, 266–271.

MTA Cooperative Group. (1999). A 14-month randomized clinical trial of treatment strategies for attention deficit/hyperactivity disorder. *Archives of General Psychiatry, 56*, 1073–1086.

Muller, E., Schuler, A., & Yates, G.B. (2008). Social challenges and supports from the perspective of individuals with Asperger syndrome and other autism spectrum.

Munk, D.D., & Bursuck, W.D. (2001). Preliminary findings on personalized grading plans for middle school students with learning disabilities. *Exceptional Children, 67*, 211–234.

Munk, D.D., & Bursuck, W.D. (2004). Personalized grading plans: A systematic approach to making the grades of included students more accurate and meaningful. *Focus on Exceptional Children, 36*(9), 1–12.

Munyofu, M., Swain, W.J., Ausman, B.D., Lin, H., Kidwai, K., Dwyer, F. (2007). The effect of different chunking strategies in complementing animated instruction. *Learning Media and Technology, 32*, 407–419.

Murphy, B., & Pushor, D. (2004). Parent marginalization, marginalized parents: Creating a place for parents on the school landscape. *Alberta Journal of Educational Research, 50*(3), 221–235.

Murray, C., & Greenberg, M.T. (2006). Examining the importance of social relationships and social contexts in the lives of children with high-incidence disabilities. *The Journal of Special Education, 39*, 220–233.

Myers, P.A. (2005). The princess storyteller, Clara clarifier, Quincey questioner, and the wizard: Reciprocal teaching adapted for kindergarten students. *Reading Teacher, 59*, 314–324.

Myles, B.S., Ferguson, H., & Hagiwara, T. (2007). Using a personal digital assistant to improve the recording of homework assignments by an adolescent with Asperger syndrome. *Focus on Autism and Other Developmental Disabilities, 22*, 96–99.

Nachshen, J.S., Garcin, N., & Minnes, P. (2005). Problem behavior in children with intellectual disabilities: Parenting stress, empowerment and school services. *Mental Health Aspects of Developmental Disabilities, 8*, 105–114.

Nachshen, J.S., & Minnes, P. (2005). Empowerment in parents of school-aged children with and without developmental disabilities. *Journal of Intellectual Disability, 49*, 889–904.

Nagel, L., & Brown, S. (2003). The ABCs of managing teacher stress. *Clearing House, 76*(5), 255–258.

Nagle, K., (2001). Transition to employment and community life for youths with visual impairments: Current status and future directions. *Journal of Visual Impairment & Blindness, 95*, 725–738.

Nagler, M., & Nagler, A. (1999). *What's stopping you? Living successfully with disability*. Toronto: Stoddart.

National Center for Education Statistics (NCES). (2007). *Indicators of school crime and safety*. Washington, DC: NCES. Retrieved from [http://nces.ed.gov/programs/crimeindicators/crimeindicators2007/]. (April 10, 2008).

National Center for Homeless Education. (2007). *School help for children with disabilities: Information for parents*. National Center for Homeless Education.

National Clearinghouse on Family Violence. [http://www.phac-aspc.gc.ca/ncfv-cnivf/familyviolence/]. (November 15, 2008).

National Reading Panel (2000). Publications and materials. [http://www.nationalreadingpanel.org/]. (November 15, 2008).

Naylor, M. (2006). From one to one hundred. *Teaching pre K-8, 36*(5), 36–38.

Nelson, J.R., Martella, R.M., & Marchand-Martella, N. (2002). Maximizing student learning: The effects of a comprehensive school-based program for preventing problem behaviors. *Journal of Emotional and Behavioral Disorders, 10*, 136–148.

Nesbit, J.C., & Adesope, O.O. (2006). Learning with concept and knowledge maps: A meta-analysis. *Review of Educational Research, 76*(3), 413–448.

New Brunswick Department of Education (1988). *Working guidelines on integration*. Fredericton: New Brunswick Department of Education.

New Brunswick Department of Education (2002a). *Guidelines and standards: Educational planning for students with exceptionalities*. Fredericton: New Brunswick Department of Education. [www.gnb.ca/0000/publications/ss/sep.pdf]. (October 27, 2005).

New Brunswick Department of Education (2002b). *Positive learning environment policy*. Fredericton: New Brunswick Department of Education. [www.gnb.ca/0000/publications/ss/1542-brochureE4.pdf]. (October 27, 2005).

New Brunswick Department of Education (2003). *A quality learning agenda: Policy statement on K–12 quality schools, high results*. Fredericton: New Brunswick Department of Education.

New Brunswick Department of Education (2004). *Inclusive Education: A review of programming and services in New Brunswick*. Fredericton: New Brunswick Department of Education.

New Brunswick Department of Education. (2006). *Report on the population of public school students with exceptionalities* (Anglophone sector, school year 2004–2005). Fredericton: Student Services Unit, Educational Programs and Services Branch.

New Brunswick Department of Education (n.d.). *Keeping our schools safe: A protocol for violence prevention and crisis response in New Brunswick schools*. Fredericton: New

Newfoundland and Labrador Department of Education (1995). *Balancing students' rights and responsibilities: K–12 curriculum*. St. John's: Government of Newfoundland. [http://www.edu.gov.nf.ca/rights/background.html]. (November 15, 2008).

Newfoundland and Labrador Department of Education (1997). *Individual support services handbook: Coordination of services to children and youth in Newfoundland & Labrador*. St. John's: Government of Newfoundland and Labrador.

Newfoundland and Labrador Department of Education (1998). *Pathways to programming and graduation: A handbook for teachers and administrators*. St. John's: Government of Newfoundland.

Newfoundland and Labrador Department of Education (2000). *Programming for individual needs: Communication disorders handbook*. St. John's: Government of Newfoundland.

Newfoundland and Labrador Department of Education. (2002). *Handbook for profiling the needs of children and youth*. St. John's: Government of Newfoundland.

Newfoundland and Labrador Department of Education. (2006). *Safe and caring schools policy*. St. John's: Government of Newfoundland.

Newfoundland and Labrador Department of Education. (2007). *Focusing on students*. St John's: Government of Newfoundland.

Nieto, S. (2003). *What keeps teachers going?* New York: Teachers College Press.

Noddings, N. (1991). Caring and interpersonal reasoning. In C. Witherell & N. Noddings (Eds.), *Stories lives tell: Narrative and dialogue in education* (pp. 157–171). New York: Teachers College Press.

Noddings, N. (1996). On community. *Educational Theory, 46,* 245–267.

Norris, M.J. (2007). Aboriginal languages in Canada: Emerging trends and perspectives on second language acquisition. *Canadian Social Trends* (Statistics Canada-Catalogue No. 11-008), 20–28.

Northfield, S., & Sherman, A. (2003). Acceptance and community building in schools through increased dialogue and discussion. *Children and Society, 18,* 291–298.

Northwest Territories Department of Health and Social Services (2004). NWT Disability framework. Yellowknife: Northwest Territories Department of Health and Social Services.

Northwest Territories Department of Education, Culture, and Employment. (2006). *The ministerial directive on inclusive schooling.* Yellowknife: Northwest Territories Department of Education, Culture, and Employment.

Norwich, B. (2008). Dilemmas of difference, inclusion and disability: International perspectives on placement. *European Journal of Special Needs Education, 23*(4), 287–304.

Nova Scotia Department of Education (1997). *Special education policy manual.* Halifax: Nova Scotia Department of Education. Halifax: Nova Scotia Department of Education.

Nova Scotia Department of Education (2001). *School code of conduct.* Halifax: Nova Scotia Department of Education.

Nova Scotia Department of Education. (2002). *Supporting student success: Resource programming and services.* Halifax: Nova Scotia Department of Education.

Nova Scotia Department of Education. (2006). *The program planning process: A guide for parents.* Halifax: Nova Scotia Department of Education.

Nowacek, E.J., & Mamlin, N. (2007). General education teachers and students with ADHD: What modifications are made? *Preventing School Failure, 51*(3), 28–35.

Nunavut Department of Education, Curriculum, and School Service. (2002). *Statement on inclusive education.* Iqaluit: Nunavut Department of Education, Curriculum, and School Service.

Nunavut Department of Education, Curriculum, and School Service. (2006). *Inclusive education in Nunavut schools: Student support handbook.* Iqaluit: Nunavut Department of Education, Curriculum, and School Service.

Nyman McMaster, K., & Fuchs, D. (2002). Effects of cooperative learning on the academic achievement of students with learning disabilities: An update on Tateyama-Sniezek's review. *Learning Disabilities Research & Practice, 17,* 107–117.

Obenchain, K.M., & Abernathy, T.V. (2003). 20 ways to build community and empower students. *Intervention in School and Clinic, 39*(1), 55–60.

Oberlink, M.R. (2006). *Creating livable communities.* Report of the National Council on Disability, Washington, DC.

O'Connor, M.C. (1996). Managing the intermental: Classroom group discussion and the social context of learning. In D.I. Slobin, J. Gerhardt, A. Kyratzis, & J. Guo (Eds.), *Social interaction, social context, and language: Essays in honor of Susan Ervin-Tripp* (pp. 495–512). Mahwah, NJ: Lawrence Erlbaum Associates.

Odom, S.L., Zercher, C., Li, S., Marquart, J.M., Sandall, S., & Brown, W.H. (2006). Social acceptance and rejection of preschool children with disabilities: A mixed method analysis. *Journal of Educational Psychology, 98,* 807–823.

Olson, C.B., & Land, R. (2007). A cognitive strategies approach to reading and writing instruction for English language learners in secondary school. *Research in the Teaching of English, 41,* 269–303.

Olson, H.C., Jirikowic, T., Kartin, D., & Astley, S. (2007). Responding to the challenge of early intervention for fetal alcohol spectrum disorders. *Infants and Young Children, 20,* 172–189.

Olweus, D. (2003, March). A profile of bullying. *Educational Leadership,* 2–17.

Ontario Ministry of Education (1994). *Violence-free schools policy.* Toronto: Ontario Ministry of Education. [http://www.edu.gov.on.ca/eng/document/policy/vfreeng.html]. (November 15, 2008).

Ontario Ministry of Education (1999). *Choices into action.* Toronto: Ontario Ministry of Education.

Ontario Ministry of Education (2000a). *Individual education plans: Standards for development, program planning, and implementation.* Toronto: Ontario Ministry of Education. [http://www.edu.gov.on.ca/eng/general/elemsec/speced/iep/iep.html]. (November 15, 2008).

Ontario Ministry of Education (2000b). *Standards for school boards' special education plans.* Toronto: Ontario Ministry of Education. [http://www.edu.gov.on.ca/eng/general/elemsec/speced/iepstand/iepstand.html]. (November 15, 2008).

Ontario Ministry of Education (2001). *Special education: A guide for educators.* Toronto: Ontario Ministry of Education. [http://www.edu.gov.on.ca/eng/general/elemsec/speced/guide/specedhandbooke.pdf]. (November 15, 2008).

Ontario Ministry of Education (2004). *The individual education plan (IEP): A resource guide.* Toronto: Ontario Ministry of Education. [http://www.edu.gov.on.ca/eng/general/elemsec/speced/guide/resource/iepresguid.pdf] (February 28, 2008).

Ontario Ministry of Education. (2005). *Education for All (The report of the expert panel on literacy and numeracy instruction for students with special education needs, kindergarten to grade 6).* Toronto: Queen's Printer for Ontario.

Ontario Ministry of Education, 2006. *Finding Common Ground: Character Development in Ontario Schools, K–12.* [http://www.curriculum.org/secretariat/december11.shtml]. (November 15, 2008).

Ontario Ministry of Education. (2007). *First Nations, Métis, and Inuit education policy framework.* Toronto: Ontario Ministry of Education.

Ontario Ministry of Education, Regulation 181/98. [http://www.edu.gov.on.ca/eng/general/elemsec/speced/hilites.html]. (November 15, 2008).

Ontario Public Health and Epidemiology Report (2000). Volume 11(5). [http://www.health.gov.on.ca/english/providers/pub/phero/phero_052600.html]. (November 15, 2008).

Oravec, J. (2002). Virtually accessible: Empowering students to advocate for accessibility and support universal design. *Library Hi Tech, 20,* 452–461.

Ostad, S.A., & Sorensen, P.M. (2007). Private speech and strategy-use patterns. *Journal of Learning Disabilities, 40,* 2–14.

Osterman, K.F. (2000). Students' need for belonging in the school community. *Review of Educational Research, 70*(3), 323–367.

Owen, R.L., & Fuchs, L.S. (2002). Mathematical problem-solving strategy instruction for third-grade students with learning disabilities. *Remedial and Special Education, 23,* 268–278.

Padden, C., & Humphries, T. (2005). *Inside deaf culture.* Cambridge, MA: Harvard University Press.

Palfrey, J.S., Tonniges, T.F., Green, M., & Richmond, J. (2006). Introduction: Addressing the millennial morbidity, the context of community pediatrics. *Pediatrics, 115,* 1121–1123.

Palincsar, A.S., & Brown, A. (1984). Reciprocal teaching of comprehension-fostering and comprehension-monitoring activities. *Cognition and Instruction, 1,* 117–175.

Palincsar, A.S., & Herenkohl, L.R. (2002). Designing collaborative learning contexts. *Theory into Practice, 41*, 26–32.

Palincsar, A.S., Magnusson, S.J., Collins, K.M., & Cutter, J. (2001). Making science accessible to all: Results of a design experiment in inclusive classrooms. *Learning Disability Quarterly, 24*(1), 15–32.

Palmen, A., Didden, R., & Arts, M. (2008). Improving question asking in high-functioning adolescents with autism spectrum disorders: Effectiveness of small-group training. *Autism, 12*, 83–98.

Palmer, H. (1997). *. . . . But where are you really from? Stories of identity and assimilation in Canada*. Toronto: Sister Vision.

Panitch, M. (2008). *Disability, mothers, and organization: Accidental activists*. New York, NY: Routledge.

Parrila, R., Kirby, J.R., & McQuarrie, L. (2004). Articulation rate, naming speed, verbal short-term memory, and phonological awareness: Longitudinal predictors of early reading development. *Scientific Studies of Reading, 8*(1), 3–26.

Paro, K.M., Pianta, R.C., & Cox, M.J. (2000). Teachers' reported transition practices for children transitioning into kindergarten and first grade. *Exceptional Children, 67*, 7–20.

Parr, J., & Ward, L. (2006). Building on foundations: Creating an online community. *Journal of Technology and Teacher Education, 14*, 775–793.

Paterson, D. (2007). Teachers' in-flight thinking in inclusive classrooms. *Journal of Learning Disabilities, 40*(5), 427–435.

Paterson, K.M. (2006). *Differentiated learning: Language and literacy projects that address diverse classrooms*. Markham, ON: Pembroke Pub. Ltd.

Patterson, D. (1996). Becoming a change agent in your elementary classroom. In J. Andrews (Ed.), *Teaching students with diverse needs: Elementary classrooms* (pp. 14–37). Scarborough: Nelson Canada.

Pearson, P.D. (1998). Reclaiming the center. In M.F. Graves, P. van den Broek, & B.M. Taylor (Eds.), *The first r: Every child's right to read*. New York: Teachers College Press.

Peavy, V. (1993). Constructivist career counseling. [http://www.ericdigests.org/1997-3/counseling.html]. (November 15, 2008).

Peavy, V. (1994). *Counselling of First Nations students*. Vancouver: Ministry of Education.

Pedersen, K.S., & Kitano, M.K. (2006). Designing a multicultural literature unit for gifted learners. *Gifted Child Today, 29*(2), 38–49.

Peel Board of Education (1990). *Looking at assessment, more than marks: Adapting tests and assignments for exceptional students* (Book 4). Mississauga: Peel Board of Education.

Pepler, D., Jiang, D., Craig, W., & Connolly, J. (2008). Developmental trajectories of bullying and associated factors. *Child Development, 79*(2), 325–338.

Perner, D.E. (2007). No Child Left Behind: Issues of assessing students with the most significant cognitive disabilities. *Education and Training in Developmental Disabilities, 42*, 243–251.

Peterson, L.D., Young, K.R., Salzberg, C.L., West, R.P., & Hill, M. (2006). Using self-management procedures to improve classroom social skills in multiple general education settings. *Education and Treatment of Children, 29*, 1–21.

Peterson, J.S. (1993). *Talk with teens about self and stress: 50 guided discussions for school and counseling groups*. Minneapolis, MN: Free Spirit.

Peterson-Badali, M., Morine, M., Ruck, M.D., & Slonin, N. (2004). Predictors of maternal and early adolescent attitudes towards children's nurturance and self-determination rights. *The Journal of Early Adolescence, 24*, 159–179.

Pewewardy, C., & Hammer, P.C. (2003). Culturally responsive teaching for American Indian students. *ERIC Digest*. (ERIC Document Reproduction Service No. ED 482325).

Phelps, L.A.C. (2003). High schools and authentic and inclusive learning practices; Selected features and findings. *Research to Practice Brief*. (ERIC Document Reproduction Service No. ED 481547).

Philpott, D. (2007) Assessing without labels: Inclusive education in the Canadian context. *Exceptionality Education Canada. 17*(3), 3–34.

Philpott, D.F., & Cahill, M. (2008). *A pan-Canadian perspective on the professional knowledge base of learning disabilities*. Unpublished paper, Memorial University of Newfoundland, St. Johns's NF.

Philpott, D.F., & Dibbon, D. (2007). A review of the literature on Newfoundland and Labrador's model of Student Support Services: A global perspective on local practice. (Appendix G, Literature review). In *Focusing on students: A report of the ISSP & Pathways Commission* (pp. 177–219). St. John's: ISSP & Pathways Commission.

Pierangelo, R., & Giuliani, G.A. (2007a). *Special education eligibility: A step-by-step guide for educators*. Thousand Oaks, CA: Corwin Press.

Pierangelano, R., & Giuliani, G. (2007b). *Understanding, developing, and writing effective IEPs: A step-by-step guide for educators*. Thousand Oaks, CA: Corwin Press.

Piggott, A. (2002). Putting differentiation into practice in secondary science lessons. *School Science Review, 83* (305), 65–71.

Pletsch, V.C. (1997). *Not wanted in the classroom*. London, ON: Althouse Press.

Pohl, A. (1997, April). Teaching Native studies. *OPSTF News*.

Polloway, E.A., Bursuck, W.D., & Epstein, M.H. (2001). Homework for students with learning disabilities: The challenge of home-school communication. *Reading & Writing Quarterly, 17*, 181–187.

Pompeo, M. (2004). *When your "problem" becomes mine: Siblings' perspectives on having a brother or sister with disabilities*. Unpublished master's thesis York University, North York, ON.

Porter, G. (2007). Making Canadian schools inclusive: A call to action. *Education Canada, 47*(1), 62–66.

Powers, L.E., Sowers, J., Turner, A., Nesbitt, M., Knowles, A., & Ellison, R. (1996). *Take charge*. Portland, OR: Oregon Health Sciences University.

Preiss, R.W., & Gayle, B.M. (2006). A meta-analysis of the educational benefits of employing advanced organizers. In B.M. Gayle, M. Allen, M., R.W. Preiss, & N. Burrell, *Classroom communication and instructional processes: Advances through meta-analysis*. Mahwah, NJ: Lawrence Erlbaum.

Premji, S., Benzies, K., Serrett, K., & Hayden, K.A. (2006). Research-based interventions for children and youth with fetal alcohol spectrum disorder: Revealing the gap. *Child: Care, Health and Development, 33*, 389–397.

Pressley, M. (2002). *Reading instruction that works: The case for balanced teaching* (2nd ed.). New York: Guilford.

Pressley, M., Roehrig, A., Bogner, K., Raphael, L.M., & Dolezal, S. (2002). Balanced literacy instruction. *Focus on Exceptional Children, 34*, 1–14.

Prevatt, F.F., Heffer, R.W., & Lowe, P.A. (2000). A review of school reintegration programs for children with cancer. *Journal of School Psychology, 38*, 447–467.

Prince Edward Island Department of Education (2001). *Minister's directive No. MD01-08, 2001: Special education*. Charlottetown: Prince Edward Island Department of Education. [http://www.gov.pe.ca/educ/index.php3?number=79894&lang=E]. (November 15, 2008).

Prince Edward Island Department of Education. (2003). *School administrators education handbook*. Charlottetown, PEI: Prince Edward Island Department of Education.

Prince Edward Island Department of Education. (2005a). *Individualized educational planning (IEP)*. [http://www.gov.pe.ca/photos/original/ed_ieplanning.pdf] (November 15, 2008).

Prince Edward Island Department of Education. (2005b). *Teachers and support staff working together.* [http://www.gov.pe.ca/photos/original/ed_tssworktog.pdf] (November 15, 2008).

Prior, J., & Gerard, M. (2004). *Environmental print in the classroom: Meaningful connections for learning to read.* Newark, DE: International Reading Association.

Punch, R., Hyde, M., & Creed, P.A. (2004). Issues in the school-to-work transition of hard of hearing adolescents. *American Annals of the Deaf, 149,* 28–38.

Punch, R., Creed, P., & Hyde, M. (2005). Predicting career development in hard-of-hearing adolescents in Australia. *Journal of Deaf Studies and Deaf Education, 10*(2), 146–160.

Purcell, J.H., & Leppien, J.H. (2004). Building bridges between general practitioners and educators of the gifted: A study of collaboration. In C.A. Tomlinson & S.M. Reis (Eds.) *Differentiation for gifted and talented students* (pp. 117–132). Thousand Oaks, CA: Cowin Press.

Purdie, N., Hattie, J., Carroll, A. (2002). A review of the research on interventions for attention deficit hyperactivity disorder: What works best. *Review of Educational Research, 72*(1), 61–99.

Pyryt, M.C. (1992). *Career development for the gifted and talented.* Proceedings of the SAGE, 6th Canadian Symposium.

Pyryt, M.C. (2000). Finding "g": Easy viewing through higher order factor analysis. *Gifted Child Quarterly, 44,* 190–192.

Pyryt, M.C. (2007). The giftedness/perfectionism connection: Recent research and implications. *Gifted Educational International, 23*(3), 273–279.

Pyryt, M.C., & Romney, D.M. (2002). Social giftedness: Evolution of the concept and its application for life. *Gifted Education International, 16,* 127–132.

Pyryt, M.C., Sandals, L.H., & Begoray, J. (1998). Learning style preferences of gifted, average-ability, and special needs students: A multivariate perspective. *Journal of Research in Childhood Education, 17*(1), 71–76.

Quick, P.M., & Normore, A.H. (2004). Moreal leadership in the 21st century: Everyone is watching, especially the students. *Educational Forum, 68,* 336–347.

Rabby, R., & Croft, D.L. (1989). *Take charge: A strategic guide for blind job seekers.* Boston: National Braille Press Inc.

Rafferty, Y. (1998, January). Meeting the educational needs of homeless children. *Educational Leadership,* 48–52.

Rakow, S. (2007). All means all: Classrooms that work for advanced learners. *Middle Ground, 11*(1), 10–12.

Ramsay, J. (2007). *A case study of an effective working relationship involving an educational assistant and an educator.* Unpublished master's thesis, Queen's University at Kingston, ON.

Randolph, J.J. (2007). Meta-analysis of the research on response cards: Effects on test achievement, quiz achievement, and off-task behavior. *Journal of Positive Behavior Interventions, 9,* 113–128.

Raver, C.C., Jones, S.M., Li-Grining, C.P., Metzger, M., Champon, K.M., & Sardin, L. (2008). Improving preschool classroom processes: Preliminary findings from a randomized trial implemented in head start settings. *Early Childhood Research Quarterly, 23,* 10–26.

Reed, V. (2005). *An introduction to children with language disorders.* Boston: Allyn & Bacon.

Regan, K., & Page, P. (2008). Character building: Using literature to connect with youth. *Reclaiming Children and Youth, 16*(4), 37–43.

Reilly, A. (2003). Families and their children with disabilities. In G. Olsen & M.L. Fuller (Eds.), *Home-school relations: Working successfully with parents and families.* Boston: Allyn & Bacon.

Reinke, W.M., Herman, K.C., & Tucker, C.M. (2006). Building and sustaining communities that prevent mental disorders: Lessons from the field of special education. *Psychology in the Schools, 43,* 313–329.

Reis, S.M., & Renzulli, J.S. (2002). *The secondary triad model: A practical plan for implementing gifted programs at the junior and senior high school levels.* Heatherton, Australia: Hawker Brownlow Education.

Reiss, J. (2008). *102 content strategies for English language learners: Teaching for academic success in grades 3–12.* Upper Saddle River, NJ: Pearson/Merrill Prentice Hall.

Reithaug, D. (1998a). *Orchestrating academic success by adapting and modifying programs.* West Vancouver: Stirling Head Enterprises.

Reithaug, D. (1998b). *Orchestrating positive and practical behaviour plans.* West Vancouver: Stirling Head Enterprises.

Renzulli, J.S. (2005). Applying gifted education pedagogy to total talent development for all students. *Theory Into Practice, 44*(2), 80–89.

Renzulli, J.S. (2008). Teach to the top: How to keep high achievers engaged and motivated. *Instructor, 117*(5), 34–38.

Renzulli, J.S., Gentry, M., & Reis, S. (2003). *Enrichment clusters: A practical plan for real-world, student-driven learning.* Mansfield, CT: Creative Learning Press.

*Report of the Royal Commission on Aboriginal Peoples.* (1996). Ottawa: Government of Canada. [http://www.parl.gc.ca/information/library/PRBpubs/prb9924-e.html]. (November 15, 2008).

Reschly, A.L., Huebner, E.S., Appleton, J.J., & Antaramian, S. (2008). Engagement as flourishing: The contribution of positive emotions and coping to adolescent' engagement at school and with learning. *Psychology in the Schools, 45*(5), 419–431.

Reynolds, C. (2004, December 27). Children of war. *Maclean's, 118*(1).

Rhone, A.E. (2006). Preparing minority students for high-stakes tests: Who are we cheating? *Childhood Education, 82,* 233–237.

Richardson, J. (2005). Steeped in study: Remote Canadian district approaches professional learning with a passion. *Journal of Staff Development, 26*(4), 50–60.

Ridgway, A., Northup, J., Pellegrin, A., LaRue, R., & Hightshoe, A. (2003). Effects of recess on the classroom behavior of children with and without attention-deficit hyperactivity disorder. *School Psychology Quarterly, 18*(3), 253–268.

Riendl, P.A., & Haworth, D.T. (1995). Chemistry and special education. *Journal of Chemical Education, 72,* 983–986.

Riley, M. (1997). Teaching French in a school for children with moderate learning difficulties. *British Journal of Special Education, 24,* 66–70.

Rimm-Kaufman, S.E., La Paro, K.M., Downer, J.T., & Pianta, R.C. (2005). The contribution of classroom setting and quality of instruction to children's behavior in kindergarten classrooms. *The Elementary School Journal, 105,* 377–394.

Roach, A.T., Niebling, B.C., & Kurz, A. (2008). Evaluating the alignment among curriculum, instruction, and assessment: Implications and applications for research and practice. *Psychology in Schools, 45*(2), 158–176.

Robbins, P.R. (2000). *Anger, aggression, and violence: An interdisciplinary study.* Jefferson, NC: McFarland & Co.

Roberts, C.A., & Lazure, M.D. (1970). *One million children: A national study of Canadian children with emotional and learning disorders.* Toronto: Leonard Crainford.

Roberts, G., Torgeson, J.K., Boardman, A., & Scammacca, N. (2008). Evidence-based strategies for reading instruction of older students with learning disabilities. *Learning Disabilities Research and Practice, 23*(2), 63–69.

Roberts, J. (2006). *First Nations, Inuit, and Metis Peoples: Exploring their past, present, and future: Teacher's resource*. Toronto: Edmond Montgomery Publications.

Roberts, J., & Cairns, K. (1999). *School children with HIV/AIDS*. Calgary: Detselig Press.

Roberts, M., White, R., & McLaughlin, T.F. (1997). Useful classroom accommodations for teaching children with ADD and ADHD. *B.C. Journal of Special Education, 21*(2), 71–90.

Robertson, H.J. (2004). In Canada: Litigating literacy. *Phi Delta Kappan, 85*(9), 714–715.

Robinson, C.S., Menchetti, B.M., & Torgesen, J.K. (2002). Toward a two-factor theory of one type of mathematics disabilities. *Learning Disabilities Research & Practice, 17*, 81–89.

Robinson, D.H., Funk, D.C., Beth, A., & Bush, A.M. (2005). Changing beliefs about corporal punishment: Increasing knowledge about ineffectiveness to build more consistent moral and informational beliefs. *Journal of Behavioral Education, 14*, 117–139.

Robinson, N.M. (1996). Counseling agendas for gifted young people: A commentary. *Journal for the Education of the Gifted, 20*(2), 128–137.

Roets, G., Goodley, D., & Van Hove, G. (2007). Narrative in a nutshell: Sharing hopes, fears and dreams with self-advocates. *Intellectual and Developmental Disabilities, 45*(5), 323–334.

Rogers, C. (2007). Experiencing an 'inclusive' education: Parents and their children with special educational needs. *British Journal of Sociology of Education, 28*, 55–68.

Rosenberg, M., & Jackman, L. (2003). Development, implementation, and sustainability of comprehensive school-wide behavior management systems. *Intervention in School and Clinic, 39*(1), 10–21.

Ross, D., Scott, K., & Smith, P.J. (2000). *The Canada fact book on poverty 2000*. Ottawa: Canadian Council on Social Development. [www.ccsd.ca/pubs/2000/fbpov00]. (October 25, 2005).

Rothery, T.G. (2007). Stepping up your game. *Mathematics Teacher, 100*, 526–528.

Rothstein, R. (2008, April). Whose problem is poverty? *Educational Leadership, 65*(7), 8–13.

Rotter, K.M. (2004). Simple techniques to improve teacher-made instructional materials for use by pupils with disabilities. *Preventing School Failure, 48*(2), 38–43.

Rubie-Davies, C.M. (2007). Classroom interactions: Exploring the practices of high- and low-expectation teachers. *British Journal of Educational Psychology, 77*(2), 289–306.

Rubin, D.H., Erickson, C.J., San Agustin, M., Cleary, S.D., Allen, J.K., & Cohen, P. (1996). Cognitive and academic functioning of homeless children compared with housed children. *Pediatrics, 97*, 289–294.

Ruck, M., Keating, D., Abramovitch, R., & Koegl, C. (1998). Adolescents' and children's knowledge about rights: Some evidence for how young people view rights in their own lives. *Journal of Adolescence, 21*, 275–289.

Rucklidge, J.J., & Tannock, R. (2001). Psychiatric, psychosocial, and cognitive functioning of female adolescents with ADHD. *Journal of the American Academy of Child and Adolescent Psychiatry, 40*, 530–540.

Running Wolf, P., & Rickard, J. (2003). Talking circles: A Native American approach to experiential learning. *Journal of Multicultural Counseling and Development, 31*, 39–43.

Rusby, J.C., Forrester, K.K., Biglan, A., & Metzler, C.W. (2005). Relationships between peer harassment and adolescent problem behaviors. *Journal of Early Adolescence, 25*, 453–477.

Russell, F. (2005). Starting school: The importance of parents' expectations. *Journal of Research in Special Educational Needs, 5*, 118–126.

Rustique-Forrester, E. (2005). Accountability and the pressure to exclude: A cautionary tale from England. *Education Policy Analysis Archives, 13*(26). [http://epaa.asu.edu/epaa/v13n26/]. (April 20, 2008).

Ryan, R., & Deci, E. (2000). Self-determination theory and the facilitation of intrinsic motivation, social development, and well-being. *American Psychologist, 55*, 68–78.

Ryder, J.F., Tunmer, W.E., & Greaney, K.T. (2008). Explicit instruction in phonemic awareness and phonetically based decoding skills as an intervention strategy for struggling readers in whole language classrooms. *Reading and Writing: An Interdisciplinary Journal, 21*, 349–369.

Rynders, J.E., & Horrobin, J.M. (1990). Always trainable? Never educable? Updating educational expectations concerning children with Down syndrome. *American Journal on Mental Retardation, 95*, 77–83.

Sabatella, M.L. (2003). Role of programs: Relationships with parents, schools, and communities. In J.F. Smutny (Ed.), *Designing and developing programs for gifted students*. Thousand Oaks, CA: Corwin Press.

Sacks, G., & Kern, L. (2008). A comparison of quality of life variables for students with emotional and behavioral disorders and students without disabilities. *Journal of Behavioral Education, 17*(1), 111–127.

Saewyc, E.M., Skay, C.L., Pettingell, S.L, Reis, E.A., Bearinger, L., Resnick, M., Murphy, A., & Combs, L. (2006). Hazards of stigma: The sexual and physical abuse of gay, lesbian, and bisexual adolescents in the United States and Canada. *Child Welfare, 85*(2), 195–213.

Salend, S.J. (2005). Report card models that support communication and differentiation of instruction. *Teaching Exceptional Children, 37*(4), 28–34.

Salend, S.J., Duhaney, L.M.G., Anderson, D.J., & Gottschalk, C. (2004). Using the internet to improve homework communication and completion. *Teaching Exceptional Children, 36*, 64–73.

Salend, S.J., & Gajria, M. (1995). Increasing the homework completion rates of students with mild disabilities. *Remedial and Special Education, 16*, 271–278.

Salmon, A. (2007). Adaptation and decolonization: Unpacking the role of "culturally appropriate" knowledge in the prevention of fetal alcohol syndrome. *Canadian Journal of Native Education, 30*, 257–274.

Salvia, J. & Ysseldyke, J. (2007). *Assessment in special and inclusive education* (10th ed.). Boston, MA: Houghton Mifflin.

Sandieson, R., (1997). Linking instructional design and developmental capabilities for persons with developmental disabilities: Monetary calculations, evaluations, and transactions. *Exceptionality Education Canada, 7*(3), 32–16.

Sandiford, M. (Director). (2006). *Why white people are funny* [video-recording]. Charlottetown, PEI: Beachwalker Films & National Film Board of Canada (in association with CTV). [Accompanying teacher's resource guide and student worksheets available online: http://www.onf.ca/sg/100494.pdf]

Sands, D.I., Guzman, L., Stephens, L., & Boggs, A. (2007). Including student voices in school reform: Students speak. *Journal of Latinos and Education, 6*, 323–345.

Sankar-DeLeeuw, N. (2007). Case studies of gifted kindergarten children part II: The parents and teachers. *Roeper Review, 29*, 93–99.

Sarason, S.B. (1993). *You are thinking of teaching? Opportunities, problems, realities*. San Francisco: Jossey-Bass.

Saskatchewan Children's Services Branch. (2008, April). *Ministry of Education intensive needs pupil guidelines 2008/2009*. Regina: Saskatchewan Ministry of Education.

Saskatchewan Education (2000a). *Community education*. Regina: Saskatchewan Education.

Saskatchewan Education (2000b). *Directions for diversity: Final report of the Saskatchewan Special Education Review Committee*. Regina: Saskatchewan Education.

Saskatchewan Education (2000c). *Strengthening supports: Minister's response to the report of the Special education Review committee*. Regina: Saskatchewan Education.

Saskatchewan Education. (2004). *Caring and respectful schools: Ensuring student well-being*. Regina: Saskatchewan Education.

Saskatchewan Learning (2001). *Aboriginal elders and community workers in schools: A guide for school divisions and their partners*. Regina, SK: Saskatchewan Education.

Saskatchewan Learning (2004). *Building communities of hope: Effective practices for meeting the diverse learning needs of children and youth*. Regina: Saskatchewan Learning.

Saskatchewan Learning (2005a). *ACCESS 2005–06 (Assistance, Collaboration, Consultation, Evaluation, Support Services)*. Regina: Children's Services and Programs Branch. Regina: Saskatchewan Learning.

Saskatchewan Learning (2005b). *Anti-bullying strategy*. Regina: Saskatchewan Learning.

Saul, J.R. (2001). *On equilibrium*. Toronto: Penguin Group.

Schalock, R.L., Luckasson, R.A., & Shogren, K.A. (2007). The renaming of mental retardation to the term intellectual disability. *Intellectual and Developmental Disabilities, 45*(2), 116–124.

Schirduan, V., & Miller, R. (2002). Why must a child's first encounter with school be filled with worries, misgivings, and fears, and not wonder, magic, and fun? *Journal of Early Education and Family Review, 9*(5), 6–17.

Schlachter, S. (2008). Diagnosis, treatment and educational implications for students with attention-deficit/hyperactivity disorder in the United States, Australia, and the United Kingdom. *Peabody Journal of Education, 83*, 154–169.

Schmid, C., & Hutchinson, N.L. (1994). *The role of the family in programs for preschoolers with special needs: A case of three Canadian families*. Paper presented at annual conference of American Educational Research Association, New Orleans, LA.

Schmidt, M., & Cagran, B. (2006). Classroom climate in regular primary school settings with children with special needs. *Educational Studies, 32*, 361–372.

Schneider, W., Ennemoser, M., Roth, E., & Kuspert, P. (1999). Kindergarten prevention of dyslexia: Does training in phonological awareness work for everybody? *Journal of Learning Disabilities, 32*, 429–436.

Schnell, L.J. (2001). *Teachers and teacher assistants: Exploring the meaning of their working relationships*. Unpublished doctoral dissertation, University of Alberta, Edmonton.

Schroedel, J.G., & Geyer, P.D. (2000). Long-term career attainments of deaf and hard of hearing college graduates: Results from a 15-year follow-up survey. *American Annals of the Deaf, 145*, 303–314.

Schumaker, J.B., & Deshler, D.D. (2003). Can students with LD become competent writers? *Learning Disability Quarterly, 16*, 129–141.

Schwartz, K., Mactavish, J., & Lutfiyya, Z.M. (2006). Making community connections: Educator perspectives on transition planning for students with intellectual disabilities. *Exceptionality Education Canada, 16*(2), 73–100.

Scott, F.B. (2001). *Teaching in a multicultural setting: A Canadian perspective*. Toronto: Prentice Hall.

Scorgie, K., Wilgosh, L., & Sobsey, D. (2004). The experience of transformation in parents of children with disabilities: Theoretical considerations. *Developmental Disabilities Bulletin, 32*(1), 84–110.

Scott, N.H. (2001). *Mentoring new teachers: A report on the 2001 beginning teacher induction program in New Brunswick*. Unpublished report, University of New Brunswick, St. John, NB.

Searcy, S. (1996). Friendship interventions for the integration of children and youth with learning and behavior problems. *Preventing School Failure, 40*(3), 131–134.

Segers, M., Gijbels, D., & Thurlings, M. (2008). The relationship between students' perceptions of portfolio assessment practice and their approaches to learning. *Educational Studies, 34*(1), 35–44.

Seidel, J.F., & Vaughn, S. (1991). Social alienation and the learning disabled school dropout. *Learning Disabilities Research and Practice, 6*, 152–157.

Sencibaugh, J.M. (2007). Meta-analysis of reading comprehension interventions for students with learning disabilities: Strategies and implications. *Reading Improvement, 44*(1), 6–22.

Shankweiler, D., & Fowler, A.E. (2004). Questions people ask about the role of phonological processes in learning to read. *Reading and Writing: An Interdisciplinary Journal, 17*(5), 483–515.

Shaw, S.R., & McCabe, P.C. (2008). Hospital-to-school transition for children with chronic illness: Meeting the new challenges of an evolving health care system. *Psychology in the Schools, 45*, 74–87.

Shaywitz, S.E., Morris, & R. Shaywitz, B.A. (2008). The education of dyslexic children from childhood to young adulthood. *Annual Review of Psychology, 59*, 451–475.

Sheetz, A.H., et al. (2004). Guidelines for managing life-threatening food allergies in Massachusetts schools. *Journal of School Health, 74*(5), 155–160.

Shogren, K.A., Wehmeyer, M.L., Palmer, S.B., Soukup, J.H., Little, T.D., Garner, N., & Lawrence, M. (2007). Examining individual and ecological predictors of the self-determination of students with disabilities. *Exceptional Children, 73*, 488–509.

Shore, B.M. (2000). Metacognition and flexibility: Qualitative differences in how children think. In R.C. Friedman & B.M. Shore (Eds.), *Talents unfolding: Cognition and development*. Washington, DC: American Psychological Association.

Shriberg, L.D., Tomblin, J.B., & McSweeney, J.L. (1999). Prevalence of speech delay in 6-year-old children and comorbidity with language impairment. *Journal of Speech, Language, and Hearing Research, 42*, 1461–1481.

Shriner, J.G., & Destefano, L. (2003). Participation and accommodation in state assessment: The role of individualized education programs. *Exceptional Children, 69*(2), 147–162.

Siegel, L.S. (1999). Issues in the definition and diagnosis of learning disabilities. *Journal of Learning Disabilities, 32*, 304–319.

Siegle, D. (2002). Creating a living portfolio: Documenting student growth with electronic portfolios. *Gifted Child Today Magazine, 25*(3), 60–65.

Siegle, D. (2005). Six uses of the internet to develop students' gifts and talents. *Gifted Child Today, 28*(2), 30–36.

Silliman, E.R., & Wilkinson, L.C. (Eds.) (2004). *Language and literacy learning in schools*. New York: Guilford Press.

Silva, M., Munk, D.D., & Bursuck, W.D. (2005). Grading adaptations for students with disabilities. *Intervention in School & Clinic, 41*(2), 87–98.

Simmons, B. (2002). Facilitative conferences: Parents and teachers working together. *Clearing House, 76*, 88–93.

Simmons, D.C., Dickson, S.V., & Chard, D. (1993). *Integrating narrative reading comprehension and writing instruction for all learners*. Paper presented at the annual meeting of the National Reading Conference, Charleston, SC.

Simpson, D. (2001). The impact of breakfast clubs on pupil attendance and punctuality. *Research in Education, 66*, 76–83.

Skyler, A.A., Higgins, K., & Boone, R. (2207). Strategies for adapting webquests for students with learning disabilities. *Intervention in School and Clinic, 43*(1), 20–28.

Slater, W.H., & Horstman, F.R. (2002). Teaching reading and writing to struggling middle school and high school students: The case for reciprocal teaching. *Preventing School Failure, 46*, 163–166.

Slavin, R.E. (1990). Research on cooperative learning: Consensus and controversy. *Educational Leadership, 47*(4), 52–54.

Slee, R. (1998). The politics of theorizing special education. In C. Clark, A. Dyson & A. Milward (Eds.), *Theorising special education*. London: Routledge.

Sloane, M.W. (2007). First grade study groups deepen math learning. *Young Children, 62*(4), 83–89.

Smith, C.R. (2004). Advocating for our students in the current sociopolitical climate: One perspective on the challenges we face. In L.M. Bullock, R.A. Gable, & K.J. Melloy (Eds.), *Effective Interventions for classrooms, schools, and communities* (pp. 1–9). Tampa, FL: Council for Children with Behavioral Disorders.

Smith, J. (2006). Every child a singer: Techniques for assisting developing singers: All children can sing if you take the time to teach them. *Music Educators Journal, 93*(2), 28.

Smith, P. (2007). Have we made any progress? Including students with intellectual disabilities in regular education classrooms. *Intellectual and Developmental Disabilities, 45*(5), 297–309.

Smith, P.K., Smith, C., Osborn, R., & Samara, M. (2008). A content analysis of school anti-bullying policies: Progress and limitations. *Educational Psychology in Practice, 24*, 1–12.

Smith, T.E.C., Polloway, E.A., Patton, J.R., & Dowdy, C.A. (1995). *Teaching students with special needs in inclusive settings*. Needham Heights, MA: Allyn & Bacon.

Smith, W.J., & Foster, W.F. (1993). Educational opportunity for students with disabilities in Canada: A platform of rights to build on. *Education and Law Journal, 5*, 193–223.

Smith, W.J., & Lusthaus, C. (1994). Students with disabilities in Canada: What rights do they have? *Education Canada, 34*(3), 4–9.

Snair, S. (2008). Are your students critically reading an opinion piece? Have them RATTKISS it! *English Journal, 97*(3), 52–55.

Snow, C., & Juel, C. (2005). Teaching children to read: What do we know about how to do it? In M.J. Snowling & C. Hume (Eds.), *The science of reading* (pp. 501–519). Malden, MA: Blackwell Pub (InterWiley).

Solomon, R.P. (1992). *Black resistance in high school: A separatist culture*. Albany: State University of New York Press.

Solomon, R.P. (1996). Creating an opportunity structure for Blacks and other teachers of colour. In K.S. Brethwaite & C.E. James (Eds.), *Educating African Canadians* (pp. 216–233). Toronto: James Lorimer & Co.

Solomon, R.P., & Levine-Rasky, C. (2003). *Teaching for equity and diversity: Research to practice*. Toronto: Canadian Scholars' Press.

Somers, C.L., Owens, D., & Piliawsky, M. (2008). Individual and social factors related to urban African American adolescents' school performance. *High School Journal, 91*(3), 1–11.

Song, Y., Heo, M., Krumenaker, L., Tippins, D., et al. (2008). Cartoons, an alternative learning assessment. *Science Scope, 31*(5), 16–21.

Sonnier-York, C., & Stanford, P. (2002). Learning to cooperate: A teacher's perspective. *Teaching Exceptional Children, 34*(6), 40–44.

Sparrow, L., & Swan, P. (2001). *Learning math with calculators: Activities for grades 3–8*. Sausalito, CA: Math Solutions Publications.

Specht, J., Howell, G., & Young, G. (2007). Students with special education needs in Canada and their use of assistive technology during the transition to secondary school. *Childhood Education, 83*, 385–396.

Spencer, B.L. (2004). *Another look at "accountability": Towards a conceptual framework for education policy research*. University of Alberta unpublished manuscript.

Special Education Technology British Columbia. *Students with visual impairment*. [http://www.setbc.org/default.html]. (November 15, 2008).

Stairs, A. (1991). Learning processes and teaching roles in Native education: Cultural base and cultural brokerage. *Canadian Modern Language Review, 47*, 280–294.

Stanovich, K.E. (1994). Constructivism in reading education. *Journal of Special Education, 28*, 259–274.

Stanovich, K.E. (1996). Toward a more inclusive definition of dyslexia. *Dyslexia, 2*, 154–166.

Stanovich, K.E. (2000). *Progress in understanding reading: Scientific foundations and new frontiers*. New York: Guilford Publications.

Stanovich, K.E. (2005). The future of a mistake: Will discrepancy measurement continue to make the learning disabilities field a pseudoscience? *Learning Disability Quarterly, 28*(2), 103-1-5.

Stanovich, K.E., & Stanovich, P.J. (1995). How research might inform the debate about early reading acquisition. *Journal of Research in Reading, 18*, 87–105.

Stanovich, P.J. (1999). Conversations about inclusion. *Teaching Exceptional Children, 31*(6), 54–58.

Stanovich, P.J., & Jordan, A. (1998). Canadian teachers' and principals' beliefs about inclusive education as predictors of effective teaching in heterogeneous classrooms. *Elementary School Journal, 98*, 221–238.

Stanovich, P., & Jordan, A. (2004). Inclusion as professional development. *Exceptionality Education Canada, 14*(2&3), 169–188.

Statham, L. (2008). *Counting them in: Isolated bilingual learners in school*. Hernden, VA: Stylus Pub. (Trentham Books).

Statistics Canada (2006) Census trends [http://www12.statcan.ca/english/census06/data/trends/index.cfm]. (November 15, 2008).

Statistics Canada (2007a). [http://www12.statcan.ca/english/census06/data/highlights/Immigration/index.cfm?Lang=E]. (November 15, 2008).

Statistics Canada (2007b). [http://www12.statcan.ca/english/census06/data/profiles/aboriginal/Index.cfm?Lang=E]. (November 15, 2008).

Statistics Canada (2007c). [http://www12.statcan.ca/english/census06/data/highlights/Language/index.cfm?Lang=E]. (November 15, 2008).

Steckler, P.M., Lembke, E.S., & Foegen, A. (2008). Using progress-monitoring data to improve instructional decision making. *Preventing School Failure, 52*(2), 48–58.

Steele, M.M. (2008). Helping students with learning disabilities succeed. *Science Teacher, 75*(3), 38–42.

Steer, M. (1998). Family-focused developmental planning for students with multiple disabilities including deafness and hearing impairment. *CAEDHH Journal, 25*, 97–107.

Steiner Bell, K. (1998). *Teaching emotion and belief as adapted curriculum for children with autism: A first step in addressing mind-blindness*. Unpublished master's thesis, Queen's University, Kingston, ON.

Steiner Bell, K. (2005). *Social understanding in the friendships of persons with a developmental syndrome*. Unpublished doctoral dissertation, Queen's University, Kingston, Ontario, Canada.

Stenhoff, D.M., & Lignugaris/Kraft, B. (2007). A review of the effects of peer tutoring on students with mild disabilities in secondary settings. *Exceptional Children, 74*, 8–30.

Sterling, S. (2002). Yetko and Sophie: Niakapamux cultural professors. *Canadian Journal of Native Education, 26*, 4–10.

Stevens, K. (2006). *The development of virtual educational environments to support inter-school collaboration*. Paper presented at the International Open and Distance Learning Conference, Eskisehir, Turkey.

Stewart, J. (1999). Career counselling for the academically gifted student. *Canadian Journal of Career Counselling, 33,* 3–12.

Stichter, J.P., Randolph, J., Gage, N., & Schmidt, C. (2007). A review of recommended social competency programs for students with autism spectrum disorders. *Exceptionality, 15,* 219–232.

Stoch, S.A. (2000). *Zak: An adolescent with learning disabilities at home, at camp, and at school.* Unpublished master's thesis, Queen's University, Kingston, ON.

Stojanovik, V., & Riddell, P. (2008). Expressive versus receptive language skills in specific reading disorder. *Clinical Linguistics and Phonetics, 22*(4–5), 305–310.

Stones, R. (2005). *Don't pick on me: How to handle bullying* (3rd ed.). Markham, ON: Pembroke Publishers.

Stott, K.A., & Jackson, A.P. (2005). Using service learning to achieve middle school comprehensive guidance program goals. *Professional School Counseling, 9*(2), 156–159.

Stough, L.M., & Palmer, D.J. (2003). Special thinking in special settings: A qualitative study of expert special educators. *The Journal of Special Education, 38,* 174–186.

Streissguth, A. (1997). *Fetal alcohol syndrome: A guide for families and communities.* Toronto: Brookes.

Strickland, C.A. (2007). *Tools for high quality differentiated instruction.* Alexandria, VA: Association for Supervision and Curriculum Development.

Strike, K.A. (2008). Small schools: Size or community? *American Journal of Education, 114*(3), 169–190.

Stringer, R.W., Toplak, M.E., & Stanovich, K.E. (2004). Differential relationships between RAN performance, behavior ratings, and executive function measures: Searching for a double dissociation. *Reading and Writing: An Interdisciplinary Journal, 17*(9), 891–914.

Stronge, J.H., & Reed-Victor, E. (Eds.). (2000). *Educating homeless students: Promising practices.* New York: Eye on Education.

Strough, J., & Cheng, S. (2000). Dyad, gender, and friendship differences in shared goals for mutual participation on a collaborative task. *Child Study Journal, 30,* 103–126.

Stuart, C.H., & Smith, S.W. (2002). Transition planning for students with severe disabilities: Policy implications for the classroom. *Intervention in School and Clinic 37*(4), 234–236.

Sturm, J.M., & Rankin-Erickson, J.L. (2002). Effects of hand-drawn and computer-generated concept mapping on the expository writing of middle school students with learning disabilities. *Learning Disabilities Research and Practice, 17,* 124–139.

Sugai, G., & Horner, R.H. (2002). The evolution of discipline practices: Schoolwide positive behavior supports. *Child and Family Behavior Therapy, 24,* 23–50.

Sugai, G., & Horner, R.H. (2008). What we know and need to know about preventing problem behavior in schools. *Exceptionality, 16*(2), 67–77.

Sugai, G., Horner, R.H., & Gresham, F.M. (2002). Behaviorally effective school environments. In M.R. Shinn, H.M. Walker, & G. Stoner (Eds.), *Interventions for academic and behavior problems II: Preventive and remedial approaches* (pp. 315–350). Bethesda, MD: National Association of School Psychologists.

Sullivan, N.A. (2004). *Walking with a shadow: Surviving childhood leukemia.* Portsmouth, NH: Praeger Publishers.

Sullivan, N.A., Fulmer, D.L., & Zigmond, N. (2001). School: The normalizing factor for children with childhood leukemia. *Preventing School Failure, 46*(1), 4–13.

Sundmark, J. (2003). *Voices from the field: The practice of educational assistants working with students with severe behaviour disorders.* Unpublished doctoral dissertation, University of Alberta, Edmonton.

Super, D.E. (1957). *The psychology of careers: An introduction to vocational development.* New York: Harper & Row.

Super, D.E., Savickas, M.L., & Super, C.M. (1996). The life-span, life-space approach to careers. In D. Brown, L. Brooks, & Associates (Eds.) *Career choice and development* (3rd ed., pp. 121–178). San Francisco: Jossey-Bass.

Swain, M., Brooks, L., & Tocalli-Beller, A. (2002). Peer-peer dialogue as a means of second language learning. *Annual Review of Applied Linguistics, 22,* 171–185.

Swanson, H.L., & Deshler, D. (2003). Instructing adolescents with learning disabilities: Converting a meta-analysis to practice. *Journal of Learning Disabilities, 36,* 124–135.

Sweeney, D.P., Forness, S.R., Kavale, K.A., & Levitt, J.G. (1997). An update on psychopharmacologic medication: What teachers, clinicians, and parents need to know. *Intervention in School and Clinic, 33*(1), 4–21, 25.

Swiatek, M.A. (2007). Gifted students' self-perceptions of ability in specific subject domains: Factor structure and relationship with above-level test scores. *Roeper Review, 27*(2), 104–109.

Szatmari, P., Bartolucci, G., Bremner, R.S., Bond, S., & Rich, S. (1989). A follow-up study of high-functioning autistic children. *Journal of Autism and Developmental Disorders, 19,* 213–226.

Talbot, R.P. (2002). Carpe diem: Andy's story. *Reclaiming Children and Youth, 11*(1), 47–51.

Tam, K.Y., Nassivera, J.W., Rousseau, M.K., & Vreeland, P. (2000). More than just a field trip: Using the museum as a resource for inclusive secondary science classrooms. *Teaching Exceptional Children, 33*(1), 70–78.

Tannock, R. (2007). The educational implications of attention deficit hyperactivity disorder. *What works? Research into practice* (Research Monograph No. 3). Toronto: Literacy and Numeracy Secretariat & the Ontario Association of Deans of Education. [http://www.edu.gov.on.ca/eng/literacynumeracy/inspire/research/whatWorks.html]. (November 15, 2008).

Tannock, R. (1998). Attention deficit hyperactivity disorder: Advances in cognitive, neurobiological, and genetic research. *Journal of Child Psychology and Psychiatry, 39,* 65–99.

Tannock, R., & Martinussen, R. (2001, November). Reconceptualizing ADHD. *Educational Leadership,* 20–25.

Taylor, J.A. (2008). *Social competence and collaborative guided inquiry science activities: Experiences of students with learning disabilities.* Unpublished doctoral thesis, Queen's University, Kingston, ON.

Test, D., Fowler, C., Wood, W., Brewer, D., & Eddy, S. (2005). A conceptual framework of self-advocacy for students with disabilities. *Remedial and Special Education, 26,* 43–54.

Terepoci, M., Kruk, R.S., & Willows, D.M. (2002). The incidence and nature of letter orientation errors in reading disability. *Journal of Learning Disabilities, 35,* 214–233.

Terpstra, J.E., & Tamura, R. (2008). Effective social interaction strategies for inclusive settings. *Early Childhood Education Journal, 35,* 405–411.

Test, D.W., Fowler, C.H., Brewer, D.M., & Wood, W.M. (2005). A content and methodological review of self-advocacy intervention studies. *Exceptional Children, 72*(1), 101–114.

Thapar, A., Langley, K., Owen, M.J., & O'Donovan, M.C. (2007). Advances in genetic findings on attention deficit hyperactivity disorder. *Psychological Medicine, 37,* 1681–1692.

Theisen, T. (2002). Differentiated instruction in the foreign language classroom: Meeting the diverse needs of all learners. *Communiqué LOTE CED* Issue 6 [http://www.sedl.org/loteced/communique/n06.html]. (November 15, 2008).

Thiessen, D., Bascia, N., & Goodson, I. (Eds.) (1996). *Making a difference about difference: The lives and careers of racial minority immigrant teachers*. Toronto: Garamond Press.

Thornberg, R. (2006). Hushing as a moral dilemma in the classroom. *Journal of Moral Education, 35*, 89–104.

Thurlow, M.L., Elliott, J.L., & Ysseldyke, J.E. (2003). *Testing students with disabilities: Practical strategies for complying with district and state requirements* (2nd ed.). Thousand Oaks, CA: Corwin Press.

Thurlow, M.L., & Thompson, S.J. (2003). Inclusion of students with disabilities in state and district assessments. (ERIC Document Reproduction Service No. ED480047)

Tobias, J. (2003). Information technology and universal design: An agenda for accessible technology. *Journal of Visual Impairment & Blindness, 97*, 592–601.

Tobin, R., & McInnes, A. (2008). Accommodating differences: Variations in differentiated literacy instruction in grade 2/3 classrooms. *Literacy, 42*, 3–9.

Tomlinson, C.A. (1999). *The differentiated classroom: Responding to the needs of all learners*. Alexandria, VA: Association for Supervision and Curriculum Development.

Tomlinson, C.A. (2003). *Fulfilling the promise of the differentiated classroom: Strategies and tools for responsive teaching*. Alexandria, VA: Association for Supervision and Curriculum Development.

Tomlinson, C.A., & Cunningham Eidson, C. (2003). *Differentiation in practice: A resource guide for differentiating curriculum, grades K-5*. Alexandria, VA: Association for Supervision and Curriculum Development.

Tomlinson, C.A., & Strickland, C.A. (2005). *Differentiation in practice: A resource guide for differentiating curriculum, grades 9–12*. Alexandria, VA: Association for Supervision and Curriculum Development.

Topping, K.J. (2005). Trends in peer learning. *Educational Psychology, 25*, 631–645.

Touchette, N. (2000). Kids and Type 2: Type 2 diabetes, the kind that only adults used to get, is on the rise among America's youth. *Diabetes Forecast, 53*(11), 79.

Tough, S., Clarke, M., & Cook, J. (2007). Fetal alcohol spectrum disorder prevention approaches among Canadian physicians by proportion of Native/Aboriginal patients: Practices during the preconception and prenatal periods. *Maternal and Child Health, 11*, 385–393.

Trautwein, U. (2007). The homework-achievement relation reconsidered: Differentiating homework time, homework frequency, and homework effort. *Learning and Instruction, 17*, 372–388.

Trent, S.C., Artiles, A.J., & Englert, C.S. (1998). From deficit thinking to social constructivism: A review of theory, research, and practice in special education. *Review of Research in Education, 23*, 277–307.

Triplett, C.F., & Hunter, A. (2005). Talking circle: Creating community in our elementary classrooms. *Social Studies and the Young Learner, 18*(2), 4–8.

Tsuji, L.J.S. (2000). Modified school years: An important issue of local control of education. *Canadian Journal of Native Education, 24*, 158–168.

Tungland, M. (2002). *Unlocking potential: Key components of programming for students with learning disabilities*. Edmonton: Alberta Learning.

Turnbull, A.P., Pereira, L., & Blue-Banning, M. (2000). Teachers as friendship facilitators. *Teaching Exceptional Children, 32*(5), 66–70.

Turnbull, R., Turnbull, A., Shank, M., Smith, S., & Leal, D. (2002). *Exceptional lives: Special education in today's schools* (3rd ed.). Columbus, OH: Merrill, Prentice-Hall.

Turley, S., Powers, K., & Nakai, K. (2006). Beginning teachers' confidence before and after induction. *Action in Teacher Education, 28*, 27–39.

Tyler, K.A., Johnson, K.A., & Brownridge, D.A. (2008). A longitudinal study of child maltreatment on later outcomes among high-risk adolescents. *Journal of Youth and Adolescence, 37*(5), 506–521.

Udvari–Solner, A., & Kluth, P. (2007). *Joyful learning: Active and collaborative learning in inclusive classrooms*. Thousand Oaks, CA: Corwin Press.

Underwood, M., & Buhrmester, D. (2007). Friendship features and social exclusion: An observational study examining gender and social context. *Merrill-Palmer Quarterly, 53*, 412–438.

Ungar, M. (2000). Drifting toward mental health: High-risk adolescents and the process of empowerment. *Youth & society, 32*(2), 228–252.

Ungar, M. (2004). A constructionist discourse on resilience: Multiple contexts, multiple realities among at-risk children and youth. *Youth and Society, 35*(3), 341–365.

Unger, M. (2005). Pathways to resilience among children in child welfare, corrections, mental health and educational settings: navigation and negotiation. *Child & Youth Care Forum, 34*(6), 423–444.

Ungar, M. (2006). *Strengths-based counseling with at-risk youth*. Thousand Oaks, CA: Corwin Press.

Ungar, M. (2007). The beginnings of resilience: A view across cultures. *Education Canada, 47*(3), 28–32.

United States Department of Education. (2007). *In their own words: Schools and students overcoming adversity*. Jessup, MD: US Department of Education.

Upitis, R. (Ed.) (2000). *Who will teach? A case study of teacher education reform*. San Francisco: Caddo Gap Press.

Urdan, T., & Schoenfelder, E. (2006). Classroom effects on student motivation: Goal structures, social relationships, and competence beliefs. *Journal of School Psychology, 44*, 331–349.

Uwah, C., McMahon, H.G., & Furlow, C.F. (2008). School belonging, educational aspirations, and academic self-efficacy among African-American male high school students: Implications for school counselors. *Professional School Counseling, 11*(5), 296–305.

Vacc, N.N. (1995). Gaining number sense through a restructured hundreds chart. *Teaching Exceptional Children, 28*(1), 50–55.

Vail, K. (2005). The medicated child. *American School Board Journal, 192*, 26–28.

Valeo, A., & Bunch, G. (1998). Teachers, attitudes, inclusion, and the curriculum. *B.C. Journal of Special Education, 21*(3), 6–19.

Valverde, L.A. (Ed.). (2008). *Latino change agents in higher education: Shaping a system that works for all*. San Francisco: Jossey Bass.

Vandenberghe, R., & Huberman, A.M. (Eds.) (1999). *Understanding and preventing teacher burnout: A sourcebook of international research and practice*. New York: Cambridge University Press.

Van den Bos, K.P., Nakken, H., Nicolay, P.G., & van Houten, E.J. (2007). Adults with mild intellectual disabilities: Can their reading comprehension ability be improved? *Journal of Intellectual Disability Research, 51*, 835–849.

Van Dongen-Melman, J.E.W.M., Van Zuren, F.J., & Verhulst, F.C. (1998). Experiences of parents of childhood cancer survivors: A qualitative analysis. *Patient Education and Counseling, 34*, 185–200.

Van Garderen, D. (2004). Reciprocal teaching as a comprehension strategy for understanding mathematical word problems. *Reading and Writing Quarterly, 20*, 225–229.

VanDeWeghe, R. (2007). What about vocabulary instruction? *English Journal, 97*(1), 101–104.

Van Reusen, A.K., & Bos, C.S. (1990). I PLAN: Helping students communicate in planning conferences. *Teaching Exceptional Children, 22*(4), 30–32.

Van Reusen, A.K., & Bos, C.S. (1994). Facilitating student participation in individualized education programs through motivation strategy instruction. *Exceptional Children, 60*, 466–470.

VanWeelden, K. (2001). Choral mainstreaming: Tips for success. *Music Educators Journal, 88*(3), 55–60.

Varga-Toth, J. (2006, February). *Meeting the needs of children and adolescents with special needs in rural and northern Canada: Summary report of a roundtable for Canadian policy-makers* (Research Report F 54). Thunder Bay, ON/Ottawa, ON: Lakehead University/Canadian Policy Research Networks, Inc.

Vass, E. (2002). Friendship and collaborative creative writing in the primary classroom. *Journal of Computer Assisted Learning, 18*, 102–110.

Vaughn, S. (1991). Social skills enhancement in students with learning disabilities. In B.Y.L. Wong (Ed.), *Learning about learning disabilities* (pp. 407–440). San Diego, CA: Academic.

Vaughn, S., Elbaum, B., & Boardman, A.G. (2001). The social functioning of students with learning disabilities: Implications for inclusion. *Exceptionality, 9*, 47–65.

Vaughn, S., Gersten, R., & Chard, D. (2000). The underlying message in LD intervention research: Findings from research syntheses. *Exceptional Children, 67*, 99–114.

Ven der Molen, M.J., Van Luit, J.E.H., Jongmans, M.J., & Van der Molen, M.W. (2007). Verbal working memory in children with mild intellectual disabilities. *Journal of Intellectual Disability Research, 51*(2), 162–169.

Venter, A., Lord, C., & Schopler, E. (1992). A follow-up study of high-functioning autistic children. *Journal of Child Psychology and Psychiatry, 33*, 489–507.

Versnel, J. (2001). *Self-determination in career education: A journey toward a proposed curriculum framework.* Unpublished paper, Queen's University, Kingston, ON.

Versnel, J. (2005). *Transition preparation program: Linking motivation and learning strategies for youth facing challenging transitions.* Unpublished Ph.D. dissertation, Faculty of Education, Queen's University.

Villa, R.A., Nevin, A.I., & Thousand, J.S. (2007). *Differentiating instruction: Collaborative planning and teaching for universally designed learning.* Thousand Oaks, CA: Corwin Press.

Villegas, A.M., & Lucas, T. (2007). The culturally responsive teacher. *Educational Leadership, 64*(6), 28–33.

Vissing, Y. (2003). The yellow school bus project. *Phi Delta Kappan, 85*, 321–323.

Vitto, J.M. (2003). *Relationship-drive classroom management: Strategies that promote student motivation.* Thousand Oaks, CA: Corwin Press.

Vo, G. (2004). Speaking from experience. In P. Travers & G. Klein (Eds.), *Equal measures: Ethnic minority and bilingual pupils in secondary schools.* London: Trentham Books.

Volkmar, F.R. (Ed.). (2007). *Autism and pervasive developmental disorders* (2nd ed.). Cambridge, UK: Cambridge University Press.

Volkmar, F.R., & Lord, C. (2007). Diagnosis and definition of autism and other pervasive developmental disorders. In F.R. Volkmar (Ed.), *Diagnosis and definition of autism and other pervasive developmental disorders* (pp. 1–31). Cambridge, UK: Cambridge University Press.

von Karolyi, C. (2006). Grappling with complex global issues, issue awareness in young highly gifted children: "Do the claims hold up?" *Roeper Review, 28*, 167–174.

Voytsekhovska, S. (2008). *Reading in a grade 9 mathematics classroom: A case study.* Unpublished master's thesis, Queen's University, Kingston, ON, Canada.

Vygotsky, L. (1978). *Mind in society.* Cambridge, MA: Harvard University Press.

Vygotsky, L.S. (1986). *Thought and language.* Cambridge, MA: MIT Press.

Vygotsky, L.S. (1996). *Thought and language* (Revised). Cambridge, MA: MIT Press.

Wagner, M., Newman, L., Cameto, R., Levine, P., & Marder, C. (2007). *Perceptions and expectations of youth with disabilities: A special topic report of findings from the National Longitudinal Transition study-2 (NLTS2). NCSER 2007-3006.* National Center for Special Education Research, Washington, DC. (ERIC Document Reproduction Service No. ED 498185)

Walczyk, E.B. (1993). Music instruction and the hearing impaired. *Music Educators Journal, 80*, 42–44.

Walker, P., & Cory, R. (2002). *Shifting from empowered agency to empowered people.* Center on Human Policy, Syracuse University, NY.

Walker, A., & Nabuzoka, D. (2007). Academic achievement and social functioning of children with and without learning difficulties. *Educational Psychology, 27*(5), 635–654.

Walker, D.R., Thompson, A.M., Zwaigenbaum, L., Goldberg, J., Bryson, S.E., Mahoney, W.J., Strawbridge, C.P., & Szatmari, P. (2004). *Child and Adolescent Psychiatry, 43*, 172–180.

Walker, K.T. (2008). *A bittersweet existence: The lived experiences of four young women with diabetes mellitus.* Unpublished master's thesis, Queen's University, Kingston, Ontario.

Walls, C.A. (2003). *Providing highly mobile students with an effective education.* (ERIC Document Reproduction Service No. ED 482918).

Walpole, S., & McKenna, M.C. (2007). *Differentiated reading strategies for the primary grades.* New York: Guilford Pub.

Ward, A., & Bouvier, R. (2001). *Resting lightly on Mother Earth: The Aboriginal experience in urban educational settings.* Calgary: Detselig Press.

Warren, J.S., Bohanon-Edmondson, Turnbull, A.P., Sailor, W., Wickham, D., Griggs, P., & Beech, S.E. (2006). School-wide positive behavior support: Addressing behavior problems that impede student learning. *Educational Psychology Review, 18*, 187–198.

Wasburn-Moses, L. (2003). What every special educator should know about high-stakes testing. *Teaching Exceptional Children, 35*(1), 12–15.

Watanabe, Y., & Swain, M. (2007). Effects of proficiency differences and patterns of pair interaction on second language learning: collaborative dialogue between adult ESL learners. *Language Teaching Research, 11*(2), 121–142.

Webb, N.M., Nemer, K.M., & Ing, M. (2006). Small group reflections: Parallels between teacher discourse and student behavior in peer-directed groups. *The Journal of the Learning Sciences, 15*, 63–119.

Webb, N.M., & Palincsar, A.S. (1996). Group processes in the classroom. In D. Berliner & R. Calfee (Eds.), *Handbook of educational psychology* (pp. 841–873). New York: Macmillan.

Webster, A.A., & Carter, M. (2007). Social relationships and friendships of children with developmental disabilities: Implications for inclusive settings, a systematic review. *Journal of Intellectual and Developmental Disability, 32*, 200–213.

Wehmeyer, M.L. (1992). Self-determination and the education of students with mental retardation. *Education and Training in Mental Retardation, 27*, 302–314.

Wehmeyer, M.L. (2002). *Teaching students with mental retardation: Providing access to the general curriculum.* Baltimore, MD: Brookes Publishing.

Wehmeyer, M.L., & Palmer, S.B. (2003). Adult outcomes for students with cognitive disabilities three years after high school: The impact of self-determination. *Education and Training in Developmental Disabilities, 38*, 131–144.

Weinstein, C.S., Tomlinson-Clarke, S., & Curran, M. (2004). Toward a conception of culturally responsive classroom management. *Journal of Teacher Education, 55*, 25–38.

Weisgerber, R.A. (1993). *Science success for students with disabilities.* New York: Addison–Wesley.

Weiss, N.R. (2005). Eliminating the use of behavioral techniques that are cruel and dehumanizing. *Exceptional Parent Magazine, 35*(10), 42–43.

Welch, A.B. (2000). Responding to student concerns about fairness. *Teaching Exceptional Children, 33*(2), 36–40.

Wellman, H.M., et al. (2002). Thought-bubbles help children with autism acquire an alternative to a theory of mind. *Autism, 6*, 343–363.

Western and Northern Canadian Protocol for Collaboration in Basic Education (2000). *Common curriculum framework for aboriginal language and culture programs, Kindergarten to Grade 12.* [http://www.edu.gov.mb.ca/ab_languages/wncp_framework.html]. (November 15, 2008).

Whitehead, B.D. (1998). *The divorce culture: Rethinking our commitments to marriage and family.* Mississauga, ON: Random House of Canada.

Whiting, G.W. (2006). Enhancing culturally diverse males' scholar identity: Suggestions for educators of gifted students. *Gifted Child Today, 29*(3), 46–50.

Whitley, J., Lupart, J.L., & Beran, T. (2007). The characteristics and experiences of Canadian students receiving special education services for a learning disability. *Exceptionality Education Canada, 17*(3), 85–109.

WHO (World Health Organization) (1980). *International classification of impairments, disabilities, and handicaps.* Geneva: WHO.

WHO (World Health Organization). (1990). *International classification of disease* (10th ed., ICD-10; Diagnostic criteria for research). Geneva: WHO.

WHO (World Health Organization) (1997). *ICIDH-2: International classification of impairments, activities, and participation: A manual of dimensions of disablement and functioning, beta 1 draft for field trials.* Geneva: WHO.

WHO (World Health Organization) (2001). *International classification of functioning, disability, and health: Final draft.* [http://www.who.int/classifications/icf/en/]. (November 15, 2008).

Wiener, J., & Tardif, C. (2004). Social and emotional functioning of children with learning disabilities: Does special education placement make a difference? *Learning Disabilities Research and Practice, 19*, 20–32.

Wiggins, G.P. (1993). Assessment: Authenticity, context, and validity. *Phi Delta Kappan, 75*(3), 200–214.

Wiggins, G.P., & McTighe, J. (2005). *Understanding by design.* Alexandria, VA: Association for Supervision and Curriculum Development.

Wihak, C., & Merali, N. (2007). Racial/cultural identity: Transformation among school-based mental health professionals working in Nunavut. *Canadian Journal of Education, 30*(1), 291–322.

Wilgosh, L. (1990). Issues in education and daily living for families of children with disabilities. *The Alberta Journal of Educational Research, 36*, 299–309.

Wilgosh, L., & Chomicki, S. (1994). Parents' views on inclusive education for young people with disabilities. *Developmental Disabilities Bulletin, 22*(2), 29–35.

Wilgosh, L., Nota, L., Scorgie, K., & Soresi, S. (2004). Effective life management in parents of children with disabilities: A cross-national extension. *International Journal for the Advancement of Counseling, 26*, 301–312.

Wilgosh, L., & Scorgie, K. (2006a). Fostering teacher understanding of parent issues when a child has a disability: A brief report. *Developmental Disabilities Bulletin, 34*, 127–136.

Wilgosh, L., & Scorgie, K. (2006b). Theoretical model for conceptualizing cross-cultural applications and intervention strategies for parents of children with disabilities. *Journal of Policy and Practice in Intellectual Disabilities, 3*, 211–218.

Wilgosh, L., Scorgie, K., & Fleming, D. (2000). Effective life management in parents of children with disabilities: A survey replication and extension. *Developmental Disabilities Bulletin, 28*(2), 1–14.

Wilhelm, J.D. (2006). The age for drama. *Educational Leadership, 63*(7), 74–77.

Willard, N.E. (2007). *Cyberbullying and cyberthreats: Responding to the challenge of online social aggression, threats, and distress.* Champaign, IL: Research Press.

Williams, D. (1992). *Nobody nowhere: The extraordinary biography of an austistic.* New York: Avon.

Williams, L., Henderson, M., & Marcuse, G. (1998). *First Nations: The circle unbroken: The teacher's guide (videos 5, 6, 7).* Montreal: National Film Board of Canada.

Williams, T., Connolly, J., Pepler, D., & Craig, W. (2005). Peer victimization, social support, and psychosocial adjustment of sexual minority adolescents. *Journal of Youth and Adolescents, 34*(5), 471–482.

Willms, J.D. (2002a). *Vulnerable children: Findings from Canada's National Longitudinal Study of Children and Youth.* Edmonton, AB: University of Alberta Press.

Willms, J.D. (2002b). *Vulnerable children and youth* [Vulnerable children: Findings from Canada's National Longitudinal Study of Children and Youth.] *Education Canada, 42*(3), 40–43.

Willows, D. (2002). The balanced literacy diet. *School Administrator, 59*, 30–33.

Wilson, R.J. (1996). *Assessing students in classrooms and schools.* Scarborough, ON: Allyn and Bacon Canada.

Winebrenner, S. (2007). *Teaching gifted kids in the regular classroom: Strategies and techniques every teacher can use to meet the academic needs of the gifted and the talented* (3rd ed.). Minneapolis: Free Spirit Publishing.

Winfree, C., Williams, R., & Powell, G.M. (2002). Children with cancer: Positive benefits of camp. *Camping Magazine, 75*(6), 26–33.

Winzer, M. (2007). *Children with exceptionalities in Canadian classrooms* (7th ed.). Toronto: Pearson Education Canada.

Winzer, M.A. (2005). The dilemma of support: Paraeducators and the inclusive movement. *Exceptionality Education Canada, 15*, 101–123.

Witzel, B.S., Riccomini, P.J., & Schneider, E. (2008). Implementing CRA with secondary students with learning disabilities in Mathematics. *Intervention in School and Clinic, 43*(5), 270–276.

Wodrich, D.L., & Cunningham, M.M. (2007). School-based tertiary and targeted interventions for students with chronic medical conditions: Examples from Type 1 Diabetes Mellitus and epilepsy. *Psychology in the Schools, 45*(1), 52–62.

Wolfensberger, W., Nirge, B., Olshansky, S., Perske, R., & Roos, P. (1972). *The principle of normalization in human services.* Toronto: National Institute on Mental Retardation.

Wolford, P.L., Heward, W.L., & Alber, S.R. (2001). Teaching middle school students with learning disabilities to recruit peer assistance during cooperative learning group activities. *Learning Disabilities: Research and Practice, 16*, 161–173.

Wolraich, M.L. (2006). Attention-Deficit/Hyperactivity Disorder: Can it be recognized and treated in children younger than 5 years? *Infants & Young Children, 19*(2), 86–93.

Wong, B.Y.L. (1996). *The ABCs of learning disabilities*. Toronto: Academic Press.

Wong, B.Y.L. (2000). Writing strategies instruction for expository essays for adolescents with and without learning disabilities. *Topics in Language Disorders, 20*(4), 29–44.

Wong, B.Y.L., & Hutchinson, N.L. (2001). *Learning disabilities in Canada*. In D.P. Hallahan & B.K. Keogh (Eds.), *Research and global perspectives in learning disabilities: Essays in honor of William M. Cruikshank* (pp. 197–215). Mahwah, NJ: Erlbaum.

Wong, J. (2000, May 6). Alisha is not a genius, but she is smart. *The Globe and Mail*, p. R7.

Wood, T., & McCarthy, C. (2002). *Understanding and preventing teacher burnout. ERIC Digest.* (ERIC Document Reproduction Service No. ED 477726).

Woods, D., & Brook, B. (2005). Controlled evaluation of an educational intervention used to modify peer attitudes and behavior toward persons with Tourette's syndrome. *Behavior Modification, 29*, 900–912.

Working Forum on Inclusive Schools. (1994). *Creating schools for all our children: What 12 schools have to say*. Reston, VA: Council for Exceptional Children.

Wormeli, R. (2006a). *Differentiating for tweens. Educational Leadership, 63*(7), 14–19.

Wormeli, R. (2006b). *Fair isn't always equal: Assessing and grading in the differentiated classroom*. Portland, ME: Stenhouse Pub.

Wright, P.M., White, K., & Gaebler-Spira, D. (2004). Exploring the relevance of the personal and social responsibility model in adapted physical activity: A collective case study. *Journal of Teaching in Physical Education, 23*, 71–87.

Wright, R. (2003). *Stolen continents: Conquest and resistance in the Americas*. Toronto: Penguin Canada.

Wysocki, T., & Gavin, L. (2006). Paternal involvement in the management of pediatric chronic diseases: Associations with adherence, quality of life, and health status. *Journal of Pediatric Psychology, 31*, 501–511.

Xin, Y.P., Grasso, E., Dipipi-Hoy, C.M., & Jitendra, A. (2005). The effects of purchasing skill instruction for individuals with developmental disabilities: A meta-analysis. *Exceptional Children, 71*, 379–402.

Xu, Y., Gelfer, J., & Perkins, P. (2005). Using peer tutoring to increase social interactions in early schooling. *TESOL Quarterly, 39*(1), 83–106.

Yamaki, K., & Fujiura, G.T. (2002). Employment and income status of adults with developmental disabilities in the community. *Mental Retardation, 40*, 132–142.

Yau, M. (1995). *Refugee students in Toronto schools: An exploratory study*. Toronto: Toronto Board of Education.

Ysseldyke, J., Nelson, R.J., Christenson, S., Johnson, D.R., Dennison, A., Triezenberg, H., Sharpe, M., & Hawes, M. (2004). What we know and need to know about the consequences of high-stakes testing for students with disabilities. *Exceptional Children, 71*(1), 75–95.

Yukon Education (2007–2008). *Handbook for teachers*. Whitehorse: Yukon Education.

Zajac, R.J., & Hartup, W.W. (1997). Friends as coworkers: Research review and classroom implications. *Elementary School Journal, 98*, 3–13.

Zentall, S. (1990). Fact-retrieval automatization and math problem solving by learning disabled, attention disordered and normal adolescents. *Journal of Educational Psychology. 82*, 856–865.

Zhou, Y.R., Knoke, D., & Sakamoto, I. (2005). Rethinking silence in the classroom: Chinese students' experiences of sharing indigenous knowledge. *International Journal of Inclusive Education, 9*(3), 287–311.

Zinga, D., Bennett, S., Good, D., & Kumpf, J. (2005). Policy and practice: Acquired brain injury in Canadian educational systems. *Canadian Journal of Educational Administration and Policy, 43*, 1–23.

# Name Index

Note: Entries for footnotes are followed by "*n*."

# Subject Index

Note: Entries for tables and figures are followed by "*t*" and "*f*," respectively.

# Photo Credits

**Chapter 1:** p. 1: Bernard Clark, p. 5: Eric Hayes, p. 21: Canadian Press/Anne-Marie Beaton, p. 28: Globe & Mail/Francine Bellefeuille, p. 33: istock photo.com

**Chapter 2:** p. 37: Angela Solar, p. 41: istock photo.com, p. 50: istock photo.com, p. 56: Bayne Stanley, p. 63: Christopher Grabowski

**Chapter 3:** p. 68: Winnipeg Free Press, p. 75: Globe & Mail/Francine Bellefeuille, p. 80: istockphoto.com, p. 102: Angela Solar, p. 112: Kingston Whig-Standard

**Chapter 4:** p. 117: Bernard Clark, p. 122: Globe & Mail/Francine Bellefeuille, p. 132: Ian MacAlpine/Kingston Whig-Standard, p. 142: Kevin Leong (arranged by Jaclyn Law at *Abilities* Magazine), p. 158: Angela Solar

**Chapter 5:** p. 165: Angela Solar, p. 169: Canadian Press/Anne-Marie Beaton, p. 182: Christopher Grabowski, p. 189: Karen Kilbride, p. 191: istockphoto.com

**Chapter 6:** p. 201: Bernard Clark, p. 205: istockphoto.com, p. 214: istockphoto.com, p. 224: Angela Solar, p. 230: Angela Solar

**Chapter 7:** p. 233: istockphoto.com, p. 237: Kingston Whig-Standard, p. 255: Kingston Whig-Standard, p. 266: istockphoto.com, p. 271: Kingston Whig-Standard/Ian MacAlpine

**Chapter 8:** p. 274: Canadian Press/Anne-Marie Beaton, p. 280: Angela Solar, p. 291: Kingston Whig-Standard, p. 296: Kingston Whig-Standard, p. 297: Globe & Mail/Francine Bellefeuille

**Chapter 9:** p. 303: Pete Gaffney, p. 306: Kingston Whig-Standard, p. 326: Bernard Clark, p. 329: Harrison Smith, p. 331: Kingston Whig-Standard

**Chapter 10:** p. 335: Vancouver Sun, p. 339: Kingston Whig-Standard, p. 342: Kingston Whig-Standard, p. 346: The Gazette/Patricia Desjardins, p. 358: Globe & Mail/Francine Bellefeuille